# Colonial Modernity in Korea

Harvard East Asian Monographs, 184

Harvard-Hallym Series on Korean Studies

## The Harvard-Hallym Series on Korean Studies

The Harvard-Hallym Series on Korean Studies, published by the Harvard University Asia Center, is supported by the Korea Institute of Harvard University and by Hallym University in Korea. It is committed to the publication of outstanding new scholarly work on Korea, regardless of discipline, in both the humanities and the social sciences.

Professor Carter J. Eckert
Director
Korea Institute
Harvard University

Dr. Soong Jong Hyun
President
Hallym Academy of Sciences
Hallym University

# Colonial Modernity in Korea

Gi-Wook Shin and

Michael Robinson, editors

Published by the Harvard University Asia Center
and distributed by Harvard University Press
Cambridge (Massachusetts) and London, 1999

Printed in the United States of America

The Harvard University Asia Center publishes a monograph series and, in coordination with the Fairbank Center for East Asian Research, the Korea Institute, the Reischauer Institute of Japanese Studies, and other faculties and institutes, administers research projects designed to further scholarly understanding of China, Japan, Vietnam, Korea, and other Asian countries. The Center also sponsors projects addressing multidisciplinary and regional issues in Asia.

Library of Congress Cataloging-in-Publication Data

Colonial Modernity in Korea / Gi-Wook Shin and Michael Robinson, editors.
       p.   cm. -- (Harvard East Asian Monographs ; 184) (Harvard-Hallym series on Korean studies)
    Includes bibliographical references and index.
    ISBN 0-674-14255-1 (cloth : alk. paper)
    1. Korea--History--Japanese occupation, 1910–1945.   2. Nationalism--Korea--History.   3. Japan--Politics and government--1912–1945.   4. Imperialism.
I. Shin, Gi-Wook.   II. Robinson, Michael Edson.   III. Series: Harvard-Hallym series on Korean studies.

DS916.54. C65 1999
951.9'03--dc21                                    99-037149

Index by the editors

♾ Printed on acid-free paper

Last figure below indicates year of this printing
09  08  07  06  05  04  03  02  01  00  99

# Contents

*Part II: Colonial Modernity and Identity*

*Reference Matter*

# *Preface*

Over the last fifteen years there has been a burgeoning interest in the study of colonialism. The rise of post-structuralist theory and its critique of the dominant mode of history writing has led to a torrent of new studies that have challenged many of the core subjects of this body of historical work. The nation as a subject and the concepts of nationalism, anti-colonialism, national liberation, development, modernization, and de-colonization that provided the frame for national narratives are all constructs that are being contested and re-thought. New approaches to the study of power, collective identity, culture, and modes of representation have opened an entire field of postcolonial studies. In one sense at least, postcolonial studies seek to destroy the artificial break imposed by the closure historical narratives create in "ending" colonialism after World War II and beginning a new era of nation-states in the non-Western world. It seeks continuities and causal relationships between the forces active during the colonial era and the social, political, and cultural experience of postcolonial nations. In the case of Korean studies, this is a wonderful development. The study of postcolonial North and South Korea offers innumerable possibilities for understanding important global, cultural, political, economic, and transnational phenomena in the late twentieth century.

For those focusing on the Korean post-colony, however, the fact that theory runs ahead of our basic historical understanding of Korea's colonial period hampers scholarly progress. Among East Asian societies, core historical, social, and cultural knowledge of Korea in the West lags considerably behind research on Japan or China. This fact is particularly troublesome for postcolonial studies because in order to examine the post-colony it is necessary to have some historical grounding on the forces that shaped the "precolonial" period. Thus revisionist arguments about power, politics, interstate relations, political identity, cultural flows, cultural hybridity, class, and gender in postcolonial Korea easily fall prey to an inadvertent ahistoricism. As we point out below, there is no lack of historical literature on twentieth-century Korea. Its utility, however, given the transformation of our ideas about the nature of nationalism, modernity, and colonialism, remains suspect. Too often, imaginative studies of postcolonial Korea draw from a highly truncated representation of the historical forces that shaped Korea before 1945.

This volume emerged from the idea that historical studies of the Korean colonial period needed a jump start in order to join more successfully the scholarly conversations in other fields of study. We hoped to gather scattered revisionist studies already under way in the United States, Japan, and Korea and discuss as a group different methods for resifting our historical understanding of colonial Korea in response to the changing discourse on nation, colonialism, and modernity at this moment. This volume presents the fruits of that discussion.

The project began as a rough idea in the summer of 1993, and the generous support of a number of institutions and individual scholars made this volume possible. The initial idea was incubated by a grant from the Social Science Research Council (SSRC) and American Council of Learned Societies (ACLS) sponsorship of a conference planning workshop. We met with Bruce Cumings, Chungmoo Choi, and Clark Sorensen in Chicago in October 1993 to thrash out the outlines of our original conference proposal. The generous advice and criticism received at this workshop expanded our original thinking and were crucial in our search for further support.

The excitement generated by this workshop ultimately attracted the interest of a diverse group of funders, and for their support we are profoundly grateful. The National Endowment for the Humanities provided a major grant (RX-21592–95) for the original conference at UCLA in the spring of 1996. The SSRC-ACLS, University of California Pacific Rim Research Program, Yonsei Institute of Korean Studies in Seoul, Korea, and the UCLA Center for Korean Studies provided additional welcomed support. We are especially indebted to the enthusiasm of Dean Jamison of the UCLA Center for Pacific

Rim Studies, Robert Buswell and Eileen Sir at the Center for Korean Studies at UCLA, and Young-Shin Park of Yonsei University.

The generous funding of our project allowed us to design a conference that joined scholars from North America, Korea, Japan, Europe, and Australia. An original group of invited studies was augmented by a call for papers from junior scholars a year before the conference. This open call located original and exciting work in progress by younger scholars from a number of disciplines. We were also able to select four graduate students representing major Korean Studies centers in the United States to participate in the general conference discussion. The ultimate conference succeeded beyond our wildest dreams. The discussion was multidisciplinary and theoretically informed, and it subjected our essays to sustained criticism that greatly aided the authors in their subsequent revisions. Ultimately, the supportive tone of the conversation and enthusiasm generated by insightful critiques motivated the assembly of the final volume in what seems to us record time for such a project.

As important as our individual authors was a wonderful group of discussants culled from different disciplines in both Japanese and Korean studies. Peter Duus, Stephen Vlastos, Hori Kazuo, Sung Young Cho, Chungmoo Choi, Carter Eckert, Donald Clark, and Carolyn So acted as conference discussants, and they pushed our often very preliminary work to another level. We were aided as well by timely commentary from John Duncan and James Matray.

We wish to thank our research assistants James Freda, Jennifer Jung-Kim, and Grace Lim of UCLA and Todd Munson of Indiana University for helping in innumerable ways. Thanks are due as well to Elizabeth Underwood and Cho Sŏkkon for their participation in the original conference. Finally, we owe a special debt of gratitude to John R. Ziemer, Executive Editor of the Harvard University Asia Center Publications Program. He arranged for two extraordinarily helpful anonymous readings of the manuscript, expertly edited our often confused prose, and generally breathed life into what had become a rather unwieldy and complex manuscript.

Gi-Wook Shin, University of California, Los Angeles
Michael Robinson, Indiana University

# Contributors

KYEONG-HEE CHOI is Assistant Professor of Modern Korean Literature in the Department of East Asian Languages and Civilizations at the University of Chicago. Her article "'Mother's Stake 1' and Female Modernity" appeared in *Minjok munhaksa yŏn'gu* (Study of national literary history) in 1996. She is currently working on a manuscript on motherhood and colonial modernity, and her research interests include the relationship between gender and the formation of public (and literary) space in colonial Korea.

HENRY H. EM, Assistant Professor, teaches modern Korean history in the Department of Asian Languages and Cultures at the University of Michigan. Since the publication of his article "'Overcoming' Korea's Division: Narrative Strategies in Recent South Korean Historiography," *positions: east asia cultures critique* 1, no. 2 (Fall 1993), he has continued his research on Korean historiography in the modern period. Currently, he is writing a book on historians and history writing in modern Korea.

DO-HYUN HAN is Assistant Professor of Sociology at the Academy of Korean Studies in Korea. His publications include *Tradition and Change of a Lineage Village in Korea* (co-author), "Environmental Movements against the Golf Course Development Since the Late 1980s in Korea," "Rural Reform and Welfare in Vietnam," and "A Historical Review of Agrarian Nationalism in Contemporary Korea." His research interests lie in the areas of community studies, environmental studies, and comparative studies of Korea and Vietnam.

JOONG-SEOP KIM is Professor of Sociology, Gyeongsang National University, Korea, teaching social movements and historical sociology. He spent a year at the Essex University completing research on human rights. His publications include *Hyŏngpy'ŏng undong yŏn'gu* (Study of the Hyŏngpy'ŏng movement) (1994), and several articles on social movements under Japanese colonial rule. He continues to do research on social movements and human rights in colonial and contemporary Korea.

CHULWOO LEE is Assistant Professor of the Sociology of Law and Legal History at the Sungkyunkwan University School of Law, Korea. He received his degrees from Seoul National University (LL.B./ LL.M.), Georgetown University (LL.M.), and the London School of Economics (Ph.D.). His publications include essays on the politics of legal culture, law and colonialism, and law and development. His current research interests are focused on the relationship between legal culture and social action.

SOON-WON PARK is a lecturer at the International Center, Keio University. She is the author of *Colonial Industrialization and Labor in Korea: The Onoda Cement Factory* (1999) and is currently conducting research on the sociocultural aspect of colonial modernity in interwar Korea focusing on the year 1929.

MICHAEL ROBINSON is Associate Professor in the Department of East Asian Languages and Cultures at Indiana University. He is the author of *Cultural Nationalism in Colonial Korea, 1920–1925* (University of Washington Press, 1988) and coauthor of *Korea Old and New: A History* (Ilchogak and Harvard University Korea Institute, 1990). His recent publishing interests have focused on Korean popular culture of the 1930s and issues of historical representation.

MICHAEL A. SCHNEIDER is Associate Professor of History at Knox College in Galesburg, Illinois, USA. He has just completed a book-length manuscript on Japanese colonial ideology in the 1920s tentatively entitled "The Future of the Japanese Colonial Empire." His current research focuses on cultural cosmopolitanism and Japanese foreign policy in the twentieth century.

GI-WOOK SHIN is Associate Professor of Sociology at UCLA. He is the author of *Peasant Protest and Social Change in Colonial Korea* and numerous articles on popular activism, nationalism, and capitalism in Korea. Recent publications include "Agrarian Conflict and the Origins of Korean Capitalism" in *American Journal of Sociology* and "The Politics of Ethnic Nationalism in Divided Korea" in *Nations and Nationalism*. He is currently working on two books, one on ethnic nationalism and the other on authoritarian industrialism in Korea.

MICHAEL D. SHIN is a Ph.D. candidate in the Department of History, University of Chicago. He is working on a dissertation on nationalist thought during the Japanese occupation period. He is also collaborating with Korean scholars to translate works on the intellectual response to the agrarian crisis in modern Korea for an edited volume.

CLARK SORENSEN is Associate Professor and Director of the Korean Studies program at the University of Washington. He is the author of *Over the Mountains Are Mountains: Korean Peasant Households and Their Adaptations to Rapid Industrialization* and numerous articles. Among his recent publications is "Folk Religion and Political Commitment in South Korea in the Eighties" in *Render unto Caesar: The Religious Sphere in World Politics*. He is currently working on the social history of Korea in the twentieth century.

KENNETH M. WELLS is a Fellow of the Pacific and Asian History Division of the Research School of Pacific Studies and Senior Lecturer (Associate Professor) in the Asian History Centre, Faculty of Asian Studies at the Australian National University. He is also Director of the ANU Centre for Korean Studies. His major publications include *New God, New Nation: Protestants and Self-Reconstruction Nationalism in Korea, 1896–1937* and, as editor and contributor, *South Korea's Minjung Movement: The Culture and Politics of Dissidence*. At present he is working on a monograph on Korean women's movements in the early twentieth century and is engaged in a collaborative project with Professors Boudewijn Walraven and Koen De Cesuter of Leiden University on religion and social change in Korea during the same period.

DAQING YANG is Assistant Professor of Japanese History at George Washington University in Washington, D.C. His publications include "Between Lips and Teeth: Ideals and Self-interest in Chinese-Korean Relations, 1910–1950," *Chicago Occasional Papers on Korea*, ed. Bruce Cumings (1991), and most recently, an essay in the August 1998 issue of the Japanese monthly *Shisō* on the Rape of Nanjing. He is currently completing a book manuscript on telecommunications networks in Japan's Greater East Asian Co-prosperity Sphere.

*Colonial Modernity in Korea*

# INTRODUCTION

# *Rethinking Colonial Korea*

## Gi-Wook Shin and Michael Robinson

Until the past decade, the national politics of division and the international politics of the Cold War have directly or indirectly constricted our understanding of modern Korean history. With liberation from colonial rule in 1945 and the emergence of two competing Korean states, history itself became part of the competition between the two Korean states. As a by-product of political competition, history fell hostage to the truth claims of two very different political systems. Abroad, the polarized politics of the Cold War also influenced historical writing on Korea. Thus, even in societies in which historians were not subject to political pressures, the story more often than not was imbedded in a frame of reference that supported or denied the generalized truth claims of political regimes in the bipolar world order.

This situation is not unique. History is precisely the site of contention and conflict over the meaning and significance of the past. When different narratives are free to compete, a general consensus often emerges only to be challenged anew in a process of continual revision. In the case of the two Koreas, however, the struggle over the past has been particularly difficult. Much of the difficulty arises from the particular connection between history and the politics of nationalism. Different versions of history can naturalize highly diverse contemporary political and social arrangements. Yet, until recently the logic of nationalism as it has informed the writing of modern Korean history assumes there can be only one legitimate outcome of national becoming. The binary logic of true nation / anti-nation restricts historical inquiry. The emergence of two competing Korean states in 1948 created an artificial break in the historical record. Rather than fearlessly probe the historical record of the pre-1945 Korean experience, nationalist histories of the North and South cast their gaze backward with tunnel vision in order to create a story that most coherently signified the telos of the separate political/social systems.

With the end of the Cold War and the transformation of domestic politics on the Korean peninsula, there has been a renaissance in historical research on the Korean colonial period. This volume was created to encourage this trend toward the reshaping of our understanding of colonial history, one that challenges the unitary focus, artificial unity, and binary-producing tendencies of older assumptions about nationalism that have too often dominated Korean historiography. The goal is not, however, to deny the important contribution that nationalist scholarship has made in effectively refuting colonialist interpretations of Korean history, nor is the purpose to reject nationalism as a variable of analysis. We do not intend to create a new historical paradigm or claim these studies as exemplars of a "correct" view of Korean history. Rather, we wish to offer a wealth of new questions and tentative answers to issues that have been obscured by the relentless politicization of the historical record that emerged after the division in 1945. In short, our collective purpose is to see how writing around, beneath, and beyond the nationalist approaches so prominent in Korean history writing can enhance our understanding of the Korean colonial period.

By understanding nationalism as a fluid, constructed, and changeable category that is neither predetermined nor fixed on a unitary pathway of development, we are able to ask different questions of the period of colonial rule. We are not interested in the historical legitimation project of either Korean state—although we are mindful that we are helpless to prevent the appropriation of this work by those who fashion such narratives. By placing these studies within a self-consciously different frame—one that emphasizes dynamism, multiple possibilities and causal connections, and various (often competing) contemporary ideas of nation, modernity, and colonialism—we hope to stimulate the process of historical rediscovery already under way within the field of modern Korean studies in the West as well as Korea.

## Nationalist Historical Narratives and
## Korea's Twentieth Century

The nationalist paradigm has dominated the historical presentation of modern Korea. It presupposes an unproblematized sense of the Korean nation, a nation that is assumed to have existed in a "natural" form in the premodern era and emerged in the late nineteenth century coeval with the modern stimuli of external political pressures, especially Japanese aggression. The process of rethinking Korean politics and culture in national form accelerated with the failure of the ancien régime's reforms and inability to defend its sovereignty. With formal colonization in 1910 by the Japanese, nascent Korean nationalism flowered in different directions—as cultural, political, and social revolutionary impulses—all focused on a reshaping of Korean society and consciousness in order to create an independent nation-state.

Early twentieth-century Western accounts of Korea either accepted the social Darwinian judgments manifest in traditional Korea's fall in the face of superior Japanese/Western political and social evolution or championed the right of the assumed Korean nation to exist. Concurrently, Korean nationalist historians constructed a nation from the repository of traditional historical narratives and cultural memories in order to have the Korean people think their way toward a new collective identity. After 1910, Japanese colonialist historians countered with elaborate justifications for seeing Korea as a part of Japan in order to legitimate Japanese political, economic, and cultural domination. Both the Korean and the Japanese narratives produced a prodigious amount of information and presented Korea, in effect, to the gaze of the global community. In their fidelity to dominating causal theories, however, they also began an equally powerful process of obfuscation. Such thinking imposed on Korean history a system of binaries that produced an exceedingly limiting historical narrative: failed tradition in the face of modernity, backwardness overcome by progress, righteous national pride obscured by evil external domination, collaboration of the rich (Korean and Japanese/Western monopoly capitalists) over the pure, impoverished (Korean) masses, Japan–Korea, Asia–the West, and so forth. The resulting verbiage created a mound of information about Korea: events, people, ideas, movements, social and economic development, and atrocities. However, the causal connecting of this cornucopia of facts remained limited by its own rationalist and bifurcating logic—the logic of linear development that undergirds modern History, itself a product of the telos of advanced, Western nation-states.[1]

Post-1945 histories of Korea's past century added more facts to the pile while further blurring causes and connections that might better illumine the full experience of humanity on the peninsula. Three powerful master narratives, like broadcast-jamming beacons, emanate from the two postwar Korean states and, to a lesser extent, linger within the political overtones of Cold War politics. Both Korean states have a powerful interest in history—their stories support their claims to legitimacy. They have woven a version of its ancient and modern memory into master narratives that justify their respective claims to be the true representative of the nation in the world community. In both cases, the state has used considerable force to repress counter-narratives. Each polices the writing of history and shapes public opinion around a general common understanding of why its system should be recognized as the true expression of Korean collective identity. A third master narrative, that of the Cold War, compounds the competition between the national stories of North and South Korea. Essentially this is a narrative created by the United States that fits the problematic of the Korean peninsula into its own concept of the post–World War II era—a story that legitimates the American struggle against global communism. These politicized narratives constrict understanding by aligning historical inquiry to the present imperatives of national and international politics.[2] The problems this poses for Korean historians in the North and, until recently, the South are obvious. Western historians have fared little better; they have often found themselves taking sides, making moral judgments, or writing between these narratives, only vaguely aware of the dominating logic that constricts their own narratives.

This volume seeks to escape from such politicized master narratives by examining colonial history from more inclusive, pluralist approaches. In recent years, a number of scholars in both Korea and the West have begun to challenge the simplistic binary of colonial repression/exploitation versus Korean resistance by attending to the interworkings of colonialism and modernity as well as to multiple representations of the national community.[3] This volume aspires to stimulate this new trend of historical scholarship with a focus on the complex relations among colonialism, modernity, and nationalism. The essays presented here were written by Korean and non-Korean authors representing a number of different academic disciplines. Despite these differences, however, we share an interest in a group of questions, and our work grows out of certain assumptions.

## An Interactive Approach to Colonial History

Our inquiries are conceptually grounded within a triangular field bounded by three interlocking and mutually influencing ideas: colonialism, modernity, and nationalism (see Fig. 1).[4] This spatial metaphor allows us greater flexibility to pursue what might be called an ecological handling of historical traces. Rather than artificially draining the flood of historical experience through channels in linear fashion — forcing the flow of events through straight canals of modernization, the rise of nationalism, or colonial repression / national resistance — it might be better to reclaim the land with a mind to restoring some of the density, richness, and complexity of the original ecosystem. Such an idea is in line with the conviction that turn-of-the-century nationalism was not a pent-up reservoir of pre-existing Koreanness ready to flow along the deep new channel provided by imported concepts of the nation-state; nor was Korea's experience of modernity bound to course inexorably within existing channels of Western or Japanese construction. Moreover, Japanese colonial domination (hegemony) must be considered a unique phenomenon; it resembled other colonialisms, yet its construction and evolution in Korea provided multiple stimuli for other processes. Colonial evolution was dynamic: it had to adapt to the responses of Korean society and, in doing so, reflected this experience back into the construction of Japanese identity and modernity.

Colonialism, modernity, and nationalism mark the borders of our field of inquiry. Each carries its own unique cluster of concepts while holding within its individual frame important constituents of the other two. By seeing them as mutually reinforcing frames, we can deepen our current understanding of colonial history, which is based largely on binary constructions: imperialist repression versus national resistance, colonial exploitation versus national development, or Japanese culture versus Korean culture. Most of the existing nationalist narratives discussed below posit a disjunction between colonialism and modernity because they assume that colonial rule either destroyed or distorted Korea's effort to modernize. Similarly, nationalism by definition must be counterposed to colonialism. It rejects any image of political community that is not explicitly anti-colonial. In other words, current nationalist narratives treat colonialism, modernity, and nationalism as

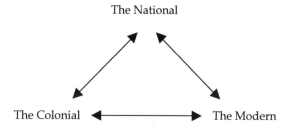

Fig. 1 The historical field

separate and isolated variables without appreciating the multiple possibilities of their interrelationship. Losing the interactive resonance of these ideas diminishes our appreciation of such important and complex issues as colonial modernity, cultural hegemony, and the formation of non-national identities. It is now time to move beyond such dichotomizing conceptions of colonialism, modernity, and nationalism, and we believe this can be done by holding a view in which all three variables interact. The twelve chapters contained in this volume attempt to examine the colonial period accordingly.

## Colonialism

The first border of our historical field is colonialism. There have been some attempts to grapple with the unique nature of Japanese colonialism in Korea.[5] Secondary histories of the colony, however, generally assume a unitary, homogenized view of colonialism. Japanese interests and domination are assumed to be uncomplicated, and there is no sense that the Japanese might have been affected by their experience in Korea or that the lines between resistance and collaboration might have been blurred and permeable throughout the period of Japanese rule. Even more fundamentally, the fact that Japan as a latecomer to the business of imperialism had the advantage of learning from Western colonialism and thus created uniquely effective control strategies is seldom discussed. In economic relations, the colony-metropolitan relationship is seen as a zero-sum game for Korea; like the other colonial powers in their respective dominions, Japan plundered Korea—this in spite of what we know about the uniqueness of Japanese economic policy and the extraordinary infrastructural development in Korea between 1910 and 1945. Soon-Won Park explicitly demonstrates this point in her analysis of labor class formation and infrastructural development in Chapter 5. In politics, one surmises, after reading most Korean-language treatments of the period, that all good Koreans organized their lives for 40 years around the single issue of resisting Japanese political domination. This is a rather narrow reading of human responses to their environment. The narratives of North and South Korean historiography on colonialism often seem a simple mud-slinging contest; this unitary focus on the memory of colonialism explains, in Bruce Cumings's phrase, "why one Korea indulges in a myth that everyone resisted and the other in a myth that no one collaborated."[6]

We are, therefore, mindful of the disproportionately dominant role Japanese colonial repression plays in historical narratives on Korea. Anti-colonialism and national liberation struggles did play key roles in the Korean pre-1945 experience; excessive emphasis, however, on a uniquely coercive Japanese political repression, economic exploitation, and its debilitating cultural policies has obscured our understanding of more complicated historical processes that emerged in this period. In the Manichean divide between nationalism and colonialism, all anti-Japanese behavior is nationalist; there are no shades of gray. North Korean and leftist historiography is equally myopic, favoring a dichotomy that divides the national liberation struggle between those who fought colonialism and everyone else who collaborated. Such thinking deflects primary historical agency from Korean society to outside forces. We propose to consider Japanese domination within the broader lens of cultural hegemony.

A major feature of modern domination is its pervasiveness in everyday life beyond political/economic realms. The modern nation-state mobilizes not only police and state apparatus but also the "culture industry" to obtain dominance over its subjects. The Foucauldian notion of discourse and the Gramscian conception of hegemony point to the modern nature of domination-subordination relations. Hegemony is essentially a concept that helps to explain how political and civil society, with institutions ranging from education, religion, and family to the microstructures of the practices of everyday life, shapes the meaning and values that produce, direct, and maintain the "spontaneous" consent of the various strata of society to domination. Nationalist narratives neglect the "hegemonic" aspects of Japanese colonialism by focusing exclusively on economic domination and political repression. We argue that such a focus obscures more subtle and complex processes within Korea's experience of colonial domination, particularly in

the *bunka seiji* (Cultural Rule) period after 1920 and before the war mobilization of the late 1930s. It turned out to be, in retrospect, a more
effective strategy than naked repression, and it encouraged reformist
rather than revolutionary/popular responses within Korean society.[7]

Japan sought to obtain cultural hegemony in Korea with a divide-
and-rule strategy developed after the failure of the *budan seiji* (Military
Rule) in the first decade of the colonial era. The policy of Cultural Rule
co-opted nationalist leaders and channeled popular anti-Japanese sentiments into institutionalized forums. By the end of the 1920s, this strategy had paid dividends, as the nationalist movement waned and as
politicized elites and the small urban, literate, middle class were subsumed in a more ambiguous culture of colonial modernity. As Gi-Wook
Shin and Do-Hyun Han point out in Chapter 3, Japanese efforts to
obtain hegemonic power also included state-initiated ideological programs, such as the Rural Revitalization Campaign, that emphasized
"mental awakening." Although the colonial government initiated
the campaign as a corporatist social policy to save rural households
(over three-quarters of the population) from poverty, it simultaneously
sought "friendly feelings and hearty cooperation between Japanese and
Koreans" and "sympathy, harmony, and mutual help between officials
and the people."

The "spiritual" (to use the term favored by Japanese officials) nature
of the campaign set it in the context of a larger colonial hegemony to
obtain what Chulwoo Lee in Chapter 1 calls "domination over the
soul." Following the beginning of Japan's war with China in 1937, the
colonial government formalized a program to assimilate Korean culture
and thought into Japanese forms in its pursuit of "total war." This shift,
encapsulated in the well-known slogan *naisen ittai* (Korea and Japan as
a single body), brought a number of state initiatives in the cultural,
economic, and social arenas together in an intensive indoctrination
program of education and participation in the rites and symbolism of
Japanese Shintoism and imperial rule. In Chungmoo Choi's words,
Japan attempted to "colonize consciousness" by imposing its own
worldview, cultural norms, and values on Koreans in the hope that
they would adopt an alien system of thought and disparage indigenous
culture and identity.[8] Did Japan's efforts to obtain cultural hegemony
succeed?

Despite its significance, the question of Japan's success has not yet
been adequately investigated in Korean historiography. The nationalist
narrative assumes, rather than proves, that such hegemonic efforts

failed, characterizing any and all social and political resistance during the colonial period as nationalist and anti-colonial. Conversely, others assume that the "colonization of consciousness" indeed occurred. We argue that such polarized views fail to capture the dynamic nature of colonial hegemony. Colonial hegemonic policy, while trying to "colonize" Korean culture and consciousness, provided "space" for groups to reconstruct their own being—some took an oppositional stance, others reformed, still others supported colonial hegemony. Accordingly, we must view colonial hegemony as a historical process continuously negotiated, contested, defended, renewed, re-created, and altered, by challenges from within and without. Proper understanding of any hegemonic process must consider its dialectical relations to counter-hegemonic voices. Although Japanese colonialists promoted the dominant ideology through their schools and mass media, Koreans—aware of earlier social, intellectual, and political forms and in the process of creating their own response to the multiple stimuli of modernity, colonialism, and national politics/identity—contested (though not necessarily as nationalist narratives portray) colonial hegemony. This response was complicated further by the rapid and telescoped change characteristic of the twentieth century—for Korea, this change occurred in the context of "colonial modernity."

## Modernity

In recent years there has been a great deal of discussion and debate over the concept of modernity among scholars in Korea as well as the West.[9] Terms like "East Asian modernity,"[10] "colonial modernity,"[11] "high modernity,"[12] and "postmodernity"[13] illustrate the diversity and scope of such debates. Modernity is a phenomenon that first appeared in eighteenth-century Western Europe and then spread to other parts of the world. It is frequently associated with the Enlightenment, rationalism, citizenship, individualism, legal-rational legitimacy, industrialism, nationalism, the nation-state, the capitalist world-system, and so on. The industrial revolution of England and the social revolution of France as well as rationalist Enlightenment thought are considered major events that shaped the rise and growth of European modernity. In short, in its origins and nature, modernity is inherently a historical and Western phenomenon.

Although modernity originated in the West, it has taken different forms as it spread to other parts of the world. Contrary to earlier modernization arguments, which held that societies develop along the line of Western modernity, it has now become clear that there are multiple paths to modernity. Barrington Moore's classic work on diverse paths to modernity — West European bourgeois democracy, German/ Japanese fascism, and Russian/Chinese communism — clearly established this idea. In a similar context, scholars of East Asia have posited an "East Asian modernity" distinct from the West European version.[14] Nonetheless, non-European modernity, such as the East Asian version, did not develop in isolation from Western Europe — it was influenced by the model of the Western nation-state and affected by power politics and economic relations in its transmission. In fact, Moore makes it clear that the German/Japanese path or Russian/Chinese path to modernity cannot be conceived without considering the Western European experience: the former were largely a response to the latter.[15] Similarly, Liah Greenfeld's recent work on nationalism shows that the existence of the model of individualistic British nationalism was to a great extent responsible for the rise of collectivist nationalism in Germany.[16] East Asia's form of modernity, while quite distinctive, has similarly been, as Tu Wei-ming points out, the result of a conscious response to the challenge of the modern West.[17]

The rise of modernity in Korea was also closely associated with external influences. In particular, it was the emergence of modern Japan and its intrusion into Korea that stimulated and provided a direct model for the effort to build a nation-state in the late nineteenth century. Efforts from above like the Kabo Reform (Kabo kyŏngjang, 1894–96) movement or from below such as the Tonghak peasant rebellions (1894) reflected the situation that Korea faced — a twofold task of modernization and the preservation or reconstruction of national identity. Thus, as the processes associated with modernity developed, they were entwined with outside economic and political influence, and ultimately they evolved in a context of colonial domination. Moreover, although the sources of what became modernity in Korea were Western in origin, Korea's reception of modernity was mediated by a complicated filtering mechanism — a process of translation begun a generation earlier in Japan and one that continued in Korea under colonial rule.

Any discussion of Korean modernity, therefore, must confront the fact of colonialism. Some scholars, especially those in Korea, are reluctant to examine modernity in the colonial context. For them, modernity signifies historical progress, and as such it cannot possibly be associated with such retrograde phenomena as colonialism; the latter hinders the creation of a "true" modernity or at best produces a "distorted" development.[18] In the nationalist perspective, the colonial state as agent of change delegitimizes the "modern" itself. This is a value-laden, essentialist use of the concept, because modernity is neither a universal good nor a historical necessity.[19] This conception of modernity denies Koreans agency in the construction of their own modernity. Colonialism intervened in Korea's path to modernity, but this did not automatically make Koreans mere passive recipients of modernity. Koreans participated directly and indirectly in the construction of a unique colonial modernity—a modernity that produced cosmopolitanism (a sense of shared universals) without political emancipation. Colonial modernity possessed liberating forces and a raw, transformative power, and it affected the more nuanced forms of domination and repression in the colony. Its sheer complexity must be recognized.

Furthermore, modernity in Korea evolved unevenly across diverse social groups and regions. Colonial modernity meant the loss of vested interests for some social groups, but it provided opportunities for social mobility for others. Moreover, modern technologies and institutions provided multiple possibilities for increased political and cultural oppression or "governmentality" by the colonial state while concretely creating new spaces for political resistance and cultural expression. In Chapter 2, Michael Robinson begins a discussion of the spaces for cultural expression opened by the explosion of consumed forms of leisure. In Chapter 8, Kyeong-Hee Choi examines the issue of new avenues of mobility through education explored by women during the period. In Chapter 11, Joong-Seop Kim analyzes the linkage of the modern idea of equality to the *paekchŏng* liberation movement of the 1920s and 1930s. These studies demonstrate the utility of examining the multiple sites of change characteristic of colonial modernity rather than assuming it to be a general universalizing process. An attention to the diverse effects of modernity enables us to explain how the uneven spread and perception of colonial modernity created a potential for competing versions of political community among diverse social groups *within* the colony.

Japan's extensive use of modern means of cultural production such as education and media for domination further complicates the effort to understand colonial modernity and hegemony. As the Frankfurt school's analysis of modernity demonstrates, the increasing rationalization of the process of cultural production can intensify hegemonic efforts. In fact, both modern education and media and their support for a modern popular culture interacted to create, transform, and maintain colonial hegemony, particularly in the 1930s. The Japanese authorities closely monitored and controlled the news media and school curriculum and also used them to socialize Koreans as good colonial subjects. This served to normalize the colonial status quo. The popular culture's connection to modernity, to new styles of leisure and consumption, indirectly legitimized colonial rule by associating colonial social and political relations with participation in the modern world. Indeed, from the inception of Korean nationalism, internalizing the idea of the nation-state meant counterpoising a "backward" traditional society with aspirations (defined first in Western terms, and later in comparative terms to Japan's modernity) to create a "modern" Korea. The issue of Korean participation in a colonial modernity is finessed in most nationalist histories by isolating the "true" national form of modernity from any connection to "tainted" Japanese modernity. Korea's unique modern experience, however, cannot be broken into discrete Japanese, Western, or Korean parts.

Moreover, the new technology's potential for producing counter-hegemony should not be overlooked. Modernity can both assist and endanger a prevailing hegemony. For example, the emergence of the modern culture industry — print capitalism, the recording industry, radio broadcasts, and cinema — provided Japan with powerful weapons to reinforce colonial hegemony. As Robinson argues, however, these new media also created oppositional spaces within the new popular culture. Allegorical readings of Korean film, imported popular magazines, popular songs, and stand-up comedy on the radio challenged centralized cultural controls in intriguing ways. Similarly, Japanese expansion of modern education to promote assimilation offered social (co-optive) mobility for some, for others it was central in forming a modern Korean nationalist consciousness, and perhaps for many it was of no consequence at all. Indeed, in Chapter 9, Michael Shin points to the fact that even though modern literature emerged in the colonial context, it was vital to the genesis of Koreans' search for national identity. The complex, double-edged nature of modernity suggests the failure of Korean nationalism to overthrow the colonial regime should be understood in part as a result not only of Japanese political repression but also of the *interaction* of inclusive forces within Japanese cultural hegemony. In the end, the fact that Japanese colonialism successfully denied Koreans liberation does not negate the force of nationalism in the colony. Ignoring, however, the complexity of cultural hegemony obscures the causes that have shaped postcolonial Korean political and cultural development.

## Nationalism

The nationalist paradigm reads Korea's recent historical experience as a narrative of emerging national self-consciousness, the resulting struggle for expression against outside forces, and, finally, the achievement of political and cultural independence as a sovereign nation. In lockstep fashion, this reading links modern nationalism to external political and economic intrusion and its maturation into the ultimately "successful" liberation from Japanese colonial rule. The process is assumed to be natural and a revelation of a pre-existing Korean nation.[20] In this view, Korean nationalism is always a "progressive" force deployed first against the corrupt ancien régime and later against "repressive" Japanese imperialism. A simplistic Korea-Japan binary overlays all such narratives. To wit, the Japanese repressed nascent Korean modernity in favor of economic exploitation and cultural assimilation. Koreans who were successful in the colonial polity, economy, or society "collaborated" and became non-Koreans, and their constructions of wealth or cultural property are labeled "anti-national." Women's liberation is appropriated as a story of resistance to Japanese oppression. Economic growth, infrastructural development, education, the creation of human capital, and institution building are decontextualized and dismissed as by-products of Japanese exploitation.

These politicized narratives obscure a rich and pluralistic discourse on representation of the political community during the colonial period. Recent scholarship shows that during the period there were a number of alternative narratives of political community that rejected modernity, denied the nation-state form, or pushed beyond traditional peninsular physical boundaries to claim a trans-Yalu territory for Korea. For example, Gi-Wook Shin shows that Korean agrarianists attempted to construct a new Korea based on a "utopian agrarian nation" uncontaminated by Western capitalism, Japanese colonialism, or Marxist ideology.[21] Andre Schmid and Henry Em reveal a number of alternative readings of the famously ambiguous Korean nationalist historian, Sin Ch'aeho; the struggle in both North and South Korea to appropriate Sin's intellectual legacy in order to legitimate their respective visions of the nation solidifies their point.[22] However, current nationalist narratives leave no space for such alternative imaginings of political community because they contradict definitions of the nation and its physical boundaries—an example of what Prasenjit Duara calls "the repressive connection between history and the nation."[23] We can no more speak in the singular of nationalism than we can of colonialism or colonial modernity. We have to specify complex and overlapped relations among multiple layers of colonialism, competing versions of nationalism, *and* alternative narratives of political community.

We chose, therefore, to emphasize a more open approach to Korea's modern history by writing away from the political narratives and within the overlapping paradigms of modernity and colonialism. Rather than simply destroy a naturalized Korean identity, as nationalist narratives most commonly assert, the merger of colonialism and modernity created a condition of ambiguity and contingency for existing identities. In particular, colonialism's merger with modernity facilitated negotiation and modification of old identities and construction and reconstruction of new identities. Adapting Eugene Weber's famous statement on the French, we might assert that colonialism transformed "peasants into Koreans." The category, *Chōsenjin* (Koreans), thus created was a bureaucratic, essentializing, and derogatory classification applicable to all Koreans. Furthermore, colonial modernity's effect was not uniform but highly uneven across diverse social groups and over different regions. The uneven spread of colonial modernity created a potential for constructing diverse and competing forms of identity within the complex field of cultural hegemony maintained under Japanese rule.

Current nationalist narratives, nonetheless, subsume all competing forms of identities under the category of the nation. In Chapter 7, Kenneth Wells provides a trenchant critique of how nationalism represses the consideration of other categories in its drive to enshrine a single, inherent identity of value. The nation becomes a whole in relation to the colonial Other and thus overrides alternative collective identities such as class, gender, region, and status. Accordingly, all social movements under colonial rule become nationalist and anti-colonial. Yet contributors to the volume warn against the danger of subsuming all other identities within the rubric of the nation. Kim's chapter shows that colonial modernity not only brought the notion of human rights and social equity to Korea, but it also offered *paekchŏng* the opportunity to engage in activism in order to gain social upward mobility. Henry Em (Chapter 12) and Clark Sorensen (Chapter 10) examine ambiguities and tensions within the process of constructing the Korean nation or Kore-anness. Em demonstrates how multiple meanings underlay the writings of Sin Ch'aeho; rather than fix the idea of the nation, Sin's seminal writings provide grist for widely varying political interpretations of the nation in postwar, divided Korea. Sorensen examines different concep-tions of peasantness and its relationship to the idea of nation; under-standing the malleability of this category sheds light on postwar efforts to recast the nation around the category of *minjung* (agrarian masses) in the 1980s. In short, the notion of the nation was not an immutable given, despite Korea's long history of maintaining a unified political community. It was contested, negotiated, reformulated, and recon-structed during the colonial period, and the process continues today in different form.

The exploration of gender is weakly represented in the narratives of twentieth-century Korea. Women's issues are treated in separate histo-ries that are often divorced from the dynamic and changing context of their genesis. As Kenneth Wells points out in Chapter 7, the feminist issue of repression under Korean patriarchy was submerged and redi-rected as the larger, male-dominated nationalist movement mobilized women's groups for political purposes. Moreover, the imperatives of nationalist and social revolutionary politics further divided women's groups by marginalizing those focused exclusively on feminist social (non-national) issues. Like modernity or nationalism, gender is also a complex variable. Kyeong-Hee Choi tackles the issue of gender by ex-amining the different experiences of women over time and between generations. The new possibilities for women in colonial Korea were not all political, and women of different generations responded vari-ously. Choi examines Pak Wonso's autobiographical novel "Mother's Stake 1" to show how the private sphere of women was altered by co-lonial modernity. Social mobility strategies, educational opportunity, and new economic roles transformed family child-rearing practices in the colonial city. Women caught between their traditional upbringing and new avenues of mobility began to realize their own dreams in the guise of guiding their daughters into the world of the "new woman."

We are not suggesting a deconstruction in a post-structuralist vein of all essentialist notions of identity in order to simply capture "differ-ence." Rather, we continue to recognize the utility of general categories such as nation, gender, and class as we attend to the historical and so-cial processes that construct these identities. To understand a dynamic process such as identity formation, we must consider that identities coexist, rise, and fall in significance depending on circumstances, context, and their relationship to large and/or small structures in society. In particular, it is important to pay close attention to the complex process in which tradition and modernity or indigenous and alien values interact to produce a particular form of identity in a historically given situation.

It is now well recognized that modernity does not necessarily efface tradition; tradition is often revitalized or even re-invented in reaction to modernity as another resource in identity formation. Nationalist intellectuals articulate the nation by drawing from the pool of culture and memory; ideologues working for the nation-state have the power to mobilize the resources of centralized educational systems and military training to socialize vast numbers of people into a re-invented tradition. The well-known work of Eric Hobsbawm and Terence Ranger and Liah Greenfeld's study on nationalism were influential in showing how this process works.[24] More recently, Takashi Fujitani's *Splendid Monarchy* has provided another example of the constructed nature of rituals used to encourage national identity formation; one wonders how the lessons learned by Japan's authors of "traditional" imperial pageantry influenced later constructions of colonial authority in Korea.[25] Under colonial rule, Koreans were also searching for indigenous sources from which to formulate or reformulate Korean national identity. Research on folklore, shamanism, and mythology that could reveal indigenous Korean roots or Koreanness constituted a key part of the Korean nationalist project during the period.[26] In this volume, Michael Shin's analysis of Korean intellectuals' embrace of *chŏng* or Sorensen's description of various constructions of peasantness as the basis of Korean nationalism are further illustrations of the process of appropriation and redeployment of tradition in identity formation. The *minjung* nationalism of the 1980s provides a contemporary example of the reappropriation of tradition in the service of identity formation.[27]

That Koreans turned to tradition in their identity formation, however, should not prevent us from appreciating the equally important influence of the larger context of imperial political culture. As a number of scholars have pointed out, nationalists often include alien influences in their articulation of national identity even as they profess the national purity of their own sources. Greenfeld, for instance, points out that Germans could not but borrow the idea of the nation from France in their formulation of collectivist nationalism in response to the individualist French rationalism.[28] Partha Chatterjee goes further by indicating the inherent contradiction faced by nationalists in accepting the logic and languages of the colonizers that they try to repudiate.[29] A number of chapters in the volume grapple differently with this issue by analyzing Korea's integration into the Japanese imperial system and its effects: technology transfer (Chapter 6, by Daqing Yang), the regional market (Chapter 5, by Soon Won Park), the culture industry (Chapter 2, by Michael Robinson), and regional colonial policy (Chapter 4, by Michael Schneider). Em's analysis of Sin Ch'aeho's nationalist oeuvre and Sorensen's discussion of the appropriation of peasantness as a source of Korean identity reveal how the metropolitan culture influenced the thinking of Korean intellectuals in their construction and reconstruction of new conceptions of nation, class, and gender. However, this should not be interpreted as suggesting that a mere "colonization of consciousness" occurred; instead, we must examine the complex ways in which indigenous and alien sources were intertwined to produce a historically distinctive form of identity. The chapters in this volume attempt to focus on such interactive processes in the formation of national, class, and gender identities.

## What Is Ahead

This volume is the outcome of a collective effort to move beyond the current nationalist master narratives operative in both North and South Korea by focusing on the complex relations among colonialism, modernity, nationalism, and identity formation. Its primary goal is to stimulate the process of recognizing more inclusive, pluralist approaches to the historical record of twentieth-century Korea and deepen the insights of Korean and Western historians working on this period. Such an approach can counter both binary conceptions and essentialist readings of colonialism, modernity, and nationalism as they have been applied to Korea's recent experience. It will also encourage our understanding of the constructed and contingent characteristics of these important concepts. Moreover, the recovery of silenced voices and subjects of history held hostage by master nationalist narratives will provide the material for the construction of a more complex and nuanced picture of colonial society. We hope that this volume will be a step in a constructive direction and facilitate a richer and freer public discourse on many of the controversial issues imbedded in the memory of colonialism that have occupied the minds of Korean intellectuals into the postwar era.

The volume is divided into two parts. The first deals with the formation of colonial modernity in areas ranging from the legal system to the mass media to industrialization and their linkage to cultural hegemony in Korea. The authors avoid the value-laden use of modernity as historical progress by focusing on its ambiguous qualities in the context of colonial domination. They also explicitly place their discussion in a larger geographic context, whether it be imperial political culture, technology transfer, or the regional market. As a whole, the chapters in this part aspire to show how various aspects of modernity emerged in the colonial context and how they were mobilized by Japanese for colonial domination in Korea, with often unexpected results.

The second part examines the impact of colonial modernity on the formation of various forms of identity from nation to gender to class. The authors do not assume these categories of collective identity as "natural" but focus on how aspects of colonial modernity facilitated the process of their formation through negotiation, contestation, and redefinition. In doing so, they also refuse to subsume this diverse array of collective identities under the name "nation"; rather, they focus on the tensions and contradictions in the process of coming to terms with multiple identities in the colonial context. In addition, some of the authors in this part have chosen to examine closely the ways in which indigenous resources were selected and mobilized in constructing these modern forms of collective identity. Collectively, the twelve chapters in this volume seek to show the complexity and diversity of colonial modernity, hegemony, and identity formation so as to capture the rich history of Korea's cultural, social, and political evolution in the twentieth century.

# PART I

*Colonial Modernity and Hegemony*

ONE

# Modernity, Legality, and Power in Korea Under Japanese Rule

Chulwoo Lee

Discussing the question of whether Japanese rule contributed to the modernization of Korea is like stepping into a minefield. The pompous claims of Japanese colonialists that they were modernizing Korean society and the use of those claims to justify colonial rule are vivid memories for Koreans, as is the support many contemporary Westerners gave Japanese imperialism for bringing the blessings of modernity to Asia. Moreover, under the sway of modernization theory, postwar Western scholars have tended to credit Japanese rule for the material and institutional changes that occurred during the colonial period. Japanese apologists also defend their nation's record by arguing that Japanese rule paved the way for modernization in the colonies. In this discussion, the concepts of modernity and modernization have become not so much tools for describing certain societal phenomena as subjects in a symbolic struggle. For both critics of and apologists for Japanese rule, modernization is a good thing, and any admission that modernization took place under Japanese rule is an acknowledgment that Japanese rule was beneficial to Korea.

Should, however, the question of modernization continue to possess such heavy political implications? We are now freer than ever before to reappraise the value traditionally attached to modernity and modernization. Modernization theory has been discredited over the past two decades, and the meaning of modernity is being relativized. If we do not condemn modernity for all the disastrous consequences brought about by the untrammeled sway of instrumental rationality, at least we employ greater reflection in examining the achievements of modernity and the discursive creation of the modern world.

Further, we are becoming increasingly skeptical about the assumed unity of the diverse phenomena subsumed under the rubric "modernity" — industrialization and capitalist development; the systematization of law and rationalization in thought; popular sovereignty, liberal legality, and democracy; and so forth. Yet these features do not necessarily form a package, nor can any one of them be essentialized, given primacy over the others, and empowered to explain the rest. The persisting diversity of political and cultural forms despite the global ascendancy of capitalism raises doubts that modernity has a fixed shape.

This rethinking of modernity enables us to move away from the excessively value-laden and essentialistic use of the terms *modernity* and *modernization* that has characterized Korean historiography. Until now, nationalist historians have overlooked the significant changes that took place during the colonial period in favor of stressing the "premodern" character of Japanese rule. They presuppose an archetype of modernity, constructed on the basis of the Western experience and equated with the combination of a capitalist economy and bourgeois democracy. They then judge the colonial experience not on its own terms but against this archetype of modernity. The transformation that took place under Japanese rule has been cast as a reproduction of the premodern because both capitalist development and bourgeois democratization were hindered or described as a "colonial modernization," a deviation from "normal" development because bourgeois democracy was not achieved despite capitalist transformation.[1]

In contrast to a conception of modernity as a fixed, unified whole or as a total, universal process, I suggest that we posit a multiplicity of kinds and fields of modernity[2] and attempt to discern features of modernization in particular fields of practice, rather than trying to define the nature of a society as a whole on the basis of one or two criteria. In this study, I focus on the features of modernization that relate to the power and domination the Korean populace found itself subjected to under the colonial legal-governmental system.

The preoccupation of Korean legal historians with the "premodern" or "distorted" character of the legal-governmental process under Japanese rule has resulted in a disregard of the important changes in the nature of power and mode of domination that accompanied colonial legal-governmental change. Japanese rule has been described as "brutal" and "arbitrary," but little effort has been made to discern the logic of power and domination underlying that governmental practice. If Japanese rule was repressive, we must ask what kind of repression there was, specify its characteristics, and identify its differences from the repression experienced by precolonial Koreans. Instead of implying a deviation from modernity by stressing the nonexistence of democratic control of power under Japanese rule, this study shows that modernization took place in the sense that the legal-governmental system was organized and implemented in such a way that the state was able to extend its power and control to minute details of life untouched by the traditional Korean state. Such intensification of control may be a common feature of modern states, whose preoccupation with internal pacification has led to the extensive reach of administrative power coupled with enhanced knowledge of the population,[3] but the particularities of Japanese colonial practice led to unique features in Korea. Again, the intent is not to highlight the anomalous nature of the Japanese governmental style vis-à-vis a presupposed archetype of modernity. Rather, by bringing together a description of the distinctive features of Japanese colonial rule and an interpretation of the ethos of Japanese colonialism, this study seeks to identify the characteristics of Japanese rule in its particular politico-social and discursive contexts.

## Devising a Colonial Legal System

Japanese control over Korea's legal and judicial affairs began when Korea became a Japanese protectorate in 1905. The Japanese had secured extraterritorial rights through the Treaty of Kanghwa in 1876 and had exercised influence in Korea's Reform of 1894–95. However, up to 1905 Japanese intervention had been neither unbroken nor cumulative. From 1896 through 1905, while enjoying a relative independence from Japan, Korea made a number of autonomous attempts to reorganize itself. In 1899 a nine-article constitution called the *Taehan'guk kukche* was promulgated, and in 1905 a 680-article criminal code called the *Hyŏngpŏp taejŏn* came into force. Although these laws did not reflect such ideas as popular sovereignty, they marked a change in the way of codifying rules. Further, the government took a series of measures to clarify landownership and increase land-tax revenue. Yet some programs of the Kwangmu Reform, as these steps are known, including the land survey (*yangjŏn*) and the issuance of title deeds (*chigye*), remained unfinished, and others were discontinued or put to selective use as Japan secured its grip on Korea's internal affairs.

During the Russo-Japanese War of 1904–5, Japan forced Korea into an agreement that provided for Japanese financial and foreign-affairs advisors within the Korean government. Although not stipulated in the agreement, Japanese advisors were also placed in other important government departments. This "rule by advisors" was strengthened under the residency-general system created by the Treaty of 1905 and continued until the Treaty of 1907, which formalized the resident-general's control over Korea's internal administration.

Under the treaties, Japanese judges and procurators were appointed to major courts as "legal-affairs advisors." This was followed by the Court Organization Law of 1907, which implemented an article in the Treaty of 1907 stipulating that judicial affairs be distinguished from general administrative affairs. The idea of functional differentiation between the judicial and executive powers had been outlined in the Court Organization Law of 1895, issued during the Reform of 1894–95, but the idea had not been fully realized. By 1898 only two courts—the Court of Seoul and the Court of Kyŏng-gi—had been separated from the executive; the High Court (Kodŭng chaep'anso) remained under the direction of the justice minister, an administrative bureaucrat, who sat on the court as chief justice, and local courts (*chibang chaep'anso*) were part of provincial administrative offices. And in 1898 even the Courts of Seoul and Kyŏnggi were abolished as independent tribunals. With the amendment of the Court Organization Law in 1899, the name of the High Court was changed to the Court of Cassation (P'yŏngniwon), but it remained under the control of the justice minister. And local courts continued to be part of the territorial administrative bodies. Therefore, with the new Court Organization Law of 1907, the Japanese declared their intent to accelerate differentiation between the judicial and administrative powers. This law introduced a trilevel judicial system modeled on that of Japan, with the Supreme Court (Taesimwŏn) at the top and local and ward (*ku*) courts at the bottom.

In 1909 the Japanese forced the Korean government to sign the Korea-Japan Memorandum on the Delegation of the Administration of Courts and Prisons. Korea lost all judicial autonomy, which had already existed only in name. The Korean courts became the Courts of the Residency-General and heard cases that previously were under extraterritorial jurisdiction. Yet, apart from changing the name of the Supreme Court to the High Court (Kōdō hōin), the Japanese by and large left the structure of the court system alone until 1912, when the courts of first instance were reorganized into district courts (*chihō hōin*) and their branches.[4]

The establishment of new courts went hand in hand with a new legislative initiative. The Residency-General set out to design rules of private law to be applied to Korea. Perhaps the most noteworthy during the protectorate period were the Land and Building Certification Regulations (T'oji kaok chŭngmyŏng kyuch'ik) of 1906, which were designed to promote the commodification of land by enabling those who obtained certifications of their real property transactions to enforce the agreements directly. Like their Western counterparts, Japanese colonial policymakers regarded the form of landownership as the most crucial indicator of where a society stood on the scale of evolutionary development and insisted on the urgent need to introduce a system of private law that would guarantee and clarify private interests if Korea was to achieve any progress.[5] With a view to drafting a civil law code, the Residency-General began to collect information on Korea's civil customs.

The government-sponsored research on customs began in 1906. In the area of private law, the researchers collected information on 180 civil-law issues and 48 commercial-law issues, selected in accordance with the concepts and structures of the Japanese civil and commercial codes. The result of the investigation was published after annexation under the title *Customs Survey Report* (*Kanshū chōsa hōkokusho*).

Underlying the customs survey was a question that the Japanese decision makers confronted in almost every administration issue throughout the colonial period: namely, how much semblance there was between Korea and Japan, which was crucial in determining the balance of assimilation and discrimination in colonial policy. Japanese colonialists had believed that Koreans had only a vague notion of private rights. The findings of the researchers, however, did not confirm this belief. Korea was found to have customs that conformed with the juridical categories for which the Japanese civil code provided.[6] This had significant bearing on the question of how much uniformity in civil law there should be between Korea and Japan. Ume Kenjirō, the civil-law expert in charge of the research, envisioned a single code of civil and commercial law separate from the Japanese civil and commercial codes. The idea was supported by Resident-General Itō Hirobumi. Opponents of this idea argued that lack of uniformity in civil law between Korea and Japan would cause trouble for investors. In the end, the idea of drafting a separate code lost momentum with Itō's death in 1909 and disappeared with Ume's death in 1910. Ironically, Ume's research was invoked by radical assimilationists in arguing against Koreans having rules different from those in the Japanese civil code.[7]

With annexation, all ideas of separate codification were abandoned; an imperial edict issued on the day of the annexation laid down a structure for the system of rules by which Korea was to be governed. This edict was replaced the following year by a Diet act entitled the Law Concerning Laws and Regulations to Be Enforced in Korea, better known as Law 30. This arrangement gave the governor-general the power to issue ordinances (*seirei*) having the same effect as Diet acts. Under this power, in 1912 the governor-general issued the Ordinance on Civil Matters in Korea (*Chōsen minjirei*) and Ordinance on Penal Matters in Korea (*Chōsen keijirei*), which introduced major Japanese codes, such as the Civil Code, Code of Civil Procedure, Commercial Code, Criminal Code, and the Code of Criminal Procedure.

Although Japanese codes were imposed on Koreans, the Ordinance on Civil Matters, not the Civil Code, was the official civil law, and the Ordinance on Penal Matters, not the Criminal Code, was the official criminal law for Korea. The Civil Code and Criminal Code were in effect only because the governor-general introduced them by way of ordinances.[8] The ordinances contained substantive and procedural rules that prevailed over the rules in the codes. Therefore, although the idea of separate codes was abandoned, full assimilation did not take place. Indeed, many laws continued from the past. Laws made during the protectorate period for controlling speech and political activity, such as the Security Law, the Publication Law, and the Newspaper Law, continued to be in force until the end of Japanese rule. The last criminal code of the Yi dynasty, the *Hyŏngpŏp taejŏn*, amended in 1908 to eliminate 270 provisions, lost effect as the

Criminal Code was introduced, except with regard to cases of homicide and armed robbery, to which the *Hyŏngpŏp taejŏn* applied because it provided for heavier penalties. As for civil law, the Ordinance on Civil Matters in Korea left room for Korean customs to apply to a wide range of practices. Between Koreans, customs were given priority over statutory rules that did not concern public policy (*ordre public*), and the Civil Code's rules on capacity, kinship, and succession did not apply to Koreans. Further, whereas the Civil Code stipulated that property rights could be created and enjoyed only in accordance with statutory rules, the Ordinance on Civil Matters in Korea recognized customary property rights.

This policy met with criticism from Japanese jurists. Critics argued that the Ordinance on Civil Matters in Korea left too much room for Korean customs to survive, that it gave the Korean legal system excessive independence, and that it caused confusion in economic transactions.[9] In fact, the judiciary took every precaution not to recognize Korean customs too generously. And, as the colonial administration stepped up its efforts for assimilation, particularly during the 1930s under the slogan of *naisen ittai* (Japan and Korea as a single body), the Ordinance on Civil Matters was amended a number of times. These changes introduced Japanese practices into even the most indigenous field of social life, the most striking example being the 1939 amendment regarding the adoption of Japanese name patterns. Nevertheless, at least in theory, Korea had a separate legal system and Japanese laws did not simply "extend" to Korea, as might be suggested by the principle of *naichi enchō*, a logical corollary of the policy of assimilation. Korea differed from Taiwan in this respect.

## Civilization, Assimilation, and Discrimination

When Japan acquired Taiwan in 1895, Japanese colonialists noted the cultural proximity between Japan and Taiwan and instituted an assimilation policy. Hara Kei (Takashi), who played an important part in drafting the Taiwan policy and later became premier, argued that Taiwan formed part of Japanese territory in the same way that Shikoku or Kyūshū did, and compared the Japanese occupation of Taiwan to the German occupation of Alsace-Lorraine.[10] The Japanese justified the annexation of Korea on the same grounds and made assimilation their governing principle.

Yet alongside this emphasis on cultural proximity lay a belief in the racial superiority of the Japanese. It was believed that although akin to the Japanese the Koreans and Taiwanese had a different "level of civilization," "degree of culture," or *mindō* (standards of popular consciousness), which accounted for the different places the three peoples occupied in the international hierarchy and justified a different treatment of the colonial populations within the Japanese imperial order. This mixture of semblance and difference in the Japanese vision of Koreans and Taiwanese rationalized a colonial rule in which assimilation and discrimination were mixed in ways that served Japan's interests in particular contexts.[11] Yet there was no uniform way of inferring semblance and difference and linking expectation, interpretation, and practice. Japanese jurist Asami Rintarō, for example, found his expectations betrayed when the customs survey of 1906–10 found that Korean legal customs did not differ that greatly from the institutions of Japanese civil law, but at the same time he was happy because this testified to the feasibility of assimilation.[12] On the other hand, although the customs survey recognized private landownership in traditional Korea, studies after the Cadastral Survey of 1912–18 tended to deny that private landownership had existed; these claims served to highlight the progressive character of the Cadastral Survey.[13] Moreover, there were various permutations in linking interpretation and policy. Those who saw only a small difference in the level of civilization between Japan and Korea were more likely to support assimilation, as is seen in the arguments of Hara Kei, but some called for a radical assimilation because the Korean national character was so inferior to that of the Japanese. By contrast, such critics of assimilationism as Yanaihara Tadao contended that assimilation was neither possible nor desirable because Koreans were highly civilized.[14]

Besides, although Japan's Taiwan policy had much in common with its Korea policy, the two colonies were not treated in exactly the same way, and the differences displayed the gap between the ideal and reality, theory and practice, in implementing assimilation. Shortly after the annexation, Nitobe Inazō, who pioneered Japanese academic studies of colonial policy, predicted that it would be easier to implement assimilation in Korea than in Taiwan because racially the Koreans were more akin to the Japanese than were the Taiwanese.[15] What happened was, however, quite the opposite; the principle of *naichi enchō*, and therefore the policy of assimilation, was more strictly enforced in Taiwan than in Korea. Although Taiwan had a law similar to Law 30 in Korea, known as Law 63, the power of its governor-general to issue executive ordinances was more restricted than that of the governor-general of Korea. After 1921, the governor-general of Taiwan could exercise legislative power only when no Japanese statute was appropriate or the enforcement of a Japanese statute was difficult "in the light of the prevailing conditions of Taiwan." On the other hand, apparently because of the strategic importance of Korea, the governor-general of Korea was free of such restrictions and had greater discretion in issuing ordinances. Therefore, the governor-general of Korea issued the Ordinance on Civil Matters as the civil law for Korea, whereas the Civil Code was simply extended to Taiwan.[16] Nitobe's expectation was betrayed further as Koreans in general showed little interest in ameliorating their condition by assimilating themselves to the Japanese, whereas many Taiwanese drew on the notion of assimilation in struggling to improve their situation within the colonial order.[17]

In the face of unrest in Taiwan, the Imperial Diet decided to give the governor-general of Taiwan the power to issue ordinances having the same effect as Diet acts. Yet, the bill incorporating this provision, Law 63, brought with it a serious constitutional question: whether the Japanese constitution applied to Taiwan. The Japanese government and the colonial administration explained that the law-making device in question was constitutional since it was a form of "delegated legislation." But many contemporary jurists disagreed, because Law 63 gave the governor the general power of legislation rather than mandating him to issue an executive ordinance on a specific issue. Law 63 was therefore unconstitutional, they argued.[18] Law 30 for Korea involved the same problem. Yet in Korea, unlike in Taiwan, no attempt was made to curb the sweeping legislative power of the colonial executive.

A similar constitutional question arose when the Japanese had to explain why colonial inhabitants were denied the political right to elect representatives to a legislature. The idea of establishing a colonial legislative council independent of the Imperial Diet was less consistent with the policy of assimilation than was allowing colonial inhabitants to elect representatives to the Diet. Many Japanese feared that independent assemblies might lead to loss of control over the colonies. Therefore, Japanese policymakers rarely supported this idea. Neither was the second formula without risk. Matsuoka

Shutarō, a public-law expert, estimated that if universal male suffrage were introduced to Korea, 150 representatives from Korea would have seats in the House of Representatives of the Imperial Diet alongside 460 from Japan. The Japanese were not prepared to cope with such a consequence, he said.[19]

The issues of the lawmaking power of the governors-general and political representation for the colonial peoples plunged Japanese constitutional interpretation into disarray. The Meiji Constitution had been drafted before Japan became a colonial power and therefore made no mention of colonial rule. Accordingly, the question whether the constitution applied to the colonies had to be settled by interpretation, and there were conflicting interpretations. The Japanese government took the stance that the constitution applied to Taiwan. As for Korea, the Imperial Diet acknowledged that the constitution applied.[20] The official explanation for the fact that the colonial subjects were not represented politically was that the necessary legal arrangements for actually bringing colonial voters to the ballot box had yet to be made and that such an arrangement would be made when the requisite conditions had been met.[21]

The opinions of legal scholars regarding the reach of the constitution varied. Hozumi Yatsuka, who represented the strongest nationalistic view among Japanese jurists, argued that the constitution applied to the colonies because those territories had come under the authority of the emperor. He was not, however, saying that the same rights had to be granted to the colonial subjects. He pointed to a number of constitutional provisions, including that on martial law and the emergency prerogative, as good devices for limiting the rights of the colonial subjects. He criticized the debate on the constitutionality of Law 63 and all the arguments concerning "delegated legislation" as a waste of time and even harmful because those discussions were informed by the idea of parliamentary supremacy, which he said was at odds with imperial sovereignty. On the other hand, Minōbe Tatsukichi, who represented the so-called constitutionalist school, argued that the constitution had been drafted with only metropolitan Japan in mind. Since conditions in the colonies differed markedly from those to which the constitution was attuned, he said, the constitution did not apply to those territories; it would apply only when the colonies had been assimilated to a degree that would make application feasible. Later, Minōbe modified this argument in a minor way. He acknowledged that the provisions enunciating the basic principles of government, such as imperial sovereignty and the functions of the Imperial Diet, applied to the colonies "by their own nature." The provisions on the rights of the citizen, on the other hand, did not apply by their own nature, because those rights presupposed "a substantial development of culture" and "loyalty to the state." He added that the will of the state would determine whether to apply the constitution to the colonies and that when the state so decided, it could simply implement relevant statutory arrangements without amending the constitution.[22]

## A Different Kind of Body

When explaining Japan's colonial policy to a Western audience, Nitobe Inazō referred to a "free society" and a "firm government" as two primary tenets of Japanese colonial rule. He declared on another occasion that the Japanese had become the "torch-bearers" of "the English idea of liberty" on the Asiatic continent.[23] In the event, however, the colonial rulers never offered "the English idea of liberty" to the colonial subjects. By contrast, they were not so reluctant to extend "firm government."

The colonial government attributed what it saw as the negative features of Korean society to a lack of order and discipline and declared that it was its mission to establish order and implement discipline. Essential to "firm government" was systematic law enforcement. Nitobe insisted that although "people unaccustomed to the protection of law feel as though it were despotism," the Japanese had to "teach in Korea as well as in Formosa what government and what laws are."[24]

The law thus imposed, however, lacked liberal legality, as "firm government" pushed aside "free society." Although the Japanese colonialists emphasized judicial independence as a feature that distinguished civilization from barbarism and a prerequisite without which "the evils and abuses" of Korea's old system "could not be fully removed," they implemented it in Korea to only a limited extent. The judiciary was a branch of the Government-General and was under the supervision of the governor-general, which was amenable to no legal restriction. Furthermore, an ordinance issued by the governor-general empowered local police and gendarmerie chiefs to deliver summary judgments on a wide range of minor offenses and punish the offenders without a court trial. The colonial government explained that because Koreans had little conception of legal rights, they hardly appreciated the difference between standing trial in court and being arraigned before an ordinary administrative officer.[25]

The Japanese were not exceptional in giving prominence to law in maintaining order and simultaneously withholding liberal legality. Their language and practice closely resembled those of many European colonialists, who, informed by the philosophy of the Enlightenment, identified "law with civilization and the absence or attenuation of law with untamed nature." For both European and Japanese colonialists, one mission of colonialism was to tame the "untamed nature" of primitive peoples by means of law. At the same time, the colonized were portrayed as being an opposite other to the colonizers and as occupying "a different position in the scale of civilization or in evolutionary development." Therefore, they warranted different treatment. The universalistic claims of liberal legality were withdrawn and various forms of direct and physical coercion endorsed as customary practices were invited to fill that vacuum.[26] In the case of Korea, nothing stands as a better example of this than the Flogging Ordinance.

The colonial government in Korea took pride in its elaborate prison system, but at the same time it preserved corporal punishment and substituted it for incarceration on a wide range of occasions. The Flogging Ordinance, issued in 1912, provided that flogging could replace imprisonment for up to three months or fines of ¥100 or less. In addition, if an offender failed to pay a fine within five days, the procurator or police chief in charge of the case could substitute flogging for the fine.

Flogging had been practiced previously in Japan as well as Korea, but it had been abolished in Japan in 1882. In Korea, the *Hyŏngpŏp taejŏn* specified flogging for many offenses. The Flogging Ordinance was issued in order to preserve flogging for many of the crimes to which the *Hyŏngpŏp taejŏn* ceased to apply in 1912. As justification, the colonial government said that flogging had been practiced in Korea "for ages past."[27]

Flogging was not, however, a mere remnant of the past with a marginal place in the new penal system. It soon became the central method of punishment. In 1911 only 21 percent of all convicted persons were flogged. By 1916 the ratio of offenders flogged had increased to 47 percent (compared with 43 percent imprisoned). Moreover, those who were flogged on the basis of court sentences formed only a small minority of all flogged. The majority were flogged upon summary judgments; out of 52,546 cases of flogging in 1916, 36,960 (70 percent) were the result of summary justice.[28] My analysis of the 1919 Criminal Cases Register of the Kwangju District Court shows that 684 persons out of the 1,359 prosecuted that year, that is, 50 percent, were flogged. Those flogged for theft numbered 228; another 185 were flogged for gambling. Other crimes that led to flogging included fraud, embezzlement, assault, causing injury to others, buying and selling pilfered goods, and violations of "administrative rules" such as the Forest Ordinance, the Liquor Tax Ordinance, and the ordinances regulating firearms, the slaughtering of livestock, and gravesites.

The Government-General justified flogging on the grounds that it was suitable for a people with a low *mindō*. As mentioned above, the Japanese believed that the cultural capacities of every people could be graded and that treatment had to correspond to the grade thus accorded. Colonial administrators argued that their subjects were so helplessly "unenlightened" that they were not motivated by the same considerations as the "enlightened" Japanese. To keep them in line, therefore, different inducements were needed. Flogging was regarded as a far more effective way of motivating colonial subjects than incarceration. The Government-General of Korea modeled its flogging law on the Taiwanese experience and explained that flogging had been adopted in Taiwan because a large number of people there "lacked any sense of shame and capacity for reasonable thinking" and because "particularly those with low living standards would not feel any pain from imprisonment."[29] In other words, for people whose *mindō* was not high enough for them to "regard injury to the mind and honor as a greater shame than physical suffering,"[30] punishment had to be geared toward inflicting direct physical pain rather than acting "in depth on the heart, the thoughts, the will, the inclinations."[31]

Yet it was not some sublime virtue that colonial rulers in Taiwan and Korea regarded their subjects as lacking; what mattered above all was the inability of the colonial subjects to adjust themselves to the mundane rhythms of a new kind of economy. The generalization of incarceration as the dominant mode of punishment requires a sense of time as a form of measurable economic value. Incarceration gives no pain to those whose lives do not follow the cadence of the clock. Therefore, a certain degree of time discipline is a prerequisite for incarceration to be a workable method of punishment. Japanese colonialists depicted the Koreans as lacking such discipline.[32] In a society that did not know how to "economize the time of life, to accumulate it in a useful form and to exercise power over men through the mediation of time," punishment could not be transformed from "an art of unbearable sensations" to "an economy of suspended rights." The bodies of the colonial subjects were untamed and undisciplined; they were not "subjected and practiced bodies," or what Foucault calls "docile bodies."[33] They were part of nature, which had to be acted on directly. Hence the punishment-body relationship in such a society had to differ from that in enlightened penal systems.[34]

The colonial authorities argued that this deficiency in economic rationality was the greatest obstacle to a universal application of carceral punishment. Because of many colonial subjects' "low standards of living," that "enlightened" method of punishment was unable to achieve what it was supposed to achieve. Accordingly, "economic development" was stressed as a precondition for changing the flogging law.[35] The assumption behind this became clear when the Government-General of Korea ascribed the less frequent resort to flogging in Taiwan compared with Korea to the "unbridled spirit of money-worship" among the Taiwanese, which had made it possible to replace imprisonment with fines.[36]

It was not only the behavior of colonial subjects that the authorities explained in economic terms. They also explained their policy in the same way. The Government-General of Korea openly encouraged the commutation of imprisonment to flogging because flogging cost 40 percent less.[37]

The benefits of flogging, however, did not outweigh the political damage incurred by maintaining this "barbaric" method of punishment in the face of criticism from both the Korean public and sympathetic Westerners. In the end, the March First movement in 1919 forced the Japanese to reconsider some of their most repressive policies and repeal the Flogging Ordinance in 1920. The official explanation was that the abolition of flogging was made possible by the "remarkable awakening and progress of the Korean people."[38]

## A Modernization of Power

The implementation of a new legal system, Korea's place within the Japanese constitutional order, the discriminatory treatment of colonial subjects, and the exclusion of liberal legality are familiar subjects in the historiography of Korea's colonial legal system. My account may not appear different from conventional accounts, which hold that although modernization may have taken place in form, in the sense that law and justice were systematized, no modernization occurred in content, since power was exercised in a "brutal" way and the people did not enjoy democratic protections. However, I suggest that we sensitize our inquiry to changes in the modality of domination behind the facade of this so-called distorted modernization. Conventional historiography underlines the continuation of premodernity in the exercise of power *in spite of* modernization in the legal form, but it does not take issue with the modernization of the legal form itself. Consequently, it loses critical sight of the systematization of law. As we will see, the systematization of law and justice entailed a greater reach of power and subjected the population to more meticulous and tighter control. Simultaneously, conventional historiography overlooks the change in the nature of power behind the veneer of premodern methods of repression.

One might, for example, take flogging as an illustration of a premodern mode of repression. Yet the Flogging Ordinance introduced some novel practices. Although flogging in precolonial times had not been without strict rules, the Flogging Ordinance laid down more detailed rules regarding the way in which flogging was to be executed. A physician was required to attend to check the health of the flogged. Although flogging in precolonial times had not necessarily been practiced in full public view, the ordinance stressed that punishment had to be executed in a closed cell in the presence of a strictly limited number of officials. The government said it had adopted this "reformed" rule so as not to damage the flogged's sense of honor, which contradicted its claim that flogging was suitable for those who "lacked any sense of shame" and "had no honor to lose."[39] Despite this logical flaw, the paternalistic language of justification, the sheer violence, which often led to severe injury and even death, and the discriminatory treatment of colonial subjects, the new flogging rules reflected a new approach to the body. The new flogging practice, which exposed the body of the offender to physical violence, ironically implied an idea in which the human body was made an object of attention and professional concern. The involvement of medical personnel in the practice of punishment is a good example of this. To be sure, this is not to assert that Japanese rule was humane and Koreans benefited from a reduction of brutality in punishment. What is important is the introduction of an idea and ritual that implied a shift in the notion of power involved in punishment.

This was one instance of a series of changes through which new disciplinary techniques and mechanisms were deployed across the society. Recent studies by Korean sociologists, in a book entitled *The Modern Subject and Colonial Disciplinary Power*, show how Koreans were placed under newly introduced disciplinary arrangements and were transformed into "docile bodies." The expansion of a mass schooling system, factory production, a health service, and the control and segregation of particular groups created and categorized as "social others," such as vagabonds and lepers, internalized in individual bodies discipline and a notion of normal behavior.[40] With these changes a growing number of Koreans found themselves placed under systematic behavioral control, close surveillance, direction informed by professional knowledge, and complex arrangements of observation and registration.

For Foucault, the disciplinization of a society is not a project deliberately orchestrated by the state but the unfolding across the society of authorless programs through which social behavior is normalized without the presence of a unidirectional command. Yet what we are concerned with here relates to the changes in the state's governmental practice, which includes its appropriation of disciplinary techniques. The aspect of transformation we will look at here relates to the advent and refinement of disciplinary power as "a subtype of administrative power" in the state's initiative for internal pacification,[41] in which disciplinary power is enmeshed with coercive forms of state power and direct sanctions.

One characteristic of Japanese rule in this connection was the extension of state power to encompass very minute details of social life. The police were the main instrument for this task. The violence of armed gendarmes under the *budan seiji* (Military Rule) of 1910–19 constitutes only part of the picture of the colonial police. During the *bunka seiji* (Cultural Rule) era of the 1920s, the police expanded in size and government spending on police more than tripled. By 1925, 250 police stations had been established in the 233 counties and municipalities, and patrol stations installed in 2,339 out of the 2,504 districts (*myŏn*). This resulted in a ratio of over nine policemen for every 10,000 people, a figure greater than that for many regions of Japan and almost as high as the ratio in England. New police personnel numbered 18,500, whereas a total of only 4,000 men had been engaged in regular policing immediately after the Reforms of 1894–95.[42]

Lengthy detention, physical abuse, and torture in police stations are the images that postcolonial Koreans harbor about the colonial police. However, equally important was the intensification of control through heavy police involvement in people's daily lives. The police were in charge of a multiplicity of programs and campaigns against indigenous lifestyles. They conducted surveys, supervised public hygiene, directed residents in road building and repair, gave instructions on farming, exhorted people to take side-jobs and to save money, acted as conciliators in private disputes, enforced court judgments, organized meetings for ideological propaganda, and so on. Indeed, the term *police* in the *Polizeiwissenschaft* of early modern Europe, which may have informed Japanese thinking about police, encompassed a large variety of responsibilities.[43] Yet, whereas "police" in that notion denotes an art of government in general and is not confined to a particular type of organization, under Japanese rule many of the administrative tasks enveloped in this broad notion of police were assigned to the organization of uniformed men. Whether or not inspired by the broad, original idea of police power of early modern Europe, which minimizes "the distinction between government by law and government by decree,"[44] colonial law gave the police only a vague mandate to act on the populace. In 1912 the Government-General issued Rules on the Punishment of Police Offenses (*Keisatsuhan shōbatsu kisoku*), which gave the police virtually unlimited power to regulate people's behavior: "Any person shall be detained or fined if he or she . . . violates an instruction or order of the police authorities."

The dense presence and extensive functioning of the police were symptoms of the "excessive attention" that Hyman Kublin underlines as a unique characteristic of Japanese colonial rule.[45] This attention entailed a refined system of collecting and storing information and was based on the idea that the state could and ought to engineer society in ways to guarantee order and achieve material progress, the two greatest gifts of civilization that the Japanese claimed they were bringing to the colonial population. To be sure, any government stores information for administrative purposes, and this function was by no means a novelty for Koreans, who had long had a highly organized bureaucratic government and a literate tradition. But the breadth and accuracy of information collected by the precolonial Korean state were no match for those achieved by the colonial state.

The Chosŏn state collected and filed information on land and people, primarily for the purpose of taxation, by carrying out surveys and compiling registers. But the surveys were frequently skipped. Further, the registers reflected only the information at the time of the survey and failed to track change. By contrast, the land register after the Cadastral Survey of 1912–18 and the household register under Japanese rule were permanent records and were continually updated to reflect diachronic changes. It became mandatory for each household to report any change in the family—deaths, births, marriages, and so forth. People were induced to record changes in their land rights, as the land records were sufficiently refined to function as proof of property rights as well as tax references, whereas the evidential function of the traditional land register was more or less a byproduct of its main use as a tax reference and was limited because the state failed to undertake surveys as regularly as dictated by law. The institutionalization of such registers was a sign of the elaboration of the judicial function of the state. The state now claimed to be the supreme overseer of a transactional society.

The logic behind censuses also reflects a significant change in the notion of government. The purpose of the colonial censuses was to collect general information on the population and was not limited to taxation. In fact, the Japanese term for population censuses was "surveys of national strength" (kokusei chōsa), which implies the constitution of the population as the ultimate target of government and a conception that demography, territory, and material resources are to be observed, accounted for, and acted on as a totality, the phenomenon that Foucault terms "governmentality."[46] Underlying this notion is a concern with the general health of society, which competes with other societies on universal criteria. Under Japanese rule, each population census was followed by a statistical report on issues that had not been of so much interest in the past, including the landownership situation of the entire population, output in each economic sector, the spatial and occupational distribution of the population, religious beliefs, the incident of crime, the divorce rate, morbidity and mortality, labor and tenancy disputes, and educational levels, in addition to such traditional concerns of censuses as the size of the population and the total number of households, births, deaths, and marriages.

The statistical data published by the Government-General were still crude, narrow in scope, and not sufficiently detailed to give information on every locality. Nevertheless, the increasing use of statistics marked a novel phenomenon: the convergence of *savoir* and *pouvoir*, "knowability" and "governability."[47] It reflects the novel conception that a state's performance could be measured and assessed in figures. The state drew on statistical data to assert its legitimacy and to decide what it should do next. Government agencies and their staffs became concerned with statistical indexes, which were used to judge their performance and achievements. The interest of the state, government bureaus, and officials in good results added to pressure to "improve" current conditions. That pressure was transferred to the populace, bringing greater intrusion and closer observation.

Yet what Hyman Kublin means by "excessive attention" involved more than an intensification of supervision. It involved vigorous campaigns to expunge traditional ways of life in the name of civilization and, later, of imperialization (*kōminka*). Again, many of those campaigns reflected a new concern with the body and a preoccupation with producing "docile bodies" amenable to a tighter work ethic. The colonial administration resumed the campaign for short hair for males, which had been suspended after the collapse of the Chosŏn reform cabinet of 1895, and tried to enforce the wearing of colored clothing instead of Korea's traditional white dress on the grounds that topknots and white dress were unhygienic and obstructed hard work. The intensity of such campaigns culminated during the Rural Revitalization Campaign of the 1930s, one objective of which was to promote work discipline (see Chapter 3).

The campaign to regulate Korean burial practices reflected a similar preoccupation. Since the Japanese had no lineage tradition and did not place as great importance on gravesites as Koreans, they had few scruples about regulating the choice of burial grounds and forcing the people to sequester graves from daily sight.[48] In 1912 the

Government-General decreed the Rules on Gravesites, Crematoria, Burials, and Cremation. This law made it mandatory either to bury the dead in public cemeteries or to cremate, and allowed private gravesites only in "special" circumstances and by permission of the county police chief. According to the government, "Korea's archaic custom of unregulated burial has not only been harmful to moral order and hygiene but also been responsible for frequent outbreaks of civil dispute and the deterioration of land, which has had bad consequences for the productive potential of the people."[49] To avoid resistance, the government implemented the rule in one province after another rather than immediately enforcing it nationwide. And in 1919 it amended the rule to allow one gravesite for each family; extra sites had to be approved by the provincial governor.

If the control of gravesites was one attempt to sequester from daily life what the government regarded as sources of displeasure, the control of the slaughtering of livestock was another. Claiming to promote hygiene, the Government-General made it illegal to slaughter animals in any place other than slaughterhouses.[50] Indeed, the government's paranoia about cleanliness subjected every household to police inspection.[51] Instruction on hygiene was based on a plethora of sanitation rules, some of which were issued by the central government, others by provincial offices. But the most powerful instrument of control was the Rules on the Punishment of Police Offenses.

By controlling the slaughtering of livestock, the government suppressed an economic activity that had been undertaken at home and, consequently, contributed to the occupational differentiation of society. Nothing exemplified this better than the regulation of liquor and tobacco production, introduced a year before annexation. The Tobacco Tax Law and the Liquor Tax Law made it mandatory for tobacco cultivators and brewers to obtain a government license and imposed taxes on their produce. These controls were subsequently elaborated in the Tobacco Tax Ordinance (1914) and the Liquor Tax Ordinance (1916).

As for tobacco, cultivators had to meet a minimum field-size requirement if they wanted to market their produce, and cultivation for home consumption was limited in terms of maximum field size. In 1921, the Tobacco Monopoly Ordinance replaced control by taxation with a state monopoly, binding licensed commercial cultivators to grow tobacco in designated areas and in accordance with strict rules on method, and to sell their produce only to the government. Further, the 1927 amendment of the Tobacco Monopoly Ordinance prohibited cultivation for home consumption, forcing all smokers to purchase tobacco products only from the government. Brewing was controlled in a similar way—by licensing and imposing minimum and maximum quantities of production. The minimum-quantity requirement forced small breweries to shut down, and the maximum-quantity requirement severely restricted brewing for home consumption, which was prohibited altogether in 1934.

The enforcement of liquor and tobacco rules were harsh and thorough. Liquor offenses could be punished with fines of ¥2,000. Both the vendor and purchaser in a private transaction of tobacco products could incur a fine ranging from 50 to hundreds of yen. It is no exaggeration to say that dealing with liquor and tobacco offenders became the primary responsibility of local courts. My analysis of criminal records of the Sunch'ŏn Branch of the Kwangju District Court shows that 241 of the 675 prosecutions filed in that court in 1926 were related to the Liquor Tax Ordinance and 221 to the Tobacco Monopoly Ordinance; the comparable figures for 1931 are 472 and 1,370 out of 2,345; for 1936, 396 and 247 out of 1,262; and for 1941, 451 and 30 out of 1,160.[52]

The government's desire to control liquor and tobacco production and sales was stimulated by the increasing significance of these two commodities in the finances of the colonial state. The land tax, which had accounted for 65 percent of all tax revenues at the beginning of colonial rule, became less important, amounting to only 30 percent of revenues in the early 1920s and less than 20 percent in the mid-1930s. By contrast, liquor and tobacco taxes together increased from 5 percent of revenues at the time of annexation to 29 percent in 1920. After the state implemented the tobacco monopoly, liquor-tax revenues increased remarkably, alone accounting for almost 20 percent of all tax revenues.[53]

Yet of greater interest than the fiscal significance of liquor and tobacco controls is their instrumentality in the interjection of state power into the daily lives of people. They were media through which the state penetrated the routines of the rural population. The tobacco monopoly bureau, for example, set a production target for every cultivator after surveying his field, production capacity, and facilities. The authorities launched raids at the least suspicion that tobacco was being produced without a license or beyond the licensed limit.[54] Historians collecting oral histories often meet informants who recall that the authorities prepared raids against unauthorized brewing of liquor by studying household registers. These files gave the government information on birthdays, anniversaries, and dates for ancestral rites. Officials launched raids during or immediately after such ceremonies, when there was the best chance of discovering secretly brewed drink. People suspected commercial brewers, who benefited from the government's outlawing of home brewing, of cooperating with the authorities by informing them of violations. Interestingly, in his best-selling novel *T'aebaek sanmaek* (1989), Cho Chŏngnae portrays a commercial brewer as a symbol of greed and unpopularity and an example of the *nouveaux riches* who made fortunes by collaborating with colonial rulers.

## Domination over the Soul

When Japanese colonialists gave priority to the establishment of order as the supreme goal of their self-imposed mission of civilizing Asia, they entertained a notion of order that was opposite to lawlessness, disarray, and governmental malfunctioning. Their programs for promoting order were geared toward remolding the behavior of the colonial populace so that it was amenable to the new economic conditions and economy of governmental power. Their programs and techniques of domination may not display a great difference from those for internal pacification found in the histories of many modern states. Yet Japanese practices of colonial domination had many peculiarities that cannot be understood simply in terms of efforts to promote internal pacification. One of those was a striking preoccupation with spiritual integration. Conventional legal historiography has tended to focus on the idiosyncrasies of the thought control practiced by the colonial government without relating them to the ideological climate of metropolitan Japan. I suggest that the focus be widened, insofar as the colonial initiatives for spiritual integration were informed by the process of constructing Japanese national identity itself and the Japanese preoccupation with its enforcement across the empire.

In Japan, orthodox imperial ideology, which we call *tennōsei* (emperor system) ideology, was not fully structured in law from the beginning. Rather, it stood outside formal law and, indeed, was given the status of a supra-law standing above a formal legal order. Yet it claimed a place within formal law as the Japanese and colonial authorities stepped up their efforts to integrate the thought of imperial subjects to an ideological orthodoxy.

The first wave of political and ideological control in colonial Korea was marked by a series of laws modeled on Japan's Newspaper and Publication Law of 1887 and Public Peace Police Law of 1890. Korea's Newspaper Law of 1907, Newspaper Regulations of 1908, and Publication Law of 1909 instituted pre-publication censorship of articles that "defamed the imperial households of Korea and Japan," "jeopardized public peace," "disturbed morals," and so on. Newspaper publishers had to obtain a general permit before publishing and faced suspension for various reasons. This system of control continued after annexation and throughout the colonial period, and the Government-General refused to issue a permit to a single Korean newspaper during the first decade of colonial rule.[55] Another significant control device was the Security Law of 1907, which was designed to control acts of association and expression by punishing "politically disquieting speeches or acts." Compared with its model, Japan's Public Peace Police Law, the Security Law gave the government broader power to disband associations outright and prohibit meetings beforehand. It operated as a powerful instrument of repression after annexation and was applied to a large number of people prosecuted for involvement in the March First demonstrations. Shortly after March 1919, the governor-general issued an ordinance entitled Ordinance on the Punishment of Political Crimes, often called Ordinance 7, which provided for imprisonment of up to ten years for organized acts of "disturbing or attempting to disturb public peace and order under the purpose of undermining the government."

The Security Law, Ordinance 7, and all other control laws previously implemented, as well as the Meiji control laws on which they were modeled, did not contain a distinctive ideological point of reference. Accordingly, the court found that Korean nationalists who orchestrated the declaration of independence in March 1919 had "disrupted public peace" and "disturbed the constitutional order of the state" (*kokuken*), but made no mention of what constituted that peace and that order.[56] Some court decisions against organizers of local demonstrations condemned defendants for "ignorance of the changing trends of the times" as well as defiance of the "new administration" and disruption of "peace."[57] But the "trends of the times" could hardly be a focus for juridico-ideological instruction.

Yet the lack of a clear ideological point of reference in formal law did not mean that the Japanese neglected to define what their sociopolitical order was to be. A variety of ideological resources made up the order that the Meiji control laws were supposed to protect, but the Japanese derived its rationales in indoctrinating the population from a unique notion of national ideological orthodoxy. As is well known, the Imperial Rescript on Education, which laid down the highest guidelines for moral instruction, placed loyalty and filiality at the apex of values all imperial subjects were to uphold. These and others regarded as typical Japanese values were to constitute the Japanese national essence captured by the term *kokutai*.

The relationship between law and this declaration of national orthodoxy was subtle in two respects. First, the declaration of the orthodox national values was, for the Japanese, not an unfamiliar and overpowering injunction but a reiteration of what had been constantly inculcated in the form of either codified or tacit knowledge. As Carol Gluck points out, those values were readily intelligible to the Japanese as ideological symbols of national unity, and their overt declaration was nothing more than a reaffirmation of shared nation-mindedness. Hence, those orthodox values "scarcely seemed to require active belief; the avoidance of overt disbelief was for the most part sufficient."[58] In other words, external sanction by means of law was redundant. Second, Meiji leaders were concerned about an "over-reliance on law," as the speedy institutional transformation of the Japanese polity introduced an abundance of new laws. It was feared that the rising significance of the law in maintaining social order might generate a belief in the omnipotence of rule by law, let alone the rule of law. Leaders like Yamagata Aritomo stressed that "society must also be maintained with morals and customs."[59] The declaration of the Imperial Rescript on Education simultaneously with the promulgation of the Meiji Constitution expressed this anxiety and aimed to remind people of traditional values that transcended codified law.

Yet this complacency with orthodox imperial ideology as an extra-legal moral doctrine did not last very long. For a while, the values subsumed in that moral doctrine were so "unexceptionable and exceedingly general" that they could coexist with a diversity of ideological formulations and partisan interests.[60] The supremacy of nation that the orthodox values symbolized did not actually suppress what was going on in society, including the social differentiation accompa-

nying capitalist transformation and clashes between conflicting interests. Yet, as conflict intensified, anxiety over the possibility of social
troubles and disorder spilling over into the realm of nation and state
grew. While calls were made for the realm of nation to be protected
against discord and for the orthodox imperial ideology to be more
consciously enforced, the growing awareness of social conflict revealed the gap between the vague ideological doctrine and the con-
flict-laden reality of social life. In Gluck's words, "this increasing dis-
parity between ideology and experience meant first that parts of the
ideology were not as unexceptionable as they once had been," and "as
the imperial ideology lost its 'apparent invisibility,' it became more
obtrusively present, more insistent, and more intolerant of diversity
than it had needed to be." Now "more artifice and force were required" to enforce it.[61] Law was called on to do the job.

The Japanese government most feared new thought trends such
as socialism that challenged the socioeconomic base on which the
imperial order stood. Until the end of the Meiji era, left-wing distur-
bances were rather exceptional and manageable within the framework of control devices against general unrest. Yet, facing spiraling
new forms of subversion, the government found insufficient the language and penalties of the Meiji control laws. Aghast at massive unrest during the Taishō era, government leaders and right-wingers
called for a tougher stance, prompting the Bill for the Control of
Radical Social Movements. The bill brought the radical ideas and
activities it was intended to stamp out within the scope of the phrase
"disturbing the *chōken* (constitutional order of government)." It also
provided for punishment against inciting "alteration of the fundamental fabric of society" through violent means. However, the terms
*chōken* and "the fundamental fabric of society" were criticized as too
vague, and the bill was shelved.[62]

Although foiled, this attempt was a prelude to the notorious
Peace Preservation Law of 1925, which was applied to Korea, Taiwan, and Karafuto through an imperial edict. The significance of the
Peace Preservation Law lay in the fact that the national orthodoxy
enshrined in the concept of *kokutai* was incorporated into a Diet act.
Transposing the *kokutai* into written law may have been a way of
dispelling the unease about "overreliance on law," for such unease
derived from a conceptual antinomy between law and moral values.
There were, to be sure, differences among jurists as to the place of
*kokutai* in law, namely, between those who argued that *kokutai* was a

matter of ethics and therefore had no relevance to law, and their opponents who, defining the source of law as the confidence of a race and *kokutai* as "the crystallization of racial confidence," gave *kokutai* a central place in law.[63] The Peace Preservation Law marked the ascendance of the latter over the former.

Until that time the term *kokutai* had only occasionally appeared in judicial opinions. Now the Peace Preservation Law clearly provided for punishments against actual and attempted involvements in anti-*kokutai* organizations. The original 1925 act stipulated imprisonment for up to ten years, but in 1928 the act was so amended as to increase penalties dramatically; it became a capital offense to organize or lead an anti-*kokutai* association. And in 1941 the law was amended again to criminalize individual anti-*kokutai* acts having no connection with any organization, along with the act of organizing or working in an association having the purpose of "impairing the sanctity of the imperial household or the Shinto shrines," which could be inferred from the nature and effect of the act. Further, while the original wording of the Peace Preservation Law placed the "purpose of denying the institution of private property" beside the "purpose of undermining the *kokutai*," thus giving private property the appearance of being one of the two highest principles of social order, the 1928 amendment moved the private-property phrase to another clause and the 1941 amendment moved it to a separate article, in order to underline the supremacy of the *kokutai* over all other values, ideologies, and institutions.[64]

The insertion of the term *kokutai* into a law, however, did not supply the law with a clear ideological point of reference. The Peace Preservation Law was burdened with the excessive generality of the orthodox values that the term expressed—loyalty, filial piety, harmony, *bushidō*, and so forth. These values were meaningful only inasmuch as they symbolized Japaneseness. There was no other way of ascertaining the ramifications of the *kokutai* than condemning certain ideas and activities as its opposite, the "un-Japanese."[65] Nevertheless, the government sought to make the *kokutai* a focus of positive indoctrination, not simply a standard for negative injunction. That is to say, suppressing disbelief was insufficient; it was necessary to enforce active belief, as suggested by the term "clarification of the *kokutai*" (*kokutai no meichō*). In an effort to define the *kokutai* positively so as to dispel confusion about the national essence, theoretical studies were made, which culminated in the publication of

*Fundamentals of the Kokutai* (*Kokutai no hongi*) in 1937. With some historicist rhetoric of a Hegelian tinge, this ideological manual explained why the Japanese national spirit was destined to prevail over the ahistorical liberalism of the West and theorized about the political system of Japan and the relation between individual and emperor/state in open denunciation of "social contract," "democracy," "constitutionalism," and "government by the law."[66]

This ideological formulation was an expression of the changing Japanese view of modernity and civilization in the 1930s. The colonial authorities no longer rebuked Koreans for "uncivilizedness" or "ignorance of the trends of the times." Instead, they ascribed the spread of popular unrest and left-wing tendencies to dark effects of that new education and civilization which nourished the self-seeking tendency of modern men. Communism was not dangerous because it denied the natural human desire for self-interest but because it was the worst offshoot of Western civilization, where self-interest was enshrined. Communism, the nationalisms of the colonized peoples, and Anglo-American liberalism were viewed as equally dangerous because they stimulated the pursuit of partisan interests — class-based, ethnic, or individual — at the expense of the unity of the empire. In the 1930s and early 1940s, the Japanese government and colonial authorities waged total war against such heretical thought trends and tried to secure the spiritual unity of the empire by combining ideological indoctrination, various forms of social control, and criminal justice.

One characteristic of social and ideological control in this period was that the state was not satisfied with controlling behavior but was obsessed with mastering the minds of the subjects as well. In criminal justice, the "liberal," "individualistic," "utilitarian," or "classical" approach that located the essence of criminal justice in applying fixed rules to objective acts of violation gave way to a "totalitarian" approach preoccupied with regulating consciousness, dispositions, and sentiment in accordance with the Japanese national spirit.[67] It was not enough to lock up thought criminals to prevent them from committing anti-*kokutai* acts. Criminals had to convert. They had to reintegrate their souls with the spirit of the Japanese nation encapsulated in the doctrine of *kokutai*. The Japanese penal authorities adopted the therapeutic approach in crime control based on the idea that criminals should be rehabilitated, an approach that was gaining influence in Europe and Germany in particular.

Nevertheless, converting ideological offenders was a uniquely Japanese method, which had no parallel even in Nazi Germany.[68] One consequence of the conversion (*tenkō*) policy in Japan was a very low rate of prosecution and punishment under the Peace Preservation Law in comparison with a large number of arrests. The Japanese government adopted this approach in the belief that offenders could and had to be re-Japanized.[69]

A thought criminal was certified when he converted. However, to verify that conversion was genuine, the authorities watched his daily life closely over a lengthy period to detect his inner state of mind. In 1936 the Diet enacted the Law on the Protective Surveillance of Thought Criminals. This law applied to those who had violated the Peace Preservation Law but been freed without prosecution or released on suspended sentence, probation, or parole, or who had been released after serving their sentence. Protective Surveillance Centers were established, and their officials were empowered to watch the daily life of the offender, confine his residence to a certain place, and control his communication with others. Since the law also applied to those who were released without prosecution, anyone suspected of being potentially anti-*kokutai* could become an object of surveillance even without a court decision. Those who were released after jail terms, of course, remained under control.

In the same year the governor-general of Korea issued the Ordinance on the Protective Surveillance of Thought Criminals in Korea, which provided for the same control methods as in Japan. However, the government was concerned about the greater difficulty of Japanizing Koreans than Japanese. According to a government study of 1,200 people in Seoul under surveillance in 1936, only 20 percent were genuine converts, while non-converts and "semiconverts"[70] each accounted for 40 percent. Further, since the government found there was greater possibility of "pretended conversion" in Korea, formal judicial punishment was more common than in Japan.[71] In 1941, the colonial government issued the Ordinance on the Preventive Custody of Thought Criminals in Korea. According to this ordinance, a Peace Preservation Law offender released after serving his full prison term or on suspended sentence could be taken into custody if the court found there was a present danger that he might commit the offense again. The 1941 amendment of the Peace Preservation Law installed the same device within the Peace Preservation Law itself. The same amendment denied offenders against the *koku-*

*tai* normal legal protections such as the right to appeal to a higher court and the free choice of defense counsel.

Lengthy custody before and during trial served as a powerful means of obtaining conversion and punishing the suspect or defendant prior to, without, or alongside a court sentence. The police and a procurator could each detain a suspect for up to ten days without a court order, and the court could keep him in custody during a preliminary examination (which was held to determine whether to hold a trial). Although subject to a time limit, custody pending a preliminary examination could be renewed an indefinite number of times.

The Peace Preservation Law, however, risked overburdening the legal system because of unclear conditions of operation and targets.[72] This danger was not avoided but diffused, as the law was wielded against an extremely large variety of acts and people while the responsibilities for its enforcement were distributed to various institutions and organizations, the judiciary being only one of them. Further, the distinction between control under the Peace Preservation Law and the general surveillance and indoctrination under which the whole society found itself was unclear. The courtroom and the prison cell were not the only places where the Peace Preservation Law disciplined offenders. And it was not only those who were officially declared to be criminals that found themselves under meticulous surveillance and control. The Peace Preservation Law and all other legal devices of thought control constituted part of a broad set of programs to control the symbolic milieux of the entire population. It was not only the legal system but the entire lifeworld that was overburdened; ceremonies and rituals, exhortation and command, suasion and repression, had to be implemented endlessly in order for that lifeworld to be integrated to any degree under the supremacy of the *kokutai*. To understand the logic and ideological implications of the Peace Preservation Law, we have to look at the Japanese method of "spiritual mobilization" in its entirety, whose colonial form was the *kōminka* movement.

Some may regard the repressive and undemocratic nature of Japanese rule as representing a premodern form of governance. But it has become clear that more problems are produced than solved if we assume modernity to be a phase of a predestined trajectory of progress leading to greater human emancipation. Such a conception of modernity risks driving diverse features of a changing society into the residual category of premodern and thereby ignoring significant changes experienced by that society. Further, it might also cast all the experiences of repression that we have seen as an aberration or anomalous course of events and thus overlook the fact that they were deeply embedded in the course of history through which the Japanese empire went, a danger similar to the one against which Zygmunt Bauman warns with respect to the relation between the Holocaust and European modernity.[73] Instead of conceiving modernity as an emancipatory project, I began with a notion of modernity as a matter of power and domination and have focused on the novel modality of power and domination to which Koreans found themselves subject under Japanese rule.

One theme of my discussion has been the legal framework of Japanese rule and the logical disarray in Japanese colonial discourse that derived from the practical problem of implementing discrimination in the midst of assimilation, notably the exclusion of the colonial populace from "enlightened" forms of governance. To be sure, the question of exclusion and inclusion has been the central issue in mainstream historiography. Yet the purpose of this volume would not be served if we limited our inquiry to this traditional problematic.

A second theme of this discussion has been change in the way power and domination was organized. There was a remarkable intensification of control under Japanese rule, as is witnessed in the expansion of the police network and the extension of state power down to the most minute details of social life. This intensification of control was made possible and facilitated by refinements in the collection and storage of information. But our concerns must not be limited to the reach of power, let alone the question of whether there was more power or less power. What is important are the "targets of power" and the "points of power's application," as David Scott puts it.[74] Japanese rule (re)discovered or (re)created as targets of control various fields of social practice uncontrolled before. Power does not operate in a given space, with only its intensity changing; it shapes and creates spaces.

This reformulation of power and of the social space in which it operated was accompanied by that novel kind of rationality which Foucault terms "governmentality." Yet, although many features studied here are present in other modernizing states, some aspects of the ethos and ideology of Japanese colonial government are unique. A third issue of this chapter pertains to the imperial ideology at work in the Japanese campaign of spiritual integration. In *tennōsei* ideology, whose content was condensed in the term *kokutai*, mainstream historiography has found deviations from, and challenges to, modernity. To be sure, in the 1930s, the search for modernity was replaced by "the overcoming of modernity" (*kindai no chōkoku*) in official ideological formulas. Yet, although the campaign to enforce *tennōsei* ideology accentuated traditional Japanese values in opposition to liberal Western values, it was an outcome of the modernizing process that Japanese society had been undergoing and a strategy to cope with the consequences of that process. The colonial application of imperial ideology and the methods of thought control developed in the Japanese homeland should also be understood against the backdrop of the socioeconomic change that the colonial society was undergoing. The seemingly anti-modern ideological campaigns were carried out by means of techniques of discipline appropriated and applied by a state that was being increasingly governmentalized[75] and whose power and strategy of domination were modernized — although, of course, "modernized" in a special sense.

TWO

# Broadcasting, Cultural Hegemony,

# and Colonial Modernity in

# Korea, 1924–1945

## Michael Robinson

In February 1927, under the call sign JODK, the newly established Kyŏngsŏng Broadcast Corporation (hereafter, KBC) began regular programming in Korea. By the end of the colonial period, an estimated 305,000 radio permits had been granted for use in private homes, tearooms, restaurants, public markets, schools, and village meeting halls, and KBC had brought every nook and cranny of the colony within range of its network of stations and relay facilities for exchanging programming with Japan, Manchukuo, and China.[1] In the twentieth century, no other colony was tied to its metropole through such an extensive communications net.[2]

Standard nationalist histories of the colonial period, if they mention radio at all, interpret it as another aspect of the extensive information control system that served Japan's propaganda and cultural assimilation programs.[3] This is, of course, accurate. All communications in the colony were under tight central control, and Japanese officials recognized immediately the potential of broadcasting to further the long-range goals of spreading Japanese-language use and Japanese cultural values. In the mid-1930s, the Japanese intensified their information control and cultural assimilation campaign under the banner of *naisen ittai* (Japan and Korea as a single body). Radio played an important role in *naisen ittai* and the later Movement to Create Imperial Subjects (*kō-minka*). After 1937, KBC became an increasingly important vehicle for transmitting sanitized war news from Tokyo throughout the colony. Indeed, the domestic Japanese broadcasting network, Nihon hōsō (hereafter, NHK), played an equally important propaganda role; although, unlike its Korean counterpart, it did not have to negotiate between two languages, its programming had become similarly dominated by central censors by 1941.

Upon closer inspection, however, the story of colonial radio is much more ambiguous. Although colonial radio would be tightly controlled from the center, the problems of creating and expanding it required the Government-General of Korea (hereafter, GGK) to make some significant cultural policy concessions. Most notably, Japanese authorities were confronted with the necessity of creating a second, all–Korean-language system in order to disseminate receivers and create a mass audience. Moreover, financing the system required a broad fee-paying audience. As the experience of the first six years of broadcasting (1927–33) demonstrated, this could be done only if Koreans were attracted to buying and using radios. Thus, within six years of the inception of colonial broadcasts, the initial mixed-language channel was supplemented by the addition of an all-Korean channel, and sales of radios soared.

While still tightly controlled by Ministry of Communications officials, all-Korean radio created a unique cultural space through the diverse informational, educational, economic, and pure entertainment programming it sent over the public airwaves—a space that contradicted the cultural/political logic (if there was one) of assimilation. From 1933 until the outbreak of the Pacific War in 1941 and the imposition of even stricter censorship (Korean-language broadcasting ceased entirely in 1944), Korean radio stimulated a revival of traditional music genres, created new forms of dramatic arts, introduced Western classical music and jazz, fed its audience's insatiable appetite for modern, popular song (*yuhaengga*), and served as a vehicle for standardizing the Korean vernacular. Indeed, Korean radio became an important productive force in the creation of a modern, popular culture in colonial Korea, and even though this culture was a product of Japanese colonial political, cultural, and economic ascendancy, it also played a role in subverting Japanese cultural hegemony.

This chapter attempts to recast the story of Korean radio as a part of a dynamic colonial cultural hegemony. It is not simply the story of the creation of another Japanese-dominated, modern institution foisted on the helpless Korean people in order to serve Japanese interests. Radio should be seen as part of a more complicated colonial hegemony that entailed both physical coercion and cultural/political attraction. Japanese cultural hegemony worked so well because it provided limited space for Korean cultural autonomy.[4] In the end, allowing space for cultural autonomy acted both to sustain and to subvert the ultimate goals of Japanese cultural assimilation. I avoid calling radio a "space of resistance" because this implies that Korean-language broadcasting directly contested Japanese cultural assimilation; it did not. It did, however, construct culture, and in doing so, it resisted Japan by creating and maintaining Korean art forms with strong emotive ties to Koreans of all classes. Therefore, Koreans were able to create something of their own even within the very vortex of the colonial propaganda apparat.

## Establishing Broadcasting in Korea, 1924–27

After the massive uprisings in the spring of 1919, the GGK altered its control policies in Korea. Under Governor-General Saitō Makoto (1919–27, 1929–1931), the GGK abandoned the previous policy of Military Rule (*budan seiji*) and instituted the policy of Cultural Rule (*bunka seiji*) in order to lessen Korean resistance and co-opt Korean elites by encouraging active participation in the cultural and political affairs of the colony.[5] After 1920, the GGK allowed Korean newspaper and magazine publication, permitted political participation, and granted permits for cultural, academic, student, and citizen associations. The 1920s witnessed, therefore, a renaissance of cultural and political activism in the colony. While granting these concessions, the Japanese strove to tighten control indirectly by strengthening intelligence-gathering and oversight functions in an expanded and reorganized police system. Japan's ultimate goal in using Cultural Rule was to encourage active Korean participation in the life of the colony while slowly intensifying its long-range program to assimilate Korea culturally.[6]

Broadcasting began in Japan in 1926 and in Korea in 1927, and policies created in Japan established precedents for the colony. By 1924, the GGK had created the basic policy framework for colonial broadcasting, and officials were enthusiastic about the potential of radio as an easily controlled, centralized medium for information and education. Indeed, early radio regulations (GGK Administrative Orders of 1924) were modeled after the Japanese 1915 Wireless Telegraphic Communications Law. This transferred the Japanese government's assumptions about broadcasting (as a public-interest option controlled and regulated by the state) and its bureaucratic controls directly to Korea.[7] In spite of the restrictions on private investment, government regulations, and a very limited market, eleven separate applications for broadcasting permits representing both Japanese and Korean investors were submitted to the Ministry of Communications in 1923 and 1924. Following the pattern established with the creation of NHK in 1924, the ministry amalgamated the petitioners into one "public interest juridical person" (*kōeki hōjin*) and issued a separate permit granting permission to erect transmission facilities between 1925 and 1927.[8]

Testing by the GGK began as early as 1924. A spate of newspaper articles in the colonial press followed the testing program closely, and the public expressed tremendous enthusiasm.[9] The colonial press presented the story as a science lesson for its readers while effusively celebrating Korea's inclusion in the emerging future of electronic communications. Ignoring the reality that government controls would constrict programming freedom, the papers provided free advertising and cultivated public awareness of and excitement for the new medium. The newspapers followed KBC's slow gestation through GGK bureaucratic red tape, tracked the number of radio owners (in 1925 only 800 receivers were operating), advertised broadcast demonstrations in public parks and in their own offices, and announced the locations of mobile testing units.[10]

The testing period between 1924 and the creation of KBC in 1927 coincided with a burst of Korean cultural activity in Seoul and the growing provincial centers of the colony. It was also a period of political transition. In the early 1920s moderate nationalists used the new Korean press and organizational "freedoms" to expand the space for cultural autonomy in the colony. Without directly challenging Japanese rule, the so-called cultural nationalists mounted educational, journalistic, economic, and cultural programs designed to strengthen Korean cultural identity and economic autonomy.[11] The advent of radio in Korea fit into this larger movement. Cultural nationalists viewed radio as an indication of cultural and technological growth in Korea. They saw it as a means for spreading Korean cultural consciousness in Korea and, more broadly, the world. As one newspaper paean to the new medium put it: "Through the miracle of radio waves we can introduce our culture, music, and the sounds of our language to the world."[12]

After February 16, 1927, this was, technically, possible. On that date the newly chartered KBC began formal broadcasts after two years of testing. Using a Marconi "Q"-type six-kilowatt transmitter at 690 KHz, KBC was on the air sixteen hours a day; its range, however, was limited to Seoul and its environs, and it broadcast in Korean less than 30 percent of the time.[13] For the next six years, KBC struggled with financial, technical, and programming problems that inhibited its expansion and cultural potential. It is in this period that the conflict over the new cultural space of radio emerged.

## Problems with Early Broadcasting, 1927–33

A dual-language broadcasting policy prevailed at KBC for its first six years.[14] The original mix of languages was three hours of Japanese to one of Korean. This meant that the overwhelming majority of broadcasting was in Japanese (with Korean translation of certain news items). KBC hired, with great fanfare, two Korean announcers in late 1926. They assumed the challenge of providing on-the-spot translations (early programming used two microphones, side by side) for general announcements, programming schedules, short news items, financial reports (commodity and stock prices, etc.), and GGK bulletins. Most programming was designed and written by the Japanese staff, and the two Korean announcers were responsible only for several hours of "entertainment" programming in Korean.

The dual-language policy came under immediate criticism in the Korean-language press; it also stirred up the Japanese community.[15] Both communities were annoyed by the use of the other's language, for predictable reasons. That the GGK responded to the criticism is another illustration of how such cultural issues were negotiated during the period of Cultural Rule. By July 1927, Korean-language use was increased to 40 percent of airtime, and different methods of alternating programming began.[16] Although this helped, the ongoing use of two languages within a single broadcast day continued to fragment and confuse the listening audience.

The original dual-language policy intended that Korean should serve as a bridge language to introduce Japanese-language reports. With short news items, market reports, and GGK announcements, this was probably effective for bilingual Koreans and not too bothersome for

Japanese listeners. Responding to Korean complaints, however, within six months KBC started to alternate Japanese and Korean versions of the same programs. This diluted by half the amount of information that could be presented and forced each community (only a small fraction of the Japanese ever learned Korean) to wait its turn.

The situation with regard to radio's most popular programming, entertainment, was equally volatile. Entertainment (music, radio drama) occupied only 30 percent of the broadcast day but was clearly the main attraction of radio from its inception. Koreans complained about the lack of Korean music and the odd scheduling of programs. Eventually, the station tried alternating entertainment programs, one full day of Japanese-language music fare followed the next day by Korean to provide some unity for nighttime listeners. The dual-language policy, however, continued to complicate the programming schedule. Korean newspapers had to run detailed daily schedules so the radio audience could plan its listening around the mixture of different shows, some repeated in both languages, others only in Korean or Japanese — all made worse by the even/odd day alternation.

In 1928, KBC introduced relay programming from Japan to Korea. By using early hard-wire connections from NHK, relays increased the percentage of Japan-based radio in Korea. Construction of a ten-kilowatt relay transmitter on Kōshima in 1928 effectively jammed the more distant KBC signal from Seoul in middle and southern Korea. In 1931, NHK agreed to stop transmission from Kōshima between 9:40 and 11:00 P.M. in order to avoid blocking KBC Korean entertainment programming from reaching the small, out-of-Seoul audience; KBC also began devoting this time slot to Korean music.

It was clear that KBC's dual-language policy inhibited the spread of radio use in the Korean community while angering the Japanese audience. Indeed, the audience for radio was still predominantly Japanese in this early period. If the GGK thought that radio dominated by the Japanese language, controlled information, and Japanese music would ultimately spread to the Korean community, it was sorely mistaken. As research in this field deepens, it will be interesting to discover the effects of alternating language broadcasting on language acquisition or resistance. Some might argue that Japanese-dominated radio encouraged Japanese-language comprehension. Others could claim that alternating use, as in bad foreign-language teaching, provided instant translation and therefore no incentive to acquire Japanese. But clearly the dual-language model failed insofar as it fragmented programming, irritated listeners, inhibited the spread of radio use, and reduced revenues in the first six years of broadcasting.

## Financing Radio and Building an Audience

Lack of a broad audience was the largest problem KBC faced in its early years, since operations were financed by registration and listener fees. The GGK spent ¥30,000 for equipment and testing in 1924 and between 1925 and 1927 increased its investment in KBC to ¥400,000. Private investment provided less than 10 percent of the initial capitalization.[17] The law governing the charter of KBC limited profits for private investors to 7 percent, but the KBC did not turn a profit until the late 1930s.[18] In the early period, simple enthusiasm for the project and perquisites for investors, which included exemption from all fees and participation in KBC governance, were the main incentives for KBC's Korean and Japanese investors.

Having chosen a noncommercial option for radio, KBC depended on listener fees, initially a two-wŏn registration fee and a monthly two-wŏn listener fee. There were 1,440 registered users in February 1927 at the inauguration of KBC; after three months users numbered 3,318. This provided a mere 6,636-wŏn in monthly income for the station, which was carrying a debt of 300,000 wŏn for construction and equipment, not to mention current operations obligations running at 10,000 wŏn a month. Clearly, income had to increase if the station was to survive, let alone thrive.

KBC tried a number of incentive programs to attract listeners. The manipulation of language content, and various strategies such as alternate-day, Japanese/Korean programming and music hours at night (introduced in Korean) responded to the need to attract Korean listeners. In 1927, KBC reduced the monthly listener fee to one wŏn per month and created installment plans for rural listeners who found monthly payment inconvenient. It dispatched autos with radios to rural markets to promote radio sales, which it backed with a mobile radio sales unit. And KBC provided free radio service centers in Seoul and P'yŏngyang as well as regular traveling service units that circulated in the provinces.[19] Ultimately, KBC focused on spreading its geographical coverage by installing more powerful transmitters as an additional strategy for expanding its listener base; this, however, required more funds for equipment and construction.

In spite of these efforts, radio sales remained flat. Moreover, the Japanese community continued to constitute the overwhelming majority of the radio audience. In the mid-to-late 1920s, radios were still expensive consumer items. The cheapest crystal sets cost as much as ten wŏn, and vacuum tube radios cost more than 100. By the early 1930s, however, cheaper vacuum radios suitable for home use appeared, followed quickly by the development of more powerful units built for larger audiences (tearooms, offices, restaurants).[20] Cost alone cannot account for stagnant sales. In the end, fragmented programming and language confusion on KBC remained its biggest problems.

This conclusion is supported by the fact that radio sales and audience expansion increased after the announcement in 1931 of plans for a second, all-Korean station (Station #2). The figures in Table 2.1 provide dramatic evidence of the effect of this decision. In the first four years of radio, the number of receivers had increased to only 10,831, of which 86.8 percent were in Japanese hands. Between 1930 and 1931, the percentage of the audience that was Korean even fell from 13.3 to 12.2. After KBC's announcement of its intention to create an all-Korean station in early 1931, radio sales to Koreans rose steadily, with large increases in audience share in 1933 (the first year of Station #2) and again in 1935 and 1937. By 1940, Korean radio use had reached parity with that of the Japanese community. While the totals are unimpressive, the fact remains that the percentage of Korean radio use increased from 13.3 percent of the total audience in 1932 to 25.1 percent in 1936 to 34.1 percent in 1937 to 49.7 percent in 1940.

The overall size of the radio audience was also increasing rapidly. The Manchurian incident of 1931 and keen interest within both the Korean and Japanese communities in news about Japan's advance in China stimulated sales. With the beginning of the war in China in 1937, the radio audience increased dramatically. By 1940, the numbers of registered receivers hovered near the 200,000 mark, and best estimates of radio distribution at the end of the colonial period are approximately 305,000 receivers (slightly more than 1 percent of the Korean population) in use. This number was quite modest compared to the vast radio audience of the metropole. In 1944, 6.6 million radios were in use in Japan, the fourth largest audience in the world behind only the United States, Germany, and Great Britain.[21]

Although the increase in radio distribution between 1931 and 1936 can be attributed to the Korean response to the new all-Korean station,

Table 2.1

*Registered Radio Receivers in Korea, 1926–42*

| Year | Total | Korean (%) | Japanese (%) | Foreign |
|---|---|---|---|---|
| 1926 | 1,829 | 386 (21%) | 1,431 (78%) | 12 |
| 1927 | 5,122 | 949 (18.5) | 4,161 (81.2) | 12 |
| 1928 | 8,469 | 1,353 (15.9) | 7,102 (83.8) | 14 |
| 1929 | 10,153 | 1,573 (15.4) | 8,558 (84.2) | 22 |
| 1930 | 10,881 | 1,448 (13.3) | 9,410 (86.8) | 23 |
| 1931a | 14,309 | 1,754 (12.2) | 12,493 (87.3) | 62 |
| 1932 | 20,479 | 2,738 (13.3) | 17,641 (86.1) | 100 |
| 1933 | 26,338 | 4,517 (17.1) | 21,690 (82.3) | 131 |
| 1934 | 28,021 | 5,111 (18.2) | 22,786 (81.3) | 124 |
| 1935 | 37,500 | 8,775 (23.4) | 28,503 (76.0) | 222 |
| 1936b | 64,821 | 16,324 (25.1) | 48,089 (74.1) | 408 |
| 1937 | 86,891 | 29,683 (34.1) | 56,570 (65.1) | 638 |
| 1938 | 120,901 | 45,490 (37.6) | 74,790 (61.8) | 621 |
| 1939 | 146,637 | 60,917 (41.5) | 85,720 (58.4) | n/a |
| 1940 | 191,180 | 95,153 (49.7) | 96,027 (50.2) | n/a |
| 1942c | 277,281 | 126,047 | 149,653 | 1,581 |

NOTES: The figures given above are for the purpose of illustration only. Much remains to be done to balance different counts. The figures for registered receivers in the *GGK Ministry of Communications Annual*, the *GGK Statistical Annual*, and the privately published *Maeil sinbo's Korea Annual (Chosŏn nyŏngam)* vary from each other year to year. The number of months included in the annual figures also varies. With the exception of the figures for 1936, which represent an eighteen-month interval; all other annual figures are for varying lengths of time, all of which are less than three months, however.

a KBC announced its intention to create a second all-Korean language station in May 1931.

b Figures are for an 18-month interval.

c The figures for 1942 are taken from estimates in Han'guk pangsong chinhŭnghoe p'yŏn, *Han'guk pangsong ch'ongnam* (Compendium of Korean broadcasting) (Seoul: Han'guk pangsong chinhŭnghoe'yŏn, 1991), pp. 222–23.

SOURCES: *Chōsen sōtokufu tōkei nenpō* (Statistical yearbook of the GGK), 1926–40; *Han'guk pangsong ch'ongnam*, pp. 176, 222–23; see also Chŏng Chinsŏk, "Ilcheha ŭi radio pogŭp kwa ch'ŏngch'wija" (Radio listenership and distribution), *Sinmun kwa pangsong*, Oct. 1992: 62.

the doubling of the audience after 1937 reflected GGK interest in expanding the information net during the war. To that end it was willing to make considerable investments in facilities. The second infusion of money into the system in 1931 (a 430,000-wŏn loan from NKH) helped build facilities for Station #2 as well as more powerful transmitters to increase the station's reach. A network of regional stations was added after 1935, with an additional 543,000-wŏn loan to KBC, again squeezed out of Japanese radio revenues. The expansion of the colonial radio audience also meant increased revenues available for expansion. By 1939, a total 1,397,000 wŏn had been invested in the colonial system. And, ironically, listener fees were drawn disproportionately from the Japanese community throughout the 1930s. In a sense, the radio listeners in the metropole and the Japanese audience in the Korean colony were forced to pay for the system—a system supporting a Korean-language station.[22]

## Oversight and Radio as an Assimilation Tool

The Japanese considered this a good investment in spite of the ironies inherent in providing a cultural space for Koreans as well as financing it on the backs of Japanese listeners. It was clear that the GGK decided to provide a Korean-language station in tandem with the move to intensify cultural assimilation in the colony after 1931. Japanese educational, linguistic, and cultural control policies shifted toward promoting in Koreans an active identification with Japanese cultural values. Under the banner of *naisen ittai*, programs were designed to spread Japanese-language use, restrict use of the Korean language in schools and government offices, rewrite Korean history, and spread Japanese cultural values more generally.[23]

In 1931, the issue of whether it was wise to provide Koreans with their own station inflamed heated debate in the internal policy committee responsible for the emerging *naisen ittai* program.[24] In the end, the contradictory interests were resolved by a decision to centralize programming control, originate more programming in Japan, and, finally, increase the number of Japanese culture and Japanese-language lectures aired on the new station. Thus the Japanese restricted the station's programming autonomy from its inception. Over time, more and more programs were simple translations of Japanese news, government reports, and cultural/educational lectures.

The Ministry of Communications created a programming oversight committee (Hōsō hensei iinkai) in 1931 to monitor the new station. To ensure total control of output, it created a "cut-off" switch for Station #2 that augmented the authority Japan already exercised through direct phone lines to KBC broadcast booths.[25] In 1935, radio control also became a mandate of the powerful Korean Information Coordinating

Committee (Chōsen hōjō iinkai) that coordinated all information and censorship in the colony.[26] Controls were virtually airtight, and there is little mention of direct censorship of politically or morally offensive items over colonial radio. Such censorship proved unnecessary since dissension was precluded from programming in its very design.

The Japanese increased the percentage of Japanese-originated programming on both channels after 1931. With new relay stations and improved relay technology, direct broadcasts to Korea from Japan began in the early 1930s. This saved money on program production and fed the Japanese audience's appetite for news and familiar sounds from home. It also supported the assimilation program by creating an illusion of unified cultural programming while binding the colony electronically to the metropole.

There was also an effort to effect a transformation of cultural forms on the radio. The Japanese progressively encouraged the playing of Japanese songs and martial music, and even the Japanization of Korean music genres during the war years. Beginning in the late 1930s, KBC ran contests publicized in the colonial press that awarded substantial prizes and the promise of airtime for Japanized Korean popular songs as well as patriotic songs in Korean.[27] This focus was particularly evident after the war with China; after 1941 and the reduction of Korean-language time slots, music programming was devoted entirely to military and patriotic songs to the point of overkill.

After 1937, Ministry of Communications officials required KBC to devote more time in its educational programs to lectures on "ethics" (simjŏn), "agricultural improvement" (nongch'on chinhŭng), and "women's education" (puin kyoyuk). These three categories of lectures were integral to the formal Movement to Create Imperial Subjects begun in 1935 by Governor-General Ugaki Kazushige and intensified by Governor-General Minami Jirō after 1936. Lectures in Japanese and "radio classroom" programs for spreading Japanese added in 1938 complemented the decision to force exclusive use of Japanese in schools and government facilities. The increase in the number of these required programs left less time for autonomous Korean-language programs in the education and lecture category, but some Korean-produced cultural and educational shows remained. Finally in July 1941, the GGK banned lectures and lessons on the Korean language altogether. This anticipated the elimination of Station #2 in April 1942 as Korean-language broadcasts were folded back into the Japanese station. All Korean-language broadcasting ended in December 1944.[28]

## Korean Radio and Cultural Construction

Certainly radio in Korea supported Japanese cultural and political hegemony. This was the design of the original policy that shaped its structure, restrained programming, controlled information, and self-consciously insinuated Japanese cultural and assimilationist content into broadcasting from its inception. It is, however, still possible to find within the world of broadcasting spaces in which cultural construction evolved toward different purposes. While this construction could not directly resist Japanese rule, it could and did serve a positive function of maintaining and creating Korean cultural traditions. Centered within an important Japanese assimilationist institution, Korean radio created a counter-hegemonic niche in and of itself and stimulated other nodes of cultural construction in the colony. Its counter-hegemonic aspects were, however, ambiguous: radio also drew Korean elites (artists, writers, programmers) into the modern sphere, thus further enmeshing them within colonial cultural hegemony.

One of the most important features of Korean radio resided in its language maintenance/development function. The advent of Korean-language broadcasting in the late 1920s added an additional weapon to the movement to organize and standardize the Korean vernacular language. The permission to publish Korean vernacular newspapers after 1920 stimulated a Korean nationalist movement to create a unified grammar and orthography. Radio played an important role in this process by raising the issue of standard pronunciation (*p'yojunmal*). Intellectuals scrutinized the choice of announcers and their use of language throughout the history of colonial broadcasting.[29] The advent of the all-Korean station in 1933 coincided with the publication of the first standard Korean orthography (*Matchumbŏp t'ongil an*) and, later, the first standard Korean grammar (*Chosŏnŏ munbŏp t'ongil an*).[30] And, in 1933, one of the first series of cultural lectures produced by Station #2 was on the Korean language.[31] These lectures were not for the masses (indeed, radio distribution was still in its infancy), but served the Korean intelligentsia's agenda of standardizing the modern Korean vernacular and elevating its use in modern discourse.[32]

Lectures on the Korean language were associated in Korean programmers' minds with lectures on Korean history, traditional arts, and more modern topics such as science, economics, and world affairs.[33] Although Korean radio producers labored under the censor's control and the cut-off button, the Korean press celebrated these lectures as a forum to demonstrate the capacity of vernacular Korea to deal with modern abstract thought. They were also seen as projecting the very "sounds and cadences" of the ancient language on the global airwaves.[34] Such commentary can be viewed as a self-conscious dialogue about making the Korean language modern, like Japanese. This illustrates the use by Korean elites of the language movement to place Korean on a par with Japanese in articulating abstract thought. Their efforts were addressed to maintaining both the use and existence of the Korean vernacular and to proving that it was the equal of Japanese as an instrument of the modern. This supports a broad, nationalist reading of such activity; namely, it resisted subordination of the Korean language to Japanese within the cultural universe of the empire. Efforts were clearly directed against the assimilation program's putative goal of reducing Korean language use to, as one Japanese commentator put it, "a simple expression of the rusticated aspects of peninsular culture in the colony, while maintaining Japanese (*kokugo*) as the argot of modern life."[35]

Although this language "resistance" can be read in simple nationalist terms, it also reveals the workings of colonial cultural hegemony. Japanese dominance of the modern sphere required Koreans to justify their own language, to "elevate" or perfect its utility as a modern language. It seems clear that further work on this issue can revise our understanding of how and how far linguistic assimilation evolved. The story of radio seems to indicate that language resistance pursued not just the survival of Korean (the usual view) but its actual use within the modern sphere of discourse. One could also read this struggle as more narrowly the concern of Korean colonial elites, fighting for a particular aspect of their dual cultural identity as both Koreans and cosmopolitans within the broader compass of the empire.

Station #2 complemented the rather intellectualized discussion of Korean with children's lessons in *han'gŭl* and grammar during the popular *Radio School* (*Radio hakkyo*) program in the late afternoon after regular school hours. This program served to augment the dwindling attention to formal Korean-language study in the state-run schools after 1931. Seeming to run at cross-purposes with itself, the government permitted both *Radio School* and linguistics lectures to continue after the formal crackdown on Korean-language use in schools, offices, and quasi-governmental corporations beginning in 1938. As late as February 1940, Station #2 was running a series on the purification of the Korean language![36] The very existence of such programming in 1940 confounds the postcolonial shibboleth of forced Japanese-language use. Further research is necessary to assess the impact of these campaigns on language use, or how these programs were interpreted in the depressed atmosphere of forced assimilation, but the contradiction remains.[37]

Of equal relevance to the issue of cultural construction was Korean radio's effect on reviving and reshaping traditional music and dramatic art genres. Initially musical entertainment was broadcast "live." There was no library of phonograph recordings to draw upon, and music programs had to find artists.[38] Station #2 also had to make choices about what kinds of music were suitable for broadcast. In the early years, music programs were a combination of performances of traditional Chosŏn dynasty court music (*aak*) and folk songs (*minyo*) drawn from different regional traditions.[39] Only small ensembles and individual singers could be featured in performances originating at the station, due to limited studio space. However, between 1927 and 1933, KBC also broadcast much of its music from theaters using direct-wire feeds to the station. Live performances over the radio stimulated attendance at and excitement for the music performances and reviews that had become a permanent feature of Seoul's burgeoning entertainment industry.[40]

Radio's use of traditional performers stimulated a revival of traditional music genres, and radio exposure created new singing stars in the late 1920s and early 1930s. Traditional music programming was not without controversy within the Korean community. There were objections to radio's use of *kisaeng* entertainers from the four great *kisaeng* schools in P'yŏngyang as well as disagreements over which folk songs were "representative" of certain regions. The discussion broadened in the first years of broadcasting to a debate over radio's bias in favoring certain regional styles (the *sŏdo* [western] or *namdo* [southern], for instance) over others. The following excerpt from *Tonga ilbo* (December 17, 1933), illustrates this struggle:[41]

All walks of life are brought together in listening to the radio. . . . In this period of transition between new and old ideas [we can detect] a collision. Anonymous letters detail struggles in households all over Korea . . . between fathers who hate the sounds of the new songs (*sinsik yuhaeng*) and want more traditional songs and their sons—or between those who want only the Korean zither (*kayagŭm*) and those who want to hear Western music. The old are arrayed against the young, who hate the 'old stinking traditional songs' or 'old-fashioned instruments.' There is also regional strife as listeners complain: 'Can't we have more music from the western provinces (*sŏdoga*)?' Or, 'Can't we have more songs from the south (*namdoga*)?'

Radio clearly sparked a debate over the canonization of traditional Korean music, stimulated public performances of obscure genres, and, ultimately, helped revive endangered art forms vis-à-vis phonograph records.

In the dramatic arts, radio also served as an important catalyst. Radio melodramas and translations of Western plays became a staple on Korean-language radio. Starting with selected readings of traditional novels and stories, KBC soon established its own Radio Drama Research Association (Radio yŏn'gŭk yŏn'guhoe) to adapt novels and stories for radio actors.[42] This association worked with Korean writers who were both producing new-style plays based on Western forms as well as directly translating works from the Western dramatic canon. Early radio featured a number of Western works (Isben, Shakespeare) as well as adaptations of longer traditional Korean works such as the *Tale of Ch'unhyang* (*Ch'unhyangjŏn*). By 1933 and the advent of the Korean-language station, the Radio Drama Hour (7:00–8:00 P.M.), which preceded the most popular late-night music program, had become a standard feature. The Korean press provided summaries of radio drama programs that served to further advertise activity in the urban live-theater scene.

In the first six years of dual-language broadcasting, popular music was eclipsed by Western music and Korean music drawn from traditional high culture. By 1933, however, new forms of popular song were clearly establishing themselves as the most popular radio fare. Korean popular song (*yuhaengga*) had evolved after 1900 as a mixture of Korean folk idioms and imported Japanese *torotto* (fox trot) music. Akin to contemporary Korean *ppongjjak nori*, these pop songs were a mixture of gliding Korean tonal scales, folk singing techniques, and a standard Western beat in either 2/4 or 3/4 time. By the mid-1920s, the Korean recording industry had already created a star system and market for new recordings in this idiom. In the early 1930s, radio began to use more and more records for their programs, and the explosion of phonograph and record sales coincides with this phenomenon.[43] The Korean-language press ran daily advertisements from record companies, and new recording releases were often coordinated with performances on radio.[44] By 1935, the recording industry was big business, and the linkage among the press, the recording industry, and radio was obvious to all.

The spectacular rise in the popularity of pop songs in the early and mid-1930s placed radio in the center of controversy. Radio's middle-class audience complained that pop music was unsuitable for family listening: barroom music should stay in the bars. One vaguely leftist cultural critic put it this way in the December 1934 issue of *Kaebyŏk* (Creation):[45]

Recently, on the streets of Seoul, all we hear are the same sounds from the same people. It's a monotone/tedium, like walking in a desert. Everyday the same flutes, oboes, violins, comedy stories, etc . . ., everyone listening [because of the novelty of radio]. Drunken songs with corrupt lyrics from the mouths of *ki-saeng* come into our homes every night . . . to great harm and spiritual corruption. . . . Noisy, incessant songs of the failed Chosŏn dynasty, songs of vagrants . . . all [come into] in the sanctity of the home. Should we not be cultivating the cultural consciousness of the masses more than [worrying about] business?

Korean intellectuals also worried that the "vulgar" pop idiom was replacing an appreciation for traditional music. Soon, the Japanese authorities began to take notice of the message within pop songs — tales of tragedy and unrequited love, laments of lost traditions and partings at the Shimonoseki ferry, paeans to a sense of Korean place — all overly melodramatic, spiritually unhealthy, and vaguely unpatriotic. The GGK's Song Purification Movement of the late 1930s (following a similar campaign in Japan) was an attempt to counteract the tremendous emotive hold of this music on the Korean population.[46] Yet, by all indications, Japanese censors began to create blacklists and ban specific songs only after 1941, both in Korea and Japan.

While sketched here only in brief, the story of Korean pop songs on the radio is clearly multilayered. Korean radio had a catalytic effect on the creation and expansion of an important popular cultural medium of song. This music was "consumed" in records and radio broadcasts, but it also became the staple of, and possibly reinforced, restaurant, wineshop, and home singing — a continuation of an earlier and more "participatory" form of popular culture. It also underscored a tension within the Korean elite's program to create a national cultural identity.

The usual reading of why popular music was attractive is that it was nationalist; that is, popular music was one of the last vestiges of cultural resistance in the face of Japanese cultural suppression. However, it is clear from press reports that some radio programmers and cultural elites were worried that popular song would divert interest from their project to canonize and preserve traditional Korean music as part of a modern Korean high culture. As in the language movement, some elites' conception of cultural construction within the modern sphere "resisted" by attempting to emulate cultural norms in the metropole through the establishment and deepening of a Korean high, modern culture co-equal to that of their colonial masters. This tension illustrates the multifaceted nature of nationalist cultural construction—a divide between popular and elite identity formations. In this sense, the debates in the 1930s in Korea over culture anticipated postcolonial debates over the same issue in South Korea, with modern Western Rock representing the new enemy to a "true" Korean music culture.[47]

## Rethinking Japanese Assimilation
## and the Korean Response

This brief synopsis of radio in colonial Korea is meant to open up discussion of the meaning and effects of colonial modernity and Japanese hegemony in 1920s and 1930s Korea. The dichotomizing repression-resistance thesis, the staple of existing Korean nationalist histories of the period, interprets radio as another in a long list of impositions. The Japanese imposed radio on the Korean population, just as they imposed Japanese history, language, cultural values, and Shinto worship at the height of the forced assimilation campaigns after 1937. At its most extreme, this view goes on to vilify all modern cultural production (radio included) in colonial Korea as dominated either by the GGK directly, or, as in the case of the recording industry, indirectly by Japanese and Western monopoly capital.[48] This view privileges the productive forces behind the construction of modern, consumption-oriented, mechanically reproduced popular culture.

We know less, however, about how radio was consumed by its audience. Were the endless lectures on how to be good imperial citizens, patriotic songs, and mind-numbing GGK news and policy reports really effective in inculcating Japanese values in the Korean population? Were the Korean intellectual elite's efforts to codify the Korean language as a "language of the modern" successful despite the decreasing amount of time devoted to such programming after 1937? One difficulty in knowing arises because the content of radio programs is difficult to determine. We can use reviews of lectures and secondhand commentary from the newspapers, but these are still biased sources. Even as we uncover transcripts and recordings of the original lectures, we still must struggle to determine how they were "read" by contemporary listeners.

The colonial intellectual elite that ran the newspapers had their own spin on the significance of Korean-language radio; they were also driven by the same commercialism that spurred Japanese and Western investment in cinema and the phonograph and recording industry. On the one hand, some Korean intellectuals saw Korean radio as part of a cultural maintenance and canonization project; on the other hand, others decried radio's role in helping erode cultural values by popularizing "vulgar" popular song genres. It is important to recognize here that both interpretations hold; Korean radio did have a role in cultural maintenance, and it also represented a locus of cultural construction that neither nationalist ideologues nor GGK officials could control. Therefore, the story of Korean radio was more than one of a single Korean culture resisting Japanese assimilation. It was also a space of intra-Korean elite struggle over how their culture should evolve in modern form, a debate decisively shaped by the cultural and political structures of colonialism.

Finally, the story of Korean radio during the colonial period must also be seen as part of a more complex system of cultural construction. Colonial radio was not placed in a vacuum. Although it did represent another modern technology transferred to Korea by colonial overlords, this new medium evolved within an already developing modern, popular culture.[49] By 1900, Koreans had begun to create a modern, consumer-oriented popular culture. Music performances in theaters for fees, modern adaptations of Western drama in new theaters, cinema, and pulp fiction—all new forms of entertainment—appeared before the advent of radio.[50] Indeed, radio reinforced the consumption of leisure in all these arenas. Most dramatically, radio was quickly linked with the development of new music genres, and it served to popularize the consumption of music in record form after 1927.

It is a gross oversimplification to assert that Japanese radio was just another in a series of coercive, modern technologies imported to Korea to further Japanese political control and, ultimately, assimilation. That it did serve these purposes does not negate the possibility that it had other effects on Korean society. Radio, like other Japanese "investments" in colonial Korea, became part of a dynamic system of new cultural forms, technologies, and habits that transformed cultural life in Korea between 1910 and 1945. These had tremendous power and shaped, while Japanizing, the structure of an emerging Korean modernity. But within selected spaces of autonomous development, Koreans struggled to make part of that modernity their own. The experience of Korean radio reveals one forum of that struggle. Further work on this subject will help shape our understanding of cultural construction in the colony, and, more important perhaps, it will also illuminate important continuities between Korea's colonial past and its contemporary cultural debates.

THREE

# Colonial Corporatism: The Rural Revitalization Campaign, 1932–1940

## Gi-Wook Shin and Do-Hyun Han

This chapter examines relations between the colonial state and rural society in 1930s Korea through the Rural Revitalization Campaign (*Nongch'on chinhŭng undong* or *Nosōn shinkō undō*) of 1932–40. Even as the Japanese promoted industrialization and urbanization in the 1930s (see Chapter 5 by Soon Won Park in this volume), they did not overlook the importance of the countryside, still home to more than three-quarters of the colonial population. Faced with rural deterioration due to agricultural depression and agrarian class conflict, the colonial government adopted a social policy approach designed to appease rural discontent and enhance village stability. This was a significant change from an earlier policy that focused on agricultural production and pursued landlord-based local control to a new one stressing social stability and promoting more direct state involvement in rural affairs. A series of legal measures that constrained landlord power, such as the 1932 Tenancy Arbitration Ordinance and the 1934 Agricultural Lands Ordinance, as well as the campaign under consideration here, reflect this new policy orientation.

Launched in the fall of 1932, the campaign was aimed primarily at economic improvement in villages ravaged by agricultural depression by reducing poverty and debt and encouraging self-sufficiency. However, the scope of the campaign was not limited to raising rural living standards. It also attempted to reorganize villages torn by class conflict and to enhance state penetration of village society. To do so, the campaign created semiofficial associations that brought local villages into more direct contact with the state, eschewing earlier reliance on the landed class for local control. To obtain popular consent to colonial rule, or hegemony to use the Gramscian term, the campaign stressed "spiritual" aspects of village life as a key part of its efforts. Although the Japanese never abandoned coercion and repression as means of colonial control, they also attempted to exercise ideological/hegemonic domination by promoting "hearty cooperation between Japanese and Koreans . . . and between the officials and the people."[1]

Unlike most previous studies, in examining the campaign, we do not consider it merely a deceptive measure or the application to the Korean colony of a policy drawn from a similar experience in Japan.[2] To be sure, Meiji reform ideology expressed in social policy and agrarianism and Governor-General Ugaki Kazushige's leadership were crucial elements of the campaign. Nonetheless, we argue that the campaign also reflected the internal colonial situation, and that ideas and suggestions from its colonial subjects, particularly moderate agrarianists, were carefully and selectively incorporated in state policy. This not only made the campaign more effective but also separated the moderates from the radicals, a typical example of a "divide and rule" policy. The government even tried to mobilize Korean tradition as a cultural resource to make the Rural Revitalization Campaign effective. The campaign served as a bridge between the *bunka seiji* (Cultural Rule) of the 1920s and the war mobilization of the late 1930s and early 1940s. It was largely an extension (in intensified form) of the earlier cultural policy, and social networks and experiences formed during the campaign were mobilized for Japan's "total war" against China and the United States.

This interpretation of the rural campaign casts serious doubt on the current understanding of state-society relations in colonial Korea, whether from the perspectives of nationalism, colonial landlordism, or colonial totalitarianism. The nationalist view understands colonial state-society relations in terms of a binary opposition between colonial repression and national resistance; the colonial landlordism perspective maintains that the colonial state relied on the landlord system for agricultural production and local control throughout its tenure; and the colonial totalitarianist view depicts colonial society as a mass society in which an atomized populace was subject to the naked manipulation of the state. However, the examination of the campaign presented here shows that colonial state-society relations were not necessarily a binary opposition, that by the 1930s the colonial state had eschewed its earlier reliance on landlord-based local control and mobilization in favor of a more direct involvement in rural affairs, and that the colonial state created not a mass society but one densely organized with hierarchical and organic entities. Such shortcomings in current views require an alternative conceptualization of colonial state–rural society relations in the 1930s. We propose a model of "colonial corporatism." The corporatist policy expressed in the rural campaign not only reveals a new colonial policy orientation, adding more complexity to our understanding of state-society relations under colonial rule, but also seems to have bequeathed a crucial legacy to the post-1945 period.

## Colonial Corporatism

As outlined above, the current literature on colonial Korea suggests three general views of state-society relations under colonial rule. The *nationalist* view of state-society relations as a binary opposition between colonial oppression and national resistance understands colonial state-society relations as basically conflict-ridden ones that produced zero-sum outcomes. In its extreme form, this view argues Japan's sole activity in Korea was to apply coercion and repression to maintain a colonial order, against which *all* Koreans resisted.[3]

Although this view points to the imperialist nature of Japanese colonialism, it is too simplistic to capture the more complex pattern of colonial state-society relations seen in the Rural Revitalization Campaign. First, we cannot assume that Korean society as a whole resisted colonial rule. Colonial society was highly differentiated, and different segments of society collaborated with and resisted the colonial state in varying degrees. Second, the colonial state's relations with various sectors of society changed over time, from accommodating to confrontational or vice versa, in tandem with internal and external conditions. The changing nature of the colonial state's relations with the landed class and the peasantry, discussed below, is a good example of this. Third, colonial state-society interactions did not necessarily produce zero-sum outcomes. The colonial state's interaction with a particular sector of Korean society may have enhanced the positions of both sides, whereas its relations with other sectors may have produced outcomes in favor of one over the other. The campaign examined here is a good case in point, in that it enhanced the positions of both the state and the peasantry as a result of their interaction at the expense of the landed class. The *nationalist* view cannot capture this dynamic and changing nature of state-society relations under colonial rule.

The second major view stresses *singmin chijuje* (colonial landlordism) by associating colonialism with landlordism. This view portrays the Japanese as having little interest in promoting economic development other than increasing agricultural production aimed at feeding their homeland population, and as maintaining or even reinforcing the regressive landlord system for local control and mobilization as well as agricultural production. In its extreme form, this view claims that Korea remained a colonial semifeudal society (*singminji pan ponggŏn sahoe*) and that the landlord system was kept as the backbone of colonial rule until the liberation in 1945.[4]

To be sure, the Japanese made no radical change in Korea's land tenure system and relied heavily on the landed class for agricultural production and local administration in the early years. Although the Japanese no longer relied on the *yangban* (or traditional elite) and made the *myŏn* (district) the main administrative unit, limited resources (an average of 4.6 people per *myŏn*) forced them to use the rural elite, especially local landlords, for social control and mobilization. In Bruce Cumings's observation, the Japanese found it to "their advantage to ally with the non-entrepreneurial landed class in Korea which resided in every village," whom they could "encourage . . . to govern the countryside for them."[5] Campaigns promoting agricultural production, such as the well-known Campaign to Increase Rice Production launched in 1920, were also carried out through the traditional landlord system.

However, the Japanese effort to rule the countryside through the landed class did not fare very well, as is illustrated by the rural support of the March First nationalist movement of 1919. Shocked by this nationwide protest, Japan lessened its repression, adopting the more moderate Cultural Rule policy that allowed some space for societal action. The change in colonial policy in the 1920s led to the rise of numerous social organizations such as tenant unions and their mobilization for political actions such as tenancy disputes and red peasant union movements.[6] The politicization of rural society forced the colonial government to rethink its earlier policy and adopt a social policy approach that attempted to deal with agrarian conflict through institutionalized means and restore social harmony in villages through new land laws as well as the rural campaign examined here. Furthermore, as the Japanese promoted industrialization in the 1930s, the economic importance of agriculture decreased, whereas the demand for rural stability crucial for industrialization and war mobilization increased. Some landlords, in response to agrarian conflict and the subsequent colonial policy that constrained the landed class, converted their capital from land to nonagricultural sectors, joining the process of colonial industrialization. This shift further undermined their position and authority in villages.[7] Put another way, in the 1930s agriculture was no longer the central economic concern of the colonial government; it was more interested in industrialization and eschewed its earlier reliance on the landed class for local control and mobilization by increasing its direct involvement in rural affairs, as detailed below. In sum, *singmin chijuje* does not adequately capture colonial state-society relations in the second half of Japanese rule in Korea because beginning in the 1920s important processes involved a direct relationship between state and rural society, and not merely the colonial state and landlord class.

The third perspective, *colonial totalitarianism*, is advocated by Gregory Henderson. According to Henderson, a powerful colonial state in Korea that pursued "rushed urbanization and industrialization" and extensive "war mobilization" created a "mass society" in which people were "subject to the naked manipulation and mobilization of central government" without "intermediary social groups." The result was an "atomized" society in which "elite and masses confront each other directly, 'by virtue of the weakness of groups capable of mediation between them,' a society characterized by amorphousness or isolation in social relations." Then, this colonial pattern of state-society relations was transmitted to the postwar period to produce "the politics of the vortex" of contemporary Korea, both North and South.[8]

Although Henderson should be commended for his coherent historical view of state-society relations in twentieth-century Korea, this view is flawed in a number of ways. First, despite the presence of a strong colonial state, Korean society was not necessarily "atomized" or subject merely to "naked manipulation and mobilization." In addition to the March First nationalist movement, Korean peasants and workers actively organized and mobilized to pursue their interests, and their activism did not go unheeded by the colonial state. On the contrary, their demands were often, if selectively, translated into colonial policy. Second, colonial totalitarianism may well describe the wartime mobilization of colonial society under the militarist colonial regime, but it does not represent state-society relations during other periods of colonial rule. Japanese colonial policy and thereby state-society relations underwent several significant changes, illustrated by the shift from the harsh, militarist *budan seiji* (Military Rule) of the first decade to the more inclusive *bunka seiji* from the second decade of colonial rule, and such changes over time must be recognized. Third, the colonial state's method of societal mobilization was more organic and corporatist than Henderson depicts. The rural campaign examined in this chapter is a clear example of the colonial state's attempt to create organic and corporatist linkages with rural society, and these campaign experiences and networks proved crucial to the subsequent war mobilization. Finally, postcolonial Korean regimes seem more corporatist than totalitarian, and their historical origins can better be traced back to state-society relations of the 1930s than of the war years, the period that Henderson's depiction more closely matches.

As is apparent, none of these three views adequately explains colonial state-rural society relations in 1930s Korea. As an alternative, we propose "corporatism," with some qualifications. Corporatism is a principle or system for linking society to the state. It differs from pluralism, Marxism, or fascism. Pluralism relies on voluntary associations in linking society to the state, and Marxism relies on class and class organizations. In both cases, the state's role is minimized or considered an instrument of the ruling class. Fascism relies on direct state mobilization without intermediary associations and requires an emotional commitment to a charismatic leader. By contrast, the corporatist state encourages the formation of a limited number of officially recognized groups that interact with the state in clearly defined and regulated ways. According to a well-known definition by Philippe Schmitter, "Corporatism . . . is a system of interest representation in which the constituent units are organized into a limited number of singular, compulsory, noncompetitive, hierarchically ordered and functionally differentiated categories, recognized or licensed (if not created) by the state and granted a deliberate representational monopoly within their respective categories in exchange for observing certain controls on their selection of leaders and articulation of demands and supporters."[9] The corporatist system is often adopted by the state as a response to economic crisis and/or erosion of ruling-class hegemony due to class conflict and is employed in ways to encourage economic mobilization and political demobilization.[10] It stresses social harmony and hierarchy; Catholicism and Confucianism are said to offer cultural/ideological bases for such principles of a corporatist system.[11] Yet corporatism appears in diverse forms, such as the societal/pluralist regimes of Western Europe and the state/authoritarian regimes of Latin America and East Asia.[12]

To apply this corporatist model to a colonial context, however, we need to make some qualifications. First of all, colonialism does not as a rule require a system of representation of the interests of colonial subjects. Typically there exists neither a party system nor any other body to represent the substantive interests of the colonial subjects. This is because by definition colonialism is imperialist, and the colonizers are interested in promoting their *own* interests rather than those of colonial subjects. However, a colonial power might adopt a corporatist policy as a means of colonial control, if not as a system of interest representation. This occurs when more conventional means of colonial control, from mere repression to reliance on a certain social class, do not work out well. In such a situation, the colonizers might try to increase "governmentality" through measures that are less coercive but require more direct state involvement in colonial affairs, an example of which would be government-sanctioned intermediary associations that link colonial subjects more effectively to the regime. The state may still dictate over society, but its linkage with society is more organic and corporatist and thus more effective for colonial control and mobilization than were it to rely solely on coercion, a particular class, or ideological manipulation.

As a means of social control or a structure of state-society linkage rather than a "system of interest representation," corporatism can readily be combined with colonialism to produce what we term "colonial corporatism." Alongside coercion and ideological manipulation, a colonial power may license or create new, semiofficial, semivoluntary, intermediary associations for colonial control and mobilization. In colonial Korea, as in other corporatist regimes, economic crisis and the decline in landlord hegemony in villages necessitated such a corporatist state response as expressed in the Rural

Revitalization Campaign. A Confucian cultural heritage stressing social hierarchy and harmony also assisted the colonial state in formulating a corporatist policy; in fact, as we show below, the Japanese were well aware of the potential value of traditional Confucian village institutions such as *hyangyak* (village compact) and mobilized them in the rural campaign. The outcome was enhanced state capacity to penetrate into rural affairs, but the state's relations with local society through various semiofficial intermediary associations were more than mechanical or "naked." This strategy also proved more effective in local control and mobilization than the earlier reliance on the landed class and/or the police.

Below we first describe the structural conditions that gave rise to a corporatist rural policy in the 1930s, followed by a discussion of the process of policy formulation for the Rural Revitalization Campaign. In doing so, we pay close attention to the process by which the internal situation was intertwined with the larger colonial political culture to produce a corporatist rural campaign. We then examine the campaign's main goals and organizations, and evaluate them. We conclude with a discussion of the larger implications of the campaign for understanding colonial state–rural society relations in 1930s Korea.

## Colonialism and Agrarian Transformation

As discussed above, modern corporatism arises as a state response to economic crisis that disrupts the production process and class conflict that challenges ruling-class hegemony.[13] With direct state intervention in the production process and the reorganization of interest groups into hierarchical, government-sanctioned associations, the corporatist regime attempts to resolve economic crisis and demobilize a politicized civil society. The Rural Revitalization Campaign was similarly a colonial state response to a rural crisis precipitated by the agricultural depression that began in the late 1920s and an intensification of the agrarian class conflict of the 1920s that undermined the power and authority of the landed class in villages. The campaign was intended to bring about social stability by resolving rural poverty and depoliticizing a mobilized rural society.

When Korea became a Japanese colony, it was a predominantly agrarian nation, with more than 80 percent of its population engaged in agriculture. Although the Japanese did not promote industrialization until the 1930s, they recognized the importance of agricultural production (especially rice), primarily to feed metropolitan Japan. As a concrete step, the colonial government launched the Campaign to Increase Rice Production in 1920, encouraging the use of chemical fertilizers and improved seeds, cultivation of new lands, and irrigation improvement, and required inspection of rice and beans to enhance quality and marketability. In addition, the growing demand for Korean agricultural crops in Japan boosted their prices, stimulated exports, facilitated market growth, and promoted agricultural commercialization. Although agriculture in precolonial Korea had been subject to the forces of the market and commercialization, colonialism accelerated these trends, often with state intervention, tightly integrating Korean agriculture into the larger world market (via Japan).

The increased commercialization of agriculture brought temporary prosperity to rural society, especially for large landlords, but Korean agriculture could not escape the pressure of market forces in the late 1920s. As the world market deteriorated, agricultural earnings plummeted in Korea. In 1927, the price of brown rice fell 22 percent off that of 1925 and by 1931 it was only 39 percent of the 1925 price. Export concentration on one crop—rice—was particularly disastrous, for rice prices plunged deepest. Most rural households went into debt; a 1932 survey, for instance, revealed that two-thirds of the 26,160 farm households investigated had debts, averaging 107 yen, which amounted to more than one-third of total annual income. Starvation was common: a leading newspaper described the situation as a "starving hell" where "people live because they cannot die." Rural Korea, with few defense mechanisms, was devastated by the worldwide depression.

In addition to the economic crisis, rural Korea was torn by intensified class conflict between landlords and tenants. When the Japanese reaffirmed the existing land tenure system through the land survey of 1910–18, they took few measures to protect tenants, leaving them without any legal means to redress their discontent. The Japanese adoption of Cultural Rule in the 1920s allowed limited political participation and offered a great opportunity for the peasantry to address its discontent against the landed class through collective action. As a result, peasants organized into unions and mobilized for collective political actions such as tenancy disputes. By 1926, for instance, 83 peasant unions with 11,938 members appeared in South

Chŏlla province alone, engaging in disputes against landlords over issues of rent, tenancy contracts, and land taxes. From 1920 to 1932, a total of 4,804 disputes involving 74,581 tenants and landlords occurred nationwide to become, in the words of the colonial government, a "constant phenomenon" of rural Korea. In addition, more radical groups such as "red peasant unions" emerged to engage in direct and often violent confrontation with colonial agencies such as local government offices and police stations over issues of taxation and interference in village affairs.

By early 1930s it became evident that earlier agricultural policies, especially the Campaign to Increase Rice Production launched in 1920 and landlord-based rural control, were largely failures. Although the production campaign helped to increase rice production and grain exports to Japan in the 1920s, it was undermined by the agricultural depression and a rice surplus in Japan in the late 1920s. In addition, the growth and intensification of rural conflict in the 1920s revealed a steady decline in the power and authority of landlords in rural villages. These changes in the countryside necessitated changes in colonial agricultural policy. In particular, the colonial government recognized the rural crisis as having arisen from an "overemphasis on production and neglect of spiritual aspects" and "lack of consistent guidance for the rural economy," despite the establishment of Chosŏn nonghoe (Korean agricultural association) in 1926. In order to correct earlier deficiencies, the colonial regime designed a new rural policy around "spiritualism" (*chŏngsin chuŭi*) instead of the earlier "production-first policy" (*saengsan cheil chuŭi*). The regime also realized the need to create a new form of village leadership in place of old elite (e.g., landlords) for more effective local control and mobilization.[14] Engaged in the Manchurian adventure of 1931 and preparing for another war, Japan feared that increased rural problems would seriously hinder labor and resource mobilization.

## Formulating a New Social Policy

The campaign was launched in the fall of 1932 during the tenure of Governor-General Ugaki, who was a strong advocate of it. Like many earlier Meiji reformers, Ugaki believed a strong Japan required "social harmony," of which the "productive classes" were a crucial component. In his diary, written in the late 1910s and the 1920s, he

expressed concern that class struggles between capitalists and workers as well as between landlords and peasants were destroying social
harmony in Japan. To correct such problems, Ugaki stressed "stabilizing people's lives" and "eradicating sources of spiritual dissatisfaction," and even asserted he would "curb the power of the capitalists and landlords in order to protect the [interests of the] productive
classes."[15] He also believed "the most important source of national
strength is neither natural resources nor population size but the
spiritual strength of the nation."[16] Furthermore, for Ugaki, "thought
problems do not simply come from communism or leftism but also
from ultra-rightism, indulgence in extravagance and passivism."[17]
By protecting producers and achieving social harmony through economic and spiritual improvement, Ugaki believed, Japan could become a superpower.

When he became governor-general of Korea in 1931, Ugaki saw
the danger that a deteriorating rural economy and intensifying class
conflict in Korea posed to Japanese empire building. He (and colonial policymakers) partly attributed "this miserable condition of affairs [to] the unconscious indifference of the farmers themselves";
more important, however, was "the absence of governmental economic and educational provisions as well as a defective social organization [and] environment and lack of guidance." As a result,
they regretted, villagers had "lost any idea of self-reliance and forgotten the real character and true pride of farming communities in . . .
the pursuit of a 'money economy.'" Poverty relief and special works
such as road construction might lessen rural poverty somewhat but
only temporarily. A more fundamental program offering both economic and spiritual guidance, they believed, was necessary to "re-
trieve the rural communities from entire collapse."[18] Well-aware of
agrarian-centered movements in Japan since the early twentieth
century, Ugaki endorsed a similar campaign for rural regeneration in
colonial Korea.

The campaign also reflected a new, social policy approach (*sahoe
chŏngch'aek*; J. *shakai seisaku*) that strongly advocated state intervention to resolve social problems. Often appearing in colonial government documents and Ugaki's diary, this conception of social policy
was a key component of Meiji ideology, since Meiji leaders believed
that appropriate state action could and would avert the social conflict and dislocation that had accompanied modernization in the
West. As a result, as Kenneth Pyle points out, they promoted "pre-

ventive action" to facilitate "conciliation of all social classes" in order to achieve the "perfect unity of the entire nation." Proposals for a tenancy law regulating tenant-landlord relations and for establishment of various credit unions and cooperatives as well as the rural revitalization campaign in Japan stemmed from such policy considerations.[19]

This social policy approach was particularly directed at the countryside, which was felt to embody and preserve the essence of what was historically Japanese. Although the Meiji reformers pursued modernization through industrialization, urbanization, and centralization—means that ran counter to the agrarian, rural, decentralized character of premodern Japan—farm policy was also a key element in Japan's overall program of modernization. Traditional Japanese political thought predisposed Meiji leaders to regard agrarian society as fundamental even in the process of modernization. Accordingly, they supported agrarian-centered movements such as the *chihō kairyō undō* (local improvement movement). Furthermore, with increased urbanization and industrialization, the importance of farming went beyond simply supporting Japanese modernization. As Japan encountered tensions and conflicts arising from modernization and as it mounted war in later years, Thomas Havens points out, the farm and its virtues were increasingly considered the social, military, and ethical foundation of the Japanese nation.[20] In other words, farm and rural society constituted key parts of the Japanese nation and by extension the Japanese empire and therefore were treated as central to both national and colonial policy even during industrialization. With this historical and ideological context in mind, the Rural Revitalization Campaign in 1930s Korea can be viewed as an extension of Meiji reformist thought embodied in an agrarianist social policy under the leadership of Governor-General Ugaki.

Nonetheless, it would be misleading to deem it a mere extension of Japanese policy into a colony or an imposition from above.[21] Internal developments within colonial Korea were also crucial to shaping the campaign. Concern over the rural crisis was not confined to the colonial government; various sectors of colonial society also attempted to resolve it, although there existed little consensus on how best to do so. For the Communists, for instance, the rural crisis signified symptoms of capitalist contradictions, and agrarian conflict furthered the cause of social revolution. Accordingly, they supported agrarian struggles as a step toward a proletariat revolution.

On the other hand, bourgeois culturalists understood the crisis in personal terms, attributing it to the peasants' lack of education and enlightenment. In response, they opened rural night schools to resolve the crisis through education.

In addition, there existed another important group, which elsewhere we have termed "agrarianists."[22] Their ideological orientations ranged from the Ch'ŏndogyo (Religion of the heavenly way)–based Chosŏn nongminsa (Korean peasant society) and YMCA-led Christian movement to village-specific Confucian-oriented rural regeneration groups and even anarchist socialists such as Kim Chung-gŏn.[23] Nonetheless, they largely agreed that the destructive power of capitalist forces was responsible for the current crisis and took an anticommercial and anticapitalist stance toward resolving it. As a result, agrarianists strongly advocated the establishment of a self-sufficient agrarian economy based on mutual assistance and collective farming as a step toward rural regeneration. Korean agrarianists viewed rural problems as major "social problems" (*sahoe munje*) and even as "national problems" (*minjok munje*), claiming that "agriculture is the last lifeline of Korea and therefore a rural crisis is a national crisis."[24] They regarded the rural crisis as much spiritual and moral as economic and social and thus urged the restoration of moral strength by promoting the virtues of diligence, frugality, social harmony, filial piety, female chastity, and the like. They also exalted the value of traditional village institutions such as *tonggye* (village aid society), *tonghoe* (village association), or *hyangyak* (village compact) as having the characteristic of self-sufficiency necessary for rural regeneration. An editorial in the journal *Kaebyŏk* advocated "an utopian agrarian nation" (*yut'op'ia chŏk nongmin kukka*) as the form for "a new Korea" (*sin Chosŏn*).[25]

Although they did not initiate nationwide petition movements for government assistance as was done in Japan,[26] they organized various spontaneous "rural regeneration" groups and associations, urging the colonial government to participate more actively in resolving the rural crisis.[27] In the course of the campaign, these organizations were either dissolved or remolded into state-sanctioned, semiofficial organizations, but in the process many of their ideas and programs were incorporated into the campaign. While suppressing Communist-supported radical groups such as red peasant unions, the colonial government attempted to incorporate these moderate agrarian movements, selectively, into the government campaign. In fact, *nongch'on chinhŭng*, a term coined and circulated by Korean agrarianists, was adopted by the colonial government to distinguish the Korean campaign from *keizai kōsei* or *kyŏngje kaengsaeng*, the term used for a similar campaign in Japan. The striking correspondences between these village-level regeneration movements and colonial state campaign programs were no coincidence. The government's Rural Revitalization Campaign contained traces of the Korean agrarianists' exaltation of rural lifestyle and self-sufficiency over urban culture and capitalist integration;[28] its emphasis on spiritualism over materialism and initiation of moral crusades;[29] its stress on social harmony expressed in collectivism;[30] its recognition of traditional values and institutions;[31] and its preference for "natural villages" (*chayŏn purak or maŭl*) over administrative villages (*haengjŏng purak*) as the main units of regeneration.[32]

## The Rural Revitalization Campaign, 1932–1940

The colonial government commended the idea of a rural revitalization campaign to provincial governors at a special session in summer 1932. After several minor technical conferences, the campaign was officially launched on November 10, 1932. As concrete preparation for the campaign, county executives and other local officials met for special courses of instruction, and "classes and lecture meetings were held in each province and county for the guiding staff in the furthest outpost lines, such as public schools, credit associations, police stations, and fishery associations, to teach them the spirit and practice of this rural revival movement."[33] In March 1933, the central government sent instructions to each provincial governor detailing concrete plans, programs, and goals. These plans made each household the direct object of guidance and sought to bring about "a stable livelihood within five years" along with "spiritual regeneration." The government identified "food shortages," "indebtedness," and "cash imbalances" as three main economic disabilities and targeted "pride in labor," "self-reliance," and a "grateful attitude" for spiritual improvement.[34] From the onset, the government made it clear that rural regeneration had to be achieved in both "material and spiritual aspects" of village life.[35]

A key part of this broad campaign was the Rural Rehabilitation Plan (*Nongga kaengsaeng kyehoek*), which was similar to the Japanese *Keizai kōsei undō*. Under this plan, each county selected villages for rehabilitation from among its *natural* villages, each with 30 to 40 households. A survey was taken of the rural economy of all households in each selected village, and a detailed plan was devised to meet the main goals of economic rehabilitation. The survey was comprehensive, including information on demographics (age, education level, etc., of each member of every household); the extent of debt, savings, and food shortages; land productivity; crop production; fertilizer use; cash income; and expenses. Based on this survey, rehabilitation households were selected and given individualized five-year economic rehabilitation plans.[36]

Each selected household was encouraged to increase its economic well-being through complete utilization of available labor (e.g., taking extra jobs in the winter), crop diversification, and rational land management. The plan emphasized development of "self-reliance or self-sufficiency" through frugality and savings so that the peasant economy would not again be subject to the "market economy," as it had been during the agricultural depression.[37] It also urged improved "spiritual welfare" through pride in farm labor, mutual assistance among neighbors, colored clothes, loyalty to the emperor, and displays of the Japanese national flag. The government estimated it would take about fifteen years for the rehabilitation plan to finally reach most villages in rural Korea.[38] As Table 3.1 shows, the first two years showed slow progress; the plan was launched in only 381 villages. But after that, implementation accelerated, expanding to 28,511 villages and 597,691 households by 1939 or about 39 percent of all rural villages and 28 percent of rural households. Geographically, North Chŏlla (48 percent), North Hamgyŏng (47 percent), Kangwŏn (43 percent), and Hwanghae (41 percent) provinces showed the greatest participation but no significant regional variation appeared (see Table 3.2).

The rural campaign also had a program to increase the number of owner-cultivators. At the onset of the agricultural depression, the rural class structure rapidly polarized into large landlords and landless tenants (between 1927 and 1932, the proportion of landless tenants increased from 43.8 percent to 52.7 percent of the rural population), and the expropriated small owner-cultivators and semi-tenants became the main supporters of the red peasant union movements.[39] Deeply concerned about this trend of rural polarization and radicalization, the colonial government attempted to forestall

Table 3.1
Annual Increases in Numbers of Rehabilitation
Villages and Households, 1933–39

| Year | Villages | Households |
|------|----------|------------|
| 1933 | 161 | 3,283 |
| 1934 | 220 | 2,974 |
| 1935 | 3,603 | 70,530 |
| 1936 | 5,761 | 118,296 |
| 1937 | 5,851 | 121,406 |
| 1938 | 6,365 | 137,289 |
| 1939 | 6,550 | 143,913 |
| TOTAL | 28,511 | 597,691 |

SOURCE: Chōsen sōtokufu, *Chōsen ni okeru nōson shinkō undō no jisshi gaikyō to sono jisseki* (Keijō, 1940), p. 38.

Table 3.2
*Number of Rehabilitation Villages by Province, 1933–39*

| Province | Total villages | Rehabilitation villages (%) | |
|----------|---------------|-----------------|------|
| Kyŏnggi | 7,479 | 2,563 | (34%) |
| North Ch'ungch'ŏng | 3,695 | 1,342 | (36) |
| South Ch'ungch'ŏng | 6,448 | 2,409 | (37) |
| North Chŏlla | 5,680 | 2,739 | (48) |
| South Chŏlla | 7,599 | 2,929 | (39) |
| North Kyŏngsang | 7,916 | 2,807 | (36) |
| South Kyŏngsang | 7,220 | 2,782 | (39) |
| Hwanghae | 8,146 | 3,369 | (41) |
| South P'yŏngan | 4,513 | 1,659 | (37) |
| North P'yŏngan | 4,594 | 1,748 | (38) |
| Kangwŏn | 4,950 | 2,119 | (43) |
| South Hamgyŏng | 3,947 | 1,427 | (36) |
| North Hamgyŏng | 1,320 | 619 | (47) |
| TOTAL | 73,507 | 28,512 | (39) |

SOURCE: Chōsen sōtokufu, *Chōsen ni okeru nōson shinkō undō no jisshi gaikyō to sono jisseki* (Keijō, 1940), pp. 36–37.

further deterioration by enabling landless tenants to purchase land and become small owner-cultivators. Only when peasants owned land, it was believed, would they feel attached to village life and thus seek social stability and harmony. The government accordingly provided tax breaks and mobilized financial co-operatives that offered low-interest loans for land purchases. Between 1933 and 1940, more than one million peasant households availed themselves of such loans.[40]

In carrying out the various programs of the campaign, the government mobilized three main organizations: the councils for rural revitalization (CRR — *nongch'on chinhŭng wiwŏnhoe*), financial co-ops (*kŭmyung chohap*), and *siksan'gye* (mutual-aid associations for production). CRRs were created in every province, county, and district to execute campaign programs at the local level, often by integrating already existing official and semiofficial village organizations. The CRRs aimed to improve consistency in guidance of rural regeneration and consisted of officials and local notables including township executives, the police chief, members of the financial co-op board, public school principals, and others. The CRRs were main official organizations and oversaw the process of the campaign.

Besides the CRRs, financial co-ops also played a key role in rural economic rehabilitation, especially in resolving debt problems.[41] Established in 1907 as semiofficial rural finance institutions, as of 1933, 685 branches with one million members were operating. Between 1933 and 1940, financial co-ops extended a total of 52 million wŏn to members as low-interest loans to obviate usury, benefiting almost a half-million peasant households. Financial co-ops were also mobilized in the campaign to create owner-cultivators; they often purchased large tracts of land to distribute among several landless tenants and semi-tenants in exchange for long-term low-interest payments.

The *siksan'gye* were created by a 1935 ordinance. Since many poor, non-member peasants were excluded from participating in co-ops, the government promulgated an ordinance enabling non-members to benefit from low-interest loans through membership in *siksan'gye*. An average of 30 to 40 households formed a *siksan'gye*, and through mutual guarantees, they could also become financial co-op members. In addition, *siksan'gye* often functioned as peasant co-ops for purchasing and marketing and became the main village-level organization.

Even as the government utilized official and semiofficial organizations such as CRRs, financial co-ops, and *siksan'gye*, it did not overlook the importance of local leadership, which was considered critical to making the campaign self-sufficient beyond government guidance. Although some landlords participated in the campaign as members of CRRs, their record in tenant disputes tainted their leadership status. Recognizing this, the government initiated leadership-training programs targeting educated local youth, both male and female, to become "mainstays" (*chunggyŏn inmul*) and replace the landed class as village leaders. According to official statistics, between 1936 and 1940 about 9,600 "mainstays" (approximately 40 per county) were trained at 148 long-term (one year) and short-term (one month) training sites.[42] Candidates had to be "physically strong" and "ideologically healthy" educated young people (age 18 to 25, with at least ordinary school education). This emphasis on rural youth was based on the notion they would be more willing than their elders to embrace new ways of thinking and farming—economic rationalization, new farming methods, and changes in social life—providing a strong "elective affinity" with the campaign.[43]

Mainstay training programs reflected the campaign's overall focus on both economic and spiritual aspects. Economic training included instruction in rational land management, organization of co-ops, collective farming, and economic self-sufficiency. Spiritual training stressed Shinto worship, service to the state, pride in imperial citizenship, and frugality. Trainees were expected to serve as the social basis of colonial rule, linking the state to rural villages.[44] No comprehensive statistics profile the class background of these "mainstays," but one source indicates that among 979 trainees in three places, 32 percent came from owner-cultivator, 44 percent from semi-tenant, and 24 percent from landless tenant classes.[45] It is unlikely that children of large absentee landlords participated in training programs. Although some sons and daughters of small landlords might have enrolled, this class profile clearly suggests the government sought to replace traditional landlords with newly trained, young semi-tenants and owner-cultivators for local leadership and mobilization.[46]

In reorganizing village leadership, the government recognized the potential value of traditional Confucian culture and institutions, especially *hyangyak* (village compacts).[47] *Hyangyak* originally served local yangban elite in the Chosŏn dynasty as a means of local control, and in the nineteenth century the state also utilized *hyangyak* (in a different form) to increase its control over local villages. These compacts emphasized "mutual encouragement of morality, mutual supervision of wrong conduct, mutual decorum in social relationships, and mutual succor in time of disaster or hardship."[48] The Japanese seized the potential such village compact codes held for local control and mobilization, introducing an exemplary *hyangyak* practiced by Yi Yulgok, a highly respected Confucian yangban scholar of sixteenth-century Korea, in the inaugural issue of *Charyŏk kaengsaeng*, the official publication of the Rural Revitalization Campaign. Ugaki himself lamented the lack of "true" Confucianism among ordinary Koreans and advocated it on behalf of rural social harmony.[49]

Accordingly, CRRs and various rural organizations such as the *siksan'gye* were encouraged to organize along *hyangyak* principles. A village CRR in Yŏn'gi county of South Ch'ungch'ŏng province, for instance, specified "filial piety," "loyalty to the emperor," "respect for elders," "frugality," and "harmony between Japanese and Koreans" as virtues to promote. In North and South Hamgyŏng provinces, *hyangyak* customs were reportedly practiced in about half of all villages to "reform bad customs," "encourage savings and timely tax payments," and "form village defense units." CRRs in South Ch'ungch'ŏng province also lauded "rational management of cultivation," "land improvement," "the practice of saving and frugality," "spiritual improvement," and "moral education for imperial citizens," all largely based on *hyangyak* principles.[50] Also, many villages organized a society for moral correction (*kyop'unghoe*) based on neo-Confucian principles to promote such virtues as diligence, frugality, savings, social harmony, filial piety, and female chastity. Revival of *hyangyak* during the campaign is one clear example of the modern appropriation of Korean tradition for colonial domination.[51]

## The Campaign, State Penetration, and Colonial Hegemony

The Rural Revitalization Campaign touched almost every aspect of rural economic and social life, from food and debt problems to lifestyle and relations to the state, and involved extensive rural mobilization through official and semiofficial organizations. What did the campaign actually achieve? Or more pointedly, what did the colonial state achieve through the campaign? What can we infer from this examination of the rural campaign about Japanese rule and colonial state-society relations?

First, the campaign appears to have achieved some success in improving the economic welfare of rehabilitation program participants. As Table 3.3 shows, 36 percent of rural households who participated in the program successfully resolved food shortages, 27 percent readjusted and repaid usurious debts, and 45 percent maintained an annual cash income and expenditures balance. Also, as Table 3.4 indicates, between 1932 and 1939 a total of 18,991 tenants and semi-tenants purchased land with government assistance. Similarly, government surveys of the 3,587 tenant and semi-tenant households who participated in the rehabilitation program show that 21 percent (590 + 25 + 154 = 769) moved up to either semi-tenant or owner-cultivator status between 1933 and 1938, whereas only 1 percent (34) declined in status (see Table 3.5). Moreover, the amount of cultivated land increased for 56 percent of participants, while it decreased for 33 percent (Table 3.6).

To be sure, the positive effect of the economic rehabilitation plan should not be exaggerated. As Table 3.3 reveals, 64 percent of rural households who participated in the program still suffered food shortages as of 1939, 73 percent remained in debt, and 55 percent had cash expenditures exceeding income. The number of tenants and semi-tenants who became owner-cultivators through government assistance constituted only 0.8 percent of the entire tenant and semi-tenant class, and their purchased land amounted to only 0.5 percent of total leased land (see Table 3.4). Also, more than three-quarters of peasant households surveyed by the government experienced no mobility, up or down, through program participation (see Table 3.5). Finally, the 1930s brought a large exodus of the rural poor to Japan, Manchuria, and urban/industrial areas: between 1930 and 1940, the number of Koreans in Japan and Manchuria increased by 892,353 and 701,934, respectively.

Nonetheless, these figures do indicate modest achievements in improving rural economic welfare. Particularly clear is that the campaign, along with other legal measures such as the Tenancy Arbitration Ordinance of 1932 and Agricultural Lands Ordinance of 1934, was a key factor in bringing about village stability. Most macro-statistics of agriculture and the rural economy showed general improvement in the 1930s. Agricultural productivity and production

Table 3.3
Outcomes of Economic Rehabilitation, 1933–38
(unit = households)

| Year | Food shortage | | Indebtedness | | Cash income imbalance | |
|---|---|---|---|---|---|---|
| | pre-rehabi-litation | current (%) (1939) | pre-rehabi-litation | current (%) (1939) | pre-rehabi-litation | current (%) (1939) |
| 1933 | 2,612 | 1,174 (45%) | 3,964 | 1,929 (49%) | 2,396 | 785 (33%) |
| 1934 | 29,460 | 10,601 (36) | 40,998 | 18,830 (46) | 26,601 | 7,079 (27) |
| 1935 | 40,935 | 21,327 (52) | 54,514 | 33,381 (61) | 35,093 | 14,625 (42) |
| 1936 | 67,898 | 41,251 (61) | 88,601 | 64,470 (73) | 53,519 | 27,672 (52) |
| 1937 | 67,898 | 45,060 (66) | 91,970 | 70,329 (76) | 56,545 | 32,814 (58) |
| 1938 | 68,721 | 57,025 (83) | 99,981 | 87,799 (88) | 55,865 | 42,928 (77) |
| TOTAL | 277,524 | 176,438 (64) | 380,028 | 276,738 (73) | 230,019 | 125,903 (55) |

SOURCE: Chōsen sōtokufu, Chōsen ni okeru nōson shinkō undō no jisshi gaikyō to sono jisseki (Keijō, 1940), pp. 26–27.

Table 3.4

*Creation of Owner-Cultivators, 1932–39*

| Year | House-holds | Purchased land (*chŏngbo*) | Prices (000 ¥) | Loans (000 ¥) | % of leased land |
|------|------|------|------|------|------|
| 1932 | 2,085 | 1,527 | 1,317 | 1,311 | 56.5 |
| 1933 | 2,095 | 1,515 | 1,338 | 1,322 | 56.3 |
| 1934 | 2,540 | 1,669 | 1,685 | 1,650 | 57.4 |
| 1935 | 2,470 | 1,578 | 1,702 | 1,650 | 57.3 |
| 1936 | 2,383 | 1,582 | 1,712 | 1,626 | 57.6 |
| 1937 | 2,483 | 1,560 | 1,761 | 1,652 | 57.6 |
| 1938 | 2,486 | 1,412 | 1,790 | 1,644 | 57.9 |
| 1939 | 2,449 | 1,308 | 1,849 | 1,638 | 58.0 |
| TOTAL | 18,991[a] | 12,151[b] | 13,154 | 12,493 | |

[a] Equivalent to 0.8 percent of total tenant and semi-tenant households.
[b] Equivalent to 0.5 percent of total leased land.
SOURCE: Chōsen sōtokufu, *Chōsen nochi nenpo* (Keijō, 1940), pp. 100–101, 109.

Table 3.5

*Social Mobility Between 1933 and 1938*
(N = 3,587 households)

| Status in 1933 | Status in 1938 | | |
|------|------|------|------|
| | tenant | semi-tenant | owner-cultivator |
| Tenant (N = 1,728) | 1,113 | 590 | 25 |
| Semi-tenant (N = 1,859) | 34 | 1,671 | 154 |

SOURCES: Chōsen sōtokufu, *Nōka keizai gaikyō chōsa – kosaku nōka* (Keijō, 1940), p. 41; and Chōsen sōtokufu, *Nōka keizai gaikyō chōsa – jisaku ken kosaku* (Keijō, 1940), p. 41.

Table 3.6
*Change in Amount of Cultivated Land Between 1933 and 1938*
(N = 3,587 households)

| Status in | 1938 | | |
|---|---|---|---|
| 1933 | Increase | Decrease | No change |
| Tenants | 991 | 516 | 221 |
| Semi-tenants | 1,015 | 662 | 182 |
| TOTAL | 2,006 | 1,178 | 403 |
| PERCENTAGE | 56% | 33% | 11% |

SOURCES: Chōsen sōtokufu, *Nōka keizai gaikyō chōsa – kosaku nōka* (Keijō, 1940), p. 41; and Chōsen sōtokufu, *Nōka keizai gaikyō chōsa--jisaku ken kosaku* (Keijō, 1940), p. 41.

increased substantially, rental rates declined, food and consumption of other goods in rural households increased, the trend of rural class polarization stalled, if not reversed, and the landed class no longer wielded its previous power and authority in villages. Government statistics show that between 1935 and 1939, labor and land productivity increased by 22 percent and 29 percent, respectively; agricultural production increased by 31 percent between 1933 and 1939; rental rates declined from 48.6 percent to 47.8 percent in paddy fields and from 38.9 percent to 37.2 percent in dry fields between 1933 and 1938; per capita rice consumption returned to pre-depression levels; and the rural class structure remained virtually unchanged (the proportion of the tenant class in the rural population was 52 percent in 1933 and 51.9 percent in 1938) and the proportion of leased land likewise stabilized (see Table 3.4). In short, along with tenancy laws, the campaign played a key role in improving rural economic and social welfare.[52]

The spiritual outcomes of the campaign are more difficult to assess. For instance, although government plans to create owner-cultivators may have, as Chŏng Munjong points out, enhanced *chajangnong kwannyŏm* (the belief, among landless tenants, that one can own one's own land by working hard),[53] the extent is hard to ascertain. The campaign's success in other aspects of spiritual regeneration is even more obscure. To be sure, the colonial government extolled the campaign's spiritual achievements: "During the present conflict in China [1937] the people of this peninsula have been fired with patriotism and national spirit to a degree far exceeding that displayed at the time of the Manchuria incident [1931]. This is . . . one of the direct results from the efficient conduct of this revival movement."[54] Similarly, it proclaimed that: "Sŏngjin county of North Hamgyŏng province had previously been full of dangerous thought that provoked anti-government activities whenever possible. . . . At present[, however,] those peasants who have participated in the campaign have great hope for their future and make every effort to achieve the goals set by the rehabilitation program." It praised the exemplary Mr. Cho "who has become an ardent worshiper of the emperor" and "speaks for His grace."[55] It is quite probable that the campaign's main beneficiaries, such as the "mainstays" or local leaders, internalized many of its spiritual aspects, including emperor worship. Yet government accounts must be viewed with circumspection, and indeed oral histories describing peasants' "everyday forms of resistance" during the war years support such caution.[56] Carter Eckert's finding that after 1945 "one of the first objects singled out for retribution was the local Shinto shrine, the key symbol of the hated Naisen Ittai policy," also suggests government claims were tendentious.[57]

On the other hand, the government greatly enhanced its "infrastructural power," that is, its capacity to penetrate into villages, through extensive organizations established during the campaign. Instead of relying exclusively on the landed class and the police to maintain rural order, it could count on semiofficial organizations like CRRs, financial co-ops, and *siksan'gye* as well as new village leaders (*chunggyŏn inmul*) to bring the state and rural society together. This more direct, tight, and corporatist linkage of the state to villages was less coercive yet more effectively achieved local control and mobilization. By 1940, more than two-thirds of all rural households were members of financial co-ops, and by 1943, 83 percent were *siksan'gye* members.[58] By the time Japan declared war on the United States and other Western powers in 1941, rural Korea was organized into hierarchical, organic, and corporatist entities, ready for state mobilization.

With the outbreak of the Sino-Japanese war of 1937, the campaign's main goal shifted from rural revitalization to "supporting the nation through production (*saengŏp poguk*)." In addition, as the war progressed, increasing emphasis was put on enhancement of national spirit (*kungmin chŏngsin*), imperial citizenship (*hwangguk sinminhwa*), and *naisen ittai* (Japan and Korea as a single body). The campaign's stress on both material and spiritual improvement was highly consistent with the Japanese concept of "total war," which pursued mobilization of both economic and human resources. Furthermore, the campaign's extensive rural networks were utilized for such war mobilization programs as *kongch'ul* (extraction of agricultural crops).[59] Although it is unclear whether the colonial government launched the campaign for wartime mobilization from the onset, it clearly relied on the campaign's organizational structure and experience once war commenced.

## Conclusions: Corporatism and Rural Mobilization

Examination of the Rural Revitalization Campaign reveals the inadequacy of viewing Japanese rule simply in terms of repression and resistance and suggests a far more complex situation. Although the Japanese used coercion and repression extensively throughout the entire colonial period and Koreans in turn continuously offered resistance to colonial rule, both domestically and abroad, colonial authorities also designed noncoercive measures to cultivate consent for their rule. The rural campaign examined here typifies a major government effort to obtain colonial hegemony in villages by raising rural living standards.

Campaign policies significantly departed from the previous focus on agricultural production and reliance on the landed class for local control and mobilization. By the early 1930s, after a decade of intense tenant-landlord conflict and agricultural depression since the late 1920s, it was clear that such approaches had outlived their usefulness. The rural crisis demanded government attention, and the campaign examined here, along with tenancy laws, emerged in response. The campaign attempted both to achieve economic and spiritual regeneration in villages and to restructure village organizations and leadership by establishing various village-level associations, such as CRRs, financial co-ops, and *siksan'gye*, and training new village leaders, or "mainstays." This shift from agricultural production and landlord-based local control and mobilization to rural stability and reliance on village-level organizations led by young villagers brought the state into more immediate contact with local society.

Although the campaign was a government-initiated program, the colonial regime, which was well aware of rural discontent, carefully and selectively attempted to incorporate peasants' demands into state policy. The campaign stressed spiritual as well as economic regeneration, the use of natural villages as the main local units, the corporative approach to rural rehabilitation, the concept of self-sufficiency, mobilization of Confucian values and institutions, and promotion of owner-cultivators as a base for rural stability, all principles discussed and suggested in one way or another by Korean agrarianists in the 1920s and early 1930s. While coming down hard on radical nationalists and Communists, the colonial government tried to accommodate moderate ideas and demands, as expressed in the campaign. In addition to Meiji reform ideology in the form of agrarianism and a social policy approach, internal developments within Korea crucially shaped the course of the rural campaign.

The campaign was a colonial-state response to increased class conflict and the decline in landlord hegemony as well as to the economic crisis in rural villages precipitated by agricultural depression. In this, it shared many features with the responses of corporatist regimes in Europe and Latin America in this century, even though it occurred under colonial rule and in a rural setting. Unlike the societal or pluralist corporatism that emerged in Europe, however, peasant interests were not institutionalized through political representation by the campaign. The Japanese initiated the campaign not so much to represent the interests of colonial subjects as to enhance Japan's ability to mobilize and control Koreans. In this regard, the Korean case seems to resemble the state corporatism or authoritarian corporatism of Latin America, which encouraged economic mobilization but discouraged political mobilization, with the state dictating over society. We thus characterize the campaign as a form of "colonial corporatism," one not implemented by other colonial powers. One clear outcome of this colonial corporatism was the enormously enhanced state capacity to penetrate into society, paving the way for wartime mobilization, which heavily relied on campaign networks and experiences.

The attempt of the colonial government to reorganize rural society into hierarchical, organic, and corporatist entities requires us to rethink previous characterizations of colonial state-society relations. As shown above, the colonial government no longer supported the landlord system in the 1930s, as it had in earlier years. Besides promoting industrialization, it sought to appease rural discontent and create new village leaders who could mediate between the state and local society, even at the expense of the landed class. This study also points out that 1930s rural Korea did not witness an atomized mass society; quite the opposite, rural society was restructured into a variety of officially sanctioned, semiofficial organizations that could offer close linkages between the state and local society.

Colonial rule ended with Japan's defeat in the Pacific War, but the colonial campaign left a crucial legacy that shaped state-society relations in contemporary Korea. It seems no historical coincidence that similar corporatist state-society relations emerged in both North and South Korea after 1945.[60] For instance, the regime of Park Chung Hee launched a similar campaign known as the Saemaul (New village or New community) movement in 1971, involving some 35,000 villages nationwide. As in the colonial campaign, the movement emphasized both economic and spiritual aspects of rural improvement, including such objectives as crop diversification, improved seed selection, simplification of traditional rituals, respect for traditional norms like filial piety, and loyalty to the nation.[61] Precipitated by Park's narrow election victory earlier in the year, it was an ideological campaign, launched to enhance rural mobilization and loyalty to the state. The parallels to the colonial campaign are unmistakable, and the colonial rural campaign examined here offers a crucial historical basis for understanding patterns of state-society relations in contemporary Korea.

FOUR

# The Limits of Cultural Rule:

# Internationalism and Identity in Japanese

# Responses to Korean Rice

Michael A. Schneider

In surveying articulate opinion on colonial policy in the mass media of imperial Japan (1895–1945), one is struck by the power of two organizing vortexes of thought on the content and significance of Japanese colonialism. On the one hand, the argument that Japan's activity expresses some inherent quality, identity, need, or interest of metropolitan society pulls together many and diverse justifications for colonialism. On the other hand, one finds with dulling repetition the mantra of "respect for local conditions," the plea that governing principles of colonial administration should follow from intimate knowledge of the specific societies developed by observers on the spot. Between national self-definition and bureaucratic pragmatism, however, one can discern a third stream, which saw colonialism as a global phenomenon associated with modernity and placed Japan's colonialism in an international context. A foreshadowing of the late twentieth-century interest in the forces of "globalization," this alternative stream recognized the processes of political and social self-definition aspiring to universality in a global environment, which

Arjun Appadurai has termed "modernity at large."[1] Often over-looked in the history of Japanese colonial thought is this reflection of a late twentieth-century truism: the local is international.

This chapter explores Japanese responses to colonialism in the 1920s as a period in which this third stream of thought gained special prominence not only because of changes in Japanese society but also because of the special features of Japanese colonial policy in Korea gathered under the rubric *bunka seiji*, conventionally translated "Cultural Rule." This third stream found fullest expression in 1920s Japan, where an atmosphere of political experimentation and cultural cosmopolitanism included a move to reform colonial rule in Korea and develop Korean agriculture. Precipitated by the March First protests of 1919, administrative reforms in Japanese colonial policy fed a broad desire to adapt Korea to the conditions and needs of metropolitan Japan. Although for most Koreans and later historians Cultural Rule denoted an expeditious, even cynical, set of policies to deflect direct opposition to Japan's domination, Japanese audiences saw it as much more. I thus use the expression "Cultural Rule" to refer to a nexus of related ideas about cultural and economic development that circulated in articulate Japanese opinion about Japan's colonialism in Korea during the 1920s. This usage may seem idiosyncratic today, but it would not have appeared so in 1920s Japan. Intersecting with such diverse metropolitan concerns as domestic rice markets, overseas emigration policy, middle-class management, and the questioning of national identity and international affairs associated with each of these issues, the specific policies adopted in Korea and the development of Korean agriculture under Cultural Rule were not viewed by Japanese audiences as strictly local phenomena. Understanding the significance of Cultural Rule as a complex of ideas for Japanese audiences helps us appreciate the context of Japanese colonialism, the content of Japan's colonial ideology, and, most significantly, how ideas of modern development shaped Japanese attitudes toward Korea in this period.

Important changes in international politics and Japanese society gave Cultural Rule the special force it had for Japanese audiences. Because of international criticism of the system of imperialist diplomacy on the heels of World War I and the diverse social movements known collectively as Taishō democracy, Cultural Rule captured Japanese attention as an important attempt to reconcile a tarnished and anachronistic colonialism with the realities of a global system of liberal internationalism. Recent scholarship has focused on the significance of a rising Japanese middle class in adapting ideologies of modernity to the goals of social management.[2] This class clamored for greater influence in existing institutions and struggled to create new avenues to influence political and social reform, and it is not surprising that Cultural Rule appealed to middle-class journalists, academics, and professionals. The urban middle class in Japan was at root a class of consumers. In a nation afflicted by recurrent and disruptive economic crises, the urban middle class, with its acquisitive bent and managerial talents, was frequently characterized as a pillar of stability between the capital-owning and the working classes.[3] The *idea* of Cultural Rule garnered considerable interest among the urban middle classes because, for them, Cultural Rule was more than just a collection of administrative reforms and cultural policies. Cultural Rule was about economic development, a Japanese attempt to fashion colonial economic development along the lines of emerging international standards of economic modernization. In Japan, Cultural Rule meant Korean rice and policies to develop Korean agriculture in the interests of Japanese consumers.

Despite the broad intellectual appeal of colonial reform, Cultural Rule and its specific agricultural policies left, at best, an ambiguous legacy in Japan. One of the most telling facts of Japan's economic hegemony in Korea is that Japanese consumed an increasing percentage of total Korean rice production throughout the 1920s. It is difficult to argue that they did so with a clear conception that they ate it to strengthen the bonds of empire, soothe nationalist antagonisms between Japan and Korea, or satisfy the aims of Japan's long-term economic development. Japanese middle-class commentary during the period of Cultural Rule shows deep dissatisfaction with Korean rice as the link between identity and colonialism. The idea of Cultural Rule spoke to metropolitan audiences in unpredictable, even contradictory, ways. This chapter argues that the tangible and symbolic promotion of Korean rice in a metropolitan context complicated rather than clarified the question of cultural identity within the empire. The struggles over Cultural Rule among metropolitan audiences attest to the powerful influence of the international context on the course of colonial policy.

## Metropolitan Sources of Cultural Rule

The administrative policies known as Cultural Rule were implemented in Korea after (from the Japanese perspective) the surprising nationalist protests of the spring and summer of 1919. The savagery of the Japanese response to the March First movement threw into stark relief the Government-General's limited vision of control and development in Korea at that time. Although departing Governor-General Hasegawa Yoshimichi's notions of political and economic cooperation placed all development in Japanese hands,[4] the Japanese intellectual community had far different ideas about the future of the Japanese colonial empire. The idea of Cultural Rule had emerged in the decade preceding the March First movement in ruminations among Japanese academics, journalists, and bureaucrats on the course of colonial development. Calls for a colonial policy informed by international standards of administration and sensitive to Japan's international reputation resulted in part from the growing influence of middle-class commentary on Japanese expansionism, the strong influences of Anglo-American internationalist thought on Japanese scholarship about empire, and new institutional settings for these ideas. Space limitations prevent exploration of the intellectual roots of Cultural Rule in detail, but three features of the post-1919 policy bear the unmistakable impress of ideas fashionable within informed Japanese opinion on empire in the years before 1919: the clear rationalization of colonial economic development in terms of global and regional forces, the ideological accommodation of colonial rule to Japanese professional and managerial classes, and the accommodation of policy and practice to emerging colonial nationalisms.

Cultural Rule in practice meant many things to many people. For Koreans, it meant new techniques of political mobilization, control, and surveillance combined with new opportunities in the economic, intellectual, and cultural spheres. Official pronouncements about reform in Korea envisioned a distant and gradual, rather than an immediate and aggressively engineered, assimilation of Korea. It also meant the Campaign to Increase Rice Production (*Sanmai zōshoku keikaku*, hereafter CIRP), a scheme to develop Korean agriculture and expand exports of Korean rice to Japan. Although Koreans were the principal audience of Cultural Rule, there was a metropolitan audience as well. Cultural Rule offered much to Japanese entrepreneurial elites and the working classes, and, as noted above, it spoke directly to issues long prominent in middle-class discourses on empire and expansionism, in at least three ways. First, a discourse on development, mobilized and sustained by colonial bureaucrats in Korea and by sympathetic agricultural and social scientists in Japan, addressed middle-class interests in rational and progressive administration.[5] Second, rice imports from Korea appealed to middle-class concerns about the "food problem" and related emigration policies, the cornerstones of middle-class interest in expansionism in the 1920s.[6] Finally, the cultural dimensions of economic development, the possibility of appeasing nationalist aspirations in Korea, eased middle-class anxieties over anti-Japanese nationalism in Asia.

Cultural Rule was not monolithic, however, and metropolitan commentators did not view it as such. Together, rice and the CIRP are one measure of the dynamics of colonial ideology in Japan within the cooperative international framework of the 1920s. This emphasis on the metropolitan and international contexts does not imply a writing out of Koreans from the equation of colonial rule. Quite the opposite, the wide interpretive latitude offered Japanese and Koreans within this complex nexus of attitudes on race, nation, and development allowed numerous points of convergence between Japanese and Korean ideas. I can explore only a few below; other chapters in this volume suggest many others. A relative fluidity of attitudes toward culture, race, and nation within Japanese colonialism may well be unique to the empire of the 1920s. The 1920s model of cooperative development within a framework of nationalist accommodation was quite different from the forced assimilation of *naisen ittai* (Japan and Korea as a single body) of the 1930s, in which an amalgamation of the Korean and the Japanese bourgeoisie cemented a Japanese-defined sense of national identity. As Carter Eckert has argued, the Korean bourgeoisie came to welcome industrialization as a means of achieving opportunities and privileges within Japan's imperial framework that had been blocked by racial prejudice in earlier decades.[7] Cultural Rule offered a different sort of accommodation between Japanese and Korean nationalisms.

In emphasizing the malleability of Cultural Rule in the hands of Japanese commentators, there are two arguments I do not wish to make. I am not proposing simply that a diversity of opinion existed in Japan on the proper course and content of Cultural Rule of the 1920s. Such diversity was obvious at the time and was itself the cause of discussion in Japan and Korea. Neither am I advocating the view that Cultural Rule was a genuinely "liberal" or tolerant policy. Japanese liberals did want a more tolerant colonial policy, and some features of Cultural Rule were in theory meant to accommodate Korean aspirations. But clearly the Government-General had no interest in abandoning its autonomy from metropolitan control or weakening its surveillance of nationalist political movements in Korea. The apparent duplicity of the Government-General in its thinking about, and implementation of, Cultural Rule has been the subject of much of the scholarship on Cultural Rule, which I do not dispute. On the other hand, the Government-General, while jealous of its administrative autonomy, was conscious of its international reputation and susceptible to the internationalist intellectual currents of the 1920s. As was widely recognized at the time, the international context of Anglo-American hegemony shaped any discussion of economic development.[8]

International and metropolitan contexts mattered to the formulation, application, and meaning of Cultural Rule. Cultural Rule expressed and was entirely consistent with new ideas in Japan on economic development and intercultural relations. These ideas were neither a continuation of late Meiji imperialism nor the fountainhead of the *naisen ittai* policies of the late 1930s. Indeed, the shift in Japanese colonial policy during the 1930s may, in part, have been a response to the failure of Cultural Rule to convince metropolitan classes to support colonial development. Cultural Rule languished throughout the 1920s because it simultaneously complemented and competed with prevailing notions of development and nationality current in Japan. Among metropolitan audiences, who were as likely to think about the metropolitan and international dimensions of colonialism as they were to dwell on the day-to-day impact of colonial policies on the lives of Koreans, Cultural Rule was subject to interpretations quite in contrast to those of observers with a ground-level view of Japan's colonizing activity in Korea.

## Rice in the Discourse on Development

"Development" has been a powerful idea for capitalist states in their relations with colonies or former colonies. It has allowed imperial states to frame their economic activity in the colonies, especially the transforming effects of capitalist market relations and economic dependency, in terms of progress and modernization. One strength of the CIRP was its link between the idea of "development" and a clear, urban, middle-class interest in empire. Japanese concern over stable supplies of inexpensive agricultural products as the basis for an industrialized society blossomed anew near the end of World War I. Rice riots flared in Japanese cities as consumers were caught between British and French wartime controls on southeast Asian rice and the machinations of Japanese speculators. The prevention of rice riots and labor radicalism required a broader conception of agricultural policy than the short-term remedies adopted by the Hara Kei cabinet in 1918 and 1919. Throughout the 1920s the Japanese government pursued a dual policy of rice-price stabilization and imperial self-sufficiency. Based on Ministry of Agriculture calculations of domestic supply and prices, the Diet regularly revised the rice law to manipulate imports of foreign and colonial rice.[9] The heyday of colonial rice coincided with shifts in exports from Japan's textile industry. After 1925, Japanese exports of cotton yarns dwindled and were replaced by finished cotton goods and silk yarns and cloth. The CIRP served as the clear link between the metropolitan middle class, particularly its managerial role in Japan's expanding international trade, and the promise of colonial economic and cultural advancement under Cultural Rule.

Although the CIRP was hailed as a fundamental solution to Japan's food problem, calls for colonial development aroused little public excitement in the 1920s. At the moment when Japanese economic involvement in Korea was placed on a realistic footing,[10] ironically the "trends of the times" (J. *jidai no taisei*) privileged individual economic achievement and international economic opportunities over government guidance and promotion. The early reactions to economic development under Cultural Rule were openly disdainful of the colonial bureaucracy. Tokyo University political scientist Rōyama Masamichi called for a genuine integration of internationalist thinking into Japanese plans for economic development. He argued that the tendency to think in "national" terms represented a "thoroughly loathsome trend" in world politics. A true internalization of an internationalist spirit among Japan's economic expansionists (frequently emigrants) required a greater vision among colonial bureaucracies than they frequently displayed. "When comparing our bureaucracies in Taiwan and Korea [to the Indian civil service], one can't help but be startled by the contrast," he lamented.[11] *Jiji* newspaper writer Yoshii Hironobu wrote that the tolerant posture of

Cultural Rule was in keeping with the "trends of the times." Nevertheless he warned of "the sorrows of Cultural Rule," likening it to a cancer, a gnawing affliction that undermined any larger economic goals. In spite of the great ambition of colonial administrators, economic growth was likely to founder on the shoals of fiscal constraints and the pervasive indifference he found among Koreans themselves. Colonial bureaucrats, he alleged, cynically furthered their own careers, contemptuous of Koreans and any possibility of real economic change.[12]

Cultural Rule and the CIRP were not the simpleminded reactions to the threat of Korean nationalism implied by contemporary critics. The CIRP was designed to increase agricultural productivity and rural income in Korea. It specifically targeted rice production by increasing and improving land under cultivation. The CIRP pursued these developments through familiar strategies and techniques that have been termed "development discourse."[13] "Development" has two distinct meanings in colonial discourse. On the one hand, development is a global historical movement, an intensification and restructuring of economic activity associated frequently with the expansion of modern capitalism. In another sense, development means conscious activity undertaken to create wealth.[14] Throughout the 1920s, Japanese conceptions of development shifted from the former to a more sophisticated grasp of the dual meaning of the term. Japanese thus increasingly viewed the colonies as sites for "exploitation and development" (*kaihatsu*) as part of a program of regional integration and resource management. The CIRP and the exploitation of southern Sakhalin forests were the most obvious features of this policy within the empire.[15] Development discourse spilled over narrow colonial boundaries. Colonial policies made sense within the wider context of Japanese commercial interests in extractive industries throughout the regional economy of northeast Asia including northern Sakhalin, Siberia, and northern China.[16]

The discourse on Korean development worked conspicuously to minimize notions of regional integration and elevate the role of the Government-General. First, development discourse in general emphasizes social arenas in which change is really possible, to the exclusion of arenas beyond its political means. It focuses on that which can be consciously and visibly developed. In Korea, Japanese administrators and analysts attributed the failure to expand cultivation and increase land productivity to technological backwardness, "feudal" attitudes, market integration, and lack of rural credit, while ignoring such problems as landlordism, economic dependency, and political oppression. CIRP resources were channeled into technical expertise and agricultural extension programs as well as rural credit agencies. Second, development discourse finds a role for the supposedly neutral development vehicles already in place. Thus, the CIRP sought to increase production through bureaucratic, technological management and semiprivate irrigation associations and paid no attention to the prominent role of Japanese capital and market pressures in drawing out rice, surplus or not, for Japanese consumers. Finally, development discourse takes a narrowly proscribed, territorial, and national perspective on economic change. Korean dependence on agricultural imports and Korean flight outside the peninsula were never seriously discussed under the CIRP. The CIRP furthered the narrow interests of Japanese colonial administration and addressed Koreans as a specific identity within an imperial framework.[17]

Cultural Rule and the CIRP offered the most clearly articulated example of development discourse up to that time in Japan. Like any discourse, it stood in a complex relationship to the policies actually implemented. Official statements of the Government-General emphasized certain features of development discourse but relied on metropolitan specialists and technicians both to generate and to spread its essential themes. The idea of development appeared in the most widely distributed media, but development discourse engaged a fairly well defined group of academics, businesspeople, journalists, and government officials. Their principal aim was to defend the newly emerging logic of development against what they viewed as an uninformed yet already skeptical and reluctant public.

In the face of public skepticism, Yamamoto Miono (1874–1941), professor of economics and colonial policy studies at Kyoto Imperial University, presented a thorough defense of the CIRP within the logic of development discourse. Having studied in the United States and adopted the views of American internationalist Paul Reinsch, Yamamoto deployed Cultural Rule as a vehicle for liberal colonial administration. Yamamoto thus simultaneously criticized overtly assimilationist cultural policies and rationalized capitalist integration of the empire. He quickly placed the CIRP in the larger context of public attitudes toward empire and attacked what he considered generally myopic and suspicious public perceptions of development and the Korean bureaucracy. Politicians and the public, he complained, lacked perspective on colonialism, and he rebuked those who irresponsibly criticized the CIRP out of misplaced idealism. Their basic mistake was to confuse a criticism of imperialism (at its high tide in 1920s Japan) with the practical demands of colonial policy. The colonies may have been acquired by questionable means and for questionable motives, but they should not be discarded. Social scientific research into questions of colonial development, he contended, permitted a new colonial "policy of mutual benefit" (*sōgo kyōeki seisaku*), which superseded both the thoroughly selfish and the unduly idealistic policies of colonial governments in previous centuries.[18]

On this basis, Yamamoto unequivocally endorsed the CIRP as a model of cooperation and mutual benefit between colonizer and colonized.[19] The program was, he argued, realistic about what was possible within budget constraints and what was politically feasible given that support for Korean farmers could not be seen as occurring at the expense of Japanese farmers. More important, the program reversed Japan's flagging reputation as a colonial power. The program would introduce new farming techniques to an "agricultural economy in its infancy," thus producing tangible increases in household incomes. Further, it would provide "intangible benefits" such as "spiritual comfort" (*ian*) and serve as an antidote against the "corruption of thought" in Korea that caused so many Japanese to use the behavior of "lawless Koreans" as a justification for colonial rule.[20] Betraying the contempt for Korean agriculture that ran throughout Japanese agricultural studies, Yamamoto's defense of the CIRP sustained the 1920s logic of Cultural Rule in economic and cultural terms.

Social scientific support for the CIRP competed with social scientific criticism, highlighting the deep fractures in middle-class support for any social issue, including empire, in Japan during the 1920s. Tokyo Imperial University professor Yanaihara Tadao (1889–1961) would become famous for his opposition to Japanese imperialism in the 1930s. Yanaihara was an adherent of Cobdenism, a pacifist ideology that found international cooperation in the cultural universalism of commodity exchange under capitalism. From Adam Smith, Cobdenites drew a deep suspicion of bureaucratic management in economic affairs and, following mid-Victorian radical Richard Cobden, imagined free-trade internationalism as a mechanism for replicating middle-class ideals across modern societies. From this per-spective, Yanaihara laid bare the operations and silences of the CIRP as evidence of the overweening nationalism of Japan's colonial de-velopment. His condemnation of Japanese policy in Korea berated the government for selling drift as mastery, crude self-interest as be-nevolence, shortsightedness as vision, in sum, colonial exploitation as a national achievement. Yanaihara's critique focused on three themes: (1) the burdens placed on the Korean economy because of a logic of nationality, (2) the role of private and semiprivate firms and the pitfalls of rural credit, and (3) the logic of the market.

Whatever the metropolitan sources of overseas expansion and the burdens placed on metropolitan classes by a policy of imperialism, Yanaihara never relinquished his belief that the costs of colonial eco-nomic policy were paid primarily by the colonies themselves. It was particularly distressing to Yanaihara that the government's statistics clearly contradicted its stated goals of improving the Korean econ-omy. That the plan might be further construed as assisting in "thought rectification" (*shisō zendo*) he regarded as fantastic. Popula-tion growth in Korea would consume any rice production increases not earmarked for export, and per capita rice consumption was al-ready a mere 60 percent of that in Japan, he complained. Dry field cultivation zones that supplemented rice with wheat and barley were to be converted to wet field rice cultivation and that produce shipped to Japan also. Other cash crops such as cotton and mulberry trees that supported Japan's industrialization were to continue to be grown. Koreans would be forced to sell their rice harvests and eat inferior grains such as millet and poorer quality rice strains from Manchuria and areas outside the empire.[21] In sum, the CIRP fash-ioned international development out of narrowly national goals and benefits.

Yanaihara's second concern was that colonial development en-trusted private and semiprivate firms with the implementation of the CIRP, such as land reclamation, irrigation works, and rural credit. Predatory capitalist firms such as the Oriental Development Com-pany (Tōyō takushoku kabushiki kaisha) and the Korean Land De-velopment Company (Chōsen dochi kairyō kabushiki kaisha), he complained, had become landowners themselves. Koreans, blinded by the allure of economic advancement, had gone into debt to Japa-nese firms and, "much like Esau who sold his birthright for a bowl of pottage," sold or mortgaged their land.[22] Yanaihara estimated that

50–80 percent of agricultural land was mortgaged to Japanese hands. He argued that Japanese could not reasonably expect renovation of the Korean economy, since any profits from expansion of the rice trade would go to "landlords, public works industries, financiers, and trading houses" rather than Korean producers.[23]

Yanaihara's broader, final complaint was with the cultural and economic impact of the CIRP, rationalized as it was, he alleged, by the dreams of bureaucrats but guided by the relentless logic of the market. All the pressures of the CIRP would fall on Koreans, and all its benefits accrue to Japanese. He predicted that under the double pressures of population growth in Korea and meager government funding, the plan would fail to increase productivity significantly while nevertheless ensuring the export of rice to Japan. Indeed the Government-General's superficial indifference to the marketing and export of rice was belied by the fact that all the mechanisms for increasing productivity required Koreans to market their rice. The real effect of the Government-General's development plan, he argued, would be to expose Korea's traditional economy to the full weight of Japan's market economy without the balancing effects of moral sentiment he had found so crucial in Adam Smith's original validation of the market. Even relatively successful Korean producers would feel the baneful effects of the CIRP. First, the inability of many small landholders to retain their land during the commercialization of the agricultural economy would lead to their "proletarianization." Even landlords would face indebtedness, since they had to pay the fees of the local irrigation association and land improvement costs. Finally, increased exports of rice would push up prices for all Korean food.[24]

Yanaihara believed the Government-General misunderstood or simply ignored the cultural consequences of the CIRP in its rush to justify the policies of Cultural Rule. He wondered how the CIRP could be automatically seen as solving either economic or cultural problems.

As long as trade and other economic dealings between Japan and Korea *are allowed to operate freely* Koreans will sell rice to Japan, which has greater purchasing power, and will buy manufactured goods from Japan where production costs are low. An increase in the volume of trade can never be the criterion for promoting the economic well-being of Koreans. It is extraordinarily difficult to propose, before any scholarly analysis, the argument that in its vague way the CIRP will solve the domestic food problem and promote the advancement of the Korean economy and is thus a policy to reconcile Japan and Korea.[25]

The net effect of the plan would be to draw rice out of Korea under market mechanisms and make Korea dependent on Manchuria, regardless of the actions of the colonial bureaucracy. Since the whole system "constrains the [Koreans'] freedom to eat the rice themselves," Yanaihara questioned whether this could be regarded as an advance in standards of living or could genuinely effect the "Japanese-Korean reconciliation" that the colonial administration and its apologists advertised.[26] In the event, Yanaihara predicted most of the results of the CIRP, and his critique presaged many subsequent criticisms.[27] More important, however, was his ability to discern the operation of development discourse. He spotted how the colonial bureaucracy implicated itself in the development process, claiming success where it was irrelevant and appearing neutral where it was politically motivated. Yanaihara was one of few Japanese to point to the swelling numbers of Koreans relocating to Manchuria during the first decade and a half of colonial rule as a function of Japanese administration itself, a serious social dislocation and national tragedy, rather than a natural process or desirable resettlement of a political nuisance. Yanaihara's critique confirmed his position as a rare internationalist critic of Japanese colonialism. Moreover, his ideas resonated throughout Japanese thinking on the association among nation, empire, and development in the 1920s. Members of the Japanese Diet, economists, and colonial publicists alike criticized the limited economic and cultural vision of Korean rice policy. For them, the CIRP contradicted the simple equation of economic hegemony with imperial identity and brought into question the effectiveness of bureaucratic administration of East Asian economic development.

## Consuming Empire

Speculations about commodities, especially food, as expressions of national identity are commonplace. In the case of Korean rice, considerable anecdotal evidence has been put to divining whether Japanese were elevated by controlling and consuming colonial foodstuffs, degraded or "Koreanized" by eating less desirable colonial rice, "proletarianized" by the experience of mass urban food consumption, or simply sated by the near-Japanese alternative of Korean rice. Rice symbolism has, moreover, been particularly prominent in Japanese exceptionalist thought (frequently labeled *Nihonjinron*, "theses on Japaneseness"). One example is Emiko Ohnuki-Tierney's startling claim that "there is no question that Yayoi (approx. 300 BCE–250 CE) agriculture laid the foundation for what became the nation-state, Japan, and for the rice cultivation that became the symbolic emblem of the nation."[28] The ease with which rice and the Japanese islands automatically constitute the modern nation-state demonstrates the tenacious appeal of rice imagery in Japanese exceptionalist thought. Ohnuki-Tierney's statement drawing a straight line between rice consumption and the authentication of the emperor-system polity (*kokutai*) echoes the logic of imperial apologists of the 1920s.[29]

Despite rice's symbolic potential, the emotive imagery of Japanese exceptionalists was muted in defending the CIRP. Japanese imports and consumption of Korean rice vaguely licensed Koreans and Japanese alike to share in the implied benevolence of imperial rule (*isshi dōjin*) and exemplified Cultural Rule's central place in the eventual political incorporation of Korea (*naichi enchō shugi*). Imperial apologists rarely ventured beyond these claims. Cultural Rule could have been fully domesticated at Japan's dining table were it not for restraints on the interpretive license of the food essentialists. First was the poor reputation of all imported rice. More broadly, imperial apologists confronted the dubious credibility of the approach of divesting from metropolitan agriculture and entrusting to Koreans the task of producing essential emblems of Japanese identity. Finally, the CIRP entailed a style of management and a theory of growth that placed itself above all private or specific interests, promoting Korean and Japanese interests simultaneously. A rigid claim of Japanese identity through empire worked at cross-purposes to the claim of disinterested, scientific administration. The fundamental constraint on grandiose rationalizations of Japanese colonialism in terms of Korean rice was that such rationalizations were neither a necessary nor a desirable component of development discourse in the 1920s.

Ultimately supporters of the CIRP were placed in the position of needing to convince Japanese consumers that what was necessary (consuming imported rice) was also desirable (consuming a project of empire). To the contrary, the international context of the 1920s, with its emphasis on free trade and multilateral cooperation in East Asia, implied that what seemed necessary was perhaps unnecessary. First, there is little evidence that the urban managerial and professional classes, whom Cultural Rule and the CIRP addressed, saw the development and commercialization of Korean rice production as the realization of a Korean-Japanese synthesis, the clarification of an updated imperial identity, or a solution to the "population problem." Overseas emigration, the prominent theme of interwar internationalists, more fully expressed metropolitan concerns over food imports and population pressures.[30] Second, metropolitan commentators drew lessons from the CIRP about Japanese and Korean national identity different from the interpretations offered by colonial bureaucrats. Middle-class development schemes frequently minimized the effectiveness of the Government-General in cultural interactions between Japanese and Koreans. What emerged was a fluid situation in which Japanese consumers were offered a number of possible interpretations of the meaning of consuming Korean rice, only one of which was an imperial ideology of Cultural Rule.

Complicating the seamless power of rice symbolism was the fact that 1920s discourse on food, with its emphasis on efficiency and cosmopolitanism, was not principally about rice, and even less about Korean rice. Thus it is difficult to generalize about Japanese consumers and their response to Korean rice except to say that they accepted it enough to consume it in ever-increasing quantities until 1934. More research is necessary into the varying responses of Japanese consumers to Korean rice over the quite brief period in which colonial rice grew to prominence in Japanese diets, but a few observations are possible. Certainly the press offered every possible approach to resolving Japan's "food problem," from fundamentally changing Japanese food preferences to spreading Japan's ecological reach through the alleged adaptability of its foodstuffs. Freer trade in foreign rice and domestic rural reconstruction were, however, the most common proposals. The Government-General attempted to prop up imported rice's flagging reputation, placing itself at the entry to the rice pipeline with an inspectorate to guarantee quality to Japanese consumers. Korean rice was shipped by private firms through large urban markets such as Osaka and Kobe before filtering to local sellers. An elaborate marketing system was necessary for Japanese rice traders to claim that they could supply Korean rice that satisfied regional variations in consumer preferences throughout Japan. Rice trade publications reported Japanese consumers' ability to discriminate the various types of Korean rice by strain and region of production.[31]

Marketing techniques, however, could not eliminate speculation that colonial rice, nevertheless, remained colonial rice. Even before the CIRP was in place, the frequently "liberal" economist Ishibashi

Tanzan advocated an interventionist role for the government in the market system to standardize the importation, blending, and distribution of colonial rice. Ishibashi's advocacy of government intervention derived from his own experiments in making colonial rice palatable. Charging that the theoreticians of rice policy were not the consumers of its second-class produce, he wondered how many of the vocal advocates of rice-importation schemes ever ate "foreign rice."[32] Much like the recent public spectacle of new cooking techniques for imported foreign rice in Japan, metropolitan responses in the 1920s emphasized the failure of Korean rice to live up to expectations. Household reference guides, the encyclopedias for the aspiring tastes of middle-class women, cautioned Japanese homemakers to add a touch of sodium bicarbonate to "foreign rice" and increase its soaking time, Korean rice being noted for its relative dryness. A later edition offered the tip that an unpleasant crunch on the tooth in otherwise pure white rice was proof of blending with inferior Korean rice or, worse yet, the small stones found in it.[33] These attitudes may explain why colonial rice was so easily excluded from Japanese diets for political reasons during 1934–39, when the gluts of metropolitan rice closed the linkage between consumer preferences and dreams of imperial development.

In isolation, the responses of Japanese consumers do not answer the question of what it meant to Japanese colonialism that Japanese ate Korean rice. Rather, we need to analyze the meanings assigned to colonial rice in the broader context of the food problem, peaceful expansionism, and internationalism as they were discussed in Japan's mass media during the 1920s. Geopolitical rationalizations and national power projection were essential to the logic of Japanese expansion into Korea at the turn of the century. Akira Iriye has termed these ideas "forceful expansion" to contrast them with complimentary ideas on emigration and overseas trade, or "peaceful expansion." Iriye's contrast highlights how Japanese ideas of expansionism in the Meiji period were contoured simultaneously by these related but quite different sets of ideas.[34] Even a cursory glance at the popular media of the 1920s shows that images of national power and formal imperialism of the late Meiji period had given way to more internationalized images of economic expansionism and exotic destinations accessible through tourism and emigration to places outside the formal empire. When the so-called population problem (*jinkō mondai*) exploded into Japanese consciousness again in 1926, colonial rice was made to seem a temporary and insufficient solution to the problem. Much of the 1920s discussion of colonial rice was therefore carried out within a larger discussion of the alternative to eating bad rice at home, overseas emigration. Based on the prominence of firms such as the Oriental Development Company, the fanciful projections of imperial publicists, the urgings of colonial bureaucrats, and later the role of the state in Japanese emigration to Manchuria, one might mistakenly conclude that emigration to the colonies was a major component of Japanese colonial ideology. However, nearly every scheme linking emigration to the colonies with national identity before the 1930s was a dismal failure. In other words, emigration was more closely allied in Japanese thinking with "peaceful," not forceful, expansion.

One manifestation of this thinking was the growth of middle-class public policy and information societies that promoted and encouraged overseas emigration. One of the most ambitious of the societies attempting to mold opinion among the urban middle classes was the Japanese Colonization Information Society (Nihon shokumin tsūshinsha). Through pamphlets, public lectures, movies, and theme nights (e.g., "Brazil Night"), the society and its journal *The Colonist* (*Shokumin*) reflected the special interest of Japanese in questions of colonial development after March First. Before the Great Kantō Earthquake of 1923, *The Colonist* had balanced colonial issues with emigration issues. After the earthquake, *The Colonist* commented on the massacres of Koreans in the Kantō region but gradually shifted away from formal colonial issues. This trend can also be observed across Japanese popular opinion journals such as *Chūō kōron*, *Kaizō*, and *Taiyō* as well as more specialized journals such as *Gaikō jihō* and the *Ekonomisuto*.

*The Colonist* blended innocuous statements from government officials with expert and scholarly opinion on colonial policy and the "population problem," travel reports from Central and South America glamorizing agricultural success in exotic lands, short stories on the immigrant experience in a foreign land, and how-to advice on going overseas. With its staunch anti-bureaucratic stance and its emphasis on private activism, *The Colonist* appealed to urban and rural middle classes. Naitō Hideo, head of the Japanese Colonization Information Society and editor of its journal, espoused an ideology of public enthusiasm and private character-building to resolve Japan's population problem through mass emigration. He called on individuals and private associations to pursue their own interests in contributing to this national achievement. Japan's colonies and Manchuria, he contended, were generally unsuited to Japanese expansion, and he was generally unsympathetic to government attempts to stimulate overseas emigration through low-interest loans to officially sanctioned companies and associations. "I generally believe that the points I wish to make to the 'powers that be' are 'an Eastern wind blowing in a horse's ear,'" that is, no more effective than offering religious incantations to a beast.[35] Thus Naitō derided government attempts to inject a bureaucratic hand into what should be left to "self-rule (*jichi*) and independence" of the Japanese "nation" (*kokumin*).[36] In a 1928 editorial, Naitō offered Japan's youth either resignation to the gloom of colonial development and angst of domestic stagnation or, in their place, resolute action to wash both away. "The root cause [of our troubles] is that [in Japan] there are no true patriots, just many sycophants, who exuding their hollow self-importance, fawn on the authorities." True patriotic duty, for Naitō, was to act self-interestedly, which was the national interest as well, thus seeking opportunities beyond the territorial confines of Japan and its colonies and expanding Japanese activity peacefully throughout South America.[37]

Inoue Masaji (1876–1947) became one of *The Colonist's* most frequent and prominent contributors in sustaining this image of emigration as an individual achievement. Inoue's colorful career included frequent trips to every corner of the globe and spanned nearly every aspect of private and semiprivate Japanese overseas activity in the first half of the twentieth century. With his election to the Diet in 1924, Inoue became a visible proponent of Japanese emigration.[38] Inoue wrote forthrightly in *The Colonist* of the limits of Japanese colonialism. In one of his harshest critiques of government policy toward the colonies and overseas emigration, Inoue dismissed the CIRP and its vision of economic development. He pointed out the Japanese failure to develop domestic agriculture and the statistical improbability of the CIRP's success and concluded that Japan was doing nothing more than "foisting its troubles off on the Koreans." As an alternative, he encouraged the Japanese to formulate different conceptions of economic development and embrace emigration outside the empire. Not only would emigration alleviate domestic population pressures, but also it would contribute to the cultural internationalist goals of increasing the geographic reach of individual cultures while promoting the global synthesis of human culture. This "internationalization of the nation" (*kokumin no kokusaika*) he called a "spiritual movement" and "sacred program" to "achieve the internationalism that is increasingly advocated nowadays."[39] Inoue's disillusion with colonial development and support for cultural and economic internationalism may seem ironic considering his participation in establishing Japanese currencies in Korea before 1910, a system that greatly facilitated the extraction of Korean rice from local markets during the years of the CIRP. He illustrates, however, how avowed expansionists viewed the problem of development in the Japanese colonial empire within the international context of the 1920s.

Similar criticisms of the colonial development apparatus continued in the next issue of *The Colonist*, criticisms imported liberally from the United States in the form of a translated short story by O. Henry. In "Helping the Other Fellow," O. Henry recounts the story of William Trotter, who joins another ex-pat in preaching the gospel of Adam Smith and the wisdom of *laissez-faire* governance to a South American despot. Trotter's friend saves the nation from economic mismanagement, for which he is duly rewarded, but falls prey to a nagging love of rum. In a fit of drunken indiscretion, Trotter's comrade shares the "secrets" of free trade with a rival banana republic, an indiscretion that costs him his life. The story broadly satirized the relationship between state power and benefit to its subjects, but in the Japanese context, it more specifically questioned bureaucratic claims about the project of colonial development. In a final reflection on the hubris of national interest, the narrator asks Trotter:

"Don't you ever desire to go back to the land of derby hats and starched collars?" I asked him. "You seem to be a handy man and a man of action," I continued, "and I am sure I could find you a comfortable job somewhere in the States."

Ragged, shiftless, barefooted, a confirmed eater of the lotos [*sic*], William Trotter had pleased me much, and I hated to see him gobbled up by the tropics.

"I've no doubt you could," he said, idly splitting the bark from a section of sugar-cane. "I've no doubt you could do much for me. If every man could do as much for himself as he can for others, every country in the world would be holding millenniums instead of centennials."[40]

The nation is, in the last analysis, the victim of the policies pursued in its interest. In offering the translation, *The Colonist* joined the theorizing of Naitō Hideo and Inoue Masaji on the national benefit of individual economic activity to a broader critique of development.[41] Japan was exhausting itself through unproductive intervention in exclusive colonial empires.

In satirizing the bureaucratic mechanisms of colonial rule as a model for cultural and economic growth, *The Colonist* argued that, for many Japanese, that vision of colonial development was a failure. In consuming Korean rice, Japanese did not consume empire. The imagery of a global and self-interested economic competition challenged the narrow vision of neo-mercantilist economic growth. In turn, it challenged Cultural Rule's assimilationist model of cultural expansion, which justified the state's drive for productivity increases in Korean agriculture. These criticisms demonstrate how difficult it became to connect the policies of colonial development to any specific national identification with empire. How this critique was applied to the problem of Korean nationalism is discussed in the next section.

## Rice for Japan and Trusteeship for Korea

If a cultural program aimed at gradual assimilation and a development program based on rice were the ideological centers of Cultural Rule, the linchpin was the idea of the nation. What was to become of the self-consciously separatist thrust of Korean nationalism? Throughout this essay, I have suggested that Cultural Rule and the CIRP were not viewed as simply suppressing questions of cultural or national identity under rational scientific management. On the contrary, official publications of the Government-General openly encouraged cultural readings of the CIRP, especially those that enabled the harmonizing and convergence of Japanese and Korean interests and identities. The faith placed in achieving harmony between specific national interests and global economic forces is emblematic of the internationalist atmosphere of the 1920s. For Japanese, such a harmony of interest and identity was more than an article of faith; the CIRP offered a concrete opportunity to achieve it. Middle-class commentators, however, remained skeptical of the CIRP's successes and were even openly critical of the project's wider impact on Japanese society. Japanese consumers purchased Korean rice, but there is little evidence they thereby purchased an attachment to empire. This final section considers the claims to a particular synthesis of Japanese and Korean nationalism under the CIRP.

The economic transformation of Japan during World War I and the shifting climate of international economic relations contributed to discussions of cultural particularity and national identity in 1920s Japan. The "official nationalism" of Meiji modernization had only vaguely theorized the connection between capitalism and nationalism, wedding individual economic success and public service to an ideology of familial reverence for the emperor. During the 1920s, by contrast, numerous alternatives to this official formulation theorized the relationship between capitalism and nationalism, suggesting different approaches to the "food problem." Kita Ikki advocated a radical rethinking of the relationship between people and emperor to foster a social regeneration superseding the restraints imposed by the liberal-capitalist economic system. Business leaders and bureaucrats hoped to employ supposed traditional patterns of benevolence in labor relations to navigate the treacherous waters of labor radicalism. Declining rural productivity, poverty, and distress gave rise to ideologies of agrarian nationalism.[42] In each, labor and national identity provided the components of a solution to the perceived malaise brought on by the uneven economic development of the 1920s.

Whatever the interest of these groups, discussion of rice's role in colonial development was found almost exclusively in the ideas of an emerging urban, managerial elite that formulated the problem of nationalism under empire on its own terms. Driven by concerns about markets and resources, this elite addressed nationalism as a problem of economic opportunities and long-term growth and development rather than a question of mass and commodity forms of national culture. Indeed, Yanaihara Tadao and Tōgō Minoru (discussed below) used commodity capitalism and nationalism to challenge assumptions about culture, race, ethnicity, and nationality that underpinned the agrarian, conservative, or radical nationalist theories of the 1920s. Of course, for Yanaihara and Tōgō, such managerial visions of nationalism had as much claim to the colonial endeavor as the other views. They argued that a managerial stance toward development and nationalism was the only reasonable response within the internationalist framework of the 1920s to nationalist and ethnic conflict within the empire. Their views are early expressions of the approach to development and nationalism in the post-1945 period called "trusteeship."

Yanaihara Tadao not only questioned specific features of the CIRP but also challenged the broader connection of commodity exchange with national identity that undergirded Cultural Rule. Yanaihara located national identity under colonialism in the "ethnic nation" (*minzoku*)[43] and tied the emergence of the "ethnic nation" to an idealization of the self-regulating market. According to Yanaihara, nations did not lose their cultural particularity through economic relationships, although they might lose their false claims to cultural holism. What he found far more dangerous and injurious to a culture than losing its alleged cultural integrity was to have its identity linked to a bureaucratic state weaving identity out of a harrowing indifference to oppression in the colonial setting. He thus analyzed the cultural implications of the CIRP as a general problem of "Cultural Rule."

Yanaihara's harsh critique of Cultural Rule united his essays on the political limitations of Japanese colonial rule. Published in the important general-interest journal *Chūō kōron*, Yanaihara's critique began with the Government-General's uncovering of a Korean "conspiracy" to use the funeral of Sunjong, the last emperor of the Yi dynasty, to launch nationalist protests on June 10, 1926. Just as the March First protests had been a Korean judgment of Military Rule (*budan seiji*), Yanaihara saw the June Tenth incident as a judgment on six years of Cultural Rule. Inevitably, it seemed to Yanaihara, Korean ethnic nationalists (*minzoku shugisha*) had cast their lot with "communists." This radicalization of the *minzoku* movement followed from the shortsighted policies of Cultural Rule. Cultural Rule had lifted the obviously repressive aspects of Military Rule without granting true political autonomy. It had done the same in the economic sphere. Korean "aspirations have been stimulated, but the means to fulfill those aspirations have not been provided. . . . Woe to those who think the superficial peace is a success of Cultural Rule."[44] Instead, Yanaihara argued, the Government-General's development policies were grounded in either an inability to see their real impacts or a simple unwillingness to respond to those impacts. Rather than real mastery, the Government-General was content with hollow language of dependency: "Japanese-Korean joint rule" (*Nissen dōchi*), "Japanese-Korean harmonization" (*Nissen yūwa*), "co-existence and co-prosperity" (*kyōson kyōei*).

Yanaihara's critique of autocratic rule and state indifference to the social dislocations of capitalist development did not lead him to advocate outright independence for Korea. Instead, he imagined a system of international cooperation that would allow for full expression of Korean national identity within a correspondingly benign framework of economic development. At the level of policy, what Yanaihara offered the colonies was a kind of "corporate liberalism," sometimes referred to as "social corporatism," as opposed to the "state corporatism" of 1930s Japan and Korea. Corporate liberals recognized a need to update classical laissez-faire political economy to accommodate the hurly-burly of organized capitalism. A limited state, incapable of defining, mobilizing, and controlling all the interests and conflicts created by capitalist development, would support the largely private activities of economic or functional groups pursuing economic growth. This state would sanction many forms of self-government in tandem with policies of social welfare and economic management. In international affairs, corporate liberals came to imagine a world culturally enmeshed in non-exclusive frameworks, politically enmeshed in multilateral frameworks, and economically enmeshed in market frameworks. A "corporatist" worldview was equally fitting for an entrepreneurial and managerial middle class.[45]

Yanaihara argued that Cultural Rule and the CIRP were, in the last analysis, vehicles of an important cultural transformation. He recognized that cultural changes were inherent to the commodities Koreans consumed under the market economy. The hierarchy of power and cultures appeared as a hierarchy of taste and texture in which the Koreans would have "less pleasure [than before] in eating but more cash. The CIRP will progressively lose its character as [a mechanism for] self-sufficiency in rice and take on the character of the commercialization" of Korean society. In their rush to convert rice to cash, Koreans would find their identity dictated by the market. "Instead of a bamboo hat, a woolen fedora; instead of straw sandals, shoes to wear or rubber boots; train and event tickets for leisure trips to the city on newly established train routes." No less than in Japan, the rise of the modern Korean consumer, Yanaihara argued, represented "Rosa Luxemburg's so-called aggressive war that capitalism wreaks on natural economies."[46] His depiction of Koreans' new commercial existence tellingly imagined Korean peasants as middle-class consumers. The commercial exchange that appropriated rice for Japan in turn replaced Korean culture with new consumer identities in a market economy integrated with that of Japan.

Yanaihara argued that a genuinely humane "cultural rule" must place this transformation of culture and economics beyond the nationalistic condescension that informed all dealings with Koreans, and restrain the self-aggrandizing capitalism of Japan's industrialization. He captured this corporatist solution to colonial nationalism in the phrase "autonomy" (*jishushugi*). "Autonomy" implied a dose of political self-rule, a Korean parliament, and cultural autonomy and colonial economic development on terms beneficial to Koreans. This shepherding of politics, culture, and economy, he reasoned, would resolve the essential failing of Cultural Rule: economic changes outpacing cultural liberalization. Outdated despotism and assimilationist rhetoric could never fully supplant the Korean "ethnic nation," he warned. Yanaihara's "autonomy" thus meant doing what more utilitarian forms of liberalism did not do: recognize the independence of the group and the historical uniqueness of social experiences. In short, economic development would work only in accord with the continued realization of the "ethnic nation."[47] Yanaihara ultimately offered something like imperial trusteeship as a path to decolonization, an idea emerging in Europe and the United States at the same time. Indeed his "autonomy" articulated the fundamental assumptions of World War II era plans for international trusteeship in Korea.[48]

Internationalist and middle-class ideologies frequently assume an isomorphism among modern societies, in other words, a uniform correspondence of social forms and cultural attitudes. Yanaihara's support for Korean cultural autonomy was based on this assumption. Market relations and rising consumerism in Korea would breed cultural attitudes that matched those found in Japan's expanding urban culture. Not least in importance was an emerging bourgeois liberal discourse in Korea on the possibilities of cultural nationalism. Yanaihara's specific calls for "autonomy" paralleled Yi Kwangsu's corporatist solution to Korea's position under Japanese rule.[49] But more broadly, through direct contacts with Protestant groups in Korea, Yanaihara shared many of the assumptions of what Kenneth Wells has termed "self-reconstruction nationalism" in Korea. Although Yanaihara did not advocate the nativist response promoted in the Korean National Production Movement under Cho Mansik, he shared with Cho and with gradualists like An Ch'angho belief in the final elimination of political and economic injustices only through the broad internalization of Christian values.[50]

Yanaihara's academic position gave his words considerable influence among the Tokyo audience for whom they were largely intended. Although his religious views may have not inspired broad acceptance, his ideas about nationalism did not emerge in isolation. In the 1920s there were many attempts to fashion the concept of "ethnic nation" (*minzoku*) as a malleable and tractable identity to manage the economic transformation of Japanese and Korean societies under capitalism. These visions of complimentary cultural relations between Korea and Japan joined the business and professional ideologies of free trade, individual opportunity, and peaceful expansionism that characterized the liberal internationalist atmosphere of the 1920s.

One prominent figure whose views paralleled Yanaihara's was former colonial administrator and Imperial Diet member Tōgō Minoru (1881–1959). Tōgō wrote extensively before World War I on the practical necessity of a program of colonial development that recognized colonialism's mortality, its vulnerability to the global historical emergence of anticolonial, ethnic nationalisms. He described an anti-assimilationist and pseudo-segregationist policy of "symbiosis" through which Japan left its distinctive cultural impress on its colonies without dislocating and antagonizing local ethnic identities. His thinking was formed largely out of his experiences in Taiwan, but after March 1, 1919, he adapted his ideas to Korea, as did many officials and colonial residents.[51] The March First protests against Japanese rule in Korea demonstrated clearly enough that an artificial separation between Japanese economic activity and the daily lives of Koreans was specious. Colonialism by its very nature creates an implacable resistance to its cultural impress, Tōgō reasoned, at the precise moment that it succeeds in the economic mobilization of the colony.

Tōgō's popular book *Colonial Policy and Ethnic Consciousness* (*Shokumin seisaku to minzoku shinri*; 1925) represented his most thorough attempt to reconcile the rise of Korean nationalism with the economic transformation created by Japanese hegemony.[52] Tōgō deeply feared Korean anticolonial nationalism, Wilsonian self-determination, and assimilationist dogma, all of which threatened Japan's ability to sustain its economic commitments. He railed against all hasty dogmatism in colonial policy that pursued reckless assimilation without regard for local and particular forms of ethnic nationalism.[53] He likened Japan's position in Korea to Britain's in Ireland, where ethnic nationalist sentiment had irretrievably tipped the scales against imperial union. The most pressing need of the day in Japanese colonial policy, for Tōgō, was to avoid the Irish solution (territorial partition) and square the political economy of Japanese expansion with the cultural implications of that expansion. For Japan to conceptualize economic development in culturally aggressive and self-aggrandizing terms, Tōgō argued, was foolish within an international context of rising ethnic national consciousness. Although Tōgō was in no danger of becoming an avowed liberal internationalist, neither did he expect the empire to be isolated from changes in the international political arena. His own ideas fully matched approaches to the "ethnic nation" or culture nationalism under a capitalist internationalist world order. Tōgō argued that great powers like Japan played a pivotal role in organizing and developing lesser economies. This view can hardly said to be at odds with the internationalism of the interwar period.

Tōgō's dual promise to colonized societies of local autonomy and Japanese leadership could appear as a "last defense of nineteenth-century colonialism,"[54] but Tōgō was operating with new conceptions of nationalism that were entirely in keeping with his attempt to fit Japanese colonialism into the new internationalism of the 1920s. He began by disassociating his central concept *minzoku* from the concept of race. Quoting the sociologist Yoneda Shōtarō (1873–1945), Tōgō defined *minzoku* as a group identity based on "a historically and culturally rooted sense of their spiritual existence." The expression of the "ethnic nation" through a state (*kokka*) was not an essential characteristic. Thus he distinguished it sharply from "race" (*jinshu*), which was ahistorical, and the "nation" (*kokumin*), which was a group created by the political and legal structure of the state. When, therefore, Tōgō referred to Japan's *minzoku* as a "historical ethnic nation" (*rekishiteki minzoku*), a polyglot of varied cultural, historical, and racial elements, he meant to dispute the notion that Japan had some special or unique place as a colonizer based on racial grounds or an ideology of extending imperial subjecthood (*kōmin*).[55] On theoretical grounds, Tōgō questioned the Government-General's reasoning that cultural assimilation was a natural complement to Japan's development strategy in Korea.

In 1924, Tōgō was elected to the Imperial Diet for the first of nine terms. From his position in the Diet, Tōgō expanded his approach to questions of colonial policy to include a broadly conceived program of international expansion. In a startling string of essays, Tōgō retreated from an optimistic vision of imperial self-sufficiency and advocated a broader vision of economic expansion. Tōgō warned against dreams of imperial cultural unity and cooperation based on faulty analogies to the British empire.[56] The first casualty of this transformation was his support for imperial self-sufficiency in rice. As metropolitan rice prices slid downward after 1927, Tōgō increasingly viewed Japan's policy of supplementing domestic production with cheap Korean and Taiwanese rice as mere degradation of metropolitan farmers. In place of an economically integrated empire, he called for a new system of tariffs to protect domestic farmers and abandonment of the policy of imperial self-sufficiency in rice.[57]

What would be the cultural framework to support this vision of international economic development? Writing in *The Colonist*, Tōgō suggested that the cultural universalism of peaceful expansionism contradicted the cultural particularism and racial condescension that informed Japanese colonial policy. He lamented the limited Japanese reservoir of historical experience of or folk wisdom on the benefits of overseas emigration. The old Momotarō (Peach Boy) legend of the superhuman boy who subdues menacing demons across the seas and returns with war booty provides a weak lead, he wrote. Tōgō's mentor, the famed internationalist Nitobe Inazō, among many others, had invoked Momotarō to capture the expansive mood of territorial expansion and colonial development.[58] This Japanese vision of expansion was narrowly self-interested and shortsighted, Tōgō complained.

Reversing the intersection of local knowledge and global structure under empire, he called on the folklore of Taiwanese aborigines to enrich Japanese knowledge of peaceful expansion. Tōgō was apparently referring to the folk tale of the Atayal, a head-hunting people of the mountains of northern Taiwan. The fable, he reported, explains the origins of the diurnal pattern of day and night. In the past, two suns visited the earth each day, bathing the land in constant sunlight but ultimately evaporating the rivers, withering the forests, and roasting the animals. One village marshaled its intellectual and material resources and launched an expeditionary force to remove one of the suns from the sky. Over the countless years it took to reach the sun, the first generation died, was replaced by a second, and from that group emerged an "aboriginal Momotarō," who "slew" the second sun with a divinely inspired arrow. This refashioning of nature upon the exhaustion of a people's natural inheritance reflected Japanese needs and experiences more accurately than did the Momotarō legend, Tōgō argued. "There is no greater enterprise than an effort such as this, carried out over not one, but two or three generations, to relieve the suffering of all living things and usher in an age of global peace."[59] The extension of nature through private, communal activity replaced the heroic image of military conquest and cultural domination.

If the lack of an innate knowledge of and experience with colonization was keenly felt anywhere among Japanese, Tōgō argued, it was in the realm of economic rather than territorial expansionism. He frequently mourned the lack of the patience, perseverance, and cross-cultural sympathy among Japanese essential to a long-term economic and cultural investment in the colonies.[60] How much less were they prepared for freewheeling economic competition outside the empire. He nevertheless called on Japanese to retain the benefits of empire—sources of raw materials and markets for manufactures—without empire. Tōgō did not exactly evoke the current imagery of tenacious Japanese businessmen, but he reminded Japanese that control of world resources was increasingly defined as economic control. Reject the old imperialism, he urged, and exploit the world's resources for the benefit of all humankind. That would be Japan's cultural impress.[61]

The ideas of Yanaihara Tadao and Tōgō Minoru (and others), in league with certain forms of Korean nationalism, provided the intellectual ingredients for Japanese "trusteeship" in Korea. Yanaihara and Tōgō imagined the future of the Japanese colonial empire in a way that separated nationalist accommodation between Japanese and Koreans from narrowly conceived colonial development projects such as the CIRP. Their conception of intercultural relations was, of course, just as deeply colored by a model of development as was the Government-General's, though quite different from it. The Government-General imagined that its stewardship in agricultural development was a natural complement to its leadership in establishing public order. Yanaihara and Tōgō framed the relationship of Japanese and Korean nationalisms in terms of a model that mimicked social relations under capitalism, organized but cooperative. Their vision of commodity exchange and nationalist accommodation, and ultimately trusteeship, postulated a degree of civilian control of Korean administration never achieved in fact. A very different model of development in the 1930s would express more strident versions of

Japanese nationalism that were less accommodating to Korean aspirations and to a metropolitan context dominated by a managerial and professional civilian elite.

## Conclusion

One frequent measure of the power of Japanese colonial hegemony is its purported ability to instill broad metropolitan acceptance of development projects that, whatever depredations they wreaked on Korea, satisfied a Japanese national consciousness of empire. I have argued that no such consensus about nationalism and colonial development existed in Japan during the 1920s. Japanese acquiescence to the plundering of the Korean peninsula did not translate into corresponding adulation of the Government-General or celebration of colonial development as a key to national development. What the colonial bureaucracy and the CIRP actually achieved in Korea is an important but separate question. Middle-class commentators believed the Government-General and the CIRP had done little to convince metropolitan classes to subscribe to a project of colonial development. Increases in Korean rice production ran at about a quarter of the Government-General's targets, but it was enough to satisfy rising Japanese domestic demand. Government-General agricultural specialists defended themselves against claims that they really had little to do with the productivity of Korean agriculture and imperial patterns of rice consumption.[62] The Government-General even argued it had been too successful, attributing the spiraling indebtedness of Korean producers to their overwillingness to market their rice immediately after harvest. To solve the problems of low market prices and irritability of metropolitan producers with the flood of cheap Korean rice, the Government-General offered the superficial remedy of warehouse construction, implying rural incomes could be propped up if more Korean producers could simply wait for the future and hedge against the market.[63]

Changes outside Korea rendered many of these issues moot. After 1931, the "population problem" lost its currency as a justification for colonial development among metropolitan audiences. Attention shifted to the problem of underemployment rather than overpopulation, and Japan's new colonial possession, Manchuria, immediately captured the imagination of proponents of Japanese emigration. The CIRP was discontinued in 1934 as metropolitan prices plunged and rice imports from the colonies were actively discouraged in order to protect Japan's depressed rural sector. These radical shifts in policy substantiated accusations by Yanaihara Tadao, Inoue Masaji, and others that the CIRP was a mere expedient with no basis in a clear conception of development or nationalist accommodation in Korea.

The end of the CIRP signaled a deep structural change in the economic and cultural practices of Japanese colonial rule. Driven by the needs of continental expansion and the defense of Manchuria, the industrialization of Korea after 1937 was coordinated under new cultural policies, *naisen ittai*. The cooperative international framework of the 1920s permitted a loose association between ethnic nationalism and a program of economic development. In contrast, *naisen ittai* envisioned a close association, one uniform imperial identity, as necessary to rapid economic development consistent with new metropolitan needs. Wartime industrialization gave the bureaucracies in Japan and Korea a new role as leaders of economic development and forged new transnational links between the Japanese and the Korean bourgeoisie. As Carter Eckert suggests, it was not simply the authoritarian politics of colonial rule that aided development but the active attempt to erase a separate Korean identity as Cultural Rule had not done. The abandonment of Cultural Rule and the CIRP as models was very much a part of what was happening in the international and metropolitan contexts. Japan's drive for autarky in East Asia not only engendered authoritarian politics at home but also attenuated the discourse on national identity within Japan.

Proponents of colonialism frequently spoke of colonialism as a "total" experience, shaping metropolitan politics and society in the interests of colonialism as much as colonialism was shaped by the priorities, interests, and needs of the metropole.[64] The dreams of imperialists just as frequently faltered in capturing the hearts and minds of the populace colonialism was meant to impress. The broad criticism of Cultural Rule and the CIRP among metropolitan audiences illustrate how deeply the international context for colonialism intervened in that process. Cultural Rule had subsumed explosive issues of race and power under broad themes of economic development and cultural accommodation. The CIRP was the principal intersection of these two themes. Metropolitan audiences were, however, deeply critical of the limited vision of the CIRP. Drawing on trends in international relations, academics, journalists, business leaders, and politicians challenged the Government-General's attempts to mobilize Japan's urban society on behalf of colonial rule. Not only did they challenge the CIRP on economic grounds, but more deeply they questioned its cultural logic. Japanese middle classes were trying to factor the empire into a broad cultural vision of modern identity. Cultural Rule and the CIRP were designed to cement an association between national identity and colonial development. This chapter has argued that, as much as these policies were conceived to strengthen the identification of the colonial empire with modern economic growth, industrial society, and regional economic integration, they ironically contributed equally to a Japanese vision of internationalism.

FIVE

# Colonial Industrial Growth

# and the Emergence of the

# Korean Working Class

Soon-Won Park

Today, in the postmodern era, every conventional concept related to "modernity" is undergoing a profound redefinition. The current theorization of "nationalism," "tradition," and "history" as fluid, changeable, and constructed conceptual categories that are neither predetermined nor fixed on a unitary trajectory is an important intellectual leap beyond conventional historiography. History is now understood not simply as one aspect of a national homogeneous culture, tradition, and nation-state, but in more inclusive, complex, and pluralistic terms. In the same vein, the focus of many studies on colonial Korea on the interactions of several interlocking, mutually influential, and competing ideas such as nationalism, tradition, modernity, and colonialism add depth to our understanding of Korea's twentieth-century experience and the modern Korean identity shaped by them.

The purpose of this chapter is to examine and summarize the research results of this revisionary colonial historiography from labor's point of view and to suggest several directions for future study. The following sections examine one of the fundamental socio-economic phenomena of colonial Korea, the substantial industrialization of the country and the growth of the workforce during the late colonial period, based on studies done since the 1980s in Korea, Japan, and the United States.

## Historiographical Development

Until the 1980s, socioeconomic studies of colonial Korea were deeply influenced by Japanese Marxist historians and their anti-imperial viewpoint, which suited the nationalistic sentiments of Koreans in general and Korean academics in particular. These studies generally presented ideologically oriented, simplistic interpretations of the colonial period—a monolithic confrontation between Japanese imperialism and the Korean struggle for national liberation—and portrayed Koreans as passive and impersonal victims of an oppressive Japanese colonial rule.

Scholars such as Kajimura Hideki, Chŏn Sŏktam, Sin Yongha, and Kobayashi Hideo, for example, described 1930s industrial growth as "enclave-style" wartime armament industrial development that exploited Koreans and had no long-term effect on the Korean economy or Korean society.[1] In the 1970s Korean economic and labor historians like Kim Yunhwan, Kwŏn Tuyŏng, Kang Tongchin, and Pak Hyŏnch'ae interpreted colonial labor and labor movements in the context of the national liberation struggle of workers. These studies depicted Korean labor as a passive victim of Japanese exploitation. Evident in these analyses are several common themes: (1) a cheap, abundant, colonial labor force was exploited by a discriminatory labor system; (2) Korean workers were limited to unskilled work because the Japanese monopolized skilled work; (3) labor surpluses continued until 1937, and workers mobilized for the war effort simply reverted into the general population after 1945; and (4) the labor movement was typically an anti-Japanese nationalist movement.[2]

Beginning in the early 1980s, these earlier studies were challenged and re-examined with iconoclastic vigor from both inside and outside the South Korean academic community. As Gi-Wook Shin and Michael Robinson point out in the Introduction to this volume, in the conventional historical understanding, colonialism produced at best a "distorted" modernity and hindered the creation of a "true" modernity. In the value-laden, nationalist perspective, the colonial state as agent of change delegitimated the "modern" itself. The newer trend of historical thinking, however, pointed out that one cannot, indeed should not, avoid colonialism in discussing Korean modernity, and it sought to articulate the interlocking relationship between colonialism and modernity as well as to discuss the complex nature of colonial modernity.

At least four factors prompted these revisionist attitudes in Korean studies. First, South Korea achieved economic success and regained national self-confidence. Second, academic interest in this impressive economic performance was spurred by the work of economists and social scientists in both the "modern economic growth" school and the "dependency" school. The influence of these scholars motivated Korean researchers to examine Korean capitalist growth from a more objective historical perspective.[3] Third, understanding the nature of colonial modernity became a prerequisite for understanding the increasingly complex and diverse modernity of present-day Korea. Fourth, the upgrading of the higher education system in Korea to a graduate school orientation under the Chun Doo Hwan government in the early 1980s brought about a surge in graduate-level research and dissertations in Korea, which intensively explored all the major topics in modern Korean history from a new point of view.[4]

One area of focus was the socioeconomic changes resulting from the intensive wartime industrial growth in the late colonial period. Many studies re-examined the previous interpretation of growth as enclave-style development, using more sophisticated social-scientific research methods. The industrialization of this period was recast as "colonial, dependent development," not sufficient for full-scale modernization but at least substantial enough to shock and dislocate the traditional society and economy and to create an early stage of capitalism that provided the historical preconditions for Korea's economic growth during the 1960s. Major research in the past decade by An Pyŏngjik, Nakamura Tetsu, Hŏ Suyŏl, Soon-Won Park, Chŏng Chaejŏng, Hori Kazuo, and Sŏn Chaewŏn analyzed both official and private statistics of the time, including the 1930 and 1940 government censuses, and discovered structural changes accompanying colonial industrial growth that transformed the traditional agrarian society and economy into a dependent and yet developing urban society and capitalist economy. Among the changes in Korea noted in these studies are (1) the penetration of the society, including the agricultural sector, by capital; (2) the rapid change in the occupational structure of the society (male employment in agriculture dropped from 80.6 percent in 1930 to 71 percent in 1945); (3) the large-scale migration of peasant farmers into urban areas and industrial work sites in both domestic and overseas areas; (4) rapid urbanization (urban population grew from 4 percent of total population in 1920 to 7 percent in 1930 to 14 percent in 1945); (5) a substantial increase in the number of male industrial workers; and (6) at least until 1940, an increase in the number of small- and medium-scale Korean capitalists and entrepreneurs.[5]

By the 1990s, after a decade of iconoclastic studies, the concept of colonial modernity became a more useful conceptual tool for illuminating Korea's unique path to modernity and the complex ways in which present-day Korean identities are formed and deformed. Scholars such as An Pyŏngjik, Nakamura Tetsu, Kim Naknyŏn, Carter Eckert, Dennis McNamara, Bruce Cumings, Hori Kazuo, and Sŏn Chaewŏn have demonstrated in their studies in the past two decades that although colonialism intervened in Korea's path to modernity, this intervention did not automatically make Koreans mere passive recipients of modernity.[6] Their studies sought to elaborate the intrinsic, non-monolithic nature of the colonial industrial growth, its diverse impacts on social differentiation and fragmentation, and the colonial modification of modernization. Karl Moskowitz, Soon-Won Park, Chŏng Chaejŏng, Michael Robinson, and Gi-Wook Shin also studied colonial white- and blue-collar workers, intellectual elites, the urban middle class, and peasant farmers, respectively, and demonstrated that Koreans participated directly and indirectly in the construction of a unique colonial modernity—a modernity that created capitalism, modern technology-oriented cosmopolitanism, an urban middle class, and a consumer culture, in the absence of political emancipation.[7]

In this era of writing new and different histories, the concept of history itself has been undergoing a significant process of redefinition because of a radical revision in the concept of human communities. As the complex and multicultural, multiethnic postmodern world increasingly matures and becomes more sophisticated at the end of the twentieth century, younger scholars have begun searching

for and rescuing many ignored and silenced historical subjects of the
colonial past, forming a new counternarrative.

## Changes in the Labor-Power Structure
## in Korea in the 1930s

It was only in the 1980s that a group of junior scholars approached
the task of uncovering structural changes in the colonial period, including the process of working-class formation, with a more developed, comprehensive handling of the source materials.[8] As previously noted, all their studies agreed that industrial growth in 1930s
Korea was a colonial, dependent development, not an enclave-style
development. According to the conventional view, growth was neither self-generated nor based on domestic needs; rather, it was forcefully transplanted in a compulsive and rapid manner that disre-
garded the rudimentary level of industry in Korea. It was based not
on small- and medium-sized native enterprises but large-scale Japanese enterprises serving armament production, such as the metallurgical, machinery, and chemical industries, industries requiring
hydroelectric power, and mining in the northern part of Korea.[9]

Most industrial centers were strategically located on the eastern
or northwestern coasts near ports to connect them efficiently with
Japan. Heavy industry was limited mainly to the production of raw
materials, semifinished goods, and war supplies, which were then
shipped to Japan for final processing and consumption. Railroad
networks ran primarily along a north-south axis, facilitating Japan's
access to the Asian mainland. Sharp contrasts among industrial
fields and a sectoral imbalance in the industrial structure and location were the inevitable results.[10] Development was also abruptly
halted by the liberation in 1945. The sudden withdrawal of the Japanese and the subsequent partition of the country created economic
bankruptcy in the post-1945 period. Research findings from the
1980s, however, have revised this picture dramatically.

The studies of Hori Kazuo, a Kyoto University economic historian,
stand out in providing a clear picture of the occupational and regional changes in labor power during the 1930s. Four of his findings
are particularly important for understanding the background of
working-class formation and consequent changes in the labor-power
structure. First, a significant segment of the rural population rapidly
found non-agricultural employment both in Korea and overseas

(mainly Manchuria and Japan). Second, a large number of rural farmers in the southern provinces moved north to Kyŏnggi, South Hamgyŏng, and North Hamgyŏng provinces. Third, migration to these provinces flowed mainly into industrial centers like Kyŏngsŏng (Seoul), P'yŏngyang, Pusan, Hŭngnam, Inch'ŏn, and Ch'ŏngjin. And fourth, among these urban centers, Kyŏngsŏng's expansion was extraordinary. These changes are examined in more detail below.

## Rural Exodus: The Shift from Agricultural to Non-agricultural Employment

The government census of 1930 shows that colonial Korea was still an agricultural society—as of 1928, 80.6 percent of the employed population was still engaged in agriculture, compared with only 2.1 percent in mining and factory work. Hori Kazuo's detailed analysis on colonial census statistics shows, however, that this rural population was rapidly changing and disintegrating in the 1920s. The same census reveals that there were 1.75 million wage-earning workers in colonial Korea, divided between over a half-million agricultural workers and 1.16 million non-agricultural, mostly unskilled, free laborers.[11] In other words, almost 7 percent of the total population employed in agriculture were landless agricultural laborers (*mŏsŭm*). An additional half-million were free laborers, desperately seeking a livelihood by floating back and forth between the urban and rural labor markets. This group developed because of the serious and rapid impoverishment and bankruptcy of both self-cultivating and tenant farmers, and the increasing number of landless agricultural laborers, especially in the southern six provinces, throughout the 1920s.[12] In other words, the traditional rural system and rural population in colonial Korea was fast disintegrating by the late 1920s.

Reports on the extremely miserable and inhumane starvation-level living conditions among peasant farmers and the urban poor, especially in Kyŏngsang and Chŏlla provinces, frequently appeared in the press and communist literature, arousing great concern among the communist-phobic colonial administrators. In the years immediately after the Great Depression hit the Japanese and Korean rural sectors in 1929, bankruptcy and unemployment rates peaked in colonial society.[13] Economic and social historians like Nakamura Tetsu, Hong Sŏngch'an, Matsumoto Takeyoshi, and Gi-Wook Shin attribute this rural crisis to several factors: (1) the deep penetration of the commercial market economy into the rural sector because of the Campaign to Increase Rice Production and the Water Utilization Union system; (2) the disappearance of traditional work-sharing labor practices in rural communities and the compartmentalization of rural households; (3) a trend toward small-scale, labor-intensive rice cultivation in rural households using wage labor to supplement household workers; (4) the rapid dissolution of the rural sector in the pre-1930 period by the rapid impoverishment and bankruptcy of both self-cultivators and tenant farmers; and (5) the accumulation of these landless, bankrupt farmers in rural areas because of the lack of a pulling factor from the industrial urban sector.[14]

The statistics in the government's 1930 national census and the government-run Railway Bureau's 1928 survey of wage earners in non-agricultural sectors provide a clear picture of urban wage earners in the 1920s.[15] Most of the 1.16 million urban workers recorded in the 1930 census were "miscellaneous workers," who were composed mainly of free day-laborers, domestic household workers, and factory and mining workers.[16] The largest group was free day-laborers, with 40.4 percent (468,000) of the total workers. This group comprised free laborers, transport laborers, A-frame porters, and long-shoremen (baggage men), all of whom can be categorized as urban informal-sector workers. The next-largest group, at 27.6 percent (319,000) of the total, worked as housemaids (senjō) or houseboys (sendō) in urban households. Third, an extremely small minority worked in factories or mines, only 5.4 percent (40,000 factory workers, 23,000 mining workers) of the total urban workers. The factory workers were mainly engaged in food-processing industries, such as rice mills and wine breweries, and in textile mills; these occupations reflect the elementary level of industry. These figures stand in stark contrast to those of the 1940s, when factory/mining/construction workers outnumbered itinerant laborers and emerged as the largest non-agricultural population group. Overall, in the absence of urban industrial development, Korean wage earners remained a huge, frequently unemployed, job-seeking, floating population and formed a pool of abundant, cheap, surplus colonial labor. Needless to say, these urban marginal poor or informal-sector workers suffered from extremely low wages, job insecurity, and often long periods of unemployment.[17]

Beginning in the early 1930s, industrial growth changed the labor structure in Korea drastically. First, it brought about a huge shift in employment from the agricultural sector to the non-agricultural sector (from 80.6 percent in 1930 to 74.8 percent in 1940 to 71 percent in 1945). This rural exodus involved two destinations, one domestic, one foreign. Within Korea, it concentrated on factory, mining, and construction work sites in the fast-rising industrial centers of Kyŏng-sŏng, P'yŏngyang, Pusan, Inch'ŏn, Chinnamp'o, Hŭngnam, and Ch'ŏngjin, leading to rapid urbanization (from 7 percent of the total population in 1935 to 13.2 percent by 1944). Additionally, the migration extended to a larger imperialist labor market in Manchuria and Japan. From 1930 to 1940, roughly 1.3 million workers (700,000 to Japan and 600,000 to Manchuria) voluntarily sought industrial employment abroad, which often paid more than the Korean labor market. In addition, another one million workers were compulsorily mobilized (0.72 million for industrial labor, 0.24 million as civilian personnel in the military) after 1939. The rural exodus was literally explosive in the late colonial period.[18]

## South to North Regional Migration and Urbanization

Between 1935 and 1944, the rural population of Korea declined from 93 percent of the total population to 86.8 percent, and the urban population nearly doubled in this period, from 7 percent of the total in 1935 to 13.2 percent in 1944. The population of cities with more than 20,000 people increased from approximately 1.6 million (7 percent of the total population) in 1935 to approximately 4 million (14 percent of the total population) in 1945. Although this percentage is far less than the comparable figure for Japan in 1944 (41.9 percent) and equals that of Japan in 1908, the initial point in the Japanese urbanization process, it represented considerable growth, remarkably rapid considering the level of urbanization in Korea before 1930 (3.4 percent of the total population in 1920, 5.6 percent in 1930).[19]

The unemployment rate, which peaked in 1931, plummeted over the next ten years, as labor demand in Korea, Japan, and Manchuria increased tremendously. Industrial growth in the 1930s created a large-scale demand for labor, especially in the mining, factory, and construction fields, throughout the Japanese empire. Formal-sector employment in factories and mines increased from 2.1 percent of the entire employed population in 1931 to 7.2 percent in 1942.[20] By 1940, the unemployment rate was negligible. After 1937 and the beginning

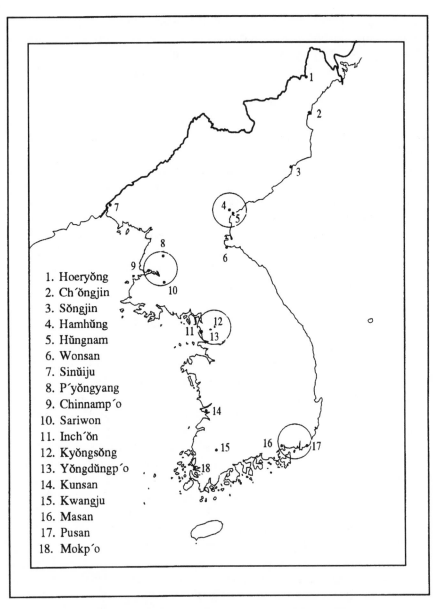

1. Hoeryŏng
2. Ch´ŏngjin
3. Sŏngjin
4. Hamhŭng
5. Hŭngnam
6. Wonsan
7. Sinŭiju
8. P´yŏngyang
9. Chinnamp´o
10. Sariwon
11. Inch´ŏn
12. Kyŏngsŏng
13. Yŏngdŭngp´o
14. Kunsan
15. Kwangju
16. Masan
17. Pusan
18. Mokp´o

Map 5.1 Industrial areas in Korea in the late 1930s

of Japan's full-scale war with China, requests for workers at urban employment offices outnumbered job seekers. Circumstances forced the government to intervene to control the labor market to cope with the acute labor shortage that resulted from the explosion in demand for factory, mine, and construction workers (see below).[21]

The movement of domestic labor was mainly from the poor, rice-growing southern provinces to northern regions like Kyŏnggi, South Hamgyŏng, and North Hamgyŏng. With the exception of Hwang-hae and South Chŏlla, where the number of agricultural workers increased 10 percent, agricultural sector employment declined by over 10 percent elsewhere and by over 20 percent in Kyŏnggi and the four northern provinces. Kyŏnggi and North Hamgyŏng provinces recorded the highest increase in non-agricultural employment, with more than 100,000 non-agricultural workers in each. By 1940, the non-agricultural employment rate stood at 25.2 percent for all of Korea, and at 47.6 percent in Kyŏnggi and 60.6 percent in North Hamgyŏng. This reflected the heavy influx of onetime agricultural workers to regions where industrial complexes were developing rapidly, such as Kyŏngsŏng-Inch'ŏn, Pyŏngyang-Chinnamp'o, Hŭngnam-Hamhŭng, Ch'ŏngjin-Najin, and Pusan (see Map 5.1).[22]

Although more concrete studies need to be done, clearly Kyŏngsŏng's growth as a large, industrial, urban center was by far the most impressive. It epitomized a growing urban space in the 1930s, with a budding urban population, popular culture, modern technology, and modern values. The lack of studies of Kyŏngsŏng in colonial historiography is an example of the politically biased historical narratives, as Prasenjit Duara had argued, that neglect and repress the complexities of the historical process of colonial modernity in which economic, social, and cultural changes intertwine.[23]

*The Expansion of Kyŏngsŏng*

From the mid-1920s to the early 1940s, the population of Kyŏngsŏng increased more than threefold, from 343,000 in 1925 to nearly 1,114,000 in 1942, and the number of households grew 2.5 times, from 76,000 in 1932 to 192,000 in 1942, for two reasons: a continuous inflow of new migrants, both Korean and Japanese, and the expansion of the administrative boundaries of the city. The latter was announced in April 1936 and resulted in a population jump from 404,000 at the end of 1935 to 677,000 at the end of 1936. The city's growth continued apace over the next six years.[24]

Although shifts in occupation structure were occurring nationwide, that of Kyŏngsŏng households changed in a unique way, with
more concentration in the industrial sector, especially factory and
mining. Whereas government employment and professional jobs increased by a factor of only 1.8, commercial and transportation jobs
increased 4.3 times, and industrial and mining jobs increased 7.6
times from 1930 to 1940.[25] Even before 1930, Kyŏngsŏng had a
unique industrial structure, based on rice processing, food processing, textile manufacturing, printing, and household goods manufacturing. Post-1930 industrial growth further developed this unique
structure, in contrast to the rapid war-related industrial growth in
northern Korea. The rice-processing industry drastically declined in
this period, especially after it came under wartime commodity controls in 1939. This contrasts with the overall industrial structure of
Korea, which was still concentrated in the food-processing (40 percent), electro-chemical (40 percent), and textile (18 percent) industries in 1940.[26] Kyŏngsŏng's industrial growth was concentrated in
the cotton textile industry, a variety of consumer goods–manufacturing industries, and the machine and machine tools industries
(which assembled, manufactured, repaired, and maintained the machines that supported textile and consumer goods–manufacturing).
This demonstrates the existence of an expanding consumer culture
and a nonmilitary market driving urban industrial growth in this
period and refutes the theory that growth was exclusively war-
related.[27] By 1940, the concentration in Kyŏngsŏng of the printing
industry and the machine and machine tools industries was remarkable, with 70 percent of the country's printing plants and 76.4 percent of the machine and machine tools industries located there.

The case of Kyŏngsŏng reveals significant changes occurring beneath the extraordinary wartime industrial growth. Until the 1970s,
these subsurface changes were largely ignored or misinterpreted by
historians influenced by the theory of enclave development.[28] The
changes in formal- and informal-sector industrial occupations in
Kyŏngsŏng and other urban centers were important in the formation
of the industrial workforce in this period and the subsequent modernization of Korea.[29] More creative research methods and new
thinking are still required to reconstruct the complex and multiple
responses of Koreans to the environment of colonial modernity.
Such labor groups as urbanized informal-sector workers, including
household workers, both male and female, urban squatters, and

miscellaneous workers, of this period and their responses to colonial modernity in an expanding urban space should be studied to shed light on the complexities of the colonial working-class communities. Attention to such sociocultural issues as workers' lifestyles, their subculture as part of urban modernity, and their transformation into colonial workers will lead us to a new frontier in colonial historiography. Beginning in the 1980s, studies along these lines focused on the growth of formal-sector workers, on factory and mining workers, and also on labor quality. The following sections summarize the findings of these studies in regard to the number of industrial workers, the labor policy of the colonial government, the quality of the workforce, and the growth in the worker consciousness and sense of identity among these workers.[30]

## Increase in the Number of Industrial Workers

### Male Full-time Workers in Industrial Workplaces

The number of industrial workers in Korea increased rapidly from 1930 to 1937 and explosively from 1937 to 1945, changing the composition and quality of the workforce. Membership in the working class reached approximately 1.75 million by 1942, if we include transportation workers and day laborers. Although half of these workers were so-called informal-sector workers such as day laborers, the number of factory, mining, and construction workers, who are generally regarded as the full-time, regular, core group of industrial workers, increased 3.3 times from 1933 to 1942, from 223,115 to 744,023 and constituted more than half the group by 1945 (see Table 5.1 and Fig. 5.1). The number of factory workers increased 3.9 times, miners 4.0 times, and construction workers a remarkable 8.7 times.

The new factor of industrial-sector employment accelerated outmigration in the rural sector remarkably, from a yearly average of 60,000 men during 1930–35 to 220,000 during 1935–45. Although roughly half this exodus was directed toward Japan and Manchuria, another half remained within Korea to meet the rapid increases in domestic labor demand. However, as noted above, the new industrial workers were not invariably freshly uprooted farmers, because a huge pool of floating labor already existed in colonial Korea by the late 1920s.[31]

Table 5.1
*Growth of the Working Class, 1933 to 1943*
(000s)

| Category | 1933 | 1943 (%) |
|---|---|---|
| Factory workers | 99.4 | 390 (22.3%) |
| Mineworkers | 70.7 | 280 (16.0) |
| Transportation workers | n/a | 170 ( 9.7) |
| Construction workers | 43.6 | 380 (21.7) |
| Miscellaneous | n/a | 530 (30.3) |
| TOTAL | n/a | 1,750 (100.0) |

SOURCES: 1943: *Shokugin chōsa geppō*, no. 38, pp. 3–4; 1943: *Daihachijūgokai teikoku gikai setsumei shiryō: Chōsen kindai shiryō kenkyū shūsei*, 1: 70.

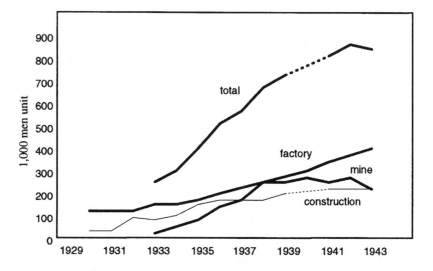

Fig. 5.1. Changes in the number of workers in Korea, 1929–1943. Sources: *factory workers*: Chōsen sōtokufu 1930–43 (1941 ed.); *mineworkers*: Chōsen sōtokufu 1944; *construction workers*: Masahisa 1941b: 3–4; *for 1941–43*: Chōsen sōtokufu, Rōmu kyōkai 1944.

The ratio of Japanese and Korean factory workers also changed between 1930 and 1945. Initially, between 1930 and 1936, Japanese workers remained a constant 10–11 percent of the entire factory workforce, doubling in number from 5,826 to 11,337. They were mostly skilled workers, concentrated in such heavy industries as the metallurgical, machine and machine tools, chemical, ceramics, and electric and gas industries. This picture changed after 1936. Although the number of Japanese workers increased from 11,337 in 1936 to 21,370 in 1941, they represented a declining percentage of total factory workers, decreasing from 11.4 percent to 7.1 percent. This decrease continued until 1943, to under 7 percent, as many Japanese workers were drafted into the military.[32]

Another change was a rapid increase in the number working in large-scale plants, mines, or construction sites. By 1939, more than 50 percent worked in factories employing over 100 workers. This phenomenon accelerated after 1939, when the industrial structure of colonial Korea shifted toward heavy industry, rendering food processing far less significant than the textile, chemical, machine and machine tools, and metallurgical industries by 1943. As noted above, these large-scale heavy industrial factories were concentrated in the five northern provinces, and the increase was much more dramatic among male workers in large-scale heavy industrial factories, mines, or construction sites in the north. The ratio of female workers peaked in 1932 at 45 percent of total factory workers and decreased to 33 percent by the end of the 1930s.[33]

## Changes in the Labor Policy of the Colonial Government

Conventional narratives of colonial Korea depict the cheap, abundant, surplus colonial workers as silent, passive victims with no legal protections or channels for grievances apart from spontaneous labor disputes. The colonial state in Korea is characterized as having an authoritarian and self-serving labor policy focusing only on Japanese interests: the uprooting of radical, communist elements, and the protection of the labor supply for large Japanese factories. Also emphasized is the government's neglect of the compelling problem of rural surplus labor until the early 1930s, when it became active and interventionist as the wartime labor mobilization got under way in the late colonial period.[34]

Many recent studies, however, have been quite critical of these

conventional interpretations, labeling them totalizing, politically biased narratives that repress and cover up the richness and complexities of the colonial drama by projecting a simple, binary ex-
ploitation-resistance theme onto colonial Korea. These studies have
tried to re-examine and re-evaluate colonial history, including the
years between the two world wars, as a product of the colonial society's own complexities and dynamics, which involved various colonial social groups, both Korean and Japanese.[35]

In the late 1920s, regional labor shortages began appearing in Korea. When Noguchi Jun, the ambitious Japanese businessman who
owned the Nihon chissō (Japan Nitrogen Fertilizer Company) group,
decided to venture into northern Korea in 1926, the remote, mountainous Hamgyŏng region experienced a sudden and rapid construction boom centering around railroad, hydroelectric dam, and
plant construction. A huge number of construction workers were
urgently demanded.[36] This tightening of the labor market continued
during the period of wartime industrial growth and ultimately
prompted the colonial government to take steps to boost the supply
of workers. In response, it approached the labor shortage in the
1930s with two goals in view: a quantitative increase in the numbers
of unskilled workers, and a qualitative upgrading of Korean workers' skills.

In contrast to its laissez-faire attitude toward the serious problem
of a surplus labor market in Korea in the early 1920s, the labor control policy of the colonial government became increasingly rigid and
authoritarian as the 1920s progressed, exacerbating labor and social
militancy in the interwar years. Legal measures for rationalizing the
authoritarian suppression by the police of labor and social resistance
were first instituted in Japan, when the Diet passed the Peace Preservation Law in April 1925. In contrast to the usual delay in implementing metropolitan policies, the provisions of this law were applied to Korea in October 1925, with colonial police raiding the
offices of the newly established Korean Communist Party. Over the
next four years, there were three more rounds of extensive raids and
arrests of Communist leaders in Korea on charges of violating the
Peace Preservation Law. In 1928, the Communist Party was dissolved, and the Government-General formed the Special Higher Police Force (Kōtō keisatsu), for thought control and the suppression of
radical elements in Korea as well as anti-Japanese Koreans in Manchuria and Siberia. The Peace Preservation Law was revised the fol-

lowing year, giving the Government-General the authority to execute the leaders of independence movements. In May 1931, the
united front organization Sin'ganhoe was dissolved by the Special
Higher Police Force.[37]

Nevertheless, the war in Manchuria from 1931 and later in China
after 1937 brought a drastic change in colonial labor policy. Government direction and control increased tremendously, to help place
the economic structure on a wartime footing. The government in Korea, led by ex-army generals Ugaki Kazushige (1931–36) and Minami
Jirō (1936–42), had to intervene in the labor supply due to the increasingly urgent demand for both unskilled and skilled workers
throughout the vast yen-bloc economy of the Japanese empire. In
September 1938, Governor-General Minami convened the Commis-
sion on the Investigation of Countermeasures for the Current Situation (Jikyoku taisaku chōsakai). Its advisory report stressed labor
market policy as the focal point of government industrial policy
for the first time since annexation. Its major points were: (1) expansion of war-related industries such as metal, machine and machine
tools, and mining; (2) reorganization of the Korean labor force for
military purposes, by training technicians and skilled workers and
mobilizing unskilled workers; and (3) transformation of small- and
medium-sized factories into subcontracting workshops for large-
scale war industries.[38] The twin labor policies were now a quantitative policy of mobilization of unskilled workers and education to
upgrade the skills of Korean workers.[39]

The government launched the first government procurement and
guidance of unskilled labor in April 1934 under the policy rubric of
"moving surplus population in the southern provinces to the northern provinces (*nansen hokuisaku*)," as part of an out-of-province employment promotion policy (*dogai shokugyō assen seisaku*). The majority of those affected were construction workers mobilized for
construction and industrial sites. This official labor mobilization
program was instituted by the Social Affairs Section (Shakaika) of
the Internal Affairs Bureau (Naimukyoku) of the Government-
General of Korea, and the internal affairs section of each provincial
administrative office. A nongovernment organization, the Kyŏngsŏng Civil Engineering and Construction Association (Keijō doboku
kenchiku kyōkai, later renamed Chōsen doboku kenchiku kyōkai),
also actively supported this undertaking.[40]

The government's efforts became more aggressive after April

1937, when it launched an employment promotion policy (*Kan assen shokugyō seisaku*) on a larger scale. For example, after announcement of the Ordinance on Korean Gold Production (*Chōsen sankinrei*) in September 1937, the colonial government included mineworkers in its official labor mobilization program after November 1938. The program mobilized 12,000 workers in 1937, 20,000 in 1938, and an average 40,000–50,000 every year between 1939 and 1944.[41]

Labor mobilization became compulsory in 1939 with the promulgation of the Ordinance on the National Draft (*Kokumin chōyōrei*). It intensified from 1941 by extension of the age range from 20–45 years to 18–45 years, as the demand for labor on mining, transportation, and construction work sites throughout the Japanese empire became desperate. The government also used the Patriotic Labor Corps for National Support (Kinrō hokokudai) system for still broader labor mobilization of students, women, and older males within Korea.

Labor affairs received special bureaucratic support in 1940. The Social Affairs Section, which was reassigned from the Education Bureau (Gakumukyoku) to the Internal Affairs Bureau in 1936, branched out to form the new Labor Affairs Section (Rōmuka) in 1940 and thereafter bore exclusive responsibility for labor mobilization and other labor affairs. The Labor Affairs Section immediately launched a new factory labor survey, not in order to implement factory law but to mobilize the labor force for the war effort. The survey results were published during 1941–43, as the *Results of the Statistical Survey of Korean Laborers and Technicians* (*Chōsen rōdō gijutsu tōkei chōsa kekka hōkoku*). Enforced enlistment (*kyōsei chōyō*) was used to mobilize rural people from 1939.[42]

As the labor shortage grew even more acute during World War II, the Association for Korean Labor Affairs (Chōsen rōmu kyōkai) was established, in 1941, exclusively for labor mobilization. By 1945, almost 750,000 workers had been compulsorily mobilized. By occupation, these workers included 340,000 coalminers, 200,000 factory and other miscellaneous workers, 110,000 construction workers, and 67,000 metallurgical workers. An additional 240,000 were mobilized as civilian workers for the military beginning in 1943.[43] In all, almost one million Koreans were mobilized by force during 1939–45.

Within Korea, 422,000 laborers were mobilized by the Government-General between 1935 and 1945 into large-scale firms for war-related or construction projects. Approximately 210,000 industrial workers, mostly rural recruits, were absorbed into major industrial areas such as Hŭngnam, Kyŏng-In, Sŏsŏn, and Pusan in the period between 1937 and 1945.[44] The outskirts of major cities in these industrial complexes developed as industrial and residential suburbs because of this rapid influx of rural workers (see Map 5.1). Thus, a full-scale interprovincial migration started for the first time in the demographic history of the colony, due to the increased openings in the expanding war economy. The labor recruitment network also became nationwide for the first time.[45]

In retrospect, the labor market in colonial Korea was rapidly integrated into the yen-bloc labor market. Demographic movements occurred both out of and into Korea. Out-migration from Korea continued between 1937 and 1945 in an explosive manner, throughout the wartime Japanese labor market. The number of Korean residents in Japan increased from 780,528 in 1936 to 2,100,000 in 1945; these figures point to the migration of approximately 1.32 million Koreans to Japan in this period, even assuming some increase through births in Japan. Similarly, though on a smaller scale, the total number of Korean residents in Manchuria increased from 1.04 million in 1938 to 1.56 million in 1944.[46] An equally significant change was the continuous influx of Japanese residents into these colonial labor markets. The number of Japanese residents in Korea increased from 527,000 in 1930 to 713,000 in 1940 to 750,000 in 1945. This Japanese migration was the important part of the urbanization process. Within Korea, around two million people moved to urban or industrial areas in the last decade of the colonial period, a remarkable change compared with that of the previous decades.[47] Historical interpretations of this mobilized labor, their sociocultural experiences, and their level of modernity as an uprooted and floating urban population, and their fate following liberation are also urgent subjects for inquiry. Bruce Cumings flagged this issue in volume one of *Origins of the Korean War*, not with reference to workers, but to the general problem of returnees in the Taegu area and southern Korea. He posits that the uprooting caused by the return of so many mobilized during the war created instability. All these fascinating topics await imaginative and innovative research and interpretation.[48]

## The Quality of Korean Workers

Given the numerical increases in Korean industrial workers, in both the formal and the informal sectors, the important question arises as to what extent and in what ways colonial industrial growth changed the quality of the labor force. Research on this issue has focused on three topics: (1) improvements in the educational level of urban factory and mining workers, who could advance their skills by several years of elementary schooling; (2) accumulation of job experience and skills at work sites; and (3) the emergence of skilled Korean workers. Research on all these points proved that conventional views of colonial labor as unconditionally abundant, surplus, and unskilled were oversimplistic and inaccurate and that the upper layers of the Korean workforce acquired greater responsibilities and improved their work skills through new opportunities afforded by wartime industrial growth.

### Elementary School Education

Until the late 1920s, the colonial government's labor policy was to use Japanese workers for all engineering, technical, and skilled work required for colonial industrial growth and Korean workers for unskilled or semiskilled work. This policy was possible because of the geographical proximity of Korea to Japan (it was an overnight ferry ride) and the surplus labor pool in Korea. The colonial government ignored and neglected the formal education and job training of Korean workers and deliberately limited their training and advance through a dualistic, discriminatory labor-management system. At the workshop level, Japanese managers maintained a certain ratio of Japanese skilled workers on the shop floor as lower-level managers. These Japanese workers had daily contact with Korean workers, controlling and supervising their work performance and, in the process, creating colonial, racial tension.[49]

The result of this policy was an extremely low level of education among colonial workers until the 1930s. The majority were rural people who had neither handicraft work experience nor a modern school education. These factors are probably behind the abundant negative descriptions of the majority of the Korean workforce, by both Korean and Japanese managers, as prone to irresponsible behavior, high absenteeism and turnover rates, and hot-tempered spontaneous violence. These characteristics were seen as lowering the quality of the labor force, especially in contrast to Japanese workers, and making adaptation to factory life difficult. The fairness of this evaluation is dubious when one considers the extreme gap between Korea and Japan, not only in the level of capitalistic development but also in the level of elementary education.[50]

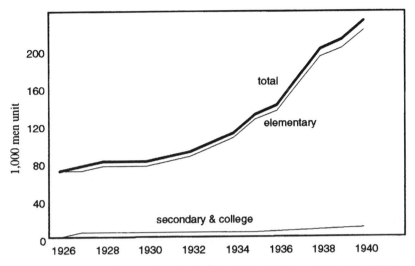

Fig. 5.2 Changes in the number of school graduates in Korea, 1926–1940. SOURCE: Chōsen sōtokufu 1941: 115–16.

In Japan, the Meiji government started compulsory elementary education of three to four years beginning in 1886, at the outset of capitalist development. The elementary school enrollment rate for male students was already 62 percent in the same year. In contrast, 50 years later in 1935, the rate in Korea was only 19.7 percent, even in the midst of rapid industrial growth.[51] The overall elementary school enrollment rate in Korea, however, increased rapidly in the 1930s, more than doubling from 14.5 percent in 1930 to 33.8 percent in 1940. A rough estimate for 1945 is around 50–60 percent.[52] In parallel with the increase in school enrollment, the number of elementary school graduates also increased slowly between 1927 and 1933 and accelerated after 1934. The numbers of middle school graduates also increased rapidly, almost doubling from 6,500 in 1934 to approximately 10,000 in 1940, and reached 13,900 by the early 1940s (see Fig. 5.2).

By 1943, factory and mining workers had a much higher educational level than other workers (see Table 5.2). Although 48.1 percent of factory workers had no school education, 49.4 percent had either graduated or attended at least several years of elementary school. Among mineworkers, 75.2 percent had no education, and only 23.6 percent either had graduated or had several years of schooling. It is

Table 5.2
*Educational Background of Workers, 1943*

| Schooling | Total | Korean (%) | | Japanese (%) | | Miscel-laneous |
|---|---|---|---|---|---|---|
| | | *Factories* | | | | |
| No education | 191,834 | 183,868 (48.1%) | | 27 | (0.1%) | 7,939 |
| Elementary, dropouts | 68,234 | 67,677 | (17.7) | 440 | (1.8) | 117 |
| Elementary, graduates | 126,868 | 121,324 | (31.7) | 5,411 | (22.7) | 133 |
| Middle school, dropouts | 1,289 | 553 | (0.1) | 736 | (3.1) | 0 |
| Middle school, graduates | 14,577 | 1,706 | (0.4) | 12,870 | (54.0) | 1 |
| Youth vocational school | 9,494 | 5,780 | (1.5) | 3,672 | (15.4) | 42 |
| Miscellaneous schooling | 2,246 | 1,582 | (0.4) | 662 | (2.8) | 2 |
| TOTAL | 414,542 | 382,490 | (100.0) | 23,818 | (100.0) | 8,234 |
| | | *Mines* | | | | |
| No education | 128,428 | 125,919 (75.2%) | | 84 | (4.7%) | 2,425 |
| Elementary, dropouts | 12,845 | 12,765 | (7.6) | 39 | (2.2) | 41 |
| Elementary, graduates | 27,317 | 26,778 | (16.0) | 479 | (26.8) | 60 |
| Middle school, dropouts | 154 | 115 | (0.1) | 39 | (2.2) | 0 |
| Middle school, graduates | 1,130 | 357 | (0.2) | 770 | (43.2) | 3 |
| Youth vocational school | 1,664 | 1,332 | (0.8) | 330 | (18.5) | 2 |
| Miscellaneous schooling | 270 | 225 | (0.1) | 43 | (2.4) | 2 |
| TOTAL | 171,808 | 167,491 | (100.0) | 1,784 | (100.0) | 2,533 |

SOURCE: *Chōsen rōdō gijutsu tōkei chōsha kekka hōkoku*, 1943. The survey included businesses that employed more than 30 employees. Construction workers are included under the category "Factories."

not possible to correlate the increasing number of school attendees and colonial industrial growth, but elementary schooling certainly would have helped upgrade the skills and learning speed of workers and meet the demand for better-quality factory workers.[53]

## Accumulation of On-the-Job Training and Skills

The employment pattern of colonial workers was diverse and complex but can broadly be divided into day labor (informal sector) and full-time permanent employment (formal sector). Factory workers were generally full-time permanent employees, whereas construction workers were commonly either day or contract laborers. In the case of miners, both employment systems were used, either the contract (*tŏkdae*) system or a permanent employment system with the mining company directly, although it is hard to judge which was more frequent. It is certain that the permanent employment system was much more widely practiced by the 1930s than previously, at least in factory, mining, and construction, if less so in the urban informal sectors of transportation services, household services, and day labor.[54]

It is now firmly established that some industrial workers permanently employed in factories and mines, such as large-scale government factories or Japanese-owned plants, had become modern industrial workers during the 1920s and emerged as the first generation of skilled workers during the post-1930 period. Several key case studies done in the 1980s provide a good picture of the growth of a skilled workforce during the 1930s industrial boom. All concur upon the following points. First, the ratio of Korean to Japanese workers increased in all large-scale industrial plants in the 1920s and 1930s. The rate of increase was gradual in the 1920s but escalated rapidly in the 1930s and exploded after 1939. In the 1944–45 period, the ratio between Korean and Japanese skilled workers in large factories reversed. In this context, some minority of Korean workers gradually established themselves as skilled industrial workers through on-the-job training in the 1930s, and some even became low-level foremen or low-level technicians after the late 1930s.[55]

The studies also find, however, that the majority of workers experienced discrimination in wages, promotion, responsibilities, and benefits. The workers' responses to social rejection and discrimination in the workshop were not simply monolithic, either resistance or collaboration, but quite varied and opportunistic, reflecting the diverse and uneven nature of modernity in colonial Korea. Accordingly, some scholars argue that the positive historical impact for Korea of this increase in skilled workers was felt more in the long run, during the post-liberation and post–Korean War era, when their intensive pre-1945 wartime experience made them valuable industrial assets.[56]

Third, the working class that Korea inherited from the colonial period in 1945 included two very different groups of workers. One consisted of the skilled industrial workers just discussed above. The other and larger group was composed of rural migrant workers who worked as unskilled labor in mining, construction, and the urban informal sector and on haphazard wartime work projects, many of whom were still half-rural and half-industrial transitional workers.[57] This complex diversity in the composition of the workforce in colonial Korea is a direct reflection of the complex diversity of colonial modernity, which spread highly unevenly across diverse social groups and regions, and varied by period.

Although not complete, labor statistics for 1943 reveal a ratio between these two groups of roughly 1:4 among factory and mining workers. Table 5.3 shows years of employment of factory and mining workers in four intervals: less than one year, one–two years, three–four years, and more than five years in 1943. The number of factory workers in these categories are 46.8 percent, 31.5 percent, 12.2 percent, and 8.6 percent, respectively; the corresponding figures for miners are 44.6 percent, 32.9 percent, 14.0 percent, and 8.4 percent. These statistics reveal that roughly half of both factory and mineworkers were new recruits with less than one year of experience, another 30 percent had only one to two years' experience, and 20 percent had more than three years' experience. We may regard the last group as full-time, steadily employed workers with enough skill and discipline to be considered skilled modern industrial workers. Several case studies also confirm that the liberation of Korea in 1945 furthered this upward movement of the careers of the upper layer of Korean skilled workers as they became skilled technical workers, engineers, or sometimes even managers in South Korean industry.[58]

Table 5.3
*Employment Seniority of Male Workers, 1943*

| Years of employment | Total (%) | Korean (%) | Japanese (%) | Miscellaneous (%) |
|---|---|---|---|---|
| | | *Factories* | | |
| Under 1 | 61,616 (44.0%) | 57,533 (46.8%) | 3,784 (23.6%) | 299 (28.5%) |
| 1–2 | 44,326 (31.6) | 38,707 (31.5) | 5,306 (33.1) | 313 (29.8) |
| 3–4 | 18,346 (13.1) | 15,049 (12.2) | 3,157 (19.7) | 140 (13.3) |
| 5 or more | 14,705 (10.5) | 10,613 (8.6) | 3,795 (23.6) | 2,972 (28.3) |
| Day labor | 1,082 (0.8) | 1,073 (0.9) | 9 (0.1) | 0 |
| TOTAL | 140,075 (100.0) | 122,975 (100.0) | 16,051 (100.0) | 3,724 (100.0) |
| | | *Mines* | | |
| Under 1 | 34,834 (44.1%) | 34,360 (44.6%) | 355 (26.2%) | 119 (20.7%) |
| 1–2 | 25,955 (32.9) | 25,344 (32.9) | 423 (31.3) | 188 (32.6) |
| 3–4 | 11,202 (14.2) | 10,757 (14.0) | 252 (18.6) | 193 (33.5) |
| 5 or more | 6,895 (8.7) | 6,500 (8.4) | 319 (23.6) | 76 (13.2) |
| Day labor | 50 (0.1) | 46 (0.1) | 4 (0.3) | 0 |
| TOTAL | 78,936 (100.0) | 77,007 (100.0) | 1,353 (100.0) | 576 (100.0) |

SOURCE: *Chōsen rōdō gijutsu tōkei chōsa kekka hōkoku*, 1943. This survey covered factories and mines employing 30 or more workers.

## Job Training by the Government

Until the mid-1930s, two government bureaus—the Railroad Bureau and the Postal and Communications Bureau—operated training schools, producing several dozen Korean trainees recruited every year exclusively for technical or skilled jobs in government factories.[59] In the private sphere, large-scale Japanese enterprises operated in-company training centers to meet their own needs for technicians and skilled workers. The largest was run by the Chōsen Nitrogen Fertilizer Company (Chōsen chissō), one of the world's largest and most advanced chemical fertilizer companies, established in Hŭngnam, South Hamgyŏng Province, in 1929. The Hŭngnam Technical Training Center annually recruited some forty trainees, of whom four to five were Koreans. Similar in-company training programs were sponsored in five Onoda Cement Company factories, branch plants of the largest cement factory in colonial Korea from 1919 to 1945, in Sŭnghori, South Pyŏngan Province. Some new recruits were selected as trainees in each branch factory and received elementary and middle-school education and basic technical training.[60]

These were, however, all limited, local, individual-level job- and skill-training programs. Only after 1937 did the government seriously intervene in industrial job training at the national level. In affiliation with the Chōsen Industrial Association (Chōsen kōgyō kyōkai), the government promoted the training of Korean technicians and skilled workers by establishing a skilled worker–training center (jukurenkō yōseisho) in 1937. The center had an electrical bureau and a machinery bureau and trained approximately 100–300 Korean youths as skilled workers in these fields every year until 1945.[61]

The acute labor shortage, especially in skilled jobs, accelerated with the drafting of Japanese skilled workers from colonial factories after 1937. The Korean workforce experienced upward mobility in two ways. First, some Korean unskilled workers were moved into skilled jobs and trained intensively, due to the industrial demand for educaied and trained workers. Many Korean workers responded aggressively to these opportunities for social advancement. Second, some Korean skilled workers moved upward into openings created by the expansion of industry and positions vacated by drafted Japanese skilled workers. The unintended (and unwanted, from the Japanese viewpoint) result of the urgent wartime labor shortage was that some workers in the upper echelons of the colonial workforce quickly moved further upward in factories, mines, and construction sites. This upward mobility was not limited to the industrial workforce but was widespread in other modern sector jobs in schools, companies, banks, and even government offices.[62]

The findings outlined above must be integrated with prevailing interpretations that have avoided ascribing any "positive" effects in the development of Korean labor to the upward mobility of labor in the wartime period. Many scholars still hesitate to admit any ameliorative effects by pointing to the dual composition of the workforce — unskilled and skilled — and the "temporary" nature of the wartime mobility. They affirm that some upper-level skilled workers received intensive work training and moved rapidly upward to supervisory and more responsible positions to meet the keen shortage of skilled workers during the emergency industrialization. They argue, however, that the opportunities were quite limited at the top of the labor force structure and that even this top layer encountered a glass ceiling: industrial relations were still tightly controlled by a small minority of residual Japanese workers and engineers.[63]

Others, such as Yi Hongrak, argue that, in contrast to this advance among upper-level Korean workers, the rapidly increasing number of rural recruits continuously diluted the overall quality of workers and reduced average labor productivity by rapidly accelerating rates of turnover, accidents, injuries, and absenteeism from 1939. In other words, a huge lower layer of urban informal-sector workers (estimated around 1 million) and wartime mobilized workers (estimated around 1.54 million) were moving in a counter-direction.[64] This is another key area for future study. Although research during the 1980s helped to clarify the urbanization of Korean labor and the upward movement at the top layer of the factory workforce, a more comprehensive and balanced understanding of the entire working class is still missing.

## The Growth in Worker Consciousness

The final question to be considered here is to what extent and in what ways these increases in the number of workers and in the quality of the upper layer of the workforce influenced workers' class consciousness ("class" in the modern identity sense of race, gender, or nation, rather than the classical Marxist sense). What kind of class identity emerged in response to the tensions and contradictions caused by working in the colonial industrial setting? And how was this connected to national identity? Did colonialism and modernity merge to create a hybrid identity? In the late colonial period, workers learned economic drive and experienced rapid social changes intensively and directly. Social changes in general took diverse and intensive forms: the penetration of capital, rapid changes in occupational structure, rapid urbanization, and the growth of both the male and the female industrial workforce, an urban middle class, and Korean capitalists. Probably due to the forced and unbalanced nature of industrial growth, the general pattern of industrial labor—increase in the number of industrial workers = a rising labor movement, with increased solidarity among the workers—does not describe 1930s Korea.

This is indicated by the fact that the colonial labor movement peaked earlier, during the 1920s and first half of the 1930s, when industry in Korea was still at an elementary level. This period between the two world wars began with the 1919–20 recession after the World War I economic boom and ended with the Shōwa depression after the 1929 Great Depression. This fifteen-year period was the only time when labor disputes and strikes increased markedly and the organized labor union movement spread aggressively in colonial Korea. The causes of this spurt in labor militancy and activity are generally linked to three trends: the economic crises of the interwar period, the Cultural Rule of the 1920s, and the Communist movement and infiltration into work sites.[65]

In the pre-1930 period, the colonial government had limited and inactive labor control policies, which concentrated only on blocking Communist agents and on supporting large-scale Japanese factories' exploitation of cheap, abundant Korean labor. Japanese labor laws were never applied to colonial Korea, and employers had a free hand to manage Korean workers as they saw fit. Colonial workers were deprived of legal protections and expressed their discontent by spontaneous strikes, work stoppages, slowdowns, and a high turnover rate. When workers became uncooperative, the Japanese police were always on hand to enforce the employer's will.[66]

Despite restrictive colonial labor policies, the number of labor disputes and participants in them doubled throughout the 1920s, and disputes grew more radical. According to official statistics, the number of disputes between 1926 and 1930 increased to 556 incidents, involving 51,531 workers. The majority of participants were non-factory workers such as day laborers or dockworkers (36.5 percent of the total) or construction workers (14.9 percent). Factory workers numbered only 12.2 percent of the participants, reflecting both the low level of industrial growth and the huge number of urban informal-sector workers at the time.[67]

Another change in the nature of labor disputes in the later 1920s was a geographic shift to the northern provinces. This was due to the major construction boom that accompanied the development of large hydroelectric dams as well as the more aggressive infiltration of Communists across the Manchurian border. Worker demands became more sophisticated, and strikes or disputes lasted longer. Although the workers were defeated in both cases, good examples of the longer, more organized, and militant pattern of disputes were the two large-scale general strikes in South Hamgyŏng Province, the first at Yŏnghŭng in 1928 and the second at Wŏnsan in 1929. By the late 1920s, workers had demonstrated unprecedented strength in organizing, as well as a new solidarity. The mystique—the sense of tradition—produced by these movements is an important element in Korean labor movement history.[68]

The frequency of labor disputes peaked in 1930–31, just after the Great Depression of 1929. In 1930 there were 160 disputes, with 18,972 participants, and in 1931, 201 disputes, with 17,114 participants. Never again under Japanese rule, however, were Korean workers to rise up and strike as they did between 1929 and 1932, the period which included the Wŏnsan General Strike.[69] According to Kobayashi Hideo's detailed study of the early 1930s labor movement in the north, Korean workers' growing militancy after the Wŏnsan General Strike was further intensified when the Comintern and Profintern adopted a new, extreme leftist line after 1929, focused on a pure proletarian movement to convert not intellectuals but laborers and farmers troubled and agitated by the Great Depression. The result was soaring dispute rates among workers in the north and more militant and revolutionary anti-imperialistic Red labor union movements in the early 1930s.[70]

The impetus for this radical surge in labor disputes and turmoil was the sudden increase in male workers engaged in heavy industry, including chemical factories, railroads, and dam construction, in the northern provinces. Communist activists and Red labor union programs targeted these workers. The basic strategy of Communist activists was to infiltrate existing labor unions, take over control of their leadership, and steer union activity into more anti-Japanese revolutionary stances. Beginning with the re-organization of a labor union in a Sinŭiju factory in October 1930, they then organized the Hamhŭng Committee of the Chosŏn Red Labor Union in February 1931. This committee formed the Hŭngnam Chemical Red Labor Union as its subgroup. Most northern industrial regions, including Sinŭiju, P'yŏngyang, Hamhŭng, Hŭngnam, and Wŏnsan, witnessed a similar surge in Red labor union organizations.[71]

Another important shift in colonial labor in the 1930s involved a change in the government's labor policy from noninterference to active intervention. The colonial police, which had been determined to eliminate any Red elements from Korea even during the pre-1930 period, launched an extensive anti–Red labor union campaign starting with the arrest of the leaders of the Hŭngnam Red Labor Union in 1931. Through 1933, several more large-scale arrests of Communist activists in Red labor unions resulted in the detention of some 1,800 activists.[72] Labor troubles rapidly subsided beginning in 1934 and finally went underground completely after 1937 during the wartime emergency rule and compulsory assimilation policies of *naisen ittai* (Japan and Korea as a single body) and *kōminka* (movement to transform the colonial peoples into imperial subjects). The historical irony is, however, that the government repression of communism during the war years unintentionally assisted the communist cause in the long run. The colonial police enhanced the image of the Communists by giving them credit for every dispute and decrying every labor disruption and all agitation as a communist plot. The Japanese sought to use the fear of communism to bind Koreans closer to the colonial system. The results were the exact opposite. The Communists' prestige was so enhanced that, when the liberation finally came, they were championed as the heroes of the underground and led an intense, yet short-lived, highly politicized labor movement, until the U.S. military occupational government crushed the movement in 1947.[73]

Another important change in labor relations, which became a fundamental and enduring legacy for Korean labor, occurred with the intensification of the Pacific War. By 1942, the empire demanded more and more sacrifice and increased output from industrial workers. The government launched the Campaign for the National Protection Corps of Industrial Workers (Sangyō hōkokudai undō; hereafter Sanpō) in late 1938 and instituted "patriotic industrial units" (*aikokuhan*) in factories in Japan, Korea, and Manchuria to increase productivity. These units were a kind of labor-management council in which rank-and-file workers, both Korean and Japanese, and managers joined together to increase production for the imperial war. Each unit in the firm chose representatives to unite as a workers' association. The association was provided office space inside the plant and funds to carry out given programs for the war effort. Full-time officers in the association were paid by the company. Together the association and managers established programs for educating workers, making production more efficient, and preventing labor-management disputes.[74]

The role of the Sanpō system in the Japanese war effort is uncertain, but one thing is sure: it became one of Japan's permanent contributions to Korea's industrial relations system. Ironically, the five years during which the wartime industrial relations program was in effect left a deep impact on contemporary Korean labor practice in several areas: (1) overpoliticization of labor, (2) government intervention in labor-management relations and a strong bond between government and business, (3) the company union system, and (4) the labor-management council system. Again, until recently these important colonial legacies have been nearly obscured by nationalist-focused narratives.[75]

Other studies have tackled the question of identity formation among colonial workers. These studies have found that as Korean workers gained more experience and skills and established themselves in higher positions, their interactions with Japanese workers and managers increased, and they inevitably confronted the most subtle, yet essential aspect of colonial modernity, namely, the conflict between colonialism and modernity. Korean workers could benefit from company-sponsored training in skills and technical know-how, the seniority-oriented incentive system, and other company benefits, but the modernization process was conditional and allowed only up to a certain point, and then in a fragmentary, filtered, incomplete way because of the colonial situation. Korean skilled workers inevitably came to realize their position in the ethnically segmented colonial labor market.

It was painful to have several ambiguous, segmented identities within oneself. Mutually conflicting individual and collective identities as well as class, gender, and national identities were entwined with each other within the consciousness of skilled workers. They were in a collective drama in which the frustrations that grew out of colonial issues of oppression and discrimination could not be settled through their efforts as individuals or as class members. Earlier theoreticians on colonialism like Frantz Fanon, Albert Memmi, and others have conceptualized this complicated, split-identity formation in colonial subjects as self-alienation, historyless-ness, or identityless-ness. Current postcolonial writers and theorists, including Homi Bhabha and Gayatri Spivak, have moved one step further by conceptualizing "hybrid identities" formed in "colonial modernity." They argue that the merger of colonialism and modernity rendered identity contingent and ambiguous, which they see as an essential element of colonial modernity.

## Conclusion

This chapter has attempted to show how Korean historians and social scientists have tried to redefine the Korean colonial experience as a bridge between late nineteenth-century premodern Korea and late twentieth-century modern Korea. Colonial industrial growth was a powerful historical earthquake. The wartime emergency situation further intensified demographic, economic, and social change. Reinterpretation of the colonial period has led to a more sober recognition of the following points: (1) the extent of the dislocation of the rural masses and traditional society; (2) the developmental shock Koreans experienced and how it fueled the postwar "catch-up-with-Japan" nationalism; (3) the extent of urbanization and changes in the family system and values; and (4) the movement of some Koreans into higher-skill modern-sector jobs. The myth of an unchanging Korean labor pool under Japanese colonial rule—cheap, abundant, unskilled, and anti-Japanese—has also been attenuated as new studies emphasize the complexity of the economic development process and the emergence of a modern working class.

Of course, some scholars remain reluctant to accept these interpretations as full proof of colonial modernization. They argue that development was excessive and unbalanced, with Koreans suffering under the *naisen ittai* assimilation policy, which tried fanatically to destroy Korean identity. They point out that (1) the *yangban*-style landed ruling class was very strong until 1945; (2) the population suffered extreme bipolarization, with a small modern sector, no middle class, and a vast number of urban poor; (3) some change occurred in the industrial sector, but serious imbalances among the different economic sectors remained; and (4) the dual structure and imbalanced nature of colonial society affected post-1945 Korea adversely.

In the end, the question of colonial industrial growth and its impact on society is ultimately unanswerable, but the debate over colonial modernization is helpful and requires us to move beyond conventional historical theories. This liberates us from nationalistic bias and the illusion that modernization was unilaterally positive. It makes us think how nationalism, modernity, and colonialism functioned in colonial society, not just in political, anti-imperialist terms, but as a more complex process of social, economic, and cultural change fostered by emerging colonial modernity. A new history is in the making.

Although beyond the scope of this paper, a critical defect of all previous studies of the colonial period should be mentioned here. Socioeconomic research has concentrated almost exclusively on the 1930–45 period, severely neglecting the next fifteen years, from 1945 to 1960, especially 1945–53. This gap seriously undermines our understanding of Korea's modern transformation. Most studies look only at the colonial period itself, stopping abruptly at 1945, and then relate it directly to 1960s or 1970s Korea, leaving out the changes that occurred in the 1950s as part of the chaos of the Korean War. Although this neglect is understandable because of the lack of source materials about this period, this critical flaw must be overcome before we can properly evaluate the changes between 1930 and 1945 and their impact on 1960s economic growth and modernization. Between 1945 and 1960, American forces penetrated liberated Korea, as another totally new, foreign, modern influence. The Korean War was an equally powerful, socioeconomic revolution and changed Korean society once again.

For example, the dislocation of the population and traditional society and values and the urbanization process that started between 1930 and 1945 continued on a more substantial scale and with accelerated speed during the Korean War and post–Korean War period. In the same manner, the legacy of Japanese labor practices was twisted and made more complex by American influence on Korean labor policy and on labor movements. Liberation from the politically oriented conventional periodization and a focus on the longer period of 1930–60 as a fundamental transition period for twentieth-century Korean society and its economy are essential for a new and better understanding of the roots nourishing Korean modernity of the 1960s and beyond.

Finally, this study points to the repressive and totalizing nature of previous conventional narratives on colonial labor in particular, and the colonial period in general, suggesting a need for a more complex, realistic, and non-monolithic approach to colonial themes. Fortunately, this compulsion to move beyond the present academic horizon and toward a more inclusive and pluralistic approach to colonial history is not an isolated one. Many studies on colonial Korea are probing into the interactive nature of several interlocking, mutually influential, and competing ideas such as nationalism, modernity, and colonialism. Some are moving even further by recovering silenced voices and ignored subjects of the colonial period, such as peasant farmers, ordinary city dwellers, workers, rural and urban women, the marginal poor, and other forgotten peoples. All these new studies and counternarratives will bring density, richness, and complexity to research on the colonial experience, adding depth to our understanding of Korea's paths to modernity in the twentieth century and the modern Korean identity shaped by them.

# SIX

# Colonial Korea in Japan's Imperial Telecommunications Network

## Daqing Yang

On a mid-January day in 1933, a group of prominent government, military, and business figures gathered in the Government-General of Korea (GGK) building in Keijō (present-day Seoul). When the clock struck half past ten, Communications Bureau Director Yamada Tadatsugu announced the long-awaited beginning of telephone service between Korea and Japan. Hundreds of kilometers away across the Japan Sea, a similar ceremony transpired simultaneously in Osaka. In a short speech read to both groups by a representative, Governor-General Ugaki Kazushige predicted that the opening of the telephone connection would further strengthen the economic and other bonds between the colony and the home islands. As if to test the soundness of this vision, officials and business leaders in the two cities took turns exchanging greetings across the newly activated line.[1]

To many historians, this was probably nothing more than one of countless, routine, and inconsequential ceremonies in the life of colonial Korea. Indeed, telecommunications—telegraph and telephone connection by means of wire, cable, or radio—has rarely been discussed in English-language works on colonial Korea. When the subject does surface, it is typically treated as an indicator of economic modernization under Japanese rule.[2]

The equation of telecommunications with modernity and progress in colonial Korea has dominated the numerous publications circulated by the Japanese government. According to this view, Japan
rapidly expanded and modernized the "primitive" communications
facilities in Korea after the takeover in 1905, to the great benefit of
economic and cultural life in the peninsula. A massive historical
survey on prewar Japanese activities in Asia, compiled by Japan's
Ministry of Finance shortly after World War II, essentially reiterated
this evaluation.[3] To be sure, Japan's tale of progress did not go unchallenged. In his pioneering 1944 work on colonial Korea, Andrew
J. Grajdanzev pointed out that telecommunications almost exclusively benefited the Japanese population.[4] Given that telecommunications in colonial Korea has not been considered to merit serious
study, it is not surprising no agreement exists on this issue.[5]

In this chapter, I consider telecommunications development as an
essential part of Japan's overall empire-building effort, not only in
the colonization of Korea but also in the establishment of an autarkic
sphere of influence in Northeast Asia. Although the modern telecommunications network emerged in Korea to a large extent as one
crucial element in Japan's apparatus for penetration and domination,
its effect on economic and social development should not be minimized, I argue, nor was its impact limited to the Japanese population. Moreover, as Japan embarked on building a new East Asian
telecommunications network in the 1930s to strengthen imperial
bonds, Korea's position in the new empire also became increasingly
contested, as manifested in a prolonged power struggle between Tokyo and Keijō over control of the network. By examining Korea's incorporation into Japan's imperial telecommunications network, I
hope to shed light on the nature of colonial modernity in Korea as
well as colonial Korea's evolving place in the Japanese empire.

## Incorporation and Consolidation

Often characterized as the "nerve of government," telecommunications networks have always been an important component of modern imperialism. As Daniel Headrick eloquently phrases it in his
study of Europe's overseas expansion, "[the] web of power that tied
the colonial empires together was made of electricity as well as
steam and iron."[6] Although it was not until the early 1930s that

Japan became connected to Korea by telephone, telegraphic links between the two date from the late nineteenth century.

In fact, autonomy in overseas telecommunications became a strategic objective for Japan after a Danish firm, the Great Northern Telegraph Company, linked Nagasaki with Shanghai and Vladivostok with submarine cables in early 1871. In exchange for transmitting romanized telegrams overseas, the Japanese government granted the company 30-year monopolistic rights.[7] During the negotiations with Korea that led to the Treaty of Kangwha in 1876, Enomoto Takeaki, Japan's minister in Russia, proposed to his government that Japan secure the rights to land a submarine cable near Pusan as well as at another site on the west coast of Korea near the Chinese border. These would allow future linkage with Chinese telegraph lines as an alternative to the Danish cable.[8] The telegraph was still a new technology then. Attributing the absence of war between Britain and the United States to the telegraph, a Japanese magazine optimistically predicted in the same year that were Japan and Korea linked by telegraph, the two would become good neighbors.[9] Such utopian visions soon evaporated, however, as Japan sought to extend and control telecommunications to Korea. In 1884, the Great Northern laid the first submarine telegraph cable across the Korean Strait at Japan's request, while Japan succeeded in establishing a telegraph office in Pusan and secured a 25-year monopoly over Korea's external telegraph traffic. Thus, although lacking the necessary technology, Japan made innovative use of the "advanced West" in facilitating its own expansion in Asia. For the first time, Japanese-language telegrams could be received and sent outside the Japanese islands, a fact of considerable importance to the growing Japanese community in Korea.

In the next two decades, telecommunications in Korea increasingly became a focus of international rivalry among Japan, China, and later Russia, each bent on establishing predominance on the peninsula. In 1885, a year after the construction of the Japan-Korea link, China extended its own telegraph line from the border city of Ŭiju to the Korean capital of Seoul, thus setting up the Western Route in Korea.[10] Protesting that this new route violated its monopoly, Japan demanded the right to construct telegraph lines inside Korea. In an effort to increase its own autonomy, the Korean government constructed a Southern Route, with assistance from foreign technicians, linking Seoul to Pusan in 1888. Although Korea set up its own telegraph office near the Japanese one in Pusan and connected them with couriers, for the first time Japan acquired an alternative route of telegraphic linkage through Korea.[11]

During the Sino-Japanese War of 1894–95, advancing Japanese troops not only took over all major telegraph lines in Korea but also constructed military telegraph lines in the south following destruction of existing lines in the peasant uprising. After the war, Japan retained control over its military lines between Pusan and Seoul, which proved to be an important asset in the war with Russia a decade later. Even before formal declaration of that war, Japan was able to outmaneuver the Russians by cutting off communication between Korea and Russia's stronghold of Port Arthur. Once war broke out, Japanese troops again quickly seized control of Korea's telegraph lines. The Russian defeat in the war signaled the end of a period of relative Korean autonomy, and Japan became the dominant power in the peninsula.

For the Japanese, control of the information network in Korea was a precondition for establishment of political and military domination. The blueprint for postwar Korea adopted by the Japanese cabinet in May 1904 stipulated permanent Japanese military and naval bases on the peninsula and Japanese supervision of Korean foreign affairs, government finances, and the railway system. Japan was also to control Korea's telegraph, telephone, and postal systems. If Japan could not incorporate Korea's communications systems into its own and standardize facilities in both countries, it was prepared to take over important lines and run them independently from the Korean government.[12] This plan was duly executed after the war, when Korea became a Japanese protectorate. Ikeda Jūsaburō, a veteran bureaucrat in charge of the Tokyo Post and Telegraph Office, led a team of Japanese technicians and officials in taking over Korea's communications facilities. The Koreans fiercely resisted, but Ikeda succeeded after applying considerable coercion.[13]

As Japan gradually assumed control of Korea's telecommunications system, it implemented several reductions in telegraph rates between Japan and Korea to facilitate its expanding scope of activities on the peninsula. These efforts brought dramatic results: traffic increased from a trickle of 3,800 telegrams in 1884 to some 100,000 per year a decade later. By 1905, some 430,000 telegrams, 98 percent of which were in Japanese, traveled between the two countries.[14]

Although the Japanese made much of their mission of developing the Korean economy, the information infrastructure in colonial Korea was not built primarily for business activities. The telecommunications network in Korea, especially long-distance telephones, developed largely to meet Japan's urgent political and military desire to consolidate control over the Korean population.

The first major challenge to Japan came in July 1907, when its forceful dissolution of what remained of the Korean army ignited a large-scale "political disturbance" across the peninsula. Telegraph and telephone lines under Japanese control were heavily damaged by Korean guerrillas, known as the "righteous soldiers." Although Japan quickly repaired them at a cost of ¥130,000, the general lack of efficient means of communication severely handicapped its response during the initial stage of the uprising. One official Japanese account cites a campaign in Kangwŏn province in which poor telecommunications caused a frequent lack of coordination among Japanese troops and generated considerable confusion.[15] Swift communication between all localities in Korea was considered crucial not only for suppressing the Korean resistance but also for future policing and security. Vice Resident-General Sone Arasuke proposed a peninsula-wide police telephone network, which would link all police stations, military barracks, postal branches, and other government offices, allowing them to be reached by telegraph or telephone within 24 hours and thus greatly strengthening control of Korea's extensive rural areas.[16]

Given the urgent need, this police telephone network had to be constructed as quickly as possible. In May 1908, Japan set up a Police Telephone Construction Department in Korea, adding telephone lines to some existing postal telegraph lines and building new routes elsewhere. Between June 1908 and September 1910, over 4,000 kilometers of new lines spanning some 3,000 kilometers were constructed. A total of 45,000 new telephone poles were erected, significantly altering the landscape of much of the peninsula. By the end of 1910, over 800 police telephone sets had been installed in security posts and post offices at a cost of ¥376,000. Although this police telephone network was far from sophisticated, the significance of its completion by 1910 cannot be overestimated.[17] That very year, Japan forced a treaty of annexation upon Korea, rendering it a Japanese colony. Control and subsequent expansion of Korea's telecommunications network had paved the way for annexation.

To complete its control of Korea's telecommunications system, Japan purchased the submarine cable in the Korean Strait from its Danish owner for ¥16 million that same year. By installing new telegraph equipment, Japan drastically reduced transmission time. On average, the time it took a telegraph to get from Seoul (now named Keijō) to Tokyo dropped from 4 hours 42 minutes to 2.5 hours.[18]

Japan's control of telecommunications in Korea, however, did not eradicate resistance. The March First movement in 1919, when Koreans staged peninsula-wide demonstrations demanding independence, took Japan by such surprise that it led to another wave of urgent expansion of its police communications network. In addition to equipping local Japanese authorities with automobiles, the new superintendent-general (seimu sōkan), Mizuno Rentarō, stressed the need to install telephone connections in every local district. As Michael Robinson reminds us, the colonial government increased the efficiency and sophistication of its control system even as it spoke of a moderate "Cultural Rule." Within two years' time, over ¥1 million was spent to extend the network in 35 districts between Pusan and Sinŭiju. The three years after March 1919 witnessed the greatest expansion of new telephone routes in Korea, as nearly 2,000 kilometers were added, a 40 percent increase. As a result, the police telecommunications network was greatly strengthened.[19]

Enhanced telecommunications soon proved to be valuable for surveillance and control purposes. In late 1919, the Korean prince attempted to join the independence movement in Shanghai. When the GGK found out that the prince was missing from his Keijō residence, it immediately cabled the police throughout Korea and also notified Japanese authorities in Japan, Manchuria, Siberia, and even Shanghai. After receiving orders by telegraph, Japanese policemen arrived at the Andong Railway Station across the border in Manchuria just as the Korean prince was disembarking from the train. The prince was escorted back to Keijō under heavy security. Speedy communication thus spared Japanese authorities a major political embarrassment not long after the March First movement.[20]

In this fashion, telecommunications in colonial Korea developed on the back of police communication facilities. Herein lies an apparent paradox that may be said to characterize Japan's colonial rule in general. What started as a police network was later opened to civilian use after the colonial government restored control. Although

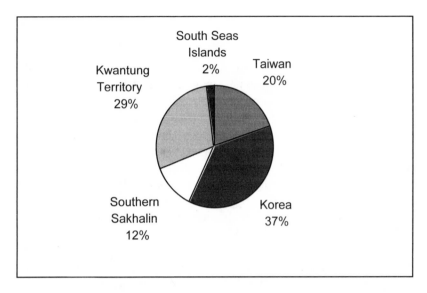

Fig. 6.1 Telegraphic traffic in the Japanese empire, 1935 (Source: Teishinshō, Denmu-kyoku, *Denpō kōryū jōkyō ni kansuru chōsa* [Tokyo, 1935], pp. 64–73).

controlled by the colonial government and despite its original inten-tion, this information network also served economic and cultural purposes. The influx of Japanese business as well as agricultural im-migrants, together with gradual economic development and urbani-zation in Korea, increased use of electronic communications. The steady advancement in telecommunications technology in the first decades of this century further contributed to this process. To give just a few examples, in 1923, the army transferred its wireless facili-ties to the GGK, and the renamed Keijō Wireless added a new di-mension to telegraphic service. The rapid development of wireless technology ushered in the age of radio, when station JODK began broadcasting in both Japanese and Korean in early 1927, and enjoyed extraordinary growth in subsequent years. Automatic exchange tele-phones were adopted during the 1920s, greatly enhancing commu-nication capabilities, and long-distance telephone service with Man-churia began in 1924. In the same year, establishment of a reduced rate for press telegrams contributed to the flourishing of newspa-pers.[21] Throughout the colonial period, Korea was the largest recipi-ent and originator of telegraphic traffic with Japan in the empire (see Fig. 6.1).[22]

## Telecommunications and Colonial Modernity

In his study of colonial Korea, Andrew Grajdanzev made an interesting observation about what may be termed the information-intensive behavior of the colonial bureaucracy in Korea. The Japanese government in Korea, he pointed out, "is a bureaucracy which is fond of mailing circulars and sending telegrams," since "in 1938, 2,206,779 telegrams out of a total of 11,710,575 were sent *muryō*, i.e. without charge, because they were official telegrams, — one-fifth of the total." In other words, he observed, "a handful of bureaucrats succeeded in sending as many telegrams as 4,300,000 of the population."[23] This preoccupation with communications on the part of the colonial government is also reflected in the numerous statistics and other publications on postal and electronic communications it compiled and issued. Table 6.1, taken from a statistical yearbook compiled by the GGK, was intended to demonstrate colonial Korea's favorable "communication capability" (*tsūshinryoku*) in comparison with other parts of the Japanese empire.

A considerable gap appears to have existed in the availability of communications facilities between metropole and peripheral areas in the empire. Generally speaking, greater urbanization and a larger Japanese population explained the highly developed infrastructure of Japan proper and the Kwantung Territory. Southern Sakhalin and the South Sea Islands, thinly populated and lacking transportation but of strategic importance, relied heavily on telecommunications. Although Korea rivaled Taiwan in the category of the telegraph, it lagged in telephone service and usage. In fact, once the police network was completed in Korea, expansion of telecommunications infrastructure slowed considerably, due less to a lack of interest than to lack of funds. The colonial government had to abandon its plan to raise public loans for telecommunications after just one year, and after 1923 telephone users had to shoulder all installation costs. As in Japan proper, telephone subscriptions in Korea became a scarce commodity and therefore a status symbol.[24]

How did telecommunications affect the Korean population? In comparing statistics on the Japanese and Korean populations of colonial Korea, Andrew Grajdanzev noted that as of 1938 only one out of every 306 Korean families had a telephone, compared to one out of every four Japanese families. Therefore, he concluded, "telephones in Korea are used almost exclusively by the Japanese."[25] Grajdanzev was certainly correct that the Japanese population in Korea enjoyed the benefit of telecommunications disproportionately, but it would be misleading to lump all Koreans together. A closer examination of telephone subscriptions during the entire colonial period suggests a somewhat different conclusion (see Fig. 6.2). Korean subscribers to telephone service increased steadily from a meager 5 percent (418 persons) of all subscribers in 1910 to nearly 30 percent—over 17,000—thirty years later. Despite the high cost of telephone installation, many considered it indispensable to their business.[26] In a limited way, those Korean subscribers were as privileged as the other 70 percent—some 40,000 Japanese—compared to the overwhelming majority of their fellow Koreans.

The fate of the Korean-language telegram may also yield clues as to how Koreans related to telecommunications (see Fig. 6.3). When Japan took over Korea's telecommunication administration in 1905, it immediately abolished Chinese-language telegram service and instituted Japanese-language service for all Korea. Both *han'gŭl* and European-language services continued, but the former was largely confined to domestic service. The share of *han'gŭl* telegrams in the overall number of telegrams sent and received in Korea between 1905 and 1940 reveals an interesting pattern. The percentage as well as the number of *han'gŭl* telegrams increased steadily for the first fifteen years after 1905, probably due to improved communications facilities and services and the standardization of *han'gŭl* telegrams. The pivotal year of 1919 registered an all-time high in *han'gŭl* telegrams sent and received in Korea. Whether or not this phenomenon was connected to the outburst of independence demonstrations, it was probably related to the growing activism of the educated Korean elite. The subsequent decline, on the other hand, reflected Japan's policy of cultural assimilation, especially the increased use of the Japanese language. The percentage of telegrams in *han'gŭl* never recovered, and its absolute number stayed largely unchanged despite a steady rise in use of the telegraph by Koreans. Following the forced adoption of Japanese names and the closing of the Korean-language press, *han'gŭl* telegrams were finally discontinued in 1941, after a similar sharp reduction in Western-language services in Korea.[27]

In justifying the pending abolition of *han'gŭl* telegram service, the

Table 6.1

Communications in Japan and Its Colonies, 1935

| Indicator | Japan proper | Taiwan | Korea | Southern Sakhalin | South Sea Islands | Kwantung Territory |
|---|---|---|---|---|---|---|
| Area (km$^2$) | 382,265 | 35,961 | 220,769 | 36,090 | 139 | 3,748 |
| Population (000s) | 69,255 | 5,316 | 21,891 | 323 | 105 | 1,637 |
| Number of post offices | 11,249 | 184 | 873 | 81 | 9 | 265 |
| Area/post office (km$^2$) | 34 | 195 | 253 | 446 | 15 | 14 |
| Population per post office | 6,156 | 28,889 | 25,076 | 3,981 | 11,653 | 6,177 |
| Telegraph offices | 8,232 | 213 | 878 | 91 | 9 | 211 |
| Area/telegraph office (km$^2$) | 47 | 169 | 252 | 397 | 16 | 18 |
| Population/telegraph office | 8,413 | 24,956 | 24,933 | 3,544 | 11,653 | 7,758 |
| Telegrams sent (000s) | 73,860 | 1,902 | 7,992 | 905 | 254 | 4,113 |
| Telegrams sent/person | 1.067 | 0.358 | 0.365 | 2.807 | 2.419 | 2.513 |
| Telephone subscriptions | 870,564 | 16,800 | 39,763 | 5,535 | 392 | 21,321 |
| Subscriptions/10,000 persons | 125.7 | 31.6 | 18.1 | 171.6 | 37.4 | 130.2 |
| Number of public telephones | 3,635 | 34 | 86 | 34 | 2 | 148 |
| Phone usage (000,000s) | 2,906 | 107 | 270 | 21 | 1 | 404 |
| Phone usage/person | 41.96 | 20.2 | 12.35 | 65.02 | 29.68 | 246.7 |

Note: Telephone usage is measured in units of three-minute calls.
Source: Chōsen Sōtokufu comp., *Chōsen teishin tōkei yōran* (1936), pp. 125–26.

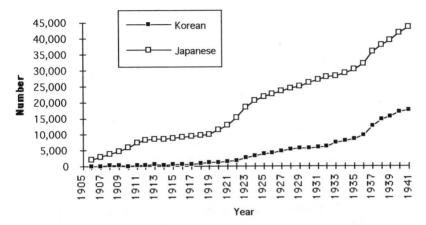

Fig. 6.2 Telephone subscriptions in Korea, 1905–41 (Source: Taehan min'guk ch'ae-shinbu, *Chŏn'gi t'ongsin saŏp p'alsimnyŏn-sa* [Seoul, 1966], p. 592).

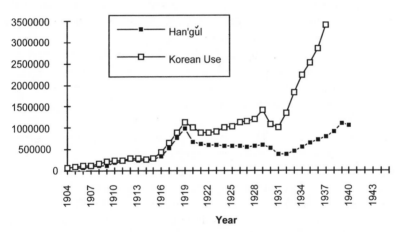

Fig. 6.3 Telegrams sent in Korea, 1904–41 (Source: Source: Taehan min'guk ch'aeshin-bu, *Chŏn'gi t'ongsin saŏp p'alsimnyŏn-sa* [Seoul, 1966], pp. 551–52).

GGK concluded from a survey that "although there are many reasons for the decline in usage of Korean telegrams, the popularization of Japanese and increasingly close ties in business transactions are most important."[28] Assimilation often is an uneven phenomenon. Japanese was the language of modern business, and an increasing number of Koreans used it. Thus, assimilation induced by modernity preceded the coercive measures and justified them in the eyes of the Japanese administrators.

Increased Korean use was even more remarkable given Japan's firm control of the communications network in Korea throughout the colonial period. Although in the 1920s the administration of Governor-General Saitō Makoto adopted legislation to "equalize" Korean and Japanese opportunities in public service, statistics for those holding offices in the communications bureaucracy indicate a continued preponderance of the Japanese, who occupied over 70 percent of all positions in the Communications Bureau. The bias was even more pronounced in the category of permanent employees, particularly among higher-ranking civil servants, with the exception of local appointments. When increasing numbers of Japanese employees in the communication services were transferred elsewhere or moved to better-paying industries in the late 1930s, demand for wireless operators surged, and the GGK belatedly undertook various programs to train Koreans. Still, high-ranking positions remained largely closed to Koreans, and only in 1935 did the first Korean rise above the rank of *hannin* (compared to 63 Japanese above this rank). As late as 1943, only six Koreans had progressed beyond this rank, compared to 93 Japanese, and no Korean reached the higher *chokunin* rank.[29] This practice seems to deviate somewhat from the general recruitment pattern in late colonial Korea.[30] One plausible reason for the exclusion of Koreans is that the secrecy of communications, as Communications Bureau Director Yamada emphasized, was especially critical for counterintelligence purposes, and all employees required appropriate supervision.[31]

In short, telecommunications in colonial Korea was simultaneously a tool of suppression and of development, since both were based on enhanced control.[32] Although more research is needed to understand its impact on Korean society, it is possible to conclude that the gradual expansion of telecommunication services in Korea, apart from the immensely popular radio broadcasting after 1927, served as a new channel of public and private interaction primarily for the Japanese population and the urban Korean elite. Even though such Koreans were only a small fraction of the entire Korean population, their incorporation into a Japanese-dominated modern information network could not but affect the development of Korean capitalism and culture during the colonial period and thereafter.

## Telecommunications and Imperial Integration

If internal political control served as the main engine for telecommunications expansion in colonial Korea during the first two decades of Japanese occupation, imperial integration assumed that role during the 1930s. As the world economy formed into increasingly autarkic trading blocs following the Great Depression, Japan's leaders not only felt the urgent need to strengthen imperial bonds with the colonies but also considered Japan amply justified in seeking a self-sufficient economic sphere in greater Asia.[33]

By "collapsing space and time," telecommunications promised to expedite the process of economic integration. The Korea-Japan telephone connection achieved in 1933, described at the beginning of this chapter, was a major step in this direction and also marked the increased emphasis on Japan's own technologies. Preparation for the connection was already under way in 1928, but technical difficulties as well as funding problems in Japan and Korea slowed progress. When the German firm Siemens und Halske succeeded in using submarine telegraph cable for telephone transmission, Japan showed particular interest and requested technical assistance. Politely turned down, Japan's Ministry of Communications (MOC) mobilized its own technical strength and enlisted the cooperation of the private firm Nippon Electric Company (NEC), in an all-out effort to develop long-distance telephone transmission technology on its own. In May 1931, a group of MOC technicians arrived in Pusan for an extended experiment to render the existing telegraph cables capable of speech transmission between Japan and Korea. The Manchurian Incident that took place in the midst of the experiment added new urgency as well as difficulty to the project. Since all cable circuits were fully utilized during the day for telegram transmissions, those technicians had to conduct their experiments at night. A year elapsed before they succeeded in installing a carrier telephone system on existing telegraph cables. In early 1933, telephone communication via submarine cables between Japan and continental Asia became possible for the first time.[34]

Events on the continent soon necessitated an expanded telecommunications network for military, political, and economic purposes.
After the establishment of Manchukuo in 1932, Japan's line of national defense was extended to the Manchukuo-Soviet border, and
the army was eager to strengthen military facilities in the north.
Meanwhile, with efforts under way to integrate Japan and Manchuria into a "Japan-Manchukuo economic bloc," communication links
between Japan and the continent became a top priority for civilian
leaders as well. Having achieved the success of cross-strait telephone
connection, MOC emerged as a chief agent of technological development in Japan and telecommunication expansion throughout the
empire. In 1934, MOC drafted plans for a new long-distance cable
that would extend from Tokyo through Korea to reach Mukden in
Manchukuo. Since the cable was considered a military link and
a matter of national policy, there would be no lack of funds.[35] In addition to cementing the special relationship between Japan and
Manchukuo, as a leading MOC engineer explained, a new Japan-
Manchuria cable would facilitate further continental expansion. It
would be less costly to connect with the prosperous regions along
the Yangtze River in central China over a land link through Manchuria than to lay a new submarine cable from Japan to Shanghai. In
addition, the land cable would help connect Japan with Europe,
since the Soviet Union was completing a trans-Siberian cable network. In short, the Japan–Korea–Manchukuo cable would be both a
highway and a byway.[36]

The emphasis on a cable network in East Asia, based on Japan's
"indigenous technology," represented a major shift in Japan's international telecommunications policy. During the previous decades,
Japan had placed its hopes for greater autonomy in international
telecommunication in the emerging wireless technology, which
promised to reduce both construction costs and the efforts needed to
acquire rights in foreign countries. Development of the non-loaded
cable carrier system for long-distance telephone transmission, by
Matsumae Shigeyoshi and other MOC technicians in Japan in the
early 1930s, tilted the balance in favor of cable over wireless.

Just as important were Japan's new empire-building requirements. As Japan gradually consolidated its political and military
presence on the Asian continent, a sharp increase in telecommunication traffic was anticipated (see Fig. 6.4). As the director of MOC's

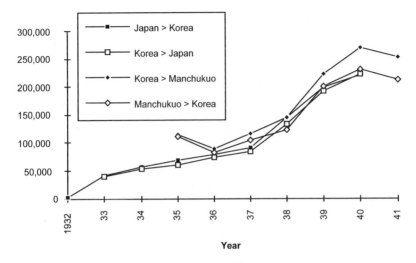

Fig. 6.4 Telephone traffic (number of calls) between Korea and Japan and Manchukuo, 1932–41 (Source: Teishinshō, Denmukyoku, *Denmu nenkan* [Tokyo, 1941], p. 393).

Telecommunication Bureau pointed out, due to the limited number of radio frequencies, wireless communication could no longer meet the requirements of a greater communications network in East Asia. In view of its strategic importance, the Japan-Manchukuo route alone, he told the Diet, could conceivably require over hundreds of channels. Thus, the limited wireless frequencies available to Japan would be inadequate and had to be reserved mainly for communication with more distant foreign countries in Europe or the Americas. Moreover, the need for secrecy had become particularly acute, as military, political, and diplomatic communications among Japan, Manchukuo, and China, now bound in a special relationship, required tightened anti-espionage measures. Here cable enjoyed a decided advantage over wireless, whose messages could easily be intercepted and deciphered. Finally, despite improvements in wireless technology, the problem of atmospheric interference with wireless communications persisted. A cable communications network provided not only tighter security but also the capacity to handle the voluminous traffic between Japan and its sphere of influence in adjacent areas. Although construction costs were higher, an underground cable would be more permanent, and therefore more appropriate, for Japan's lasting imperial enterprise.[37]

A telephone cable linking Japan and the continent proved not only strategically indispensable but also highly popular. After telephone service began in 1933 between Japan and Korea, demand soon outstripped capacity. During the first ten days after service began on January 15, an average of close to a hundred telephone calls per day was placed between Korea and Japan, nearly reaching the single circuit's maximum daily capacity of 120.[38] Later, some 30 telephone calls per day were exchanged between Japan and Manchukuo initially, but the number soared to about 130 in less than two years.[39] Here, the political-military concerns of empire-building and business's interest in what were called "nutrition lines" — profit-generating routes — coincided.

Construction of the Japan–Korea–Manchukuo cable began in the early winter of 1935 in Manchukuo and in November 1936 in Korea. MOC provided not only much of the technical expertise but also over ¥9 million of the total ¥11 million required in Korea alone. More than half a million men, the majority Korean, were mobilized. Ahead of schedule in September 1939, construction of the 900 kilometers of cable in Korea, buried one meter underground along the main north–south highway, with twenty relay stations en route, was completed.[40] The cable from Tokyo to Mukden via Keijō was some 2,600 kilometers in length, the longest underground telephone cable in the world at that time (see Map 6.1). The some ¥40 million poured into the project significantly strengthened communications among the three areas.[41] Japan–Manchukuo telephone capacity increased by 24 channels and Japan–Korea by 10, with telex and facsimile services as well, using equipment developed entirely by Japan.[42]

With another technological victory in sight, confident technocrats in the MOC in Tokyo drew up plans for unified control of the soon-to-be-completed long-distance telecommunications network in East Asia. Not surprisingly, they sought to justify such an unprecedented extension of authority largely by emphasizing the technological imperative.[43] In contrast to the open-wire line of the Meiji period, a MOC report declared, non-loaded cables were a uniquely Japanese technology, a step ahead of the advanced countries in the West, thus requiring maintenance by knowledgeable technicians to prevent interruptions. The frequency of such accidents on long-distance cables, according to MOC's own tests, increased in proportion to the square of the distance. MOC considered current maintenance levels far from

Map 6.1 The Japan–Korea–Manchukuo long-distance cable network (Source: Teishin-shō, Kōmukyoku, *Nichi-Man renraku denwa shisetsu sekkei keikaku kōyō* [Tokyo, 1937]).

sufficient for a cable stretching from Tokyo to Mukden (and soon to the Manchukuo capital, Shinkyō), and it was necessary that all maintenance technicians follow a single chain of command under MOC supervision. Also, further savings could be expected by adding use by military, railway, news, broadcast relay, and aeronautical facilities to that by the public. The MOC report argued that "for the higher purpose of future East Asian telecommunications," technical control and maintenance of the Japan–Korea–Manchukuo cable circuits should be entrusted directly to the MOC. Only under its unified control, according to MOC, could the long-distance circuits "satisfactorily fulfill the function of our important national policy of [creating] a communications artery" and forcefully advance Japan's news and information policy in East Asia.[44]

## Colonial Autonomy and Imperial Integration

Arguing that the history of telecommunications is not simply a narrative of the evolution of technical efficiencies, communications scholar Carolyn Marvin suggests shifting the focus from the instrument to the drama in which existing groups perpetually negotiate power, authority, representation, and knowledge with whatever resources are available.[45] This perspective illuminates the history of the Japan–Korea–Manchukuo long-distance cable. Japan's new imperial telecommunications network was not simply an epoch-making technological achievement; it also exacerbated political problems throughout the empire. As Japanese technocrats in MOC pursued their designs of unified control, the impact of the technological innovation, mediated by the new imperial agenda, affected bureaucracies outside the home islands as well.

Timing was important: extension of the Japan–Korea–Manchuria cable network into the peninsula coincided with fresh visions of Korea's place in the empire. The new overall plans Japan envisioned for East Asia beginning in the early 1930s necessarily meant redefining the status of colonial Korea. After Minami Jirō arrived in Korea as governor-general in 1936 and particularly following the outbreak of the Sino-Japanese War in 1937, the idea of Korea as the "forward military depot on the continent" (*tairiku zenshin heitan kichi*) gained wide currency. As Suzuki Takeo, a Japanese professor at Keijō Imperial University and major exponent of the idea, explained, given its political stability, level of industrialization, and abundant cheap energy and labor, Korea was the ideal supply base for Japan's further continental operations, be it war against the Soviet Union or expansion into China. In fact, Korea would become the "second *naichi* [homeland]," he predicted, and in case of conflict with the United States, Japan could entrust its continental enterprise to Korea and devote itself to troubles in the Pacific.[46] Such visions also guided those in the colonial government. Dōmoto Tatsuo, a Japanese official in GGK, took pains to delineate the various interpretations of the "continental base" theory, adding that, as Koreans increasingly became involved in Manchukuo, China, and Inner Mongolia, Japan's continental expansion would increasingly become a joint Japanese-Korean enterprise.[47] This implied that, after more than two decades of Japanese rule, colonial Korea had moved closer to becoming a core area in an ever-expanding Japanese imperium in Asia.

A former commander of the Kwantung Army, Governor-General Minami adopted a series of measures aimed at strengthening ties with Manchuria under the slogan "Korea and Manchuria as one" (*Man-Sen ichi'nyō*). Since colonial Korea was aspiring to project its influence beyond its borders, it must first overcome obstacles of space and time by improving means of communication and transportation. In a meeting between Minami and Kwantung Army leaders, it was decided to construct fourteen bridges across border rivers between the two areas. Korea relinquished control of telecommunications facilities in the predominantly Korean-populated Kantō (Jiandao) area across the border in Manchuria to the new Manchurian Telegraph and Telephone Company (MTT) in return for rate cuts between Kantō and Korea. Moreover, conferences for railway coordination with Manchukuo and North China were held.[48]

In addition to Manchukuo, North China was another promising economic frontier for Korea. Although still commanding a dominant position, Japan's share in Korea's external trade began to decline somewhat in the late 1930s. On the other hand, Manchukuo and Japanese-occupied areas in China became increasingly important partners, jointly claiming 83.6 percent in 1938 and 88.2 percent in 1939 of Korea's trade with the East Asia region outside Japan's formal empire.[49] The Korean population in China proper increased almost eightfold within five years after 1937.[50] The Korean Trade Association (KTA) boldly predicted that Korea would "take the initiative" in the North China trade, despite possible competition from goods produced in Japan and Manchukuo. Direct sea routes from Korean ports to North China were established, and the impact of Korea's growing trade with North China on telecommunications was noted in Korea. A KTA journal emphasized that the "capitalist world economy" was characterized by the international fluctuation of commodity prices, exchange rates, and the stock market, which made efficient communication essential for market expansion. The association stressed the urgent need for direct communication links between North China and Korea as well as low rates.[51]

Telecommunications became an increasingly important priority for the colonial government due to industrialization at home and trade activity abroad. At the 1936 Conference on Korean Industrial and Economic Policy, business leaders from Korea and Japan lamented high telegram rates and scarce telephone service.[52] Expansion of telecommunications in Korea became a major agenda at the conference convened by the GGK in September 1938 to cope with the new conditions in East Asia after outbreak of the Sino-Japanese War. The colonial government admitted that inadequate telecommunication facilities in Korea were causing numerous delays and poor service. The conference recommended a wide range of expansions of telecommunication facilities: extension of telegraph and telephone lines, conversion of bare wires to more secure cables, adoption of high-speed telegraphic equipment, and improvement of special communication services for aviation, weather forecasting, and shipping. In the meantime, control over all forms of communication by means of censorship and radio intelligence gathering was to be strengthened. Given radio's great role in educating the people, unifying opinion, and stabilizing the public order, the GGK pointed out, broadcast facilities must be greatly expanded, and public radio receivers and high-power radio stations to broadcast to the Soviet Union and to interfere with Soviet broadcasts to Asia must be established.[53] In response to the growing business concerns voiced at the conference, the GGK soon established radiotelephonic links between P'yŏngyang, Pusan, and Keijō in Korea and Beijing, Tianjin, and Shanghai in China in 1939.

Although the "second naichi" proposition, calling for industrialization of Korea as well as imperial expansion beyond it as a "forward base," generated much enthusiasm among the Japanese in Korea, it met with skepticism outside the peninsula. For instance, questions arose in the Japanese Diet as to the disruptive consequences of an aggressively expanding Korea on existing national boundaries.[54] The Kwantung Army, on the other hand, averred that the primary purpose of a "forward base on the continent" was to strengthen military preparations in Manchukuo.[55] Even those in Korea realized that Korea might assume roles other than simply being a "forward base." Given its unique geographic location, as Professor Suzuki pointed out, Korea itself could also serve as a vital strategic link between insular Japan—"the center of leadership"—and the vast continent of Asia—the subregions in the Greater East Asian economic zone. By the late 1930s, the peninsula itself supported the important Pusan-Keijō-Ŭiju-Mukden railway trunk line. The oceans on both sides of the peninsula featured sea-lanes linking Japan with Manchukuo and China, effectively turning both the Japan Sea and the Yellow Sea into "Japanese lakes." In short, Korea must also become the "route to the continent" (*tairiku rūto*).[56] The "route" theory seemed to coincide with the role of "organic link" assigned to Korea in MOC's discussions about the new cable network.

Therefore, considerable ambiguity, if not disagreement, emerged over the primary role of colonial Korea in the new empire. By coining the phrase "Korea as the *hanamichi* and Manchuria as the stage," thus comparing Korea to the runway in the kabuki theater that serves as a secondary but independent stage, Governor-General Minami did not clarify the matter.[57] As we shall see, how to make Korea function smoothly as a "route to the continent" was no simple question. In fact, Japan's attempt to establish an empire-wide telecommunications network in the late 1930s made it clear that imperial integration would not be attained as easily as technical experts in Tokyo had hoped.

## Telecommunications and Colonial Autonomy

During the months before construction of the Japan–Korea–Manchukuo cable began, MOC officials negotiated a temporary understanding with GGK that allowed MOC engineers into Korea for construction work and the use of MOC equipment. Soon afterwards, MOC began making arrangements for long-term maintenance of the cable network and proposed stationing MOC engineers on a permanent basis inside Korea. In early October 1935, shortly after construction began, MOC engineer Matsumae Shigeyoshi accompanied the chief of the newly created Japan-Manchukuo Telephone Construction Section on a visit to Keijō to discuss the matter with GGK officials. Interestingly, Matsumae's repeated allusions to unified control of long-distance networks in advanced countries in the West bolstered his call for a unified system of control and maintenance of the highly technical non-loaded cable network. Technology became an unwitting ally of MOC hegemony.[58]

The MOC plan for unified (read: centralized) control over this telecommunications system might have made perfect sense from Tokyo's perspective, but proved unacceptable to the GGK. Arguably the most important colony in the Japanese empire, Korea had legally enjoyed virtual autonomy, since its governor-general in theory reported directly to the emperor.[59] Previous telecommunications issues involving the home islands and the colony had been resolved by bilateral agreements between government agencies. This proved impossible with the MOC proposal: although the colonial administration in Korea welcomed the new network in Korea, since it would boost its own telecommunications infrastructure, it made no secret of its disapproval of MOC control. Not persuaded by MOC's justifications, GGK proposed that unified maintenance must first be implemented in the home islands and Manchukuo before being extended to Korea. This was a stumbling block for MOC, since the Kwantung Army had earlier rejected MOC's plan of unified control and proposed the new MTT be made responsible for maintenance. Thus during their meetings with GGK officials, MOC bureaucrats had to downplay the significance of the portion of the cable in Manchukuo, since Kwantung Army opposition made it impossible to carry out their plans in Manchukuo. In response to GGK insistence that Korea be allowed to attempt its own maintenance, Matsumae retorted that this would be like two good neighbors erecting high walls.[60] Tension consequently mounted between the MOC, which, largely on technical grounds, demanded centralized control and maintenance of the new cable, and the GGK Communications Bureau, which saw this as an intrusion.

In the end, MOC presented to GGK a carefully worded memorandum that noted the new cable was just "passing through Korea and would in no way affect the jurisdiction of the GGK." To make the deal more palatable, MOC promised to lease surplus circuits to GGK at favorable rates—a major enticement, given the colonial government's limited funds. The GGK Bureau of Communications relented, with the proviso that maintenance work inside Korea be entrusted to a private company.[61]

The conflict between MOC and the colonial administration in Korea involved more than quibbling among petty bureaucrats. In a private meeting, Ōno Rokuichi, superintendent-general in Korea, expressed uneasiness at the prospect that if allowed into Korea, MOC employees would be in direct contact with local administrations as well as ordinary people.[62] Disagreement over the communications network even affected the governor-general himself. On an inspection tour near Kaesŏng, Minami Jirō was apparently disturbed to see Ministry of Communications (Teishinshō) on signs for the Japan–Korea–Manchukuo cable then under construction. Yamada Tadatsugu, chief of the GGK Communications Bureau, proposed simply changing "ministry" to "bureau." When a MOC engineer in the entourage objected, asserting that the cable belonged to the Ministry of Communications in Tokyo, Minami was enraged. "Korea is under the jurisdiction of the governor-general directly appointed by the emperor. What authority on earth does the Minister of Communications have to build facilities here?" In the end, as a compromise, the word "ministry" was dropped from all signs, and construction proceeded. Only the ambiguous term "communications" remained.[63]

Why was GGK so recalcitrant on such a seemingly trivial matter? As one MOC bureaucrat bluntly stated to his colleagues in Tokyo, "extension of MOC authority to Korea is a problem of invasion of their administrative jurisdiction, which has always been feared there."[64] The colonial bureaucracy suspected that if it gave in on telecommunications, other areas under their jurisdiction, such as aviation and insurance, would be next. As a short-term solution, MOC had to secure an imperial ordinance in 1938 to make limited MOC operations in Korea legal.[65] As a more fundamental solution, however, the ministry had to modify its strategy by using a semiprivate company, the International Telecommunications Corporation, for construction and maintenance outside Japan proper.

The problem of conflicting interests could not be resolved simply by removing a character on a sign, however. The tug-of-war over the status of Korea within the empire continued till the eve of the Pacific War and moved to a different arena.

By the end of the 1930s Japan had acquired the technological capacity to link all telecommunications facilities into one single network in East Asia, promising imperial integration under Tokyo. In

reality, however, the separate operation of telecommunication services in Japan's home islands, its colonies of Korea and Taiwan, Manchukuo, and China threatened to undermine the effectiveness of the
network. In addition, facilities for the public, military, police, railway, and other purposes were often managed by separate agencies.
Such a situation was anathema from MOC's standpoint. Beginning
in 1939, a series of annual East Asian telecommunications conferences were convened to develop the necessary coordination of all
operations. Although almost all the delegates representing Japan's
colonies as well as "Sino-Japanese joint-venture" telecommunications companies in China and Manchukuo were Japanese, consensus
did not come easily. Only after much deliberation was an East Asian
Telecommunication Pact drafted in late 1940 to ensure smooth communication within Japan's newly expanded sphere of influence.[66]

A new problem arose, again with Korea pitted against the MOC.
In previous international treaties on telecommunication matters involving Japan and its colonies, Korea as well as other colonial administrations had signed under the umbrella category of "Japanese
agencies in charge of telecommunications," essentially delegating
authority to the MOC. At the Second East Asian Telecommunications Conference in October 1940, Korea's colonial bureaucrats expressed their dissatisfaction with this practice and insisted on being
treated as an independent signatory in the proposed East Asian
Telecommunications Pact. Although Korea had been represented by
MOC in previous international treaties, explained an official from
Korea, it wanted a more prominent role in the East Asian telecommunications network now that the pact included China and Manchukuo. Korea was not going to lose its relative autonomy in dealing
with such areas in the new imperium.[67]

MOC viewed the matter differently. In a memo sent to Korea before the January 1941 conference for signing the pact, it described a
"harmonious union between Japan and Korea" as the "core of East
Asia," destined to be the axis of a broader East Asia in cooperation
with Manchukuo and China. Ultimately this circle would include
Southeast Asia to form the Greater East Asian Co-prosperity Sphere.
MOC assured the GGK that under the new pact, Korea's authority
in dealings with Manchuria and China would not diminish. However, Korea's independence from the central government in external
telecommunications matters, MOC implied, would not only abro-
gate decades-old precedent but alter the "fundamentals of national

policy," with grave consequences. As a practical matter, none of the institutional adjustments required could be accomplished within the short time available before the new Telecommunications Pact took effect on April 1.[68]

Despite these efforts to persuade the GGK, MOC's worst nightmare came true at the general conference in January 1941. Korea's representative, after consulting with Keijō, refused to sign the pact. MOC officials responded by calling Korea's refusal to participate as a member of the imperial government "suspicious." It was a major embarrassment to MOC that the primary obstacle to unity in East Asian telecommunications should be Japan's own colonial government in Korea. To rescue the pact, MOC had to accede to the GGK's demand by entering into a separate agreement with Korea that promised to treat Korea as an independent entity in East Asian telecommunications matters.[69]

Clearly, the GGK's obstinacy was not just for theatrical effect. Shortly after this episode, a Japanese official from the GGK Bureau of Communications justified its action to his counterparts from other areas in the empire:

In Korea, we must pay close attention to governing an alien people (*i-minzoku*) in more ways than can be imagined in Japan proper. We must adopt special measures appropriate for the situations. Things not in accordance with this principle, even if they are extremely rational and perfectly legitimate, are considered inappropriate and even illegitimate in Korea. We public servants in Korea cannot forget even for a minute this principle of governing an alien people.[70]

Statements like this seemed incongruous with, if not contradictory to, the official policy of "Japan and Korea as a single body" (*naisen ittai*) in force since the late 1930s. That resistance to the total eradication of a separate Korean identity would come from the colonial bureaucracy itself may be ironic but not inconceivable.[71] Complete obliteration of the differences between Korea and Japan would inevitably jeopardize the separate sphere of authority the Japanese bureaucracy in Korea enjoyed. This tendency toward autonomy had been at least in part reinforced by the relative stability in personnel in the GGK bureaucracy. Although occasional lateral transfers to other colonies or even Japan proper were possible—GGK Communications Bureau Director Yamada Tadatsugu himself had served in the Kwantung Territories—those serving in the GGK tended to have grown up and stayed in Korea.[72] The lack of personnel transfers could only reinforce the growth of a separate identity for the Japanese serving in Korea vis-à-vis Japanese in Japan. In this context, even relatively mundane issues such as different pay scales might become a source of friction. Referring to the prospect of MOC operating inside Korea, a GGK official hinted that its own employees would be displeased to work side by side with MOC people since the latter's chances for promotion were better. As a bureaucrat, he was voicing a real albeit limited concern. Despite high-sounding rhetoric, the governments in both Tokyo and in Keijō were often dominated by bureaucratic self-interest.

## Conclusion

Essentially, this chapter has explored two paradoxes. The first reflects the character of Japan's colonial policy in Korea. Introduced and expanded primarily as a modern means of colonial control, the telegraph and telephone under Japanese rule not only served to strengthen the colonial administration but also provided new opportunities, however limited and unevenly distributed, to the native population. Few would deny that it was under Japanese rule that the telegraph and telephone first gained widespread use in Korea. The incorporation of Korea into a Japan-dominated telecommunications network helped create a peculiar kind of modernity that can best be called "colonial." Although Koreans in increasing number could and did send telegrams, for example, the relative decline of Korean-language telegrams reveals that colonial assimilation under the Japanese was succeeding exactly because it included not just coercion but inducement.

The second paradox arises partly from the nature of a communications network itself. Japan's new East Asian telecommunications network was a double-edged sword. Promising to collapse space and time within the imperium, it also threatened to upset the uneasy balance between the imperial center and the colonial periphery. Although in transportation and other areas coordination between Tokyo and the colonial governments was by no means smooth, the conflict between GGK and MOC over the new East Asian telecommunication network was particularly serious, in part due to the instantaneous nature of telecommunications and the issue of control and governance it entailed. This phenomenon was not entirely new in the annals of imperial history. Writing about the role of telegraphy in generating the ground conditions for urban imperialism in the late nineteenth century, James Carey has noted that the cable and telegraph, in addition to sea power, turned Western colonialism into imperialism, a system in which the center of an empire could dictate, rather than respond, to the margin.[73] The redefinition of colonial Korea is an example of such a transition: colonialism, in which power and authority rested with the domestic governor, became imperialism, in which power and authority were absorbed by the imperial capital. Essentially, the contest over telecommunications, the ultimate medium of control, illustrates the thorny political problem of imperial integration versus colonial autonomy and in turn helped redefine the future role of colonial Korea in the new empire.

Bureaucratic infighting notwithstanding, Korea's importance in Japan's imperial telecommunications network waxed during the Pacific War. As increased communications between Japan and North China occupied more and more circuits on the Japan-Manchukuo cable, construction of a second cable linking Keijō with northern Manchuria began, eventually reaching Wŏnsan by the end of the war. Domestic service in Korea had to be reduced to meet the need of through traffic and air defense. The Korean Strait in the south became the biggest bottleneck for telecommunications traffic, especially because a planned cable linking Japan and central China directly failed to materialize. Although a second non-loaded submarine cable across the strait was laid in December 1943, it soon ceased functioning due to technical problems. To ensure the vital link between Japan and the continent, an ultra-short-wave (VHF) connection was established, but the relay station in Tsushima also ceased operation, due to a fire. In a last-minute push, the Japanese undertook construction of new direct, cross-channel facilities that needed no relay points. Ironically, the work was completed on August 15, 1945, the day of Japan's surrender.[74]

The colonial telecommunications infrastructure continued to play a role in postcolonial Korea, however. An American survey in the late 1940s described the telecommunications network in southern Korea as "small and in many respects obsolete by American standards," after years of poor maintenance, but considered it "generally adequate to meet the existing needs." To supplement these rapidly deteriorating lines, the Republic of Korea government purchased wireless equipment from the American electronics giant RCA.[75]

In June 1950, five years after Japan's empire had disintegrated, the

Korean peninsula was engulfed in a new conflict. Badly in need of communication facilities, U.S. forces found the underground "Mukden cable" running through the peninsula a crucial asset. Throughout the war, American engineers repaired Japanese cables and repeater stations, to maximize the cable's use as a trunk line for troops in Korea and as the vital link between General MacArthur's headquarters in Tokyo and U.S. forces in the peninsula. As the great artery of communication, a U.S. Army officer recalled, the Mukden Cable was a "God-sent gift."[76] Interestingly, Americans were not the only ones taking advantage of Japan's imperial legacies. The same cable also served as a major communications link for North Korea and China, which joined the war in October 1950. Lacking spare parts to repair damages to the cable between Sinŭjiu and P'yongyang, Chinese engineers resorted to removing portions of the nonloaded cable the Japanese had laid along the former Manchukuo-USSR frontier.[77] Thus, in a manner that no one would have predicted, what remained of Japan's imperial telecommunications network contributed to postcolonial Korea's transition to the new Cold War world order.[78]

# PART II

## Colonial Modernity and Identity

# SEVEN

# The Price of Legitimacy: Women and the Kŭnuhoe Movement, 1927–1931

## Kenneth M. Wells

In fact, much the same sort of movement and mixture went on in old England as we find in older Herodotus, who also, in telling what had been, thought it well to take a woman's lot for his starting point.                    —George Eliot, *Middlemarch*

A growing number of historians both inside and outside Korea are becoming disenchanted with the dominance of the nationalist paradigm for interpreting Korean history in the twentieth century. Not only are the evaluative categories of nationalism unhelpful when examining the activities of the nationalists themselves, but they also hinder the historian from investigating large and important areas of experience that fall outside the interests of nationalists then and now. Recent challenges to the nationalist approach, however, have tended to demystify specific nationalist figures and movements chiefly by attacking their nationalist credentials, and thus they inadvertently reinforce the operation of nationalist categories. This chapter attempts an indirect critique of nationalist historiography and a more direct critique of the claims of nationalists during the 1920s and 1930s by raising the question: What happens when one takes the position of women as one's starting point?

This course does not enable the historian to sidestep the nationalist paradigm. On the contrary, it forces one to tackle head-on the central claim of nationalism, namely, that nationalism works on behalf of all and therefore it is in everyone's interest to work on behalf of nationalism. From their inception, women's movements and issues in twentieth-century Korea have been drawn into the orbit of this generic pretension. Moreover, unless one holds an essentialist view of "femaleness," one can hardly say that Korean women ought not to have been involved in nationalism—or become "nationalists." In this case, it might not be the nationalist paradigm that is at issue so much as a version of nationalism in which women either were or are thought to have been passive, a version that closer attention to a wider base of materials might call into question. But if it can be argued that women actively contributed to the substance of Irish nationalism, for example, it is not at all easy to do so in Korea's case.[1]

It is not easy moreover to conceive what a "female" version of nationalism might constitute, especially in the Korean case, other than a redefinition of nationalism so fundamental that it would no longer be recognized and supported by most male nationalists. Where nationalism is based on the priority of ethnic and linguistic identity, movements to reorganize in earnest the power relations between men and women seem irrelevant, or worse, a violation of the priority that will weaken the national project. It was not possible for Korean women to share jointly in whatever benefits nationalism promised without some such major reorganization of their society. But that, to the men, was not what nationalism was about. Yet if women decided not to help further the nationalist aspirations of the men, it was possible they would fare even worse in their efforts to change gender dynamics. As it was, activist Korean women had to rely on promises, in a kind of strategic deal, that once nationalist objectives were realized, women would be rewarded. But since Japan's expulsion from Korea and the reorganization of gender relations were not at all the same thing, there was no guarantee that in a politically liberated Korea women would not find themselves subjected even more firmly to reasserted precolonial traditions or some other male-centered prescription of womanhood. It is a moot point whether this was not actually the case under the two decades of Park Chung Hee's rule.

Be that as it may, what I wish to argue is not what women should or should not have done, but that the experience of many women and their movements in the 1920s and 1930s undermines the common viewpoint that by working for nationalist objectives women also worked positively on behalf of the causes they believed were specific to their historical situation. I argue, further, that although some women were conscious to a degree of this subterfuge of nationalism, they were hindered in their pursuit of an independent agenda by lack of support from other women, hostility from Korean men, the nationalists' stranglehold on debate, and the subsumption of women's liberation under the socialist agenda. They were of course also affected in many ways by the Japanese version of modernization, but this is far too large a topic to expand upon in this chapter.

Korean society historically presents an almost prima facie case for using gender as an interpretive framework. The metaphysics, mores, human functions, architectural designs, spatial divisions, and state ideology of the Chosŏn dynasty were so consciously organized with reference to gender principles that instead of a social construction of gender one might justifiably speak of a gendered construction of Korean society. This is confirmed by the fact that in the late nineteenth and early twentieth centuries when pressure for social reform intensified, gender — particularly the role of women — became a central issue. In the 1920s, when restrictions on Korean publications were relaxed, debate on gender issues exploded, a debate strangely absent from subsequent nationalist histories of the period.

Women's movements in the modern era were initially associated with religious movements such as Tonghak (later Ch'ŏndogyo) and Christianity, a finding that agrees with Gerder Lerner's "discovery" in her second volume on the history of women in the West.[2] At the turn of the century, educated Korean Protestants in particular strongly promoted reform of social practice and thought regarding women, partly for moralistic reasons but also as part of a campaign to "strengthen the nation." Thus began the tradition that spans the Ch'anyanghoe of the 1890s and the Songjukhoe of the 1910s (discussed below) and the National Debt Repayment movement of the 1910s, the various *aeguk puinhoe* (patriotic women's societies) of the 1920s and 1930s, and some religious women's groups and certain features of the Korean Women's Development Institute in contemporary South Korea. Brought into being by nationalists, it is this tradition that worked most on behalf of nationalist goals and tolerated the subordination of "women's" issues in the process.

In 1920, an alternative movement was introduced through the new journals and newspapers by some highly educated women such as Kim Wŏnju (1896–1971), the first Korean woman to found and edit a journal,[3] and Na Hyesŏk (1896–1948). This movement can in many respects be characterized as a liberal-feminist movement, and it activated a debate on gender that proved its undoing, as the discourse was taken over by males and diverted toward issues of "patriotic" virtue and "national" import: gender was treated as it had been in early Chosŏn—as a morally prescriptive endeavor. By the mid-1920s it was clear that many males, bereft of their power to rule the nation, were hostile to any move by women that would affect the gender balance of power, something "modernity" ostensibly offered women.

At this point a split ensued between the earlier religion-based (and now comparatively "conservative") groups and the newer, more iconoclastic women's groups associated with socialist organizations or ideas. Cognizant of the easy isolation of the liberal feminists, socialist women addressed basic conditions of rural and new laboring women. These rival groups joined forces in 1927 in the Kŭnuhoe, the "sister" body of the united front organization, the Singanhoe. Although numerically inferior, the socialists proved more articulate in their explication of women's conditions and requirements. In the process, however, women's issues as such lost clear definition as they were merged with generic socialist goals.

Sharing the fate of the Sin'ganhoe, the Kŭnuhoe also dissolved in 1931. Through the remainder of the decade, the image of the "new" or "future" woman was steadily transformed by the rise of commercial media, under Japanese and Korean direction, from a conscious self-determining being to a "modern" mother compliant with the fashions of glossy magazines and the obligation to support the modern advancement of her children. Heavy political pressure drove the more radical groups underground and the religious and conservative leadership into a truce with the Government-General or even into the service of its programs.

Although, given the imbalance between male and female power and resources, it is difficult to see what strategy might have been more fruitful, acceptance of the notion that women's goals could be attained by working for nationalist and, to a lesser extent, socialist agendas appears to have been a costly procedure. The severity of the struggles of South Korean women since 1948 is in part a consequence of the way in which the women's movements related to nationalist and socialist movements during the 1920s and 1930s.[4] My object is to examine the dilemma in terms of the historical data, beginning with some observations on problems surrounding the elevated status awarded the nation in analyses of modern historical experience.

## The Strength of the Nation

Prasenjit Duara has reminded us recently of the need to free modern Chinese history from preoccupations with the nation-state.[5] Hardly less must be said about Korean historiography, especially concerning the history of women on the Korean peninsula, where nationalism put down such deep roots and so successfully inculcated the utter naturalness of the nation as the basis for all else that one might reasonably doubt that any considerable importation of a Western linear-teleological mentality was required.

The primacy of "nation," however defined, is an aspect of nationalism itself. It is only *within* nationalism that the nation is considered so crucial; only *within* nationalist thought does it appear to be the self-evident basis of statehood. Social Darwinism, which is sometimes used to account for Korean nationalism in its late nineteenth-century phase, applies to nations (if at all) only if the "nation" has already been made the natural unit of competition. The same circularity is true of organic conceptions of the national community, which, as elsewhere, was (and is) espoused by most Korean nationalists, including the early Sin Ch'aeho (1880–1936): transferring the idea of the organic unity of the individual to the nation and then describing its internal and external relations in these terms is supposed to prove that the nation must be organic. "History" thus becomes the expression of that organism. If I wish to save the history of Korean women from this idea of the nation, it is not because I have no regard for the nation as such, but because I find the view that the pattern of history does or should correspond to the imaginations and ambitions of various nationalisms a demagogic one, and one that can normally fulfill itself only by curbing the expression and pursuit of other views.

What alternative, then, does a gender perspective on history offer? Here I distinguish between feminist historiography and gender

studies. A long tradition of feminist historiography interprets a
given historical experience through an analysis of gender dynamics.
Some key feminist theories attribute to gender composition the material structures and cultural form of societies in general; others are
more modest and apply feminist principles to specific, limited historical issues that might not be about gender per se.[6] This chapter is
not about feminist historiography, but I am indebted to it for many
insights and guidance.[7]

Gender studies I take to mean that which makes any of a multi-
tude of gender issues the subject of analysis. It implies an awareness
not only that gender relations, dynamics, and perceptions should be
given far more attention in historical analyses but also that those are
of the highest importance in understanding the cultural formation of
societies. In particular, gender studies in its recent manifestation entails a restatement of an older position, that ideas and culture enjoy
agency in history.[8]

As ideas of history, particularly in their approach to nationalism,
both Marxist and non-Marxist structuralisms considered gender to
be so much a matter of cultural form that it could only be admitted
as an effect for which underlying structural causes must be found.
This exclusion of cultural dynamics from the realm of causation and
from the status of structure has, in fact, handicapped Marxists in
their endeavor to topple nationalist historiography. The view that
culture is an effervescence, a derivative of movements in social and
political structures, precludes real understanding of nationalist culture. Or to put it another way, insofar as nationalism does not lend
itself to structural analysis, it has been deemed "mere" culture or
even simply emotion. Culture, it has been thought, cannot account
for things, at least not important things: it can only be accounted for.
Hence culture could not be accepted as a starting point of a historical
explanation or be treated as an agent of historical development. Nationalism thus became an enigma, Benedict Anderson's "failure" of
Marxist analysis.

It is important therefore, when treating the relationship between
gender and nationalism, to recognize that culture was being formed
and fought over and that history was being made in the process. For
understanding the nature of the cultural struggle in colonial Korea,
gender dynamics are an excellent starting point. By "gender dynamics," I have in mind the interaction among the beliefs Koreans
held about gender origins, roles, and relations, the forms gender re-

lations took in their society, and the new forms that some envisaged and proposed. To say this interaction has historical agency is to claim that the nature of societies and changes in them is in part explicable in terms of this interaction. At the same time, a cultural approach is suitable for an inquiry into the relation between gender and nationalism and as a method of unmasking the way in which nationalism operates.

## Breaking down the Myth

It is always helpful to remember that the people we study engaged in daily, repetitive rounds of work, meeting, and talking and functioned as family members, companions, and so on. It is important to realize that Koreans in the 1920s and 1930s did not relate everything to nationalist projects, as if there were no other reference points in their lives than the fact of Japanese rule. It was actually a very heady time—there was almost too much going on. Society was undergoing the structural change, with all its attendant problems, of industrialization; an urban labor force was emerging and organizing, people were moving away from hometowns to work at new things, and rural people were experimenting with innovations in agriculture and with cooperatives. There was an explosion of printing—books, journals, newspapers. Education was expanding vigorously among the populace. From the universities of the colonial power, Korean students were bringing back knowledge of new professions, new politics, and all kinds of thinkers from T. H. Green, Tolstoy, and Ibsen to Kropotkin, Smith, and Marx—and Ellen Key and August Bebel.[9] Tradition was being challenged as never before. And whenever tradition was debated, the gender question served as a catalyst.

Women had opportunities as never before. They were being educated; joining the workforce, some as journalists, teachers, and nurses; and large numbers were being drawn from rural families and herded into strictly supervised factory employment. These activities were so contrary to the traditional female prescription that both female and male writers and activists demanded revision of the received culture of gender. The sources on this are abundant, but until recently and, in most current writing on Korea under Japanese rule, still, women's concerns that are not directly linkable to nationalist or socialist movements and aims have been dismissed as frivolous. This simply repeats the accusations of the period itself. Some of the women's concerns, however, related more concretely to the changes and challenges facing Koreans than did many of the nationalist preoccupations. It is the fate of these concerns that raises the question, Did participation by women in nationalist movements and debates further their causes? (By "their causes," I mean the causes they espoused, not causes I or anyone else would prefer they had espoused.) Significantly, placing gender dynamics at the center of analysis involves a similar critique of the socialists' attitudes toward women's concerns.

## Background Movements

We can usefully distinguish two phases in women's movements between 1890 and 1920, despite some overlapping: (1) a period of modernization, 1890–1910; and (2) a period of mobilization, 1910–20. The first phase reflected two ideas: the low status of women was a symbol of national backwardness, so that raising their status through education and legal reforms would enhance the overall level of civilization and strength; and the oppression of women was seen as a hallmark of traditional society, so that their rescue from oppressive family and social customs would signify the onset of a new society. It is remarkable how explicit was the insight that Korea's society was gender-based. In the second phase, aspirations for social equality were not put aside, but the emphasis shifted to mobilizing women on behalf of independence movements.

When young activist intellectuals engaged in a critique of neo-Confucianism in the 1880s and 1890s, they immediately raised the question of women's status. A limited form of public debate commenced in 1896 with the establishment of the Independence Club (Tongnip hyŏphoe) and its newspaper, *Tongnip sinmun* (Independence newspaper). Here, the position of women was offered as an example of neo-Confucianism as a hierarchy of oppression and an enemy of progress. The first shot in this campaign, regarding women, was fired by Sŏ Chaep'il (1866–1951), founder of the Independence Club in an editorial in *Tongnip sinmun* on April 21, 1896, in which he argued that only stupidity had allowed men to believe Korean women were in any way inferior to Korean men. The antidote was equal education for males and females, from which would ensue social equality and an increase in national strength. In September of that same year, Sŏ advanced the argument that gender relations were a crucial index of a nation's degree of civilization.[10]

Some two years later, in September 1898, over one hundred wives of aristocratic intellectuals formed the Ch'anyanghoe and established a girls school. In a petition to Emperor Kojong, dated September 1, the leaders stated: "We women . . . have founded the school for the purpose of contributing to the strengthening of the nation through loyalty and patriotism."[11] In this petition begins the application of the labels "old" and "new" to Korean women and their customs. The Old are absurd, imprisoned, and subject to husband, father, and son; the New are enlightened, socially active, and partners with their husbands. Following the failure of the Ch'anyanghoe's campaign to have this school, Sunsŏng School, and other women's schools recognized and funded by the government, women's education passed into the orbit of religious movements.

In April 1907, the first of several *aeguk puinhoe*, or patriotic women's associations, was founded on the belief that if women demonstrated the will and ability to serve the country as *citizens*, men would be stripped of excuses to oppress them. The association's activities included efforts to reduce the national debt as well as promotion of female education. Although the idea of women participating in national life was a radical departure from tradition, the programs were far from revolutionary. Despite rhetoric by men about social equality, reform of customs was limited to raising the marriage age, allowing the remarriage of widows, and questioning the institution of concubinism. Korea does not seem to have had a woman as forthright as the Chinese activist Qiu Jin, who in 1906 had declaimed: "The young intellectuals are all chanting 'Revolution, Revolution,' but I say revolution will have to start in our homes, by achieving equal rights for women."[12] Perhaps Ko Hŭijun comes closest in her observation that the National Debt Repayment movement provided Korean women with an opportunity they had been awaiting for five millennia, a means of building a new world.

Shortly after Korea became a Japanese colony in August 1910, a Christian organization named the Songjukhoe (Pine and bamboo society) was formed among teachers and pupils of girls schools in Seoul and P'yŏngyang, and a national network was organized with secret monthly meetings for the inculcation in women of the "spirit of independence." Immediately before the outbreak of the 1919

March First movement, Kim Maria (1891–1944), who had studied in Tokyo and was an associate of Hwang Aedŏk (Esther Hwang, 1892–1971) and Na Hyesŏk, arranged for female students to distribute pamphlets calling for female participation in the movement.[13] Subsequently, 471 women and girls were arrested; among them were 68 teachers, 154 students, 73 in public service, 41 farmers, and 23 workers.[14] The movement produced a few outstanding female heroes, such as the martyred Yu Kwansun (1904–20), who were hailed for their dedication to the national movement. Saying that women could not leave the struggle all to men, Kim Maria in April 1919 founded the Taehan aeguk puinhoe (Korean patriotic women's society), forging links with the Korean Provisional Government in Shanghai. By 1920 the association boasted 2,000 members and a platform of national self-determination and rights identical to that of male organizations of the time.[15] But threatened with arrest, Kim Maria fled to Shanghai.

The Taehan aeguk puinhoe was representative of women's movements of the time, which, however, were few in number. Its Christian membership and inspiration, leadership by a newly educated woman, reliance on schools, and conformity to male organizations' goals typify this phase. Their participation in the national cause did raise male estimation of Korean women, just as the war efforts of the suffragettes engendered greater respect for women in Britain. Thereafter, women became active in a wide range of "public" spheres; their activities and, from time to time, their opinions were featured in publications.

However, identification with national causes appears to have been closer in this decade than during the previous one. Issues of gender reform and female social equality gave way to struggle alongside men for the same ends as men. Despite the magnitude, relative to traditional times, of the female presence in the March First movement, I have been unable to find any statement specific to women. By comparison, the 1919 Chinese May Fourth movement, which was also precipitated by Japan's imperialist activities, was explicit on women's issues. Confucianism was severely attacked for sexual inequality, filial piety, and its one-sided demand for female chastity. Why was the March First movement so silent on these issues? Was there a women's platform, or only a determination that women would do their bit for the nation? Part of the answer might be that these issues had been raised already in Korea in the 1890s, especially in connection with a Christian critique of Confucianism. But part of the answer clearly is that for the men who drew up the charter and generated the movement, the cause of national political independence, after a decade of actual rather than imagined imperial occupation, had taken precedence over the issue of gender relations.

## Gender Dynamics in the 1920s

The Government-General's reform of laws on the press and assembly after the March First movement opened up new opportunities for women to express their views. The term "New Woman" was instated, and ideas of female liberation from a liberal feminist viewpoint were printed. The initial impetus came from Kim Wŏnju's new journal, *Sin yŏja* (New woman); Na Hyesŏk presented her feminism through another journal, *Yŏja kye* (Women's world). The acumen of these and other highly educated women and their truly revolutionary views piqued male interest, and in 1920 a debate on gender burgeoned among all leading nationalist and cultural publications. In the process, men recaptured the debate and, by dint of their greater numbers and resources, quickly steered it in their preferred direction. Before long, Kim Wŏnju, Na Hyesŏk, and other feminist women such as the novelist Kim Myŏngsun (1896–?) were ostracized,[16] and the women's movements split.

Much more than among men, the split in women's movements was basically between, on the one hand, Christians and nonsocialist nationalists who identified with the Korean YWCA (founded in 1922), church social programs, and the various women's patriotic societies and, on the other hand, the socialists and communists who identified with the Chosŏn yŏsŏng tonguhoe (Korean women's socialist league; founded in 1924) and the organizations of their husbands. A general characterization of the two sides has arisen, according to which the nonsocialist women were conservatives whose politics consisted of financial support for the Provisional Government and affiliation with groups such as the Patriotic Youth Corps (Ch'ŏngnyŏn aegukdan) and whose object was the amelioration of women's conditions through education and reform. By contrast, the socialist camp is seen as radical and feminist, pursuing class revolution and thoroughgoing female liberation. This, generally, has been considered to be the basic situation when the two streams merged in the Kŭnuhoe in 1927.[17]

Christian and nonsocialist activists were numerically far stronger than those in left-wing women's groups. Their views were also less susceptible to censorship and, in contrast to the liberal feminist viewpoint, which was anathematized by males and conservative women and almost immediately smothered by the preponderance of male writings, enjoyed much wider and more frequent publication. Male psychology was clearly an influence on the plot throughout this period, but is too large a subject to analyze in this chapter except incidentally. Suffice it to say that the humiliation engendered by the Japanese removal of the traditional male elite's prerogative to rule and the consequent subjugation of Korean men rendered them extremely sensitive to any suggestion of loss of prerogatives in the home, let alone any call for Korean women to assert themselves against Korean men.

Women's liberation was, however, a topic over which Korean men and their journals competed energetically. The editorial of the second volume of *Kaebyŏk* (Creation) identified three areas in which Koreans must pursue major reform: labor, women's status, and race. The poor treatment of women in Korea was blamed on the "Chinese" principle of *namjon yŏbi*, whereby women were designated male possessions. To rectify this, two main courses were advocated: to persuade men that the *namjon yŏbi* construct was artificial, not a law of nature, and to effect recognition of the sanctity of female personhood (the editorial having already urged recognition of the sanctity of labor). On this basis, and "for the sake of the times, for the sake of Korea," men should support women's liberation. If young women actively promoted female education throughout the land and led the "ignorant," women would understand and act upon their own personhood. The editorial was cautionary, however: given that developments in women's rights in Korea "lag far, far behind" those in European nations, immediate demands for application of women's rights were deemed impracticable. What was envisaged was "natural liberation," something that required men and women to grow in awareness together, even if it took 100 years or more.[18] Presumably the term "natural liberation" signified a repudiation of any radical social reform.

A subsequent article on family systems repeated the castigation of *namjon yŏbi* and the call for recognition of a woman's complete, free personhood (*in'gyŏk*). It is significant, I believe, that in both this article and the editorial, the lack of female personhood was linked to the general order and health of society. In the editorial, it was made responsible for a pathological social formation; in the article it was the reason for the suppression of individuality altogether.[19] But neither writer could refrain from pointing out that female liberation should be supported for the sake of the strength of the nation. This was hardly a feature of the interests of men in Korea only. Much of the discussion of women's rights in China concerned practical arguments. Luo Jialun (a male), for example, argued in 1919 that women's liberation would make the nation strong, since slavery of 50 percent of the population prevented formation of an independent spirit and individual self-determination for men and women alike.[20]

In its September issue, *Kaebyŏk* included a survey of twenty prominent figures, all male, on the subject of female liberation. Only one respondent, Yi Pyŏngjo, president of the culturalist Munhŭngsa, expressed reservations about the idea, fearing it would open up a can of worms—free love, debate on chastity, and so on—and claimed it was secondary to democratic and legal reforms. Others stressed the theme of personhood (*in'gyŏk*) and the artificiality of gender prescriptions, and two respondents even stated that women should enjoy absolute equality with men. Two others opined that the whole issue was for women to decide. One of these, Yu Chinhŭi, considered it curious that men should be calling for female emancipation, since that surely implied liberation from male oppression, which could therefore only ensue from women's own consciousness and action. Nevertheless, he observed that women could enjoy complete liberation only after a revolution of society had been accomplished (but what this meant was not explained).[21] The other, the linguist Kwŏn Ch'igyu, simply thought men had no business inquiring into women's issues. It was, he said, "like barging in on someone else's dinner party."

Kwŏn's response does point up a crucial problem in the debate on women's issues in this period, a problem that soon crippled ideas and movements trying to address female concerns on their own merits. It is one thing to express modesty in relation to others' affairs, quite another to disclaim responsibility and push them aside. For those men who avoided the "woman" question, the latter appears to have been the dominant reason: it was too uncomfortable and they balked at incorporating these women's demands into their visions of a new society and nation. These demands, after all, went far beyond reform of kitchens, or other so-called women's quarters. It is noticeable how interest fell off among *Kaebyŏk* contributors after the fourth issue, and nothing significant appeared again until an item on divorce in the thirty-fifth issue. Likewise, news items and thoughtful articles on gender in the Shanghai *Tongnip sinmun* (1919–25) simply disappeared as soon as something "vital" arose, such as formation of the Kungmin taep'yohoe (National delegates conference) or submission of Korea's case to the Washington and Pacific conferences of the League of Nations.

Nevertheless, it is possible that if more men had left the whole issue to women, the outcome might have been more positive for the women. Yet few male writers and activists could let the question lie, and in the absence of enough women who had the means and education to publicize their views, men willingly pushed their advantage when not otherwise distracted by "important" matters. It has been observed of the Chinese male domination of this debate during the same decades that one of the reasons "may be that female emancipation was used as a weapon directed as much toward destroying the existing society as for creating real independence for women."[22] This applies much more neatly to Korea in the late nineteenth century, when men perceived that their society was a concrete expression of traditional gender ideals and could not be changed without gender reform. But Japan's direct colonial occupation complicated the situation. Although social change was still desired, most Korean male activists felt obliged to resist the social changes that the colonial regime was effecting and became intolerant of women's movements that could not readily be used to discomfort the enemy or aid national liberation. In addition, the normal male reluctance to surrender traditional prerogatives over women was exacerbated by the perception — or reality — that under the colonial system women, unlike men, stood to gain from social change.

The greatest continuity between the late nineteenth century and the 1920s was a belief in education. The twenty male public figures cited above uniformly subscribed to the omnipotence of education as a means of female emancipation. This can be related to the intense energy expended on education during the first half of the 1920s following the rescinding of the more draconian colonial educational policies. Education was, for the culturalists especially but by no means exclusively, expected to enhance greatly the Koreans' chances of gaining national independence. For women, or more accurately, for the nonsocialist activists among them, education was valued supremely as a means of raising the economic and social status of women and improving their life in the family. Through local church networks, these women conducted widespread activities among rural women. The object of their reformist education was health and hygiene, kitchen management and diet, home economics, and child-rearing practices. Many leaders in this enterprise, such as Kim Hwallan (Helen Kim, 1899–1970), gained prominence nationally and later provided leadership for the Kŭnuhoe. But their faith in education and seemingly nonpolitical approach brought them into conflict with the small but growing number of socialist women, for whom education signified raising women's political consciousness and whose object was not reform but revolution.

## The Kŭnuhoe Experience

The Sin'ganhoe (February 1927 to May 1931) was a united front movement, designed to pool the resources of socialists, communists, and other left-of-center nationalists in a bid to wrest back some self-determination for Koreans and ultimately to restore political independence. The idea was to bury ideological hatchets to the degree necessary to unite around the common goal of national liberation. It may be a measure of the impact of female education programs that women decided in July 1927 to organize an affiliate body, the Kŭnuhoe (Friends of the rose of sharon), in order to ensure that women's concerns were represented and addressed in the united front. They also published a journal, *Kŭnu*. Probably on account of the organization's socialist elements, the 530-page history of Korean women from the Enlightenment period to 1945, published in 1972, disposes of the Kŭnuhoe in one sentence as an early movement for women's liberation.[23] Yi Kyun'yŏng's recent 650-page work on the Sin'ganhoe mentions the Kŭnuhoe a mere ten times in passing, without analysis.[24]

The genesis of women's socialist movements between 1924 and 1927 was unpropitious. Male socialists' views of the proper understanding of the "woman" question had already been clarified in the March 1923 general meeting of the left-wing coalition, the Chosŏn ch'ŏngnyŏn tang, when a program of action on women's issues was proposed. Among the 150 delegates present from 80 organizations, only eight were women, who represented four nascent socialist women's groups. Of eight items proposed, four (reform of the family system, resistance to the good mother / virtuous wife ethic, freedom in marriage and divorce, and abolition of prostitution) were approved, and four (resistance to male violence, reform of women's social system, support for women's economic independence, abolition of customs disadvantageous to women) were rejected. All the rejected items concern problems that concerned women primarily or required males to change their habits and attitudes. The approved items all involved aspects of reform that were believed to have national implications. The first item had long belonged to the attack on Confucian or, more aptly for socialists, "feudal" tradition, the second repudiated the Japanese prescription of the time, the third was equally congenial to male interests, and the fourth was an aspect of anti-Japanese ideology, since the new, generalized, urban prostitution trade was attributed to colonial policy.

The women's socialist league, the Chosŏn yŏsŏng tonguhoe, was founded in May 1924 by 30 women under the watchful eyes of 50 males and 10 police agents. When the relationship between female liberation and class liberation was raised, it was agreed that feminism was a logical corollary of socialism and that female liberation therefore depended on class liberation. As Marxist-Leninist theories of imperialism took hold in the socialist movement, especially after the Comintern instructed Korea's communists, from 1926, to form the united front, all Koreans bar collaborators were deemed a class under the Japanese, with the consequence that women's liberation was made secondary also to national liberation.

Yet the issue was not entirely closed. In founding the Kŭnuhoe three years later, its leaders made it clear that they wished to reassert the urgency of the woman question and reinstate the principle that gender change was vital to genuine social transformation. The July 1927 manifesto proclaimed that the reason women were putting aside schism was to unite behind two major struggles, one against "feudal legacies" and the other against "modern contradictions." As in the Sin'ganhoe, the Kŭnuhoe platform and prospectus strategically refrained from mentioning Japan directly, but unlike the Singanhoe the issue of modernity was raised as a specific area for attention. The manifesto claimed that, contrary to men's impressions, the lot of women had deteriorated in recent times. "Far from having been eradicated, the former legacies of the old era remain potent as ever, and on top of this are piled the stresses of modern times." Although it conceded that all problems were interrelated so that one could not solve one without mending the whole, this did not mean, it argued, that particular women's issues should be submerged under a general viewpoint: only by addressing women's problems in their own terms could anything effective be done. Less cautiously, the manifesto ended with the flourish, "The day women liberate themselves, the world will be liberated!"[25]

The prospectus outlined seven specific objectives.

1. Complete abolition of all social and legal discrimination against women;

2. Eradication of all feudal customs and superstitions regarding women;

3. Abolition of early marriage and the institution of free marriage;

4. Abolition of female slavery and licensed prostitution;

5. Amelioration of the economy of rural women;

6. Abolition of wage discrimination and the institution of paid maternity leave;

7. Abolition of dangerous labor and night work for women and boys.[26]

By 1929 membership in the Kŭnuhoe had risen to 2,970 women, including 260 residing abroad, mostly in Tokyo. The largest provincial concentration of members was in South Kyŏngsang (623 members), followed by South P'yŏngan (502) and Kyŏnggi (224) provinces. Between them, North Hamgyŏng and South Hamgyŏng provinces accounted for 489 members, and the organization was well represented throughout the peninsula. The heaviest metropolitan concentration was in P'yŏngyang (452), followed by Seoul (224), Pusan (127), Tongnae (117), and Tokyo (105).[27] The relatively large Japan-based contingent accounts for the growth in influence of socialist women by 1929 and suggests familiarity with Japanese feminist ideas.

According to a report submitted early in 1929, the Kŭnuhoe had by that time focused mainly on educational, social, and political-economic activities, as well as membership drives. Social activities included relief for flood victims in the northeast and assistance in hygiene reform; political-economic action involved promotion of debating societies, lecture tours, instruction in handcrafts, and support for women involved in labor disputes, particularly in the Wŏnsan area. But by far the greatest amount of energy had been expended on educational work: literacy campaigns, construction of kindergartens and schools for women and poor children, night classes for women, and so on. In connection with education, campaigns were mounted to eradicate what was called "superstition" (*misin*).[28]

Although education was always deemed vital, impatience was evidently growing over the weak focus on social and economic activism, an impatience that reflected the ideological division within the movement. The general meeting in Seoul in July 1928, attended by 50 delegates from around the country, was marked by mutual recriminations, threats to leave the organization, and resignations by some elected officers.[29] After two years of domination by the nonsocialist women, socialist leaders in 1929 had gained enough influence to effect a limited radicalization of the movement. The prominent socialist Hŏ Chŏngsuk (1902–91), an executive officer of the Kŭnuhoe from July 1928 till her arrest in December 1930 during the Kwangju movement, published an article in 1929 in *Kŭnu* in which she suggested that the Kŭnuhoe ought to be the key to opening up the whole women's liberation enterprise to the masses.[30] A significant number of other articles pushed the same line. Chŏng Ch'ilsŏng (1897–1958), a founding member of the Kŭnuhoe, delivered a powerful, satirical critique of the "lucky" women who talked glibly of the new age for women while remaining blind to the mass of women for whom conditions had only deteriorated.[31] Chang Rin, a male Kŭnuhoe adviser, called for a campaign to unite female farmers and laborers.[32] As a result of this pressure, the prospectus was revised in July 1929, with four principal additions: (1) abolition of sexual discrimination in education and expansion of women's higher education; (2) freedom of divorce; (3) freedom of speech, press, and assembly; and (4) establishment of medical facilities and child-care centers for laborers and farmers.[33]

Friction among Kŭnuhoe members came to a head during the November 1929 Kwangju student movement and its aftermath. Under Sin'ganhoe and Kŭnuhoe sponsorship, this protest by middle- and high-school students expanded into a major national movement. The Government-General acted swiftly to forestall the uprising, arresting the leadership of both united front organizations. Nonsocialist Kŭnuhoe members thereupon urged that the movement be depoliticized and concentrate on the elevation of women's conditions through education and other "safe" avenues. But as in the Sin'ganhoe, the Kŭnuhoe socialists campaigned for the dissolution and reorganization of the united front. Both bodies were dissolved, but neither was permitted to reorganize by the Government-General.

## Meaning of the Experience

In a study of women's movements, Nam Hwasuk advances the thesis that the lack of progress with their objectives was in large part due to the insufficient consciousness of the numerically superior "conservative" Christian female leaders. In particular, the cause of the stagnation by 1925 of education-based enlightenment activities is to be found "in the ideological limitations of the [enlightenment] groups themselves." Religious and educational programs "could not hold out any promise at all to rural women, who were in a condition of absolute poverty."[34] It is not clear that the evidence bears this out, since any decline in enthusiasm or the pace of development of schooling in city and town after 1925 was relative only to the extraordinary energy and expansion of the previous four years. The "decline" was a feature rather of elite education, such as attempts to establish a university. There is evidence in Nam's own work that conservative women were not as irrelevant to the masses as she claims. Although she tends to portray the "new" group of left-wing women as potters and the "old" group of Christian reformist women as their clay, she indicates that the socialist women divided over pressure to include nonsocialist women in their membership in order to secure a wider base[35] — as later occurred in the Kŭnuhoe.

There is in any case no question that membership in educational and religious-based women's organizations far outnumbered that in their socialist counterparts. The issue is their relation to the Kŭnuhoe and the wider women's movement: their position on liberation, their aims, and whether any progress was made toward those aims. The "conservative" women appear, on examination, to be far more radical, indeed iconoclastic, than has often been supposed. In contrast to many of the socialist leaders, who gained influence largely through their marriages to male socialist activists, the more influential among the nonsocialists, usually Christian women, made the very antitraditional choice of remaining single. Moreover, they cut their hair short and often refused to follow restrictive female clothing traditions, for which they published their reasons.[36] They intruded on male occupations and became self-supporting. Although they were happy enough to support, with modifications, the good mother / virtuous wife ethic that Confucian tradition and modern Japan supported, they insisted on a good father / virtuous husband ethic as well: the first Korean woman to divorce her husband for infidelity was the Christian educator Pak Indŏk (1897–1940).[37]

However, there was no single viewpoint or clear-cut position among the nonsocialist women on the meaning and methods of women's liberation. Of the Christians it may be said that they believed in self-determination and self-respect, and that this was predicated on a "spiritual" liberation that redefined the ethics of gender relationships. The suppression in the early 1920s of the "liberal-feminist" stand of Kim Wŏnju and Na Hyesŏk robbed the other nonsocialists of a precisely defined position. Elements of Kim's and Na's principles were, of course, retained, but not so much as part of a coherent, proactive viewpoint as part of a response to changed circumstances in education and employment. Their external inspiration was drawn chiefly from the writings on freedom of love, marriage, motherhood, and divorce of the Swedish reformer Ellen Key, who was also popular among Japanese women activists. References to Key appear repeatedly in most of the cultural and nationalist journals of the 1920s, particularly in *Sinyŏsŏng, Tonggwang, Pyŏlgŏn'gon,* and *Hyesŏng.*

This interest disposed nonsocialist women to focus on female self-determination and equal rights in marriage, family, and occupation for which their new educational attainments were judged to equip them: this was what it meant to be a "new woman."[38] It was also the rationale behind their sense of mission to those who had not yet benefited from the new education, and this meant campaigns among rural women. It is important not to underestimate the extent of nonsocialist activity among rural women. There was a network of YWCA organizations throughout the peninsula and a corresponding network of secular women's youth organizations called *yŏja ch'ŏngnyŏnhoe* (not to be confused with the Yŏja ch'ŏngnyŏn tongmaeng, which was affiliated to the socialist Yŏsŏng tonguhoe).

As for work among poor rural women, Kim Hwallan, a Kŭnuhoe officer and a spokesperson for the YWCA philosophy and activities, became increasingly convinced that rural education was the most pressing task. In the late 1920s she was perhaps the most widely respected female leader in the country. When in November 1927 she spoke in Seoul on the topic of women's rights, the auditorium was reportedly filled one hour before her address and an equal number of people had to be turned away.[39] In mid-1930, she left for Columbia University in New York to complete her doctoral dissertation, "Rural Education for the Regeneration of Korea."[40] At the welcome dinner held on her return in January 1932, 118 guests attended, "the largest crowd ever seen for such occasions."[41]

Here, of course, we run up against a central problem: given this general perception of the need for rural education and reform, what specific place did rural women occupy? Were women taken as a starting point, or were they subjects of an overall national mission, in which women's activities were simply parallels of men's in an enterprise spearheaded by men? There is no reason why women *should not* have promoted education: in fact, given the previous exclusion of women from education, this promotion ensured that women would not be left without a voice in the new form of society that was perforce developing around them. And the very emergence of educated women campaigning for women's education and social reform was a clear break with the past that opened up new possibilities for women in the future. The question remains, however, whether the leaders of these developments were operating within a "patriarchal" framework of programs and vision. If *gender* issues are to take central stage here, then this is not a minor concern.

But was there awareness of this in the debates of the time? In a sense, there was. The socialist women's critique of the educational campaigns break down into two broad charges: first, that they maintained the traditional male view of gender relations; and second, that they were complicit in the Japanese colonial regime's modernization programs. In relation to the first charge, it is evident that prominent male leaders were eager both to support the educational campaigns and to keep them within proper bounds. Yun Ch'iho (1865–1945), for example, founder of the Korean YMCA, educator, and arguably the most influential Methodist leader since the 1890s, not only approved but actively supported the educational and rural activities of nonsocialist women. He looked upon the training of female physicians such as Dr. Esther Kim (1876–1910; Korea's first female physician; also known as Esther Pak and Kim Chŏmdong) with great satisfaction, commended Kim Hwallan highly for her educational work for women through the YWCA and Ewha College, and used his influence to ensure Pak Indŏk was given every support in her successful experiment with the "folk high schools,"[42] a rural education venture modeled closely on a Danish educational experiment that continues in Scandinavia today.

More interested in working directly for the improvement of Koreans' spiritual, mental, and material well-being than in political work against Japan, Yun was also more positive than many national leaders about women's efforts to emancipate themselves from traditional marriage culture. Familiar with Judge Lindy's companionate theory of marriage, which stressed the importance of sexual fulfillment and compatability, Yun was prepared to give his children considerable choice in their marriage partners.[43] While viewing the condition of many wives as one of slave-like drudgery, Yun was prepared to intervene on behalf of his daughters when they were treated disrespectfully by their husbands, refused to participate in the spread of rumors of sexual misconduct leveled against Kim Hwallan and Pak Indŏk,[44] and resolutely defended Pak Indŏk against attempts to ostracize her for divorcing her husband. His comments on this last case in October 1931 are worth quoting at some length:

What do I think of it? (1) In the first place, I think she has as much right to divorce her husband as hundreds of young men who divorce their wives, many of them, for no other reason than to marry more attractive girls. To pass by these heartless young men uncensured but to revile and say all manner of evil things against P.I.D. [Park Indŏk] is another way of saying "women ought to remain men's slaves for ever." (2) Then again what is it that a man—a Korean man—cannot do or enjoy without divorcing a disagreeable wife? . . . But a woman must be chaste, must bear all the hardships and drudgery of a wife, of a mother, of a sewing woman, of a washer woman, [and] face the danger of being kicked, beaten and dragged about by the hair without anybody to appeal to."[45]

On the other hand, Yun assumed that women, even as doctors and teachers, were to be confined to work among women, and he chimed in with the chorus of men who denounced women's independence as "frivolous" when it was not clearly directed toward furthering the welfare of other women. Busying themselves with other matters was "going off on a tangent."[46] He urged young women to retain the traditional feminine virtues of "modesty, reticence, thoughtfulness, and politeness" and of "reverence, faith, and unselfishness."[47] And when at the commencement ceremonies of Ehwa Women's College in March 1935 the center-left nationalist Yŏ

Unhyŏng (1885–1967) advised the students to discard the old ethics for women, Yun expressed concern that his speech contained "unwise advice to young girls."[48]

Although cautious, Yun Ch'iho was in fact more liberal in his views on female aspirations than many of his nonsocialist peers. In early 1929, the Kŭnuhoe solicited written comments from male national leaders on the organization and their expectations of it. It would be tedious to analyze all the responses, and I will cite only the more thoughtful and representative ones.

Yi Chongnin (1885–1950), a well-known Ch'ŏndogyo leader and Sin'ganhoe officer, described the Kŭnuhoe in prose filled with metaphors from nature as a tender, green shoot that one day would mature and blossom. But remarking on the negative reactions of many men to the Kŭnuhoe, he offered this advice: "Rather than crying 'Liberation, liberation, struggle, struggle,' first strive to fulfil your appropriate duties," for "rights are the wages of responsibilities," and "all complaints and discontentment in human society derive from asserting only one's rights and failing to carry out those duties that lie within one's means." Preparing food and clothing, he continued, are not functions belonging solely to "old women," and making speeches and studying books are not the only functions of the "new women." If women carried out their duties according to their abilities or condition without demanding rights, he concluded, these rights would follow of their own accord even if people deliberately worked to prevent this.[49] It is difficult to imagine how any real change in gender relations could ever ensue from this advice, especially given the fact that, as Yi acknowledged at the beginning of his article, Korean women had fulfilled their duties for centuries with nary a right (in the sense meant here) in sight.

The newspaper editor Song Chinu (1890–1945) opined that the most pressing task was to provide the kind of education for housewives and women in "old-style" households that was required to enlighten them concerning the "modern world."[50] This sentiment was seconded by one Kim Tonghyŏk, who also placed it in the context of the "overall" national movement: Korea was cursed with mass ignorance, and the first priority was to cultivate "real strength" with enlightenment education. The same applied to women, the masses of whom required education as their part in the struggle to eradicate the "feudal" customs of Old Korea.[51] Undeniably, most of the funding and effort behind women's education even by 1929 (when approximately 70, 000 Korean females were in schools) was contributed by Christians.[52]

These male leaders failed to spell out their expectations of the Kŭnuhoe, but the implicit message was that women's movements were to operate alongside or in partnership with male nationalist enterprises. In fact, for many educated nonsocialist women, independence from Japan was a primary concern, and so the same sort of tension existed in their movements as existed in Protestant nationalist movements. Vis-à-vis males' expectations, however, these women were damned if they did not engage in nationalism and damned if they did. A Ch'ŏndogyo leader of the Chosŏn nongminsa (Korean peasant society), Yi Sŏnghwan, attacked the alleged preoccupation of educated women with opportunities for more active participation in national life for the neglect of the vast majority of Korean women.[53] Another male, Yi Siwan, remarked that women's movements needed to face up to the great gulf that education had opened up between the few and the many.[54]

It is small wonder, then, that many nonsocialist women did depoliticize their activities following the Kŭnuhoe's dissolution, as articles in Tonggwang after May 1931 indicate. Their activities, however, addressed issues that were certainly specific to women: factory work, economic independence, clothing, and family. But the gender debate had lost its pointedness; the sense of excitement, urgency, danger even, had dissipated. It became not quite incidental but certainly subordinate to "broader" issues. The December 1931 issue of the cultural-nationalist journal Tonggwang reviewed the year from many angles, one of which was the woman question. "The women's movement," it opened, "is a sectional movement (pumun undong). Therefore the direction its growth and development take is always determined by the general state of the whole movement."[55]

Whatever the complexity of the relationship between the nonsocialist women's movements and nationalism, the socialists were more concerned with their relation to the Government-General, that is, to the forces of imperialism. There was a double sting to their accusation that the "conservatives" indulged in reformism. In the first place, it pointed to the effect of half-measures in diluting women's consciousness of their true, oppressed condition. This, of course, is a standard insight of revolutionary socialist thinking. As William Morris put it so well, "Though making a great many poor people, or even a few, somewhat more comfortable than they are now . . . is not in itself a light good; yet it would be a heavy evil, if it did anything towards dulling the efforts of the whole class of workers towards the winning of a real society of equals."[56]

In the second place, it raised an uncomfortable possibility, especially for nationalist-oriented women, that their programs differed in no important respect from the colonial power's programs, especially in the educational area. There is some substance to this charge. The Japanese monthly journal, *Chōsen ihō*, for example, carried a number of articles between June 1920 and October 1936 on Korean women's "progress" — in labor mobilization, hygiene, clothing, education, textile production, marriage and family customs, and childcare. But the charge that the Government-General's promotion of certain activities concerning women automatically ruled them out was not accepted by the "conservatives," who were not incapable of firing back acerbic retorts. In January 1931 *Pyŏlgŏn'gon* published an article by Chŏng Ch'ilsŏng, a centrist whose initial sympathy for socialism appears to have waned after dissolution of the Kŭnuhoe, in which she accused the socialist group of abandoning meaningful activity altogether: "Those who now find themselves with nothing to do after all their clamor for the dissolution of the Kŭnuhoe are whiling away their time doing knitting. Is *this* the transition to socialism?" (Chŏng employs a pun on characters here, using, instead of the actual Sino-Korean compound for *sahoe* [meaning society or social as in "socialism"], a pair of characters pronounced "sahoe" but meaning "drawing thread.")[57] This brings us to discussion of the relationship between women's issues and socialism in the Kŭnuhoe.

Yi Siwan, a male critic of the nonsocialist group, pointed out that there was an apparent contradiction between the "necessary" socialist principle that all parts of the social organism are affected by the same cause-and-effect relationship and the idea that there is something inherent in the women's question that makes it a special category under the oversight of a separate organization. How, he asked, was one supposed to understand its contribution toward the ideals of the whole of humanity, even if as an interim body?[58] Another male socialist, Pae Sŏngnyong, translator of Bebel's writings on female liberation, provided a revealing metaphor on the relationship between women's liberation and socialist liberation. The two are, he wrote, as inseparable as the warp and woof of a fabric.[59] In practice, this enabled the men, who after all controlled debate, publication, and most activities, to determine the weave of the relationship so that women's issues would serve the overall pattern the men desired.

Socialist women proved susceptible to this pressure. Hŏ Chŏngsuk argued that the woman question was part of a global situation and that its solution was bound up with this general situation. The "correct" socialist position can hardly be said to be clear at any stage of socialist debate. Engels wrote that the monogamous family was an original expression of division of labor systems and private property and that gender inequities grew in tandem with them, but he was ambiguous about whether gender as such or rather economics was the crucial issue.[60] More forthrightly, Plato advocated communal sexual relations, and Christian monks took vows of celibacy out of a sure belief that sexual exclusivity was the door to the concept of private property, not vice versa.[61] Latterly, feminist historiography and anthropology have to some degree dethroned the classical Marxist attribution of structural depth to class and its correlative ambivalence toward feminist politics. It is now impossible not to acknowledge that gender—or the family—is something around which many societies are explicitly arranged or that it can serve as a catalyst for major change.

However, the Korean debate was pursued well before feminism had prompted changes in many Marxists' views on gender. Despite some ambiguity in the Kŭnuhoe manifesto on this point, as mentioned above, in the end Hŏ Chŏngsuk proffered a straightforward materialist analysis of women's status as a dependent feature of the economic organization of society. Before the advent of "civilization," under a system of public ownership, women were equal with men. Their relegation to inferior status and oppression by men developed as a consequence of private ownership and economic diversification. Women's fate was related to the rise of classes through the transfer of ownership rights from feudal landlords to capitalists (women as commodity exchange). Hence the present ferment over women's position was not accidental but a result of historical necessity and must be solved according to this same historical necessity.[62] The influence of Bebel on socialist women's thinking was decisive: the "lecture" in the Kŭnu journal in 1929 by the pseudonymous Tusŏng, for instance, was a paraphrase of Bebel's *Woman and Socialism*.[63]

This construction of the past set the stage on which the Korean women's movement was cast in a supporting role in the overall socialist drama. The feature article of the 1929 issue of *Kǔnu* was written under a pseudonym, presumably by a high-ranking officer of the Kǔnuhoe, who explained the relation in some detail.[64] The Kǔnuhoe was founded, she wrote, for the specific purpose of releasing women from the fetters of the anti-female past and the capitalist present. What then of its relation to the Sin'ganhoe? The existence of a gender-specific body was not legitimate, she answered, in terms of the general principle of unity, but only as "an interim body responding to the special subjective and objective conditions of Korean women and aimed at unifying all levels of the women's movements, including thought, religion, education, church, and so on." It was not to be considered a vanguard movement of an ideological group. Nor, as a movement for the liberation of women, was its meaning to be sought simply in a struggle against Korean men, for "insofar as women, too, are one part of society, it is a necessary fact that they must act in tandem with men in the whole movement."[65]

The socialist literary leader, Yi Kiyŏng (1895–1984), argued energetically that the women's movement should focus on the "broader" aim of socialist revolution. "In a sense," he stated, "we may say that women and laborers share the same destiny. That is, just as in the absence of liberation of the laboring classes one cannot hope for women's liberation either, so without proletarian literature one cannot establish a wholesome women's literature." Simply resisting men in society and in literature was meaningless. Instead, if women joined the proletarian struggle, they would gain considerable strength. The more women writers the better, he said, but they had to be proletarian writers before all else, joining the stream of the "ardent human liberation movement." For the real struggle was not between men and women but between the proletariat and the bourgeoisie.[66] It would be hard to find a clearer dismissal of a feminist gender position.

## Conclusion

It is far from evident, however, that women activists of either persuasion were more than dimly aware of any serious contradiction between their objectives and nationalist or socialist objectives. One can find little explicit discussion of this in the sources. The non-socialists were more apt than socialists to blame the lack of improvement in status and rights on male incorrigibility, which they did often enough. But they rarely questioned the nationalist mode of operations itself: they did not link it with the fact that they had to run the gauntlet of a hostile press whenever they cut their hair, re-formed their dress, or made independent decisions about their work, lifestyle, or marriage status. Logically, they were right not to make such a link, but nationalism forced the link in any case. For as long as women's activities that were not approved as "patriotic" duties were deemed irrelevant, frivolous, or anti-male, not only was the whole "woman question" itself rendered suspect, but those women who did actively support nationalist movements were unable to exert any independent influence on the definition and aims of nationalism such as would, when Korea became independent, favor a reorgani-zation of gender relations in the interests of women.

The nationalist focus on the restoration of political rights to Kore-ans left little opening for activism on behalf of women's social rights. To be sure, when their menfolk lacked meaningful political rights, Korean women could expect them even less, and so the continuation of this situation was hardly to their advantage. However, the vast majority of men in Korea were not seeking to restore political rights but to gain them for the first time: only a very few Korean men—perhaps only 3 percent—had had such rights (or hereditary, aristo-cratic privileges, to be more accurate) before the Japanese annexed Korea in 1910, and not a great many more were in a position to grasp them if the Japanese were to get up and go. Moreover, universal suffrage was rare throughout the world in the 1920s and 1930s and was only just being extended to women in many Western states. Political rights were thus not the most pressing issue for Korean women. Greater social self-determination and reform of gender relations were, however, goals for which they had been striving actively since at least the 1890s.

Socialist women, as we have seen, placed blame for difficulties in gaining social rights on class factors and imperialism, and disap-pointments often led to mutual recriminations. Yet to the historian's eye, it is apparent that the strong, clear position on women's libera-tion articulated in 1920 and again in 1927 was progressively relativ-ized in the course of the nationalist and socialist debates until it be-came a pale, ineffectual image of its former self. The Kŭnuhoe experience, after which much of the women's movement became nonpolitical, or prey to commercial modernity, or implicated in Japanese schemes, was crucial in this development.

Part of the reason undeniably lies in the difficulties the leadership faced in securing support from other women. There was considerable confusion over the nature of the Kŭnuhoe, for example, with debates over whether it was a religious, socialist, educational, enlightenment, or feminist movement, let alone its relation to other women's movements and to nationalism and socialism generally. The Kŭnuhoe was, moreover, grievously short of financial backing. Its only real revenue source was from subscriptions, but even in its third year, only three branches had paid their dues. Consequently, not a single tour of the branches had been possible.[67] Other activities, such as reports on the condition of female labor in the new factories, were likewise hampered by this dire financial situation.[68]

However, although the logic of female liberation had first been published by women such as Na Hyesŏk and Kim Wŏnju in 1920, the terminology used thereafter was in the main formulated by male nationalists in relation to their own aims. On this issue there was certainly some awareness. The silence in the media concerning the Kŭnuhoe was of great concern to its members. The feature article of their journal in 1929 complained that when the media did on occasion speak of the women's movements, its comments were characterized by a dismissive tone and cheap criticism. The only way to interpret the "unscientific, irresponsible, and mostly groundless construction of women's issues," the writer claimed angrily, "is as a deliberate policy of publicity seeking and self-advertising." Since the function of the media was to inform, she continued, why was there so little news of this new movement in Korean society—and why were not women given the opportunity to write concerning their own movements and issues?[69]

Linking women's liberation with nationalist and socialist liberation was perhaps the chief strategy adopted by women to gain recognition for their movements. As noted above, the most accommodating idea at the time was that women's issues were related to the "whole" in the sense that their solution depended on the solution of the "whole." But by accepting this linkage, women activists increasingly surrendered, perhaps unwittingly, their original goal of a new gender arrangement in which women enjoyed self-determination in all personal, social, and, eventually, political relations to core nationalist and socialist priorities. Few males and not many more women took seriously the idea that national change *was* gender change, which would have made perfect sense in Korea and had been hinted at as early as the 1890s. In effect, whatever their desires regarding their own political liberation, in gender relations nationalist and socialist men favored cultural continuity, not real independence, for women. So long as nationalism and socialism focused on an external enemy, the logic of female liberation inherent in the Kŭnuhoe movement was masked and at best served as a handmaiden. Only recently have women's groups in South Korea been able to offer effective resistance to male-centered perspectives on national culture and history.[70]

# EIGHT

# Neither Colonial nor National:
# The Making of the "New Woman" in
# Pak Wansŏ's "Mother's Stake 1"

## Kyeong-Hee Choi

Forgetting, I would even go so far as to say historical error, is a crucial factor in the creation of a nation, which is why progress in historical studies often constitutes a danger for [the principle of] nationality. — Ernest Renan

All nationalisms are gendered, all are invented, and all are dangerous. . . . Nowhere has feminism in its own right been allowed to be more than the maidservant to nationalism. — Anne McClintock

It is only when we do not forget ourselves that we will be able to love others genuinely. It is only in the unforgetfulness of ourselves that women's liberation, freedom, and equality exist, our love will become thorough, the foundation will be laid on which to improve our lives, and the desire for financial independence will arise.

— Na Hyesŏk

## "Disjunct Spaces and Divergent Time-Lines":
## Gender and Colonialism

In his 1994 article "Anxious Nations, Nervous States," Homi K. Bhabha, one of the leading theorists in postcolonial studies, posed a series of far-reaching questions: "What if the nature of historical experience produces tiles that have incommensurable, jagged dimensions? What if different social experiences occupy disjunct spaces and divergent time-lines?" Bhabha continues: "What if the 'big picture' of national culture has always dominated and silenced the anxious, split truths and double destinies of those who are minoritized and marginalized by the inequities of modern society?"[1] For women, Bhabha's critical questioning is not wholly new. In her 1938 work, *Three Guineas*, for instance, Virginia Woolf (1882–1941) addressed her grave concern about the war efforts, identifying them as men's business. Through the voice of a member of what she called the "Outsider's Society," Woolf asked, "What does 'our country' mean to me an outsider?" She replied: "In fact, as a woman, I have no country. As a woman I want no country. As a woman my country is the whole world."[2] On the other side of the world, Xiao Hong (1911–42), a woman writer from Manchuria, addressed a similar concern at the outbreak of the war between Japan and China in 1937. In her essay "Shimian zhi ye (The night of insomnia)," Xiao Hong quarreled with the notion of home in response to the wish of her patriotic lover, Xiao Jun, to take her to his parents' village after their country had been liberated from the Japanese. "As far as I am concerned," she says, "it always comes down to the same thing: either riding a donkey and journeying to an alien place, or staying put in other people's homes. I am never keen on the idea of homeland. Whenever people talk about home I cannot help but be moved, although I know perfectly well that I had become 'homeless' even before the Japanese set foot on that land [Manchuria]."[3] Both Woolf's and Xiao Hong's statements anticipate the increasing consensus of present-day feminist scholars about women's relationship to the nation-state and civil society. In "Identity and Its Discontent: Women and the Nation," Deniz Kandiyoti puts it simply: "The integration of women into modern 'nationhood,' epitomized by citizenship in a sovereign nation-state, somehow follows a *different* trajectory from that of men."[4]

Like many other national groups of women, Korean women have certainly been subject to a disjunctive and differential national identification. For any Korean as well as for any sensitive observer of Koreans and Korean society, it is indisputable that the neo-Confucian principle of gender differentiation summed up in the rubric *nam-nyŏyubyŏl* (distinction of men and women) still permeates the daily lives of the Korean people. Yet the rather obvious truth of this enduring legacy has rarely been acknowledged in scholarly writings about Koreans' experiences of modernity and colonial relations or about the nature of the Korean national subject. To redress this neglect, we need to consider the important role Korea's tradition has played in shaping and conditioning the ways in which Korean men and women experienced the modern or colonial period differently. In the neo-Confucian tradition, Korean women's womanhood was defined only in relation to the other sex: that is, by what they are not. But in the early decades of the twentieth century, women were suddenly invited to become equal members with men in a modern nation-state, a state that failed, however, to materialize under colonial rule. Since then, far from having too little, Korean women perhaps have had too much of the nation. In fact, they have lost their face as women in order to wear the mask of nationality, only to find that in everyday life they must function only as women.[5]

The gendered dimension within colonialism, nationalism, and nation-building projects has been a quintessential object of feminist inquiry in recent postcolonial studies in the West and the rest of the world.[6] In teasing out complex issues of the colonial and the national, scholars have faced the need to tackle questions of modernity and modernization as they study colonial and national experiences.[7] By questioning views that see a linear temporal displacement in the trajectory from tradition to modernity, some have stressed the often false duality between tradition and modernity that permeates discussions of the metropolis and colony as well as nation-building efforts. The instability surrounding the category of modernity itself has been recognized, and tradition has come to be viewed as a highly complex and continuous process of reconstruction carried out in the present.

Amid these discussions, the relationships among nationalism, gender, and the colonial past of Japan and Korea have also begun to draw feminist attention.[8] In the 1990s the study of "Comfort Women," colonized women who were mobilized as sex slaves for the Japanese Imperial Army during World War II, has led to important discussions about the relationship between colonialism and women as well as between patriarchy and the official nationalism of the postcolonial period.[9] What has been little discussed in the debate over women's lives in colonial Korea is the relationships among the colonial, the national, and the modern as experienced by women in their everyday lives before the war, and one of the most neglected areas of study is Korean women's experiences as mothers in colonial Korea.

This chapter examines "Mother's Stake 1," an autobiographical narrative by Pak Wansŏ (1931– ), one of the most renowned contemporary South Korean writers, exploring the intersection of the colonial, the modern, and the maternal as demonstrated in Pak's literary representation of her own mother's as well as her life in colonial Korea. "Mother's Stake 1" addresses what it meant for a traditional Korean mother to modernize her daughter and what it was like for a Korean girl to be modernized during the colonial period by a mother who was neither strictly traditional nor wholly modern.

Pak's representation of her mother in "Mother's Stake 1" shares several characteristics of many female writers' narratives about their mothers, as analyzed by Marianne Hirsch, an American feminist literary critic: "the distancing and objectification of mothers, the nostalgia that surrounds them, the tone of celebration and mystification, and the inverse degradation with which they are shaped."[10] Set in 1930s colonial Korea, Pak's story of her girlhood was not published until 1980, when she was nearly fifty years old. The temporal distance between the daughter-writer's girlhood and her writing seems to be a literary and psychological factor that serves to explain the characteristic qualities of women writers' representation of mothers. What is notable about "Mother's Stake 1" is that the same interval of time enables this writer to look back on the colonial historical context, in which her girlhood was spent, with a scrupulous sense of distance and not to be carried away by any one ideological stance such as nationalism.

In examining Pak's literary analysis of the influence of her mother's mothering in "Mother's Stake 1," I identify both the presence and absence of the colonial experience in the representation of a colonized woman's modern mothering. In this story, the maternal protagonist's mind is characterized as neither colonial nor national. Taking into full account the importance of "disjunct spaces and divergent time-lines" in relation to women's experiences, I investigate the historical forces that seep into the everyday life of Omma (mom) and Na (I; the first-person singular pronoun in Korean), who happen to be colonized women in the Japanese Empire.

## Silence on Colonialism in "Mother's Stake 1"

The "Mother's Stake" trilogy (1980, 1981, 1991) encompasses a remarkable historical spectrum from the colonial period through the Korean War to the contemporary era.[11] The temporal settings of the trilogy's three divisions correspond roughly to the three major phases of South Korea's modern nationhood: Part 1 is set in the period of Japanese colonial rule (1910–45); in Part 2 the memory of the Korean War (1950–53) is drawn into the narrative present, the era of South Korea's much-heralded success as a newly industrialized nation; and Part 3 is set in the time of its writing (early 1990s), when the nation's economy is stable and the division of the nation is seemingly permanent. The temporal progression of the work suggests that it might be read as a modern Korean national epic.

Any attempt to read "Mother's Stake" as a national allegory, however, encounters frustration from the outset. The opening segment, which one might expect to read as a reflection on family life in colonial Korea, is oddly lacking in explicit colonial signification. No Japanese character appears in person, nobody uses the names associated with Korea's colonial past — Chōsenjin (people of Chosŏn) or pando/pandoin (peninsula / people in the peninsula or Korea / Koreans) — and there is no indication in the text of active nationalist struggles or of the ruthless Japanese suppression of them.[12]

Instead of portrayals of the colonial realities of nationalism and racism, most of the narrative is devoted to the trials and tribulations of a single mother and her daughter. Focusing on the year in which Na is six years old, "Mother's Stake 1" consists of a series of vignettes that apparently occur outside the great public events of history: Na's carefree childhood at Grandfather's house in the countryside; Omma's unexpected cutting of Na's long hair; their move to Seoul; Na's preparation for school and Omma's prohibition of Na's learning how to sew; Na's encounter with a local girl who seems to know everything about the female body and their neighborhood; Na's entrance to school "inside the gates," the center of Seoul; her alienation both at school and in the neighborhood; and vacations spent in Grandfather's house. Although participants in Korea's colonial history, neither daughter nor mother in "Mother's Stake 1" has much consciousness of the workings of colonial power; in any event, they do not think nationalistically, or at least in the way that the nationalist assumes every colonized person should. Na's school is the only public sphere in the story and a potential site of colonial confrontation, but even there we read only of Na's preschool days and her first year of primary school, when her political conscious-ness has not been developed; her pressing concerns at school are whether or not she touches her teacher's hand or plays with other children.

Only in the penultimate section of Part 1, in which Pak depicts the life of Na's family during World War II, does it become evident to the reader that Korea is ruled by Japan and that Omma and Na are colonized women in their own land. Here, colonial violence reveals itself in such events as the Japanese monopoly of the rice crop, bru-tally enforced thorough surveillance and policing, and the mobiliza-tion of comfort women. Nonetheless, this violence is experienced secondhand and generates anxiety and terror but no actual physical damage to Na's family. Most notably, this account of colonial vio-lence runs for only five paragraphs. Pak's silence about colonialism is even more striking because most of "Mother's Stake 1" is set around 1938, when, historically, the Japanese colonial regime began resolutely to pursue a policy of forced assimilation.[13]

In her much longer and less fictionalized autobiographical narra-tive, *Kŭ mant'ŏn singa nŭn nuga ta mŏgŏsŭlkka* (Who has eaten up all the *singa*?, 1992), Pak makes it clear that from her entrance to pri-mary school in 1938 on she received all her formal education in Japanese. The first word she learned upon entering school was *hoan-den*, the place in which the Japanese emperor's edicts and words were stored and displayed.[14] "Mother's Stake 1," however, never engages in this kind of explicit colonial reference. The seeming ab-sence of colonial signification in most of the text makes us wonder whether "the pervasiveness and will of Japanese rule" ever suc-ceeded in penetrating the family to which this particular mother-child dyad belonged.[15]

This lack of colonial identification on the part of female characters in "Mother's Stake 1" gives rise to two questions. The first is how relevant the nationalist interpretation is to understanding the lives of traditional and transitional women like Omma. By tracing Omma's relative autonomy in what might be called a New Home building, I show that Omma's identity as a colonial and a national subject is minimal, yet she nevertheless plays an important role in subjecting her daughter to colonial cultural forces. The second question, which I pursue through the daughter's narrative, is whether Pak's critique of modernity, in terms of the making of the *sinyŏsŏng* (New Woman), is also a critique of the shaping of the "New Korea" under colonial rule and, if so, in what ways. I argue that the relative autonomy observed in Omma's maternal space is not stable at all. In fact, I suggest that the narrative of Na's tension and struggle with Omma as the mother imposes the ideal of New Womanhood on the daughter embodies certain quintessential aspects of the logic and contradiction of colonial modernization imposed upon Korea as a nation.

## A Portrait of the Artist as a
## Little Girl: The Plot

"Mother's Stake 1" starts *in medias res* with a description of the author herself as a six-year-old girl trudging up the last hill to a train station. Leaving her birthplace of Pakchŏk, a small village in the country, Na is being taken to Seoul for her primary school education. The idea of sending a girl to Seoul for schooling, practically unimaginable to her rural but high-class grandparents, arises from her mother's unusual boldness. In the opening scene, Na's hands are literally and symbolically held on either side by her mother and grandmother as she is led onward and upward. Halmŏni (grandmother) initially does not approve of Omma's ambition for Na's education, but she crucially assists her daughter-in-law not only by taking the resisting Na by the hand to the train station but also by inducing her granddaughter to separate herself psychologically from her ties to her hometown. The opening of the narrative thus enacts the march of three generations of women in the Pak family toward the modernization of the youngest.

A flashback reveals that since the death of her husband Omma has been determined to take her children, Na and Oppa (older brother), to Seoul for a proper education. The mother has already started a journey away from traditional ways of life—away from superstition, ignorance, and domestic duties as the eldest daughter-in-law—by taking her son to Seoul and devoting herself to his "success" there, leaving Na, for the time being, in the care of the grandparents. Returning to the novelistic present, she has now returned to Pakchŏk Village to take her daughter with her as well, declaring that "girls should learn, too."[16] This declaration is followed by a concrete, deliberate measure, which overcomes both the parents-in-law's objections and Na's resistance to her mother's determination to take her to Seoul. One morning, as Na sits waiting for Omma to comb her long hair into braids, the mother suddenly cuts off most of Na's hair and fashions it into a bob, a sign of modernity. Na is forced to give in to her mother's will and finally bids farewell to her grandmother in the station, stepping aboard the train for Seoul.

In the train Omma fills Na's head with fantastic expectations about city life, but Na is jolted out of her fantasies at the first sight of her mother's residence at Hyŏnjŏ-dong. The shabby rented room that her mother and older brother share lies not in the heart of Seoul but on the outskirts. Omma ekes out a living by sewing for professional female entertainers (kisaeng), the lowest class of people. For the sake of her aspirations concerning her children, Omma endures poverty and social degradation.

Omma's ambition is to make her daughter a New Woman, the ideal modern image for women in the early decades of twentieth-century Korea.[17] In the train carrying the two to Seoul, Na asks two urgent questions about Omma's dream: What is a New Woman? and What does she do? Omma, however, can only explain what a New Woman looks like but *not* what she is or what she does. Pretending "to know something which she actually didn't" (188), she defines the New Woman as a woman with limitless freedom and knowledge: according to Omma, a New Woman is "a woman who studies so much that she is knowledgeable about everything, and can do freely whatever she sets her heart on" (188, 149).[18] This episode simultaneously reveals Omma's vicarious excitement over the prospect of Na's future and her inadequacy as the engineer of her daughter's achievement of New Womanhood.

Learning is the vehicle Omma has chosen for making her daughter a New Woman. In its name, Na is initially confined to her mother's room to learn the alphabet, prior to entering primary school. Omma's vigilance, however, fails to prevent Na's exposure to the outside world, a world inhabited by those Omma views as "people too lowly and worthless for our acquaintance" (206). In this neighboring world of "the lowlies," Na meets the Welder's Daughter, the most important agent for her widening knowledge about the surrounding reality. Upon discovering that her daughter has been associating with "the lowlies," Omma sends Na to a school "inside the gates" of Seoul, the center of modernity, by fabricating a residential record. At the school inside the gates, Na suffers as an outsider. Yet when she returns to her neighborhood outside the gates, the neighborhood children also treat her as an outsider. Her isolation and loneliness deepens, increasingly disenchanting her with her mother's ideal of the New Woman. At this point, the narrator intrudes to analyze the relationship between her mother and her ideal: Omma's devotion to the ideal stems from her own sense of deprivation; the sacrifices the mother makes for her daughter's "modern" education is a way of attaining vicarious fulfillment. While awaiting the accomplishment of her ideal, the mother supplies such modern commodities as a Western dress and ice skates to make her daughter what might be called a New Girl.

As the Japanese war effort intensifies, sheer survival becomes an issue. Omma takes dangerous trips to the countryside to obtain rice for her children and even faces the possibility of Na's conscription as a comfort woman. Toward the end of the war, Omma has to move back to her parents-in-law's house, not because she has exhausted her physical, emotional, and economic resources but because the Japanese colonial government has issued a wartime eviction order. The story ends with the author's critical reflections on her mother's ideal of New Womanhood: how pretentious the project was and, nonetheless, how integral in shaping her life.

## Colonial Coding and New Womanhood

Given the predominance of apparently "ordinary" and trivial subject matter in the text, it is perhaps not surprising that critics of Pak's work so far have taken little notice of the context of Japanese colonialism in "Mother's Stake 1." In the work's most detailed textual study to date, Kang Insuk, who examines the urban life and modernity represented in the piece, refers to Seoul simply as "prewar Seoul" — the war in this case is the Korean War — rather than as colonial Seoul and never discusses the reality of colonialism.[19] Even more notable is the fact that Part 1 has received little attention as a separate narrative in Pak's well-known autobiographical trilogy.[20] Although emerging feminist critics have recognized the importance of Pak's rendering of the mother-daughter relationship here, no critical writings have studied the colonial coding in "Mother's Stake 1."[21] The critical elision of colonial issues in "Mother's Stake 1," however, can be attributed to the implicit nature of the text's colonial coding and its explicit preoccupation with the mother's and daughter's involvement in female modernity.

Omma's New Woman project as represented in "Mother's Stake 1" is a belated expression of the historical New Woman movement of the 1920s and early 1930s; belated not merely because this maternal project started more than a decade later, but also because by 1938, when she began it, the ideal had lost its radical edge as a movement and been transformed into a commercial fad. Pak's narrative about her mother's obsession with New Womanhood indicates that this model had been known and spread at the grassroots level as it underwent changes in political implications.

The failure of critics to recognize the literary and cultural significance of the representation of New Womanhood in "Mother's Stake 1" is not just an accidental and isolated instance of critical negligence. This lacuna echoes within a larger silence in the historiographical canon regarding Korean women's modern and colonial experience as women. In my view, this silence is deeply related to the premature closure of the New Woman debates during the last decade of the colonial period and the subsequent subsumption of feminist discourse into the nationalist and socialist discourse in the post-independence era.[22] While a nationalist perspective has dominated the study of Korean history, literature, and culture, the post-liberation study of the New Woman movement has been notably scanty. The few studies largely stress the bourgeois nature of the culture of New Women and their failure to provide a full-scale feminist collective movement for the majority of Korean women.[23] Alternatively, they focus on the colonial co-optation of New Woman figures into the war mobilization effort.[24] Meanwhile, little has been written about how New Womanhood was received and internalized by ordinary Koreans, a process at work in Pak's excellent portrayal of her mother in "Mother's Stake 1."

What gives Pak's story not only psychological depth but also historical breadth is the division and merging between the maternal and daughterly narratives. Although the two narratives are interwoven, it is useful to keep the maternal and the daughterly analytically separate. My proposed reading of the modern and colonial codings within "Mother's Stake 1" rests on this interplay between these discursive layers. The key to understanding the two narratives in this story is the merging of the two women's modernization in the New Woman project. This interdependence manifests itself in the splitting of the subject and the object of modernizations: the mother performs as the subject imposing modernization on her daughter, and the daughter, the object of modernization, gradually comes to terms with her own modernization as a subject.

While focusing on the thoughts and feelings of the six-year-old Na, the narrative is substantially infused by the perspective of the middle-aged authorial narrator. Within this daughterly narrative, Na's separation from her mother effects an internal critique of Omma's mothering. The middle-aged narrator enunciates in the narrative present what she, as a growing girl, failed to or was not ready to articulate or express in the past. Distinctively, in "Mother's Stake 1" this narration is not marked by what Brenda O. Daly and Maureen T. Reddy call "daughter-centricity," a tendency many feminist critics in the West have observed within women's autobiographical and fictional writings.[25] Rather, although Omma's experience and words are filtered through Na's observations, the central daughterly perspective is balanced by an equivalent mother-centricity of the narrated events. The reader both sees the effects on the daughter of Omma's mothering, toward which Pak adopts a highly critical stance, and comes to understand the motives behind the mother's strivings toward modernity and a presentation of them as seen from her own perspective.

To be sure, Omma and Na live under the same roof and are intensely involved in the same project of making a New Woman, but they occupy different time-lines. Roughly speaking, Omma largely resides in a prenational or precolonial space, whereas Na increasingly enters a colonial space. This mother-daughter relationship leads to tensions, frustration, and psychological wounds because they have different points of departure and goals on their path to female modernization. Although the New Woman project in "Mother's Stake 1" is surely subject to colonial and national coding, a reading that I will undertake later, I would argue that, prior to any examination of its possible connection to national or colonial issues, it first needs to be understood in terms of gender, particularly in the terms of different phases of female modernization.

At the core of Pak's study of modernity and coloniality is the theme of the pursuit of self-knowledge, self-affirmation, and self-reclamation. This theme is precisely one that Korea's pioneering New Women such as Na Hyesŏk (1896–1946) called for, as is shown in the epigraph of this chapter. Korea's New Women writers emphasized the act of affirming one's own *female* self, a self discriminated against under the neo-Confucian Law of the Father. As part of this critical tradition, "Mother's Stake 1" evokes the importance of gendered and sexual identity in the making of Na's modern subjectivity.

## Omma's New Motherhood and
## New Home Building

Omma's New Woman project is part of her larger attempt to make a New Home, in which a new kind of mothering takes place. This traditional woman sets herself the goal of forming her daughter into her ideal New Woman and her son into a New Man. Through the New Woman project, both Omma and Na enter the time of the modern: as Omma pursues the ideal of the New Woman through her daughter, Na is made into a New Girl, who differs from a traditional girl—by, to begin with, attending a modern school. At the same time, Omma also becomes a new kind of mother, one who resists the traditional patriarchal law, the native Law of the Father.

Crucial to Omma's New Home building is the absence of the father, both literally and metaphorically. Father's sudden death when Na is little is a blow to the family name, for he was to be the next head of the extended household.[26] Subsequently, and symbolically, Grandfather is left semiparalyzed by a stroke and secludes himself in his own room. Although Father's illness and Grandfather's partial paralysis are not linked directly with larger political events, the crisis of the male order within this family is symptomatic of the crisis and transformation of the traditional *yangban* (upper-class) rule of the literati. Behind the weakening of the patriarchal authority of this family is a larger restructuring of the class system under colonial rule and increasing modernization.

One of the foremost factors in the crisis of the *yangban* patriarchal order is the shift from sinocentric to Western-oriented order of power and knowledge, something that Omma quickly grasps in her search for a new future for her family after her husband's death. Father's illness and death proves to her that the "old" system of knowledge and technology is unreliable. The healing methods used in vain to cure Father were comprehensive: the traditional medicine man's acupuncture and herbal medicine, Grandmother's folk medicine, Grandfather's Chinese pills, and Grandmother's final resort to a shaman for divination and a healing ritual. After his death, while the others superstitiously attribute Father's death to the disturbance of the spirit of the land, Omma nourishes her dream of "an exodus to the city" (178), believing that she has lost her husband to the backwardness of country people and the tradition of the countryside. She is certain that Father's life could have been saved had he undergone surgery by a doctor of Western medicine in the city.

Na sees her grandfather's house prior to her father's death as "a paradise" (176). Enclosed by his favorite flowers, symbolically named "the *t'ojong* [native] chrysanthemum shrubs" (177, 140; italics added), Grandfather's house in Pakchŏk Village represents the landed establishment of the ruling class of the previous dynasty. Characteristically marked by spaciousness, affluence, nature, and high traditional culture, Grandfather's house represents the precolonial space untouched by intrusive modern, colonial forces.[27] In this indigenous space, Grandfather's voice embodies the Old Name / Law of the Father in the precolonial order, repeating by heart Chinese poems, "which had been all the more clear during the blooming season of those chrysanthemums" (177).

Father's death deals a blow to the way things are, causing the drastic weakening of Grandfather's power, both physical and symbolic. By the time Na heads off to Seoul to study the New Learning (*sinhangmun*, or modern Western learning), Grandfather's loud recitation of Chinese poems had since ceased, to be replaced by his intermittent rasping and silence. Once an active man, he now secludes himself in his own room. In an implied concession to the "New Learning," Grandfather no longer opposes Na's journey to Seoul but rather silently tries to be supportive. Startled by her husband's unexpected behavior, Grandmother expresses her surprise by saying "He's all but dead! All but dead!" (182, 144).

Whereas Father's physical death and Grandfather's symbolic death mean the loss of paradise for Na, for Omma they open a path toward independence and autonomy as a mother. Omma's Law of the Mother is established in the interregnum, during which the Old Law of the Father is dying or dead and the New Law of the Father is yet to be born. She takes the crisis caused by her husband's death not as reason for despair but as an opportunity to be met with strength and affirmation: she decides to "make all things new," in the words of the modernists. Omma's modernity as a New Mother resides in her decision to create a new basis of patriarchal authority within the family by educating her son in the New Learning rather than in Grandfather's Old Learning. Even before the obligatory three-year mourning period for her husband is over, Omma "left home in dignity, holding only the hand of her young son" (178). Omma's determination is crucially forged by "the rumors about civilization" she heard from relatives before her marriage—rumors that cultural hegemony was shifting from China to the West. Pak's depiction of Omma's maternal project even suggests the possibility that the colonial crisis of the nation, which unavoidably led to a crisis for Korean males and particularly threatened the rule of Korean male elites, may have affected some Korean women differently, even benefiting them at a certain stage of colonial rule.[28]

Omma's modern move does not imply the abolition of patriarchal authority within her family. On the contrary, she decides after her husband's death to commit herself fully to her son, the patriarch-to-be. The main purpose of Omma's urban migration is social and economic mobility, which she believes can be achieved by getting her son a Western education, which might then secure for the family a house inside the gates of Seoul. Omma is the catalyst in transforming the class status of her family, acting as the mother of the next head of the family. The ultimate goal of Omma's sacrificial devotion to her son is the family's integration into what she considers to be the ruling class in a modern urban society; her strong desire for having a "house inside the gates of Seoul" signifies a desire for higher social status. And yet the process requires a replacement of traditional patriarchy with a modern one. Omma's decision that her son's learning should differ from that of Grandfather anticipates a certain modernization of patriarchy. According to Carole Pateman, the transition from the traditional to the modern world can be explained as "a change from a traditional (paternal) form of patriarchy to a new *specifically modern* (or *fraternal*) form: patriarchal civil society"—what Juliet Flower MacCannell in a similar context calls "the regime of the brother."[29] The new family to be established in Seoul will be marked by this modern patriarchy, a "regime of the brother." In fact, after Father's death Oppa (older brother) assumes the responsibility for reviving the family's name.

Omma's devotion to Oppa is thus instrumental to this transition from the paternal to the fraternal form of patriarchy, helping what appears to be an ultimately conservative move. Yet it also allows a totally new possibility for Omma: her service in strengthening the Name-of-the-Father in the family is precisely what makes it possible for her to embark upon a journey to modernity. The account of Omma's exodus shows that the pretext of giving the future head of the family a modern schooling frees her from her duties as the eldest daughter-in-law and allows her fully to become a mother.

A woman's complete absorption into motherhood has been often viewed as negative and debilitating for the mother herself. In Omma's case, however, the condensation of her identity into "mother" paradoxically coincides with, and aids, her liberation from the intergenerational legislation of her duties by other members of the family. Although set in the colonial period and amply describing the difficulties that Omma has to confront — which I have no intention to underestimate — "Mother's Stake 1" is optimistic and positive in tone. Significantly, the maternal narrative in the story enacts the theme of liberation rather than of subjugation — by liberation, that is, from the custom of *sijipsari* or patrilocal residence. This process of entering the husband's parents' household requires that the woman shed her identities as daughter, sister, and grand-daughter and assume new roles and identities as wife, daughter-in-law, sister-in-law, and aunt-in-law. *Sijipsari* also involves the wife's complete subjection to her superiors' authority. In the text, it is only after Omma leaves her parents-in-law's house and establishes her own nuclear family that the maternal role becomes her primary identity.[30]

If Omma's "first exodus" marks her birth as a "New Mother," her second exodus with her daughter, which opens "Mother's Stake 1," constitutes a truly modern moment, not only for the mother, but also for the whole family: it completes the disintegration of Grandfather's extended family in the country and the formation of Omma's nuclear family in Seoul. Omma's New Mothering is characterized by iconoclastic behavior for her times. She abandons her *yangban* lifestyle as well as any claims to property and then voluntarily becomes a manual laborer. The mother endures not only poverty but also social degradation, since she sews for *kisaeng*, professional female entertainers who are considered to occupy the lowest stratum in the social hierarchy. By doing so, however, she secures a certain amount of financial independence, which is indeed the foremost condition for her independent mothering.

The first house the family owns in Seoul has a "triangular yard" (214), which symbolically exteriorizes the triangular nuclear family. Omma's words of triumph, "Finally, I have placed a stake in Seoul," are followed by Na's observation that "the house was very tiny, with six tiny rooms, but we had everything" (214). The family's feelings toward this house can metaphorically be extended to express Omma's feelings of pride and plenitude. While the mother earns the money, playing the role of breadwinner, Oppa, who is eight years older than Na, assumes the roles of both surrogate father for Na and surrogate husband for Omma. Ironically, in the absence of the father, Omma comes to have an ideal partner, a modern man, for building her own home. Between mother and son, in the absence of the father, there exists an unusual degree of intimacy and mutual respect.[31] Raised jointly by Omma and Oppa, Na undergoes her second infancy—this time a cultural one—in the new independent family.

In the early decades of colonial Korea, the idea of public education for young girls signaled a radically new culture for females. Until the late nineteenth century, Korean women learned from their mothers—or maternal figures such as aunts, grandmothers, or sisters—within the private, female sphere. After the turn of the century, however, the need for girls' schooling was emphasized, and what had been normative womanhood was categorized as Old Womanhood (*kuyŏsŏng*), against the image of the New Woman. In Pak's story, Omma's decision to make her daughter different from herself implicates a shift in role models for Na. The ideal figures for Na are no longer a traditional woman like Omma or Grandmother but rather Oppa, the figure of a modern man, and ultimately, the first-grade teacher at her school, a New Woman who has versatile knowledge and a modern female appearance.

In fact, the most radical aspect of Omma's New Motherhood is her active support of her young daughter's education, not just her son's. Omma's granting of equal educational opportunity to her daughter not only promotes an antitraditional principle of gender equality, but also recognizes female individualism. "Look! Giving schooling to a girl is not like giving schooling to a son" (212, 168), Omma says to Na. She continues: "It's just for your own good, not for the family. When your brother succeeds, our family will enjoy the fruits of his success. But when you study hard and become a New Woman, it's only for your own good. Do you understand?" (212). Omma's intense desire for her girl's education comes from her "vengeful rancor and longing for knowledge and freedom" (212, 168). At the core of Omma's maternal efforts resides her proto-feminist complaint against precolonial patriarchy, which had deprived women of knowledge and freedom for hundred of years.[32] Although presented as being solely for Na's future interests, the New Womanhood is Omma's own fantasy. As she supports her daughter's realization of New Womanhood, Omma's desire for modernity is vicariously fulfilled.

In mothering her daughter toward New Womanhood, Omma moves from the past through the present to the future. First, Omma relives and reprocesses her past, haunted by her repressed desire for knowledge and freedom, in the very act of negating it through her zeal for her daughter's education. At the same time she lives in the present and partakes of modernity by becoming a consumer in the middle-class urban culture emerging in colonial Korea. In order to make her daughter a proper Seoulite, for instance, Omma visits a department store in the center of Seoul to have a close look at Western clothes; being a seamstress by vocation, she then reproduces them for her daughter. When she sends her daughter to Pakchŏk Village to spend her vacation, she provides a pair of skates to create an impression that her daughter is a real Seoulite. Even as Omma equips her daughter's body with these visible signs of Western modernity, she tries to cram Na's mind with knowledge about urban landscapes by taking her to a zoo and by showing her around the city in a streetcar. The new urban culture that she imitates and inscribes on the surface of her daughter's body and mind is something she herself would never have experienced on her own. Indeed, Omma's New Motherhood is what enables her to taste this culture of modernity: for her, Na is a channel leading to the public, urban space as well as to modernity. While replaying her past as she denies it, she appropriates the new opportunities for women and lives anticipating a future in which her daughter will become the subject of freedom and knowledge.

Omma launches her project of making a modern home at a time when nationalist elites, mostly male, are excluded from public offices under colonial rule. In Omma's prime, modernization and colonialism were happening simultaneously. Yet, she develops little sense of being a colonized woman. To understand both Omma's lack of political awareness and the modern nature of her maternal devotion, one has to consider the profound impact of the traditional division between the female and male spheres, which kept colonialism from having much effect on Omma's private sphere.

Japanese colonialism in Korea did not erase but rather reinforced indigenous patriarchal authority within the family; the colonial government implemented various administrative measures such as *hojuje* (literally, the household-master system) for more efficient rule. Not originally derived from Korean tradition, *hojuje* was imposed on Korean family law in 1909 on the eve of annexation. The Japanese used this system as "a way to take control of the existing Confucian social patriarchy in Korea along with the traditional land-based economy."[33] A product of the traditional female, inner, and private space, Omma rarely enters the space that is colonially conditioned; despite her formal identity, she does not perceive her times as the colonial era. For her, the "new" does not translate into the "colonial." In this respect, she lives in a unique temporal state: she is able to escape traditional time and enters into modernity, and yet her entrance into the colonial order is relatively delayed. In this state, Omma's pursuit of the new, the modern, and the foreign is derived largely from her class and gender positions, as she performs her identity as an upper-class female and mother. Her disposition to appropriate the new is reinforced by her anxiety about her insecure position, not only as a single mother, but also as a member of the declining *yangban* class. For her, the struggle for modernity comes down to a struggle for pride, making her adhere more avidly to upward mobility and class distinctions. As Omma struggles in her adverse living conditions to make a brave new world her own, however, the precolonial neo-Confucian ideologies of class and sexuality generally continue to exist and are even reinforced.

So far, I have read "Mother's Stake 1" from the perspective of the mother's emergence as a New Mother, arguing that her New Woman project should be understood in the context of what might be called her New Home project. Seen from Omma's standpoint, her New Woman project is a proto-feminist transgression—"proto-" in the sense that she is not politically conscious—that aims to rescue her daughter from possible imprisonment within the inner section of the house, *anch'ae* (the female sphere). In order to achieve this purpose, Omma moves from the countryside to the city and struggles to enter the center of Seoul, at that time called the "area inside the gates" (*munan*). Her maternal project metonymically involves the act of opening various doors for her daughter, doors that were not open to traditional girls, especially those from the country: the front door (*taemun*) as well as the middle door (*chungmun*) of Grandfather's house; the four gates of Seoul (*sadaemun*) leading into its center; and, ultimately, the gate of the school (*kyomun*), the site of forbidden fruit for women. Omma does her utmost to transform Na from someone restricted to the private sphere into an occupant of the center of civilization.

## The New Woman Project and Colonial Modernity

But what if the area inside the gates, which Omma views as the heart of Enlightenment, is the heart of colonial darkness? What if the place in which the cultivation of the mind occurs is a locus of the colonization of the mind? What if Na's schooling inside the gates is simply a shortcut to her colonial subjecthood? The problem is that in a colonial situation, the "new" in the notion of the New Womanhood is inseparable from the colonial. Not being fully aware of the colonial implication of her modern ideal, Omma ends up pushing her daughter into the colonial order.

Omma's preoccupation with the area "inside the gates" of Seoul resonates curiously with the Japanese colonialist distinction between the imperial metropolis and the periphery of the Empire: that is, the *Naichi* ("inner land"; i.e., Japan), and the *Gaichi* ("outer land"; i.e., Japan's colonies).[34] Korea was the most important portion of Japan's outer land. In this colonial mapping, Hyŏnjŏ-dong, where Na's family resides is a microcosm of urban colonial Korea, which is denied the benefits of the culture of the colonial center. Described by Omma as being "not the real Seoul" (192), the family's residence is located in a "dirty and messy" area in which the urban poor live along squalid paths in crowded, boxy, makeshift houses that seem to "spit out dirty entrails" and "endless brawls" (191, 151). Considering this new world as low and backward, just as she did their hometown in the countryside, this self-determining mother tries to rescue Na from their immediate world and transplant her inside of the gates. The modern culture inside the gates of Seoul was, however, a colonial mimicry of the culture of Tokyo, the center of *naichi*. In the colonial space, the culture inside the gates of Seoul is a center not just of modernity but of *colonial* modernity — as Na experiences it. Hence, it is important to examine how Omma's ideal of New Womanhood is marked by *colonial* modernity, however subtly it may be.

Na first hears about the ideal of New Woman while her mother cuts her hair to fashion it into a bob. Later, Na hears more on the train heading for Seoul. The train runs "at a terrible speed" (189), heralding Na's imminent accelerated modernization. In this symbolically charged space, Na asks her mother: "What's a New Woman?" Omma replies: "You can't become a New Woman just by living in Seoul. You must study a lot. When you become one, you won't have your hairdo like mine, *tchok*, but will have *hisashikami*. You'll wear a short skirt and high-heeled shoes, showing your legs, and will carry a *handobaku*" (187–88, 148). For Omma, modernity is a matter of fashion as well as knowledge.[35] Among various elements of the New Woman appearance, Omma then makes special efforts to explain the *hisashikami* and the *handobaku* to Na, assuming, correctly, that, because both names are Japanese, her daughter is "completely ignorant of" them (188, 148). The *hisashikami*, a half-modernized hairstyle, is a direct cultural import from Japan, and the *handobaku*, the handbag, is a Western product imported through Japan.

Language, scripts, and external cultural markings such as fashion are pivotal to understanding the colonial relationship between the Japanese and the Koreans, given that the differences between them are far less biologically marked than those between whites and other races. Women's hairstyle and clothing at first glance appear to be incidental and insignificant, and yet they are crucial for studying Korean women's relationship to modernity and colonialism. In the text, the word *handobaku*, a Japanese pronunciation of "handbag," brings into view the way in which Korea is exposed to Western and transnational culture through its colonizer, Japan. Furthermore, Omma's stress on the *hisashikami* and the *handobaku* reveals the process by which these foreign cultural products and their Japanese names emerge as proper objects of knowledge necessary for Na's New Womanhood.

Omma's description of the look of the New Woman helps us understand her relationship to this ideal. The appearance of the modern woman is articulated in terms of what her own appearance is *not*: neither high heels nor *handobaku* are part of Omma's apparel. Rather than skirts exposing a woman's calf, Omma wears skirts that completely cover her legs; the *hisashikami*, a short hair style, would obliterate the markings of marital status, which Omma's chignon, *tchok*—with its long hairpin—serves to signify. In this regard, Omma's stress on the foreign items and their names gains added importance because her explanation neglects the single traditional Korean element in what is known as the New Woman's apparel: that is, the *chŏgori* (Korean indigenous blouse). That Omma takes no notice of this familiar item while expressing her excitement about the new items such as short hair, handbags, and high heels is emblematic of the process of cultural selection in her making of New Womanhood.

If clothing is a form of language written on the surface of the body, then traditional Korean female clothing inscribes confinement, concealment, and constriction.[36] The New Woman's clothing styles and hairdo, in contrast, tended to remove the visible signs of marriage and promoted more physical mobility and exposure. Underlying Omma's enthusiasm about the New Woman is the spirit of freedom and convenience that characterized the reforms of Korean female clothing in the early decades of the twentieth century.[37] For Omma, national identity is not national subjectivity, and hence what she notices about New Woman's apparel is the new and liberating as opposed to the old and familiar. She sees neither the national distinctions nor the colonial contradictions.

Given the complex coloniality of the ruling culture, however, the demand for visible signs of female modernity entails a certain degree of colonization of the mind. For Na, studying at school means learning how to read and write in Japanese—that is, in the colonizer's language, although she is now fully conscious of the colonial relationship between Japan and Korea. Na's admittance to an elementary school (*kungmin hakkyŏ*) places her on the path of the imperial policy of assimilation.[38] Her studies include copying *kana* (the Japanese syllabary) and Chinese characters (ultimately to be used as *kanji*, the Chinese portion of the Japanese script) as well as arabic numerals. In contrast, the Korean vernacular script is excluded from the curriculum.

Na's female modernization is complicated by her forced dissociation from traditional womanhood combined with her gradual entrance into colonial space. Unconsciously, Omma becomes deeply implicated in the colonial power structure as she persistently indoctrinates Na with the importance of studying for school. For Omma, it is an act of liberation for a woman to study. For Na, however, *what* to study is as important as whether to study. Na is already literate in *han'gŭl* when she begins studying the Japanese script. Traditionally regarded as appropriate only for women and for the lower classes, the Korean vernacular script had never been used as an official script since its promulgation in 1446. Only toward the end of the nineteenth century did newspapers begin to be published in it. Omma's staunchly traditional bent leads her to completely ignore this script for Na. Despite her literacy in *han'gŭl*, Na is not encouraged to express herself through the script she knows. Here again, the class and gender hierarchy of precolonial, premodern society wields power over Omma's mind, reinforcing the suppression of Korean vernacular script under the colonial system. Symptomatic of its degraded status, throughout the story it is called *ŏnmun*, an old name meaning *"vulgar* script," not *han'gŭl*, a name bestowed and used by nationalist intellectuals during the colonial era. Since Omma's promotion of the new knowledge is accompanied by suppression of knowledge about the old and familiar and about one's own self in the present, the daughterly narrative increasingly makes it clear that there are two main areas of knowledge suppressed under Omma's New Woman project—knowledge about the female sexual body, the object of patriarchal suppression, and knowledge about the national body, the object of colonial suppression—that can be crucial to the shaping of one's self-knowledge.

In her journey in modernity, Na is primarily concerned with the self-expression and self-determination that she lacks, and from the beginning of her journey in the center of modernity, she presents herself mostly as a resisting subject. The source of her resistance is her vivid memory of the freedom she enjoyed—as an Old Girl—in the countryside as well as her knowledge of the indigenous tradition alive there. In the mother's eyes, New Womanhood is a symbol of freedom, and her six-year-old daughter is a tabula rasa on which her New Woman ideal can be written. However, the paradox within Omma's pursuit of her daughter's New Womanhood is that her mothering totally contradicts the principle of self-determination, which is essential to this modern ideal. Na perceives the ideal as "a noose" (179, 141), which is "set by Omma in complicity with the city" (182, 143). Omma's and Na's positions on modern womanhood are in striking contrast, the mother being coercive and self-righteous and the daughter ambivalent and resisting. By juxtaposing Omma's forward coercive step with Na's responsive resisting backward step,

Pak shows us the risk in Omma's self-determination at the expense of Na's self-determination.

From early on, Na complains about the intervention of powerful adults who deprive her of the right to decide her own destiny. When Omma returns home to take Na to Seoul, Omma and Grandmother constantly quarrel, for Grandmother does not want to send her granddaughter away. As Na comments, however, "neither of them had asked me where I wanted to live" (176). In a curious way, Na's relationship with her mother as the object of forced modernization tangentially, though not fully, mirrors the Koreans' status as colonized people under Japan. In the larger political picture, the "West 'taught' Japan. Japan in time was to 'teach' the rest of Asia," as Masao Miyoshi succinctly puts it.[39] Unlike Japan, Omma is never fully integrated into the modern world, except vicariously. This marks the crucial difference between Japan and Omma: the latter is not in a position to "teach." The fundamental problem is that Omma has no substantive idea about what the New Woman is or what she does.

Na's recurrent criticism of Omma centers on the latter's ignorance: ignorance of the specifics of the New Woman ideal on the one hand and ignorance of the psychological pain and emotional lack that Na suffers on the other. Although an absolute, utopian quality shines through Omma's definition of the New Woman, the faltering and hesitant manner with which she tries to mentor her daughter proves to Na, as well as to the reader, that Omma does not fully grasp her ideal. By insisting on the superiority of the culture inside the gates, however, Omma, in fact, ironically undermines her own authority as the guardian of her daughter. At the same time, having never experienced modern schooling and thus the process of modernization, Omma's understanding of its psychological cost is extremely limited. Omma, a traditional woman who has spent her whole life under strict patriarchal restrictions, cannot comprehend the very different frustrations experienced by Na, whose freedom has never been restricted by gender discrimination.

Thus, Na's seemingly childish complaint about Omma's blind imposition of modern ideals blends seamlessly into the author's mature critique of scrambling after the appearance of modernity at the expense of actually understanding what is at stake psychologically and physically for a child. The critique in "Mother's Stake 1," however, does not reject modernization *per se* but critically interrogates on whose terms and for whose sake modernization is pursued, asking who pays the price for its so-called benefits. Although Na is made to live through a temporality different from that of her mother, her New Girlhood (and later New Womanhood) is not just hers but her mother's as well. In fact, the two women's projects of modernity are interdependent: imposing the New Woman project on Na is itself the form of her mother's vicarious modernization. Indeed, the daughterly narrative closely examines the psychological price the daughter has to pay in order to pursue her mother's modern aspirations. One may suspect that the daughter will experience complicated problems on her way to modernity because she carries her mother's ideal. In the end, Na comes to realize that "Whether knowingly or unknowingly Omma used her children to ease the contrast between her unattained utopia and the actual reality she faces. But she was fairly ignorant of what kinds of conflicts her children underwent" (215, 170).

The juxtaposition of the maternal and the daughterly perspectives in "Mother's Stake 1" allows us to see that at the initial phase of the modern project Omma benefits more from the making of Na's New Girlhood than does this New Girl herself. Omma's pursuit of her fantasy through her maternal function helps us understand why mothering may be so attractive to a woman who has few viable options for her own self-fulfillment in making a transition to the modern. The daughterly narrative yields the unsettling insight that through her mothering a mother unwittingly pursues her own goals, and inflicts unintended violence on her child in the name of love.

## The Incomplete New Woman Project
## and Colonial Conditioning

As suggested above, Omma's agency in modernizing her daughter's womanhood roughly doubles Japan's position in modernizing Korea. But in Pak's depiction of the last phase of Japanese colonial rule, the analogy between the colonial and the maternal loses its relevance. The text makes clear that in the last years of the colonial era the ultimate agency determining the direction of New Womanhood is neither Omma, the mother outside the gates, nor even the teacher, the new mother inside the gates, but rather the imperial government in Japan.

Revealing for the first time how directly Omma's life is subject to Japanese colonial rule, this penultimate part of the narrative integrates Omma's private life into public historical events. For the purpose of this discussion, the most important threat posed by the colonizer's agency is its power to undo what Omma has been doing: namely, the making of the New Woman and the New Home. First, the Japanese monopoly over the rice supply in Korea forces Omma to go on long trips to smuggle rice. To Na, Omma's frequent trips mean a possible danger to her mother from the Japanese police. The loss of Omma, the agent of modernization, would end this family's project of modernity. Second, the conscription of comfort women threatens not only Na's schooling (thereby potentially making her retreat to the Old Womanhood) but also her whole future. Out of fear, Omma even contemplates the possibility of marrying her daughter off; that is the point of Na's bitterest despair. Finally, the evacuation of Seoul at the end of the war, which Pak calls "the last order issued by the Japanese" (224), forces the family to leave its house with the triangular yard, the ground for their modern project. The family is driven back to its old home in the countryside, which Omma had deserted in her pursuit of the "new."

Even while depicting the relative autonomy that a Korean mother might have under colonial rule, Pak's narrative shows convincingly how Omma's maternal struggle for modernity is destined to be circumscribed by colonial power. Omma's domestic sphere is no longer unaffected by the whole nation's depressing colonial ordeal. In this short wartime narrative, the illusion of benign colonialism is shattered; the family is no longer revealed through its relation to schools, which are part of what Louis Althusser calls the "Ideological State Apparatus," but through its relation to the military and police, elements of the "Repressive State Apparatus."[40] The three episodes about the risks posed to the family are preceded by a series of vignettes dramatizing Omma's tight control over Na's knowledge and behavior. This sequence of presentation highlights how powerless Omma's overprotective mothering is in the face of indisputable colonial reality. In terms of control over her daughter's personhood, Omma's colonized position bears on the course of her daughter's modernization. Losing her leading role in determining the particulars of new knowledge to be acquired and the female modernity to be embodied by Na, Omma is reduced to the role of pushing her daughter to school as well as policing and coercing her at home. This narrative of the threatened maternal project suggests that under colonialism mothers and daughters are almost systematically denied the ability to sustain a fantasy of an omnipotent mother.

I cannot resist concluding with a final question: Did the New Woman project, which survived colonialism, come to fruition in the post-liberation era? The text gives us no clear answer, though it appears Omma's New Woman project never reached completion. In the epilogue, the middle-aged narrator revisits Hyŏnjŏ-dong and the hill that she climbed every day to go to primary school.

Musing on the hill, Na articulates the different positions of herself and her mother on their way to modern womanhood: "To me the hill had been a commuting path, but to Omma it had been the wall, which separated the 'inside' from the 'outside the gates'" (226). What, then, the text seems to ask in a final note, is the final consequence of Na's commuting between the "inside" and the "outside" of the gates? Na points to the uneven path of modernization and a gap between appearance and reality. On the surface, she is far more stylish, therefore far more "advanced," than Omma ever dreamed of her being. Yet Na laments the unrealized ideal: "How far was I from the things Omma thought possible for a New Woman?" (227, 179). Here it is useful to remember what Omma thought a New Woman was: "a woman who studies so much that she is knowledgeable about everything, and can do freely whatever she sets her heart on" (188, 149). "The things Omma thought possible for a New Woman" were thus limitless freedom and knowledge, which the middle-aged narrator thinks she is far from attaining.

At the end, the narrator expresses a simultaneous will toward forgetting and remembering the New Woman ideal as a whole. Although she "won't restore it again in the future, since it was just something of the past," Na insists that "the days that passed by should not be denied, even when the trajectory might be no more than a short length of rope" (227, 179). What she decides not to restore is the problematic quality within Omma's project of modernity, which also characterizes her own consciousness in the present: "the conflict between the too outmoded appearance and the absurdly high ideal, the contradiction between the ground of decency and the snobbish vanity, and the eternal outsider consciousness" (227, 179). However, Pak's actual revisit to the hill in the narrative and, more important, her writing itself signals a renewed engagement with her mother's New Woman project, a project of female modernity that seems to remain incomplete.

What is remarkable about Pak's narrative is that while dealing with the mother's and daughter's seemingly narrow life within a domestic space, it points to the question of colonial modernity, which is not only important for understanding colonial Korea but also crucial to the postcolonial debate on modernity in Korea. In their New Woman project, as in Korea's colonial modernity, although the goal to be pursued is certain, the understanding of what that goal actually involves is not. In both cases, aspirants strive for the visible appearance of advanced modernity, even though they fail to achieve much of substance. In this sense, both Na's and Omma's relationship to the New Woman ideal is emblematic of a larger process of modernization experienced by many latecomers. While the ideal has become theoretically accessible—though in many cases only through colonial rule—to those outside so-called advanced civilizations, that very condition guarantees that it remain unreachable. That the hands of the teacher seem untouchable and are untouched by Na is a subtle but telling detail: Omma's New Woman ideal is not, and cannot be, grasped in a colonial context.[41]

"Mother's Stake 1," whose author appears to have little interest in depicting larger issues such as Japanese colonialism, brings to light Korean women's keen feminist concern about modernity, a concern that happened to gain currency during the Japanese colonial period. Addressing complex issues of modernity through the mother-daughter relationship, Pak's autobiographical narrative brings forth Korean women's "anxious, split truths" and their "double destinies," which have been marginalized and silenced in the dominant discourses of nationalism and modernization. This focus on the "small" dyadic world of mother and daughter allows Pak to achieve all the more penetrating scrutiny of the ideology and reality of colonial modernization.

NINE

# Interior Landscapes: Yi Kwangsu's "The Heartless" and the Origins of Modern Literature

## Michael D. Shin

Yi Kwangsu is like a wound that grows more painful the more one touches it.

— Kim Hyŏn

I am not denying that we received the influence of European and American literature and of the Japanese literary world, but ... as long as [literary] works are not viewed as imitations, it is not true that trends formed and developed through either importation or a deliberate act. — Yŏm Sangsŏp

The [literary] work has no interior, no exterior; or rather, its interior is like an exterior, shattered and on display. Thus it is open to the searching gaze.

— Pierre Macherey

On February 9, 1949, newspapers in Seoul reported the arrest of Yi Kwangsu (1892–1950?) under the law on antinationalist activities, marking the end of the career of one of the best-known figures of the colonial era.[1] Yi was an impoverished but precocious young orphan who earned a scholarship to study in Japan and then became one of the pioneers of modern literature by writing, at age 25, the first mature modern novel in Chosŏn,[2] *Mujŏng* (The heartless; 1917). He solidified his status as a nationalist hero with his participation in the overseas independence movement. Just a few weeks before the March First movement in 1919, he wrote the Declaration of the Chosŏn Independence Youth Corps in Tokyo and later participated in the Korean Provisional Government in Shanghai. After he returned to Chosŏn in 1921, his fame continued to grow, as he worked as an editor of the newspaper *Tonga ilbo* and serialized several popular novels, such as *Chaesaeng* (Rebirth, 1924–25) and *Hŭk* (Earth, 1932–33). By the time he resigned from the *Tonga ilbo* in 1933, no more than a handful of intellectuals had attained a similar stature within Chosŏn. However, because of his collaboration with the Japanese authorities, which began around 1940, Yi Kwangsu has become the archetypal traitor of "Korean" nationalism. Ever since his arrest, usually in conjunction with commemorations of Chosŏn's liberation from Japan on August 15, 1945, newspaper articles and television programs have occasionally recounted the story of his collaboration. Although such efforts at catharsis have tried to exorcise the "pain" of his betrayal, the debate on Yi Kwangsu continues to this day, as scholars are still obsessed with explaining how someone so seemingly nationalistic turned into a collaborator.[3]

Part of the dilemma is rooted in the difficulties of reconciling his life with his writings. In fact, research on Yi Kwangsu often has the drama of a detective story: a search of his writings for clues to a shocking and unforgivable real-life crime. Although many scholars have suggested that the roots of his pro-Japanese leanings can be found in the gradualist, nonconfrontational views of his political writings from the 1920s,[4] few would deny his importance in the development of nationalist literature. Among his many literary works, *Mujŏng* has received by far the most scholarly attention. Despite some contrary opinions,[5] the serialization of the novel is considered to represent the true beginnings of the modern novel, heralding the rapid growth in literary activity after the March First movement. Another motive behind research on *Mujŏng* and Yi Kwangsu's other writings from the 1910s seems to be the hope of finding evidence that his nationalism was not genuine, in the period when he was apparently a "true" nationalist; such evidence would discredit him and end the controversy once and for all.[6] Although these efforts to find explanations of his life in his writings have provided valuable insights into both Yi Kwangsu and his works, such research has still not exhausted the possible approaches to understanding *Mujŏng*'s role in the origins of modern literature.

Literary histories generally consider *Mujŏng* to be the culmination of developments that began around 1905. During the years 1905–10, the growth of newspapers stimulated the production of what are now seen as the first attempts at modern literature by writers such as Yi Injik (1862–1916), who is considered to be the first modern novelist, and Yi Haejo (1869–1927). Fiction from this period was later categorized as *sin sosŏl* (new novel), a genre seen as a transitional stage between classical and modern literature.[7] The vernacular was used more widely but was not yet standardized, and plots still resembled the good-versus-evil approach of traditional literature and allegories more than "realistic" fiction. When newspapers were shut down and political works were censored following the formal annexation by Japan in 1910, the literary world reverted to more traditional melodramas and pulp fiction.[8] What little "new literature" (*sin munhak*) there was in the early colonial period was published virtually through the efforts of one man, Ch'oe Namsŏn (1890–1957), the founder of influential journals such as *Sonyŏn* (Boys, 1908–11) and *Ch'ŏngch'un* (Youth, 1914–18). A close colleague of Ch'oe Namsŏn, Yi Kwangsu published many of his early experiments at short fiction in these journals. It would only be a slight exaggeration to say that the "new literature" of the 1910s was dominated by Ch'oe Namsŏn and Yi Kwangsu. Yi Kwangsu had already become famous enough that, as novelist Kim Tongin (1900–1951) later recollected, "issues of *Ch'ŏngch'un* that did not have a story by Yi Kwangsu did not sell as many copies."[9]

The debate on the origins of modern literature usually revolves around the relative importance of external versus internal factors. On the one hand, many facts from Yi Kwangsu's life seem to suggest that early modern writers in Chosŏn merely imported the literature of the West. Both Yi Kwangsu and Ch'oe Namsŏn, as well as many future writers who debuted in the 1920s,[10] studied in Japan, where they were exposed to both Western literature and the developing Japanese literary world. The many references to Western thinkers and artists such as Beethoven, Byron, Gorky, Maupassant, and Socrates in Yi Kwangsu's early writings indicate that he read widely in Western literature. In 1908, while he was studying at Meiji gakuin, a Christian school, a Japanese friend gave him a copy of Tolstoy's "My

Religion," and he later recollected that it was a revelatory and transforming experience for him both as a person and as a writer.[11] Furthermore, he wrote *Mujŏng* not in Chosŏn but in Japan while he was studying at Waseda University. On the other hand, it is difficult to deny the importance of internal developments. Throughout *Mujŏng*, there are references to the tale of Ch'unhyang, a popular *p'ansori* folktale. His other stories and historical novels reveal a thorough knowledge of classical Chinese and historical texts going as far back as the thirteenth-century *Samguk yusa* (Memorabilia of the Three Kingdoms). In addition, an audience for vernacular literature developed through urbanization and the rise of markets during the previous centuries as well as more recent movements to promote the use of the vernacular.

Yi Kwangsu himself commenced the debate on these issues with "Munhak iran hao" (What is literature?"; 1916), the first work of literary theory in Chosŏn, which appeared just weeks before *Mujŏng*'s serialization began.[12] Previous attempts at literary theory were limited to Yi Haejo's brief comments in the prefaces and epilogues of some of his novels[13] and short essays published by Chosŏn students in Japan, among which was Yi Kwangsu's "Munhak ŭi kach'i" (The value of literature; 1910).[14] Seemingly emphasizing the influence of external factors, Yi Kwangsu argued that translations of Western literature would play a critical role in the origins of modern literature.[15] Translation is generally viewed as a technical process that is supposed to produce an almost exact imitation of the original, but for Yi Kwangsu, translation was more a creative act that produced a work that was qualitatively different from yet clearly resembling the original.[16] Instead of choosing between internal or external factors, Yi Kwangsu sought to promote a literature that was like a translation: both unmistakably modern and, at the same time, uniquely "Chosŏn."

When a writer does double duty as a theorist, it is common to view the creative work as an attempt to put the theory into practice. In the case of Yi Kwangsu, it might be more accurate to see his fiction as an extended discussion of his theory. Since Japanese censorship severely restricted the freedom of intellectuals to discuss politically charged issues, one strategy they used was to carry out such discussions under the guise of fiction. Years later, Yi Kwangsu acknowledged that "rather than consciously trying to write literary works," he wrote novels as a "substitute for articles (*nonmun*)."[17] His stories ostensibly avoided political topics and treated various social issues of the time, such as arranged marriages, the traditional family system, and new-style (*sinsik*) education. However, the fact that almost all the protagonists were aspiring young writers suggests that the stories can also be read as reflections on writing itself and contain a second narrative about the difficulties of writing literature under colonialism. One of my objectives in this chapter is to make these "coded" narratives on writing explicit and to examine how Yi Kwangsu, consciously or not, elaborated his conception of literature-as-translation within the stories themselves.

The "definitive" study of Yi Kwangsu is Kim Yunsik's three-volume work, *Yi Kwangsu wa kŭŭi sidae* (Yi Kwangsu and his age),[18] which literally covers his life and writings from the cradle to the grave. Its objective was to write the "psychological history of Korean people in the modern age" by examining "the relationship between a person and his texts and between that person and his age."[19] In addition to its thorough archival research and creative interpretations, Kim Yunsik's book is notable for its methodology and synthesis of various literary theories. As shown by his use of the term "internal landscape" (*naemyŏn p'unggyŏng*), he incorporated the ideas of Japanese literary critic Karatani Kojin,[20] who has argued that modern Japanese literature originated in a process of the simultaneous discovery of landscape and "interiority."[21] Following Kim Yunsik's example, this chapter will attempt to apply Karatani's ideas to an analysis of Yi Kwangsu's early writings. Rather than seeking to uncover a psychological history, my purpose is to use the trope of landscape and the concept of interiority to decode the secondary narratives on writing embedded within his stories.

"Interiority" is not an exact synonym for "identity"; more accurately, it is a *form* of identity: identity as unchanging essence. Encompassing concepts such as the psyche, imagination, and emotional life, "interiority" refers to what remains constant despite changes in the external world. According to Karatani, landscape was "discovered" when humans were torn and alienated from their natural environment. Lacking human connection, landscape acted as a blank screen on which interiority could be projected and then "discovered" as if it had a visible, objective reality; a crude example would be a description of a landscape endowed with human qualities. Landscape was a dominant motif in Yi Kwangsu's early works as well, not just in *Mujŏng* but also in his lesser-known writings. The plots of these stories were relatively conventional narratives about lonely characters searching for love in cold, alienating environments. I will try to show that landscape functioned as a metonym for Japan and that the efforts of his characters to move to a new landscape can be read as a search for an interiority that expresses an identity distinct from that of the colonizer. My argument will be that the discovery of interiority was also a process of translation—from Japan to Chosŏn—and that it was not until *Mujŏng* that the discovery of interiority was accomplished.

Karatani and other critics have pointed out that a sense of interiority is essentially a linguistic effect of using the vernacular. For both Chosŏn and Japan, one of the principal obstacles to modern literature was the lack of a suitable vernacular *written* language. Yi Kwangsu's linguistic innovations in *Mujŏng* represented a qualitative leap in the development of a literary vernacular. More than just a matter of standardizing spelling rules, its development also involved finding "neutral" forms of expression within an extremely hierarchy-conscious language. A recording of the spoken language, vernacular writing creates and is based on a textual "metaphysics": seemingly imprisoned behind the black bars of the text is a speaking subject, an inner being that authenticates the meaning of what is "said."[22] By narrating the discovery of interiority as if it has a "real" and objective existence, literature is able to obscure its origins as an effect of language. Through such narration, literature seems to become a transparent medium that allows direct access to the interior life, thus giving it the illusion of realism. The discovery of interiority allows the transformation of literature from technique to art form, and this process, in part, can be seen in Yi Kwangsu's writings from the 1910s.

This chapter covers Yi Kwangsu's writings from 1915 to 1918; rather than presenting them in a strict chronological order, however, I have divided them according to genre in order to trace more clearly the connections between his literary theory and his fiction. The first section examines "What Is Literature?" to see how Yi Kwangsu introduced and reinterpreted Western literary theories to produce a conception of a unique Chosŏn literature. The second focuses on a reading of Yi Kwangsu's short stories in *Ch'ŏngch'un* as allegories of colonialism and as discussions of the difficulties of writing modern literature. To put them in context, I also discuss the literary contest sponsored by the journal, for which Yi Kwangsu was one of the judges. The last section is an extended reading of *Mujŏng* to show how it succeeded in overcoming the obstacles to the discovery of interiority that the short stories could not. Ultimately, the term *minjok* (nation) was the name given to the intangible and mysterious "reality" of interiority. Although the term *minjok* was not widely used until after the March First movement, the discovery of interiority can be understood as one of the necessary preconditions to the expression of a national identity. Such an analysis will, I hope, contribute to a greater understanding of the significance of *Mujŏng* in the history of nationalist literature in Chosŏn.

## Literature as Translation: Yi Kwangsu's "What Is Literature?"

When Yi Kwangsu enrolled in Waseda in 1915, the turmoil of the war in Europe was causing Japanese intellectuals to reflect on the value of the Western ideas they had been introducing into Japan. Chosŏn students in Japan were also involved in this re-examination, as is shown by the articles they published in journals such as *Hak chi kwang* (*Lux Scientiae*). In the 1917 article "*Uri ŭi isang*" (Our ideals), Yi Kwangsu himself expected that "after this war, there will be tremendous confusion and significant reforms in modern civilization (*hyŏndae munmyŏng*)."[23] As intellectuals began to harbor doubts about Western ideas introduced earlier, many new ideas were introduced and debated, such as neo-Kantian philosophy and Bertrand Russell's theories of "social reconstruction."[24] One of the most significant results of such intellectual ferment was the shift in emphasis in the intellectual world from "civilization and enlightenment" to "culture."

In "Our Ideals," Yi Kwangsu even defined the task of intellectuals as the "establishment of a new culture" (*sin munhwa*).[25] Although he did not explicitly define the difference, his writings from this period suggest that he did make a distinction between "civilization" (*munmyŏng*) and "culture" (*munhwa*). In his usage, "civilization" encompassed areas ranging from literature and art to industry, commerce, and politics,[26] whereas the term "culture" referred only to the four areas of philosophy, religion, literature, and art.[27] He noted that although Chosŏn did not have its own philosophy or religion, this lack was not a serious problem because only a few countries could claim to have their own.[28] Of the four areas of culture, he considered the development of a unique literature to be the most important because "the spirit of the nation that has been transmitted from the time of our ancestors . . . will be the center of literature."[29] The objective of "What Is Literature?" was to provide a theory on how to write such a literature. Serialized in the *Maeil sinbo*, the vernacular daily of the Japanese Government-General, it was the first discussion of the general principles of literature to be published in Chosŏn. Written in Yi Kwangsu's usual straightforward prose, the eleven sections of "What Is Literature?" proceed from a broad definition of literature to a section on "Chosŏn literature."[30]

Almost two decades after the publication of this article, Yi Kwangsu wrote, "The person who most influenced my view of art was Tolstoy."[31] Yi had been introduced to Tolstoy's writings during his days at Meiji Gakuin (1907–10) and immediately became a devoted follower.[32] It is clear that he read Tolstoy widely, including the Russian writer's theoretical work *What Is Art?*[33] In later works on literary theory, Yi Kwangsu listed several Japanese texts that would be useful for understanding literature such as Natsume Sōseki's *Theory of Literature* and Tsubouchi Shōyō's *Essence of the Novel*,[34] but Tolstoy was the one figure he consistently mentioned and was associated with throughout his career. The strong similarities between the two have masked equally strong differences. Yi Kwangsu did not blindly accept Tolstoy's views, and what occurred in the process of translating Tolstoy's ideas to Chosŏn's situation was a recoding of the theory. Tolstoy did not just function as an "influence"; rather, Yi Kwangsu was engaged in a dialogue with Tolstoy's ideas in "What Is Literature?" I will attempt to trace this process of recoding to demonstrate how Yi Kwangsu arrived at a conception of national literature.

Right at the beginning of "What Is Literature?" Yi declared that literature had broken with its past: "The word 'literature' (*munhak*) is not the literature of the past; what is called 'literature' has the meaning of literature as defined in Western languages."[35] Initially, he defined literature as "that which expresses the thought (*sasang*) and emotions (*kamjŏng*) of human beings within a specific form" (507). But "emotion" (*chŏng*) was the central term in his definition, since it was the factor that most distinguished modern from premodern literature. For Yi Kwangsu, *chŏng* was a general term; he intended it to cover as broad a range of emotions as possible, including "love, rage, sorrow, evil, hope, and courage" (509). At the same time, Yi Kwangsu believed that the importance of *chŏng* was also tied to the emergence of the individual: in the past, emotion had been ignored because "humanity did not have a clear conception of individuality (*kaesŏng*)" (508). In short, he used *chŏng* to designate the range of individual human emotions. Yi Kwangsu's views on the centrality of emotion in literature sound similar to those of Tolstoy, who stated that "whereas by words a man transmits his thoughts to another, by means of art he transmits his feelings."[36]

Yi Kwangsu's advocacy of Western theories of literature was based on his critique of traditional literature. "What Is Literature?" can be seen as a complement to his social criticism from the 1910s that attacked Confucianism for obstructing Chosŏn's modernization.[37] Yi Kwangsu felt that "the greatest reason that [modern] literature did not develop in Chosŏn" was the domination of literature in classical Chinese (509). Although the human mind consists of three factors—knowledge (*chi*), emotion (*chŏng*), and will (*ŭi*)—people in the past "regarded *chŏng* as lowly and considered only knowledge and will important" (508). More specifically, emotion was viewed as "a supplement to or subordinate of" morality and religion (508). As a result, literature was used to instill a Confucian morality based on "encouraging good and punishing evil" (*kwŏnsŏn chingak*) (509). Such an emphasis on morality had long limited the range of emotions that could be portrayed in literature: "The thoughts and emotions of the Chosŏn people were restricted by an intolerant moral code for around five hundred years after the founding of the Yi dynasty" (510). Yi Kwangsu believed that the reason that Western countries were able to produce great literature was that Westerners had the freedom to express their thoughts and emotions (510); in those countries, *chŏng* became the equal of *chi* and *ŭi* (508) in the modern age.

Rather than promoting a specific morality, Yi Kwangsu called for a literature rooted in Western (more specifically, Tolstoyan) notions of realism. In theorizing such a literature, he had to elaborate on his initial definition of literature. Literature does more than express emotions: it also "enables the fulfillment of emotions" (508). After initially defining the "fulfillment of emotions" as "interest" (*hŭngmi*), he explained that what interests people are "things about themselves" (508). These "things" should come from people's lives (509) but do not necessarily have to correspond with the outside world or empirical reality. Literature enables readers to "escape real society and walk in the ideal world of a free imagination . . . to be able to experience various aspects and kinds of life, thought and emotions, that one would not normally be able to experience" (511). The "fulfillment of emotions" involves the creation of an imaginary world so vivid that it is shared between writer and reader. For Yi Kwangsu, the novel is especially suited for this function since it "opens up to the reader's eye vividly and realistically a world that exists within the author's imagination and makes the reader feel as if he or she is living inside that world" (513). Yi Kwangsu's views on the relation between writer and reader echoed Tolstoy's conception of the "infectiousness of art": "Art is a human activity consisting in this, that one man consciously, by means of certain external signs, hands on to others feelings he has lived through, and that other people are infected by these feelings and also experience them."[38]

As his discussion of literature became more complex, Yi Kwangsu turned to the metaphor of landscape to illustrate his ideas. Landscape made its first appearance in the following line: "If one intends to build a new literature (*sin munhak*) in Chosŏn, one has to exert oneself to select materials freely and to depict the infinite and unlimited thoughts and emotions of life by *standing them on a field* (*kwangya*)" (510; emphasis added). Yi Kwangsu was comparing the writing of literature to a process of imbuing a landscape with *chŏng*, and following Karatani, I will try to show that it is this process which enables the discovery of interiority. The relation between interiority and landscape becomes clearer in another aspect of literature that Yi Kwangsu and Tolstoy share. Generally speaking, Tolstoy's art in his later years combined two movements: it was meant to elevate humanity to a religious ideal and, at the same time, penetrate daily life. As a result, the conduct of daily life would be thoroughly imbued with this ideal and enable its realization. One example of this connection is the last lines of Tolstoy's *Resurrection*, a novel that was tremendously popular in both Japan and Chosŏn but is accorded a minor place in the Tolstoy canon in the West: "After that night a new life did begin for Nekhludof, not because he entered new conditions, but because all the happenings of his daily life assumed a different aspect and a new significance. The future alone will prove how this new stage of his life will end."[39]

The common view of Yi Kwangsu as a moralistic, preachy writer[40] generally attributes these qualities to the influence of Tolstoy, ignoring the connection of Tolstoy's art to daily life.[41] "What Is Literature?" also sought to bring art closer to daily life. First of all, Yi

Kwangsu argued that in order to fulfill human emotions, "literature must completely take its material (*chaeryo*) from life. Such material is namely the conditions of daily existence and the thoughts and emotions of life (*insaeng*)" (508–9). Furthermore, he stressed the use of the vernacular because it is the "language of daily usage" (*ilyongŏ*; 515).[42] Despite his emphasis on the creation of an ideal world, Yi Kwangsu believed that depiction and description (*myosa*) in literature must be realistic or, more specifically, "correct and vivid" (509). The relation between reality and the ideal world corresponds to that between landscape and interiority: just as literature enables readers to perceive an ideal world through its depiction of the "reality" of daily life, interiority is made visible through its projection onto a landscape.

What Yi Kwangsu tried to make visible to the gaze of the reader was the nation (*minjok*). His emphasis on the nation represented a clear break from Tolstoy. Tolstoy sought to create an ideal world of universal Christianity and abhorred all forms of patriotism; as Yi Kwangsu later acknowledged, his "path diverged from Tolstoy's concerning the religious way of life."[43] In the section "Literature and Nationhood" ("Munhak kwa minjoksŏng"), Yi Kwangsu stated that "the thought, emotions, and way of life of a generation were the result of the study, cultivation, and training of the earlier people (*minjok*) and a crystallization of their innumerable sufferings and efforts" (511–12). Believing that this legacy constitutes the "spiritual civilization of a people and the basis of its nationness (*minjoksŏng*)," he argued that "the most effective way to transmit this valuable spiritual civilization [to future generations] is the literature of the people (*minjok ŭi munhak*)" (512). Literature was uniquely suited for this function because it allowed the seemingly unmediated expression of the emotions and thoughts that constituted the legacy of the nation. When the "excesses of the age" (512) threaten this crystallization with extinction—that is, in a colonial situation—it becomes even more necessary to pass this legacy to a future generation who can "add" to it and continue passing it on for generations until it becomes fuller and more productive (512). The task of literature is no less than to preserve the nation and ensure its continued survival for "hundreds and thousands of generations" (512). Although Yi Kwangsu was clear about the function of literature, he did not specify what was supposed to be transmitted. An expression of identity taking the form of interiority, the *minjok* had to be "discovered" through literature before it could be preserved through its transmission. He stated that Chosŏn "must in the future build its first-ever legacy that can be transmitted to later generations by expressing the renewed thoughts and feelings of a growing new literature" (512).

Yi Kwangsu believed that to create such a literature, writers need to have "genius" (*ch'ŏnjae*). Influenced by Carlyle's idea that "the civilization of a country is the accumulation of the works of its great figures (*uiin*),"[44] Yi made genius a central part of his social theory in the 1910s. In his 1917 article "O Genius! O Genius!" he even named ten aspects of civilization in which Chosŏn urgently needed to develop geniuses. In "What Is Literature?" he defined a "literary genius" as someone who "possesses sharp insight, free imagination, passionate emotions, and full powers of expression" (515). With "an imagination [that], in an instant, can create a world," such a genius must have the ability to "make vivid in front of the readers' eyes what one has observed and created in one's imagination" (515–16). But Yi Kwangsu warned that genius alone does not make one a great writer. "What Is Literature?" combined two different conceptions of the author: the possessor of inborn genius and a trained and devoted craftsman who labors at creation. Yi Kwangsu believed that a person without genius could not acquire it through cultivation; however, genius had to undergo rigorous training in order to produce great literature (516). He emphasized that even for such a developed genius, the act of writing itself involved a great deal of pain and labor; it was a repetitive process of "writing and erasing . . . of tens of revisions" (516). For such efforts, the writer should receive both spiritual rewards (respect) and material compensation (prize money or earnings from the sale of books) (517). In later critical writings, Yi Kwangsu emphasized the character of the author more and more, and by the mid-1920s, the word "genius" disappeared from his texts, replaced by the word *ingyŏk* (character)—a transition to a conception of the author as the possessor of a special kind of interiority, rather than a heaven-sent genius.[45]

In "O Genius! O Genius!" Yi Kwangsu emphasized that geniuses do not simply appear; society must summon and nurture them.[46] To enable the development of literary geniuses, Yi Kwangsu sought to promote the establishment of literary institutions. He and Tolstoy had diametrically opposed views on the value of modern literary institutions. Not only was Tolstoy opposed to all forms of patriotism, but he also rejected institutionalized art, believing that remuneration for artists, the professionalization of art, and art criticism were the main causes of what he called "counterfeit art."[47] By contrast, Yi Kwangsu considered critics to be the equal of writers (515) and noted that "among manuscript fees, literary manuscript fees are the highest" (517), arguing for the necessity of compensating writers. In the section "Literature and Literary Figures," he advocated a division of labor into writers, readers, and critics, explaining the functions of each one (515). Furthermore, he had a conventional view of literary genres; in the section on "The Types of Literature," he mentioned only criticism, novels, drama, and poetry, leaving out all forms of oral literature (513–14). Yi Kwangsu apparently felt that such institutions were necessary because of the obstacles created by colonialism; they would provide the conditions that would allow writers to devote themselves to the production of modern literary works.

In the last section of "What Is Literature?" Yi Kwangsu declared that "Chosŏn literature has no past; it has only a future" (518). Examining Chosŏn's situation using his new theory of literature, he both lamented the lack of previous achievements and mapped out a vision for its future development. Yi Kwangsu defined "Chosŏn literature" as "literature that is written by Chosŏn people in Chosŏn writing" (517). The term "Chosŏn" designated a transhistorical identity; it encompassed not just the last dynasty (1392–1910) but all previous dynasties and historical periods all the way back to Tan'gun, the mythical founder of the country. Significantly, he used the term *Chosŏn mun* (Chosŏn writing) rather than *Chosŏn ŏ* (Chosŏn language), clearly privileging textual over purely oral forms of communication. Later writing that "language is the soul of the nation,"[48] Yi Kwangsu made vernacular language the central aspect of his definition of literature. He then gave a brief history of such literature, beginning with the invention of the *idu* transcription system in the Three Kingdoms period. For Yi Kwangsu, the origins of a genuine Chosŏn literature dated from the creation of *han'gŭl* by King Sejong in the mid-fifteenth century (518). All literature written in classical Chinese was discounted, including all the literature from the Koryŏ period up to King Sejong's time. In his discussion of recent literary developments, it is striking that he included translations in the category of Chosŏn literature, noting particularly translations of the New Testament and other Christian works (518). This inclusion would not be acceptable today, but it is understandable if the introduction of modern literature is viewed as a process of recoding or translation. Yi Kwangsu appears to have seen fundamentally little difference between the act of translation and the writing of "new literature" because both involved writing in the vernacular. Although the plots and characters remained the same, the act of translating into the vernacular produced a qualitative difference that transformed a foreign story into a work of Chosŏn literature.

"What Is Literature?" ended with a vision of the future of Chosŏn literature that was described in terms of landscape: "Chosŏn literature . . . must in the future produce several geniuses who will cultivate Chosŏn's *field of literature* (*munhakya*), which is as yet unmarked by human traces" (518, emphasis added). Although Yi Kwangsu himself was perhaps not aware of it, the references to landscape scattered throughout the article were not random but fell within a consistent pattern. Humanity was set apart from an inhuman landscape, and the task of writers was to write stories that endowed the landscape with *chŏng*. Although his historical overview yielded few works that satisfied his definition of literature, Yi Kwangsu had hope for Chosŏn's future. Whereas Western literature had few areas left to explore, "all the aspects and various human emotions (*injŏng*) of Chosŏn society await great poets and great novelists just as the gold, silver, and bronze in the mountains are waiting to be excavated" (519). Readers could thus overcome their alienation by experiencing the *chŏng* that was simply waiting to be discovered in the landscape. In "What Is Literature?" Yi Kwangsu juxtaposed two conceptions of the origins of modern literature: literature as translation and literature as the discovery of interiority; the relations between the two were unclear in his literary theory but were further elaborated within his fiction.

## Literature as Literary Theory: Short Stories in *Ch'ŏngch'un*

When Ch'oe Namsŏn, himself a pioneer in modern poetry, returned from Japan in 1907, he founded a publishing company, the Sinmun'gwan, through which he published *Sonyŏn* and *Ch'ŏngch'un*. These all-purpose journals covered a wide variety of topics from science to the arts and religion, and they are especially known for their contributions to the modernization of the Korean vernacular (ŏnmun ilch'i). As its name suggests, Ch'ŏngch'un was aimed at a young student audience; it emphasized the new and introduced Western knowledge in a variety of fields. Originally sold only in Seoul, it quickly found outlets in other cities, mainly those along the main railway lines such as Pusan, Taegu, Ch'ŏnan, P'yŏngyang, and Ŭiju.[49] Early issues contained articles on baseball, student life in Japan, and tips on how to study, including one on memorizing Western numerals. To promote modern literature, there were articles on the vernacular language and abridged translations of Western classics such as Victor Hugo's Les Miserables (issue no. 1) and John Milton's Paradise Lost (no. 3). Although Ch'ŏngch'un suffered its first shutdown by Japanese authorities just a few months before Yi Kwangsu left for Waseda in 1915, it was the first arena in which he took an active role in shaping the early literary world.[50] In addition to contributing his own writings, Yi Kwangsu was also the judge of a literary contest sponsored by the journal, and such activities can be seen as part of an effort to further develop the conception of literature he put forth in "What Is Literature?"

Unlike literary contests that seek submissions in established genres, the contest in Ch'ŏngch'un attempted to stimulate the production of works of a "new literature" that was still in its early stages; accordingly, the format of the contest provides a glimpse into the state of the literary world at the time. When Ch'ŏngch'un resumed publishing with its seventh issue in May 1917, it announced the beginning of a continuous literary contest, the results of which would be published in every issue. In the same issue, the journal also announced a one-time "special" literary contest, whose results would appear in the ninth issue.[51] They were the first such contests in the Chosŏn literary world[52] and were essentially exercises in modern forms of writing. In the absence of institutional support, the journal itself assumed the role of teacher; in fact, it enforced its pedagogy by requiring that contestants had to be readers of Ch'ŏngch'un and affix their "reader card" (tokjajŭng) to the first page of their manuscripts. It was training its own readers to become writers—an indication of the lack of differentiation in the literary world at the time. To promote the use of the vernacular, the use of classical Chinese was forbidden, although the occasional use of Chinese characters was permitted within the modern style (simunch'e). Prize money, with the amounts explicitly noted, was given out, to give financial support to young, unknown talent.[53] As Yi Kwangsu wrote in "What Is Literature?," "poverty has been the companion of writers since ancient times" (517).

The format of the "special" contest suggests that vernacular writing was more than just a matter of recording the spoken language. Whereas the "regular" contest included categories in traditional genres such as *sijo* and classical Chinese poetry, the "special" contest had three categories: (1) "writings recording and transmitting the conditions in one's hometown"; (2) "writings explaining one's current situation"; and (3) short stories; the short stories were judged by Yi Kwangsu, and the other two by Ch'oe Namsŏn. The distinction between fiction and nonfiction was somewhat ambiguous; at this stage, the emphasis seemed to be on just getting people to write in the modern vernacular without regard to genre. The categories were not genres but descriptions of situations that would provide a context to help potential writers express themselves in such a style. For the first category, contributors were supposed to write as if "reporting to a friend who lives far away the natural scenery of one's hometown or the many and various conditions and aspects of its people." For the second category, they were asked to write "to a close friend, depicting in a style with sentiment (*chŏngch'ui*) something one has experienced, felt, or seen recently in one's daily life." Short stories were supposed to have a student as the protagonist, and submissions in all three categories were to avoid "exaggeration and confusing styles."

The fact that such contrived situations were necessary implies that for writers of that time, vernacular writing was hardly spontaneous or natural. It is not the results of the contest but the lack thereof that testified to the difficulty. In the ninth issue (July 1917), instead of announcing the results of the contests, there appeared a notice saying that, for both contests, "in terms of quantity and of content," the results had been disappointing, and the announcement would be postponed until a later issue.[54] Despite the emphasis on the "current style" and a more conversational writing, modern literature apparently required more than the technical development of writing. Such difficulties suggest that the origins of modern literature also required a change in the "metaphysics" of language, and it is this aspect of writing that I am calling "the discovery of interiority." Literature or, rather, literary situations acted as a pretext to stimulate such writing, and it is this mediating role of literature, clear at its origins, that the discovery of interiority was meant to obscure.

The stories Yi Kwangsu selected were eventually published in the eleventh issue (Nov. 1917), and his comments on them appeared in the following issue (no. 12, Mar. 1918). Both the selected stories and his comments suggest a conception of literature consistent with his literary theory. In "Hyŏnsang sosŏl kosŏn yŏŏn" (Comments on the selection of the prize-winning novels), Yi Kwangsu discussed five things that "surprised" (97) him about the stories that were submitted; in reality they seem more like the criteria he used to pick the winners. Although there were no fundamental differences with "What Is Literature?" he did comment on more technical aspects of writing for the reader-writers of the journal. In stressing the use of the "current style" (simunch'e; point no. 1), he mentioned various usage and punctuation errors made in the submissions, such as confusion of question and exclamation marks and of commas and periods (97). There were also a few, seemingly minor, elaborations of points made in the article that introduced elements that were amplified in his later discussions of literary theory. First, he noted that everyone "wrote with sincerity" (98; point no. 2), and this emphasis on sincerity became part of an emphasis on personality that supplanted earlier notions of genius in his conception of the author. Second, Yi Kwangsu repeated his criticisms of didacticism (point no. 3) and praised the general movement from the idealistic to the realistic (point no. 4). Again, what is important is the new status of chŏng in literature; for example, "if jealousy is used as material [for a story], it should not be for the purpose of eliminating jealousy; ... by making the emotion called jealousy the basis [of the story], it should faithfully portray and just put in front of all the readers the comedies and tragedies it causes in daily existence" (98). To this familiar conception of literature, he added a new argument, the eternalness of emotion: "moral lessons [same characters as those for "didacticness"] change according to the times, but the flow of human emotions is always the same going back ten thousand generations" (99). The eternalness of emotion later became the basis for claims of the antiquity of the minjok.

Although he apologized at the beginning of "Comments" for having had low expectations (97), his faint praise for the winners suggests that he was disappointed with the results. There were twenty-odd submissions; Yi Sangch'un's "Kiro" (The fork in the road) won first prize, Chu Yohan's (writing under the name Chu Nagyang) "Maŭl chip" (Village home) came in second,[55] and Kim Myŏngsun's "Ŭisim ŭi sonyŏ" (Suspicious girl) was awarded the third prize. However, the only story in which "the sprouts of new thought can be seen" (101; point no. 5) was "Village Home." The other two stories were praised mainly for "technical" achievements in character portrayal and story structure. Conspicuous by its relative absence in "Comments" was the term *chŏng*, and its absence suggests that what disappointed Yi Kwangsu was the stories' failure to create a sense of interiority. Yi Sangch'un's story centered on a student from the countryside who comes to Seoul and gets involved with a dissipated youth; the country boy manages to straighten out his life, but the other one ends up in jail and brings about the ruin of his family. Yi Kwangsu noted that "its descriptions and development of events did not have any unnatural points" (99) and that the dissipated youths had good as well as bad qualities (100). Kim Myŏngsun's story was about a beautiful young girl who moves into a town with her grandfather; they keep to themselves, leading the townspeople to wonder about their background, which is not revealed until the end when they suddenly have to leave.[56] Yi Kwangsu especially remarked that this story "had absolutely no trace of didacticism" (99), calling it one of only three stories to have achieved this quality—the other two being his own *Mujŏng* and Chin Sunsŏng's "Purŭjijim" (A shout) (99).[57] This lack of didacticism also revealed itself in her balanced character portrayals; as Yi Kwangsu noted, Director Cho, the father of the young girl, whose unfaithfulness led his wife to commit suicide, also had a tremendous love for his daughter (100).

Chu Yohan's story was distinguished by its "intense contact with the modern" (p. 101). It was about the "sadness, anger, and defiance" a young student feels when he returns to his hometown, and Yi Kwangsu praised it for "trying to show the weak but vital hope [he felt]" (101). One aspect of its modernity was the protagonist's rejection of his past. The people of his village are still the same despite outward improvements in the village (54, 57). Lamenting that "there is no emotion or passion in their eyes" (62), he decides to leave his hometown, "even though [he] may be called unfilial" (62). Chu Yohan's story probably came in second because "there were some points where [he] tried to preach" (99). What is unique about the story is that it ends at the point where the main character begins to be able to write. Writing became possible at the moment of the most intense alienation; he writes a letter to his friend that begins, "I can't stand it. I can't bear it. Everything is all blocked up" (62). The last lines show him struggling to write: "He grasped the brush to write more. His hand was shaking." The ending to this story suggests that the prizewinning stories lacked not interiority but the *discovery* of interiority. Although they achieved a certain degree of technical sophistication, interiority must not be seen as a performative effect of such techniques. Literature must narrate the "discovery" of interiority, not its performance, if the interior world is to seem "real" and "objective." Chu Yohan's story left readers at the brink of that discovery.

Writing was more centrally problematized in Yi Kwangsu's short stories from *Ch'ŏngch'un*, and in these stories, the connection between literary translation and the discovery of interiority is clearer. From the sixth to the thirteenth issue, he wrote almost one story per issue, beginning with "Kim Kyŏng"[58] and ending with "Yun Kwangho."[59] These stories are the best known of his short fiction, and for many future writers and critics, they were their first exposure to vernacular literature.[60] On first glance, they seem to have much in common with Yi's stories of the previous decade because many were set in Japan with students as the main characters. Some of the stories also had long, almost claustrophobically personal passages with abstract ramblings on love and death that suggested the confessional style of the Japanese "I-novel," which was in its heyday during this period.[61] In fact, some of the incidents resembled events from his own life so much that over a decade later he still had to deny that they were autobiographical.[62] What distinguished these stories was their self-consciousness; almost all the protagonists were writers. By writing about people trying to learn how to write, Yi Kwangsu turned the stories into reflections on the origins of modern literature. Taken as a whole, the stories in themselves reveal a considerable amount of experimentation with the short-story form. Both "Kim Kyŏng" and "Yun Kwangho" used third-person flashbacks; "Panghwang" (Wandering)[63] used first-person narration; and "Ŏrin pŏt ege" (To my young friend)[64] was written in an epistolary style. These narrative techniques and other devices such as dream sequences and diary excerpts were an advanced form of the contrived situations from the literary contest; they were used in an effort to project emotions outwardly in order to evoke a sense of interiority. Rather than mechanically imitating these pre-existing forms in the modern vernacular, it seems that Yi Kwangsu was trying to rewrite and "translate" these forms to discover a new mode of writing.

What the novelist Kim Tongin said about "To My Young Friend" applies to all of Yi Kwangsu's short stories; they were about an "intense longing for love."[65] The stories involved a simultaneous search for *chŏng* on two levels. On one level, all the main characters are lonely, isolated men searching for *chŏng*. On the second, Yi Kwangsu was searching for a literary form (the "expression" and "fulfillment" of *chŏng*) within which he could narrate a character's attainment of the desired object of love. The discovery of interiority was the solution to both of these searches. In almost all the stories, the characters fail to attain the love-object, suggesting that the stories are allegories about the inability to write modern literature. At this point, Yi Kwangsu seemed able only to gesture at his failure to discover interiority, at his frustration. The stories themselves have only a minor place within the Yi Kwangsu canon. Part of the reason for his "failure" is his misunderstanding of the short-story form; as Kim Tongin wrote, "By nature, Yi Kwangsu was very incompetent as a short-story writer."[66] Such criticism is somewhat misplaced because it judges him by a literary standard that was only beginning to emerge at the time. Because of their self-conscious, reflective nature, these stories can be seen as historical snapshots that captured various attempts at the process of recoding that ultimately led to the discovery of interiority. Instead of trying to uncover the hidden meaning of these stories, my reading focuses on their depictions of landscape and their relationship to *chŏng* to show how they were reflections on the failure to discover interiority.

These stories mentioned above, plus "Sonyŏn ŭi piae" (Sorrows of a youth),[67] are usually the only ones mentioned when discussing Yi Kwangsu's fiction from this period, but a focus on interiority and landscape enables an examination of a wider range of writings, in particular, "Kŏul kwa majo anja" (Sitting across from a mirror)[68] and "Tonggyŏng esŏ Kyŏngsŏng kkaji" (From Tokyo to Seoul).[69] With the exception of the prizewinning stories, *Ch'ŏngch'un* did not have a special section for fiction, nor were short stories identified as such in the table of contents. The ambiguity of their status as fiction or nonfiction further suggests that there is no reason to distinguish these two "stories" from his other works. Although they in a sense failed like the other short stories, I will begin with a brief examination of them because they mapped out the path that the discovery of interiority had to follow.

"From Tokyo to Seoul" was a fictionalization of the literal meaning of the word "translation": "to carry from one place to another."[70] An epistolary story, it consisted of a series of eleven letters written as the narrator traveled from Tokyo to Seoul by train and boat to a friend he left behind in Japan. Since the letters recorded his thoughts as he looked out the train window, the story provides an opportunity to compare landscapes, thus illustrating the difficulties in "translating" modern literature from Japan to Chosŏn. Like Yi Kwangsu's other protagonists, the narrator was fundamentally lonely; as he left, he "almost cried. . . . the only one who noticed me was you" (73). But once the train left the city, he began to notice "great Nature" and "truly realized the happiness of life" (73). Traveling through the landscape of Japan was so bewitching an experience that it moved him to write. When he heard a "chorus of frogs" (74), he "wanted to join the frogs and make noise. However, since it would not be polite to do so, I cried out with my hands and made the sounds of writing (*munja sori*)" (75). Later, when looking at flowers on a mountain, he "wrote a song because it was so beautiful" and then mentioned that "it was so much fun to sing this song as I looked out the train window" (79). These images are all signs that Japan was a land with a modern vernacular literature.

When he arrived in Chosŏn, the landscape was the complete opposite of that of Japan: "When the sun rose, Chosŏn's shabby appearance became clear to the eyes. Look at the bare mountains. Look at the dried-up streams. Because of a long drought, the flowers and trees are so dried up that they appear pitiful like a child raised by a stepmother" (80). Interestingly, the desolate landscape made the narrator realize the necessity of art. The last letter ended with the narrator urging his friend to create art: "Aren't you now in the middle of drawing a plan for a new world? Yes, you are. But there is no need to rush. Please take your time and draw us something that is great and eternal" (80). The narrator himself was moved to write, but all he could do was point out the failure of Chosŏn's landscape to inspire the writing of literature. The train ride, a type of translation, was a metaphor[71] for the literature that Yi Kwangsu was trying to create, but it failed to reach its desired destination, a beautiful landscape that would stimulate a literature testifying to the existence of interiority.

"Sitting Across from a Mirror" can be read as an examination of the relationship between literature and language, turning the mirror into another metaphor for literature. It was a short, first-person account of the narrator's impressions as he looks at his face in a mirror—apparently a rare event, since he was surprised at what he saw. He was so dissatisfied that he "hit [his] head with [his] two fists" (80). Then, paraphrasing the cliché that the eyes are the mirror of the soul—"the eyes are the window to a person"—he noted that human eyes are able to perceive things that are *not* visible: "When [eyes] look at a person . . . they can discover a person's state of mind and changes in emotion" (82). In the context of Yi Kwangsu's emphasis on *chŏng*, the mirror can be viewed as a metaphor for literature; it is supposed to enable the beholder to "see" an interiority that is simply there. The narrator began to wonder, "What have my eyes seen?" (82) and even called out to them in despair: "Ah, my eyes, in the decades since you have appeared, what have you done?" (82). Comparing his eyes to those of a cow resting on a board in a *sŏllŭngt'ang*[72] shop, he concluded, "it probably is because my head is completely empty" (82). The problem was one of language, of signification. He sees things but not their meaning, or, in other words, he sees landscapes but not ideal worlds. Interestingly, he attributed his inability to grasp meaning to a lack of interiority, his "empty head." Since literature is meant to obscure the fact that interiority is an effect of language, it seems as if it is interiority that gives things meaning. The narrator was unable not only to perceive but also to convey meaning. When he examined his ears and lips, he noted that although they can emit sounds in various languages, his lips just make "meaningless sounds" (83). He wondered why his lips cannot say things like "the earth is round" or "living things evolve" and cannot make sounds like those in *Hamlet*, *Faust*, and *The Divine Comedy* or the ones that come out of Beethoven's lips (84). If he could find a literature-as-mirror that would enable his eyes to see the inner essence of things (make signification possible), he would then be able to make discoveries and produce art. Literature had to narrate the discovery of interiority, but that discovery would, in turn, inspire the production of more literature.

In the canonical stories in *Ch'ŏngch'un*, the presence of landscape dominates the two stories set in Japan—"Wandering" and "Yun Kwangho"[73]—suggesting that landscape can be viewed as a metonym for Japanese imperialism. These landscapes are nightmarish versions of the dream-like one depicted in "From Tokyo to Seoul." The main character of "Wandering" is another lonely student with ambitions of becoming a writer. Narrated in the first person, the story records the main character's thoughts as he lies alone in bed one day while recovering from an illness. However, right at the beginning of the story, it is clear that his physical condition is not really what is bothering him. "My fever has gone down, and I have no more headaches. This morning, I could have gone to school. However, I am still lying here" (74). What troubles him is the sky; he looks at the gray-colored sky and notices that "the cold sky is stealthily looking down on me" (74), a phrase repeated several times throughout the story. He covers himself up and pulls a curtain over the window, but the sky is still able to reach him: "It seems as if the cold sky, covered with gray clouds, is turning into powder like snowflakes, flying in through the edges of the window, *tatami*, and wall, and gathering inside my blanket." (75). It makes him feel that his "life force (*saengmyŏng*) is cold" (75), leading him to reflect on loneliness and death (pp. 76–77). These "I-novel"-ish passages could be interpreted as signs of paranoia or depression, but the menacing landscape suggests an interpretation of the story as an illustration of the difficulties of writing under colonialism. Seemingly ubiquitous, the colonizer's presence is inescapable and threatens the narrator's very existence, rendering him incapable of writing. The love-object is not a person but Chosŏn itself, explicitly demonstrating the connection between interiority and nationalism. The narrator recollects that a friend had tried to comfort him by telling him, "Please remember that your body is no longer yours alone. And remember that all the people of Chosŏn have great expectations of you" (79). The narrator mentions that he had tried to devote himself to teaching and writing (80) but "could not 'marry with Chosŏn' as the great patriots do" (80). Whenever he feels lonely or cold, he "tries to think of Chosŏn as my lover (*aein*)," but "my love for Chosŏn is not that intense, and Chosŏn also does not seem to respond to my love" (80). The story ends as it began: the narrator concludes, "I am all alone," yet again feels the sky looming over him (82). The act of writing produced the same paradox: the narrator is moved to write but only ends up affirming his inability to write. All he can do is depict the landscape he cannot overcome.

"Yun Kwangho" is a story of the failure to find *chŏng* within such a threatening landscape. The title character is a sophomore studying economics at a university in Tokyo who has just received the top prize in his class, earning him the praise of all the Chosŏn students there (68). However, he begins to feel "loneliness and sorrow" (69), a feeling described as a lack of interiority: "In Kwangho's heart, there was a kind of deficiency. It was a large and deep cavern that seemed difficult to fill" (68). Like many of Yi Kwangsu's protagonists, Yun Kwangho is a loner. He has one close friend, Kim Chunwŏn, but as the "cavern in Kwangho's mind became more evident day by day, his loneliness and sorrow became more severe. . . . Even if [he] listened to Chunwŏn's words, not only did [he] not get comfort as he did before, but his loneliness and sorrow grew even deeper" (70). To fill this cavern, he begins a search for *chŏng*. He starts staring at young girls and boys on trolley cars (69), but after a while, this amusement ceases to satisfy him: "He was not satisfied with a mild, superficial love and demanded a passionate, concrete love. His cavern would be filled only by such a love, and his loneliness and sorrow would be relieved only by such a love" (72). As in "Wandering," it is when the search for *chŏng* fails that Japan is depicted as a loveless, inhuman landscape: "To Kwangho, the whole world was cold like an ice world and lonely like an uninhabited land" (72). In this state, Kwangho sees a student identified only as "P.," and "without being aware of it, his whole soul was moved toward P." (72). Failing to catch P.'s attention by dressing up and being too shy to confess his love in person, Kwangho writes P. a letter in his own blood. Rejected, he descends into despair and finally commits suicide. The story ends with the revelation that P. is a man, but what is also significant is that Chunwŏn, who is a helpless but pained spectator to the tragedy, writes the epitaph for Kwangho's grave: "This is the grave of Yun Kwangho who was born in an ice world, lived in an ice world, and died in an ice world" (82). Yun Kwangho's unrequited love reminds Chunwŏn of a similar incident years ago when he was in P.'s position (78–79), an event that now has a totally different meaning for him. Although he was not a direct participant in the events, he was the one who was moved to write. The spectator who becomes a writer is a theme that was fully developed in *Mujŏng*. His writing is literally an act of inscription into a landscape, but again, all it does is point out the failure to discover interiority.

Although the presence of Japan-as-landscape is more distant in the stories set in Chosŏn, "Sorrows of a Youth" and "Kim Kyŏng,"[74] it remains a formidable obstacle to modern writing. "Kim Kyŏng" concerns another character in a process of "translation." The title character is a young teacher returning to his school in the country-side after a short trip, and the story narrates his thoughts as he walks from the train station to the campus. Although he is an orphan and as lonely as the characters in the other short stories, he seems in harmony with the landscape. He "deliberately slowed down his steps" to savor the walk through the rice paddies, looking at the poplar forest (118), and then "with an even greater joy and happi-ness, Kim Kyŏng sat down, spreading his legs in the shade of the willow tree that he always sat under and smoked a cigarette" (119). Part of the reason for his happiness is that he hopes to fulfill his am-bition of becoming a poet. Instead of continuing his own studies, he decides to "return to his hometown and, remaining in the country-side, attempt to investigate the way of life of real society and the se-crets of the heart of the Chosŏn *minjok*" (119). The discovery of inte-riority can be understood as a kind of homecoming; Kim Kyŏng was trying to write a literature that would narrate a return to one's true self. At this point, the story is interrupted by a flashback to his days as a middle school student in Tokyo that names his literary influ-ences: "the ones who first influenced him emotionally were Tolstoy, Kinoshita Naoe, and Tokutomi Roka" (120), but later he also became an avid reader of Byron (121), so that "in the young Kim Kyŏng's soul, a good angel and evil angel were fighting for dominance" (121). The struggle between "Byronism" and "Tolstoyism" "almost drove him crazy" (122), and it was in this state that he returned to Chosŏn and began teaching. But despite the intensity of his literary influ-ences, it was at "Osan [the name of the school] where he became a person of Chosŏn (*Chosŏnin*)" (122). Yi Kwangsu was again sug-gesting that the origins of modern literature were not a matter of imitating the West but of rewriting and *translating* it.[75]

When the story returns to the narrative present, everything begins to change, and gradually the apparent harmony is lost. Kim wonders "whether it was worthwhile to sacrifice his freedom for Osan" (124). His writing also suffers; he is constantly making resolutions such as "writing one composition or poem a day and reading one hundred pages" (124), but he "did not complete even one-third of his planned compositions and reading" (124). His students were the main object of his affections, and as someone who "grew up not knowing the warmth of a family with brothers and sisters," he regarded the students as his "brothers, sisters, and beloved ones (*chŏngin*)" (p. 123). In the end, he loses faith even in them. Hearing their voices as he nears the campus, he rushes to meet them, but by the time he gets there, they had already gone by, leaving him to reflect, "What is my relationship to them?" (126) and lamenting, "Is there anyone who would not be able to forget me?" (126). It is Japan that literally interrupts the process of translation, turning his homecoming into an experience of almost total alienation. Yet again, the narrator finds himself at the wrong destination, having failed to discover interiority.

"Sorrows of a Youth" can be read as an allegory of modern versus traditional literature. It begins promisingly as the story of a young student, Munho, who is a favorite of his female cousins because he "liked amusing them with interesting stories he read [to them] when he came home from school" (106). Munho's foil is his male cousin Munhae, who is more "distant and logical" (108) and does not like playing with the female cousins. The two also embody different conceptions of literature:

Munho praised Chinese poets like Li Po and Wang Ch'ang-ling, and Western poets such as Tolstoy, Shakespeare, and Goethe. Munhae, however, berated such poets as being good-for-nothing idlers whose literature was of no use in life. He esteemed men such as Confucius, Mencius, Chu Hsi, or, among Westerners, Socrates and Washington. . . . Whereas Munho loved literature with aesthetic, emotional qualities, Munhae preferred literature that was intellectual and morally good.[76] (109)

Munho is clearly the embodiment of the principles expounded in "What Is Literature?" When both Munho and Munhae write stories for their cousins, the women, not surprisingly, prefer Munho's (109). The object of Munho's affections is his young cousin Nansu, his favorite among all his cousins (106). In Nansu is combined Munho's search for *chŏng* and his love of literature; he "believed that she had the natural talent to become a poet" (110) and planned to take her to Seoul for her education (111). However, Nansu's parents arrange a marriage for her with the young son of a yangban family. The marriage proceeds although everyone becomes despondent when they learn the son is mentally deficient (112). Even on her wedding day, Munho urges Nansu to run away with him to Seoul, but she says that she cannot disobey her parents (115). The story then jumps ahead three years to Munho's return from studying in Japan. Although his female cousins gather around him as before, "the happiness he felt three years ago had disappeared forever" (117). The experience in Japan has clearly changed him; he is no longer the happy storyteller he once was. A critique of the traditional family system on one level, "Sorrows of a Youth" can be read as yet another illustration of the paradoxical nature of writing in the early colonial period.

Kim Tongin called "To My Young Friend" "the first [literary] work in Chosŏn that was influenced by Western literature."[77] Serialized over three issues of Ch'ŏngch'un,[78] it consisted of four letters from a young student in Shanghai to an unidentified friend that contained "I-novel"-ish reflections on topics such as love, marriage, and art and related his pursuit of a young woman with whom he fell in love when he was a student in Tokyo years ago. A widely read and influential story, it became "the standard of the letter form for men and women in love."[79] The epistolary form in itself demonstrated that the narrator had acquired the ability to write, and its partial "success" at overcoming the obstacles to writing was perhaps one of the reasons why Kim Tongin distinguished it from the rest of Yi Kwangsu's short fiction of this period. The first letter is reminiscent of "Wandering"; the narrator, yet another lonely student, writes about a recent serious illness. Unlike the characters in the other stories, the narrator "believes that though my body may die, my spirit will live in the spirit of many fellow countrymen, maintain its life, and, by being passed on to their descendants, will be able to preserve its life forever" (no. 9, p. 96). Seemingly referring to the relation of literature to the nation in "What Is Literature?" the narrator is expressing a faith in literature itself, more specifically, in its ability to transmit his spirit to others. This faith is also a belief in the importance of chŏng, and not surprisingly, the narrator says that "what a person values when he thinks of and fears death . . . is simply love" (98). Such emotion is juxtaposed against a stark landscape: "I try to live in order to experience the exquisite pleasure of . . . holding you in my arms and being held by you on the cold and bitter fields of humanity" (99). When a young woman and boy come to nurse him, he feels "as if I had met a comrade on an uninhabited field" (100). The cold world that Yun Kwangho cannot bear to live in became tolerable because of his "faith" in chŏng; it is an experience that is close to, but not quite yet the same as, the discovery of interiority.

Considered in isolation, the second letter would be no different than Yi Kwangsu's other stories from this period; it is about yet another failed attempt at love. Toward the beginning of the letter, the narrator notes that "the men and women of Chosŏn have not yet met each other through love," and this statement describes as much a literary reality as a social one. The first half of the letter is a long digression on various aspects of love, including an almost scholarly-like analysis of its three "practical benefits" (107–8). Significantly, only after writing these thoughts down is the narrator able to continue with his story. In his weakened state, he did not recognize the woman he now calls his "savior," and he goes looking for her to thank her for her help (104)—another *cherchez-la-femme* as a search for *chŏng*. When he receives a note from her asking about his health, he learns her name and remembers that they had met in Tokyo six years ago (110–11).

The second half of the letter is a flashback to their first encounter. The woman turns out to be Kim Illyŏn, the younger sister of a close friend from his days at Waseda (111). He had immediately been captivated by her, and what was interesting is that they interacted mainly through writing. Though married, he sent her a letter that was, in effect, an abridged Yi Kwangsu short story. Confessing that he was a "lonely person," he wrote that he "thinks it strange that his soul has not shriveled up and died from the long winter" (114) and entreated her just to tell him, "I love you," the "one phrase [that] would give me eternal hope, pleasure, and passion" (115). When he received her reply, he rushed out of his room because "it seemed right to read it in the fresh and wide Nature under the clear sky and shining sun" (116), but her rejection apparently shocked him so deeply that he cannot even quote it to his friend. Contrary to what he had expected, he was not saved from the chilly landscape that he felt was menacing his very soul. Later, she sent another note asking for his forgiveness (116), leading to a romantic meeting in a park, but the whole episode turns out to have been a dream (117–20). The dream itself is also a literary encounter; it is about the fulfillment of *chŏng* on both the personal and literary levels. He felt that "all the cells composing my body tingled with happiness and fulfillment" (118) and told her that "thoughts of you will give me unlimited poetic inspiration" (119). What is unique about this story is that the literary devices that are mainly used to express a single character's emotions in the other stories are used here to further the relations *between* the characters. If the story had ended with the narrator's waking up from his dream, it would have been virtually the same as the other stories, but the fact that he relates those events as part of his past foreshadows that something different is about to happen.

Although the story loses some of its narrative coherence in the third letter, the relation between landscape and *chŏng* remains the same. The letter begins as another story of "translation"; the narrator was traveling on a Russian ship, headed to Manchuria on his way to America (26). A mysterious accident causes it to sink, and most of the letter recounts the narrator's thoughts as the ship slowly became enveloped by the sea. By an incredible coincidence, Kim Illyŏn was on the same ship, and although other people were also in danger, he decided to save her from drowning because "it is natural to save my fellow countryperson" (32). In the end, they are saved by a boat called "Korea" (33); finally, a character finds himself in a vehicle of "translation" that protects him from the threatening landscape. But instead of recounting their return home, the fourth letter continues the journey; the narrator is writing on a train with the woman he loves sleeping next to him, while outside is the Siberian forest, a "sacred sanctuary where no two-footed animal has tread" (134). Initially, it seemed that the discovery of interiority was complete; after the tumultuous past few days, he now has had the time to "read" her. Believing that "if one looks at a person's face while sleeping, one can judge fairly accurately their character," he states that "the best opportunity for such an examination is on a train or a boat" (130). The way Kim Illyŏn sleeps "revealed the grace and calmness of her heart (*simjŏng*)" (131).

He begins to remember all he has suffered because of his love for her and realizes that "since the hearts of two people who have overcome such difficulties are like two different worlds, they cannot approach each other before communication is established between them" (131). Saying that "the best means of communication are language and emotions (*kamjŏng*)" (131), he resolves to tell her everything when she wakes up (132). In other words, they still need one more literary moment to complete their "love story." They begin to talk, but the narrator soon wanders into his own thoughts in a state of blissful confusion. He wonders, "For what reason are people riding in this car, and where are they headed? . . . Why do flowers bloom and wither, and why do the sun and the moon rise and set? . . . How, among all people, did she and I meet and fall in love?"

(136–37). His only answer is: "I do not know. I do not know" (137). The story ends with the narrator anxious but expectant: "Now I cannot predict what will happen tomorrow. . . . We will bring our bodies wherever this train takes us, and we will take our souls to wherever they are brought" (147). Despite all the hope he feels, his uncertainty suggests that the process of "translation" is incomplete; he is not sure whether the train is taking him to a place where the landscape would be imbued with *chŏng*.

## Birth of a Writer: The Discovery of Interiority in *Mujŏng*

Written while Yi Kwangsu was studying at Waseda, *Mujŏng* was serialized in the *Maeil sinbo* beginning on January 1, 1917, and was an immediate sensation. There are stories of people walking miles to buy a copy of the paper to get their daily installment.[80] Soon after the serialization ended, it was published in book form by Ch'oe Namsŏn's Sinmun'gwan[81] and went through several reprintings in succeeding decades. In early issues of the journal *Chosŏn mundan* (The Chosŏn literary world) in the mid-1920s,[82] advertisements for the novel noted that it was the only book in Chosŏn to have sold more than ten thousand copies.[83] I feel that one reason for its popularity was that it narrated the discovery of interiority, and this discovery entailed the overcoming of the obstacles that disrupted Yi Kwangsu's short stories: eyes could see the invisible; meaning could be understood and conveyed; landscape became beautiful; and the love-object was obtained. The plot of *Mujŏng* is the archetypal love-triangle of a young man, the schoolteacher Ri Hyŏngsik, who is torn between two women: Yŏngch'ae, the virtuous daughter of his early benefactor who became a *kisaeng* when her family was ruined and has now suddenly reappeared in Hyŏngsik's life, and Sŏnhyŏng, the beautiful daughter of a rich church elder to whom Hyŏngsik is giving private lessons in English. Since Yŏngch'ae's father, the founder of the school Hyŏngsik attended, occasionally joked that he wanted her to marry Hyŏngsik, he feels obligated to obey her father's wishes. Before he can act, she is raped and apparently heads to P'yŏngyang to commit suicide. It turns out that Sŏnhyŏng's father arranged for him to teach his daughter English because he views him as a potential son-in-law, planning to send them both to college in the United States—a longtime dream of Hyŏngsik's. He agrees to marry Sŏnhyŏng, and he and Yŏngch'ae pursue separate paths until all the characters meet by chance on a train.

The preceding discussion of Yi Kwangsu's literary theory enables a different interpretation of the novel's title. If *chŏng* is the basis of interiority and thus of modern literature itself, then the term *mujŏng* (no *chŏng*) can be understood literally as a lack of interiority or even as a lack of literature. The novel can be read as a *Bildungsroman* in which the characters gradually attain interiority, and the full-length novel apparently provided Yi Kwangsu with the form to accommodate such narration in a way that the short story could not. It should be remembered that it was not until *Sarang* (Love; 1939) that Yi Kwangsu wrote a novel completely before its publication; *Mujŏng* was written as it was being serialized. The text shows the traces of having been a process of exploration for Yi Kwangsu as well; the style of narration changes slightly as the story progresses. At first, the narration, always in the third person, is a little awkward; characters generally do not reveal things about their past until they tell someone about it, as in Yŏngch'ae's initial meeting with Hyŏngsik. But after Yŏngch'ae's departure, the narration becomes more "confident," directly relating various flashbacks without dialogue. About a third of the way through the novel, the storyteller begins to appear in the text, announcing shifts in the story (e.g., pp. 117, 256).

There were at least two ways in which Yi Kwangsu overcame the obstacles to writing modern literature and became able to narrate the discovery of interiority. First, he made *Mujŏng* a quasi-historical novel. Years later, he revealed that in *Mujŏng*, he was trying to depict a "Chosŏn that had awakened during the Russo-Japanese War."[84] It is set before the formal annexation by Japan in 1910, during the formative period of modern journalism in Chosŏn. This is also the time that Yi later identified as the beginning of Chosŏn literature: "The beginning of modern literature . . . was the end of the Russo-Japanese War."[85] These conjunctions suggest that the novel was about a search for origins, the origins of modernity. This move enabled him to project the search for interiority onto the recent past. Second, the various devices used in the short stories were naturalized by "sublimating" them into the relations among the characters; that is, the way the characters interacted with each other was fundamentally *literary*. The use of the epistolary form and other such techniques perhaps made the artifice of literature too apparent to make the discovery of interiority seem believable. Devices such as letters, daydreams, and flashbacks still appeared in *Mujŏng*, but they had a secondary, subordinate role to the relations among the characters, which dominated the narrative. The characters found *chŏng* in and projected their interiorities onto each other; another way of putting it is that the characters functioned as landscapes (and as love-objects) for each other. In this way, the discovery of interiority became natural, and its relation to landscape as well as its source as a performative effect of language became obscured. I will try to demonstrate how this second aspect worked by showing how the "inner person" (*sok saram*) of the characters is awakened. The phrases "inner person" and "true person" (*ch'am saram*) are used repeatedly and are interchangeable synonyms for "interiority," again suggesting that it is the interior life that is the authentic source of a person's identity.

The very first scene of the novel—in which Hyŏngsik is walking to Sŏnhyŏng's house for the first time from his school—establishes him as what should by now be seen as the prototypical Yi Kwangsu protagonist; he is shy, awkward, and studious. When he bumps into his carefree journalist friend Sin Usŏn, it takes some prodding before Hyŏngsik admits who he is going to teach, "embarrassedly and rubbing the back of his neck with his hand" (23). Like Kim Kyŏng, he is an orphan who became a teacher, but he continues to be lonely because he has never been able to find anyone of his own age to befriend, even when he was studying in Japan (205). All his affection is showered onto his students, and it is again expressed through the trope of landscape: "When he became a teacher and came into contact with all the young boys, Hyŏngsik's love, which had been locked up and starved for twenty years now, came forth like the blades of grass that shoot up in the spring wind after being covered by snow" (207). Only after the main characters are introduced and meet each other is it mentioned that both Hyŏngsik and Sŏnhyŏng have not matured yet and do not possess an interiority. Sŏnhyŏng, "having been raised in a Christian family, already received the baptism of heaven. However, [she] still had not received the baptism of fire called life (*insaeng*). . . . A person like Sŏnhyŏng can become a true person for the first time only after [she] has received the baptism of fire called life and the 'person' inside her has awakened" (94). And even though "Hyŏngsik called himself an awakened 'person,' [he] too had not yet received the baptism of fire called life" (95). In "What Is Literature?" Yi Kwangsu stated that modern literature must be rooted in life; this "baptism" need not be literal nor involve direct suffering—it can be a literary experience. Thus, the plot of *Mujŏng* can be understood as a series of literary encounters that constitute a "baptism of fire."

Hyŏngsik's transformation begins when Yŏngch'ae suddenly reappears in his life and tells him her story. The meeting occurs on the day he begins teaching Sŏnhyŏng and seven years after Yŏngch'ae's father's school was forced to close down because he was wrongfully imprisoned. She relates how she had been tricked into becoming a *kisaeng* and how her father's shame led him to commit suicide in prison. Her story moves all her listeners to tears, and after she leaves, Hyŏngsik notes that she has a "literary bent" (*munhak chŏk saekch'ae*; 51)—emphasizing that their interaction is literary, that of a storyteller and a listener. After hearing her story, Hyŏngsik's "inner person" is awakened, and this awakening is described as an opening of eyes, a gaining of sight: when he looks at people on the street, he

smelled a fragrance and saw a light inside them that he could not see before. In other words, they seemed to have a new light and new significance. . . .

It seemed as if a layer had been removed from his eyes. However, it was not that a layer had been removed from his eyes, but in reality, an eye that had been closed up to now had newly opened. . . .

Only now did the "person" inside Hyŏngsik open his eyes. Through his "inner eyes," he came to see the "inner meaning" of all things. Only now did Hyŏngsik's "inner person" become liberated. (96–97)

Although she herself does not realize it until later in the novel, Yŏngch'ae's "inner person" had already been awakened because of her sufferings over the preceding seven years (see, e.g., p. 163), and indeed, she is a virtual repository of stories. The reason that she was not aware of her "inner person" is that "the *Classic of Virtuous Women*, which her father had taught her when she was young, . . . completely ruled her life" (102). Because she lived according to traditional morality, she was incapable of recognizing *chŏng*. All the main characters eventually hear Yŏngch'ae's life story, and before their final transformation into patriots dedicated to Chosŏn's future, what unites them all is Yŏngch'ae and her stories.

As he learns more about her life, Hyŏngsik continues to have "literary" experiences that nurture the development of his "inner person." When Yŏngch'ae went to P'yŏngyang, her hometown, intending to commit suicide, she left Hyŏngsik a letter (156–59) explaining that she saw no reason to live now that she had lost the virginity that she had been preserving for him. Her letter affected not only Hyŏngsik but also his friend Sin Usŏn and the old *kisaeng* madam (only identified as *nop'a*—"old woman"): "Hyŏngsik's shaking hand dropped the letter on his lap. And large teardrops fell onto the letter on his lap. The fallen tears made the characters written on the letter all the more clear. Usŏn also wiped away tears with his sleeve, and the old woman covered her face with her skirt and fell to the floor" (159).

Hyŏngsik has another transforming experience as he rides the train to P'yŏngyang with the *nop'a* in pursuit of Yŏngch'ae; it shows that Hyŏngsik has gained the ability to perceive the "inner person" in others. As he looks at the old woman, he thinks, "'That old woman did not have opportunities to see a 'true person' and so did not even think of becoming a true person.' . . . . While absorbed in these thoughts, Hyŏngsik looked again at the old woman's face. Now thoughts of her as dirty and evil disappeared, and in fact he began to pity her. . . . The old woman saw Yŏngch'ae's determination to die and for the first time discovered the 'true person'" (168–69). Riding on the train through the barren landscapes that inspired no songs in "From Tokyo to Seoul" now enables Hyŏngsik to have a revelatory, and literary, experience. After arriving in P'yŏngyang, he heads to the grave of Yŏngch'ae's father, thinking that she would at least stop there one last time before committing suicide. He does not find her there, but "standing before the grave, Hyŏngsik was not sad" (197) and returns to Seoul alone. On the train back, "Hyŏngsik's mind . . . was in a most confused state" (199), and his reflections lead him to conclude: "Am I not being too heartless (*mujŏng ham*)? Shouldn't I have stayed longer and found out where Yŏngch'ae is? Even if she is dead, shouldn't I have at least looked for her body?" (203). Although the opening of his "inner eye" has enabled him to see the intangible and to gain a compassion for others he did not have before, he himself does not think that he possesses *chŏng*.

Although it is Yŏngch'ae who makes him realize his lack of *chŏng*, it is in his relationship with Sŏnhyŏng that Hyŏngsik seeks love. The first time he saw her, he "thought of her as his sister" (28), showing that initially he does not know how to deal with her as an individual. Their relationship develops faster than their emotions; it essentially begins with their engagement. After his return from P'yŏngyang, Sŏnhyŏng's father arranges a dinner to formalize their engagement, but it turns out to be a comic and empty ritual rather than an affirmation of love. Wanting to do things according to the "new style" (*sin sik*), he gathers the family together and in turn asks his wife, Hyŏngsik, and Sŏnhyŏng if each agrees to the engagement; instead of being moved, the young couple find it funny (246–47). Not only are they not in love, but they are also not able to "read" each other: "Of course, both Hyŏngsik and Sŏnhyŏng did not understand each other. Their love was like the love of a beautiful flower. ... It was an extremely superficial love. ... When they looked at each other, they wondered, 'What is going on inside that person's mind (*saram ŭi sok*)?'" (244). After their engagement, Hyŏngsik is a regular visitor at Sŏnhyŏng's house, giving both of them a chance to examine each other more closely. Sŏnhyŏng finds that he is far from her ideal type (see p. 282), and she "tried to alter his face in several ways. Pull up his eyelids, push in his cheek bones, make his hands smaller . . . and slowly Hyŏngsik's face became likable. However, after a while, the drawn-in cheek bones popped out again ... his eyes became very narrow" (283). What was a solitary experience in "Sitting Across from a Mirror" now occurs between two people; Hyŏngsik is acting as Sŏnhyŏng's mirror, reflecting her lack of an "inner eye" in the features of his face. Ultimately, Hyŏngsik is so confused by her that he asks her directly if she loves him, but this only causes more misunderstanding (288). Like the lovers in "To My Young Friend," they need a literary experience in order to fall in love.

Fittingly, the novel concludes with a train ride, a "translation" that resolves all the relations among the characters, and a meeting on the train brings the tensions among them to a climax. When Hyŏngsik and Sŏnhyŏng board a train on their way to America, Hyŏngsik and Usŏn, who is accompanying them part of the way, discover that Yŏngch'ae is still alive. She has boarded the same train with her friend Kim Pyŏnguk, who talked Yŏngch'ae out of committing suicide and is taking her to Tokyo to study together. Finding out that she is alive causes Hyŏngsik to waver again between the two women, and he imagines that Yŏngch'ae's spirit appears in front of him, saying, "You heartless (*mujŏng*) creature, receive my eternal curse!" (327). Again, it is Yŏngch'ae who makes him realize his lack of *chŏng* and that his "love is only a love of appearances. ... He did not understand Sŏnhyŏng's personality one bit" (332–33). For Sŏnhyŏng, it is on the train that her *ch'am saram* begins to awaken; this occurs somewhat later for her than it does for the other characters— which is not surprising since she is the last to meet Yŏngch'ae. Sŏnhyŏng's "baptism of fire" occurs when Hyŏngsik goes to talk to

Yŏngch'ae: "Sŏnhyŏng's heart was not calm. While Hyŏngsik was away to find Yŏngch'ae, her mind became scattered. . . . As if [she] were about to burst into tears, her nose quivered. ... This is how jealousy and melancholy are learned" (335–36). Although she does not see the two of them together, she imagines the scene in her mind; again, the experience is a literary one. In fact, her restlessness is attributed to her lack of life experience and, more specifically, her lack of literature: "In the school of life, Sŏnhyŏng was now entering the middle-level course. She was beginning to learn love, jealousy, rage, hate, and sadness. ... If she had learned what love and jealousy are by studying life through religion or literature, she would have definitely known what to do in this situation" (339–40).

Before their journeys of "translation" are completed, the train ride is interrupted by an intrusion of landscape; rain has flooded the tracks, making it impossible to go any further. Unlike the trains in the other stories, this train has uncannily brought them to the proper destination, the place where a final transformation becomes possible. As they leave the train, they see people covered in mud fleeing into the hills, and "thoughts of the flood, the sound of the water, the gathering clouds, and the people climbing the steep hills who had lost their houses made them forget about themselves as individuals and made them have the thoughts that are common to all human beings" (344). When they see a pregnant woman collapse, all rush to help her, taking her to an inn and getting her a doctor (347–49). Instead of being overwhelmed by the flood, they are moved to action. Pyŏnguk, a female music student, organizes an impromptu concert to raise money for the flood victims, and everyone contributes. Pyŏnguk plays the violin, Yŏngch'ae sings a hymn accompanied by Pyŏnguk, and then all three women sing a song together that Yŏngch'ae had written in classical Chinese and Hyŏngsik translated into the vernacular. Once connected only through personal ties, they "become much closer while working together" (355) and now form a nascent artistic community.

Hyŏngsik is the one who makes the others realize that the flood has given them a glimpse of the Chosŏn *minjok*. Back at the inn, a pensive Hyŏngsik talks at length about the necessity of helping the Chosŏn people by devoting themselves to education: "Who gives us the money to ride this train and pay for our tuition? It is Chosŏn that gives it to us. To gain strength, to gain knowledge. ... Let's devote ourselves to seeing a much better Chosŏn by the time we grow old and die" (357–58). When he asks the others what they intend to do to achieve this goal, they are so moved that "each tried to imagine their future" (360). In contrast to the protagonists of "To My Young Friend," they now know exactly where the train will take them. The carefree and irresponsible Usŏn declares, "Today, I also have become a person of this land. ... Remember that I am now no longer the Sin Usŏn of old" (361), and Sŏnhyŏng "felt sorry about the thoughts she had had about [Yŏngch'ae]. Now she wanted to love both Hyŏngsik and Yŏngch'ae" (357). Hyŏngsik's transformation is perhaps the most subtle. Initially, he was a giver of language; he taught English at school and to Sŏnhyŏng, and when he was a student, he had written the complete vernacular alphabet on a sheet of paper for Yŏngch'ae that is one of her most prized possessions (160). The attainment of *chŏng* enables him to become a true writer: a translator into the vernacular and a giver of *chŏng* who enables others to visualize the future of the *minjok*. The train finally arrives at a place where interiority permeates and transforms the landscape itself; as the narrator notes at the very end of the novel, "Ah, our land is becoming more beautiful every day" (364).

## Conclusion

It is not true that I consciously entered the literary world with a naturalist work. ... What I am trying to say is that both our naturalist literature and our realist literature are neither imitations nor imports but naturally arose from their own foundations and that it was the era and the life environment that gave birth to writers and works that had naturalist tendencies.                    —Yŏm Sangsŏp[86]

When he betrayed the *minjok*, the reason that readers were so enraged and hurt was that they themselves had become Yi Kwangsu. They were not criticizing Yi Kwangsu but were criticizing, crying over, and pained at their own selves.        —Kim Yunsik[87]

Despite various efforts to "banish" Yi Kwangsu, his figure continues to haunt the margins of the *minjok*. He is often called back to and conjured up at its center, only to be exiled again, the fate of all those who betray the *minjok*. It is in this repetitive, ritual movement between the margins and the center that the *minjok* defines and reproduces itself. Ironically, this movement is based on a form of narration whose origins can be traced in Yi Kwangsu's writings. The persistence of Yi Kwangsu can be explained, at least partially, by his intricate relation to modernity.

The discovery of interiority was a reaction to Japanese hegemony, which sought to deny Chosŏn a distinct identity and to "monopolize" the modern, including modern literature, within the colony. Although the modern works Yi Kwangsu read in Japan expressed an interiority, they did not express *his* interiority. They were foreign and thus "exterior," making him self-consciously aware of Chosŏn's lack of both modern literature and a distinct identity. Yi Kwangsu's texts documented, in part, the introduction of a conception of literature in which identity took the form of interiority. One of my objectives has been to show that the conditions of writing at the time were imbricated within the texts themselves. Borrowing terms from Karatani Kojin's analysis of Japanese literature, I have tried to show that in Yi Kwangsu's works, the presence of Japan was internalized through the trope of landscape. He then conceptualized the origins of modern literature as a process of "translation": literally to move from the cold and alienating landscape of Japan to an ideal world where the land was humanized by being imbued with *chŏng*. Rather than merely imitating Western or Japanese literature in the vernacular, modern literature in Chosŏn sought to produce a difference within the same, a literature that was modern yet expressed an identity unique to Chosŏn. What this act of translation produced was the discovery of interiority. For Yi Kwangsu, it was modern because only modern literature could express the emotions of interiority that had supposedly been suppressed in traditional literature. It was unique to Chosŏn simply because it had always been there, waiting to be discovered; as something nonphysical and immaterial, it captured the aspects of identity that were unaffected by tumultuous changes in the outside world.

As Yi Kwangsu and other intellectuals discussed and debated the term *minjok* in the 1920s, it became conceived as the essence of the Chosŏn people. If the term *sok saram* (inner person) in *Mujŏng* represented interiority on the level of the individual, then *minjok* represented a community of "inner people," a *sok nara* (inner country), if you will. By narrating its discovery, as if it had an existence prior to its expression, literature enabled the nation to "forget" its origins in language. Another objective of this chapter has been to show how writing itself was a central concern of Yi Kwangsu's short stories and how this aspect later became obscured in *Mujŏng* through its displacement into the relations among the characters. Rather than being seen as a form of mediation that created a sense of interiority, literature seemed to become a transparent medium that depicted a nation that was "real" and "objective." It is this moment—the moment that the "new literature" transformed the "metaphysics" of writing—that is one of the markers of literary modernity. The discovery of interiority can also be seen as one of the bases for a new type of history; namely, the history of the *minjok*. In trying to break with traditional literary forms, Yi Kwangsu felt that he was writing not within a history but as if he were trying to find his true history. It was a search for origins in a past that was thought to be pure and timeless. Although it was only in modern times that such a search became possible, literature enabled the nation to mask its newness by giving it an aura of pristine authenticity.[88]

Through the discovery of interiority, *Mujŏng* enabled readers to "visualize" an emerging national community. Although at the beginning of the novel Ri Hyŏngsik seems no different from the protagonists of Yi Kwangsu's short stories, he transforms into a completely different person at the end by discovering his "inner person." He is able to marry the woman he loves and to "write" words that move others to devote themselves to the future of Chosŏn. But *Mujŏng* only gave readers a glimpse of the existence of interiority; it was the task of later writers to describe and fill in the details of Chosŏn's identity. Yi Kwangsu's second novel, *Kaech'ŏkcha* (The pioneers; 1918), is centered on a character who has returned from studying abroad, apparently starting at the point that *Mujŏng* ended.

Yi Kwangsu continued to pursue his vision of nationalist literature in the early 1920s, although the March First movement completely transformed the literary world. The explosion of mass-level resistance led the Japanese to loosen publication laws, and with the establishment of privately owned vernacular dailies and several new journals, the once relatively small and unitary literary world both expanded and fragmented. Western literary schools such as naturalism, symbolism, and dadaism were introduced, and proletarian literature became a major force among intellectuals, mainly through *Kaebyŏk*, the leading intellectual journal of the early 1920s. In this period, Yi Kwangsu was most famous for stirring up a controversy over the gradualist politics he advocated in articles such as "Minjok kaejoron" (On national reconstruction, *Kaebyŏk*, May 1922),[89] but he also was the editor-in-chief of the journal *Chosŏn mundan*, which he helped to found in 1924.[90] His writings in this journal bore many similarities to those of the pre-1919 period. He serialized a much longer and more sophisticated exposition of his literary theory under the title "Munhak kangjwa" (Lectures on literature), and his short stories still contained familiar elements such as letter writing and lonely male protagonists.[91] Just like his stories in *Ch'ŏngch'un*, his short fiction from the early 1920s can also be seen as textbooks on writing.[92] However, at the same time, Yi Kwangsu's conception of literature came under attack from a new generation of writers and critics.[93] Modernity itself became the issue of debate: Did the March First Movement enable the fulfillment of nationalist literature or demonstrate its impossibility?[94]

# TEN

# National Identity and the Creation

# of the Category "Peasant"

# in Colonial Korea

### Clark Sorensen

In the twentieth century, Korean agrarian nationalists have often treated the cultivators, or *nongmin*, as a self-evident natural category that embodies the essence of the Korean nation. Although the term *nongmin* is ancient, thinking of the *nongmin* as a natural group within the Korean stratification system and privileging the relationship of that group to Korean national identity emerged only in the 1920s in conjunction with the introduction of Western class models of society. In this chapter, I argue that this discursive practice is a historically contingent strategy to carve out a space for a Korean identity within an assimilative empire, rather than a belated recognition of the primordial base of the Korean people, as promoters of class models of Korean society tend to assert. In fact, investigation of a range of popular written sources from the 1890s through the 1930s suggests that changes in discourse about social stratification in which cultivators, or *nongmin*, are conceptualized as peasants was part of a struggle to capture politically and discursively the process of restructuration of class relations taking place as a result of colonialism. Although a similar process in China led to the creation of the category *nongmin* at approximately the same time, because China retained national sovereignty the discursive uses to which this category were put are distinct from those of Korea. The evidence here points to a model in which social categories are contingent and discursively constructed rather than things in themselves, but constructed in relationship to goal-directed political activity.

One of the literary phenomena of the 1970s, during the period that the South Korean economy began surging ahead and Korea transformed itself within a single decade from a predominantly rural, peasant country to a predominantly urban-industrial one,[1] was the serialization beginning in 1971 in the literary journal *Hyŏndae munhak* (Contemporary literature) of Pak Kyŏngni's novel *T'oji* (Land). This *taeha sosŏl*, or *roman-fleuve*, dealing with the inhabitants of a small village on the Sŏmjin River that divides the two southern provinces of South Kyŏngsang and South Chŏlla, had reached twelve long volumes by 1979, when it was published as a whole, and was continued into the 1980s with three more volumes, bringing the story into the present.

Although by no means the only South Korean *roman-fleuve* from the 1970s to focus on traditional Korean life,[2] *Land* epitomizes a certain kind of Korean thought about the importance of peasants to Korean culture. The book begins with an extraordinary invocation of a village festival on the feast of the Autumn Moon, 1897, where "no matter who [the peasants performing the ceremony] are . . . they are the handsomest men with the best carriage in the village, who free the very pith of their minds with joy beating out the rhythm [of the dance on gongs and drums]."[3]

These peasants contrast with the effete local *yangban* landlord, Undersecretary Ch'oe (Ch'oe *ch'amp'an*), who is immersed unproductively in books, and for whom "all the nervous complaints of the world and the melancholy outlined in his profile stand up." Nevertheless, these handsome peasants and this effete *yangban* have a relationship:

After performing for a spell in the threshing ground, the peasants (*nongbu*)[4] enter into the final phase of the ceremony (*kut*), and snake out—not to the riverbank or mountain shrine—but onto the road, and throng into a compound with a large wooden gate [Undersecretary Ch'oe's compound]. There they do a spell of earth spirit treading (*chisin palpki*) and, wiping the sweat from their brows with hook-like hands, are fed liquor and rice.

Ceremonies analogous to this earth spirit treading were designated by the South Korean state in the 1970s and 1980s as "intangible cultural treasures" (*muhyŏng munhwajae*) that express the Korean essence. In the novel, however, all was not well for these 1897 peasants, who were living the Korean essence, for the impending decline of Korea into colonial subjugation is foreshadowed:

Could the autumn moon of the eighth lunar month be sorrow, like the transparent yet obscure Hansan ramie screens? . . . [For] while this harvest moon festival like Hansan ramie goes on, from the mountain slopes to the emptying fields an evening glow appears and lies emptily over them. The mountain of mixed forest behind the village, and the darkly rising mountain crest slowly withers to yellow. A dry wind will blow over the memorials praising men's past deeds, the moss-covered monuments to womanly virtue, and the one or two crape myrtle trees standing beside the devil posts. And so, the sound of the approaching long winter night can be heard.

*Land* is an example of "peasant literature" (*nongmin munhak*),[5] a literary genre created in the 1930s and revived in the 1970s that expresses the extraordinary and special role the peasantry, or *nongmin*,[6] have occupied in Koreans' twentieth-century constructions of their national identity. As late as the 1960s, half the Korean population were still small-scale cultivators, of course, but even as Korea became predominantly urban and industrial in the past thirty years, the peasantry has continued to occupy an important place in the Korean national imagination. The extraordinary success of *romans-fleuves* centering on the peasantry, of which *Land* is an example, is well known. And well into the 1990s Korean folklorists and anthropologists have continued to comb the countryside to find in the peasantry a source of authentic Koreanness that, properly packaged, has come to be widely consumed by urbanites in folklore games, "national art" shops, and so forth—including even the "transparent yet obscure" Hansan ramie screens that symbolize the tragedy of the Korean peasantry in *Land*, and whose makers have been designated "intangible national treasures." As the basis of the Korean *minjung*—the popular masses envisioned as the "agents of social transformation and progress"[7]—populist historians continue to privilege the peasantry as the site of construction of modern Korean national identity. The historian Cho Tonggŏl, for example, has written:

Korea's modern national consciousness came to maturity in the course of a survival movement to oppose Japanese penetration. In particular, what was hastened by the struggle to oppose the damage due to Japanese penetration in the late Han empire [1897–1910] was the growth into a nation of the *minjung* composed largely of peasants. More than anybody else, it was the peasants who could feel the Japanese penetration. . . . So the Tonghak revolutionary movement from the beginning of Japanese penetration developed into a peasant revolutionary movement. . . . The anti-feudal, anti-imperialism promoted by the Tonghak Army was precisely the demand of the peasantry, and the Tonghak revolutionary movement came to maturation just as it was as a peasant movement.[8]

It is not my purpose here to investigate whether authentic Korean national consciousness is *really* found pre-eminently among the Korean peasantry, or whether the development of modern Korean nationalist consciousness can indeed *really* be traced to an anti-Japanese Tonghak movement, which was fundamentally a peasant movement as Cho claims. Nor is my concern with the "scientific" description of social reality—for example, whether I as an observer and analyst of Korean society would choose to describe rural Korean agriculturists as peasants. My concern here, rather, is how the categories Koreans themselves have used to classify themselves and each other have contributed to the structuration of Korean society. Specifically, how and in what historical circumstances did Koreans begin imagining and promulgating an image of the Korean "peasantry" as the basis of Korean ethnicity, and what are the implications of this for our understanding of social stratification in Korea?

Many have attributed the importance of the notion of peasantry in twentieth-century Korean nationalist discourse to the numerical importance of rural cultivators in Korean society and assume that since there have always been farmers in Korea, the notion of *nongmin* arose long ago as a natural description of reality. As with all categories of social classification, however, invocation of the *nongmin* bundles together, to some degree arbitrarily, a number of separate notions—that agricultural management and agricultural labor are rarely done by the same persons, that only some members of rural society are thus true *nongmin*, that relations of production are more important for understanding society than kinship and other kinds of relations, that those engaged in agricultural labor thus constitute not simply one of a number of possible social categories but an organic group of people who form a bounded community with internal solidarity, that historical consciousness is a superstructural expression of an underlying economic base, and so forth.

The task is not simply to improve our classification of rural Korean social strata. Classification of rural Korean agriculturalists as *nongmin* by "objective" criteria without interrogating rural Koreans' own classificatory practices, no matter how carefully done, easily becomes anachronistic and makes the *nongmin* objects rather than subjects of history. From an almost limitless array of possible definitional criteria, conscious subjects construct social categories such as *nongmin* using a limited number of features that, once chosen, define which groups these subjects deem important, which groups they wish to link and oppose discursively, and which fields of contrast they find most socially salient. One cannot assume *a priori* that the characteristic "being a rural cultivator" should be a main dimension of a social classification system, and as we shall see, this has not always been the case in Korea. Invocations of the "peasantry" are not simply descriptions of Korean social reality; rather, they are active political and cultural acts that create a social reality. Rather than existing as such, a class is better seen as constituted at least in part by discursive practices through which "social subjects comprehend the social world which comprehends them"[9] and act accordingly.

During periods of social change such as Korea experienced in the early twentieth century when various new social, intellectual, and ethnic groups began contesting for power, one expects systems of social classification to be contested ground. Those whose classifications triumph will also triumph politically as leaders of the "imagined communities"[10] they have thereby created. The emergence of a new category such as peasant, then, should not be conceived in the Marxist sense as an "actually existing class" coming into consciousness of itself. The notion of *nongmin*, after all, was promoted by the intelligentsia. Rather, its appearance signals a political and cultural struggle over the particular social characteristics that, among a number of possibilities, should be used to classify people, and what relationship the groups so classified should have to the existing nation, or in a colonial context, the imagined nation to come. Politically engaged works of peasant literature such as Pak Kyŏngni's *Land*, thus, are not simply reflections of this classifitory struggle; they are part of it.

The terms of social classification, of course, do not exist in isolation; they are part of a larger semantic field. Those categories rejected, as well as those selected, are part of the struggle. I argue below, for example, that imagining a social category that can be termed the "peasantry" in Korea began after the Japanese takeover in 1910 and did not take hold fully until after the March First movement in 1919. This term was not introduced as an isolated discursive event but was part of a wholesale re-imagining of the Korean nation in which the previously most salient status-group categories were rejected and replaced with economic class categories. Late nineteenth-century Koreans operated in terms of the status groups of *yangban* (officials, their families, and descendents of officials, who thereby were eligible for high office if qualified), *sangnom* (commoners, who were subject to military service, corvée, corporal punishment, and taxation), and *ch'ŏnnom* (the unfree and those who engaged in polluting occupations such as butchering).[11] Up until 1895, each of these status groups wore distinctive clothing enforced by sumptuary regulations and had distinctive rights and duties vis-à-vis the state. At the turn of the twentieth century, however, Koreans begin to talk in terms of peasant, landlord, tenant, and worker, with clothing reflecting not so much ascriptive status categories as access to wealth and contacts with style setters. The re-imaging of social stratification was accompanied by a re-imagining of national identity: what had previously been imagined in terms of *yangban* mastery of a Chinese culture that was a marker of civilization began to be imagined in terms of primordial ethnic community epitomized as the peasantry.

The new social categories of the early twentieth century such as landlord or worker did not necessarily refer to social positions that in and of themselves were new. However, these positions came to be socially salient in a new way because of the particular political and economic context of Korea's incorporation into the world political economy as the colony of a close neighbor. In this context the older distinctions of honor based on lineage, access to government office, and mastery of Chinese culture became irrelevant due both to indigenous modernization based on Western and Japanese models begun in the 1890s and to the near-total monopolization of high government office during the colonial period by Japanese. Koreans found themselves caught in a system of ethnic stratification in which they had became peripheral agriculturalists in relation to a rapidly expanding Japanese industrial core. The market became the most important force differentiating urban Japanese from rural Koreans, and rural Koreans from one another. Those able to take advantage of new market opportunities could sidestep former status categories to express new modern identities through consumption patterns made possible by market-based success, but in a colonial context in which Koreans had little control over modern spaces, the Koreanness of these new identities could always be contested. Paradoxically, then, although peasants in the sense of people for whom "agriculture is a livelihood and a way of life" have existed in Korea for thousands of years, the invocation of peasants as a salient social category is modern and came into vogue only in the

1920s along with the introduction of conflict models of society and class analysis.

## "Peasantry" as a New Concept

The invocation of farmers, or *nongmin*, as the basis of the state is an ancient trope in East Asian civilization. The Guliang Commentary on the *Spring and Autumn Annals*, which dates to China's Warring States period (third century B.C.) mentions the "four people" (*sa-min*) as officials, farmers, craftsmen, and merchants (*sa-nong-gong-sang*).[12] At an even earlier period, Kuanzi (seventh century B.C.) observed that "the four people—officials, peasants, craftsmen, and merchants—are the stone people," since "if a state has these four people, it will be firm and hard." Similar statements underlining the fundamental economic importance of farmers as the basis of the dynastic state can be found throughout the traditional Chinese and Korean historical record.[13]

When we consider the semantic field within which these Confucian valorizations of the importance of farmers for the state must be contextualized, however, it is clear that these ancient usages of the term *nongmin* do not correspond precisely either to the twentieth-century Korean usage of the *nongmin* as the foundation of a specifically *Korean* nationhood or to the modern English notion of "peasant." Whether in the evolutionary sense of subsistence farmers who have some relationship to cities, states, and markets and are thus more advanced than tribal agriculturalists, or the more literary sense related to its derivation from the Old French term *paissant*, "inhabitant of a district, or *pay*," *peasant* in English points less to farming as an activity than to a close connection with the soil of a particular rural district and agriculture as an independent and traditional way of life. John Stuart Mill, who was content to use the term to denote the sharecropping *metayers* of the European mainland, did not use it for English tenant farmers, since, he noted, in England the owners of the land, the owners of capital, and the cultivators of the soil were different classes.[14]

And as is well known, the pious Confucian notion of the fundamental importance of farmers was combined in traditional times with an ideology that valued mental over manual labor and elevated officialdom to the "fathers of the people," who, through their education, had achieved moral superiority and the right to govern. The classical *nongmin*, although the foundation of society, could exist within a variety of relations of production, and their rootedness (or lack of rootedness) to a particular place is not what made them *nongmin*. Korea's traditional claim to civilization, in any case, lay not in the distinctiveness of its *nongmin* — something that was scarcely considered relevant to Korea's nationhood — but, as the missionary James Scarth Gale noted, in the Korean upper-class's adherence to the Confucian proprieties derived from China.[15] What classified one socially in nineteenth-century Korea was not whether one was a farmer (however defined) or even whether one engaged in manual or nonmanual labor, but whether one had a pedigree as an official family with a tradition of education, propriety, and access to government office,[16] whether one was owned by another (i.e., a slave regardless of type of work), and whether oneself or one's relatives engaged in polluting occupations (such as entertainment, clairvoyance, or butchery). Whom one married was more important for social classification than the amount of wealth one possessed.

Until the 1920s, in fact, the term *nongmin* seems not to have been a particularly salient social category in Korea, and to have been rarely, if ever, used in the sense of "peasant." In 1891 the famous early progressive statesman Yu Kilchun (1856–1914), for example, wrote a long memorial to the throne in *hanmun* (Koreanized Classical Chinese) about the land system and agriculture without once using the term *nongmin*, although he freely used other terms to designate the common people engaged in agriculture such as *inmin* (people), *hamin* (low people), or simply *min* (people).[17] Although the particularities of Yu's linguistic usage might be explained by his use of Classical Chinese as a written medium, the evidence from vernacular sources is equally decisive. Korea's first vernacular daily newspaper, *Maeil sinmun*,[18] published for a year in 1898, is full of discussions about social status and classification, but I have found no use of the term *nongmin*. The most common status term used in this publication is *paeksŏng* — "hundred names" or the "common people" — and it is used in contrast with "officials" (*kwal-lyo*) or "official families" (*sajok*). The common people had become important at this historical moment because the "enlightenment" party was arguing that reforms on Western and Japanese models were imperative, and the Western model involved citizen participation in public affairs. The recently enacted Kabo Reform of 1895 and the movement of the Independence Club (several of whose members were involved with the newspaper) to assert that common people who are not officials have the right and duty to discuss public policy and express their opinions thereon were major inspirations for *Maeil sinbo*. As the lead editorial of March 3, 1898, asserts: "The responsibility of those in a country who are the common people (*paeksŏng*) is enormous, so that the rise and fall, success and failure, of a country are completely dependent upon the common people." People whom foreigners at that time might have termed "peasants" are in this newspaper simply described as "countrymen" (*sigol saram*)[19] or "common people who farm" (*nongŏp hanŭn paeksŏng*),[20] a form of reference parallel to "common people who do day labor" (*mangnil hanŭn paeksŏng*) used for laborers in the capital. The status of being a common person, or *paeksŏng*, is clearly the socially salient distinction here, with the way one makes a living secondary.

Although people's occupations are often described, primary classification of people by occupation or ownership categories is absent from *Maeil sinmun* in spite of the fact that it abounds with a rich variety of terms for distinguishing social status. One could be "a famous scholar of south Seoul" (*namch'on myŏngsa*), a country gentleman (*sigol sŏnbi*), a Seoul neighborhood leader (*sŏngnae tumok*), a slave (*chong, ha-in*), or a ruffian (*chamnyu*). And disputes over social status are described again and again. Messrs. Chŏn and Kim, both day laborers in the warehouse district along the Han River near Seoul, for example, are reported on April 18, 1898, to have gotten in a fight over social status:

In riverside custom, making a living carrying an A-frame carrier (*tchok chige*) is yangban. Making a living carrying the backpack (*tŭngt'e*) is perfectly clearly sangnom. Backpack Chŏn was going somewhere, and A-frame Kim said [using language reserved for social inferiors], "How are you doing today (*nŏ yosai chal innŭnya?*)" Backpack Chŏn replied [using the same speech level] "You or I (*ne wa nae*) both stick our necks in two by two rooms and our life is about the same, so what is this using of low speech with me?" A-frame Kim got extremely angry and reproached Chŏn saying "Do you rudely speak roughly to a yangban?" Backpack Chŏn's father came out attempting to restrain him, but they say A-frame Kim's three brothers were sent out and thrashed him without mercy.

What was the difference between the two men? A-frame Kim, in spite of the fact that he lived in a hovel and made a living carrying things for hire, had a locally recognized claim to descent from an official's family.[21] As a *yangban*, he had a right to assert his status through the use of condescending language to those without that claim. This claim was enforced not only by A-frame Kim himself but by his whole family, who rushed out to defend his honor when challenged by Backpack Chŏn, even though the economic positions of Chŏn and Kim were identical. Reports of fights over levels of linguistic usage are common in *Maeil sinmun,* as are disputes over burial sites that expressed elite status and according to geomancy (*p'ungsu chirihak*) were thought to affect the fortunes of descendants.[22] Clearly the social classifications on people's minds in the late nineteenth century had more to do with what Weber termed "status honor"[23] (*myŏngnye*) than relationship to the market and means of production. The connection between status and one's relationship to the means of production, though by no means absent, was at best only approximate, as was noted by the iconoclastic historian Sin Ch'aeho as late as 1908:

From olden times in our country, official families (*sajok*) that have produced famous persons, if they merely come across another's secret burial among their family tombs, they think it is a stain on their family honor (*kamun ŭi ch'iyok*). And although the family be ruined and have lost its fortune, they take this [insult] deeply to heart, so that though they cut off their head or break their arm they must make amends. Whether living, dying, or injured, they do not consider anything else. This might in the end be reliance on some magic power. Nothing more comes out of it than a worm-eaten family genealogy (*kabo*) inside a dusty box.[24]

Truly, as mentioned in *Maeil sinmum* concerning the fight between A-frame Kim and Backpack Chŏn, "Our country's various lineages (*chich'e*) indeed cannot be known in their entirety."

## The Introduction of the Term *Nongmin*

Although familiar from its classical associations, as we have seen, the term *nongmin* seems not to have been used colloquially as an important social category prior to the colonial period. The earliest vernacular use of this term I have found comes from the colonial government's official Korean-language newspaper *Maeil sinbo*[25]—the only Korean-language daily allowed in Korea between the annexation in 1910 and the March First Independence movement in 1919. Typically, its first page was devoted to a major editorial and official announcements, the second page to international and economic news, the third page to internal Korean news (often human interest or crime stories), and the fourth page to a serialized story and regional news. Each page had a distinctive linguistic profile. Whereas the third and fourth pages were written in pure Korean with no admixture of Chinese characters (except for proper names given in parentheses), the front-page editorials and announcements, particularly before 1915, were clearly often translated directly from Japanese. In many cases these editorials and announce-

ments can be understood only if the Chinese characters are given distinctively Japanese readings rather than their usual Korean readings.
The second page, though not obviously translated from Japanese, still
uses a technical, sinified vocabulary that introduced many Sino-
Japanese neologisms into Korean. Later, the first page began to include
essays by well-known Korean intellectuals, though still in sinified style.

The lead editorials on the front page often discuss colonial policy —
justifying the colonial presence in terms of protecting the peace in East
Asia and the "yellow race," introducing new thought and reforms, and
so forth. Social problems (clothing, social stratification, adoption, relations between the races, evils of gambling) are frequently mentioned
with government-approved solutions, but lead editorials also focus on
self-improvement and promotion of capitalist relations of production.
The editorial for February 2, 1915, for example, attempts to counter
Korean Confucian prejudices against commerce:

What we call commerce (*sang*) is exchanging goods and money between those
who have them and those who do not and, with the profit coming from this,
adding riches to one's private life, and, by providing for oneself in this way,
supplying what other people want. So commerce, even though it be a mere
moment in our lives, is something we cannot do without. Therefore, even at the
end of the ancient period, the fact that the *tàpú* [Han dynasty procurement
official for the emperor] went during the day to the market and returned after
trading was considered a good thing.

New, more Western, terms of social classification current in Japanese, such as *hai k'alla* (high collar) and *jyent'ŭlmaen* (gentlemen) (Feb.
2, 1915) also appear in contexts that clearly indicate some Koreans, at
least, aspired to these new statuses.[26] A report from June 1918 mentions
the down-at-the-heels mountebank in "worn shoes with broken-down
heels and rumpled out-dated clothes" who, after swindling people
selling phony mining shares, "firmly decks himself out as a gentleman
(*sinsa*) in a customary neat Western suit, gold-rim spectacles, and a
wristwatch. And having taken care of his debts through a wad of
money, in this time frame, he has his picture taken in Chinese restaurants and acts as if he is on watch at *kisaeng* houses" (June 1, 1918, p. 3).

It is in the formal, Japanese-influenced first and second pages of this
newspaper that the term *nongmin* first begins to appear, along with
other linguistic usages enforced by colonial authorities (for example
using *china*[27] rather than "Middle Kingdom" for China, and *naeji* [inte-
rior] to refer to Japan). The usage of *nongmin* is not remarkable. It occurs in articles promoting savings and diligence in agricultural house-

holds, or encouraging the cultivation of potatoes among "ordinary farmers" (*ilban nongmin*) (May 18, 1911), and was a natural outgrowth of the statistical and classificatory practices of the colonial authorities — dividing households into agricultural and non-agricultural, and classifying the agricultural households by size of farm (*sonong, taenong*). In fact, beginning in 1913 a precise system of classifying farm families for statistical purposes was adopted in which households were listed as landlord, owner-cultivator, cultivator-tenant (own more than 50 percent), tenant-cultivator (less than 50 percent), or tenant. This system was refined after completion of the new cadastral survey begun shortly after formal Japanese annexation of Korea in 1916 to distinguish between non-cultivating landlords (Landlord A), and cultivating landlords (Landlord B), with the category "fire field farmers" added in 1925.[28]

## Korean Appropriation of the New Terminology

Although the period between 1910 and 1920 when independent newspapers were not allowed in Korea is often thought of as a dark age in which no significant Korean intellectual activity took place, indigenous discussion of social issues did not suddenly stop when the Chōsen sōtokufu was established by the Japanese in 1910. In fact, although direct expression of anti-imperialist or nationalist goals was not allowed, significant social discussion took place even within the pages of *Maeil sinbo*. Its major reporters were Korean, and well-known literary figures such as Yi Injik had some of their "new fiction" (*sin sosŏl*) serialized in its pages. Alongside the government announcements and editorials, essays by such intellectual figures as Chang Chiyŏn, Ch'oe Namsŏn, and Yi Kwangsu dealt with Korean cultural and social questions. Many of these authors were known for their criticism of Korean tradition and advocacy of modernity.

In fact, in *Maeil sinbo* and elsewhere, we can glimpse the introduction of new intellectual frameworks that began changing the grounding of Koreans' understanding of rural agriculturists. As is illustrated below, the term *nongmin*, while retaining its denotation of "people who farm as an occupation," came to be framed within an evolutionary notion of social development and a sense of preserving a distinctive way of life. Among some intellectuals the Korean nation came to be identified primarily with the *nongmin*. The *nongmin*, in turn, came to be conceived in a distinctive way as *inside* history, because of their significance in schemes of evolutionary development, but as *outside* history, because of their significance for preserving an essentialized Korean ethnic identity. Within the ethnic division of labor set up by the Japanese empire Korea was assigned the role, at least until the 1930s, of agricultural hinterland supplying raw agricultural products to Japan and consuming Japanese manufactures.[29] This left only rural areas as ethnic Korean space even within Korea itself.

In this context the *nongmin* came to be conceptualized as something very similar to peasants in the Anglo-American sense of the term. Their way of life had not yet changed radically from how it had been in the past. Moreover, incorporation of the *nongmin* more completely into market relations did not make them *objectively* peasants in a way they had not been in the past. Rather, at this historical moment, the idea of *nongmin* as peasants had become useful as a discursive signifier for a Korea conceived of as a people with a distinctive way of life (that implicitly deserves self-determination) regardless of political and economic arrangements. The imagining of the *nongmin* as a peasantry thus must be understood as part of the re-imagining of Korea as a nation in the context of the development of colonial modernity.

An early example of this reimagining of Korea as residing in the *nongmin* comes from a "fictionalized story" titled *The Enlightenment and Development of the Villages* (*Nongch'on kyebal*), serialized in *Maeil sinbo* starting on November 26, 1916. Yi Kwangsu, soon to become an eminent writer of modern fiction during the colonial period, wrote it while still a student resident in Tokyo. It is premised on the idea that Korea must develop on the basis of commerce and industry. Yi recognizes, however, that since Korea is made up of *nongmin*, the development of agriculture must precede the development of commerce. The *nongmin* in this essay are no longer simply the foundation upon which the state is built; they represent the Korean people itself. "The *nongmin*'s poverty and servility is the entire Korean people's (*Chosŏnin chŏnch'e*) poverty and servility." Yi goes on to imagine the "enlightenment and development" of the peasantry through leadership by enlightened local notables (*yuji*).

The line of thought Yi was developing in the 1910s continues in his other writings of the period. Not only does Yi begin to conceive of the peasantry as the epitome of the Korean nation, but he also focuses on "class" as a source of Korean national weakness. In a 1917 essay published in *Ch'ŏngch'un*, for example, he criticizes Korean Christians for being "classist" (*kyegŭpchŏk*) so that "classes[30] like the former yangban factions become stern and cannot extricate themselves from this [classist] prison. The relationship among pastor, elders, and ordinary church members comes to be just like the relationship between officials and people, older and younger, teacher and disciple; the pastor and elders always will stand above the ordinary church members, and the ordinary church members receive the direction and interference of the pastor and elders."[31]

It is in his famous 1922 essay "Theory of National Reconstruction" ("Minjok kaejoron"), however, that all the elements of the reconceptualization of the Korean nation fall into place. "What is reconstruction of the nation?" he writes. "Since a nation (*minjok*), like other natural phenomena, is something that takes a particular direction and changes every second, a particular nation's history can be said to be the record of that nation's changes." Reconstruction is necessary when, Yi thought, a nation concludes that its goals, plans, and characteristics are not in accord with the welfare of the nation and in fact may lead to its extinction. "From this realization and conclusion comes the proof that [the nation] has already acquired a high level of civilization, so that nations without it are unable to realize their danger and end up extinct amid benighted ignorance."[32]

Yi's equation of the nation, or *minjok*, with an organism "like other natural phenomena," which progresses or declines in competition with other similar entities is typical of the Spencerian notions introduced into Korea in the early decades of the century through Sin Ch'aeho's translations and writings, as well as direct reading of the works of the Chinese journalist Liang Qichao, who promoted social Darwinist notions of evolution and competition among nations. Although not the only East Asian social Darwinist of the period, Liang was especially influential in Korea during the first decade of the twentieth century. In this period, when most members of the educated elite still had a command of written Chinese, Liang's works were read both in the original Chinese and in Korean translation. He was frequently mentioned in newspaper editorials.[33]

Yi likely derived his evolutionary notions from multiple sources. He may well have become acquainted with concepts of national organicism and national character from such Japanese writers mentioned in "Theory of National Reconstruction" as Katō Hiroyuki (organizer of the Minyōsha, which published the magazine *Kokumin no tomo* [Friend of the people]) and Miyake Setsurei. The only source directly cited in his work, however, is the French social-psychologist Gustave Le Bon, who is quoted regarding the notions of racial soul, national character, and evolution. Whatever the source, Yi Kwangsu pins the blame for Korea's sorry state on the *yangban* and identifies Korea's national character as the element most critically in need of reconstruction.

## The *Nongmin* as a Class

By 1922 when the "Theory of National Reconstruction" was published, however, Yi was no longer on the cutting edge of Korean social thought. As a result of the March First demonstrations, Japanese authorities had been forced to relax their "Military Rule" policy and replace it with a "Cultural Rule" (*bunka seiji*) policy that allowed more room for Korean intellectual activity, and numerous, more radically inclined journals had emerged. Among the most prominent was *Kaebyŏk* (Creation). Published by a group of progressive intellectuals, many of whom were associated with the syncretistic Ch'ŏndogyo religion, *Kaebyŏk* began publishing in June 1920, with the mission of introducing new thinking into Korea. This new thinking placed great emphasis on the importance of the peasantry. Thus, the "agricultural question" was cited by Pak Talsŏng in the first issue of *Kaebyŏk* as one of the two most urgent questions facing Korea. As Pak argued, "Chosŏn has been purely dependent on the agriculture of the *nongmin*. Therefore Korea is a specialized agricultural country for the world. . . . It is an unavoidable fact that Chosŏn's future is tied to the development of the villages and encouragement of agriculture." Noting that the rural poverty of the villages could not be attributed to the laziness of the *nongmin*, Pak indicted "exploitation by the capitalist landlords" and advocated rent reduction and tenant organization.[34]

From the first number of *Kaebyŏk* until its suppression by colonial authorities five years later, hardly an issue went by without discussion of rural problems and of the relationship of the rural folk to the nation. Although intellectuals such as Yi Kwangsu recognized the demographic importance of the rural population and realized that Korea could not progress without raising their level of productivity and culture, he and his fellow cultural nationalists saw these tasks primarily as a matter of making better use of them as human capital. They did not in general deem peasants to have an intellectual importance beyond their numbers. For these nationalists, the Korean nation, while made up of rural agriculturists, did not *reside* in these agriculturists.[35] The writer

Yi Sŏnghwan, however, soon began arguing for a more central role for the peasantry.

Yi Sŏnghwan hit the cultural scene in a January 1925 with an article in the literary journal *Chosŏn ŭi mundan* (Korean literary world) in which he made a heartfelt plea for peasant literature. In "Toward the New Year's Literary World, Raise Peasant Literature,"[36] he argued, partly on grounds familiar by then, that since Korea was 90 percent rural, literature must be *for* the *nongmin*. Citing Tolstoy and Dostoevsky, he credited the influence of peasant-centered literary works for Alexander II's freeing of the serfs. Beyond the education and leadership that Yi Kwangsu advocated for peasants, Yi Sŏnghwan called on writers to express the Korean spirit and "exert yourselves to make [us] taste the flavor of actual life amid the hoe and plow, awakening in the *nongmin* a Korean soul, a mission and spiritual values for all of life." For "strong reactions are necessary for today's Korean *nongmin*. A violent awakening is necessary."

These *nongmin* are not simply rural raw material; rather, they have been conceived of as peasants in the European sense. For Yi Sŏnghwan, at least, they have begun to become the repository of Korean ethnicity, where the "soul" (*kibaek*) of the Korean people can be nurtured. Yi Sŏnghwan ended his essay by noting, "I have ceaselessly lamented the absence in Korea of tasting-the-earth (*chijijŏk*) peasant literature that flows with Korean emotions, that is ripe with Korean feeling, that is alive with the soul of the peasants (*nongmin*). . . . I say this is where Korea's poets and writers who hope for the best for Korea and Korean people should put their effort."

Yi Sŏnghwan, though never himself a major fiction writer, spent the next years of his life promoting his ideal of peasant literature, which in the next twenty years became one of the major genres of Korean prose writing. His major vehicle for promoting this idea was the journal *Chosŏn nongmin* (The Korean peasant), published from December 1925 until June 1930 under his leadership. This journal, designed to be circulated broadly among the peasantry itself, was a vehicle for raising peasant consciousness, literacy, and self-esteem. As such, it propagandized for the central role of the peasantry in Korean national identity.

## The Korean Peasant Society

The Korean Peasant Society (Chosŏn nongminsa), which published *Chosŏn nongmin*, was organized by intellectuals involved with the journal *Kaebyŏk*, together with members of the Ch'ŏndogyo Youth Party (Ch'ŏndogyo ch'ŏngnyŏndang), a political arm of the Ch'ŏndogyo religious movement with relatively strong contacts with the rural population. Later members of the YMCA (Kidokkyo ch'ŏngnyŏn hoegwan) took part as well, but the Ch'ŏndogyo religion was always recognized as the main midwife of the publication, to which it gave substantial logistical support. Yi Tonhwa and Kim Chijŏn, two of the regular contributors to *Chosŏn nongmin*, were adherents of the Ch'ŏndogyo religion and also important writers for *Kaebyŏk*.

Conceived as a major vehicle to mobilize and educate the Korean peasantry, the fifty pages of each issue included hortatory essays by well-known figures, reports on agricultural matters, a peasant-oriented primer, articles on hygiene and scientific agriculture, short stories, and poems. Several leading intellectuals outside the radical *Kaebyŏk* circle, such as Song Chinu, An Chaehong, and Han Kiak (all associated with the *Tonga ilbo* and the *Chosŏn ilbo*—two leading newspapers of the day), also contributed to the journal. Among the many educational and political aims of the journal, one finds a major preoccupation with defining and defending the importance of the peasantry (*nongmin*) as an important social category superseding older social categories still used in speech and newspaper writing such as *yangban* and *sangmin*.

This can be seen in the lead article of the first issue of *Chosŏn nongmin*, which was written by Yi Sŏnghwan. Yi noted the economic importance of the peasantry but then observed, "The peasantry in Korea play the most vital role, but have lived without being treated as important. They're abused with 'those farmer beasts,' 'those bumpkins,' 'those ferryboat beasts.'"[37] In the same issue Yi Tonhwa mentioned that the teaching of the four peoples (officials, farmers, artisans, and merchants), while seeming to give farmers an important and respected role, actually "teaches that the class of officials, perhaps as the group who have knowledge, have a right to be officials so that they can put down farmers." The habit the *yangban* have of referring to the peasants as the *paeksŏng* "hundred names," he notes, is actually derogatory.[38]

Yi Sŏnghwan and Yi Tonhwa agreed that the solution for Korea's problems was to make the peasants the "owners of society." This is only just, they argued, because peasants actually produce most of the wealth of Korea. More important, however, was that all Koreans are kinsmen, not just the same ethnic group (*minjok*) but brethren (*tongp'o*).[39] Here we can see the locus of Korean ethnicity being changed. If the nation is an organism, as Yi Kwangsu argued in

"Theory of National Reconstruction," then all organs must be healthy and evolving for the whole organism to survive. The *nongmin* are no longer the rocks on which society are built, but rather the very body of the nation.

*Chosŏn nongmin* promoted strains of class analysis along with the organic analogy. The second reading lesson of the first issue introduced class analysis in a very didactic way: "What we call *nongmin* are those people who are actually engaged in agriculture. Among those we call *nongmin*, those who have land are landlords (*chiju*) and those who borrow land from others to cultivate it are tenants (*sojagin*). Those who hire themselves out to another house to do farming are *mŏsŭm*, *ilkkun*, or *nongbu*. However, *nongbu* is also used as a general term for all those actually engaged in agriculture, whether landlord or tenant."[40] The lesson continues with a discussion of the statistical categories used by the colonial government to classify the rural Korean population: landlord A (non-cultivating landlord), landlord B (cultivating landlord), owner-cultivator, owner-tenant, and tenant, noting that non-cultivating landlords are also called "big landlords" or "absentee landlords." Finally, the question of European serfdom is introduced so that emancipation movements and the trend of history can be discussed.[41]

The categories introduced in the first issue of *Chosŏn nongmin* are everyday terms today and thus seem commonsense descriptions of social reality. It is clear, however, that the editors expect these class categories—which just happen to be the categories used for statistical purposes by the Chōsen sōtokufu—to be unfamiliar to their readers and in need of explanation. In fact, rural residents had probably not been in the habit of explaining social stratification in terms of "relationship to the means of production" before this time. We have already seen that status categories such as *yangban*, *paeksŏng*, and so forth had been the socially salient terms of newspaper writing from the 1890s, rather than class categories. Peasants today, moreover, describe social differences in terms of wealth, kinship, and social role and tend to avoid class terms (which they all know). In colloquial conversation among peasants, a rich peasant might be a *paeksŏkkun* (hundred bagger) and a really rich peasant a *ch'ŏnsŏkkun* (thousand bagger). In speaking of the past, rural Koreans note certain families were *mansŏkkun* (ten thousand baggers) (only a few dozen families in all of Korea harvested as much as 10,000 bags of rice a year during the colonial period, and since land reform in the 1950s none have), but rarely volunteer the category landlord. A landlord's agent could be a *marŭm*; a big rice trader a *kaekchu*;

a seasonal live-in laborer a *mŏsŭm*; a person who borrowed rice from a rich peasant and paid off the debt in labor a *kojikkun*; a wage laborer a *p'ump'arikkun* or *nongbu*. A prominent family might be the main house of such-and-such a lineage (*mo ssi ŭi k'ŭn taek*), and a local leader a *yuji*. Although the custom of sharecropping (*paemegi, pyŏngjak*) has a long history in Korea, "tenant" was not used as a social status term before the 1920s. In fact, the terms now most commonly used for tenancy and tenants (*sojak, sojagin*) are terms of Japanese origin used for statistical purposes during the colonial period.[42] The colloquial Korean categories, although related to productive roles as Korean peasants perceived them, were not ones on which the Japanese collected statistics and thus did not become important analytic categories for the peasant class theorists.

The early issues of *Chosŏn nongmin* did not address the colonial situation of Korea directly. However, there are many indirect references in *Kaebyŏk* and *Chosŏn nongmin* to Korea's role as an agricultural nation in the international division of labor and the significance of this for Korea's ethnicity. Some modernizers, such as Yi Kwangsu, reacted to this by trying to figure out ways to develop commerce and industry while preserving the peasantry. Others point to the peasantry itself as the repository of Korean ethnicity. Sŏnu Chŏn, however, pointed to the nub of the dilemma of Korean ethnicity: "The great majority of our *tongp'o* are farmers, and the largest amount of our productivity is agricultural. No matter what city or town you enter, if you except the great amount of power controlled by foreigners, the power of Koreans has reached the virtual point of extinction. In rural villages, however, the power and life of Koreans still remains."[43] For Korea to develop, Korea must have modern commerce and industry, but it is only among the *nongmin* that true Koreanness remains. Will the coming urban society be Korean any more?

## The Dilemma of Colonial Modernization

Yi Kwangsu, in his essay "Theory of National Reconstruction," advocated modernization and the development of the Korean people to prepare them for independence. In any country on the periphery of the world economy, however, such modernization must involve appropriation of elements from more developed foreign cultures, which creates problems for ethnic identity. Colonial modernization compounds this problem. The loss of sovereignty deprives the nation of a source of identity. The discourses the occupying power inevitably develops to shore up its legitimacy impoverishes national myth-making. Control of institutions essential for spreading new, modern national identities — schools in particular — fall to the colonial power, who uses them for its own purposes. In a colony like Korea where an expatriate community of some 700,000 Japanese formed a significant proportion of the urban population,[44] the urban areas where modern values and institutions were present was also the area that was most foreign. In such circumstances, the assimilation of modern culture becomes doubly problematic: "modern" becomes conflated with "colonial." Modernizers in colonies are always in danger of collaboration. Under such conditions, it is only natural that people look toward rural areas as a source of distinct ethnic identity.

Traditional Korea had very weak urban development. In 1905 less than 2 percent of the ethnic Korean population was urban, yet by the 1920s, the beginnings of a lively, modern, urban life were apparent. Magazines were being published, and movies shown; streetcars and multistory buildings were appearing. These big urban centers, as Sŏnu Chŏn noted above, however, were largely Japanese in style. By the end of the colonial period in 1945, more than 15 percent of the residents of most important Korean cities were ethnic Japanese, and most of the ethnic Koreans who lived in cities could speak Japanese. Those most enmeshed in the advantages and opportunities of modern life became those most enmeshed in the "tentacles" (as understood in nationalist rhetoric) of Japanese culture and, rightly or wrongly, became vulnerable to denunciation as collaborators.

Japanese propaganda during the colonial period trumpeted that only Japan could lead Asia into the new millennium. Japan's control of Korea was warranted, it was alleged, by Japanese modernity. Koreans, while they justified their desire for independence on the basis of Korean ethnic distinctiveness and the morality of self-determination, at the same time recognized that only development and modernity would give them sufficient power to maintain independence. It was in this specifically colonial context that the lifestyle of rural Koreans needed to become the marker of Korean ethnicity per se and that the peasantry was conceived of as the social group who were the definition of what was Korean. Although what was urban might be conceded to be advanced, even necessary, it was also foreign, dangerous, and seductive. How to combine the urban and advanced with the rural and Korean was the question.

This sounds schematic, but much of the peasant literature written during the 1920s and 1930s conforms to this point of view. Yi Kwangsu, in his classic peasant novel *Soil* (*Hŭk*) of 1933, for example, cast the main conflict in terms of the protagonist Hŏ Sung's love for the pure, rural, Korean maiden Yusun versus his attraction to the modern, sophisticated urbanite Sullye, whose rich father could send him to Japan for further training and a future of upward mobility. This work, which conceptualizes peasants as the repository of Korean ethnicity, uncannily foreshadows the opening of Pak Kyŏngni's *Land* written some forty years later, in which the peasants express their Koreanness through folkish ceremonies and the venal *yangban* represents decay.

## Peasantry, Modernity, Colonialism

Korea is not the only country, of course, where "peasant" as a discursive category has appeared in tandem with the beginnings of modernization. Myron Cohen has pointed out a similar process of naming and ideologizing the peasantry in China.[45] As in Korea, the term *nongmin* seems to have been introduced as a "return graphic loan"[46] from Japanese in the early twentieth century as part of a process of reconceptualizing the nation. As in Korea, journals devoted to the peasantry were published[47] in which the intelligentsia noted that since 80 percent of the population were peasants, peasants must be part of the solution to national problems. But the similarities stop there. The discursive complex Cohen identifies in China does not treat the Chinese peasantry as both inside and outside history, as was done in Korea. The peasants are not glorified as the repository of Chineseness. Rather, the peasants are stigmatized as backward, feudal, and the cause of China's backwardness. Journals, such as *The Chinese Peasant* that was published in Canton in the mid-1920s focus on mobilization of the peasants for revolution, not on modernizing the peasantry as a way of modernizing the Chinese nation. Liao Zhongkai wrote in typical fashion in 1926:

We must know that the most important element of the revolution is the people (*guomin*), and among the people nothing compares with the peasants (*nongmin*), the largest group. Therefore, the one important thing of the people's revolution is that we must get the majority who are peasants to clearly understand and gather under the banner of this party [the Guomindang]. If the peasants do not clearly understand gathering under the banner of this party, then we can definitely say the revolution will not succeed.[48]

The differences between the early twentieth-century Chinese and

Korean discourses on the peasantry point to the difference between modernization in colonized countries and modernization in countries that maintained national sovereignty (however hemmed in by imperialism that sovereignty might be). The colonial situation in Korea led many intellectuals[49] to cast questions of national identity in a characteristic form that equates Koreanness with the peasantry and modernity with foreignness. Until recently, the possibility of a Korean modernity was not considered. And one can still see echoes of this dilemma, which was forged during the colonial period. When the Koreans created a system of "intangible cultural treasures" (*muhyŏng munhwajae*) to define what landmarks of Korean ethnicity should be conserved, they turned largely to rural rituals and rural crafts, which account for some 80 percent of Korea's intangible cultural treasures (unlike Japan, where traditional urban and court-centered arts are heavily represented).

Today, Korea is an overwhelmingly urban country, and only a small part of the present population have rural experience. Nevertheless, the tradition of identifying the rural population with Korean ethnicity remains. A politician, for example, recently published a book under the title *The Eternal Bumpkin* (*Yŏngwŏnhan ch'onnom*), in which the claim of being a village bumpkin is used positively to express the politician's artless sincerity and true Koreanness, in spite of his long years in Korean urban politics.[50]

The relationship of Korean ethnic identity to the peasantry remains a central issue that must continue to be interrogated to understand Korean culture. What is important in this context, however, is not the reality of the peasantry, however defined, but the process of reimagining Korean identity in which peasant, or *nongmin*, became for the first time a meaningful category for Koreans. The contours of this reimagining show clear influences of the particular time and place in which it occurred. The colonial context of Korea's modernization made problems of ethnic identity especially acute and made urban models of Korean ethnicity relatively unavailable. It was logical that some would turn to the peasantry.

Rural nostalgia is a common trope of modern life, but it is not inevitable that modernization leads to valorization of rural models of ethnicity. When the English wax nostalgic about the "true English Yeoman," images of peasants do not come to mind (though such a yeoman might well be a rural cultivator). England did not industrialize under the control of a colonial power, however, and urban life, whatever its joys or despair, was not disqualified as English. However, although

Korea has always had rural cultivators, these cultivators have not always been conceived as an "actually existing class" nor have they usually been considered an important repository of Korean civilization. The category *nongmin* was defined and promoted as important for understanding Korean society at a particular historical moment. Accordingly, to understand Korean society we need to consider the process by which such social categories were defined and promoted, the groups by whom they were promoted, and the political consequences of these processes.

ELEVEN

# In Search of Human Rights:
# The Paekchŏng Movement
# in Colonial Korea

Joong-Seop Kim

The advent of "modern society" and the struggle toward modernization in Korea began in the late nineteenth and early twentieth centuries, as diverse influences, both internal and external, came to bear on the peninsula. Next to Japanese colonialism, the most powerful and enduring force was Western culture and ideology, including both socialism and liberalism, whose penetration of Korea predates the colonial era. In addition, internal developments such as the Tonghak peasant rebellions of 1894, the Kabo Reform movement of 1894–96, and the Independence Club of the early 1900s shaped Korea's transition to modernity. Accordingly, each must be considered in explaining Korea's approach to the modern world.

Deserving of particularly close attention is the historical coincidence that Korean modernization took place under colonial rule. Japan, as the main channel of Korean contact with foreign culture, provided opportunities for Korea's advent to modernity. Yet, Japanese colonialism disrupted and even discouraged Korean modernization through harsh authoritarian repression, and the Korean resistance to colonialism determined the course of social development during the period.

The double-edged nature of colonial modernity, its enabling and constraining effects, is evident in social movements. Although Japanese colonialism repressed every anticolonial, nationalist movement, it also facilitated "modern" social movements organized around issues of gender and class (for a study of women's movements during the colonial period, see Chapter 7, by Kenneth M. Wells, in this volume). This chapter studies colonial modernity by examining the liberation movement of the *paekchŏng*. After centuries of discrimination and repression during the Chosŏn dynasty (1392–1910), this group of hereditary outcastes formed the Hyŏngp'yŏngsa (Equity society) in 1923, which lasted more than a decade. The *hyŏngp'yŏng* (equity) movement proclaimed as its primary aims and purposes the abolition of the traditional bondage of the *paekchŏng*, their liberation from repression and social discrimination, and above all, the universalization of equal rights and dignity within an egalitarian society. The Hyŏngp'yŏngsa was a human rights movement and derived the notion of liberation from its conception of modern society, in which the rights of citizens as equal members of the society are realized through the institutionalization of practices in the social and political spheres.[1]

The history of the Hyŏngp'yŏngsa clearly illustrates the transition from tradition to modernity in Korea, as well as the social experience of colonial rule and its effects. Although the movement has received little attention from scholars until recently, a close examination of this human rights movement will help to unveil the complex relations between colonialism and modernity in Korea.

## Historical Background of the *Paekchŏng*

The *paekchŏng* occupied the lowest rung in traditional Chosŏn society. A stigmatized minority, comparable to the "untouchables" in India or the *burakumin* in Japan,[2] they were regarded as inferior even by low-status slaves and *kisaeng* (female entertainers). Therefore, the appellation "*paekchŏng*" conveyed contempt and reflected the rigid hierarchical structure of the traditional *sinbun* (hereditary status) system in Chosŏn Korea. The origins of the *paekchŏng* and the reasons for their degradation before and throughout the Chosŏn period remain largely unknown, but it is indisputable that they were severely discriminated against by ordinary people throughout the Chosŏn period.[3]

The *paekchŏng* suffered from numerous discriminatory restrictions. They could not live in the villages of ordinary people. They had to observe strict restrictions on decorations and ornaments. For example, the use of roofing tiles was forbidden, as was the wearing of ordinary hats and clothes. Their behavior was to be extremely modest and to show utmost humility. This humiliation and segregation extended even to their wedding and funeral services and burial sites. Social discriminations against *paekchŏng* ranged from the Chinese characters permitted for use as names to the social actions required in everyday life. The names of *paekchŏng* could include no Chinese characters with noble meanings, only degrading ones. Self-derogation was necessary in their conversation and personal interactions. The status forms of the Korean language further confirmed their inferiority: regardless of age, the *paekchŏng* were obliged to address ordinary people in honorific forms and to use humble forms in reference to themselves.

Even into the twentieth century, the *paekchŏng* continued to be stigmatized, unlike other despised groups such as slaves. However, new social and ideological forces at the turn of the century began to transform the *paekchŏng*. In particular, two channels introduced the *paekchŏng* to human rights concepts and subsequently encouraged them to organize and mobilize in defense of their interests—the indigenous religion, Tonghak, and a foreign faith, Christianity.

Religious leaders of the Tonghak (a coinage meaning "Eastern learning" adopted to contrast the movement with Christianity's "Western learning") focused on the abolition of unjust *sinbun* conventions.[4] During the 1894 peasant uprisings, rebel leaders with Tonghak religious backgrounds championed human rights, particularly for the society's lowest groups. In a statement calling for social reform by the government, they demanded, among other things, that the *paekchŏng* no longer be required to wear discriminatory hats and that widows be permitted to remarry. Advocating these causes challenged traditional Confucius-based social customs, which legitimized the humiliation of the *paekchŏng* and women. Although the uprisings were defeated, the peasant demands were reflected in governmental initiatives promulgated in the Kabo Reform of 1894–96. The peasant leadership of the revolt and the consequent change in government policy helped topple the *sinbun* structure and liberate most despised groups. Slaves were obvious beneficiaries. Although some progress in their status had occurred since a gov-

ernment proclamation in 1801, only in 1894 were they officially man-
umitted. The government outlawed slave ownership and the slave
trade. Compared with that of slaves, however, the social situation of
the *paekchŏng* was less improved. Social convention continued to
segregate them from ordinary people in residence and clothing and
restrict them to hereditary occupations, such as slaughtering and
butchering, perpetuating unjust social practices toward them. Nonetheless, Tonghak ideas and the Kabo Reform, which undermined the
social status system, implicitly and explicitly helped the *paekchŏng*
recognize the injustice of their social situation.

In addition, the *paekchŏng* encountered egalitarian ideas through
Western culture, particularly through Christianity. Unlike Catholic
efforts in Korea in the eighteenth century, the Protestant missions of
the nineteenth century were rather successful right from the beginning.[5] Some missionaries developed close contacts with the *paekchŏng*, exposing them to the concepts of human rights and social
equality. For example, Samuel F. Moore, an American Presbyterian
missionary in a *paekchŏng* village in Seoul, successfully converted a
large number of them to Christianity.[6] Among the converts was the
village leader, Pak Sŏngch'un, an impressive speaker at the People's
Rally in Seoul organized by the Independence Club in 1898.

However, even though conversion made them equal before God,
*paekchŏng* did not become equal in the eyes of other members of
Moore's congregation. In 1895 non-*paekchŏng* believers protested
Moore's inclusion of *paekchŏng* in worship services. They boycotted
services, and some threatened to quit the church altogether. The
reluctance of non-*paekchŏng* converts to Christianity, generally regarded as rather progressive by Korean standards, to sit beside *paekchŏng* believers shows how far the *paekchŏng* remained from freedom. A similar incident occurred at a Presbyterian church in Chinju
in 1909: the attempt of *paekchŏng* to attend services with other converts met with protest and attack.[7] The non-*paekchŏng* believers
chastised the missionary for being insensitive to Korean customs,
and left the congregation in protest. The confrontation obviously
undermined Christian preachings of egalitarianism and presumably
reinforced traditional hierarchical distinctions as well as social discrimination against the *paekchŏng*. Yet in both cases, the missionaries
clearly conveyed to the *paekchŏng* that all people have equal rights
under God. Although no direct evidence connects these episodes
with the birth of a *paekchŏng* organization, it is conceivable that the

evangelism of missionaries contributed to transformations in concepts of the status of the *paekchŏng*. And exposure to Western egalitarian ideas probably heightened the *paekchŏng*'s desire to participate in society on an equal basis and introduced them to the changing social norms.

Thus, whether from Tonghak or Christianity, the *paekchŏng* were exposed to egalitarian ideas in the late nineteenth and early twentieth centuries. This exposure paralleled the rapid, uneven, and enormous changes in Korean society, and these also affected the *paekchŏng* in their everyday life.

## The *Paekchŏng* in Transition

The dramatic changes permeating Korea in the late nineteenth and early twentieth centuries inevitably affected the *paekchŏng*'s position in society. They no longer silently tolerated social discrimination and began to protest their situation even before the Hyŏngp'yŏngsa emerged in 1923. In 1900, for example, *paekchŏng* leaders from sixteen counties around Chinju, South Kyŏngsang province, presented petitions to the mayor of Chinju seeking permission to wear the same clothes and hats as ordinary people.[8] In 1901, when government officials in Haeju, Hwanghae province, demanded bribes in return for their emancipation, *paekchŏng* leaders appealed to the central government in Seoul. Similarly, in 1901, when some *paekchŏng* in Yech'ŏn, North Kyŏngsang province, were jailed for their refusal to comply with the mayor's order to wear the humiliating traditional garb, Pak Sŏngch'un (thought to be the same person as the speaker at the People's Rally in 1898 mentioned above) responded by bringing a case seeking their release before the government.[9]

Two features of social movements help explain *paekchŏng* activism at this time. First, "social enabling" environments and resources assist people in establishing and sustaining movements.[10] The various experiences discussed above clearly schooled the *paekchŏng* in resource mobilization and collective action. Such events demonstrate how the *paekchŏng* continued to absorb egalitarian ideas that stimulated a desire for a transformation of their status. In addition, the *paekchŏng*'s social environment changed enormously—for example, the strict residential segregation loosened to the point that the *paekchŏng* came into more frequent personal contact with ordinary people through cohabitation in more open, progressive communities. And a small number of wealthy *paekchŏng* families were able to educate their offspring in private and public schools. Also, the tight *paekchŏng* community network long built up through marriage and occupation proved an asset in organizing and mobilizing resources. Such social environmental factors, outside as well as inside the *paekchŏng* community, unquestionably enhanced their ability to launch the *hyŏngp'yŏng* movement.

Second, "social constraints"—the injustices a social movement seeks to redress—were another factor behind *paekchŏng* activism. Social constraints comprise not only externally enforced social conventions but also internalized norms and attendant emotional judgments. That is, structural conditions may encourage or, conversely, strain internal perceptions of oneself and others. The inner conflicts produced by social deprivation and status inconsistency are often studied by sociologists and social psychologists.[11] As noted above, despite the official abolition of the *sinbun* hierarchy in the Kabo Reform legislation of 1894, the government continued to discriminate against the *paekchŏng*. For example, on several occasions in the late 1890s the minister of internal affairs ordered lower-ranking officials to punish members of the despised class who displayed a disobedient attitude toward noble people.[12] Such social constraints continued to operate, and the *sinbun* ethic and structure was maintained, into the 1920s. In 1922, the year prior to foundation of the Hyŏngp'yŏngsa, for example, *kisaeng* who accompanied *paekchŏng* on a picnic in Taegu were publicly criticized and then stripped of their guild membership for consorting with *paekchŏng*.[13] Clearly the *paekchŏng* continued to suffer social discrimination, unlike members of other menial groups such as slaves and craftpersons, against whom discrimination had eased somewhat.

These complex aspects of the modernizing process, that is, the social constraints and enabling that generated the *hyŏngp'yŏng* movement, characterized the economic sphere as well. Although still embryonic, industrialization affected and altered the *paekchŏng* community as a whole in the late nineteenth and early twentieth centuries by causing the expansion of urban areas and an enormous reshuffling of the occupational structure.

The *paekchŏng*'s traditional occupations—slaughterers and butchers, tanners and leather workers, wicker craftsmen, and on occasion executioners—had been exclusive and hereditary to them. They consequently held a monopoly over such industries, although these occupations marked them as menial outcasts in both Buddhist Koryŏ and Confucian Chosŏn. However, their monopoly was broken when their occupations became profitable during industrialization. In the late nineteenth and early twentieth centuries, the Chosŏn government and the subsequent Japanese colonial administration passed legislation that brought slaughtering and butchering under close state surveillance.[14] Following the first regulations in 1896, the state gradually eliminated the *paekchŏng's* monopoly of meat processing. As the meat trade expanded among the burgeoning urban population and became lucrative, increasing numbers of non-*paekchŏng* assumed jobs in the industry. Dominant among them were Japanese residents in Korea, who were encouraged to do so by the Japanese colonial administration.

As a result, *paekchŏng* slaughterers became the employees of Japanese-owned slaughterhouses and worked in conditions largely controlled by the colonial administration and Japanese associations. *Paekchŏng* butchers procured their meat from Japanese-controlled slaughterhouses and became subject to Japanese price and quantity manipulation as well as government surveillance. Once again, the *paekchŏng* seemed to occupy the lowest rung. As shown in Table 11.1, many found work in slaughterhouses and leather factories, and some, deprived of their traditional occupations altogether, became peasants or joined the ranks of the unemployed, even though there were regional variations. As capitalism destroyed the *paekchŏng's* traditional monopoly, their living conditions deteriorated. Although a fortunate few, particularly in the south, maneuvered themselves into the profitable aspects of the meat industry, such as butchering animals and trading leather products, the unsuccessful adjustment of the great majority brought a sense of crisis to their community. Urbanization and the increased profitability of the packing industry attracted non-*paekchŏng* investors, particularly well-financed and government-backed Japanese entrepreneurs, and the resulting loss of hereditary monopolies brought long-simmering grievances to a head and provoked a crisis of identity. The *hyŏngp'yŏng* movement of the 1920s emerged from this crisis.

Alongside these constraining forces, however, were enabling factors in the economic sphere. These included increasing differentia-

Table 11.1

Population and Occupation Breakdown of Paekchŏng, 1926

| Province | a | b | c | d | e | f | g | h | i | j | k | l | m | Total | % |
|---|---|---|---|---|---|---|---|---|---|---|---|---|---|---|---|
| Kyŏnggi | 477 | 25 | 1,114 | 176 | 334 | 98 | 168 | 142 | 2 | 0 | 72 | 193 | 439 | 3,240 | 8.8% |
| N. Ch'ungch'ŏng | 129 | 2 | 870 | 239 | 286 | 32 | 74 | 2 | 8 | 0 | 33 | 41 | 338 | 2,054 | 5.6 |
| S. Ch'ungch'ŏng | 237 | 54 | 1,592 | 498 | 444 | 109 | 236 | 8 | 52 | 0 | 36 | 144 | 389 | 3,799 | 10.3 |
| N. Chŏlla | 289 | 43 | 1,557 | 134 | 864 | 156 | 349 | 5 | 29 | 1 | 19 | 153 | 194 | 3,793 | 10.3 |
| S. Chŏlla | 556 | 84 | 1,309 | 21 | 403 | 99 | 539 | 33 | 11 | 0 | 45 | 82 | 50 | 3,232 | 8.8 |
| N. Kyŏngsang | 381 | 156 | 1,037 | 681 | 2,480 | 136 | 286 | 229 | 77 | 0 | 34 | 529 | 1,384 | 7,410 | 20.2 |
| S. Kyŏngsang | 239 | 146 | 1,005 | 302 | 496 | 134 | 74 | 58 | 61 | 0 | 71 | 44 | 32 | 2,662 | 7.2 |
| Kangwŏn | 281 | 3 | 210 | 326 | 787 | 110 | 209 | 4 | 16 | 0 | 11 | 29 | 59 | 2,045 | 5.6 |
| Hwanghae | 232 | 553 | 78 | 674 | 3,406 | 189 | 40 | 278 | 26 | 0 | 1 | 211 | 0 | 5,688 | 15.5 |
| N. Pyŏngan | 505 | 106 | 76 | 229 | 295 | 29 | 80 | 40 | 71 | 0 | 11 | 39 | 1 | 1,482 | 4.0 |
| S. Pyŏngan | 136 | 0 | 16 | 157 | 283 | 45 | 1 | 0 | 46 | 0 | 3 | 43 | 189 | 919 | 2.5 |
| N. Hamgyŏng | 24 | 0 | 0 | 1 | 0 | 0 | 0 | 0 | 0 | 0 | 0 | 0 | 0 | 25 | 0.1 |
| S. Hamgyŏng | 211 | 3 | 3 | 1 | 47 | 16 | 18 | 12 | 0 | 0 | 2 | 9 | 7 | 329 | 0.9 |
| Total | 3,697 | 1,175 | 8,867 | 3,439 | 10,125 | 1,153 | 2,074 | 811 | 399 | 1 | 338 | 1,517 | 3,082 | 36,678 | 100% |
| % | 10.1 | 3.2 | 24.1 | 9.4 | 27.5 | 3.1 | 5.7 | 2.2 | 1.1 | 0 | 0.9 | 4.1 | 8.4 | 100% | |

KEY: a = slaughterer; b = leather worker; c = butcher; d = wicker worker; e = farmer; f = laborer; g = restauranteur; h = leather shoemaker; i = basket maker; j = public servant; k = merchant; l = miscellaneous; m = jobless
SOURCE: Chōsen sōtokufu, Keimukyoku, Chōsen no chian jōkyō (1927), p. 2–9.

tion of the *paekchŏng* community into haves and have-nots and the concomitant growth of economic resources available for collective activities. Wealthy *paekchŏng*, who despite economic success did not escape their inherited status, were potential resources as members and supporters of the new human rights movement. In particular, *paekchŏng* in the southern region were more successful in adapting to industrialization than their counterparts in the north, and it is no coincidence that the *hyŏngp'yŏng* movement started and was most active in the south.

In short, two contrasting forces drove the transformation of the *paekchŏng* in social and economic spheres as industrialization took hold. On the one hand, long-standing social constraints continued to block the liberation of *paekchŏng* from traditional bondage, even as they were deprived of their traditional sources of income. On the other hand, these social changes exposed them to the concept of human rights and equality in modern society. Additionally, those few *paekchŏng* who prospered in the midst of these rapid changes boosted the social and economic resources of the *paekchŏng* community. These dynamic social conditions contributed to the initiation and subsequent activities of the *hyŏngp'yŏng* movement for human rights in the 1920s and 1930s.

## Toward Social Equality: Development of the *Hyŏngp'yŏng* Movement

The Hyŏngp'yŏngsa was not the first attempt to organize the *paekchŏng* in the twentieth century. In 1910, some *paekchŏng* had already sought to organize a national trade union for butchers. To this end, Chang Chip'il, one of the most important founders of the Hyŏngp'yŏngsa, tried to convene a gathering of *paekchŏng* leaders from South Kyŏngsang province in Chinju.[15] He was not, however, able to establish an enduring organization, presumably because of hostile reactions from social superiors.[16] The Chipsŏng Chohap (Success union), founded in 1921 in Seoul under the leadership of Korean and Japanese entrepreneurs, aimed to provide social-welfare services, mainly for butchers in the Seoul area.[17] The organization did not press a broad human rights agenda on behalf of *paekchŏng* but focused on economic interests. It lasted several years until coming into conflict with the Hyŏngp'yŏngsa in the late 1920s.[18]

The Hyŏngp'yŏngsa was the first organization whose initial and ongoing purpose was to improve the *paekchŏng*'s human rights. The Hyŏngp'yŏngsa was officially launched in Chinju, South Kyŏngsang province, on April 24, 1923, through the cooperative efforts of well-known non-*paekchŏng* social movement activists and wealthy or educated *paekchŏng* in the Chinju community.[19] For example, Kang Sangho, a key founder, came from a landowner's family and had a relatively advanced education. He had previously been involved in various social activities. His leadership of protests in the Chinju area during the March First movement of 1919, for example, resulted in his detention in prison for one year and his appointment as director of the Chinju office of the *Tonga ilbo*, a nationalist newspaper, in 1920. Among the social associations with which he had been affiliated before the Hyŏngp'yŏngsa were peasant and laborer groups and a committee for establishing a private high school. He was one of many social movement activists within local communities, who, as a group, exerted a major influence over the course of social matters throughout the country after the March First movement.[20] Such activists took a significant part in leading the *hyŏngp'yŏng* movement.

Among the wealthy *paekchŏng* who helped launch and lead the society was Yi Hakch'an, an influential member of the *paekchŏng* community who owned a large butcher shop at a newly founded marketplace in Chinju. Such wealthy contributors had successfully adjusted economically to the "great transformation" of society, and in some cases had been able to move to residential areas previously closed to them. They still suffered from social prejudice and discrimination at many levels, but, as noted above, their contact with social superiors exacerbated their sense of grievance and consciousness of human rights. Their wealth helped support the *hyŏngp'yŏng* movement, at least in its initial organizing process, throughout the country.

A third significant element in the *paekchŏng* community that played a key role in organizing the movement was the rare, educated, intellectual *paekchŏng*. Chang Chip'il, for example, who came from a *paekchŏng* family in Ŭiryŏng, 30 kilometers east of Chinju, had attended Meiji University in Japan.[21] He had applied for a post at the Government-General Offices in Seoul, but withdrew his application after discovering his *sinbun* status embedded on the government register records submitted with his application.[22] Chang and others like him supported the movement throughout its history.

Thus, non-*paekchŏng* activists and wealthy or intellectual *paekchŏng* joined forces to launch and develop the *hyŏngp'yŏng* movement; this diversity eventually gave rise to friction among association members in later years.

The foundation of the society was enthusiastically welcomed by *paekchŏng* communities nationwide. About three weeks later, over 400 leaders of *paekchŏng* communities, mainly from southern regions, gathered to celebrate the society's foundation in Chinju.[23] Among them were well-known leather traders, owners of slaughterhouses, and butchers from major cities. In the wake of the celebration in Chinju, numerous branches opened in other major cities, mainly in Kyŏngsang, Chŏlla, and Ch'ungch'ŏng provinces. According to Japanese records, the Hyŏngp'yŏngsa had twelve regional headquarters and 67 local branches in 1923–24.[24] The number of branches expanded over the years, peaking in the early 1930s (see Table 11.2). This increase in branches reflected a vitality in membership unprecedented among social movements at the time. Although the Hyŏngp'yŏngsa's official claim of 400,000 members is probably inflated,[25] its size and ability to mobilize active and potentially supportive members throughout the country during the long period of Japanese colonial rule was unmatched. In fact, Japanese documents, which grossly underestimated the Hyŏngp'yŏngsa's organizational capacity, credited it with 7,681, 9,688, and 7,439 members in 1926, 1928, and 1929, respectively.[26] Its success in the 1920s and the early 1930s reflects the dynamic social circumstances surrounding the *paekchŏng* and their organization, including the social constraints and enabling conditions described above.

The *paekchŏng* and their sympathizers focused on social and economic injustices. As noted earlier, urbanization and colonization and the transition from a traditional to a modern society created enormous social and economic tensions for the *paekchŏng*, even in the 1920s. Regardless of their economic achievements, however, they still faced strong resistance when they attempted to enroll their children in public schools, and, if enrolled, the children suffered from their schoolmates' scorn. The Ipchang incident in 1924, which was caused by a protest among non-*paekchŏng* students against *paekchŏng* in the classroom, followed by a six-week conflict between non-*paekchŏng* and *paekchŏng* villagers, is one example of this.[27] Therefore, high on the agenda of the national and local organizations were

Table 11.2
*Number of Hyŏngp'yŏngsa Branches, 1923–35*
(1923 = 100)

| Year | Number | Index | Year | Number | Index |
|------|--------|-------|------|--------|-------|
| 1923 | 80 | 100 | 1930 | 165 | 206 |
| 1924 | 3 | 104 | 1931 | 166 | 208 |
| 1925 | 9 | 23 | 1932 | 161 | 201 |
| 1926 | 30 | 162 | 1933 | 146 | 183 |
| 1927 | 50 | 88 | 1934 | 113 | 141 |
| 1928 | 53 | 91 | 1935 | 98 | 123 |
| 1929 | 162 | 203 | | | |

SOURCES: The figures for 1923 are from Chōson sōtokufu, *Chōsen no gunshū* (Seoul, 1926), p. 183. The survey appears to have been conducted between late 1923 and early 1924. All other figures are from Chōsen sōtokufu, Keimukyoku, *Saikin ni okeru Chōsen chian jōkyō* (1933, 1935).

access to public schools and the eradication of ostracization of *paek-chŏng* students. Hyŏngp'yŏngsa members also met obstacles when seeking to join in public activities and use facilities available to ordinary citizens. For instance, when a *paekchŏng* ran for town council in Kimch'ŏn, fierce opposition from villagers forced him to withdraw his candidacy.[28] For *paekchŏng*, gravesites remained segregated, participation in local meetings was prohibited, and discriminatory customs remained. Despite fierce protests, *paekchŏng* had great difficulty ridding themselves of the despised appellation.

An external impetus to *paekchŏng* organization was no doubt the establishment of the social movement sector throughout the country following the March First movement.[29] The historical experience of massive nationwide protests in 1919 stimulated Koreans to organize in order to address political and social discrimination at local and national levels. Such protests led to changes in colonial policy and energized activists to launch a diverse set of social mobilization campaigns, capitalizing on the new policy of "Cultural Rule." These "professional" social movement activists at the national and local levels came from wealthy families and had higher educations, at least in the early 1920s. They were leaders in a general cultural movement that aimed to transform colonized Korea into a modern society. With their support and active participation, the *hyŏng-*

*p'yŏng* movement rapidly became one of the main social movement groups in the 1920s and 1930s.

The movement's fortunes, of course, fluctuated. Within a year of its foundation, factional dispute erupted among the leading members, ostensibly over the location of the national headquarters. Some considered Chinju too far from Seoul to serve as the headquarters of the society and urged relocation to a more central site. Chinju leaders who had launched and led the society objected that the situation was not yet ripe for such a move. However, the controversy over the location of the headquarters masked more important differences over leadership and strategy.[30] Leaders of the Seoul faction, who came mostly from central Korea and had intellectual backgrounds, were obviously discontented with the Chinju leaders. The Chinju leaders still controlled the national movement, but most of them were from *non-paekchŏng* or wealthy *paekchŏng* backgrounds. In addition, although members of both factions hoped to abolish social discrimination against the *paekchŏng* and to establish an egalitarian society, the leaders of the Chinju faction stressed enlightenment of members through education, whereas the Seoul group was more interested in economic issues associated with traditional *paekchŏng* trades. As a result, Chinju leaders advocated establishing night schools and a publishing firm, and Seoul leaders sought to establish a leather firm, protect slaughterers' wages, and promote corporative sale of members' products. Such divergences cast the Chinju leaders as "moderates" and the Seoul leaders as "progressives."

The factional dispute resulted in a split national leadership and headquarters. Although the annual national convention of 1925 was co-hosted by the two groups in order to paper over the split, their conflicting views continued to affect the movement. For instance, the Seoul leaders, who assumed the national leadership after the 1925 convention, reunified the movement by emphasizing economic issues and closer contact with other social movements. Accordingly, Hyŏngp'yŏngsa members began to join other social movements at the national and the local levels, and when national concerns such as flood relief and Japanese control of newspapers arose, Hyŏngp'yŏngsa leaders mobilized their members in support. Meanwhile, other groups such as peasant, labor, and youth movements supported the Hyŏngp'yŏngsa's drive against social discrimination. *Paekchŏng* problems often rose to the fore at regional and national meetings of groups such as the Chosŏn Youth League and Chosŏn Labor and Peasants League.[31] Thus, the *hyŏngp'yŏng* movement became a major force in the national social movement sector.

Reunification of the national leadership and the successful establishment of the social movement sector encouraged the geographical spread of the *hyŏngp'yŏng* movement and an increase in the number of local branches. With this, subgroups for youth, women, and students emerged between 1924 and 1928. Even though their character varied widely, from the Chŏngwidan (Righteous Defense Unit), a small militant unit, to the Hyŏngp'yŏng Youth League, a national organization of youth, these subgroups energized the movement as a whole.

The Chŏngwidan, launched in 1925, aimed to protect members and the organization against external attacks. Young leaders active in several local branches led the group, but how long it endured and how widely it spread remain unknowns. In contrast, the Hyŏngp'yŏng Youth League, which first appeared in 1924 in Chinju, rather quickly sponsored several local branches, although no systematic network coordinated them. Despite the diverse character of local branches, however, the league provided a unifying social network for young members as a whole. It became the largest subgroup within the Hyŏngp'yŏngsa, with over 25 groups cited in newspapers, and the parent organization proceeded to found regional organizations in some provinces in 1926. Apparently, their effective and varied campaigns, such as unofficial schooling for Hyŏngp'yŏngsa members, proved attractive and encouraging to rank-and-file members. Another major subgroup, the Hyŏngp'yŏng Student League, launched in 1925, consisted of members' children who were enrolled in public schools. Considering the powerful barriers to *paekchŏng* access to public education, the league was an important outcome of the *hyŏngp'yŏng* movement. When the organization visited local areas and campaigned for the enlightenment of members and the education of their children, local members applauded and collected funds for their activities.[32] These three subgroups were able to launch nationwide organizations and received the endorsement of and support from the national headquarters. Numerous other subgroups arose in various local branches such as in Kunsan, North Chŏlla province, in Kanggyŏng, South Ch'ungch'ŏng province, and in Chinyŏng, South Kyŏngsang province, with specific goals like temperance, thrift, and support for women and children. Such narrowly focused groups failed to expand or develop national bases. Nonetheless, they show that Hyŏngp'yŏngsa rank-and-file members, while autonomous and diverse in local focus, sought to improve their social life and the lot of particularly deprived groups, such as children and women. Indeed, the development of such subgroups with diverse purposes was the source of Hyŏngp'yŏngsa's energy and success in the latter part of the 1920s. Some subgroup leaders were promoted to key positions in executive committees at the national headquarters in the late 1920s and early 1930s. As a result, relatively younger leaders gradually came to share national leadership with the professional, relatively older activists who had initiated the movement.[33]

To be sure, relations between the two generations were not always harmonious. They particularly clashed over the issues of future direction and strategy. Younger leaders leaned toward the radical ideology of socialism, particularly attractive at the time among social movement activists, whereas older leaders were relatively less radical in terms of political orientation and sought mainly to retain their indigenous identity. Despite such divergences and conflicts, however, they continued to share national leadership and focus on human rights as a primary issue of the movement, at least until the end of the 1920s.

## The *Hyŏngp'yŏng* Movement in Search of Human Rights

The Hyŏngp'yŏngsa was the longest-lasting social movement under colonial rule, and its activities fluctuated over time in terms of strategy and political stance, depending on internal and external circumstances. Throughout its history, nonetheless, it consistently protested social discrimination against and stigmatization of *paekchŏng*, and fought to abolish all unequal treatment based on *sinbun* conventions. Its efforts explicitly and implicitly championed an egalitarian society that respected the divine human dignity of all members, and thus clearly distinguish the Hyŏngp'yŏngsa as a human rights movement.[34]

The constitution of the Hyŏngp'yŏngsa, passed at the inaugural meeting in 1923, stated the aims of the association as "the abolition of classes and of contemptuous appellations, the enlightenment of members, and the promotion of mutual friendship among members."[35] This message of basic human dignity also resounds in the first sentences of the declaration establishing the society in Chinju in 1923: "Equity is the basis of society, and love is the essential idea in the human mind. Therefore, we want to overthrow unequal social classes, to put an end to contemptuous appellations, and to enlighten people. Thus, we, too, will become truly human beings. This is the main principle of the association."[36] The issue of equity repeatedly appears in the statements and agenda of meetings at local and national levels. For example, soon after the Chinju meeting in May 1923, the local branch at Kimje in North Chŏlla province issued a similar statement: "[We seek] to recover our rights, to regain our liberty, to escape from repressive institutions, to abolish traditional customs, to dismantle national discrimination, and to put an end to contemptuous 'paekchŏng' appellations, so that we can build our history in a fresh form and construct our life in a form of truth, goodness, and beauty."[37] To realize these goals, Hyŏngp'yŏngsa members began collective protests against social "superiors" who used the appellation "paekchŏng" as an insult in conversation. Members of some branches resolved to abandon their traditional hairstyle, a key symbolic expression of their inferior social status in the Chosŏn period. National leaders successfully demanded that government officials efface all indications of paekchŏng status in government registers.[38]

The concept of human equality in the hyŏngp'yŏng movement was not confined to individual rights. From the beginning, Hyŏngp'yŏngsa programs were designed to improve human dignity by instilling a sense of communal fellowship among paekchŏng. Its constitution promoted enlightenment, mutual friendship, and righteous behavior among members.[39] Clearly the movement's conception of human rights was communitarian, attributing to all members a common responsibility to improve the life of their fellows. This tempering of the pursuit of individual freedom with community responsibility as constituents of human dignity made the Hyŏngp'yŏngsa's concept of human rights socially constructive.[40] Members considered education the key to human dignity and therefore placed it foremost on the agenda at local and national meetings. When new school terms began, movement leaders campaigned to enroll members' children in public schools. Many local branches also ran night schools for illiterate members. Members were urged to read newspapers and magazines to enhance their commonsense and general knowledge. The organization attempted to publish its own journal several times, although with little success due to severe Japanese censorship.[41]

Two mutually reinforcing circumstances of the *paekchŏng* community facilitated support and friendship among Hyŏngp'yŏngsa members. One was the traditionally strong community bonds forged over a long history by the circumscribed choices available for occupation and marriage. The other was the fear that industrialization and urbanization might gradually lead to the disintegration of their community. Though long isolated from the broader society, even the *paekchŏng* community felt the drastic changes affecting it. Change compelled them to reaffirm their group identity and solidarity, already perceived as a treasured tradition. This did not entail pride in the demeaning *sinbun* status of their ancestors; rather, it meant valuing their tradition of caring for their fellows, especially the deprived, as the foundation of a worthwhile group identity.

Reinforcement of group identity helped overcome the social divisions arising from increased economic differentiation within the community. Despite such differentiation, all members of the *paekchŏng* community sensed their shared social and economic vulnerability and need to promote group solidarity. Economic cooperation was reinforced as they witnessed the gradual loss of exclusive privileges in their traditional industries. Even though different economic priorities initially fostered factional disputes, as noted above, once the national leadership shifted to the Seoul faction, economic cooperation among members accelerated. The national headquarters mounted programs to found a leather firm, promote the collective sale of products, and improve slaughterhouse working conditions, especially through a regular salary system and minimum wage. Later projects included plans to seek direct management of slaughterhouses and regain ownership of hide-drying firms forcibly appropriated by Japanese residents after Japanese intervention in the industry.[42]

This focus on economic interests and activities gradually transformed the group into a sort of trade union movement, especially in the late 1920s. Members in some areas sought to form trade unions for slaughterers and to promote close relations among butchers. Their demands for improved working conditions and an increase in meat prices often resulted in industrial protest actions. Such actions in local branches drew attention from colleagues in the national headquarters as well as at other branches. National headquarters often dispatched delegates to support local members in trouble.[43] The economic focus also transformed the Hyŏngp'yŏngsa's conception of human rights. At the national convention in September 1926, delegates passed a resolution restating the aims and policies of the movement: "Our basic mission is to improve human rights, which requires improving economic conditions."[44] This emphasis on economic concerns, however, aroused severe antagonism among opponents in the broader community. Conservatives mounted attacks on the *hyŏngp'yŏng* movement itself and on its members. On some occasions, they organized violent raids on villages of Hyŏngp'yŏngsa members, at times over several days, devastating the villages and causing members to flee. These attacks often generated defensive support from Hyŏngp'yŏngsa colleagues nationwide.[45]

The Yech'ŏn incident, the harshest attack in the history of the *hyŏngp'yŏng* movement, is a case in point.[46] It occurred in August 1925, just after a meeting commemorating the foundation of the branch. At the meeting, a non-*paekchŏng* speaker insensitively argued that social discrimination against the *paekchŏng* had been an inevitable historical phenomena, inciting *paekchŏng* members in the audience. Although the meeting ended as scheduled with the restoration of order, some incensed non-*paekchŏng* town residents, bridling at the "insult" to the non-*paekchŏng* speaker, mobilized an attack on the office of the Hyŏngp'yŏngsa branch and its members' village. Local police made no attempt to curb the violence, and the riot lasted more than a week. Several casualties resulted, some requiring urgent transport to facilities in a larger city for emergency operations, and one Hyŏngp'yŏngsa member died from injuries six months later.

Confrontations between supporters of the *hyŏngp'yŏng* movement and their opponents transpired in numerous cities and towns across the country, incited by diverse causes. Among the 110 incidents reported to the national headquarters from 1923 to April 1926 (see Table 11.3), 52 were caused by members' reactions to social discriminations practiced by the (former) *yangban* class and commoners. Thirty-three were ignited by government officials' discrimination, and ten by schoolchildren's contemptuous verbal abuse of members'

Table 11.3

*Immediate Causes of Incidents, 1923 to April 1926*

| Causes | No. |
| --- | --- |
| Discrimination by the upper class | 28 |
| Discrimination by officials | 33 |
| Discrimination by "commoners" | 24 |
| Discriminating language against pupils | 10 |
| Economic issues | 15 |
| TOTAL | 110 |

SOURCE: Hirano Shoken, "Chōsen kohei undō no kogai," *Jinruiai,* no. 2 (May 1927): 221.

Table 11.4

*Discrimination Against Hyŏngp'yŏngsa Members, 1923–35*
(n = number of incidents)

| Year | n | Year | n | Year | n |
| --- | --- | --- | --- | --- | --- |
| 1923 | 17 | 1928 | 60 | 1932 | 31 |
| 1924 | 10 | 1929 | 68 | 1933 | 26 |
| 1925 | 14 | 1930 | 67 | 1934 | 27 |
| 1926 | 14 | 1931 | 52 | 1935 | 27 |
| 1927 | 44 | | | | |

SOURCE: Chōson sōtokufu, Keimukyoku, *Saikin ni okeru Chōsen chian jō-kyō* (1933, 1935).

children. Also notable are fifteen incidents caused by economic conflicts with ordinary people. In all, such confrontations reflected members' growing view that the injustices fostered by traditional conventions had to be redressed. The variety and number of confrontations between Hyŏngp'yŏngsa members and their opponents increased sharply in the late 1920s (see Table 11.4). Members refused to perform humiliating acts of deference to government officials, who continued to use disparaging language toward them, and resisted officials' expectation of "gifts" or bribes as well as discrimination against their children in schools. In addition to social issues, economic grievances also increasingly ignited confrontation. In particular, the organizational efforts of the Hyŏngp'yŏngsa to regain

their monopoly over inherited industries fostered tension with restaurant managers, who needed a constant supply of meat, and non-
*paekchŏng* slaughterhouse managers, who were imperiled by strikes
mounted by working members of the Hyŏngp'yŏngsa.

In short, the increased antagonism between 1927 and 1930 reflected overall changes in society wrought by modernity as well
as the spread of new human rights values. Such internal and external social and economic changes abetted the demands of Hyŏng-
p'yŏngsa members for equal human rights and their protest against
all customs and conventions perceived as unjust.

## A Setback for the Human Rights Movement

As we have seen, the Hyŏngp'yŏngsa rapidly expanded geographically and fostered the formation of vital subgroups. Moreover, it
promoted the concept of human rights among members, encouraged
members to resist unfair status conventions much more vigorously
than ever, championed communitarian fellowship through an enlightenment campaign, and urged mutual protection of *paekchŏng*
economic interests against external intrusion. Despite its broad success during the 1920s, however, the movement started to stagnate in
the first years of the 1930s and to deteriorate rapidly in the mid-
1930s, losing sight of its initial goals. Finally, it changed its name to
the Taedongsa (Fusion society) in 1935 and lost its character as a
human rights movement. The donation of a warplane and ammuni-
tion to the Japanese war effort by association leaders suggests a
swing toward overt collaboration. Meanwhile, the pursuit of economic interests through exclusive rights in the leather trade was
abandoned in the face of Japanese militarism.[47]

The decline of the Hyŏngp'yŏngsa as a human rights movement
was closely related to its historical and social context. External situations, especially shifting relations with Japanese colonial powers,
were of profound influence. In its incipient stage, when the *hyŏng-
p'yŏng* movement effectively pursued its original goal of liberating
the *paekchŏng* from discriminatory conventions, activities focused
on making Korean society egalitarian, at least ostensibly. Japanese
colonial authorities saw no need to intervene in such activities in the
first few years and enjoyed the confrontations among the Korean
people. Hyŏngp'yŏngsa leaders did not denounce the Japanese but
obeyed the law. Also, they benefited at times from the Japanese pol-

icy of nonintervention, which helped them, among other things, get marks distinguishing *paekchŏng* removed from government registers.

However, the reality of colonial rule could not but affect the *paekchŏng* along with other Koreans. From the beginning, a nationalist vein ran through the *hyŏngp'yŏng* movement because of its genesis during the patriotic upswing of the March First era. It was natural, therefore, that it resisted both unfair Korean social conventions and Japanese colonialism. Some leaders openly opposed the occupation and attempted to harmonize nationalism with their fundamental focus on *paekchŏng* human rights. The Koryŏ Revolutionary Party affair provides concrete evidence of a strong nationalist element in the *hyŏngp'yŏng* movement. Key leaders of the Hyŏngp'yŏngsa joined leaders of the Ch'ŏndogyo (Heavenly way—a descendent of the Tonghak), a nationalist religious organization, and the Chŏngŭibu (Righteous government), a Manchurian-based organization that sought Korea's independence, to launch a nationalist organization in 1926. The clandestine organization was uncovered by Japanese police in 1927 within several months after its foundation, and key members were detained. Hyŏngp'yŏngsa leaders involved in the affair consequently could not carry out their duties, and national leadership shifted from the older professional activists with a nationalist bent to younger radicals with a socialist orientation.[48]

This reshuffling brought younger socialist leaders to the fore and had an enormous impact on the course of the movement, particularly from the late 1920s to the early 1930s. The younger leaders, previously active in the subgroups, radicalized the movement. The dissolution controversy of 1931 provides clear evidence that socialist influence in the *hyŏngp'yŏng* movement grew in the late 1920s and early 1930s, although its historical background is admittedly complex.[49] As in the case of the Sin'ganhoe (United front for independence), the proposal to dissolve the Hyŏngp'yŏngsa probably originated with the Comintern. Most of the younger generation of socialist-inclined Hyŏngp'yŏngsa members at central headquarters actively endorsed the proposal. Even before this, however, socialist agendas had begun to color Hyŏngp'yŏngsa activities. Examples are proposals advanced at the national meeting in 1928 for the protection of wicker and slaughterhouse workers and for close cooperation with other social movement organizations. Socialist influence on the Hyŏngp'yŏngsa grew stronger during the dissolution controversy.

As in the Sin'ganhoe, the socialists' call to dissolve the Hyŏng-p'yŏngsa was based on the claim that bourgeois leaders controlled the movement and exploited their proletarian fellows. Therefore, they urged that the Hyŏngp'yŏngsa be dissolved and replaced by trade unions so that proletarian members could better pursue their interests.

A distinct division among leaders as well as rank-and-file members arose over the dissolution proposal, reflecting both a generational gap and differences in political ideology. Older members who had struggled to establish and develop the association generally opposed the proposal, whereas the younger leaders supported dissolution. Heated debates over dissolution dominated the *hyŏngp'yŏng* movement at the local and national levels throughout 1931. When Suwŏn branch members passed the first resolution to dissolve the local Hyŏngp'yŏngsa in the spring of 1931, their fellows in other towns such as Yangyang, Kangwŏn province, and Ipchang, South Ch'ungch'ŏng province, endorsed the decision.[50] In contrast, members in other towns such as Wŏnju, Kangwŏn province, objected to the proposal. The Yesan branch in South Ch'ungch'ŏng province proposed that a definitive decision would be deferred until the national meeting in Seoul, and this proposal was adopted.[51] The dissolution proposal was, of course, the most hotly contested issue at the national conference in Seoul in April 1931. Tension first arose during the election of the national leadership. The older, founding leaders, who opposed dissolution, prevailed, prompting the faction supporting dissolution to leave the conference hall after alleging improper handling of the vote. The dissolution proposal was subsequently rejected by the remaining delegates without debate.

Nevertheless, the issue remained on the agenda of both local and regional meetings throughout most of 1931. At the South Kyŏngsang and Kangwŏn regional meetings in May and July 1931, respectively, socialist members unsuccessfully raised the resolution for dissolution.[52] Ultimately the dissolution proposal was rejected by rank-and-file members as well as the founding leaders. Their experience of social discrimination and isolation from the broader society prompted them, regardless of ideology, to prefer the continued existence of the Hyŏngp'yŏngsa to ensure group survival.

Despite its apparent resolution, the dissolution controversy had an enduring impact on the *hyŏngp'yŏng* movement. Ideological differences among the leaders, especially between the younger socialist radicals and older founding moderates, continued to plague the movement. Attempts to repair the split invariably failed, abetting a rapid decline in the activism and number of members and local branches (see Table 11.2). The ninth and tenth annual national conferences in Seoul in April 1932 and 1933 were attended by only about 110 delegates from some 40 branches, a dramatic decline from the 220 delegates from 58 branches in 1928 and the 230 delegates in 1930.[53] Rank-and-file members, especially wealthy ones, seemed gradually to withdraw support. Typical was Yi Sŏngsun's ineffective stewardship as head of the national executive committee. Yi, a wealthy Pusan leather merchant, was elected to the post at the national conference in April 1932. He presumably was expected to remobilize the resources of wealthy members to remedy financial difficulties and membership inactivity, especially in the South Kyŏngsang province area. Yi, however, refused to serve, and disappointed leaders at the national headquarters passed a resolution to remove Yi, citing his ineffective leadership at the national executive committee meeting in July 1932.[54]

The emergence of radicalism and the consequent split in the national leadership was a great disappointment and even embarrassment to rank-and-file members, who at the time were weathering the effects of the Great Depression. Accordingly, many local branches ceased to be active, and the drop in membership dues consequently hampered efforts to maintain previous levels of vigor. In the end, what proved fatal to the movement, however, was the intervention of Japanese colonial authorities, who dismantled and transformed the movement into a collaborationist group.[55] The so-called Hyŏngp'yŏng Youth Vanguard League affair occurred in 1933. Over a period of months, the police arrested and interrogated more than 100 Hyŏngp'yŏngsa members, mainly younger activists, on the charge of organizing an unlawful clandestine association for the purpose of forming a communist society.[56] After several months of detention without trial, many were released, but 68 were prosecuted. Although all 68 were pronounced guilty at preliminary examinations, only fourteen were formally tried on charges of organizing an illegal association, the Hyŏngp'yŏng Youth Vanguard League. The defendants were released from jail in November 1936, nearly four years following their arrest, after a Japanese judge found them innocent.[57]

Meanwhile, a resolution was passed at the national convention in April 1935 to change the name of the organization to the Taedongsa.

National leadership passed to the moderates Yi Sŏngsun and Kang Sangho from South Kyŏngsang province. With the change in name, the preoccupation with human rights was replaced by a focus on economic interests, such as retaining traditional privileges in industries like leather and butchering. This fostered collaboration with Japanese colonial powers and the final betrayal of Hyŏngp'yŏngsa, once one of the most successful human rights movements in Korean history.

## Conclusion

The *hyŏngp'yŏng* movement, the longest-lasting nationwide movement under Japanese rule, was enabled and constrained by the social conditions under which it labored. The *paekchŏng*, its beneficiaries, were social pariahs under the rigidly hierarchical *sinbun* structure. Industrialization, moreover, deprived them of their traditional monopoly over certain industries, threatening to place them under the economic control of non-*paekchŏng* and to destroy their community solidarity. However, social constraints were complemented by factors that enabled the *paekchŏng* to develop an effective social movement. Among these were a long history of strong community fellowship, increasing exposure to the concepts of human rights, liberation from oppressive social traditions, and a proliferation of economic resources for some. These factors also facilitated the geographical expansion of the organization and its development of various subgroups.

The Hyŏngp'yŏngsa was primarily a human rights movement, and as such it undertook activities designed not only to abolish externally imposed social discrimination against the *paekchŏng* but also to enhance the sense of human dignity within the community by re-establishing the sense of communal fellowship that had been attenuated by industrialization. Although plagued by internal division and ideological compromise as well as external intervention, the *hyŏngp'yŏng* movement was successful in fighting collectively against social discrimination to achieve equal human rights. It helped topple the discriminatory *sinbun* structure and thus bring Korea into the modern era as a society of equals. It is no historical accident that, in sharp contrast to the situation of the Japanese *burakumin* or the Indian untouchables, the descendents of the *paekchŏng* are not discriminated against.

Hyŏngp'yŏngsa efforts, however, inevitably invited hostile reactions from conservatives and intervention by the Japanese, who feared nationalist and socialist influences. Ideological rift fostered factional divisions, undermining group solidarity, and Japanese surveillance proved particularly inimical in the movement's final years. During the Taedongsa period, the association forfeited its initial focus on human rights and fell into passivity, disappearing without a trace in the 1940s. Even after liberation from Japanese rule, the *paekchŏng* failed to reconstruct their original community, partly because of the Korean War in the 1950s and partly because of the rapid industrialization in the 1960s. The conference of the P'yŏngusa (Equal friends society) in Seoul in 1964 was probably the last meeting of the offspring of Hyŏngp'yŏngsa members.

Examination of the Hyŏngp'yŏngsa movement reveals the complexity of colonial modernity. On the one hand, colonial industrialization undermined the economic base of the *paekchŏng*. On the other hand, colonial modernity facilitated modern social movements such as the Hyŏngp'yŏngsa that pursued the removal of social discriminations. A stress on the binary of exploitation and resistance cannot capture the complex nature of colonial modernity, which requires a more flexible approach.

TWELVE

# Minjok as a Modern
# and Democratic Construct:
# Sin Ch'aeho's Historiography

## Henry H. Em

"Korea" as a civilization, or as a cultural and social formation, has a history dating back over a thousand years. As the political and religious elite of "Unified" Silla (676–935), Koryŏ (936–1392), and Chosŏn (1392–1910) reacted to and participated in intellectual movements within the larger cosmopolitan world centered around "China," they were compelled to generate various forms of collective identity—representations of their state and their people as separate and unique. Through the practice of state-sponsored rituals, the building of monuments, and the compilation of official histories, narratives about the collective "self" were continuously generated. As such narratives were generated, other (competing) narratives were repressed or contested. That is to say, narratives on "Korean" identity did not simply accumulate over time: not all such narratives got transmitted, and even those that were, were invariably translated (reinvented) for use in the present.[1]

It is in this sense that the concept of Koreans as constituting a "nation" (*minjok*) is a modern construct, which, in the historical context of its emergence at the turn of the century, enabled more democratic, more inclusive forms of political action. The word itself (read *minzoku* in Japanese, *minzu* in Chinese) was a neologism created in Meiji Japan.[2] In the early 1880s, according to Yasuda Hiroshi, Miyazaki Muryū translated the French Assemblée Nationale as *minzoku kaigi*. But it was only in the 1890s that *minzoku* came to mean the ethnic nation.[3] As understanding of the term became more fixed in Japanese political discourse, its meaning approached the German *Volk* or *Volkschaft*.[4] And, as Andre Schmid pointed out, when intellectuals throughout East Asia appropriated the neologism, *minjok* became not only a powerful political concept but also "a powerful conceptual tool . . . to rewrite [the] historical past."[5]

This is not to ignore Lydia Liu's injunction to those engaged in cross-cultural studies to eschew a conceptual model "derived from a bilingual dictionary."[6] Although the word "*minjok*" entered the Korean vocabulary in the late 1890s and became widely used two decades later, this is not sufficient proof that the *minjok* is a modern construct. Son Chint'ae (1900–Korean War?) made this point in 1948 when he wrote, "Although the word '*minjok*' was not used in the past—because it was the quintessential character of Korea's court-centered, aristocratic states to obstruct the development of such [national] consciousness (*sasang*) and concepts—the [Korean] *minjok* certainly did exist even if the word did not."[7] Similarly, Cho Tonggŏl, in a recent book on historians and historiography in Korea, applauds the pioneer of nationalist historiography, Sin Ch'aeho (1880–1936), not for creating a historical narrative based on a new construct called the *minjok* but for creating a historical narrative based on the *discovery* of the *minjok*—suggesting that prior to its discovery the *minjok* was already (and always) present.[8] In contrast to these views, I argue in this essay that *minjok* is a modern construct, and not to recognize it as such is to miss the crucial link in early twentieth-century Korean historiography between nationalism and democratic thought.

To understand this linkage, we might begin with the question of when and how peasants of Kyŏngsang province, for example, became "Koreans." Of a very different historical context, Eugen Weber has argued that the French peasant was "nationalized" (that is, made French) only in the 1880s. "The French" were produced in the last decades of the nineteenth century through the creation of a national language (standard French) and national customs. To be more precise, the transformation of peasants into Frenchmen became possible after the establishment of universal schooling, unification of customs and beliefs by inter-regional labor migration and military service, and subordination of political and religious conflicts to an ideology of patriotism. In other words, it was only after the emergence of modern state structures that distinctive social, political, and linguistic practices became "local variations" of a newly created national culture.[9]

If the French became "French" in the 1880s, when did Koreans become "Koreans"? In asking this question, it must be emphasized that Korea, perhaps as early as the Koryŏ period, had far more linguistic and cultural unity than did pre-Revolutionary France. There were, however, significant linguistic and cultural differences among the various provinces in Korea. Even more important than these regional (lateral) differences, status distinctions between *yangban*, *chungin* (middle people), commoners, and *ch'ŏnmin* (base people) had created horizontal lines of cultural cleavage in which each status group had its own idiom, norms, and social role. It can be argued, for example, that Confucianism "belonged" to the ruling (*yangban*) class in the sense that it served to underscore, legitimize, and make authoritative the different worlds inhabited by the horizontally segregated layers in pre-modern Korean society.[10] As Carter Eckert notes, prior to the late-nineteenth century,

there was little, if any, feeling of loyalty toward the abstract concept of "Korea" as a nation-state, or toward fellow inhabitants of the peninsula as "Koreans." Far more meaningful at the time, in addition to a sense of loyalty to the king, were the attachments of Koreans to their village or region, and above all to their clan, lineage, and immediate and extended family. The Korean elite in particular would have found the idea of nationalism not only strange but also uncivilized. Since at least the seventh century the ruling classes in Korea had thought of themselves in cultural terms less as Koreans than as members of a larger cosmopolitan civilization centered on China. . . . To live outside the realm of Chinese culture was, for the Korean elite, to live as a barbarian.[11]

Eckert is not suggesting that Korean elites were ignorant of differences (political, linguistic, and cultural) between themselves and, say, the Chinese. For more than a thousand years, Korea had a central bureaucratic state that employed a class of people whose job was to maintain and articulate difference vis-à-vis competing, neighboring states (most often in Manchuria, sometimes Japan, and of course, China itself).[12] However, unlike the modern nation-state, the kingdoms of "Unified" Silla, Koryŏ, and Chosŏn were not interested in "nationalizing" their subjects. In fact, it can be argued that the pre-modern state's (extremely effective) solution to the problem of maintaining political stability was to tolerate local distinctiveness and to maintain status distinctions.[13]

The people of Chosŏn knew that they shared certain ties with other people living in the Chosŏn kingdom, as well as with ancestors they had never seen. But, as Benedict Anderson would argue, these "ties" would have been imagined particularistically—"as indefinitely stretchable nets of kinship and clientship."[14] At the turn of the century, however, a new generation of political activists and intellectuals felt they had to redefine Korea in terms of internal homogeneity and external autonomy. The historical juncture for this epistemological break came after Korea was forcibly incorporated into a nation-state system dominated by Western imperial powers, after the Korean monarchy proved itself incapable of keeping these powers at bay, and after Korean intellectuals were forced to acknowledge the strength of Meiji (Westernizing) Japan. Organizing movements for independence, self-strengthening, and people's rights, these intellectuals re-imagined Korea's collective identity in terms of a "deep, horizontal comradeship"—regardless of, or because of, the actual divisions and inequalities that prevailed in Korean society.

## Minjok and Historiography

It was ethnic-national historiography (*minjok sahak*), then, born in the early twentieth century, that for the first time narrated the history of Korea as the history of the Korean *minjok*, a category inclusive of every Korean without regard to age, gender, or status distinctions.[15] The first nationalist historian responsible for centering the ethnic nation—both as the subject of history and as the object for historical research—was Sin Ch'aeho.[16] His 1908 essay "Toksa sillon" (A new way of reading history) set forth the first and most influential historical narrative equating Korean history (*kuksa*) with the history of the Korean nation (*minjoksa*). As a history of the ethnic nation, rather than a dynastic history, Sin Ch'aeho traced the origin of the Korean nation to the mythical figure Tan'gun.[17]

The Tan'gun legend had an ambiguous place in premodern Korean historiography. It is not mentioned in Korea's oldest extant history, the *Samguk sagi* (Historical record of the Three Kingdoms) compiled by Kim Pusik in 1145.[18] In a recent book on Korean historiography, Han Yŏngu states that the political intent of Kim Pusik's *Samguk sagi* was to bolster bureaucratic authority centered around the Koryŏ court

(936–1392)—at the expense of the aristocracy. Compiled ten years after Kim Pusik suppressed a revolt led by Myoch'ŏng,[19] *Samguk sagi* also makes no reference to Parhae (699–926: P'ohai in Chinese), a kingdom, established by a former Koguryŏ general, encompassing much of Manchuria, southern Siberia, and northeast Korea.[20]

In writing the history of the Three Kingdoms (Koguryŏ: 37 B.C.E.–668 C.E.; Paekche: 18 B.C.E.–660 C.E.; and Silla: 57 B.C.E.–935 C.E.), Kim Pusik depicted Koryŏ as the successor to Silla (which by 676 had come to control the southern two-thirds of the peninsula). In contrast, the forces led by Myoch'ŏng had regarded Koryŏ as the successor state of Koguryŏ and had advocated an (incautious) expansionist policy to recover onetime Koguryŏ land.[21] The suppression of Myoch'ŏng's revolt went hand in hand with policies of coexisting peacefully with the Chin and bolstering the authority of the Koryŏ court by promoting Confucian principles, particularly, loyalty to the king. Likewise, the narrative strategy as well as the methodology of Kim Pusik's *Samguk sagi*, including the invocation of the Confucian historiographic principles of rationality (*mujing pulsin*) and fidelity to historical sources (*suli pujak*: that is, transmission without creative elaboration), cannot be understood apart from the political context of mid-twelfth-century Koryŏ.

The Tan'gun legend does appear in the thirteenth-century texts *Samguk yusa* (Memorabilia of the Three Kingdoms; 1285?) written by the Buddhist Sŏn master Iryŏn, and in *Chewang un'gi* (Rhymed record of emperors and kings; 1287) written by Yi Sŭnghyu.[22] But these histories were compiled under very different historical circumstances. Both began their histories with Tan'gun, a significant assertion that traced Koryŏ's origin directly to heaven. Because Iryŏn and Yi Sŭnghyu witnessed the suffering of the people during the Mongol invasions and its domination of Koryŏ, Yi Kibaek surmises that this "strengthened their sense of identity as a distinct race (*minjok*) and gave force to the concept of their descent from a common ancestor."[23] Among the events that Iryŏn and Yi Sŭnghyu witnessed was King Ch'ungnyŏl's marriage to a daughter of Kubilai in 1274, and the Koryŏ royal family's becoming a cadet branch of the Mongol imperial house.[24] The meaning of the Tan'gun legend in these thirteenth-century texts, then, cannot be isolated from the historical context of the Mongol domination of Koryŏ from 1259 to 1356. Indeed, it is reasonable to interpret Iryŏn's narrative strategy of making Tan'gun as ancient as the legendary Chinese Emperor Yao, and his willingness to talk about "extraordinary forces and capricious spirits" and "wondrous tales" (religiously ignoring the Confucian principle of *mujing pulsin*), as a narrative of resistance.[25]

Sin Ch'aeho's use of the Tan'gun legend in a twentieth-century context was similarly a narrative of resistance, but it was also a re-invention—and not simply a revival—of this old and recurrent narrative in premodern Korean historiography. That is to say, earlier representations of Korea as a social totality in the *Samguk sagi, Samguk yusa*, or in the Confucian historiography of the Chosŏn period did not necessarily, or teleologically, develop into the secular and egalitarian imaginary called the "*minjok*." The best evidence that any "transmission" of the past must also be a re-invention is Sin Ch'aeho's "Toksa sillon" itself. If Korea as a homogenous ethnic nation had been a well-established, abiding concept, then there would have been no need to write "Toksa sillon," and it would not have caused such excitement among his readers in 1908.

By identifying the *minjok*, rather than the monarch, as the subject of an evolutionary history (where the strong survive and the weak perish), Sin Ch'aeho's "Toksa sillon" displaced traditional forms of Confucian historiography—*p'yŏnnyŏnch'e* (chronicles) and *kijŏnch'e* (annal-biographies)—with the (tragic) epic form. Sin Ch'aeho adopted a novel way of telling what Confucian historians had already known; his narrative utilized new codes to produce new structures of meaning quite different from that found in histories written in the chronicle and the annal-biography styles.[26]

Confucian historiography had constituted itself not as a separate discipline but as part of a larger body of knowledge of statecraft (*kyŏnghak*). Its function was to serve as a mirror and as a repository of knowledge that would enable the monarch and his officials to act morally and ethically in the present. As a pedagogical tool, Confucian histories were used to educate scholar-officials in the art of governing; as a political tool, history writing had the solemn ethical function of assigning praise or blame. Although both official and private histories existed, both were written by bureaucrats for other bureaucrats (either holding office or aspiring to do so).[27] Moreover, in terms of access to court documents and official histories (with the exception of the Collected Statutes), these could be consulted only by a small group of scholar-officials.[28]

Although nationalist historiography constituted itself as a separate discipline (separate from statecraft), it preserved some aspects of Confucian historiography: for example, the concept of history as a mirror for the present, and history as serving an ethical function (assigning praise and blame). But the critical difference had to do with the profound epistemic break caused by Korea's incorporation into the nation-state system dominated by the West in the late nineteenth century, and the social position of the historian and his intended readership in colonial modernity. Few of the nationalist historians came from high *yangban* status, many were regularly hounded by the colonial police, and most wrote their histories in their capacity as "public intellectuals." When Sin Ch'aeho wrote "Toksa sillon," for example, he was a member of the secret society Sinminhoe (New people's association) and employed by the newspaper *Taehan maeil sinbo* (Korean daily news), and the essay itself was serialized in the *Taehan maeil sinbo* from August to December 1908.[29]

On the eve of being colonized by Japan, to achieve political independence and to reclaim dignity and "authentic" identity in reaction to colonialist discourses on Korea, nationalists such as Sin Ch'aeho sought to arouse, unite, and mobilize the entire Korean population. In place of loyalty to the king and attachments to the village, clan, and family, and in place of hierarchic status distinctions among *yangban*, commoners, and base people, nationalist historiography endeavored to redirect the people's loyalty toward a new, all-embracing identity of Koreans as a unique ethnic group. It was with this political intent, then, that Sin Ch'aeho wrote "Toksa sillon," for an emerging "general public," tracing Korea's ethnic and cultural origins as far back as possible to a geographic area that extends far beyond the Korean peninsula into Manchuria.

In 1908, Sin Ch'aeho's indictment of Kim Pusik's *Samguk sagi* for the deletion of Manchuria from Korean history and his reconceptualization of state history (*kuksa*) as the history of the Korean nation (*minjoksa*) were radical conceptual acts.[30] Sin Ch'aeho's identification of the *minjok* as the subject of an evolutionary History marks a watershed in modern Korean intellectual history.[31] Through a reading of Sin Ch'aeho's writings, I hope to create an interpretive framework for understanding the historical emergence of nationalist historiography in Korea.

In creating this interpretive framework, I sometimes side with those who condemn nationalism and nationalist historiography and at other times side with those who defend nationalism and nationalist historiography in postcolonial societies such as Korea. To put it simply, some see nationalism as a rational attempt by the weak and poor peoples of the world to achieve autonomy and liberty, whereas others see nationalism as "one of Europe's most pernicious exports," whose inevitable consequence has been the annihilation of freedom. In contrast, I argue that, as in other nationalist movements, Korean nationalism embodies both democratic (liberating) and oppressive tendencies, and these tendencies manifest themselves most directly in the writing of nationalist historiography in Korea. Focusing on the historiography of Sin Ch'aeho, I show how nationalist historiography resisted the degrading assertions of Japanese colonialist historiography and helped to create a modern form of civil society in Korea. At the same time, I explain how this nationalist historiography has inhibited the deepening of democracy by suppressing heterogeneity and discontinuity in Korean history.

## "Toksa sillon" (1908)

Because of space limitations and the existence of superb studies of Sin Ch'aeho, here I do not attempt an exhaustive interpretation of his historiography.[32] Instead, I present interpretive readings of selected passages in "Toksa sillon" and later works such as *Chosŏn sanggosa* (History of ancient Korea) and the political manifesto "Chosŏn hyŏngmyŏng sŏnŏn" (Declaration of the Korean revolution). "Toksa Sillon" begins:

[Para. 1] The history of a state is that which renders a precise record of the rise and/or fall, prosperity and/or decay of the *minjok*. Without the *minjok*, there is no history; without history, the *minjok* cannot have a clear perception of the state—and thus, the historian has a heavy responsibility. . . .

[Para. 3] A state is an organic entity formed from the national spirit (*minjok chŏngsin*). That is to say, even in a state formed by various tribal groups (*chongjok*), not to mention a state formed by one tribe with a single blood line, there is always a special tribal group that assumes the primary role. . . .

[Para. 4] Examining history books used at different schools, I've found hardly any of value. In the first chapter, Koreans (*minjok*) are described as if they were part of the Chinese people; in the second chapter, Koreans appear almost like part of the Hsien-pi (Sŏnbijok); and reading the entire book Koreans are variously made out to be part of the Moho (Malgaljok), part of the Mongols (Mongojok), part of the Jurchen (Yŏjinjok), or part of the Japanese (Ilbonjok). If this were true, our lands, which encompass several tens of thousands *li*, would be in pandemonium, with barbarians from north and south milling around, and [our] accomplishments of four thousand years would be credited to the Liang in the morning and in the evening to the Ch'u.[33]

[Para. 5] Incomplete as our ancient history may be, if we examine it carefully, we can clearly discern the true likeness of those who constitute the primary ethnic composition of our country—the descendants of Tan'gun. That being so, what is the reason for the confusion over who our ancestors are? As we try to dispel the ignorance of the entire citizenry through nationalism (*minjokchuŭi*) and train the minds of our youth with concepts of state so that they may guard our country's last remaining pulse, history is an indispensable instrument. But bad histories are worse than no history.[34]

The textbooks referred to by Sin Ch'aeho were published by the Bureau of History (P'yŏnsaguk: established in 1894 under the aegis of the Japanese minister to Korea). Although these books listed Kim T'aegyŏng, Hyŏn Ch'ae, and others as authors, many of them were translations of history books on Korea written by Japanese scholars.[35] In criticizing these textbooks, Sin Ch'aeho (1) identified the history of Korea with the fortunes of the *minjok* as constituted by the descendants of Tan'gun; (2) gave the geographic size of Korea as about ten times the customary 3,000 square li, thus appropriating nearly all of Manchuria; (3) took great pains to assert a distinct, separate ethnicity for the Korean people, tracing a precise, singular genealogical history beginning with Tan'gun through Old Chosŏn-Puyŏ-Koguryŏ-Parhae-Koryŏ-Chosŏn; and (4) characterized, without equivocation, history as an instrument or a vehicle for instilling patriotism among youth.

Sin Ch'aeho's identification of a country's history with the history of the people (*minjok*) parallels the revolutionary shift that occurred with the French Revolution, the shift from *L'état c'est moi* to *L'état c'est le peuple*. The opening sentence of "Toksa sillon" reflects the republican ideal held by Sin Ch'aeho and many other leading nationalist intellectuals of that time. Later in this text, Sin Ch'aeho stated, "A state does not belong to one individual, it belongs to the entire people."[36] As a tactical matter, however, Sin Ch'aeho did not attack the Korean monarch.[37] Nevertheless, the nationalist position staked out in "Toksa sillon" gives evidence of what Kang Man'gil has described as the shift from patriotism based on loyalty to the king to a nationalism based on popular sovereignty.[38] This *democratic* predisposition became much more manifest in Sin Ch'aeho's later writing (see the discussion below of the *minjok* in relation to the *minjung*).

As Andre Schmid has pointed out, when Sin Ch'aeho asserted a distinct, separate ethnicity for the Korean people that originated with Tan'gun and descended through Puyŏ, his aim was to subvert weak and limited conceptions of Korea's national space.[39] Schmid notes that confrontations over territorial access—such as resource concessions to foreign powers, circulation of foreign currencies, extraterritoriality, unregulated Japanese immigration—had already undermined inherited conceptions of territorial authority. Sin Ch'aeho's "Toksa sillon" "became the first in a long line of Korean history writing that wielded the Manchurian connection to create a nationalist history that reveled in the grandeur of an ancient past."[40]

In thus problematizing orthodox conceptions of Korea's national space, Sin Ch'aeho drew on irredentist themes from earlier historiography.[41] It is also important to note that, two decades prior to Sin Ch'aeho's "Toksa sillon," Japanese historians had begun to question the "limited" conception of Japan's national space. In an article published in 1889, Kume criticized the notion of "Japan as an island nation that had not changed in thousands of years," and he reminded his readers of an ancient Japan that had encompassed Korea and southeastern China. Eventually, as Stefan Tanaka notes, "arguments like Kume's [served] as a historical justification for the annexation of Korea."[42] The spatial imagining of a greater Japan and Sin Ch'aeho's greater Korea shared a similar strategy, but their political aims were diametrically opposed—Kume was creating a historical framework for Japanese colonialism, and Sin a historical framework for Korean resistance.

With this defensive motivation, then, Sin Ch'aeho identified the Korean *minjok* as the descendants of Tan'gun and privileged the northern line of descent over the southern one, thus making Manchuria the birthplace of the *minjok* and a powerful reminder of Korea's past glory. Although Sin Ch'aeho's appropriation of Manchuria can be seen as a defensive response, this historical narrative also sustained and duplicated a potent totalizing tendency.[43] Below, I elaborate on these issues in my discussion of *minjok* as a totalizing discourse, but first we need to examine more closely what Sin Ch'aeho was reacting against.

## Colonialist Historiography

Colonialist historiography, written mostly by Japanese historians but also by a number of Korean historians, provided justification for Japanese control over Korea by narrating Korean history in terms of "lack"—for example, Koreans lacked the capacity for autonomous development, or Koreans lacked a progressive spirit. Colonialist historiography suggested (and at times stated unequivocally) that because of such inherent deficiencies Japan had no choice but to lead Korea into the modern world. Present-day South Korean historians identify four characteristics of colonialist historiography: *t'ayulsŏng-ron*, external forces (Chinese, Manchurian, and Japanese) had determined Korea's historical development; *chŏngch'esŏng-ron*, Korean history was stagnant (the late Chosŏn had not even reached the feudal stage of development); *tangp'asŏng-ron*, factionalism is deeply ingrained into the Korean political culture (as evidenced by successive literati purges and factional strife during Chosŏn); and *ilsŏn tongjo-ron*, Japanese and Koreans shared common ethnic origins, and thus Japan's colonization of Korea represented the restoration of ancient ties.[44]

According to Hatada Takashi, the origins of what many contemporary Korean historians characterize as colonialist historiography can be traced to mid-Meiji efforts to write a national history for Japan.[45] One influential work was *Kokushi gan* (A survey of Japanese history), published by Tokyo Imperial University in 1890. Written by Shigeno Yasutsugu, Kume Kunitake, and Hoshino Hisashi, *Kokushi gan* was intended as a pointer in the teaching of Japanese history, and it was long used as a university textbook. According to Numata Jirō, Shigeno played the leading role in establishing the "modern Tokyo tradition" of history writing. Stressing the native origins of "mainstream" historiography in modern Japan, Numata argues that the Tokyo tradition resulted from a fusion between the critical methods of Western historical science (as introduced by the German historian Ludwig Riess starting in 1887) and the scholastic tradition of evidential research, or *kōshō-gaku* (*kochŭnghak* in Korean, *k'ao-cheng* in Chinese), which had been well established during the Tokugawa period.[46]

The narrative framework for Japan's national history was also greatly influenced by the Tokugawa nativist (*kokugaku*) views on Japan's origins. According to Hatada, *Kokushi gan* drew on the nativist reading of the *Kojiki* and the *Nihon shoki*, which asserted that Japanese and Koreans had a common ancestry (*Nissen dōso-ron*): in the sense that Susano-o (the Impetuous-Male-Deity, or the Storm God) had ruled Korea before settling in Izumo (in western Honshu); Inapi no mikoto (brother of Jinmu, the mythical first emperor of Japan) had become king of Silla; his son Ama no hi hoko had returned to Japan in submission; and Empress Jingu (Jingū kōgō) had led a punitive expedition against Silla, forcing its king into submission.[47] Ko-

*kushi gan*, as intended, provided the narrative framework for the national history textbooks used in primary and secondary schools in Japan. This, along with media portrayals of Korea following Japan's victory in the first Sino-Japanese War (1894–95), created a historical imaginary (*rekishi zō*) whereby the Japanese came to believe that Japan had ruled Korea in ancient times, and the Japanese colonization of Korea in modern times represented the restoration of an ancient relationship.[48]

This nationalist imaginary in Japan's national histories was reproduced in histories of Korea. Hayashi Taisuke's *Chōsenshi* (History of Korea), published in 1892, argued that in ancient times the northern part of Korea had been a colony of China (the Four Chinese Commanderies of Lo-lang, Chen-fan, Lin-t'un and Hsüan-t'u: 108 B.C.E.–313 C.E.), and the southern part of Korea had been controlled by Mimana (Kaya), a Japanese colony. Hayashi's *Chōsenshi* set the framework for other studies on Korea that sought to explain Korea's historical development as having been determined by external forces. Hyŏn Ch'ae's *Tongguk saryak* (1906), which was used as a Korean history textbook in the newly established public schools, was pretty much a translation of Hayashi's *Chōsenshi*. But what truly scandalized Sin Ch'aeho was that Hyŏn Ch'ae did not know what he had done wrong—both in terms of historical scholarship and in the political sense.[49] To cite one more example, Fukuda Tokuzō's *Kankoku no keizai soshiki to keizai tani* (Economic units and economic organization in Korea), published in 1904, asserted that the most salient characteristic of Korean history was its stagnancy, itself a reflection of Korea's failure to have a feudal period. Thus, Fukuda found late-nineteenth-century Chosŏn comparable to tenth-century Japan (Fujiwara period).[50]

These studies of Korea in turn set the tone for other studies on the Orient. Stefan Tanaka has shown how late-nineteenth-century Japanese historians created the category of Tōyōshi (Oriental history) so as to narrate Japanese history as different but equal to European history. One strategy used by Tokugawa intellectuals to deal with the prevailing China-centered East Asian world order and to assert Japan's equivalence with China had been to replace "Chūgoku" (Middle Kingdom) with "Shina" as the Japanese appellation for China. This term allowed nativist (*kokugaku*) scholars to separate Japan from the barbarian/civilized or outer/inner implications of the term "Chūgoku."[51] However, after Japan's victory in the first Sino-Japanese War, historians such as Shiratori Kurakichi employed the term "Shina" to signify China "as a troubled place mired in its past, in contrast to Japan, a modern Asian nation."[52] The symbolic shift in names for China had its counterpart in Korea as well. Sin Ch'aeho's use of "China" rather than "Chungguk" reflects what Andre Schmid has called the "decentering of the Middle Kingdom." After Japan's victory in the first Sino-Japanese War, this decentering reversed inherited notions of "civilization" and shifted the locus away from China and toward Japan and the West. This point is illustrated by a revealing editorial in the *Tongnip sinmun*, the organ of the Independence Club, uncovered by Schmid:

The only thing [we Koreans] knew was to revere China as the central plain (*chongwŏn*), scorn Japan as the country of *wae*, and call all other countries barbarians (*orangk'ae*). Now, for more than ten years, our doors have been open, and we have welcomed guests coming from all places. With our ears we can hear, and with our eyes we can see the customs and laws of western countries. We can now generally judge which countries are the civilized ones and which countries are the barbarous ones.[53]

In Japanese historiography, the substitution of "Shina" for "Chūgoku" and the creations of a new spatial category called Tōyō (the Orient) and a new academic discipline called Tōyōshi (Oriental history) marked the emergence of a comprehensive ideological system regarding Japan's position and destiny vis-à-vis the West and the rest of Asia.[54] Behind the creation of Tōyōshi was the political desire to portray the Japanese as uniquely capable (among non-white peoples) of meeting the European nations on an equal plane and thus uniquely capable of leading Asia. Tōyōshi enabled Japanese intellectuals to conceptualize the West as "merely another culture (though in some aspects still a superior one), a fellow competitor on [the] rocky path toward progress."[55] The creation of Tōyōshi, then, was motivated by defensive considerations in that it sought to deflect notions of permanent Western superiority. At the same time, Tōyōshi had its aggressive side. In the hands of Japan's Orientalists, China and Korea came to embody all the negative aspects of the West's Orient.

As argued by Tanaka, "modern" Japanese historiography emerged as a response to the Orientalism of the West—that is, as an attempt to de-objectify Japan and Asia. The strategy adopted by historians like Shiratori (and institutions like the Department of Oriental History at Tokyo Imperial University) was to prove that the Japanese were not "Oriental," as defined by the West, by using the *same* [Orientalist] epistemology.[56] As a new academic field, Tōyōshi legitimated itself on the basis of its "scientific," "rationalistic" methodology, and on the basis of its practical application in the "administration of southern Manchuria" and the "protection and development of Korea."

For historians like Sin Ch'aeho, the violence of imperialism (and colonialist historiography) was justification enough for writing a nationalist historiography. Sin Ch'aeho's historiography came to set the themes for much of later nationalist historiography, which insisted that Korea has always had a distinct culture and society, testified to the veracity of the Korean nation by chronicling the long history of the Korean people's resistance to foreign aggression, and narrated the emergence of the Korean nation as an essential part of world history.

At the same time, we can detect in Sin Ch'aeho's adoption of categories like China (Shina) and Tongyangsa (Tōyōshi), a paradox inherent to nationalist discourse in the colonial world: the subjugated people, in the very act of resisting colonial rule, speak the language of their oppressors—the language of competition, democracy, and progress. The problematic in nationalist thought forces it relentlessly to demarcate itself from the discourse of colonialism, but even as nationalist discourse seeks to assert the feasibility of entirely new political possibilities, it remains a prisoner of the modes of thought characteristic of rational knowledge in the post-Enlightenment age—thus the lack of autonomy of nationalist discourse.[57]

## *Minjok* as a Totalizing Discourse

If, however, *minjok* is a twentieth-century construct, and a derivative discourse at that, how was it that Korean nationalism (*minjokchuŭi*) became such a powerful mobilizing force? Although acknowledging the power (and achievements) of the Korean nationalist movement, we should be on guard against the appropriating and totalizing power of nationalist historiography. As Elie Kedourie cautions, not being wary of nationalist categories in historiography can result in deception: "Men who thought they were acting in order to accomplish the will of God, to make the truth prevail, or to advance the interests of a dynasty, or perhaps simply to defend their own against aggression, are suddenly seen to have been really acting in order that the genius of a particular nationality should be manifested and fostered."[58] Or, as argued more recently by Prasenjit Duara, while in reality the "nation" is a contested and contingent identity, national (as well as nationalist) historiography secures for the nation "the false unity of a self-same, national subject evolving through time."[59] Kedourie's and Duara's critiques of national historiography are pertinent to the Korean case.

With easy confidence, contemporary Korean national historiography (*minjok sahak*) secures for the nation a long list of "national" heroes from as early as the Three Kingdoms period, military heroes like Ŭlchi Mundŏk (mid-sixth century–early seventh century) of Koguryŏ. But, as John Duncan points out, it is "extremely unlikely that the peoples of Koguryŏ, Paekche, and Silla all thought of themselves as members of a larger, 'Korean' collectivity that transcended local boundaries and state loyalties."[60] Nevertheless, on the basis of certain assumptions made about blood and soil, national (and nationalist) historiography endows these military heroes with a common "national" identity. As explained by Etienne Balibar, this national identity "is always already presented to us in the form of a narrative which attributes to [this entity] the continuity of a subject. The formation of the nation thus appears as the fulfillment of a 'project' stretching over centuries, in which there are different stages and moments of coming to self-awareness."[61] Through the power of this ideological form, national histories can portray even Paleolithic inhabitants of the peninsula as "early Koreans," their culture as "pre-national," and the modern Korean nation-state as the culmination of a long process of development.[62] But, as Etienne Balibar reminds us, we should not read this history as "a line of necessary evolution but [as] a series of conjunctural relations which has inscribed them after the event into the pre-history of the nation-form."[63]

Even as some historians acknowledge the discontinuities and breaks in Korean history, nearly all still accept the nation-state as the "normal" or "natural" form of political community.[64] This, Prasenjit Duara argues, is a central facet of Western hegemony: the assumption that the nation-state is the only legitimate form of polity.[65] We are as yet unable to imagine alternative political forms, and by writing narratives of the nation, which constitute much of modern historiography, historians help maintain the illusion of a nation's necessary and unilinear evolution. The nation form, as ideology, presents itself to us as ontological necessity—our desire that history will confirm our belief that the present rests on profound intentions and necessities prompts the production of a linear, continuous history that begins in the Paleolithic period and culminates in the establishment of (depending on one's politics) the

Republic of Korea (South) or the Democratic People's Republic of Korea (North Korea).[66]

It remains for a democratic historiography, then, to show how the nation threatens to impose immutable articulations in an authoritarian way. And strange as it may sound, the basis for a much less totalizing historiography may, I think, be found in Sin Ch'aeho's later historiography and certainly in his anarchist writings. But first, we need to look more closely at the relationship between colonialism and nationalism.

## Colonialism and Nationalism

The proliferation of discourses on Korean identity, which emanated from both the Korean nationalist movement and the Japanese colonial state, stemmed from the *necessity* to "nationalize." For both Koreans and Japanese, the necessity of producing Korean subjects was prompted by the development of the global nation-state system.[67] In the process of trying to compete, or simply survive, in the nation-state system, *both* the colonial state and the Korean nationalist movements and organizations had to study, standardize, and thus re-invent (or just invent) everything we now associate with the Korean nation, including such "essential" elements as the Korean language and Korean ethnicity.[68]

In terms of language, it was only in 1894 that the syllabary created by King Sejong in 1446 acquired the status of "national script" (*kungmun*). Had it not been for the Tonghak uprising in the countryside and the "reform" cabinet installed by the Japanese military (1894–96), it would have taken much longer for the Korean syllabary to overturn the privileged status of literary Chinese. Until the very end of the nineteenth century, the *yangban* opposed the use of the syllabary (*hunmin chŏngŭm*: instructing the people on the correct sounds) on epistemological grounds—that is, they considered *hunmin chŏngŭm* (or *ŏnmun* as it was disparagingly called) a vulgar script, and they felt popular use of this syllabary would mean turning away from a whole universe of knowledge.

What is interesting, however, is that, when *ŏnmun* was raised to the status of the "national script" in 1894, and the spoken vernacular became the "national language" (*kugŏ*), the rationale given for dropping literary Chinese was that it was *Chinese*. After annexation in 1910, of course, the national script and the national language became *kokugo* and *kokubun* — Japanese. To avoid confusion, Korean nationalists later changed the appellation for the Korean vernacular writing system to *han'gŭl* to distinguish it from Japanese script (*kokubun*; *kungmun* in Korea).[69] The esteem suddenly accorded *ŏnmun* in the late nineteenth century gives evidence of a certain "racialization of knowledge" which followed the breakdown of the China-centered East Asian order.

As Yi Kimun notes, without a revolution it would have been impossible for *ŏnmun* (*han'gŭl*) to overturn the privileged status of literary Chinese. The revolution came in the form of a royal edict in 1894 which decreed that all laws and edicts be published in the national script (that is, in the *han'gŭl* syllabary), with Chinese appended for clarification. (The edict also allowed the "occasional" use of mixed script: *han'gŭl* along with Chinese ideographs.)[70] Outside the official realm, newspapers and books were being published in the vernacular. As Benedict Anderson argues, the use of the vernacular in writing (imparting dignity to spoken speech) and the emergence of print capitalism created the institutional base that made imagining the "nation" possible. The royal edict of 1894 and the proliferation and dissemination of vernacular newspapers like the *Tongnip sinmun* enabled the production of that "homogenous time" and "homogenous space" within which one could imagine the simultaneous existence of fellow Koreans inhabiting a shared geographic space bounded by distinct borders.[71]

The revolution that allowed *han'gŭl* to overturn the privileged status of literary Chinese drew its energy from the various centrifugal movements within Korea that were undermining the authority of the Yi dynasty.[72] This particular revolution also had foreign sponsorship. The edict was announced as part of a larger "reform" effort under the auspices of the Japanese forces in Korea.[73] Imperialist rivalry over Korea and eventual colonization by Japan intervened in the nation-building process, and the process of nationalizing Koreans was assumed by the Japanese colonial state.

It was the Japanese colonial state that went on to establish controls over print capitalism as well as national systems of schooling, transportation, and communication.[74] Compelled to deny any "constructive" role to Japanese colonialism, contemporary Korean nationalist accounts draw attention to the last decade of the colonial period when the colonial authorities, under the banner of *naisen ittai* (Japan and Korea as a single body), pursued a policy of forced assimilation: eliminating the use of Korean in school instruction (1934), requiring attendance at

Shinto ceremonies (1935), and mandating the adoption of Japanese surnames (1939). The slogan of *naisen ittai*, however, reveals the ambivalence of Japan's racist policy throughout the colonial period, the ambivalence marked by the combination of exteriorization and internal exclusion. Japan, as the interior (*nai*), excludes Korea (*sen*) as the "outside"; at the same time, this outside (Korea) must become one with the interior, which is always already there.[75] It was in this sense that Japanese colonialism was "constructive" for both the colonizer and colonized: the construction of Japanese superiority as demonstrated by the inferiority of Koreans, and the superiority claimed by the colonizer generating a self-image of inferiority among Koreans.

Coercion, prohibition, and censorship, then, were not the only (or even primary) forms through which colonial power was exercised. The Japanese colonial state did establish new rules and controls over the enunciation of Korean national identity. Areas, if not of utter silence, at least of tact and discretion, were established—for example, in newspaper editorials and the school curriculum. At the same time, there was a steady proliferation of discourses concerning Korean identity emanating from the Japanese colonial state itself—including studies of Korean history, geography, language, customs, religion, music, art—in almost immeasurable accumulated detail. What are we to make of this?

For the Japanese colonial state, the goal of exploiting Korea and using it for its strategic ends went hand in hand with the work of transforming peasants into Koreans, or "Chōsenjin." In other words, the logic of its racist colonial policy compelled the Japanese colonial state to reconstitute (disparate) Korean identities into a homogenous "Chōsenjin." Thereafter, "Chōsenjin" became both a bureaucratic and derogatory classification that applied to all Koreans regardless of gender, regional origin, or class background.

Thus, contrary to conventional nationalist accounts that argue that Japanese colonial authorities pursued a consistent and systematic policy of eradicating Korean identity, we should see that the Japanese colonial state actually endeavored to produce Koreans as subjects—subjects in the sense of being under the authority of the Japanese emperor, and in the sense of having a separate (and inferior) subjectivity. This, in turn, led to a bifurcated national (and racial) discourse, because Korean nationalist historians, in competition with the Japanese colonial state, were engaged in the project of recovering/producing an autonomous Korean subjectivity. Nationalist historians would find evidence of this subjectivity in history, but in necessarily incomplete or disfigured form:

only political independence could render possible the full realization of true Korean subjectivity.

Thus we have both the Japanese colonial state and revolutionary Korean nationalists researching and writing Korean history, preserving and interpreting Korean customs and religious practices, and laboring to create a standard Korean language. Although the power of the repressive and ideological apparatuses of the Japanese colonial state far surpassed that of the Korean nationalist movement, the contradictions inherent in Japan's racist colonial policy, along with the capacity of the Korean nationalist movement to (re)generate discourses of identity and liberation, ensured that the discourse on nation remained a contested field throughout the colonial period.[76] Thus, *any* "Korean" subjectivity created under such conditions—whether loyal to the Japanese empire or defiant of it—had to be profoundly unstable and constantly threatened by the contradictions of colonial experience.[77]

## The Nation-State System

In analyzing discourses that are hegemonic on a global scale, such as the nation form, we must consider non-discursive macro-processes, processes that have to do with the capitalist world-economy, or what Wallerstein has called the "World System." According to Wallerstein, hegemony in the World System has to do with "productive, commercial and financial preeminence of one core power over other core powers," a pre-eminence that is not enduring because there is both upward and downward mobility in core-periphery relations.[78] The nation-state system emerged as the political superstructure of this World System. The interstate system is competitive because nation-states in the periphery may succeed in attaining core status, and core nations can slip to semi-periphery status.[79]

Bruce Cumings makes use of World Systems theory to argue that for most of the twentieth century (with the exception of the seven months from Pearl Harbor to the battle of Midway), Japan has been a subordinate part of either a trilateral American-British hegemony or a bilateral American hegemony.[80] In other words, even as it ruled Korea, Japan was a sub-imperial power—that is, a "core" power vis-à-vis Korea and China but a dependency of Britain and the United States in both the regime of technology and in world politics. Cumings illustrates this by citing the example of Japanese textile firms, the leading sector in Japan's first phase of industrialization, which bought their machines from

England until about 1930. In the 1930s Japan began producing better machines and quickly became the most efficient textile producer in the world. In the mining industry, however, Japan was still dependent on American technology throughout the 1930s, allowing American gold-mining companies to profit from Korean gold mines. In sum, according to Cumings, Japan's position in the world-system changed according to the following timeline:

1900–22: Japan in British-American hegemony
1922–41: Japan in American-British hegemony
1941–45: Japan as regional hegemon in East Asia
1945–70: Japan in American hegemony[81]

Cumings is not proposing a reduction of national narratives to some abstract capitalist relations of production. Rather, along lines suggested by Etienne Balibar, Cumings's approach to understanding national narratives might be described as "bound up not with the abstraction of the capitalist market, but its concrete historical form: that of a 'world-economy' which is always already hierarchically organized into a 'core' and a 'periphery,' each of which have different methods of accumulation and exploitation of labor power, and between which relations of unequal exchange and domination are established."[82] In other words, as Etienne Balibar explains, it is "the concrete configurations of the class struggle and not 'pure' economic logic which explain the constitution of nation states."[83]

On the relationship between discourses on ethnic identity and the logic of the World System, Wallerstein notes that the capitalist system is based not merely on the capital-labor antinomy but on a complex hierarchy within the labor segment. This hierarchy within labor generates the "ethnicization" of the workforce within a given state's boundaries. There are certain advantages to the ethnicization of occupational categories—because different kinds of relations of production require different kinds of "normal" behavior. The advantages have to do with the fact that the state need not do all the work—the oppressed group will *voluntarily* defend its ethnic identity and socialize its membership. This resolves "one of the basic contradictions of historical capitalism—its simultaneous thrust for theoretical equality, and practical inequality."[84]

The concrete, historical form of this World System—which is always hierarchically organized into a core and periphery—provided the framework for the hegemony of the nation-state system. The ability of historians such as Shiratori to define, limit, and authorize a certain view of the rest of the Orient and then impose it was made possible by an emerging industrial mode of production in Japan whose success was verified in Japan's victories over China (1895) and Russia (1905). And yet, Japan's version of Orientalism could not achieve full hegemonic status in the sense that even as Japan colonized Korea, established a puppet state in Manchuria, and controlled parts of North China, Japan remained a dependency of Britain and the United States. Thus, we might say that there were overlapping and competing "hegemonies" operating in Korea, producing competing discourses on race, nation, gender, modernity, and culture. Moreover, these hegemonies dissipated as one moved from the core (London, Washington, Tokyo) to the major intellectual centers in the periphery (Beijing, Shanghai). From the periphery, intellectuals like Sin Ch'aeho succeeded in subverting and/or displacing the dominant framework in important ways.[85]

## Minjok and Minjung

In Sin Ch'aeho's anarchist writings (1925 on), the all-embracing identity of *minjok* is replaced by the more partisan category of *minjung*. In historical studies written in the 1910s and early 1920s, Sin had begun to present a less essentialist way of conceptualizing the nation. Perhaps as a self-critique of his earlier position in "Toksa sillon," Sin Ch'aeho's "Introduction" to the *Choson sanggosa* (hereafter *CS*) has moments of ambivalence in signifying the *minjok*, moments of slippage in the opposition of self/Other. But before we examine the text itself, it is relevant to note how and why *CS* came to be published in Korea in 1931, about a decade after it was written.

In 1931, the general crisis in the world economic system had pushed the Soviet Union toward a policy of "socialism in one country," the United States toward the New Deal, and Europe and Japan toward fascism (which presented itself as an alternative to the problems of a market economy). In 1931, the Sin'ganhoe voted to dissolve itself—acknowledging its failure to create an effective united front linking Korean Communists, nationalists, and anarchists within Korea. That same year Japanese forces invaded Manchuria, and Korea began to be transformed into an economic and military base for Japanese penetration of the Chinese mainland. On the intellectual scene, the Chōsenshi henshūkai (Society for the compilation of Korean history; hereafter SCKH), whose work was directed and funded by the office of the governor-general in Korea, was about to begin publication of its massive, detailed study of Korean history—the outcome of a project begun by Governor-General Saitō Makoto in 1922.[86]

It was at this historical juncture that Sin Ch'aeho's *CS* was serialized in Korea in the *Chosŏn ilbo*.[87] The day after publication of *CS* ended, the *Chosŏn ilbo* began running Sin's *Chosŏn sanggo munhwasa* (Cultural history of ancient Korea; hereafter *CSM*), in 40 installments. An Chaehong (1891–1965), a historian in his own right and the president of the *Chosŏn ilbo*, was instrumental in publishing Sin Ch'aeho's work inside Korea.[88] Because Sin Ch'aeho had not compromised with the Japanese—at the time Sin was incarcerated in a Japanese prison in Lüshun (Port Arthur)—and because the work itself had been written (geographically and intellectually) outside the perimeter of Japan's hegemony, Sin Ch'aeho's historiography was presented as a much needed corrective to colonialist historiography's distortions of Korea's ancient past.

But in "writing from the periphery," Sin Ch'aeho succeeded in subverting not only colonialist historiography but many of the assumptions associated with the nation form. Ironically, this counter-hegemonic move was made possible through Sin Ch'aeho's appropriation of Hegel's subject-object distinction. It is worth quoting at length from Sin's introduction to *CS*.

What is history? It is the record of the state of mental activity in human society wherein the struggle between the "I" (*a*) and the "non-I" (*pi-a*) develops through time and expands through space. World history, then, is a record of such a state for all of mankind, whereas Korean history is a record of such a state for the Korean people (*Chosŏn minjok*).

Who do we refer to as "I" and the "non-I"? Simply put, we call the person situated in the subjective position "I," and all others we call "non-I." For example, Koreans call Korea "I" and call England, America, France, Russia, and others the "non-I." But the people of England, America, France, Russia, and other countries call their countries "I" and call Korea a "non-I." The proletariat refers to itself as "I" and to landlords, capitalists, and others as the "non-I." But the landlords, capitalists, and others refer to their own group as "I" and to the proletariat as the "non-I." Not only this but in learning, in technology, in occupations, and in the intellectual world—and in every other area—if there is an I there will be a non-I as its opposite; and just as there is an I and the non-I within the I position, so there is an I and the non-I within the non-I position. Therefore, the more frequent the contact between I and the non-I, the more heated will be the struggle of the I against the non-I. And so there is no respite in the activity of human society, and there will never be a day when the forward advance of history will be completed. It is for this reason that history is the record of struggle between I and the non-I. . . .

[Para. 7] If the people of Myo, China, etc.—the non-I—constituting the other (*sangdaeja*) had not existed, it is unlikely that "I" would have existed. That is, naming the state as Chosŏn, building the three capitals, keeping the five armies, etc.—this manifestation of the "I" would not have occurred.[89]

Here, in reference to "China" (Shina in Japanese), we might detect the presence of Japanese Orientalism. But although Sin Ch'aeho may have used "China" rather than "Chungguk" to distance Korea from the barbarian/civilized, outer/inner implications of China as the Middle Kingdom, Sin Ch'aeho's use of China in *CS* did not (indeed could not) invoke the kind of Orientalist assumptions present in Shiratori's historiography. The national subject (Korean, English, or French) is historically constructed,[90] and it lacks essential unity: national identity may have been constructed in opposition to a foreign other, but it is also (necessarily) fragmented from within. Thus, we find the subject-object distinction made by Hegel, but it is clear that the philosophical structure "which uncannily simulates the project of nineteenth-century imperialism," as Robert Young puts it, has been taken over, made "universal" from the point of view of the colonized.[91]

Immersed in the intellectual ferment of Shanghai and Beijing (especially in the wake of the May Fourth movement), Sin was able to appropriate Hegel's dialectic in a way that produced not a chauvinist historiography (based on the triumphant, rational subject), but a contingent and open-ended one. Even if we did not know that Sin Ch'aeho became an anarchist after writing these histories, the texts themselves suggest moments of ambivalence in signifying the *minjok*: that is, moments of slippage in the opposition of self/Other.[92] "If there is an I there will be a non-I as its opposite; and just as there is an I and the non-I within the I position, so there is an I and the non-I within the non-I position."[93]

In his later anarchist writings, Sin tried to construct a new collective subjectivity capable of subverting the modernist program, which he saw as oppressive, exploitative, and brutal. The nation form as imagined by the West was hegemonic—hegemonic in the sense that the global nation-state system set the boundaries of political discourse, defining the nation-state as the "normal" or "natural" form of political community. And yet, no construct can be completely or permanently hegemonic, and hegemony dissipated as one moved from the core to the periphery. From the periphery, then, intellectuals like Sin Ch'aeho succeeded in subverting and/or displacing the dominant framework in important ways.

Nationalist readings of Sin Ch'aeho focus on the anti-Japanese aspects of his writings. In the "Chosŏn hyŏngmyŏng sŏnŏn" (1923), Sin Ch'aeho did list "bandit Japan" (*kangdo Ilbon*) as the primary target of the revolution, understood as the Japanese emperor, the governor-general of Korea and other high officials, "traitorous politicians," and any and all facilities belonging to the enemy. By smashing Japan, Koreans could recover an "indigenous Korea" (*koyu ŭi Chosŏn*), which lay beneath Japan's despotism. (Korea and Japan are in brackets in the original). But the recovery of an indigenous Korea did not mean the restoration of old social forms. Along with foreign rule, "slavish culture and servile mentality" were to be destroyed. All religious beliefs, ethics, culture, art, customs, and habits of traditional culture produced by the strong for their enjoyment had to be dismantled so that the people (*minjung*) could break out of their abject fate and construct a people's culture (*minjungjŏk munhwa*).

Sin Ch'aeho excoriated those Koreans who were lobbying for an "independent domestic administration" (*naejŏng tongnip*), "participatory government" (*ch'am chŏnggwŏn*), or "self-rule" (*chach'i*). They were forgetting how Japan had devoured Korea "even as the ink was drying on [Japanese] slogans that had guaranteed 'Peace in Asia,' and the 'Protection of Korean Independence.'" Sin also ridiculed those nationalists who advocated a "cultural movement" (*munhwa undong*). Writing editorials that would not offend the colonial authorities was all the cultural movement amounted to. For Sin, one hundred million pages of newspapers and magazines could not equal the power of one uprising in awakening the *minjung*.

Sin also denounced those nationalists who advocated "diplomacy" (*oegyoron*) or "preparation" (*chunbiron*). He did not name specific individuals, but it would have been clear to his readers that the targets of Sin's polemics were Syngman Rhee and An Ch'angho. Syngman Rhee was "stupid" (*ŏlisŏkgo yongryŏl hada*) for banking on foreign intervention to solve the problem of national survival. As for An Ch'angho and others who argued for "preparation," Sin Ch'aeho reminded them that they should be preparing for a war of independence. Arguing that Koreans must ready themselves for independence, the advocates of *chunbiron* actually advocated political quietism, turning their energies to education, industry, and a whole list of things that had to be "prepared." These activists made the rounds in Beijing, Siberia, Hawaii, and the United States to collect money for their programs, but all they could show for their efforts were a few precarious schools and inept organizations.[94]

What did Sin Ch'aeho advocate in the 1920s? As Sin Yongha argues, Sin's disgust with nationalists in the Korean Provisional Government, plus his reading of Pyotr Kropotkin, turned Sin from nationalism to anarchism.[95] Today, most conservative intellectuals in South Korea gloss over the fact that rather than the nation (*minjok*), the historical subject in Sin Ch'aeho's revolution was the people (*minjung*), a broad political grouping of the oppressed and exploited "propertyless masses" (*musan taejung*).[96] The *minjung*, as Sin Ch'aeho used the term, was a more amorphous category than Marx's proletariat, but it was not synonymous with the Korean people as a whole, that is, *minjok*. As Marx did for the proletariat, Sin Ch'aeho granted ontological privilege to the *minjung*.

Throughout Korean history, argued Sin, the *minjung* had formed the wretched majority — exploited, beaten, starved, lulled into subservience and obedience. For that very reason, the *minjung* was uniquely capable of sweeping away all oppressive and exploitative institutions and practices, and in that sense the *minjung* was a universal subject. But unlike the Marxist-Leninists, Sin Ch'aeho refused to distinguish between the vanguard and the masses, or between leaders and the led, and the revolution was therefore a "*minjung* revolution" or a "direct revolution." The *minjung* formed the "the grand headquarters" of the revolution (*Minjung ŭn uri hyŏngmyŏng ŭi taebonyŏng ida*). Through a program of assassinations, bombings, and uprisings, Sin Ch'aeho believed, the "conscientized" segment of the *minjung* could succeed in imparting "resolve" (*kago*) to the *minjung*. When the *minjung* as a whole resolved to take the path of revolution, all the cunning and savagery of the colonial state would not be able to stop the revolution.

Thus, Sin Ch'aeho differentiated between the "awakened" *minjung* and the "not awakened" *minjung*, but this distinction was not at all similar to the kind of external and manipulative relationship that characterized the Leninist conception of relations between the "vanguard" and the "masses." Sin Ch'aeho resisted the Leninist idea that the "for itself" of the revolutionary subject was accessible only to the enlightened vanguard. And indeed, even as he called for a revolution, Sin Ch'aeho's language echoed the moralistic tone of Kropotkin. The exploitative economic system swallows up the people (*minjung*) in order to fatten thieves, but this system of plunder must be destroyed in order to improve the lives of the people. In all societies with inequalities, the strong oppress the weak, the high-born stand above the humble, and the people have to plunder, excoriate, and envy one another. At first the majority of the people are harmed for the happiness of a few. But later, the privileged few struggle among themselves so that the people are harmed even more. Thus, the happiness of *all* the people can be attained only with the eradication of social inequalities.[97]

In spite of this seemingly immutable commitment to an egalitarian ideal, many conservative intellectuals assume that had Sin Ch'aeho lived to see Korea liberated, he would have abandoned anarchism.[98] But it was Sin Ch'aeho's assertion that an unfettered people would construct communities based on equality, cooperation, and reason. Although Korea's liberation from colonial rule was a fundamental goal of the revolution, "privileged classes" (*t'ŭkkwŏn kyegŭp*), which oppress the "Korean people" (*chayujŏk Chosŏn minjung*—with *Chosŏn minjung* in brackets in the original text), including the colonial administration, were to be overthrown so as to recover an "unfettered people" (*chayujŏk Chosŏn minjung*). The emergence of an unfettered people, and the communities they would create based on equality, cooperation, and reason, could not be brought about through the power of any nation-state.

Here, then, was a political program that went beyond nationalism, and a historical view that undermined the continuous, unified narrative of the nation. To those who fear the unraveling of this narrative, Sin Ch'aeho might say: "Those who do not know how to build do not know how to destroy, and those who do not know how to destroy do not know how to build. Construction and destruction are different only in appearance. In the mind, destruction is immediately construction."[99] After the Korean War, state-nationalism as it emerged in both North and South Korea all but overwhelmed and swamped such autonomous forms of imagination. Sin Ch'aeho's turn to anarchism (where the all-embracing identity of *minjok* is replaced by the more partisan category of *minjung*) suggests that *minjok*, by itself, can no longer serve as a democratic imaginary.

# Exorcising Hegel's Ghosts: Toward a Postnationalist Historiography of Korea

## Carter J. Eckert

*Shadow and Substance*, a short story by South Korean writer Hyon Kilon (Hyŏn Kirŏn) first published in 1986,[1] is eloquent testimony to the timeliness and importance of the essays collected in this book by Gi-Wook Shin and Michael Robinson. In Hyon's story, set in the present, a scholar has just published a historical study of the diving women of Cheju Island that recounts an uprising against the official colonial divers' union in 1937. The book becomes a national sensation, fueled by the media, and there are even plans under way by the regional government to honor the women as "ideal traditional females"[2] and to memorialize their patriotic act with the erection of a group statue. Complications develop, however, when the reputed former leader of the uprising, an old woman now living in Pusan, sends letters to the scholar and the island's local newspaper describing the incident in detail and protesting that she was in fact not the leader, that the revolt was completely spontaneous, and that it was motivated not by nationalism but by simple anger at repeated poaching in the divers' territory by pirate Japanese fishing vessels. She wants nothing to do with the congratulatory projects being planned and asks the newspaper to print her letter to set the record straight. The newspaper ignores her request and the construction of the statue continues.

In the meantime, Hyon's chief protagonist, a reporter named Song, has done some checking and discovered that the scholar's depiction of the affair is seriously flawed, based on an ideologically motivated article written ten years after the fact in a recently partitioned and politically polarized Korea. A subsequent interview with the old woman and her daughter convinces him beyond doubt of the veracity of her account, and he feels compelled to air what he knows. Since his newspaper refuses to print the old woman's letter, he prepares a paper for a public symposium being held as part of the ongoing commemoration of the incident. When he delivers the paper, however, he is greeted with open hostility, and he eventually walks out of the meeting in disgust. The story ends eight months later with the unveiling of a monumental sculpture of the heroic women divers by one of the country's leading artists and an abortive special award ceremony for the old woman, who refuses the honor and declines to appear.

Hyon's story is a telling exposé of the power and pervasiveness of what might be called a nationalist intellectual discourse in Korea. Several points are worth noting. First, it is clear that the nationalist paradigm is so deeply rooted in the mental life of the community that it has become in effect an *a priori* discursive framework for interpreting historical events that brooks no opposition. To think differently is to challenge, in Gramscian terms, the "common sense" of the community, in effect to speak nonsense, to be considered recalcitrant toward reason itself. Thus the scholar and the local Cheju newspaper are baffled by the old woman's insistence on her story, and in the end they simply dismiss her as stubborn and troublesome.

Second, the nationalist historical discourse is buttressed by strong vested interests throughout the community. The region basks in its new glory as a national historical site, an elevation in status that also holds potential economic benefits through increased tourism and related commercial development. The local and national media also profit from a popular story. And virtually everyone appreciates the nationalistic version of the women divers' story. Among other things, it is an unequivocal celebration of Korea and Korean identity — precisely the kind of narrative of the colonial past, perhaps the only kind, that nearly everyone can and does enjoy hearing about. As one of the local Cheju newspapermen says about the old woman's attitude: "Isn't it odd . . . that she's acting this way, when everybody's feeling so good about what she and her colleagues have supposedly done . . . and even when people are thinking of erecting a monument in their honor?"[3]

A third aspect of the nationalist discourse that stands out in Hyon's story is its imperviousness to contrary empirical evidence. When Song presents his paper at the symposium, he is harangued by a young man who says, "We're concerned not so much with what is *truthful* as with what is *meaningful* about a particular action or event or person in the progress of history" (italics added).[4] The implication here is clear: what matters is correct ideology, not facts. Facts are malleable or even irrelevant. Indeed, the facts have to be countered or suppressed if they conflict with the ideology. They are a tempting but insidious snare that can subvert meaning and weaken political resolve and action. As the young man puts it, "What we have heard today from Mr. Song is only the inevitable conclusion of a sentimentalist or a defeatist who has no faith in the people as the subject of history. His approach to the divers represents the kind of intellectual trap we too can fall into if we don't stand firm."[5]

Finally, and perhaps most important, Hyon's story also considers the price that must be paid for such avoidance or distortion of the truth. Accurate history is not the only casualty. Assigning meaning and value to the old woman's story only insofar as it affirms a readymade ideological stereotype denies the old woman her humanity by reducing her to a caricature. Hence Song's retort to the young man who berates him: "If you were she [the old woman], wouldn't your individual life be more precious to you than history? We become blind to the truth of individual life as soon as we start theorizing about history, with abstract concepts replacing concrete reality. Then we let ourselves be part of a scheme for the destruction of individual lives."[6]

Song's statement, as Hyon's readers know, is not empty rhetoric. In investigating the old woman's story, he has discovered from her daughter that the original account of the incident, written for a radical leftist magazine shortly after Korea's liberation from colonial rule and depicting the women divers as imbued with a spirit of revolutionary communism, has indeed ruined the old woman's life. The magazine article in fact led directly to her arrest and imprisonment as a communist by a local right-wing terrorist regime, from which she was released only by giving in to the sexual demands of one of her captors. News of her acquiescence led in turn to rejection by her family and eventually the loss of her husband. Song learns, moreover, that the old woman's daughter is actually the child not of her husband but of her rightist tormentor, and that the daughter, too, has therefore been a victim of ideological zeal and falsified history. In speaking to Song, the daughter vents her anger and bitterness: "How could people make up stories that hurt other people? All they think about is what they want to say themselves. . . . These men, obsessed with their ideology . . . they'd give any interpretation to what others do as long as it suits them."[7]

Although Hyon's story is fictional, it captures an undeniable part of the reality of Korean historical understanding and writing in the twentieth century. As the chapters in this book repeatedly and effectively argue, nationalist paradigms have so dominated intellectual life in Korea that they have obfuscated, subsumed, or obliterated virtually all other possible modes of historical interpretation. Whatever the topic—social groups and classes, political or cultural movements, governments or other institutions, individual figures, novels, poems, films, scholarship, even ideas themselves—all have been screened through a myopic nationalist lens that is as judgmental as it is pervasive. Thus have valorizations been bestowed, condemnations meted out, and heroes, traitors, victims, and perpetrators designated. It is a narrow and unforgiving gate through which the facts of history, as well as the historian must pass. Any interpretation that lies outside the nationalist framework, let alone one that dares to challenge the relevance or validity of the framework itself, is often ignored as unimportant or castigated as morally deficient, regardless of the evidence. Nowhere is this pattern more prevalent than in studies of the Japanese occupation of Korea from 1905 to 1910, the focus of this book. How did we reach this point? Where do we go from here? How can we escape from this intellectual panopticon and begin to fashion a more liberal, postnationalist historiography of Korea?

The answer to the first of these questions lies in history itself. Nation-states and nationalism, of course, developed first in Europe, and nationalist history was their handmaiden, especially in the nineteenth-century heyday of nation-building and imperialism. Hegel, whose intellectual influence proved in time to be as profound in East Asia as in Europe, regarded nation-states as the vehicles of reason and freedom in the universal progress of world history. The Hegelian view was in fact quite unequivocal on this point: no nation-state meant no freedom and no history.[8] From the beginning, therefore, nationalist historical thinking was part and parcel of a modern consciousness that would spread from Europe throughout the world.

In Korea nationalist discourse was spawned in the late nineteenth century as the Chosŏn dynasty was beset by internal dissensions and imperialist encroachments from foreign countries, many of which, including Japan, had organized themselves into powerful nation-states that could effectively mobilize material, social, and cultural resources to defend and advance its own interests. Late Chosŏn reformists, who were the first to articulate a nationalist discourse, saw themselves living in a savage new world of Social Darwinian conflict where Korea's only hope for survival lay in emulating its imperialist aggressors. Their goal was to transform the dynasty into a strong nation-state along Western or Meiji Japanese lines and to encourage nationalism as a primary value that would transcend debilitating traditional status, factional, and regional divisions and thereby unify the populace against outside threats.

This nascent nation-building effort was still a radical enterprise in the late nineteenth century, and its novelty is reflected in the work of Yu Kilchun (1856–1914), the most prolific of the early reformists, especially in his famous 1895 work *Sŏyu kyŏnmun* (Things seen and heard in travels to the West). There in a separate chapter Yu painstakingly laid out the definition of "nation" (*kungmin*) and explained the modern meaning of "patriotism" (*aeguk*) for a public to whom these were still alien ideas. Even more to the point is the fact that even in this very early introduction and advocacy of nationalist thought, written more than a decade and a half before the Japanese seizure of the peninsula, one can already find nationalism being held up as an *ultimate* identity and loyalty for Koreans. In a sense one can say that nationalism both incorporated and superseded Neo-Confucianism as a discursive moral framework, and for Koreans steeped in moralistic Confucian histories, it was but a small step from there to the idea that the proper task of the modern historian was the writing of nationalist history, where the morality of Confucianism was mixed with and submerged by the morality of nationalism. Hegel's insistence on the moral *telos* of the nation-state blended perfectly with this early post-Confucian sensibility, and in 1908, one of Korea's first great nationalist historians, Sin Ch'aeho (1880–1936), echoing the master of Jena, wrote that "without the nation there is no history" and argued for a new kind of historical writing, one that would celebrate the nation-state and instill nationalism to allow Korea to compete on an equal basis with other countries in the world for its share of reason and freedom. It is a view that would reverberate in manifold ways throughout the course of the new century.[9]

Korea's subsequent occupation by Japan intensified this burgeoning nationalist sentiment to an unprecedented degree. To appreciate the depths of the feelings involved, one must remember that for well over a millennium, civilization in Northeast Asia had flowed largely from China through Korea to Japan. Indeed, from the seventeenth century, when China was invaded by the Manchus who would establish the Qing dynasty, many in the Korean elite had come to see their country as "the last bastion of civilization on earth."[10] Japan, on the other hand, had always been regarded as an inferior country in the sinocentric cosmos. For that reason alone, its occupation and colonization of the peninsula were psychological shocks for many Koreans, provoking mixed feelings of shame and wrath. Yu Kilchun had warned that insufficient nationalism would lead to Korea's becoming a "slave" among nations,[11] and for many leading intellectuals of the next generation, who came of age under Japanese rule, it became an article of faith that nationalism was the value above all others that needed to be promoted to regain political independence. Unfortunately and ironically, the ubiquitous "ultra-nationalism" of prewar Japan was also transmitted directly to Koreans through the colonial education system and helped make Korean nationalism all the more militant and xenophobic.[12]

Inequities and brutalities during the forty-year occupation also further inflamed Korean nationalism. Already by 1919 it was clear from the March First movement that nationalism was spreading throughout the populace. Although somewhat less repressive colonial governments in the 1920s and early 1930s dampened the nationalist fire to some extent, the flames were reignited in the late 1930s. The last eight years of Japanese rule were in fact especially severe, characterized by a relentless mobilization of the Korean population for "total war" against China and the Allies and by a forced cultural assimilation policy, both of which led to numerous excesses and atrocities. By 1945, when the colony finally came to an end, nationalism, whether to the right or left of the political spectrum, had become a widely shared value, and a principle around which political and intellectual activities were increasingly being organized and legitimated.

After 1945 a number of factors commingled to produce a historiography of the Japanese occupation in which a nationalist discourse reigned supreme. First, historians in both halves of the peninsula, infused with the nationalist perspective of Sin and other intellectual predecessors, were understandably eager to expose and condemn the injustices of colonial rule and to erase the shame of colonization by celebrating the heroic resistance of Korean nationalists. The tendency of such writing was toward a diachronic depiction of good and evil, exploitation and resistance, Korean victims/heroes and Japanese villains. In this stark parquetry of blacks and whites, there was little room for a spectrum of shades and colors, for the differences, singularities, exceptions, contradictions, ambiguities, subtleties, and ironies of colonial life, most of which were relegated to the background or actively disremembered.

In both Koreas, moreover, nationalism was used to legitimate state power and functioned as a kind of state religion in the postcolonial nation-building process. The full panoply of resources of both states was mobilized in a deliberate promotion of nationalism in the educational system, as well as in intellectual and cultural circles, especially from the 1960s on, and the states themselves took an active role in the fostering of nationalist history through the publication of official Korean histories. Decades of extensive state-led reconstruction and economic development that eventually affected all segments of the population were launched, carried out, and justified under the rubric of nationalism. Over and over again the state authorities preached nationalism as an ultimate civic virtue for which no sacrifice was too much.

As Shin and Robinson note in the Introduction to this volume, the political partition of the country along ideological lines in 1945, cemented by a bitter and destructive civil war in 1950–53, further narrowed the range of permissible historical writing in both Koreas. It was not enough for historians simply to have a nationalist perspective; the nationalist perspective also had to be ideologically correct. In the North this eventually came to mean focusing almost exclusively on the Manchuria-based, anti-Japanese guerrilla activities of Kim Il Sung in the 1930s. Other nationalist efforts by Koreans during the colonial era, especially those in Korea itself, were dismissed in the North as futile or in some way tainted by accommodation to Japanese rule, and the founding political, economic, social, and intellectual elite of South Korea were branded as anti-nationalist collaborators, who had sold out the country first to the Japanese and later to the Americans. Even the nationalist efforts of the Communist party in Korea during the Japanese occupation were obscured by the North's fixation on Kim Il Sung. In the South, one found a mirror image of the North. There for years Kim Il Sung was incorrectly portrayed as a Soviet lackey named Kim Sŏngju who had appropriated the name of a famous anti-Japanese guerrilla fighter; the issue of elite collaboration during the colonial period was covered up and surrounded by taboos as a subject of discussion; and the Korean Provisional Government, founded in 1919, and the cultural nationalist activities associated with An Ch'angho, Kim Sŏngsu, and others were officially designated and promoted as the only legitimate political and intellectual lines of descent of the Korean nationalist movement.

Nationalism and Cold War ideologies have thus severely constrained intellectual life in both Koreas during the past half-century. And not only in Korea. Indeed, most scholars of Korea in the last fifty years, regardless of nationality, including this author, have been captive to these double sirens to a greater or lesser degree. During the past decade or so, however, generational change, the collapse of communism and the end of the Cold War, and the retreat of militarism and opening up of the political system to democratic influences in South Korea have all worked to open an aperture for the emergence of a more liberal historiography of the colonial period and for Korean studies scholarship in general. Not surprisingly, South Korean artists and scholars have courageously led the way, and Hyon's short story is in fact a reflection of this growing new sensibility. This book, together with the conference that preceded it, has brought together both younger and older scholars from a number of different countries, including the United States, South Korea, and Japan. All of us who have participated in the project have been invigorated not only by the new work being presented but also by the sense that our desire to break through the historiographical confines of the past is a common perspective that knows no national boundaries. We have every reason to expect that this broad cooperative international effort will continue, and it is exciting to anticipate the scholarly landscapes that still lie before us. In the writing of history, for example, we can envision a number of possibilities, some of which may have relevance for other disciplines as well.

We can imagine, first of all, a scholarship that is *pluralistic* in its focus and approach. To be sure, nationalism will forever remain a crucial aspect of colonial history, indeed, of the larger history of late Chosŏn and twentieth-century Korea, and we owe much to earlier historians, especially in Korea, for laying the groundwork here. It may also be noted that even in our post–Cold War world of increasing globalization, politics often continue to have a strong national character, even as we become ever more enmeshed in an international web of economics, technology, and information; it is therefore not at all unlikely that nationalism will extend its influence into the next century as well.

But we must distinguish here between nationalism or nation-building as a modern historical phenomenon worthy of study, and nationalist scholarship, which seeks to exalt the nation and subordinate all scholarly inquiry to that purpose. Postnationalist scholars may choose to study nationalism or not. They may argue that a particular person, group, institution, or event is best understood in the historical context of modern Korean nationalism, or they may not. They may contend, for example, that a feminist approach brings us closer to understanding the dynamics of a women's group, that a focus on material concerns is equally or more important than nationalism in explaining why workers and peasants rise up against colonial factory owners and landlords, and that colonial policies in Korea must be placed in the context of Japanese domestic politics and intellectual trends or more broadly conceived imperial goals. In any case, what is essential is that scholars feel empowered to range as freely and widely as they choose, wherever their individual interests or perhaps differing notions of what is historically significant may lead them.

Pluralism in the writing of history also implies a recognition of the multi-dimensional quality of human life and societies, including the existence of such diversity and contradiction even within a single life. Like the old diving woman in Hyon Kilon's story, we all perceive the complexity of our own persons only too clearly and chafe at having the meaning of our lives distorted and diminished by facile categorizations. Whatever the topic at hand, the postnationalist scholar should take this self-knowledge to heart and resist the temptation of trying to smooth out what Kant called the "crooked timber of humanity."[13] Rather, we should relish all the crooks and irregularities of our subject and strive to capture them as fully and accurately as possible for the historical record.

A pluralistic scholarship also assumes that conclusions about the historical meaning and legacy of the Japanese occupation will be various and different. The postnationalist, liberal historian will embrace all these differences with an open mind and welcome the debates they provoke as an integral part of a collective and public scholarly enterprise. A distinction should be made, however, between historical interpretation and mere personal opinion. There can be little constructive discussion on the basis of personal opinion. Historical interpretation, on the other hand, assumes an accompanying body of corroborative evidence, and both the evidence and any interpretations based on it can and should be subject to vigorous public debate. It is unlikely that all interpretations put forward will survive this kind of scrutiny and interrogation. With respect to some questions, moreover, it is possible that even with all the best available evidence spread out on the table, there will still not be enough to support one view decisively over another. On other questions, the complexity or ambiguity of the evidence, or differing intellectual perspectives on the part of historians, may lead to multiple or conflicting interpretations. So be it. Such is the nature and limitation of scholarly inquiry.

But evidence does matter. Postnationalist historiography on the colonial period will ideally be not only pluralistic but also *inductive*. Writing inductively implies accepting the reality of history, that something actually happened, being passionately curious about it, and aspiring, like Ranke, to pierce through the barrier of time and get as close as possible to it through research and empathy. This is not to voice a slavish paean to empiricism. While the idea is hardly new, postmodern historians are certainly right to call attention to the inherent limits and biases of historical source material, and even of human knowledge itself. Historical understanding can never equal the certainty of a demonstrable scientific theorem. But to say that any given historical phenomenon cannot be known fully or absolutely is not to say that it cannot be known at all. All knowledge, even scientific, is partial. But unless one wants to assert that history has no objective reality at all and that therefore all interpretations are equally valid (which would include, for example, in an absurd extension of this logic, the view that Japan never colonized Korea), then one must conclude that some interpretations are better than others, even if the knowledge they impart is ultimately only partial and subject to further scholarly discussion and debate. In that sense the study of history cannot be directly equated with the study of literature. Although literature can often reflect and illuminate the past, the past itself is not fantasy or fiction. It is not an unbounded "text" subject to unrestrained semiotic speculation and play. The best historians always write creatively, but they do so within the compass of the totality of the evidence available to them. Such, indeed, is the thrill of the profession: knowing that something happened and trying to capture it in all its complexity, not by imagining the facts, but by using the facts to discipline the imagination.

For that reason, it will behoove the inductive historian to begin research with a simple what-how-why question about a particular historical phenomenon rather than with a general theoretical framework or set of assumptions. It is, of course, easier to work deductively, starting with a premise and marshaling the facts to support it. The result may also be very impressive in terms of the sheer quantity of material one can bring to bear on the argument. But the problem with this approach is that the research itself is then driven by the premise and not by the unfettered curiosity of the historian about the historical phenomenon itself. The consequence here all too often is that the premise, or some modification of it, simply gets "proved" or "disproved," while the lush reality of the phenomenon is lost. One is reminded here of Isaac Newton's modest description of himself as a boy at the seashore looking at pebbles and shells "whilst the great ocean of truth lay all undiscovered before me."[14]

Although the question that informs the research must be genuine, something to which the historian does not have a ready-made or predisposed answer, there is of course nothing wrong with pursuing tentative hypotheses that emerge naturally in the course of the research. The historian must be prepared to abandon them in an instant, however, if they prove subsequently untenable. The guiding principle here should be one of fierce loyalty to the discipline of history, not to any particular viewpoint, however emotionally satisfying or popular. The incomparable richness of Korean history itself is sufficient justification for its study, and a presentation of that history in all its unruly fullness is ultimately what will fascinate readers and provoke further interest about Korea. And to capture this history, the scholar must be governed by an intrepid dedication to the truth, a willingness to follow the questions and facts down whatever roads they may lead, however dark or strange.

Such dedication obviously requires a certain level of scholarly impartiality. And despite the fact that some postmodernist scholars have turned it into virtually a dirty word, the postnationalist, liberal scholar also must strive to be as *objective* as possible. Again, it is a question of degree. No historian of merit would ever claim unqualified objectivity on any subject. We all bring to our work a bundle of attitudes and assumptions that reflect our personalities and personal histories, our political predilections, and the times in which we live. But just as an assertion of complete objectivity seems both extreme and contrary to an honest appraisal of our own mental processes, so, too, does a rejection of the possibility of any degree of objectivity seem excessive and alien to our sense of ourselves as creatures of choice and will. Although the effort is sometimes a bit like Sisyphus pushing his rock up the hill only to see it roll down again and again, the liberal historian must at least struggle and aim for objectivity. Even if the scholarly result is imperfect, which, of course, it will always be, it is still likely to be relatively more objective than a work whose author has consciously or unconsciously made no attempt to discipline his or her prejudices.

But how should such a struggle be waged? One might begin by carefully choosing a subject of study. Ideally the historian is well advised to avoid topics where there is significant emotional investment, palpable or potential, like the biography of a family member or a close friend, or the study of a political, social, or cultural movement to which one feels personally committed or opposed. Premodern Chinese and Korean historians, for example, were well aware of the dangers such attachments posed and sought to guard against them by various conventions, including the practice of composing a dynastic history only after that dynasty had come to an end.[15] To be sure, such scrupulousness is not always possible. Indeed, one often feels impelled to study a particular subject or period precisely because it touches one so deeply. But even as the filial son or daughter who is motivated to go into medicine to uncover the etiology and cure for a disease that has killed a beloved parent must adhere to clinical procedures to be successful, so must the historian who defies prudence and decides to work on a subject close to the heart try to develop a certain professional detachment if the history that is produced is to have any credibility.

Whatever the focus of inquiry, however, the historian must engage in an uncompromisingly frank process of self-examination and criticism. This involves, first of all, ferreting out and acknowledging the influences, assumptions, and biases that perhaps have shaped one's own thinking and attitude toward the subject of study. Although total self-knowledge is again impossible, and readers will undoubtedly still detect unconscious biases in the work, such self-reflection is crucial to the goal of nurturing historical objectivity. The process of reflection must also be continuous. Throughout the entire course of research and writing, the historian must consciously stand vigilant against personal biases in the sifting and selection of evidence, the structuring of arguments, and the overall tone of the work.

The objective historian would also do well to cultivate a genuine respect for what Simon Schama has called the "the obstinate otherness of the past."[16] In projecting our own *mentalité* and preoccupations backward in time, we assume a familiarity with the past that is more often than not false and misleading. To be sure, respecting the essential strangeness of the past in this way is easier, perhaps even goes without saying, if we are talking about distant periods and events whose impact on us today seems remote and inconsequential. But we need look no further than our own childhoods to realize how quickly and powerfully time and memory work to distance us from the reality we ourselves once experienced. For the historian aspiring to objectivity, there can be no past that is not remote, and the "integrity of its remoteness"[17] should not be violated. And the reward for such professional restraint is immense: an opportunity to challenge our minds and expand our consciousness by escaping from the intellectual and emotional strictures of our own time and exploring a world that is surprisingly and sometimes fundamentally different from our own, or from what we had imagined the past to be. One of the great intellectual pleasures in reading the chapters in this book is that they reveal a history that is not only more complicated than we had been led to believe but also filled with unfamiliar and sometimes quite unexpected new people, groups, events, and ideas.

Pluralistic, inductive, objective, the new postnationalist historiography gives hope at last of exorcising the stubborn ghosts of Hegel, whether of the idealistic or materialistic variety, that have haunted scholarship on Korea for so long. But there are some who may object that the new scholarship, for all its virtues, will in the end be sterile, devoid of the things that most give life and value to any historical writing: viewpoint, passion, and moral vision. I would beg to differ. Thinking pluralistically, inductively, and objectively does not mean eschewing a point of view. Indeed, the presentation of a reasoned interpretation or narrative lies at the core of all good historical writing. It is the structure in which all the information gathered finds its home and the mortar that ultimately holds the edifice together. But interpretation or narrative must be constructed on the basis of a fair assessment of all the available evidence, including (especially) evidence that may be subversive of the thesis or that suggests the possibility of other interpretations. Instead of being built from elaborate blueprints, the main argument and its corollaries should take form gradually and naturally in the course of the research and writing and be carefully checked at every step along the way for any trace of bias. One might say that the aim of the liberal historian in the postnationalist era is to *discover* a persuasive interpretation in the mass of evidence rather than to impose one from the outside.

There is also no reason why the new historiography should lack passion. The question, however, is where that passion should be directed. The historian who indulges in a passionate hatred or affection for some figure, movement, government, or country is likely to compromise the scholarly enterprise, however inadvertently, and wind up producing a one-dimensional history that only the likeminded will want to read. At worst, such passion, especially if it is in the service of an idea or movement that society deems morally admirable and therefore applauds, can tempt one to rationalize an act of deliberate distortion so long as it promotes the sanctioned moral principle or goal. Here the case of Rigoberta Menchú is a cautionary tale. Menchú, a Quiché Indian from Guatemela, won the Nobel Peace Prize in 1992 for an autobiography that focused on her personal survival and triumph over racist oppression. But a meticulous decade-long investigation by an American anthropologist working in Guatemala revealed that much of Menchú's story was simply untrue, based on "experiences she never had herself." The fact that Menchú's work brought international attention to the miserable plight of Guatemala's indigenous Indian population did not justify her breach of professional ethics as an author. She would have been better advised to confine her passion to a political movement dedicated to the good cause she sought to advance or to present her work more honestly as a fictional representation of Mayan experience.[18]

The passion of the historian, I would suggest, is twofold. The first, and perhaps fundamental passion, is one of curiosity about history itself. It is an intellectual passion for the truth, a zeal for finding out what happened, how, and why. Anyone who lacks this primal passion should not become a historian. The second passion is for the historical interpretation being put forward. Again, this is an intellectual passion, and it is also directly related to the search for truth. It is satisfied only when the historian feels he or she has developed a clear and elegant argument that is both sustainable on the basis of the sum total of evidence and also so deeply layered as to make the history not only lucid but real and human. One is tempted here to draw a metaphor with a fine piece of music, a late Mozart piano concerto, perhaps, where the themes are always crystalline, yet so creatively played out in the course of the work as to display a full range of musical variation and human feeling. There is an important difference, however. The historian's creativity must always be tempered by the available evidence. The passion for graceful argument must never become a blind passion for a *particular* argument. The historian must always be open to public debate, to the possible validity of alternative interpretations based on new or better documentation. In that sense a work of history is never complete. It is at best only a glimpse at the truth, an enticing prologue to further study.

Finally, we come to the issue of morality. There is no doubt, in my mind at least, that the writing of history is a moral undertaking. But what does this mean? It does not mean, I would suggest, approaching history with an explicit intention to praise or blame, especially on the basis of a narrow, highly judgmental criterion of right and wrong that may reflect no more than the historian's personal religious or political convictions, or the various moral prejudices of the era in which he or she lives. Eulogies and polemics have their place in life, but they make for bad history. They diminish the historical reality and demean the historical profession.

The morality of the historian is ultimately humanistic. It might be described as a fearless commitment to knowledge of the human condition in all its complexity, a factual, honest, and richly detailed exploration of the things human beings have done, why and how they have done them, and their impact on human life. When the historian renders judgment, let those judgments be made not merely with the vision of hindsight, but also from a scholarly, empathic understanding of the full temporal and psychic context of the human lives and actions being studied. One could say that the historian should aim to be no less than a Shakespeare of facts, and the accolade bestowed on the Bard's work by Samuel Johnson in the eighteenth century might still serve today as an inspiration to us all: "These characters are so copiously diversified, and some of them so justly pursued, that his Works may be considered as a Map of Life, a faithful Miniature of human Transactions."[19]

There is no guarantee, of course, that greater knowledge of *la condition humaine* will always be personally liberating for historians and their readers or that it will lead to greater tolerance of human differences. But unless we wish to remain encased in modes of thinking and living that are all in some way less than fully human or even dehumanizing, what choice do we have but to know ourselves as deeply and fully as we possibly can? As Isaiah Berlin once wrote: "Yet what solutions have we found, with all our new technological and psychological knowledge and great new powers, save the ancient prescriptions advocated by the creators of humanism — Erasmus and Spinoza, Locke and Montesquieu, Lessing and Diderot — reason, education, self-knowledge, responsibility — above all, self-knowledge? What other hope is there for all men and women, or has there ever been?"[20] Indeed. It is in this hope that one finds the moral vision and promise of an emerging postnationalist historiography of Korea.

*Reference Matter*

# Notes

## Introduction: Gi-Wook Shin and Michael Robinson, "Rethinking Colonial Korea"

1. For a critique of nationalist narratives based on a linear, evolutionary history of the Enlightenment model in China and India, see Prasenjit Duara, *Rescuing History from the Nation* (Chicago: University of Chicago Press, 1995).

2. Michael Robinson, "Narrative Politics, Nationalism, and Korean History," *Papers of the British Association of Korean Studies* 6 (1996): 26–40.

3. See, e.g., Kim Chin'gyun and Chŏng Kŭnsik, eds., *Kŭndae chuch'e wa singminji kyuyul kwŏllyŏk* (Seoul: Munhak kwahaksa, 1997); and Andre Schmid, "Rediscovering Manchuria: Sin Ch'aeho and the Politics of Territorial History in Korea," *Journal of Asian Studies* 56 (1997): 26–46.

4. One might go further with this metaphor to consider the three paradigms as seas bounding the Korean peninsula.

5. See, e.g., the chapters in Ramon Myers and Mark Peattie, eds., *The Japanese Colonial Empire, 1895–1945* (Princeton: Princeton University Press, 1984).

6. Bruce Cumings, "The Legacy of Japanese Colonialism in Korea," in ibid., pp. 479–96.

7. For further discussion, see Michael Robinson, *Cultural Nationalism in Colonial Korea, 1920–1925* (Seattle: University of Washington Press, 1988); and Gi-Wook Shin, *Peasant Protest and Social Change in Colonial Korea* (Seattle: University of Washington Press, 1996).

8. Chungmoo Choi, "Discourse of Decolonization and Popular Memory: South Korea," *positions: east asia cultures critiques* 1 (1993): 77–102.

9. For recent debates in Korea, see the special issue "Han'guk kŭndaesa-hoe ŭi hyŏngsŏng kwa kŭndaesŏng munje," _Ch'angjak kwa pip'yŏng_ 21, no. 4 (1993): 1–91; and Hanguksa yŏn'guhoe, ed., _Kŭndae kungmin minjok munje_ (Seoul: Chisik sanŏpsa, 1995).

10. Tu Wei-ming, ed., _Confucian Traditions in East Asian Modernity_ (Cambridge, Mass.: Harvard University Press, 1996).

11. See the inaugural issue of _positions: east asia cultures critique_ (1993), which was devoted to the question of colonial modernity.

12. Anthony Giddens, _The Consequences of Modernity_ (Cambridge, Eng.: Polity, 1990).

13. David Harvey, _The Condition of Postmodernity_ (Cambridge, Eng.: Blackwell, 1989).

14. For studies that pursue this theme, see Tani E. Barlow, ed., _Formations of Colonial Modernity in East Asia_ (Durham, N.C.: Duke University Press, 1997).

15. Barrington Moore, Jr., _Social Origins of Dictatorship and Democracy_ (Boston: Beacon Press, 1966).

16. Liah Greenfeld, _Nationalism: Five Roads to Modernity_ (Cambridge, Mass.: Harvard University Press, 1992).

17. Tu Wei-ming, "Introduction," in Tu, ed., _Confucian Traditions_.

18. "True" modernity here could mean that an independent and discrete Korean modernity was interrupted by the imposition of Japanese colonial rule. Yet this precolonial modernity is also described using a Western-centered conception of the key elements of modernity. It is thus impossible to separate different models of modernity in such a manner.

19. As Kim Chin'gyun and Chŏng Kŭnsik (_Kŭndae chuch'e wa singminji kyuyul kwŏllyŏk_) rightly point out, both _singminji kŭndaehwaron_ (perspective of colonial modernization) and _sut'alnon_ (perspective of exploitation), despite their contrasting views of Japanese rule, regard modernity in the same way, as representing historical progress. For the recent debate, see Cho Sŏk-kon, "Sut'alnon kwa kŭndaehwaron ŭl nŏmŏsŏ," _Ch'angjak kwa pip'yŏng_ 97 (Summer 1997): 355–70; Chŏng T'aehŏn, "Sut'alnon ŭi songnyuhwa sog'e sarajin singminji," _Ch'angjak kwa pip'yŏng_ 97 (Fall 1997): 344–57; Sin Yongha, "'Singminji kŭndaehwaron' chaejŏngnip sidoe taehan pip'an," _Ch'angjak kwa pip'yŏng_ 97 (Winter 1997): 8–38; An Pyŏngjik, "Han'guk kŭnhyŏndaesa yŏn'gu ŭi saeroun p'aeradaim," _Ch'angjak kwa pip'yŏng_ 97 (Winter 1997): 39–58; and Kim Dongno, "Singminji sidae ŭi kŭndaejŏk sut'al kwa sut'al ŭl t'onghan kŭndaehwa," _Ch'angjak kwa pip'yŏng_ 99 (Spring 1997): 112–32.

20. Earlier social science theory attempted to "predict" the emergence of nationalism. Such theory privileged structure over content (the content of the nation was assumed to be natural) and placed the emergence of nationalism with a modernization framework. Thus, Karl Deutsch's classic _Nationalism and Social Communication_ measured linguistic development and literacy

and other forms of social mobilization that attended economic and social change. Ernest Gellner's work is more sophisticated but still a structuralist explanation of the phenomenon (see, e.g., his *Nation and Nationalism*). In the end, no single structuralist theory satisfies us beyond establishing a connection between the demands of the industrializing state and national mobilization. By not considering the infinite possibilities within a subjective process of national identification, this sort of theory ends up privileging the cultural and political version of whoever comes to power over the nation-state. The historical process, the contested nature of the content – who is included and excluded – of nationalism is lost.

21. Gi-Wook Shin, "Agrarianism: A Critique of Colonial Modernity," ms, UCLA, Department of Sociology, 1997.

22. See Schmid, "Rediscovering Manchuria"; and Chapter 12 by Henry Em in this volume. See also Henry Em, "'Overcoming' Korea's Division: Narrative Strategies in Recent South Korean Historiography," *positions: east asia cultures critique* 1, no. 2 (Fall 1993): 450–85.

23. Duara, *Rescuing History*.

24. Eric Hobsbawm and Terence Ranger, eds., *Invention of Tradition* (Cambridge, Eng.: Cambridge University Press, 1983). See also Stephen Vlastos, ed., *Mirror of Modernity: Invented Traditions of Modern Japan* (Berkeley: University of California Press, 1998).

25. Takashi Fujitani, *Splendid Monarchy: Power and Pageantry in Modern Japan* (Berkeley: University of California Press, 1996).

26. See, e.g., Chizuko Allen, "Northeast Asia Centered Around Korea: Ch'oe Namsŏn's View of History," *Journal of Asian Studies* 49 (1990): 787–806; and Roger Janelli, "The Origins of Korean Folklore Scholarship," *Journal of American Folklore* 99 (1986): 24–49.

27. See Kenneth M. Wells, ed., *South Korea's Minjung Movement: The Culture and Politics of Dissidence* (Honolulu: University of Hawaii Press, 1995).

28. Greenfeld, *Nationalism*.

29. Partha Chatterjee, *Nationalist Thought and the Colonial World* (Minneapolis: University of Minnesota Press, 1986).

*Chapter 1: Chulwoo Lee, "Modernity, Legality, and*
*Power in Korea Under Japanese Rule"*

1. For an example of this conception of modernization, see Chŏng T'ae-hŏn, "Han'guk ŭi singminjijŏk kŭndaehwa mosun kwa kŭ silch'e," in Yŏksa munje yŏn'guso, ed., *Han'guk ŭi 'kŭndae' wa 'kŭndaesŏng' pip'an* (Seoul: Yŏksa pip'yŏngsa, 1996), p. 242.

2. Michel Foucault adopted this approach in conceptualizing rationality; see his "*Omnes et Singulatim*: Towards a Criticism of 'Political Reason,'" in Sterling McMurrin, ed., *Tanner Lectures on Human Values* (Salt Lake City:

University of Utah Press, 1981), 2: 226; and "Questions of Method," in G. Burchell, C. Gordon, and P. Miller, eds., *The Foucault Effect: Studies in Governmentality* (London: Harvester Wheatsheaf, 1991), p. 79.

3. See Anthony Giddens, *The Nation-State and Violence* (Cambridge, Eng.: Polity Press, 1985), chap. 7.

4. For the changes in the judicial system before annexation, see Pak Pyŏng-ho, *Kŭnse ŭi pŏp kwa pŏpsasang* (Seoul: Chinwŏn, 1996), chap. 4; and Edward Baker, "Establishment of a Legal System Under Japanese Rule," in Sang Hyun Song, ed., *Introduction to the Law and Legal System of Korea* (Seoul: Kyung Mun Sa, 1983).

5. See Baker, "Establishment of a Legal System Under Japanese Rule," p. 204.

6. See Chōsen sōtokufu, *Kanshū chōsa hōkokusho* (1912).

7. See Chŏng Chonghyu, *Kankoku minpōten no hikakuhōteki kenkyū* (Tokyo: Sobunshi, 1989), pp. 89–92.

8. Nakamura Akira, "Shokuminchi hō," in Ukai Nobushige et al., eds., *Nihon kindaihō hattatsu shi* (Tokyo: Keiso shobō, 1958), 5: 199–200.

9. Chŏng Chonghyu, *Kankoku minpōten no hikakuhōteki kenkyū*, pp. 103–10.

10. Akihara Gensan, "Nihon tōchika ni okeru Chōsen no hōsei," *Yōhō shirizu* 14 (1971): 1–26.

11. This reflected the discursive creation of *tōyō*, or what Stefan Tanaka has aptly termed "Japan's Orient." This intellectual enterprise was a discursive strategy for putting Japan on a par with the West while highlighting difference and according Japan a privileged position vis-à-vis the rest of Asia. See Stefan Tanaka, *Japan's Orient: Rendering Pasts into History* (Berkeley: University of California Press, 1993).

12. See Asami Rintarō, "Chōsen hōkei no rekishiteki kenkyū," *Hōgaku kyōkai zasshi* 39, no. 8 (1921): 34; cited in Chŏng Chonghyu, *Kankoku minpōten no hikakuhōteki kenkyū*, p. 90.

13. See Wada Ichirō, *Chōsen tōchi chizei seido chōsa hōkokusho* (Tokyo: Sōkō shoten, 1920).

14. Aoyagi Tsunatarō, *Chōsen tōchi ron* (Seoul: Chōsen kenkyūkai, 1923), pp. 125–29; Mark Peattie, "Japanese Attitudes Toward Colonialism, 1895–1945," in R. Myers and M. Peattie, eds., *The Japanese Colonial Empire, 1895–1945* (Princeton: Princeton University Press, 1984), pp. 109–10.

15. Inazō Nitobe, "Japan as a Colonizer," *Journal of Race Development* 2 (1912): 360.

16. See Edward I-te Chen, "The Attempt to Integrate the Empire: Legal Perspectives," in Myers and Peattie, eds., *The Japanese Colonial Empire, 1895–1945*, p. 252; and Nakamura Akira, "Shokuminchi hō," pp. 198–99.

17. For a comparison of these contrasting attitudes, see Edward I-te Chen, "Japan: Oppressor or Modernizer?," in Andrew C. Nahm, ed., *Korea Under Japanese Colonial Rule: Studies of the Policy and Techniques of Japanese Colonial-*

*ism* (Kalamazoo: Western Michigan University, Institute of International and Area Studies, Center for Korean Studies, 1973).

18. See Nakamura Akira, "Shokuminchi hō," pp. 175–89; Suzuki Keifu, "Pŏp ŭl t'onghan Chosŏn singminji chibae" (Ph.D. diss., Korea University, 1988), pp. 63–64; Kim Ch'angnok, "Ilbon esŏŭi sŏyang hŏnpŏp sasang ŭi suyong e kwanhan yŏn'gu" (Ph.D. diss., Seoul National University, 1994), pp. 132–53.

19. Matsuoka Shutarō, "Shokuminchi seido to Chōsen," *Chōsen* 139 (1926): 1–17.

20. Kim Ch'angnok, "Ilbon esŏŭi sŏyang hŏnpŏp sasang ŭi suyong e kwanhan yŏn'gu," p. 134.

21. Akihara, "Nihon tōchika ni okeru Chōsen no hōsei," p. 10; Matsuoka, "Shokuminchi seido to Chōsen," p. 9.

22. See Kim Ch'angnok, "Ilbon esŏŭi sŏyang hŏnpŏp sasang ŭi suyong e kwanhan yŏn'gu," pp. 134–50, for Hozumi's and Minōbe's arguments.

23. Nitobe, "Japan as a Colonizer," p. 361; and "The Influences of the West upon Japan," in Shigenobu Ōkuma, ed., *Fifty Years of New Japan* (London: Smith, Elder, 1909), 2: 469.

24. Nitobe, "Japan as a Colonizer," p. 359. As for Taiwan, Gotō Shimpei, the architect of colonial administration in Taiwan, said: "The greater part of the inhabitants are Chinese; but most of these being, so to speak, descendants of rebels and insurgents, they lack the character of a people who have lived an orderly life under an hereditary government" (Shimpei Gotō, "The Administration of Formosa," in Ōkuma, ed., *Fifty Years of New Japan*, 2: 533).

25. Baker, "Establishment of a Legal System Under Japanese Rule," pp. 187–95.

26. Peter Fitzpatrick, " 'The Desperate Vacuum': Imperialism and Law in the Experience of Enlightenment," *Droit et societé* 13 (1989): 347–58; see pp. 350 and 354 for quoted remarks.

27. Baker, "Establishment of a Legal System Under Japanese Rule," p. 201.

28. Chōsen sōtokufu, "Taikei ni tsuite, I," *Chōsen kihō*, Oct. 1917, p. 55.

29. Chōsen sōtokufu, "Taikei ni tsuite, II," *Chōsen kihō*, Nov. 1917, p. 82.

30. See *Tong'a ilbo*, April 1, 1920, p. 3.

31. Michel Foucault, *Discipline and Punish: The Birth of the Prison* (New York: Vintage Books, 1979), p. 16.

32. One Japanese report during the Russo-Japanese War stated: "Koreans do not have clocks . . . and do not feel any shame in not keeping time. . . . When they want to get up early in the morning, they simply drink jars of water so that they wake up when they feel like urinating" (cited in Pak Hyŏn-su, "Ilche ŭi ch'imnyak ŭl wihan sahoe munhwa chosa hwaltong," *Han'guksa yŏn'gu* 30 [1980]: 136).

33. See Foucault, *Discipline and Punish*, pp. 11, 138, 162.

34. "The body now serves as an instrument or intermediary: if one intervenes upon it to imprison it, or to make it work, it is in order to deprive the individual of a liberty that is regarded both as a right and as property. The body, according to this penalty, is caught up in a system of constraints and privations, obligations and prohibitions. Physical pain, the pain of the body itself, is no longer the constituent element of the penalty" (ibid., p. 11).

35. Chōsen sōtokufu, "Taikei ni tsuite, II," p. 83.

36. In Taiwan flogging accounted for 24 percent of all sentences from summary justice between 1913 and 1915, compared with 45 percent in Korea, whereas fines were imposed in 70 percent of the cases, compared with 48 percent in Korea (Chōsen sōtokufu, "Taikei ni tsuite, I," p. 56).

37. Chōsen sōtokufu, "Taikei ni tsuite, II," p. 81.

38. Baker, "Establishment of a Legal System Under Japanese Rule," p. 202.

39. Chōsen sōtokufu, "Taikei ni tsuite, II," p. 85.

40. Kim Chin'gyun and Chŏng Kŭnsik, eds., *Kŭndae chuch'e wa singminji kyuyul kwŏllyŏk* (Seoul: Munhwa kwahaksa, 1997).

41. See Giddens, *The Nation-State and Violence*, chap. 7.

42. See Chōsen sōtokufu, *Chōsen sōtokufu shisei nenpō*, 1940, pp. 84–87; Chōsen sōtokufu, *Chōsen keisatsu shi gaiyō* (1925), pp. viii, 25–44; Ronald Dore and Tsutomu Ōuchi, "Rural Origins of Japanese Fascism," in J. Morley, ed., *Dilemmas of Growth in Prewar Japan* (Princeton: Princeton University Press, 1971), p. 187.

43. One list of police responsibilities in Europe included (1) religion; (2) morals; (3) health; (4) supplies; (5) roads, highways, town buildings; (6) public safety; (7) the liberal arts; (8) trade; (9) factories; (10) manservants and laborers; and (11) the poor (Foucault, "*Omnes et Singulatim*," p. 249).

44. Colin Gordon, "Governmental Rationality: An Introduction," in G. Burchell et al., eds., *The Foucault Effect*, pp. 10–11.

45. Hyman Kublin, "The Evolution of Japanese Colonialism," *Comparative Studies in Society and History* 2 (1959): 80.

46. Foucault, "Governmentality," in G. Burchell et al., eds., *The Foucault Effect*.

47. Jack Goody, *The Logic of Writing and the Organization of Society* (Cambridge, Eng.: Cambridge University Press, 1986), p. 116.

48. According to Giddens (*The Nation-State and Violence*, pp. 195–96), the modern state sequesters death from the ordinary activities of daily life, whereas in premodern societies death is closely integrated with the continuity of social activities through moral sources deriving from tradition.

49. Chōsen sōtokufu, *Chōsen sōtokufu shisei nenpō*, 1914, p. 79.

50. Ibid., 1915, pp. 324–25.

51. For an interesting account of police inspections of animal sheds and toilets, see Han'guk nongch'on kyŏngje yŏn'guwŏn, ed., *Kurye yussiga ŭi saenghwal ilgi* (Seoul: Han'guk nongch'on kyŏngje yŏn'guwŏn, 1991), p. 473.

52. Criminal Cases Registers 1926, 1931, 1936, and 1941, Sunch'ŏn Branch, Kwangju District Court.

53. Chŏng T'aehŏn, *Ilche ŭi kyŏngje chŏngch'aek kwa Chosŏn sahoe* (Seoul: Yŏksa pip'yŏngsa, 1996), p. 44.

54. In his diary, Yu Hyŏngŏp of Kurye lamented that many public places, from financial cooperatives to shops run by Japanese settlers, had become places where information was collected and channeled to the authorities. Yu, too, experienced a house search by tobacco monopoly officials and was fined for secretly possessing tobacco (see Han'guk nongch'on kyŏngje yŏn'guwŏn, ed., *Kurye yussiga ŭi saenghwal ilgi*, pp. 670, 796).

55. For a review of colonial publication policy in Korea, see Michael Robinson, "Colonial Publication Policy and the Korean Nationalist Movement," in Peattie and Myers, eds., *The Japanese Colonial Empire, 1895–1945.*

56. Criminal Appeal Cases 522 and 523 (1920), Keijō Court of Appeals; trans. in Kim Pyŏnghwa, *Han'guk sabŏpsa* (Seoul: Ilchogak, 1982), 2: 594–621.

57. Criminal Cases 456 and 457 (1919), Sunch'ŏn Branch, Kwangju District Court.

58. Carol Gluck, *Japan's Modern Myths: Ideology in the Late Meiji Period* (Princeton: Princeton University Press, 1985), p. 262.

59. Ibid., p. 119.

60. Ibid., chap. 7.

61. Ibid., p. 282.

62. Okuhira Yasuhirō, *Chianijihō shōshi* (Tokyo: Tsukuma shobō, 1977), chap. 1; Richard Mitchell, *Thought Control in Prewar Japan* (Ithaca: Cornell University Press, 1976), pp. 44–53.

63. Richard Minear, *Japanese Tradition and Western Law: Emperor, State, and Law in the Thought of Hozumi Yatsuka* (Cambridge, Mass.: Harvard University Press, 1970), pp. 66–69.

64. Han Insŏp, "Ch'ianyujibŏp kwa singminji t'ongje pŏmnyŏng ŭi chŏn'gae," in Pak Pyŏngho kyosu hwangap kinyŏm nonch'ong kanhaeng wiwŏnhoe, ed., *Han'guk pŏpsahak nonch'ong* (Seoul: Pagyŏngsa, 1991), p. 429; Suzuki, "Pŏp ŭl t'onghan Chosŏn singminji chibae," pp. 351–52.

65. Minear, *Japanese Tradition and Western Law*, p. 68.

66. See Robert Hall, ed., *Kokutai No Hongi: Cardinal Principles of the National Entity of Japan* (Cambridge, Mass.: Harvard University Press, 1949), pp. 161–62.

67. See Naka Sechiō, *Zentaishōgiteki keihōkan* (Ōsaka: Daidō shoin, 1941).

68. Mitchell, *Thought Control in Prewar Japan*, p. 190.

69. Ibid., pp. 121, 141–42.

70. "Semiconverts" had not renounced their deviant beliefs but were expected to do so in the future or had pledged not to engage in any form of activism (ibid., p. 128).

71. Suzuki, "Pŏp ŭl t'onghan Chosŏn singminji chibae," p. 309. In Japan only 8 percent of the approximately 66,000 arrested between 1928 and 1941

were prosecuted, compared with 47 percent of all thought suspects arrested in Korea in 1937 and 1938 (Chōsen sōtokufu, *Saikin ni okeru Chōsen no chian jōkyō* [1938], pp. 15–17; Mitchell, *Thought Control in Prewar Japan*, pp. 141–42).

72. Overburdened because so much discretion was needed and because the content of the law was so deduced from extra-legal axioms that the legal system became entangled with its environment and its autonomy was impaired. See Niklas Luhmann, *The Differentiation of Society* (New York: Columbia University Press, 1982), chaps. 5–6.

73. Zygmunt Bauman, *Modernity and the Holocaust* (Cambridge, Eng.: Polity Press, 1989).

74. David Scott, "Colonial Governmentality," *Social Text* 43 (1995): 191–220.

75. "The pastoral, the new diplomatic-military techniques and, lastly, police: these are the three elements that I believe made possible the production of this fundamental phenomenon in Western history, the governmentalisation of the state" (Foucault, "Governmentality," p. 104).

### Chapter 2: Michael Robinson, "Broadcasting, Cultural Hegemony, and Colonial Modernity in Korea, 1924–1945"

Research for this paper was supported, in part, by a Korea Foundation Fellowship for research in Korea during summer 1994.

1. See Table 2.1 for yearly statistics on radio receivers (permits) by ethnicity in Korea.

2. French Algeria is the closest analogue to Japanese-dominated Korea. However, French Radio Algeria focused on broadcasts to urban centers and their immediate hinterlands, where the French population was centered. Only near the end of French rule did it spread its net to counter resistance broadcasts (also spoken in French). See Frantz Fanon, *A Dying Colonialism* (New York: Grove Press, 1965), chap. 2.

3. Andrew Nahm put it this way: "A vast majority of Korean families had no radios, and to them the wireless communication system was irrelevant"; see Nahm, *Korea: Tradition and Transformation* (Seoul: Hollym Press, 1988), p. 247. The exhaustive histories of communications published in Korea generally share this sentiment, yet contain data that might support new interpretations were different questions asked. See Han'guk pangsong kongsa, *Han'guk pangsongsa* (Seoul: Han'guk pangsong kongsa, 1977), hereafter *HPSS*; and Han'guk pangsong chinhŭnghoe p'yŏn, *Han'guk pangsong ch'ongnam* (Seoul: Han'guk pangsong chinhŭnghoe p'yŏn, 1991), hereafter *HPSCN*.

4. Other spaces I have in mind are the Korean-language press, recording industry, and cinema. I have argued this case in a general way in my paper "Mass Media and Popular Culture in 1930s Korea: Cultural Control, Identity, and Colonial Hegemony," in Dae-Sook Suh, ed., *Korean Studies: New Pacific Currents* (Honolulu: University of Hawaii Press, 1994), pp. 54–73.

5. The best narrative of the Cultural Policy reforms is Frank Baldwin, "The March First Movement: Korean Challenge and Japanese Response" (Ph.D. diss., Columbia University, 1969).

6. The period of Cultural Rule is generally set at 1919–31, ending with the Manchuria Incident and intensification of Japanese assimilation programs. I would argue that Cultural Rule set important parameters within the overall Japanese cultural hegemony in Korea. Although the policy co-opted Korean cultural, social, and political leaders, it also created autonomous cultural spaces that undermined later assimilation programs of the middle-to-late 1930s. See Baldwin, "The March First Movement"; and in Korean, Kim Kyuhwan, *Ilche ŭi taehan ŏllon sŏnjŏn chŏngch'aek* (Seoul: Iu ch'ulp'ansa, 1982), p. 162.

7. Gregory Kasza, *The State and Mass Media in Japan, 1918–1945* (Berkeley: University of California Press, 1988), pp. 72–83. For a description of GGK policy linkages and administrative orders on radio, see *HPSCN*, pp. 137–39.

8. Formal permission was granted on November 30, 1926; broadcasts began Feb. 16, 1927. For the distinction between public interest corporations and for profit companies, see Kasza, *State and Mass Media in Japan*, p. 80.

9. Both the *Chosŏn ilbo* (Korea daily) and *Tonga ilbo* (Eastern daily) followed the testing program closely. See, e.g., "Chadongch'a ro chilchu hamyŏnsŏ musŏn pangjŏn silsi," *Tonga ilbo*, Dec. 17, 1924; and "Kŭnse kwahak ŭi iltae kyŏng'i," *Chosŏn ilbo*, Dec. 17, 1924.

10. *Chosŏn ilbo*, July 2, 1925, Apr. 20, 1926, July 8, 1926; *Tonga ilbo*, June 26, 1925, July 15, 1926, Nov. 6, 1926.

11. Michael Robinson, *Cultural Nationalism in Colonial Korea, 1920–1925* (Seattle: University of Washington Press, 1988), chap. 3.

12. *Chosŏn ilbo*, "Chungyohan munhwa chisik ŭi hanain radio kangsŭphoe," Jan. 12, 1927.

13. *HPSS*, pp. 18–20.

14. The dual-language policy for KBC is, as far as I can see, unique to the pre-1945 colonial world. At least the standard Korean histories claim this to be the case.

15. Even before formal broadcasts began, there was sniping in the press; see "Pangsong kwa Chosŏn ch'wiji ŭi ch'ŏlchŏga p'ilyo," *Maeil sinbo*, Dec. 8, 1926. In 1927 criticism focused on how the language mix inhibited the spread of radios; see *Chosŏn ilbo*, Jan. 7–9, 1927, Mar. 23, 1927; and *Tonga ilbo*, May 21, 1927. Dec. 16, 1927. A useful, but not exhaustive compilation of news articles bearing on broadcasting in Korea is contained in Chŏng Chinsŏk, *Han'guk pansong kwangye kisa moŭm* (Seoul: Kwanhŭn k'ŭlŏp sinyŏng yŏn'gu kigŭm, 1992).

16. *HPSS*, pp. 38–40.

17. Figures on the financing of KBC before 1933 are drawn from the secondary histories, *HPSS*, and *HPSCN*. More detailed year-by-year budgets for

KBC are contained in the GGK Ministry of Communications annual, *Chōsen sōtokufu teishinkyoku nenpō*, yearly after 1933.

18. Government Directive (*furei*) no. 380, *Chōsen sōtokufu kampō* (Feb. 1926). This directive set profits, registration, and listener fees.

19. *HPSS*, pp. 33–35.

20. Chŏng Chinsŏk, "Ilcheha ŭi radio pogŭp kwa ch'ŏngch'wija," *Sinmun kwa pangsong*, Oct. 1992, pp. 54–61; *HPSS*, pp. 122–30.

21. Gregory Kasza, *State and Mass Media in Japan*, p. 88. Japan broke the million mark in the early 1930s.

22. Expansion of the radio audience meant that listener fees could be reduced. The basic monthly fee was lowered again to 75 chŏn in 1939. This section on finances is based on figures given in *HPSS*, pp. 30–35.

23. The assimilation movement is well chronicled in English-language sources. See Chong Sik Lee, *The Politics of Korean Nationalism* (Berkeley: University of California Press, 1964); Dae-Sook Suh, *The Korean Communist Movement* (Princeton: Princeton University Press, 1967); Gregory Henderson, *Korea: The Politics of the Vortex* (Cambridge, Mass.: Harvard University Press, 1968); Wonmo Dong, "Japanese Colonial Policy and Practice in Korea, 1905–1945: A Study in Assimilation" (Ph.D. diss., Georgetown University, 1965); Nahm, *Korea*; and Wan-yao Chou, "The Kōminka Movement in Taiwan and Korea: Comparisons and Interpretations," in Peter Duus, Ramon Myers, and Mark Peattie, eds., *The Japanese Wartime Empire, 1931–1945* (Princeton: Princeton University Press, 1996), pp. 40–68.

24. *HPSCN*, pp. 198–99.

25. Early Korean broadcasts were monitored by an official of the Ministry of Communications sitting in the studio. This official had an open telephone line to the ministry and could stop broadcasting on the spot. Later, a cut-off button wired to the ministry itself replaced the need of an official in the control booth. There is no evidence that the button was ever used.

26. *HPSCN*, pp. 159, 195–97. This board, along with the programming oversight board, was made up of representatives of the High Police, Ministry of Communications, Military Liaison Office, KBC, and the Publication Office of the GGK. The Information Coordinating Committee had been established in 1920 as part of the Cultural Policy reorganization. It gradually assumed control of all printing, journalism, cinema, radio, and advertising media. The committee was charged with coordinating all information surveillance as well as the production of propaganda after 1937.

27. Singled out for particularly vehement denunciation in postwar writing on assimilation programs was the Japanese attempt to "recast" Korean folk song genres (*minyo, kasa*) in a traditional Japanese narrative song (*naniwabushi*) style. See *HPSS*, pp. 45–50; and *HPSCN*, pp. 190–95.

28. *HPSCN*, pp. 206, 220–21.

29. Radio announcers became stars during the period. The inclusion of women announcers, following the Japanese pattern, contradicted traditional

roles for women in public life. The female KBC announcers received thousands of letters, among them proposals of marriage. The voice quality, education, and erudition of the announcers was critical in "representing" the women as suitable for the new medium. See "Saek tarŭn chigŏp romansŭ," *Chosŏn ilbo*, Jan. 7, 1927; and "Kyŏngsŏng pangsongguk ŭi saeroun annaunsŏ," *Chosŏn ilbo*, Jan. 9, 1927.

30. *Han'gul hakhoe 50 nyŏnsa* (Seoul: Han'gul hakhoe, 1971), pp. 89–97; Robinson, *Cultural Nationalism in Colonial Korea*, pp. 89–92.

31. "Pangsongguk han'gŭl kangchwa kangsa nŭn Kwŏn Tŏkkyu," *Chosŏn ilbo*, Nov. 7, 1933.

32. This article illustrates a later version of the debate; see "Hansimhan radio: Chosŏnŏ algi swipge paro sayong haesŏ minjung kwa ch'in hara," *Tonga ilbo*, Dec. 14, 1938.

33. The first director of Station #2 gave his own assessment of the "unlimited potential" for cultural elevation: see Yun Paeknam, "Sinsedae ŭi sahoejŏk yŏkhal," *Sindonga*, Mar. 1934, p. 120.

34. "Ap'ŭro pogo twiro pogo," *Tonga ilbo*, Nov. 10, 1929.

35. Tsuda Takeshi, "Hantō bunka no seikaku," *Chōsen*, no. 299 (Apr. 1940): 57.

36. "Arŭmdaun Chosŏnmal ŭl Kyŏngsŏng pangsongguk chei pangsongbu esŏ sunhwa undong," *Chosŏn ilbo*, Feb. 9, 1936.

37. An important part of this research, as yet only beginning, will be to investigate the issue of Japanese-language use by the colonial population. The Japanese boasted that by 1943, 23.2 percent of the population understood some Japanese, 12.3 percent "without difficulty." The Korean population in 1944 stood at 25,133,352 (there were 712,587 Japanese in the colony that year). Further research on Korean use of radio and consumption of Japanese-language publications in the colony will help us assess these claims.

38. Yi Ch'anghyŏn, "Ilcheha munhwa sanŏp ŭi taejung ŭmak saengsan e kwanhan chŏngch'i kyŏngjehak," *Sahoe pip'yŏng* 3 (Dec. 1989).

39. Indeed, the regional mixture of material was deliberately fostered through a programming device of remote broadcasts from provincial cities, the popular "Night in P'yŏngyang" or "Night in Kwangju" broadcasts. These began during the period of dual-language radio and continued after 1933. It is interesting to speculate whether and how these broadcasts represented or stimulated regional identity during the period. See *HPSS*, p. 42, *passim*.

40. Yu Sŏnyŏng, "Han'guk taejung munhwa ŭi kŭndaejŏk kusŏng e taehan yŏn'gu: Chosŏn hugi esŏ ilche sidae kkaji rŭl chungsim uro" (Ph.D. diss., Korea University, 1992). Ch'ae Mansik satirized the popularity of "live" music reviews in his serialized novel, *Peace Under Heaven*, personified by the listening habits of the novel's odious protagonist, Master Yun; see Ch'ae Mansik, *Peace Under Heaven*, trans. Chun Kyung-ja (New York: M. E. Sharpe, 1993).

41. "Sin'gu sasang i 'ant'ena' sŏ ch'ungdol," *Tonga ilbo,* Dec. 17, 1933.

42. *HPSS,* pp. 20, 66–67, 71–74.

43. According to *Wŏlgan ŭmak* (Music monthly), "Even poor farmers can identify major record companies and different popular records" (Dec. 1935, pp. 449–50). This article claims there were 30,000 phonographs in Korea at the time. Other sources indicate that a single recording selling 50,000 copies in Korea was a "bestseller," as in the case of "The Tears of Mokp'o Harbor" ("Mokp'o ŭi nunmul") in 1935. The same source reminds us of the popularity of Korean singers and their songs in the Japanese market. In Japan, a record selling 300,000 copies was not uncommon. See Pak Ch'anho, *Han'guk kayosa* (Seoul: Hyŏnamsa, 1992), p. 276.

44. A good example of how radio and performances were linked is the well-publicized radio performance of Chŏn Ok and Kang Hongsik (both recording superstars) in May 1935. Columbia Records ran an advertisement for the radio performance and the release of a new record featuring the famous duo. See ibid., p. 255; and for other advertisements, pp. 267, 317, 371.

45. "Radio," *Kyebyŏk* 2, no. 1 (Dec. 1934): 94.

46. For one description of the Song Purification Movement (Kayo chŏnghwa undong), see "Kayo chŏnghwa ŭi ponghwa: yabi chŏsokhan norae rŭl ilso hago kŏnjŏnhan norae rŭl nŏlli mojip hayŏ," *Chosŏn ilbo,* Dec. 21, 1939. The movement took a number of forms. One technique was to sponsor song- and radio drama–writing contests with cash prizes to induce the production of new material; for one such contest, see "Radio sosŏl hyŏnsang mojip," *Chosŏn ilbo,* Sept. 1, 1937. Such attempts to create "patriotic" culture were laughable in commercial terms. A roundtable discussion by record industry executives in 1939 noted that such songs were just not commercially viable; see "Rek'o‒dŭ kye ŭi naemak tŭnnŭn," *Chogwang* 5, no. 3 (Mar. 1939): 314–23.

47. Contemporary struggles over the issue of Western popular culture and its corrosive influences in Korea are played out at both the state and grass-roots levels. The state holds Western rock music responsible for the corruption of Korean youth—its hedonism, materialism, and "untraditional" attitudes toward its elders. Young cultural nationalists are also trying to revive Korean folk music, dance, and participatory theater.

48. Yi Ch'anghyŏn, "Ilcheha munhwa sanŏp ŭi taejung ŭmak."

49. Yu Sŏnyŏng, "Han'guk taejung munhwa," *passim.*

50. The bibliography on these separate elements of popular culture is restricted to informal "histories" of various music genres, the Korean (not other) cinema, and modern literature. Mainstream historians dominating history writing in the ROK have not yet embraced this topic as relevant. Among younger scholars, however, the field is growing; the work of these younger scholars will ultimately challenge and reshape historical studies in Korea.

Chapter 3: *Gi-Wook Shin and Do-Hyun Han, "Colonial Corporatism: The Rural Revitalization Campaign, 1932–1940"*

1. Government-General of Tyosen, *Annual Report on Administration of Tyosen*, 1936–37, p. 214.

2. For representative works on the campaign, see Chŏng Munjong, "1930 nyŏndae Chosŏn esŏ ŭi nongŏp chŏngch'aek e kwanhan yŏn'gu" (Ph.D. diss., Seoul National University, Department of Economics, 1993); Chi Sugŏl, "1932–35 nyŏn kanŭi Chosŏn nongch'on chinhŭng undong–Singminji ch'eje yujich'aek ŭro sŏŭi kinŭg e kwanhayŏ," *Han'guksa yŏn'gu* 46 (1984): 117–49; Han Tohyŏn (Han Do-Hyun), "1930 nyŏndae 'nongch'on chinhŭng undong' ŭi sŏnggyŏk e kwanhan yŏn'gu" (M.A. thesis, Seoul National University, Department of Sociology, 1985); and Miyata Setsuko, "Chōsen ni okeru 'nōson shinkō undō,'" *Kikan gendaishi* 2 (1973).

3. See Pak Kyŏngsik, *Ilbon cheguk chuŭi ŭi Chosŏn chibae* (Seoul: Ch'ŏng'a, 1986).

4. See, e.g., Chang Siwŏn, "Singminji ha Chosŏn ŭi pan ponggŏnjŏk t'oji soyu e kwanhan yŏn'gu," *Kyŏngje sahak* 4 (1980): 38–139.

5. Bruce Cumings, "The Legacy of Japanese Colonialism in Korea," in Ramon Myers and Mark Peattie, eds., *The Japanese Colonial Empire, 1895–1945* (Princeton: Princeton University Press, 1984), p. 492.

6. For detailed discussion of agrarian conflict under colonial rule, see Gi-Wook Shin, *Peasant Protest and Social Change in Colonial Korea* (Seattle: University of Washington Press, 1996), esp. chaps. 4–8.

7. See Gi-Wook Shin, "Agrarian Conflict and the Origins of Korean Capitalism," *American Journal of Sociology* 103 (Mar. 1998): 1309–51.

8. Gregory Henderson, *Korea: Politics of the Vortex* (Cambridge, Mass.: Harvard University Press, 1968).

9. Philippe Schmitter, "Still the Century of Corporatism?," *Review of Politics* 85 (1974): 104.

10. See James Malloy, ed., *Authoritarianism and Corporatism in Latin America* (Pittsburgh: University of Pittsburgh Press, 1977).

11. See Harmon Zeigler, *Pluralism, Corporatism, and Confucianism* (Philadelphia: Temple University Press, 1988).

12. See Peter Williamson, *Varieties of Corporatism* (Cambridge, Eng.: Cambridge University Press, 1985).

13. The discussion in this section is based largely on Shin, *Peasant Protest and Social Change.*

14. Chŏng Inkwan, "Nongch'on kuje ŭi tanmyŏngsang," *Cheilsŏn* 2, no. 11 (Dec. 1932): 6–9.

15. See Ugaki Kazushige, *Ugaki Kazushige nikki* (Tokyo: Misuzu shobō, 1968), 1: 222 (Sept. 1919) and 231 (Oct. 1919).

16. Ibid., p. 440 (1923).

17. Ibid., p. 728 (Aug. 21, 1928).

18. Government-General of Chosen, *Annual Report on Administration of Chosen*, 1934–35, pp. 216–17.

19. See Kenneth B. Pyle, "The Technology of Japanese Nationalism: The Local Improvement Movement, 1900–1918," *Journal of Asian Studies* 33 (1973): 51–65.

20. Thomas Havens, *Farm and Nation in Modern Japan: Agrarian Nationalism, 1870–1940* (Princeton: Princeton University Press, 1974), p. 321.

21. The Japanese *Keizai kōsei undō* (Economic rehabilitation campaign) was launched in the fall of 1932, almost simultaneously with the Korean one.

22. For detailed discussion of Korean agrarianism during the colonial period, see Gi-Wook Shin, "Agrarianism: A Critique of Colonial Modernity in Korea," manuscript, UCLA, Department of Sociology, 1997.

23. See Cho Tonggŏl, *Ilcheha Han'guk nongmin undongsa* (Seoul: Han'gilsa, 1979), pp. 158–233; Min Kyŏngbae, "Han'guk kidoggyo ŭi nongch'on sahoe undong," *Tongbang hakchi* 38 (1983), pp. 179–220; the special issue "Isanghyang kŏnsŏl" (Building utopia) in *Sinmin* (New people), Mar. 1929; and Sun'guk sŏnyŏl sorae Kim Chunggŏn sŏnsaeng kimyŏm sapŏhoe, *Kaehyŏk ŭi iron kwa tongnip undong: Sorae Kim Chunggŏn ŭi ch'ŏlhak kwa sasang e taehan yŏn'gu nonch'ong* (Seoul: T'aesŏng, 1994).

24. Ma Myŏng, "Chosŏn odae chinhŭngch'aek: Chosŏn nongch'on ŭi chinhŭngch'aek," *Hyesŏng*, Jan. 1932, p. 2.

25. "Sin Chosŏn ŭi unmyŏng kwa nongmin ŭi chiwi," *Kaebyŏk* 41 (Nov. 1923).

26. For Japanese petition movements, see Kerry Smith, "A Time of Crisis: Japan, the Great Depression, and Relief Policy" (Ph.D. diss., Harvard University, 1994).

27. See, e.g., the special issue "Building Utopia" in *Sinmin*.

28. Yi Sŏnghwan, ed., "Hyŏndae nongmin tokbon—nongmin kwa tongnip chayŏng," *Nongmin* 2, no. 1 (1926): 36.

29. See the special issue of *Sinmin*, Mar. 1929, p. 55.

30. "Sin Chosŏn ŭi unmyŏng kwa nongmin ŭi chiwi," p. 8.

31. Ma Myŏng, "Chosŏn odae chinhŭngch'aek," pp. 6–8.

32. See Nonggyŏng hagin, "Nongch'on ch'aemu chŏngni munje," *Nongmin* 2, no. 6 (1931): 53; Paek Min, "Kongdong kyŏngjak ŭl silsi haja," *Nongmin* 4, no. 3 (1933): 5.

33. Government-General of Chosen, *Annual Report on Administration of Chosen*, 1934–35, p. 218.

34. Chōsen sōtokufu, *Chōsen ni okeru nōson shinkō undō no jisshi gaikyō to sono jisseki* (Keijō, 1940), p. 2.

35. Ibid., p. 1.

36. The colonial government published the results of the surveys (conducted in 1933 and 1938) for a sample of tenant (N = 1,778) and semi-tenant households (N = 1,919) selected for rehabilitation. See Chōsen sōtokufu,

Nōka keizai gaikyō chōsa – kosaku nōka, 1933–1938 (Keijō, 1940); and Chōsen sōtokufu, Nōka keizai gaikyō chōsa – jisaku ken kosaku nōka, 1933–38 (Keijō, 1940).

37. See Chŏng Munjong, "1930 nyŏndae Chosŏn esŏ," pp. 56–64.

38. Chōsen sōtokufu, Chōsen ni okeru nōson shinkō undō, p. 5.

39. See Shin, Peasant Protest and Social Change, chaps. 5–6.

40. Chŏng Munjong, "1930 nyŏndae Chosŏn esŏ," p. 125.

41. In Japan industrial co-ops played a key role in the rural regeneration movement, but in Korea their role was nominal.

42. See Chōsen sōtokufu, Chōsen ni okeru nōson shinkō undō, p. 9.

43. Even where elders took the leadership positions in the CRRs, youth organizations played a key role in carrying out the campaign in the villages. See Chōsen sōtokufu, Nōsangyoson shinkō kōsekisha meikan (Keijō, 1937).

44. See Chōsen sōtokufu, Chōsen ni okeru nōson shinkō undō, pp. 10–11; and Chŏng Munjong, "1930 nyŏndae Chosŏn esŏ," pp. 74–80.

45. See Miyata Akiko, "Nōson shinkō undō-ka no chūken jinbutsu no yūsei," Chōsenshi kenkyūkai ronbunshū 18 (1981). Another source, on the characteristics of 889 female trainees in 1936, shows 74 percent age 19 to 24; 88 percent graduates of ordinary school; and 29 percent, 45 percent, and 27 percent from the owner-cultivator, semi-tenant, and landless tenant classes, respectively. See Chŏng Munjong, "1930 nyŏndae Chosŏn esŏ," p. 76.

46. However, the government by no means excluded local landlords from the campaign and sought their support as well.

47. Even before the campaign, Japanese recognized the value of Confucianism in preserving a colonial social order. See Michael Robinson, "Perceptions of Confucianism in Twentieth Century Korea," in Gilbert Rozman, ed., The East Asian Region (Princeton: Princeton University Press, 1991), pp. 204–25; and Warren W. Smith, Jr., "Japanese Support for Confucianism in Korea," in his Confucianism in Modern Japan (Tokyo: Hokuseido Press, 1959), pp. 166–84.

48. Carter Eckert et al., Korea Old and New: A History (Seoul: Ilchogak, 1990), p. 141.

49. Ugaki, Nikki, 2: 909 (July 25, 1932).

50. Chōsen sōtokufu, Nōson wa kagayaku (Keijō, 1934); see also Han Tohyŏn, "1930 nyŏndae 'nongch'on chinhŭng undong.' "

51. See Eric Hobsbawm and Terence Ranger, eds., The Invention of Tradition (Cambridge, Eng.: Cambridge University Press, 1983).

52. See Shin, Peasant Protest and Social Change, chap. 7.

53. Chŏng Munjong, "1930 nyŏndae Chosŏn esŏ," p. 145.

54. Government-General of Tyosen, Annual Report on Administration of Tyosen, 1936–37, p. 215.

55. Chōsen sōtokufu, Nōsangyoson shinkō kōsekisha meikan, pp. 81, 109.

56. For concrete examples, see Shin, Peasant Protest and Social Change, chap. 8. Also note that tenant experience in disputes, though institutional-

ized, raised political consciousness that became a crucial resource in post-1945 peasant radicalism (ibid., chap. 9).

57. Eckert, *Korea*, p. 251. One could argue, however, that had the campaign lasted much longer, it would have been more successful in internalizing Japanese culture and thought among Koreans.

58. Chŏng Munjong, "1930 nyŏndae Chosŏn esŏ," pp. 182 and 190.

59. Chōsen sōtokufu, *Chōsen ni okeru nōson shinkō undō*, pp. 8–9.

60. See Jang Jip Choi, *Labor and the Authoritarian State* (Seoul: Korea University Press, 1989); and Bruce Cumings, "The Corporate State in North Korea," in Hagen Koo, ed., *State and Society in Contemporary Korea* (Ithaca: Cornell University Press, 1993).

61. See Park Chung Hee, *Saemaul: Korea's New Community Movement* (Seoul: Republic of Korea, Secretariat of the President, 1979).

*Chapter 4: Michael A. Schneider, "The Limits of Cultural Rule: Internationalism and Identity in Japanese Responses to Korean Rice"*

1. Arjun Appadurai, *Modernity at Large: Cultural Dimensions of Globalization* (Minneapolis: University of Minnesota Press, 1996).

2. Sheldon Garon, *Molding Japanese Minds: The State in Everyday Life* (Princeton: Princeton University Press, 1997); David R. Ambaras, "Social Knowledge, Cultural Capital, and the New Middle Class in Japan, 1895–1912," *Journal of Japanese Studies* 24, no. 1 (Winter 1998): 1–33.

3. See the series of articles entitled "Chūryū seikatsusha no fuan mondai," *Jitsugyō no Nihon* 23, no. 5 (Mar. 1, 1920): 7–25.

4. Kang Toksang, ed., *Gendaishi shiryō*, vol. 25, *Chōsen 1* (Tokyo: Misuzu shobō, 1965), pp. 481–500.

5. Sheldon Garon, "Rethinking Modernization and Modernity in Japanese History: A Focus on State-Society Relations," *Journal of Asian Studies* 53, no. 2 (May 1994): 346–66.

6. Akira Iriye, "The Failure of Economic Expansionism," in Bernard S. Silberman and H. D. Harootunian, eds., *Japan in Crisis: Essays on Taisho Democracy* (Princeton: Princeton University Press, 1974).

7. Carter Eckert, *Offspring of Empire: The Koch'ang Kims and the Colonial Origins of Korean Capitalism, 1876–1945* (Seattle: University of Washington, 1991), pp. 239–41.

8. See pp. 344–45 in Henry Em's chapter in this volume. See also Hori Kazuo, "East Asia Between the Two World Wars: Industrialization of Japan and Its Ex-colonies," *Kyoto University Economic Review* 64, no. 2 (Oct. 1994): 1–22.

9. Ōmameuda Minoru, *Kindai Nihon no shokuryō seisaku: taigai izon beikoku kyōkyū kōzo no hen'yō* (Kyoto: Minerva shobō, 1993), pp. 181–261.

10. On the fanciful plans for developing Korea before annexation, see Karl Moskowitz, "The Creation of the Oriental Development Company:

Japanese Illusions Meet Korean Reality," *Occasional Papers on Korea*, no. 2 (Mar. 1974): 74–123.

11. Rōyama Masamichi, "Shokumin seisaku no kakuritsu to kokusai kyōchō shugi," *Shokumin* 3, no. 10 (Oct. 1923): 6–9.

12. Yoshii Hironobu, "Chōsen bunka seiji no hiai," *Shokumin* 3, no. 10 (Oct. 1923): 138–43.

13. James Ferguson, *The Anti-Politics Machine: "Development," Depoliticization and Bureaucratic Power in Lesotho* (Minneapolis: University of Minnesota Press, 1994), pp. 9–21. Arturo Escobar, *Encountering Development: The Making and Unmaking of the Third World* (Princeton: Princeton University Press, 1995).

14. Ferguson, pp. 25–73.

15. Kobayashi Hideo, "Senkanki no higashi Ajia: shokuminchi kenkyū o chūshin ni," in Rekishigaku kenkyūkai, comp., *Gendai rekishigaku no seika to kadai II, 3: teikokushugi to gendai minshushugi* (Tokyo: Aoki shoten, 1982); Kobayashi, "Nihon teikokushugi ka no shokuminchi (Dai ichiji sekai taisen ikō)" in *Komazawa daigaku keizaigaku ronshū*, 3 pts., 18 (Mar. 1987): 143–70, 19 (Nov. 1987): 257–81, and 20 (Mar. 1988): 127–60.

16. Kobayashi Yukio, *Nisso seiji gaikō shi* (Tokyo: Yuikaku, 1985); Gaimushō, ed., *Nisso kōshō shi* (Tokyo: Gennando, 1942).

17. Examples of development discourse and the CIRP are so numerous I mention only two here: Chōsen sōtokufu, Shokusankyoku, *Chōsen no kome* (Chōsen sōtokufu, 1927); Ninagawa Arata, ed., *Chōsen sanmai zōshū keikaku* (Chōsen jijōsha, 1927).

18. Yamamoto Miono, "Shokumin seisaku no shintai 1," *Gaikō jihō* 45, no. 530 (Jan. 1, 1927): 96, 101.

19. Yamamoto Miono, "Chōsen sanmai zōshoku keikaku to seron," *Keizai ronsō* 22, no. 1 (Jan. 1926): 142–61.

20. Ibid., pp. 159–60.

21. Yanaihara Tadao, "Chōsen sanmai zōshoku keikaku ni tsuite," in *Yanaihara Tadao zenshū* (hereafter YTZ) (Tokyo: Iwanami shoten, 1963), 1: 709.

22. Yanaihara Tadao, "Chōsen tochi no hōshin," in YTZ, 1: 728.

23. YTZ, 1: 713. Yanaihara Tadao, "Shokumin no shōkyoku oyobi sekkyokuteki igi," *Shokumin* 6, no. 5 (1927): 7. Lecture before the Home Ministry's Bureau of Social Affairs sponsored by Ishokumin mondai kōshū kai.

24. YTZ, 1: 713.

25. YTZ, 1: 720. Emphasis in original.

26. YTZ, 1: 709–12, 721.

27. Kawai Kazuo, *Chōsen ni okeru sanmai zōshoku keikaku* (Tokyo: Miraisha, 1986); Bruce Cumings, *The Origins of the Korean War: Liberation and the Emergence of Separate Regimes, 1945–1947* (Princeton: Princeton University Press, 1981), chap. 2; Cumings, "The Origins and Development of the Northeast Asian Political Economy: Industrial Sectors, Product Cycles, and Political

Consequences," in Frederic C. Deyo, ed., *The Political Economy of the New Asian Industrialism* (Cornell: Cornell University Press, 1987), pp. 44–59.

28. Emiko Ohnuki-Tierney, *Rice as Self: Japanese Identities Through Time* (Princeton: Princeton University Press, 1993), p. 31.

29. Ohnuki-Tierney's calculation is "food consumption = ritual = agricultural production = human reproduction = polity." Based on this equation, Ohnuki-Tierney asserts provocatively that rice remains an essentially uncommodified symbol of Japanese cosmology and aesthetics and thus maintains its critical role in a telescoping commensality of family, locale, and Japan (ibid., p. 57; see also chaps. 4–6). Criticism of ahistorical readings of agriculture and identity in the Japan islands has been the life's work of Amino Yoshihiko; see, e.g., his popular work, *Zoku Nihon no rekishi o yominaosu* (Tokyo: Chikuma Primer Books, 1996).

30. Iriye, "The Failure of Economic Expansionism."

31. On the structure of rice procurement and distribution, see Hishimoto Nakaji, *Chōsenmai no kenkyū* (1938), pp. 457–592. For extensive quotations from the rice trade press that give some sense of the place of Korean rice in Japanese markets, see Iinuma Jirō, *Chōsen sōtokufu no beikoku kensa shidō* (Tokyo: Miraisha, 1993), pp. 151–63.

32. Ishibashi Tanzan, "Gaibei no tabekata," 1918; reprinted in *Ishibashi Tanzan zenshū* (Tokyo: Tōyō keizai shinpōsha, 1971), 3: 226–35.

33. *Josei hōkan* (Osaka: Ōsaka mainichi shimbunsha, 1924), p. 469; Maenami Nakako, *Shin josei hōkan* (Tokyo: Sōzōsha, 1934), p. 300. Both are reprinted in *Kindai Nihon josei seikatsu jiten*, 8 vols. (Tokyo: Ōzōsha, 1992).

34. Akira Iriye, *Pacific Estrangement: Japanese and American Expansion, 1897–1911* (Cambridge, Mass.: Harvard University Press, 1971).

35. Naito Hideo, editorial, *Shokumin* 6, no. 11 (Nov. 1927): 2–5.

36. Naito Hideo, editorial, *Shokumin* 6, no. 12 (Dec. 1927): 2–5.

37. Naito Hideo, editorial, *Shokumin* 7, no. 1 (Jan. 1928): 2–5.

38. Under the tutelage of Konoe Atsumarō, Inoue became a researcher for the East Asian Common Culture Society (Tōa dōbunkai). The resident-general of the Japanese protectorate in Korea (1905–10) appointed him to the Korean finance ministry, where he surveyed the economic potential of Korean provinces extensively. He later served as a reformer in the Korean imperial household and president of the *Korea Nichi-nichi* newspaper. After Korean annexation, Inoue set up a private rubber company in Southeast Asia and served as president of the Overseas Development Company (Kaigai kōgyō kabushiki kaisha), which advocated Japanese emigration to Southeast Asia and South America. See Nagami Shichirō, *Kō-A ichi ro: Inoue Masaji* (Tokyo: Tōkō shoin, 1942).

39. Inoue Masaji, "Shokuminchi o sakushu suru zōmai keikaku wa waga kokusaku mujun nari," *Shokumin* 6, no. 3 (Mar. 1927): 6–9; and Inoue, "Kokusai teki seishin undō toshite no kaigai ishokumin no daishimei," *Shokumin* 6, no. 4 (Apr. 1927): 6–9. For a more widely available selection of Inoue's

writings on emigration, see Inoue Masaji, *Iju to kaitaku* (Tokyo: Nihon sho-kumin tsūshinsha, 1930).

40. *Shokumin* 7, no. 2 (Feb. 1928): 57–69. Quoted from original text: O. Henry (pseud., William Sidney Porter), *The Complete Works of O. Henry* (New York: Doubleday, 1953), pp. 967–68.

41. See Inoue Masaji, "Sakoku o saran toshite," *Shokumin* 7, no. 5 (May 1928): 6–11.

42. Carol Gluck, *Japan's Modern Myths: Ideology in the Late Meiji Period* (Princeton: Princeton University Press, 1985); Sheldon Garon, *The State and Labor in Modern Japan* (Berkeley: University of California Press, 1987); Thomas Havens, *Farm and Nation in Modern Japan: Agrarian Nationalism, 1870–1940* (Princeton: Princeton University Press, 1974).

43. On the complexities of the meaning of *minzoku*, see Kevin M. Doak, "What Is a Nation and Who Belongs? National Narratives and the Ethnic Imagination in Twentieth-Century Japan," *American Historical Review* (Apr. 1997): 283–309.

44. *YTZ*, 1: 729–30.

45. Michael J. Hogan, "Corporatism: A Positive Appraisal," *Diplomatic History* 10, no. 4 (Fall 1986): 363–72; Robert Weibe, *The Search for Order, 1870–1920* (New York: Hill and Wang, 1967).

46. *YTZ*, 1: 709–10.

47. *YTZ*, 1: 733–43.

48. Akira Iriye, *Power and Culture: The Japanese-American War, 1941–1945* (Cambridge, Mass.: Harvard University Press, 1981), pp. 128–34, 203–5; Cumings, *Origins of the Korean War*.

49. Michael Robinson, *Cultural Nationalism in Colonial Korea, 1920–1925* (Seattle: University of Washington Press, 1988), pp. 137–41.

50. Kenneth M. Wells, *New God, New Nation: Protestants and Self-Reconstruction Nationalism in Korea, 1896–1937* (Honolulu: University of Hawaii Press, 1990), chaps. 5–7.

51. See, e.g., the recommendations of the 1920 convention of the Japanese Chambers of Commerce in Korea; discussed in Kaneko Fumio, "Sen-kyūhyaku nijū nendai ni okeru Chōsen sangyō seisaku no keisei: Sangyō chōsa iinkai o chūshin ni," in Hara Kaku, ed., *Kindai Nihon no keizai to seiji* (Tokyo: Yamakawa shuppansha, 1986).

52. Tōgō Minoru, *Shokumin seisaku to minzoku shinri* (Tokyo: Iwanami shoten, 1925).

53. Ibid., pp. 48–49, 293–303, 340–45.

54. Mark R. Peattie, "Japanese Attitudes Toward Colonialism, 1895–1945," in Ramon H. Myers and Peattie, eds., *The Japanese Colonial Empire, 1895–1945* (Princeton: Princeton University Press, 1984), pp. 109–14.

55. Tōgō, *Shokumin seisaku*, pp. 51–59.

56. Tōgō Minoru, "Kaigai ni shin Nihon mura o kensetsu seyo," *Shokumin* 6, no. 6 (June 1927): 6–9.

57. Tōgō Minoru, "Jinkō shokuryō mondai to sono taisaku 4," *Seiyū* 353 (Mar. 1930): 60–64. This position was not accepted in Japan until well into the Great Depression with the discontinuation of the CIRP in 1934. The decline in the productivity of metropolitan agriculture because of the importation of cheap colonial rice is analyzed in Yujiro Hayami and V. M. Ruttan, "Korean Rice, Taiwan Rice and Japanese Agricultural Stagnation: An Economic Consequence of Stagnation," *Quarterly Journal of Economics*, 84, no. 4 (Nov. 1970): 562–89.

58. Miwa Kimitada, *Nitobe Inazō and the Development of Colonial Theories and Practices in Prewar Japan* (Tokyo: Sophia University, Institute of International Relations, 1987), p. 13. Contrast Tōgō's interpretation of Momotarō with the wartime uses of the famous children's tale; see John Dower, *War Without Mercy* (New York: Pantheon, 1986), pp. 251–53.

59. Tōgō Minoru, "Kaigai hatten no kiun ni saishite 1," *Shokumin* 7, no. 1 (Jan. 1928): 6–10.

60. Tōgō Minoru, "Naichi oyobi shokuminchi no sotai hihan," *Tōyō* 25, no. 1 (Jan. 1922): 60–61; Tōgō, "Shokuminchi tochi to giseiteki seishin," *Tōyō* 31, no. 3 (Mar. 1928): 16–19.

61. Tōgō Minoru, "Jinkō shokuryō mondai to sono taisaku 5," *Seiyū* 354 (Apr. 1930): 54–59; Tōgō, "Kaigai hatten no kiun ni saishite 3," *Shokumin* 7, no. 3 (Mar. 1928): 6–10.

62. Yamamoto Hiroshi, "Seisan yori mitaru Chōsen mai no shochō to sono shōrai," in Chōsen sōtokufu, *Chōsen sōran* (Keijō: Chōsen sōtokufu, 1934), pp. 203–17.

63. Government-General of Korea, *Annual Report of the Government of Chōsen, 1933/34* (Keijō: Chōsen sōtokufu, 1934), p. 105.

64. Louise Young, *Japan's Total Empire: Manchuria and the Culture of Wartime Imperialism* (Berkeley: University of California Press, 1998).

## Chapter 5: Soon-Won Park, "Colonial Industrial Growth and the Emergence of the Korean Working Class"

1. Examples of such analyses include Chŏn Sŏktam and Ch'oe Yun'gyu, *Chōsen kindai shakai keizaishi*, trans. Kajimura Hideki (Tokyo: Ryūke shōsha, 1978 [1959]); and three works by Kobayashi Hideo: "1930 nendai Chōsen kōgyōka seisaku no tenkaikatei," *Chōsenshi kenkyūkai ronbunshū*, no. 3 (1967); "1930 nendai zenhanki no Chōsen rōdō undō ni tsuite: P'yŏngyang komu kōgyō rōdōsha no genesto o chūshin ni shite," *Chōsenshi kenkyūkai ronbunshū*, no. 6 (1969); and "1930 nendai Nihon chissō hiryō kabushiki kaisha no Chōsen e no shinshutsu ni tsuite," in Yamada Hideo, ed., *Shokuminchi keizaishi no shomondai* (Tokyo: Ajia keizai kenkyūsho, 1973). For examples of North Korean work, see Ri Kuksun, "Hŭngnam piryo kongchang nodongjadŭri kŏrŏon sŭngli ŭi kil," *Yŏksanonmunjip*, no. 4 (1963); and Kwŏn Yŏnguk, "Nihon teikokushugika no Chōsen rōdō jijō," *Rekishigaku kenkyū*, no. 303 (1969).

2. For examples, see Kim Yunhwan, *Han'guk nodong undongsa,* I (Seoul: Ch'ŏngsa, 1982 [1972]); Han'guk nodongchohap ch'ongyŏnmaeng, comp., *Han'guk nodongchohap undongsa* (Seoul: Han'guk noch'ong, 1979); Pak Hyŏnch'ae, *Minjok kyŏngjeron* (Seoul: Han'gilsa, 1978); and Kwŏn Tuyŏng, "Han-guk ŭi sanŏphwa wa nosa kwan'gye yŏn'gu" (Ph.D. diss., Korea University, 1979).

3. Among the numerous literature along this line, a pathbreaking project was the eight-volume series entitled "Studies in the Modernization of the Republic of Korea, 1945–1975," published by the Council on East Asian Studies at Harvard University in 1979–81. As for the dependency development approach, Peter Evans's, Immanuel Wallerstein's, and many other Latin American scholars' works were introduced. Within Korea, Ch'oe Changjip, Pak Hyŏnch'ae, and Im Hyŏnjin, among others, introduced these theories and issues.

4. Most junior researchers in the 1980s were concerned with contemporary historical issues, such as the post-liberation years, the Korean War, the 1950s, and the colonial period, especially 1930s industrial growth and its impact.

5. See the following studies by An Pyŏngjik: *Nihon teikokushugi to Chōsen minshū* (Tokyo: Ochanomizu shobō, 1988); "Nihon chissō ni okeru Chōsenjin rōdōsha keikyū no seichō ni kansuru kenkyū," *Chōsenshi kenkyūkai ronbunshū,* no. 25 (1988); "Shikminchi Chosŏn ŭi koyong kujo e kwanhan yŏn'gu," in Nakamura Tetsu, An Pyŏngjik, et al., eds., *Kŭndae Chosŏn ŭi kyŏngje kujo* (Seoul: Pip'yŏng ch'ulp'ansa, 1989); "Kokumin shokugyō nōryoku shinkokurei shiryō no bunseki," in Nakamura Tetsu et al., eds., *Kindai Chōsen kōgyōka no kenkyū* (Tokyo: Nihon hyōronsha, 1993). For more up-to-date, comprehensive econometric work on colonial industrial growth, see Hori Kazuo, *Chōsen kōgyōka no shiteki bunseki: Nihon shihonshugi to shokuminchi keizai* (Kyoto: Yuhikaku, 1995). Hori's other researches include "Nihon teikokushugi no shokuminchi shihaishi shiron: Chōsen ni okeru honganteki tsukuseki no ichisokumen," *Nihonshi kenkyū,* no. 281 (1986); "1930 nendai Chōsen ni okeru shakaiteki bungyō no saihensei: Kyŏnggido, Keijōfū no bunseki o tsujite," in Nakamura et al., eds., *Kindai Chōsen kōgyōka no kenkyū·* and "Shokuminchiki Keijōfū no toshi kōzō," *Keizai ronsō,* nos. 154–56 (1994). See also Chŏng Chaejŏng, "Chosŏn ch'ongdokpu ch'ŏldoguk ŭi koyong kujo," in Nakamura, An, et al., eds., *Kŭndae Chosŏn ŭi kyŏngje kujo;* Soon-Won Park, "The Emergence of a Factory Labor Force in Colonial Korea: A Case Study of the Onoda Cement Factory" (Ph.D. diss., Harvard University, 1985); Kim Nagyŏn, "Singminji Chosŏn ŭi kongŏphwa," in Kang Man'gil, et al., eds., *Han'guksa,* no. 13, *Singminjigi ŭi sahoe kyŏngje* (Seoul: Han'gilsa, 1994); Kim Kyŏngil, *Ilcheha nodong undongsa* (Seoul: Ch'angjakkwa pip'yŏngsa, 1992); and Yu Yŏngik, *Han'guk kŭnhyŏndaesaron* (Seoul: Ilchogak, 1992).

6. In addition to the works cited in note 5, see Carter Eckert, *Offspring of Empire: The Koch'ang Kims and the Colonial Origins of Korean Capitalism* (Seat-

tle: University of Washington Press, 1991); Dennis McNamara, *The Colonial Origins of Korean Enterprise, 1910–1945* (Cambridge, Eng.: Cambridge University Press, 1990); Bruce Cumings, "The Legacy of Japanese Colonialism in Korea," in Ramon Myers and Mark Peattie, eds., *The Japanese Colonial Empire, 1895–1945* (Princeton: Princeton University Press, 1984); and Sŏn Chaewŏn, "Shokuminchi to kōyō seido: 1920, 30 nendai Chōsen to Nihon no hikaku-shiteki kōsatsu" (Ph.D. diss., Tokyo University, 1996).

7. Karl Moskowitz, "Current Assets: The Employees of Japanese Banks in Colonial Korea" (Ph.D. Diss., Harvard University, 1980); Michael Robinson, *Cultural Nationalism in Colonial Korea, 1920–1925* (Seattle: University of Washington Press, 1988); Gi-Wook Shin, *Peasant Protest and Social Change in Colonial Korea* (Seattle: University of Washington Press, 1996).

8. See the works by An Pyŏngjik, Nakamura Tetsu, Hori Kazuo, Kim Kyŏngil, and Kim Nagyŏn cited above. More recent works include Matsunaga Susumu, "1930 nendai Chōsennai rōdōryoku idō ni tsuite," *Keizai ronsō* 147, nos. 1–3 (1991); and Sŏn Chaewŏn, "Shokuminchi to kōyō seido."

9. Hori, *Chōsen kōgyōka*, pp. 28–51.

10. Kim Nagyŏn, "Singminji Chosŏn ŭi kongŏphwa," pp. 59–89; Hori, *Chōsen kōgyōka*, pp. 28–51. Hori (ibid., p. 186) lists several negative legacies of this dualistic colonial industrial development for contemporary Korean capitalism: (1) the Korean economy's abnormally high reliance on the import-export trade, (2) the strong reliance on Japanese production technology, (3) the inferior position of small- and medium-sized enterprises, and (4) the almost total absence of rural industry.

11. Hori, *Chōsen kōgyōka*, p. 96.

12. Ibid., p. 94.

13. This is the time when terms such as "Spring Starvation" and "Barley Hills" were coined to symbolize colonial poverty. The pages of the *Chosŏn* and *Tonga* newspapers were filled with starvation tolls and descriptions of rural misery.

14. See Nakamura, An, et al., eds., *Kŭndae Chosŏn ŭi kyŏngje kujo*, chaps. 1 and 4; and Hori, *Chōsen kōgyōka*, pp. 91–97. For details of the rural crisis and social differentiation in this period, see Gi-Wook Shin, *Peasant Protest and Social Change in Colonial Korea*, chap. 4. For changes in the landlord class in this period, see Hong Sŏngch'an, *Han'guk kŭndae nongch'on sahoe ŭi pyŏndong kwa chijuch'ŭng* (Seoul: Chishiksanŏpsa, 1992).

15. *Chōsen ni okeru rōdōsha sui oyobi bunpū jōtai*, a survey done by the Chōsen tetsudō kyōkai, in July 1928. Other statistical sources for factory and mining workers are Chōsen sōtokufu, Social Affairs Section, *Kōjō oyobi kōzan ni okeru rōdō jōkyō chōsa*, 1933 (survey date: June 1931); Chōsen Chamber of Commerce, *Chōsenjin shokkō ni kansuru ichi kōsatsu*, 1936; and Chōsen sōtokufu, *Chōsen rōdō gijutsu tokei chōsa hōkoku*, 1941, 1942, 1943.

16. Since the 1930 census reported 2.04 million in non-agricultural em-

ployment, this means that nearly half the non-agricultural workers were urban informal-sector workers.

17. Hori, *Chōsen kōgyōka*, pp. 156–59.

18. Sŏn, "Shokuminchi to kōyō seido," pp. 51–56.

19. Hori, *Chōsen kōgyōka*, pp. 110–14. In 1920, the urban population was 3.4 percent of the total.

20. Ibid., pp. 90–91.

21. Ibid., pp. 102–4.

22. Ibid., pp. 158–59.

23. See Prasenjit Duara, *Rescuing History from the Nation* (Chicago: University of Chicago Press, 1995).

24. Hori, *Chōsen kōgyōka*, pp. 169–70.

25. Ibid., pp. 171–72.

26. Ibid., pp. 180–82.

27. Ibid., pp. 172–79.

28. Other terms for this interpretation include "continental logistics base theory" or "munitions industrialization."

29. Hori, *Chōsen kōgyōka*, pp. 182–85. See also Yi Hongrak, "Singminjigi ŭi sahoe kujo," in Kang Man'gil et al., eds., *Han'guksa*, no. 14, *Singminjigi ŭi sahoe kyŏngje II* (Seoul: Han'gilsa, 1994).

30. See An Pyŏngjik, "Nihon chissō ni okeru Chōsenjin rōdōsha keikyū no seichō ni kansuru kenkyū"; Chŏng Chaejŏng, "Chosŏn ch'ŏngdokpu ch'ŏltokuk ŭi koyong kujo"; Soon-Won Park, "Emergence of a Factory Labor Force in Colonial Korea"; and Sŏn, "Shokuminchi to kōyō seido."

31. Nakamura, An, et al., eds., *Kŭndae Chosŏn ŭi kyŏngje kujo*, pp. 395–96; Hori, *Chōsen kōgyōka*, pp. 156–60.

32. Nakamura, An, et al., eds., *Kŭndae Chosŏn ŭi kyŏngje kujo*, pp. 400–401.

33. Yi Hyojae, *Yŏsŏng ŭi sahoe ŭishik* (Seoul: P'yŏngminsa, 1980), pp. 54–56. For recent studies on colonial female labor, see Yi Chŏngok, "Ilcheha kongŏp nodong e itssŏsŏ ŭi minjok kwa sŏng" (Ph.D. diss., Seoul National University, 1990); and Kang Ihsu, "1930 nyŏndae myŏnbang taekiŏp yŏsŏng nodongja ŭi sangt'ae e kwanhan yŏn'gu: nodong kwajŏng kwa nodong t'ongje rŭl chungsim ŭro" (Ph.D. diss., Ewha Woman's University, 1991).

34. See notes 1 and 2 to this chapter.

35. Kwŏn Hyŏkt'ae, "Nihon teikokushugi to Chōsen no sanshigyō: shokuminchi tokushitsu to shite no nijū kōzō," *Chōsenshi kenkyūkai ronbunshū*, no. 28 (1991); Kim Nagyŏn, "Singminji Chosŏn ŭi kongŏphwa"; Cho Sŏngwŏn, "Shokuminchi Chōsen mensaku mengyō no tenkai kōjō" (Ph.D. diss., Tokyo University, 1993); Sin Yŏnghong, *Kindai Chōsen shakai jigyōshi kenkyū* (Tokyo: Ryokuin shobō, 1984); Gi-Wook Shin, *Peasant Protest and Social Change in Colonial Korea*; Eckert, *Offspring of Empire*; McNamara, *Colonial Origins of Korean Enterprise, 1910–1945*; Soon-Won Park, *Colonial Industrialization and Labor in Korea: The Onoda Cement Factory* (Cambridge, Mass.: Harvard University Asia Center, 1999).

36. The Chōsen Chissō construction sites in the Hŭngnam and Pujŏn River area demanded around 20,000 construction workers daily (*Tonga ilbo*, Apr. 18, 1927).

37. Kobayashi, "1930 nendai zenhanki no Chōsen rōdō undō," pp. 110–15.

38. Ibid., pp. 147–48.

39. Soon-Won Park, "The First Generation of Korean Skilled Workers: The Onoda Cement Sŭnghori Factory," *Journal of Korean Studies* 7 (1990): 84–85.

40. Hirose Seizan, "Shokuminchiki Chōsen ni okeru kan assen tōken rōdōsha: dogai assen o chūshin ni," *Chōsen gakuhō*, no. 155 (Nov. 1995): 115–32.

41. Ibid., pp. 132–35.

42. Chōsen sōtokufu, *Jikyoku taisaku chōsakai shimon toshinshō* (Keijō: Chōsen sōtokufu, 1938), pp. 103–22.

43. Recently teenage Korean women mobilized by force as "comfort girls" have received wide attention through the efforts of the Korean public, feminist groups, and international human rights organizations. They were mobilized as civilian personnel to support the military in the name of "Chŏngsindae" (Corps of volunteers).

44. Han Insu, "Han'guk ŭi kongŏp chidae hyŏngsŏng," in *Inch'ŏn Kyodae Nonmunjip*, no. 12 (1963).

45. Ch'oe Chinho, "Han'guk ŭi kungnae in'gu idong e kwanhan yŏngu" (M.A. thesis, Seoul National University, 1981), p. 21.

46. Sŏn, "Shokuminchi to kōyō seido," pp. 56–57; Hori, *Shiteki bunseki*, p. 116.

47. Hori, *Chōsen kōgyōkai*, pp. 110–14.

48. Hirose, "Shokuminchiki Chōsen ni okeru kan assen tōken rōdōsha," pp. 115–32; Sŏn, "Shokuminchi to kōyō seido," pp. 56–57.

49. Chŏng Chaejŏng's and Soon-Won Park's case studies confirm the role of Japanese skilled workers as lower-level labor managers in the Railway Bureau machinery plants and Japanese Onoda cement factory in Sŭnghori, near P'yŏngyang, throughout the 1920s and 1930s.

50. Sŏn, "Shokuminchi to kōyō seido," pp. 214–40.

51. An Pyŏngjik, "Singminji Chosŏn ŭi koyong kujo," p. 204. It was only in 1942 that the colonial government began to consider compulsory education for the first time, which it planned to implement in 1946.

52. This rate is quite similar to Japan's at the beginning stage of capitalism around 1900. Sŏn's recent study has developed further the parallels between Korean industrial growth in the late 1930s and that of Japan at the turn of the twentieth century.

53. Edward Mason et al., *The Economic and Social Modernization of the Republic of Korea: Studies in the Modernization of the Republic of Korea, 1945–75* (Cambridge. Mass.: Harvard University Council on East Asian Studies, 1980), confirms this argument.

54. Nakamura, An, et al., eds., *Kŭndae Chosŏn ŭi kyŏngje kujo*, pp. 407–9.

55. An's, Chŏng's , and Park's studies all prove these points.

56. Park Soon-Won, "Haebang hu Samch'ŏk siment'ŭ kongjang ŭi chae-gŏn kwajŏng, 1945–1960," *Kyŏngje sahak*, no. 17 (1993).

57. Park Soon-Won, "Singminji kongŏphwagi nodongja kyegŭp ŭi sŏng-jang," in Kang Man'gil et al., eds., *Han'guksa*, no. 14, *Singmijigi ŭi sahoe kyongje II* (Seoul: Han'gilsa, 1994), pp. 82–83.

58. Ibid., p. 83; Park, "Haebang hu Samch'ŏk siment'u kongjang ŭi chae-gŏn kwajŏng."

59. Chŏng Chaejŏng, "Chosŏn ch'ongtokbu ch'ŏltoguk ŭi koyong kujo."

60. See An's and Soon-Won Park's studies on the Chōsen chissō hiryō and the Onoda Cement factories, respectively.

61. An, "Singminji Chosŏn ŭi koyong kujo," pp. 416–17.

62. For a study of Korean white-collar workers in colonial banks, see Mo-skowitz, "Current Assets."

63. Yi Hyojae, *Yŏsŏng ŭi sahoe ŭisik*, p. 156; Park, *Singminji kongŏphwagi*, p. 82.

64. Hori, *Chōsen kōgyōka*, p. 105; Sŏn, "Shokuminchi to kōyō seido," p. 106.

65. Kim Yunhwan, *Han'guk nodong undongsa*, I, chap. 3. For more recent works on the colonial labor movement, see Kim Kyŏngil, *Ilcheha nodong un-dongsa* (Seoul: Ch'angjak kwa pip'yŏngsa, 1992); and Kim Kyŏngil, "Ilcheha komunodongja ŭi sangt'ae wa nodong undong," *Sahoesa nonmunjip*, no. 9 (1987).

66. Soon-Won Park, "Making Colonial Policies in Korea: The Factory Law Debate, Peace Preservation Law, and Land Reform Laws in the Interwar Years," *Korean Studies* 22 (1998): 41–61.

67. Kim Yunhwan, *Han'guk nodong undongsa*, pp. 141–48; Chōsen sōto-kufu, Keimukyoku, *Saikin ni okeru Chōsen chian jōkyo* (1933), pp. 146–47.

68. Kim Yunhwan, *Han'guk nodong undongsa*, pp. 139–43.

69. Chōsen sōtokufu, *Saikin ni okeru Chōsen chian jōkyo* (1933), pp. 149–50.

70. Kobayashi Hideo, "1930 nendai zenhanki no Chōsen rōdō undō ni tsuite," pp. 115–22.

71. Ibid., pp. 120–22.

72. Ibid., p. 122.

73. George E. Ogle, *South Korea: Dissent Within the Economic Miracle* (Lon-don: Zed Books, 1990), pp. 3–7. Ogle also explains that the United States added to this politicization of Korean labor through the anti-Chŏnp'yŏng (Communist-led General Council of the National Labor Unions) campaign by the U.S. Military Occupation Government during 1947–48.

74. Ibid., p. 6. This practice resurfaced during the period of 1960s eco-nomic growth and continues in today's Korean industrial relations. The Chun Doo Hwan government reinforced it by making the labor-manage-ment council system legally mandatory in any plant employing more than 100 workers. The Sixth Republic continues this practice. Management's

payment of union officers was still customary in Korean labor relations until the labor law reform in 1996 and was continuously criticized as a critical impairment of worker autonomy and independence at the bargain table.
75. Ibid., pp. 20–22.

### Chapter 6: Daqing Yang, "Colonial Korea in Japan's Imperial Telecommunications Network"

1. "Nai-Sen renraku denwa kaitsū shiki," *Chōsen* 213 (Feb. 1933): 156–58; "Nai-Sen denwa kaitsū shiki," *Teishin kyōkai zasshi* (hereafter *TKZ*) 294 (Feb. 1933): 32. Throughout this paper, I use Keijō to refer to Seoul under Japanese rule.

2. For example, Gregory Henderson writes of Japan's "correct" "order of priority" in building a good communications network in colonial Korea in a short time, and further notes that its efforts were "on the order of 500 times as intensive as that of the Portuguese during half a millennium in Angola or Mozambique"; see his "Japan's Chosen: Immigrants, Ruthlessness and Developmental Shock," in Andrew C. Nahm, ed., *Korea Under Japanese Colonial Rule: Studies of the Policy and Techniques of Japanese Colonialism* (Kalamazoo: Western Michigan University, 1973), p. 267. Kirk Y. K. Kim similarly refers to "Japan's impressive program to build up physical equipment in Korea after 1931," which included telegraph and telephone installation ("The Impact of Japanese Colonial Development on the Korean Economy," in C. I. Eugene Kim and Doretha E. Morimore, eds., *Korea's Response to Japan: The Colonial Period, 1910–1945* [Kalamazoo: Western Michigan University, 1977], p. 95). Michael Robinson provides a more balanced summary in Carter J. Eckert et al., eds., *Korea Old and New: A History* (Seoul: Ilchogak Publishers, 1990), pp. 269–70.

3. For example, Chōsen sōtokufu, *Chōsen teishin jigyō enkaku shōshi* (Keijō, 1914); Chōsen sōtokufu, *Chōsen teishin jigyō enkaku shi* (Keijō, 1938); and Ōkurashō, Kanrikyoku, comp., *Nihonjin no kaigai katsudō ni kansuru rekishiteki chōsa* (Tokyo, 1947–50), 9: 105–11. To my knowledge, however, no postwar scholarly work in Japanese has addressed this subject.

4. Andrew J. Grajdanzev, *Modern Korea* (New York: International Secretariat of the Institute of Pacific Relations, 1944). Not surprisingly, official histories of telecommunications published in postwar Korea regard the colonial period as an era of "ordeal and stagnation"; see, e.g., Taehan min'guk ch'aeshinbu, *Chon'gi t'ongsin saŏp p'alssimnyŏnsa* (Seoul, 1966), and *Chŏn'gi t'ongsin paengnyŏnsa* (Seoul, 1985).

5. A recent work on telecommunications development in Korea mentions the colonial period in two sentences, citing government monopoly and the installation of automatic telephones; see James F. Larson, *The Telecommunications Revolution in Korea* (Hong Kong: Oxford University Press, 1995), p. 32.

6. Daniel R. Headrick, *Tentacles of Progress: Technology Transfer in the Age of Imperialism, 1850–1940* (New York: Oxford University Press, 1988), p. 98. On the role of telecommunications in European expansion, see also Headrick, *The Tools of Empire: Technology and European Imperialism in the Nineteenth Century* (New York: Oxford University Press, 1981).

7. On European submarine cable networks to East Asia in the late nineteenth century, see Jorma Ahvenainen, *The Far Eastern Telegraphs: The History of Telegraphic Communications Between the Far East, Europe and America Before the First World War* (Helsinki: Soumalainen Tiedeakatemia, 1981).

8. Kaiteisen shisetsu jimusho, *Kaiteisen hyakunen no ayumi* (Tokyo, 1971), pp. 114–15. The 1876 treaty allowed Japan to set up a post office in Pusan.

9. *71 zahō* (Jan. 13, 1876), quoted in Nakamura Fumio, "Gunji tsūshin shiwa," *Denpa to juken*, Oct. 1983, p. 98.

10. Although China supplied the funds and technicians for construction, Koreans began to receive training for low-level maintenance work, making this the first large-scale technological infusion in modern Korea; see Kang Ung, "19-seiki matsu Chōsen no denki tsūshin gijutsu," *Kagakushi kenkyū*, 2d series, 30, no. 179 (Autumn 1991): 161–62.

11. Ibid., pp. 164–67.

12. Peter Duus, *Abacus and Sword: Japanese Penetration of Korea, 1895–1910* (Berkeley: University of California Press, 1995), pp. 184–86.

13. See Okamoto Keijirō's reminiscences at a roundtable talk in 1935 (Chōsen sōtokufu, Teishinkyoku, *Teishin shūi* [Keijō, 1935], pp. 10–16). Okamoto was one of the seven Japanese sent to Korea in May 1905.

14. Chōsen sōtokufu, *Chōsen teishin jigyō*, pp. 107–9, 133; Kaiteisen shisetsu jimusho, *Kaiteisen hyakunen no ayumi*, p. 171.

15. Chōsen chōsatsugun, Shireibu, *Chōsen bōto tōbatsu shi* (Keijō, 1913), p. 50.

16. Kangoku keibi denwa kensetsubu, *Kangoku keibi denwa kensetsubu jigyō gaiyō hōkoku* (Seoul, n.d.), pp. 1–2, 13.

17. Ibid., pp. 21–29, 53–54; Nihon denshin denwa kōsha, *Denshin denwa jigyō shi*, hereafter cited as *DDJS* (Tokyo, 1961), 6: 341; Chōsen sōtokufu, Teishinkyoku, *Teishin shūi*, pp. 16–18.

18. Taehan min'guk ch'aeshinbu, *Chŏn'gi t'ongsin saŏp*, p. 432.

19. Robinson, in Carter Eckert et al., p. 282; *DDJS*, 6: 333. The total budget for communications for the same year was ¥7 million (*Chōsen sōtokufu tōkei nenpō*, 1930, p. 320).

20. "Chōsen gyōsei" henshōkyoku, *Chōsen tōchi hiwa* (Keijō, 1937), pp. 228–46. For this and other examples of GGK's use of telecommunications, see ibid., pp. 58–59, 119.

21. *DDJS*, 6: 331.

22. This was based on a nationwide survey of nearly all 7,000 telegraph offices throughout Japan proper between July 10 and 21, 1933. The large

share of nongovernment use is noteworthy. See Teishinshō, Denmukyoku, *Denpō kōryō jōkyō ni kansuru chōsa* (Tokyo, 1935).

23. Grajdanzev, *Modern Korea*, p. 199. In fact, a large portion of "official" *muryō* telegrams dealt with telegraph operations.

24. On the telephone in prewar Japan, see Ishii Kanji, *Jōhō, tsūshin no shakaishi* (Tokyo: Yūhikaku, 1994), esp. pp. 162–201.

25. Grajdanzev, *Modern Korea*, pp. 199–200.

26. Although distribution by profession of subscribers is not certain, a rough count of the 200 Koreans with the surnames Yi and Kim in a Japanese-language "Who's Who in Korea" shows 112 with telephone numbers. Those in business and medical and legal practices were most likely to have telephones, followed by those in government service, with agriculture coming last. See Chōsen shinbunsha, *Chōsen jinji kōshiroku* (Keijō, 1935).

27. Taehan min'guk ch'aeshinbu, *Chŏn'gi t'ongsin saŏp*, pp. 551–52. This relative decline would probably have been more rapid without the efforts by Korean educators to promote *han'gŭl*. For *han'gŭl* education, see Seok Choong Song, "Grammarians and Patriots: Han'gul Scholars' Struggles for the Preservation of Their Linguistic Heritage," in Kim and Mortimore, eds., *Korea's Response to Japan*, pp. 165–87.

28. "Onmon denpō ni kansuru jikō," in Japanese Ministry of Communications Papers, vol. 249; hereafter cited MOC Papers.

29. *DDJS*, 6: 348. *Hannin* was the lowest class among all officials, whereas *chokunin* was the second highest rank in the pre-1945 Japanese bureaucracy. For a lucid explanation of these ranks, see B. C. Koh, *Japan's Administrative Elite* (Berkeley: University of California Press, 1989), pp. 16–17.

30. This is in striking contrast to the 18–25 percent of *chokunin* positions occupied by Koreans in the main government offices in Keijō during the 1930s. See Carter Eckert, "Total War, Industrialization, and Social Change in Late Colonial Korea," in Peter Duus et al., eds., *The Japanese Wartime Empire, 1931–1945* (Princeton: Princeton University Press, 1996), pp. 25–26.

31. See Yamada Tadatsugu's speech at the First Meeting of Local Communications Bureau Chiefs in Korea, *Chōsen teishin* 277 (June 1941): 11.

32. On the latter point, see James R. Beniger, *The Control Revolution: Technological and Economic Origins of the Information Society* (Cambridge, Mass.: Harvard University Press, 1986).

33. See, e.g., Michael A. Barnhart, *Japan Prepares for Total War, 1919–1941* (Ithaca: Cornell University Press, 1987), pp. 22–76.

34. For details on this development, see my unpublished Ph.D. dissertation, "The Technology of Japanese Imperialism: Telecommunications and Empire-building, 1895–1945" (Harvard University, 1996), chap. 5. See also Nihon denshin denwa kōsha, *Denki tsūhsin jishu gijutsu kaihatsu-shi: hansō denwa-hen*, hereafter cited as *DTJGKS* (Tokyo, 1972), pp. 11–12, 73–82.

35. Sakamoto Mamoru, *A Lion Aroused: Conversations with Shigeyoshi Matsumae* (Tokyo: Tokai University Press, 1986), p. 135.

36. Kajii Tsuyoshi, "Tōyō denki tsushinmō yori mitaru Manshū no chii," *TKZ* 330 (Feb. 1936): 168–76.

37. *Dai-74-kai teikoku gikai shūgiin gijiroku* (Tokyo, 1939), p. 383. Writing in *Teishin kyōkai zasshi*, Tamura estimated 47 telegraph circuits and 28 telephone circuits would be required by 1944 to link Japan, Manchukuo, and North China; see Tamura Kenjirō, "Tōa denki tsūshin seisaku to Kokusai denki tsūshin kabushiki kaisha no kakujū ni tsuite," *TKZ* 369 (May 1939): 37.

38. For their daily breakdown and destinations, see Okumura Kiwao, "Nai-Sen renraku denwa no kaitsū," *TKZ* 294 (Feb. 1933): 42–43.

39. Shindō Seiichi, "Nichi-Man denshin denwa ni tsuite," *TKZ* 330 (Feb. 1936): 147.

40. On construction of the Japan–Korea–Manchukuo route, see Kuroiwa Kōichi, "Nichi-Man renraku denwa kēburu no kensetsu ni tsuite," *Denki tsūshin* 3, no. 11 (1940): 94–95; *DTGJKS*, pp. 209–42. Murakami Motonori, then in charge of technical operations, estimated that, construction and transportation of equipment included, total manpower mobilized for the entire project in both Korea and Japan reached 2 million; see his "Nichi-Man rūto kōji kansei no higan," ibid., p. 222. On the laying of submarine cables linking Korea with Japan, see also Kaiteisen shisetsu jimusho, *Kaiteisen hyakunen no ayumi*, pp. 258–74.

41. Teishinshō, Kōmukyoku, "Nichi-Man renraku denwa shisetsu sekkei keikaku yōkō" (Feb. 1937), MOC Papers, vol. A-1; *DDJS*, 6: 400–401.

42. "Nichi-Man renraku denwa kōji shunkōsu," *TKZ* 375 (Nov. 1939): 120–26.

43. "Tōa kokusai chōkyori yūsen denki tsushinmō tōsei yōkō an," drafted by the Engineering Bureau in November 1937, as reprinted in *DTGJKS*, pp. 206–7.

44. Teishinshō, Kōmukyoku, "Nai-Sen-Man renraku kēburu kaisen no hoshu tōsei o hitsuyō to suru riyū" (Oct. 1936), MOC Papers, vol. A-1: 1–6.

45. Carolyn Marvin, *When the Old Technologies Were New* (New York: Oxford University Press, 1987), pp. 4, 5.

46. Suzuki Takeo, *Chōsen no keizai* (Tokyo: Nihon hyōronsha, 1942), pp. 296–98.

47. Dōmoto Tatsuo, "Tairiku heitan kichi shōron," *Chōsen* 296 (Jan. 1940): 43–62.

48. Mitarai Tatsuo, ed., *Minami Jirō* (Tokyo: Kankōkai, 1957), pp. 440–43.

49. "Kōi, yusō mondai no shin kyokumen," *Chōsen sangyō nenpō* (1943).

50. *Tōyō keizai tōkei geppō* 4, no. 11 (Nov. 1942): 11.

51. "Bōeki, jinkō o chūshin to suru Chōsen Hokushi keizai kankei," *Chōsen bōeki kyōkai tsūhō*, July 1938.

52. Chōsen sōtofuku, *Chōsen sangyō keizai chōsakai kaigiroku* (Keijō, 1936), pp. 555–58.

53. Chōsen sōtofuku, *Chōsen sōtokufu jikyoku taisaku chōsakai shimon tōshinsho* (Keijō, 1938), pp. 55–61.

54. Mitarai Tatsuo, ed., *Minami Jirō*, p. 443.

55. See Kwantung Army Colonel Katakura Tadashi's speech at the 1938 conference, in Chōsen sōtofuku, *Chōsen sōtokufu jikyoku*, pp. 457–58.

56. Suzuki, *Chōsen no keizai*, pp. 299–302.

57. Quoted in *Nai-Sen-Man renraku denwa no hoshu ni kansuru uchiawase kaigi gijiroku* (Oct. 5–10, 1936), MOC Papers, vol. A-0. Hanamichi may be compared to the runway in a fashion show in the West.

58. *Nai-Sen-Man renraku denwa no hoshu.*

59. On the legal framework of Japan's colonial administration and the status of the Korean GGK, see Edward I-te Chen, "The Attempt to Integrate the Empire: Legal Perspectives," in Ramon H. Myers and Mark R. Peattie, eds., *The Japanese Colonial Empire, 1895–1945* (Princeton: Princeton University Press, 1984), esp. pp. 262–66.

60. *Nai-Sen-Man renraku denwa no hoshu.*

61. Ibid.

62. Letter from Yamada Tadatsugu to Kajii Tsuyoshi, Sept. 4, 1937, MOC Papers, vol. 311.

63. Murakami Motonori, *Ichi gijitsusha no shōgai* (Tokyo: Kankōkai, 1966), pp. 373–74; Teishin gaishi kankōkai, *Teishin shiwa* (Tokyo: Denki tsūshin kyōkai, 1962), 2: 250.

64. Statement by Chief of Inspection Section of MOC Teshima at a meeting in Tokyo on Nov. 18, 1936, in MOC Papers, vol. A-0.

65. Murakami, in *DTGJKS*, p. 203; Murakami, *Ichi gijutsusha no shōgai*, pp. 374–75. An MOC official sarcastically compared issuance of the ordinance after completion of the construction in Korea to the issuance of a marriage certificate after the rape.

66. See, e.g., *Tōa denki tsūshin kyōgikai dai-2-kai kaigi gijiroku* (1940).

67. Director of GGK Bureau of Communications (Yamada) to Director of MOC Bureau of Telecommunications (Yasuda), Dec. 25, 1940, in MOC Papers, vol. 311.

68. Teishinshō, "Tōa denki tsūshin gyōmu kyōtei ni okeru Chōsen teishin no tōjisha chii ni kansuru iken" (Jan. 7, 1941), MOC Papers, vol. 311.

69. Teishinshō, Denshinkyoku, *Tōa denki tsūshin ni kansuru gyōmu kyōtei teiketsu kaigi gijiroku* (Jan. 1940), pp. 32–33, 38–41. For the agreement reached, see "Oboegakisho," dated Jan. 22, in MOC Papers, vol. 311.

70. Fukakawa Toshio, speech at a panel discussion published in Teishinshō, Denshinkyoku, *Tōa denki tsūshin* (1942).

71. For a discussion of *naisen ittai* policy implications, see Carter Eckert, *Offsprings of Empire: The Koch'ang Kims and the Colonial Origins of Korean Capitalism, 1876–1945* (Seattle: University of Washington Press, 1991), pp. 236–38.

72. "Chōsen no kansei, gyōsei mondai o Hagiwara shi ni kiku," in Chōsen shiryō kenkyūkai, *Chōsen sōtofuku kansei to sono gyōsei kikō* (Tokyo, 1962), pp. 25–27.

73. James W. Carey, *Communication as Culture: Essays on Media and Society* (Boston: Unwin Hyman, 1989), p. 212.

74. *DDJS*, 6: 245–47. The following non-loaded cable circuits remained open at war's end: Korea–Japan (17 for telegraph, 24 for telephone), Korea–Manchukuo (6, 9), Keijō–Beijing (1, 0), intra-Korea (5, 21).

75. George McCune, *Korea Today* (New York, 1950), pp. 160–61.

76. Nakamura Fumio, "Gunji tsūshin shiwa," *Denpa to juken* (Jan. 1983): 64–65; James A. Huston, *Guns and Butter, Powder and Rice: U. S. Army Logistics in the Korean War* (Selinsgrove, Penn.: Susquehanna University Press, 1989), pp. 297–98.

77. Chen Ende, "Kang-Mei yuan-Chao qiangxiu dianlan," *Yudian wenshi tongxun* 14 (Dec. 1993): 19. Chen headed the Chinese engineering group that carried out the repair work between late 1951 and early 1952.

78. This was also true of the railroad linkage to Japan. Since the Korean railroads had been built by Japan, repair and replacement items were borrowed from the Japanese National Railways and airlifted to Korea within a very short time; see Roy E. Appleman, *South to the Naktong, North to the Yalu* (Washington, D.C.: Office of the Chief of Military History, 1960), p. 261.

### Chapter 7: Kenneth M. Wells, "The Price of Legitimacy: Women and the Kŭnuhoe Movement, 1927–1931"

1. In the case of Ireland, Margaret Ward ("National Liberation Movements and the Question of Women's Liberation: The Irish Experience," in Clare Midgley, ed., *Gender and Imperialism* [Manchester: Manchester University Press, 1998], pp. 104–22) cautions against too easily accepting the position of some feminist writers that Irish nationalism was essentially masculinist or hostile to female aspirations. Ward does not find anything in the Irish experience, however, that contradicts Anne McClintock's assertion that "nowhere has feminism in its own right been allowed to be more than a maidservant to nationalism" (ibid., p. 106), and thus Ward's argument in the end amounts to little more than a plea for recognition of actions women have actually taken to put their imprint on the direction of nationalism.

2. Gerder Lerner, *The Creation of Feminist Consciousness: From the Middle Ages to Eighteen-Seventy* (New York: Oxford University Press, 1993). See especially her comments in the Preface.

3. It is sometimes claimed that the first women's journal was the educational journal *Yŏja chinam*, founded in May 1908. Whereas this journal was founded for women, it was not founded by or edited by women. See Yung-Chung Kim, ed. and trans., *Women of Korea: A History from Ancient Times to 1945* (Seoul: Ewha Women's University Press, 1976), p. 253.

4. The recent publication edited by Elaine H. Kim and Chungmoo Choi, *Dangerous Women: Gender and Korean Nationalism* (New York: Routledge,

1998), which concentrates on the South Korean experience, confirms this observation. I take Margaret Ward's point ("National Liberation Movements," p. 105) that one cannot simply assume that women's subordination in regimes growing out of nationalist struggles is an inevitable result of the way such struggles are conducted, but we are looking for patterns and connections, not inevitabilities.

5. Prasenjit Duara, *Rescuing History from the Nation: Questioning Narratives of Modern China* (Chicago: University of Chicago Press, 1995).

6. The division, of course, is not so neat: Donna Haraway's *Primate Visions: Gender, Race, and Nature in the World of Modern Science* (New York: Routledge, 1989) is difficult to situate in this sense.

7. In particular, the following works have helped me in my preparation of this chapter: Carroll Smith-Rosenberg, *Disorderly Conduct: Visions of Gender in Victorian America* (New York: Knopf, 1985); Linda J. Nicholson, *Gender and History* (New York: Columbia University Press, 1986); Gerder Lerner, *The History of Patriarchy* (New York: Oxford University Press, 1986); and Lerner, *Creation of Feminist Consciousness*.

8. This position is clear especially in Giambattista Vico's orations of 1708, "De nostri temporis studiorum ratione" (trans. Elio Gianturco as *On the Study Methods of Our Time* [Ithaca: Cornell University Press, 1990]). One wonders whether cultural Marxism is belated recognition of Marx's own debt to Vico.

9. Ellen Karolina Sofia Key (1849–1926), a Swedish feminist and reformer, wrote *Love and Marriage* (1910) and *The Renaissance of Motherhood* (1913). August Bebel (1840–1913) is the author of *Woman and Socialism* (ca. 1909), which was translated into Korean by Pae Sŏngnyong in the 1920s. Both writers were introduced to Koreans via Japan.

10. *Tongnip sinmun*, Sept. 29, 1896, editorial.

11. *Tongnip sinmun*, Sept. 9, 1898. The Sept. 27 and 28, 1898, issues of *Tongnip sinmun* give a figure of around 100 women attending the meeting, but Kim Yŏngdŏk et al. (*Han'guk yŏsŏngsa: Kaehwagi–1945* [Seoul: Ewha Women's University Press, 1972], p. 61) consider this a journalistic exaggeration. The Ch'anyanghoe was also called the Sunsŏng hakkyo puinhoe.

12. Elisabeth Eide, *China's Ibsen: From Ibsen to Ibsenism* (London: Curzon, 1987), p. 74.

13. Yi Yunhŭi, *Han'guk minjokjuŭiwa yŏsŏng undong* (Seoul: Tosŏ ch'ulp'an sinsŏwŏn, 1995), pp. 68–73.

14. Figures provided in Lee Chong-sik, *The Politics of Korean Nationalism* (Berkeley: University of California Press, 1963), pp. 113–15.

15. Chōsen sōtokufu, Keimukyoku (Government-General of Korea, Police Affairs Bureau), Dec. 5, 1919, Kokei 34497: "Daikan minkoku aikoku fujinkai kenkyo no ken"; and Jan. 22, 1920, no. 1536: "Daikan aikoku fujinkai ni kansuru ken." See also the trial records of the Taehan min'guk aeguk puinhoe and Taehan min'guk ch'ŏngnyŏn wegyodan: Taegu District Court, June

29, 1920, in *Chōsen tōchi shiryō*, 10 vols. (Tokyo: Kankoku shiryō kenkyūsho, 1970–72), 5: 739ff.

16. See Kim Yŏngdŏk et al., *Han'guk yŏsŏngsa: Kaehwagi–1945*, pp. 376–79.

17. This characterization is particularly clear in Nam Hwasuk, "1920 nyŏndae yŏsŏng undongesŏ ŭi hyŏptong chŏnsŏn kwa kŭnuhoe" (Masters thesis, Seoul National University, 1989).

18. "Segye samdae munje ŭi p'agŭp kwa Chosŏnin ŭi kago yŏha," *Kaebyŏk* 2 (July 1920), editorial.

19. Ch'anghae Kŏsa (pseud.), "Kajŏng chedo ŭi ch'ŭngmyŏn'gwan," *Kaebyŏk* 3 (Aug. 1920): 23–28.

20. Eide, *China's Ibsen*, pp. 83–84.

21. "Che myŏngsa ŭi Chosŏn yŏja haebanggwan," *Kaebyŏk* 4 (Sept. 1920): 28–45.

22. Eide, *China's Ibsen*, p. 75.

23. Kim Yŏngdŏk et al., *Han'guk yŏsŏngsa: Kaehwagi–1945*, p. 262. The same applies to Yung-Chung Kim, *Women of Korea* (Seoul: Ewha Women's University Press, 1976), p. 263, the English abridged version of the above.

24. Yi Kyun'yŏng, *Sin'ganhoe yŏn'gu* (Seoul: Yŏksa pip'yŏngsa, 1993).

25. The version of the manifesto I have translated from is reprinted in *Yŏsŏng* 3 (1989), as "Charyo: Kŭnuhoe."

26. *Tae-Il minjok sŏnŏn* (Seoul: Iru munsa, 1972).

27. "Kŭnuhoe chosabu," *Kŭnu*, 1929: 82.

28. Ibid., pp. 83–93. For a fuller account of Kŭnuhoe activities, see Nam Hwasuk, "1920 nyŏndae yŏsŏng undongesŏ ŭi hyŏptong chŏnsŏn kwa kŭnuhoe," chap 3.

29. One Kyŏnggi Province committee member, U Pongun ("Yŏsŏng kakcha ŭi ŭisikchŏk unwŏn esŏ," *Kŭnu*, 1929: 58), described this fracas as "a manifestation of ambition or of too many ideologues."

30. Hŏ Chŏngsuk, "Kŭnuhoe undong ŭi yŏksajŏk chiwiwa tangmyŏn immu," *Kŭnu*, 1929.

31. Chŏng Ch'ilsŏng, "Ŭisikchŏk kaksŏng ŭrŏ put'ŏ—musan puin saenghwal esŏ," *Kŭnu*, 1929: 35–37.

32. Chang Rin, "Nodong puin ŭi chojikhwarŭl," *Kŭnu*, 1929: 33–34.

33. "Charyo: Kŭnuhoe," *Yŏsŏng* 3 (1989).

34. Nam Hwasuk, "1920 nyŏndae yŏsŏng undongesŏ ŭi hyŏptong chŏnsŏn kwa kŭnuhoe," p. 18.

35. Ibid., pp. 24ff. Somewhat inconsistently, on p. 35, Nam remarks that the conservative program of the Christian women appealed to the masses—because of their ignorance!

36. Kim Hwallan, for example, explains her decision to bob her hair in her autobiography: Helen Kim (edited by J. Manning Potts), *Grace Sufficient* (Nashville, Tenn.: Upper Room, 1994), pp. 82–83. She also defended her action in *Tonggwang*. She was criticized not only by men (though some de-

fended her) but by women even of her own or younger generation. See *Yun Ch'iho ilgi* (Seoul: Kuksa p'yŏnch'an wiwŏnhoe, 1987): entry for Jan. 25, 1932.

37. Pak provides an account of this divorce and its significance for Korean women in her autobiography: Pahk Induk, *September Monkey* (New York: Harper Brothers, 1954).

38. One commentator remarked that although the definition of the "new woman" was not clear, generally a woman was considered such if she had received the "new" education and was regarded as an "old woman" if she had not; a "new woman" looked forward to all women being recognized as "main actors" (*chuin'gong*) in both family and society; see Hong Pyŏngsŏn, "Kajŏng puin haebange," *Kŭnu*, 1929: 27–28.

39. *Yun Ch'iho ilgi*, entry for Nov. 30, 1927. I have not been able to ascertain which auditorium was used. Kim Hwallan was the only female speaker in a week-long series of lectures on various aspects of public life.

40. Helen Kim, *Grace Sufficient*, pp. 87–88.

41. *Yun Ch'iho ilgi*, entry for Jan. 16, 1932.

42. Ibid., entries for Dec. 22, 1926, Nov. 30, 1927, Mar. 18, 1933, June 2 and Oct. 25, 1934, and Aug. 7–9, 1935.

43. Ibid., Apr. 19, 1933.

44. Ibid., Oct. 28, 1931, Feb. 12, 1932, Sept. 27, 1934, Jan. 26 and 29, 1935, Feb. 27, 1935, and Mar. 30, 1935. Yun was for many years unconvinced that Pak Indŏk and Sin Hŭngu, a principal leader of the YMCA, were sexually involved, but even when he later began to suspect they were, he did not consider it something to make an issue of. See his diary entries for Jan. 10, 1938, and Nov. 9, 1940.

45. Ibid., Oct. 26, 1931. See also the entry for Dec. 16, 1932, in which Yun argues that if she had not divorced her husband, Pak would "never have been able . . . to promote the welfare of rural women."

46. Ibid., Nov. 12, 1927, and June 29, 1929.

47. Ibid., Aug. 2, 1925, and Mar. 14, 1927.

48. Ibid., Mar. 28, 1935.

49. Yi Chongnin, "Mŏnjŏ ŭngbunŭi ŭimurŭl ta hara," *Kŭnu*, 1929: 28–30.

50. Song Chinu, "Kajŏng puin kyoyuge," *Kŭnu*, 1929: 31.

51. Kim Tonghyŏk, "Mŏnjŏ kyoyang ŭrŏput'ŏ," *Kŭnu*, 1929: 32.

52. Yi Siwan, "Kŭnu undong ŭi ŭiŭi wa chŏnmang," *Kŭnu*, 1929: 39.

53. Yi Sŏnghwan, "Kŭmhu ŭi Chosŏn yŏsŏng undong: tohoejirŭl ttŏnasŏ modŭn himŭl nongch'one," *Kŭnu*, 1929: 41–43.

54. Yi Siwan, "Kŭnu undong ŭi ŭiŭi wa chŏnmang," p. 40.

55. "Kwagŏ illyŏn'gan ŭi Chosŏn yŏsŏng undong," *Tonggwang* 3, no. 28 (Dec. 1931): 12.

56. William Morris, *Collected Works* (London: Longmans, Green, 1915), 23: 267.

57. Chŏng Ch'ilsŏng, in *Pyŏlgŏn'gon* 9, no. 1 (no. 69) (Jan. 1934): 21.

58. Yi Siwan, "Kŭnu undong ŭi ŭiŭi wa chŏnmang," p. 38.

59. Pae Sŏngnyong, "Chosŏn yŏsŏng undong ŭi hyŏnjae," *Kŭnu*, 1929: 14–20. Regarding Bebel, see notes 9 and 63 to this chapter.

60. "[Monogamy] was the first form of the family to be based, not on natural, but on economic conditions — on the victory of private property over primitive, natural communal property" (Friederich Engels, *The Origin of the Family, Private Property, and the State*, in Alice S. Rossi, ed., *The Feminist Papers: From Adams to Beauvoir* [New York: Columbia University Press, 1973], p. 482).

61. Bertrand Russell, *A History of Western Philosophy* (London: George Allen & Unwin, 1961), p. 129.

62. Hŏ Chŏngsuk, "Kŭnuhoe undong ŭi yŏksajŏk chiwiwa tangmyŏn immu," *Kŭnu*, 1929. Hŏ Chŏngsuk had earlier argued, at the end of 1927, that the policies and direction of the Korean women's movement would be determined by the participation of the female proletariat, but in her later writing she reflects more strongly the doctrine of historical stages then current in Korean socialism; see Hŏ Chŏngsuk, "Puin undong kwa puin munje yŏn'gu III: Chosŏn yŏsŏng chiwinŭn t'ŭksu," written Dec. 25, 1927, and printed in *Tonga ilbo* on Jan. 5, 1928, p. 7. Hŏ's views on the economic determination of women's position were upheld even by many nonsocialist members, such as Sin Chŏnggyun, who nevertheless advanced a Marxist analysis of the economic stages that have led to the present form of women's bondage: see Sin's "K-Hyŏng ege tŭrinŭn kŭl," *Kŭnu*, 1929: 74–81.

63. In this connection it is interesting to note that Bebel's influence also led to some indulgence in a nostalgic view of women's past, in the idea of a Golden Age in prehistoric times. The strongest expression of this nostalgia flowed from the pen of Tusŏng (pseudonym: Small Star). Tusŏng located the woman question as the central issue in the contemporary global condition of change and uncertainty. Women were related to society as an organism, and their demand for freedom and equality denoted their intention to work as useful members of society in the struggle for the eradication of poverty and exploitation. But the traditional view of womanhood as something innate and immutable had prevented women from joining this task, specifically by making them economically subservient to men. Here, Tusŏng attacked the tradition that the position and function of women were biologically determined. On the contrary, she argued, biological research indicated that men and women evolved together as the highest form of animal life. History and anthropology showed, further, that humans originally lived happily together in a primitive communist era (*wŏnsi kongsan sidae*) in which women's constitutions and mental powers were no whit inferior to men's: indeed, women were largely in control and men served them by hunting and defending them against attack, but otherwise they were not necessary. This situation lasted for several millennia. What destroyed this utopia was the development of production and consequent division of labor, leading to slavery and then wage slavery and sexual exploitation, of which women be-

came the double prey. Thus matrilocal, matrilineal society gave way to a patriarchal order; in Korea, *ch'ulga wein* (on leaving home for marriage one becomes a stranger to one's own family) originally applied to men, not women. See Tusŏng, "Puin kangjwa: kyŏngje chojik ŭi pyŏnch'ŏn kwa puin ŭi chiwi," *Kŭnu*, 1929: 44–49. These ideas find striking echoes in recent South Korean historiography. See, e.g., Han'guk minjungsa yŏn'guhoe, comp., *Han'guk minjungsa I* (Seoul: P'ulpit, 1986), pt. I.

64. H-Saeng, "P'yŏngnon," *Kŭnu*, 1929: 50–55.

65. Ibid., p. 51.

66. Yi Kiyŏng, "Puin ŭi munhakchŏk chiwi," *Kŭnu*, 1929: 63–66.

67. Han Sin'gwang, "Kŭnu undonggwa chaejŏng pangch'ime taehayŏ," *Kŭnu*, 1929: 67–69.

68. Some surveys were carried out, however, and the findings are important: it is thus all the more regrettable that the organization was not able to act on the findings in any concrete or coordinated fashion. See Pak Hosin, "Yŏjikkong pangmun'gi," *Kŭnu*, 1929: 70–73.

69. H-Saeng, "P'yŏngnon," p. 53.

70. The journals *Tto hana ŭi munhwa* (Alternative culture) and *Yŏsŏng* (Women), begun in the 1980s, and the various law-reform movements of the past decade are obvious indicators of this. See Seongsook Moon, "Begetting the Nation: The Androcentric Discourse of National History and Tradition in South Korea," in Elaine H. Kim and Chungmoo Choi, eds., *Dangerous Women*, pp. 33–66. There are similarities in the pattern of experiences of Korean and South African women; see Anne McClintock, "'No Longer in a Future Heaven': Women and Nationalism in South Africa," *Transition* 51 (1991): 104–23.

*Chapter 8: Kyeong-Hee Choi, "Neither Colonial nor National: The Making of the 'New Woman' in Pak Wansŏ's 'Mother's Stake 1'"*

This essay has been in the making for a long time, and I am grateful to many friends, colleagues, and students who have generously given me their comments and editorial assistance.

EPIGRAPHS: Ernest Renan, "What Is A Nation?" (1882), in Homi K. Bhabha, ed., *Nation and Narration* (London: Routledge, 1990), p. 11; Anne McClintock, "Family Feuds: Gender, Nationalism and the Family," *Feminist Review* 44 (Summer 1993), special issue on "Nationalisms and National Identities," p. 61; and Na Hyesŏk, "Narŭl itsiannŭn haengbok," *Sinyŏsŏng* 2, no. 6 (July 1924): 38.

1. Homi Bhabha, "Anxious Nations, Nervous States," in *Supposing the Subject*, ed. Joan Copjec (London: Verso, 1994), p. 216.

2. Virginia Woolf, *Three Guineas* (1938; rpt., New York: Harcourt Brace Jovanovich, 1966), pp. 107, 109.

3. Quoted in Lydia H. Liu, "The Female Body and Nationalist Discourse: Manchuria in Xiao Hong's *Field of Life and Death*," in Angela Zito and Tani E. Barlow, eds., *Body, Subject and Power in China* (Chicago: University of Chicago Press, 1994), p. 157.

4. Deniz Kandiyoti, "Identity and Its Discontent: Women and the Nation," in Patrick Williams and Laura Chrisman, eds., *Colonial Discourse and Post-colonial Theory: A Reader* (New York: Columbia University Press, 1994), p. 377.

5. Kandiyoti's (ibid., p. 380) description of women's general stake in nationalism also applies to Korean women: "On the one hand, nationalist movements invite women to participate more fully in collective life by interpellating them as 'nation' actors: mothers, educators, workers and even fighters. On the other hand, they reaffirm the boundaries of culturally acceptable feminine conduct and exert pressure on women to articulate their gender interests within the terms of reference set by nationalist discourse."

6. Among numerous articles, books, and anthologies, see Andrew Parker et al., eds., *Nationalism and Sexualities* (New York: Routledge, 1992); *Feminist Review*, no. 44 (Summer 1993), special issue on "Nationalisms and National Identities"; and Anne McClintock, Aamir Mufti, and Ella Shohat, eds., *Dangerous Liaisons: Gender, Nation, and Postcolonial Perspectives* (Minneapolis: University of Minnesota Press, 1997). See also three works by Partha Chatterjee: "Colonialism, Nationalism, and Colonialized Women: The Contest in India," *American Ethnologist* 16 (1989): 622–33; "The Nationalist Resolution of the Women's Question," in KumKum Sangari and Sudesh Vaid, eds., *Recasting Women: Essays in Colonial History* (New Delhi: Kali Press, 1989), pp. 233–53; and *The Nation and Its Fragments: Colonial and Postcolonial Histories* (Princeton: Princeton University Press, 1993), esp. chap. 6, "The Nation and Its Women."

7. For a collection of essays focused on women's life in colonial and post-colonial contexts, see Kalpana Ram and Margaret Jolly, eds., *Maternities and Modernities: Colonial and Postcolonial Experiences in Asia and the Pacific* (Cambridge, Eng.: Cambridge University Press, 1998).

8. Most of the contributions in Elaine H. Kim and Chungmoo Choi, eds., *Dangerous Women: Gender and Korean Nationalism* (New York: Routledge, 1998), critically examine the notion of a Korean national subject, deconstructing it as a male subject. For the relationship between the Korean nationalist movement and women's issues, see also Chapter 7 by Kenneth M. Wells in this volume; and Yung-Hee Kim, "Under the Mandate of Nationalism: Development of Feminist Enterprises in Modern Korea, 1860–1910," *Journal of Women's History* 7 (1995): 120–36.

9. Among the most recent publications, see *The Comfort Women: Colonialism, War, and Sex*, ed. Chungmoo Choi, special issue, *positions: east asia cultures critique* 5, no. 1 (Spring 1997).

10. Marianne Hirsch, "Maternity and Rememory: Toni Morrison's Beloved," in Donna Bassin et al., eds., *Representations of Motherhood* (New Haven: Yale University Press, 1994), p. 93.

11. Pak Wansŏ, "Ŏmma ŭi malttuk (Mother's stake) 1" (1980), in Pak, *Kŭ kaŭl ŭi sahŭl tongan* (Three days that autumn) (Seoul: Nanam, 1991), pp. 137–79; "Ŏmma ŭi malttuk 2" (1981), in ibid., pp. 181–222; and "Ŏmma ŭi malttuk 3," *Chakka segye* no. 8 (Spring 1991): 152–67. For English versions of parts 1 and 2, see Yu Youngnan, trans., "Mother's Stake 1," in *Pŏnyŏk iran muŏt singa* (Seoul: Taehaksa, 1991), pp. 173–227; and Kim Miza and Suzanne Crowder Han, "Mother's Hitching Post 2," *Korea Journal* 39, nos. 1–2 (1999).

12. The terms *pando* and *pandoin* were used during the Japanese colonial period to refer to Korea and Koreans. In my personal correspondence with Pak Wansŏ of July 29, 1995, I addressed the question why the name "Chosŏn" never appears in her text. She replied that at the time of her writing of "Mother's Stake 1," 1980, "Chosŏn" was still associated with North Korea and that she might have avoided using the word due to the political atmosphere.

13. "Mother's Stake 1" does not mention a specific year. According to Pak's biographical data, however, it is certain that the temporal setting of the story is 1938. For the most recently published chronology of Pak's life and work, see Pak Wansŏ et al., *Haengbokhan yesulga ŭi ch'osang* (Seoul: Ungjin, 1992), pp. 227–35.

14. Pak, *Kŭ mant'ŏn singa nŭn nuga ta mŏgŏssŭlkka* (Seoul: Ungjin, 1992), pp. 77–79.

15. "By the end of Japanese rule in 1945 there was not one aspect of Korean life that lay unaffected by the pervasiveness and will of Japanese rule" (Carter J. Eckert et al., *Korea Old and New: A History* [Seoul: Ilchogak, 1990], p. 254).

16. Pak, "Mother' Stake 1" (1980), trans. Yu Youngnan, p. 180. Further references to Pak's text are cited in the text in parentheses.

17. On New Women and modern Korean female writers, see Kim Yŏngdŏk, "Han'guk kŭndae ŭi yŏsŏng kwa munhak," in Kim Yŏngdŏk et al., *Han'guk yŏsŏngsa: kaewagi–1945* (Seoul: Ewha Woman's University Press, 1972), pp. 349–421; Sŏ Chŏngja and Pak Yŏnghye, "Kŭndae yŏsŏng ŭi munhak hwaltong," in *Han'guk kŭndae yŏsŏng yŏn'gu* (Seoul: Asia yŏsŏng munje yŏn'guso, Sukmyŏng Women's University, 1987), pp. 185–237; Han'guk yŏsŏng sosŏl yŏn'guhoe, ed., *P'eminichŭm kwa sosŏl pip'yŏng: kŭndaep'yŏn* (Seoul: Han'gilsa, 1995); Kim Mihyŏn, *Han'guk yŏsŏng sosŏl kwa p'eminich'ŭm* (Seoul: Sin'gu munhwasa, 1996); and Yi Sanggyŏng, "Yŏsŏng ŭi kŭndaejŏk chagipyŏhyŏn ŭi yŏksa wa ŭiŭi," *Minjong munhaksa yŏn'gu* 9 (1996): 55–91.

18. The English translations of passages in "Mother's Stake 1" are largely taken from Yu, unless otherwise indicated by the citation of double page numbers in parentheses. When given, the second page number(s) refer(s) to *Kŭ kaŭl ŭi sahŭl tongan* and the translation of the citation is mine. I am in-

debted to Gregory N. Evon and Kenneth M. Wells for help in finding English expressions for Korean words.

19. Kang Insuk, "Pak Wansŏ sosŏl e nat'anan tosi ŭi yangsang," in Kwŏn Yŏngmin et al., *Pak Wansŏron* (Seoul: Saminhaeng, 1991), p. 283.

20. Published separately in three parts over a decade, the parts of "Mother's Stake" trilogy have received an intriguingly uneven reception. Part 3 (1991) has attracted the fewest remarks understandably because it is the most recent publication of the three and a kind of epilogue to the earlier parts. Receptions of Parts 1 and 2 divide asymmetrically by the gender of the critics. "Mother's Stake 2" has been highly and widely praised largely by male critics as an excellent example of the "literature of the national division" and "national literature." In contrast, "Mother's Stake 1" (1980) has received little analytic attention and is treated merely as a background for Part 2.

Yi Namho, for instance, provides an analysis of the meanings of the term *malttuk* (stake or tether) in Pak Wansŏ's work, but in his actual analysis, "Ŏmma ŭi malttuk 1" is missing. He examines instead "Ŏmma ŭi malttuk 2," "Nakto ŭi aidŭl" (Children of paradise), "P'omal ŭi chip" (House of bubble), and "Yŏindŭl" (Women) (see Yi, "Malttuk ŭi sahoejŏk ŭimi," *Pak Wansŏron*, pp. 317–23). In their recent work on Korean literary history, Kim Yunsik and Chŏng Houng, for instance, do not refer to "Mother's Stake 1" and mention the "Mother's Stake" trilogy only in terms of the wounds and healing of the trauma left by the Korean War, which constitutes the theme of Part 2 (*Han'guk sosŏlsa* [Seoul: Yeha, 1993], p. 437).

21. O Seŭn, "Pak Wansŏ sosŏl sogŭi 'omoni wa ttal' motif," in An Suksŏn et al., *Han'guk yŏsŏng munhak pip'yŏngnon* (Seoul: Kaemunsa, 1995), pp. 217–41.

22. In colonial times, Korean male intellectuals such as Kim Kijin, An Hamkwang, and Paek Chŏl, who played an important role in shaping cultural and literary debates in their times, intervened in the New Womanhood debates from the 1920s on; they imposed their nationalist and socialist perspectives, giving the nation primacy over gender. See Kyeong-Hee Choi, "Colonialism and Korean Women: The Images of the New Woman in the 1920s and 1930s," paper read for the conference "After 'Orientalism': East Asia in Global Cultural Criticism," Apr. 1992, University of California, Berkeley, unpublished. Although I do not have space to elaborate on this issue in this chapter, one of the most serious consequences of the *lack* of decolonization in South Korea in the post-liberation era has been the unchallenged hegemony of state discourses and nationalist perspectives over women's issues.

23. Among others, see O Sukhŭi, "Han'guk yŏsŏng undong e kwanhan yŏn'gu: 1920 nyŏndae rŭl chungsim ŭro," M.A. thesis, Ewha University, 1988, pp. 129–52; Sin Yŏngsuk, "Ilcheha sinyŏsŏng ŭi yŏnae, kyŏrhon munje," *Han'guk hakpo* 45 (1986): 182–217; and Chŏn Taeung, "'Sinyŏsŏng kwa kŭ munjejŏm," *Yŏsŏng munje yŏn'gu* 5/6 (1976): 351–62.

24. Chang Hajin, "Yŏryu myŏngsa tŭrŭi ch'inil haengjŏk: Kim Hwallan, Mo Yunsuk, Pae Sangmyŏng, Yi Sukjong, Song Kŭmsŏng . . . ," _Yŏksa pip'yŏng_ 9 (1990): 100–11.

25. Brenda O. Daly and Maureen T. Reddy, "Introduction," in Daly and Reddy, eds., _Narrating Mothers: Theorizing Maternal Subjectivities_ (Knoxville: University of Tennessee Press, 1991), p. 2.

26. According to Pak's biographical data, this occurred when Pak was three years old.

27. In Pak's description the backyard of this house is filled with various nut trees and fruit plants and the front yard is "big" enough for all the village people to enjoy themselves in festivity (117). If the chrysanthemum and the sword—to use Benedict Ruth's formulation—describes Japan under the _samurai_ class, one might call Korea under _yangban_ rule a world of the ink brushes and Korean chrysanthemums, respectively symbolizing moral integrity and literary cultivation.

28. The incommensurability of certain historical experiences between men and women is suggested in Joan Kelly, "Did Women Have a Renaissance?," in Kelly, _Women, History and Theory: Essays of Joan Kelly_ (Chicago: University of Chicago Press, 1984), pp. 19–50.

29. Carole Pateman, "The Fraternal Social Contract," in John Keane, ed., _Civil Society and the State: New European Perspectives_ (London: Verso, 1988), p. 104 (the second emphasis is mine). For MacCannell's notion, see Juliet Flower MacCannell, _The Regime of the Brother: After the Patriarchy_ (London: Routledge, 1991), esp. pt. I: "The Theory and History of the Regime of the Brother," pp. 9–40.

30. _Sijipsari_ is an explicit example of the implementation of Neo-Confucian ideology by the Chosŏn dynasty's founding fathers beginning with Chŏng Tojŏn. For the consequences of Confucian legislation for women, see Martina Deuchler, _The Confucian Transformation of Korea: A Study of Society and Ideology_ (Cambridge, Mass.: Harvard University, Council on East Asian Studies, 1992), pp. 231–81. The nuclearization of the family system requires that women assume a greater role in child-rearing. For a sociological overview of the changes in the Korean family, see Lee Dongwon, "The Changes in the Korean Family and Women," _Yŏsŏnghak_, May 1985, pp. 376–95. For a historical analysis of the relationship between the nuclear family system and mothering in the West, see Elizabeth Fox-Genovese, _Feminism Without Illusions: A Critique of Individualism_ (Chapel Hill: University of North Carolina Press, 1991), pp. 124–31.

31. On the intense bonding between mother and son in the absence of the father, Hortense Spillers offers useful insights with her analysis of the case of slavery: "Mama's Baby, Papa's Maybe: An American Grammar Book," _Diacritics_ 17 (1987): 65–81.

32. Omma's region of origin, near Songdo, also explains her unusual zeal for modernity. As the capital of the Koryŏ kingdom, prior to the Chosŏn

dynasty, the Songdo region was not as tightly integrated into the Chosŏn dynasty's upper-class ideology as the regions around Seoul. Indeed, this region, which was well known for its commercial activities, was more open to the modern capitalist order than other areas of Korea. Although the text does not make explicit the relationship between Omma's exceptional modern endeavor and the characteristics of her region, it is useful to take into account that Omma's class consciousness and morality might not exactly represent those of typical *yangban* members of the Chosŏn dynasty and that her desire for modernity might have been colored by the progressive characteristics of her region. I am grateful to Professor Nak-chung Paik for reminding me of these points.

33. Chungmoo Choi, "Korean Women in a Culture of Inequality," in Donald N. Clark, ed., *Korea Briefing, 1992* (Boulder, Colo.: Westview, 1992), p. 107.

34. In his famous essay on adopting a Japanese-style name, Yi Kwangsu used the term *naichi*. In "Ch'angssi wa na" (The change of the name and me), originally published in the *Maeil sinbo* (Daily news) on Apr. 20, 1940, Yi wrote: "The state allowed Koreans to experience 'Japan and Korea as a single body (*naisen ittai*).' The ones who should lead this movement are indeed Koreans. What else can we desire for other than our becoming not different from those in the *naichi*" (cited from Im Chongguk, *Ch'inil munhangnon* [Seoul: P'yŏnghwa, 1966], p. 285).

35. On the study of female modernity and fashion in general, see Elizabeth Wilson, *Adorned in Dreams: Fashion and Modernity* (Berkeley: University of California Press, 1985).

36. The Korean indigenous clothing (*hanbok*) for women is characterized by complete covering of the figure of the female body with long skirts and veils, the binding of breasts, and a sharp distinction between married and single statuses through the style as well as the length of the hair.

37. In the 1920s, the reform of women's clothing was one of the main agendas of the changes in Korean women's lives taken up by both Western missionary educators as well as by *sinyŏsŏng* pioneers including Kim Wŏnju and Na Hyesŏk. For an instance of public dialogue among "principal New Women," see Na Hyesŏk, "Puin ŭibok kaeryang munje: Kim Wŏnju hyŏng ŭi ŭigyŏn e taehayŏ," originally published in *Tonga ilbo*, Sept. 28–Oct. 1, 1921; reprinted in Na Hyesŏk, *Kaja chukŭrŏ, ppari ro kaja* (Seoul: Osangsa, 1985), pp. 36–46. Although initiated by New Women pioneers, the modernization of Korean women's clothing was institutionally propagated through girls' school uniforms. For the history of modernization of women's clothing, see Yu Sukyŏng, *Han'guk yŏsŏng yangjang pyŏnch'ŏnsa* (Seoul: Iljisa, 1990).

38. The term *kungmin hakkyo* appears for the first time in the text, in place of the *sohakkyo* (elementary school) often used earlier, only when Omma decides to send Na to a primary school inside the gates of Seoul. Historically,

the term *kungmin hakkyo* was not used until 1941 when the Japanese colonial government mandated the new term for elementary school as part of its assimilation policy. Associated with Japanese imperial citizenship, the term *kungmin hakkyo* had been among the most visible vestiges of Japanese colonialism. In 1995, the Ministry of Education in South Korea decided to remove this term from public use, and *ch'odŭng hakkyo* is now used to refer to elementary school.

39. Misao Miyoshi, *As We Saw Them: The First Japanese Embassy to the United States, 1860* (Berkeley: University of California Press, 1979), p. 182.

40. Louis Althusser, "Ideology and Ideological State Apparatuses (Notes Towards an Investigation)," in Althusser, *Lenin and Philosophy and Other Essays*, trans. Ben Brewster (New York: Monthly Review, 1971), p. 143.

41. For a detailed analysis of Pak's use of the trope of hands for her portrayal of Na's transition to modernity, see Kyeong-Hee Choi, "'Omma ŭi malttuk 1' kwa yŏsŏng ŭi kŭndaesŏng," *Minjong munhaksa yŏn'gu* 9 (1996): 118–39. This piece explores Na's ambivalence about touching her teacher's hand, a point whose significance I did not sufficiently discuss in this chapter.

## Chapter 9: Michael D. Shin, "Interior Landscapes: Yi Kwangsu's *The Heartless and the Origins of Modern Literature*"

I thank the following for their assistance and helpful comments and critiques of various drafts of this article: Walter K. Lew, Paul S. Nam, and Professors Kim Yŏngmin, Michael Robinson, Carolyn P. So, and Ann S. Lee.

EPIGRAPHS: Kim Hyŏn, "Yi Kwangsu munhak ŭi chŏnpanchŏk kŏmt'o," in Kim Hyŏn, ed., *Yi Kwangsu* (Seoul: Munhak kwa chisŏngsa, 1977), p. 11; Yŏm Sangsŏp, "Na wa P'yeho sidae," *Sin ch'ŏnji* (New world), Feb. 1954, reprinted in *Yŏm Sangsŏp chŏnjip* (Seoul: Min'ŭmsa, 1994), 12: 210; Pierre Macherey, *A Theory of Literary Production*, trans. Geoffrey Wall (London: Routledge, 1978), p. 96.

1. See, e.g., *Kyŏnghyang sinmun*, Feb. 9, 1949. He was arrested on Feb. 7, together with his former colleague, the historian Ch'oe Namsŏn.

2. I use the term "Chosŏn" instead of "Korea" because it was the term used by writers at the time. "Korea" is best used as a translation of "Hanguk," which was not widely used until after 1945.

3. For survey articles on scholarship on Yi Kwangsu, see Kim Hyŏn, "Yi Kwangsu munhak"; and Kim Yŏngmin, "Nam-bukhan esŏ ŭi Yi Kwangsu munhak yŏngusa chŏngni wa kŏmt'o," in Yŏnsei taehakkyo, Kukhak yŏnguwŏn, ed., *Ch'unwŏn Yi Kwangsu munhak yŏn'gu* (Seoul: Kukhak charyowŏn, 1994).

4. See, e.g., Michael Edson Robinson, *Cultural Nationalism in Colonial Korea, 1920–1925* (Seattle: University of Washington Press, 1988).

5. Most notably, Cho Tongil, who has argued against the modernity of

*Mujŏng*; see Cho Tongil, *Han'guk munhak t'ongsa* (Seoul: Chisik sanopsa, 1989), pp. 436–41.

6. For an example of this approach, see Yi Tongha, *Yi Kwangsu* (Seoul: Tonga ilbosa, 1992).

7. In a recent monograph, Kim Yŏngmin has demonstrated that the term *sin sosŏl* was not used as a genre designation until the 1930s. Before that time, the term was not a proper noun and was mainly used in advertisements to announce the publication of new novels. See Kim Yŏngmin, *Han'guk kŭndae sosŏlsa* (Seoul: Sol, 1997).

8. Ch'oe Wŏnsik, *Han'guk kŭndae sosŏlsaron* (Seoul: Ch'angjak kwa pip'yŏngsa, 1986), pp. 11–12.

9. Kim Tongin, *Ch'unwŏn yŏn'gu* (Seoul: Ch'unjosa, 1959), p. 184. Although Kim Tongin worked with Yi Kwangsu on the journal *Chosŏn mundan* (The Chosŏn literary world) in the mid-1920s, their views of literature differed, and Kim Tongin was one of Yi Kwangsu's most vociferous critics. *Research on Yi Kwangsu* is a well-known and unsparing polemic that is extremely dismissive of Yi's literature.

10. For example, Kim Kijin, Kim Tongin, Na Hyesŏk, and Yŏm Sangsŏp.

11. Such experiences were fictionalized in some of his short stories and novels, including the 1936–37 novel *Kŭŭi chasŏjŏn* (His autobiography).

12. Yi Kwangsu, "Munhak iran hao," *Maeil sinbo*, Nov. 10–23, 1916, reprinted in *Yi Kwangsu chŏnjip* (Seoul: Samjungdang, 1963), 1: 506–19.

13. For a discussion of these prefaces and epilogues by Yi Haejo, see Cho Yŏnhyŏn, *Han'guk sinmunhak ko* (Seoul: Ŭlyu munhwasa, 1982), pp. 77–81; and Cho Tongil, *Han'guk munhak t'ongsa*, 4: 217–21.

14. The ideas in this essay were worked out in fuller form in "What Is Literature?"

15. This view seems to have some similarities with leftist critic Im Hwa's (1908–53) later theory of "transplanted literature" (*isik munhak*): e.g., "the history of modern literature in the East is, in truth, the history of the importation and transplantation of Western literature." See Im Hwa, *Sin munhaksa*, ed. Im Kyuch'an and Han Chinil (Seoul: Han'gilsa, 1993), p. 18. See also Kim Yunsik's discussion of Im Hwa's literary histories in Kim Yunsik, *Im Hwa yŏn'gu* (Seoul: Munhak sasangsa, 1989), pp. 506–27. Yi Kwangsu and Im Hwa had very little else in common. Im Hwa was an actor and poet who became one of the leading theorists of the proletarian literary group KAPF (Korean Artista Proletaria Federatio, 1925–35).

16. For an interpretation of the process of translation that has some similarities to Yi Kwangsu's view, see Walter Benjamin, "The Task of the Translator," in *Illuminations*, ed. Hannah Arendt (New York: Schocken Books, 1968).

17. Yi Kwangsu, "Yŏ ŭi chakchajŏk t'aedo," *Tonggwang* (Eastern light), Apr. 1931, reprinted in *Yi Kwangsu chŏnjip*, 16: 191.

18. Kim Yunsik, *Yi Kwangsu wa kŭŭi sidae* (Seoul: Han'gilsa, 1986).

19. Ibid., p. 10.

20. A reference to Karatani's work can be found in Kim Yunsik, "Munhakchŏk p'unggyŏng ŭi palgyŏn: Han'guk kŭndae munhak ŭi kihohakjŏk chŏpkŭn," in his *Han'guk kŭndae sosŏlsa yŏn'gu* (Seoul: Ŭlyu munhwasa, 1986), p. 55. In this essay, he devotes only a little more than two pages to *Mujŏng*, choosing to cover a range of authors including Yi Injik, Chu Yohan, Kim Tongin, and Yŏm Sangsŏp. Kim Yunsik's focus is mainly on a semiotic analysis of *ŏnmun ilch'i* (the correspondence of written and spoken language), but a linguistic treatment of the development of the vernacular is beyond the scope of this chapter. Other literary scholars mentioned in Kim Yunsik's work on Yi Kwangsu include Pierre Macherey, Georg Lukacs, and Lucien Goldmann; see Kim Yunsik, *Yi Kwangsu wa kŭŭi sidae*, p. 685.

21. See Karatani Kojin, "The Discovery of Landscape" and "The Discovery of Interiority," in his *Origins of Modern Japanese Literature*, trans. Brett de Bary (Durham: Duke University Press, 1993), pp. 11–75.

22. Karatani here was following on the ideas of semioticians and theorists such as Roland Barthes. Probably the clearest exposition of these ideas can be found in Roland Barthes, *Elements of Semiology*, trans. Annette Lavers and Colin Smith (New York: Hill and Wang, 1967).

23. Yi Kwangsu, "Uri ŭi isang," *Hak chi kwang*, no. 14 (Nov. 1917): 5.

24. Pak Ch'ansŭng, *Han'guk kŭndae chŏngch'i sasangsa yŏn'gu* (Seoul: Yŏksa pip'yŏngsa, 1992), p. 181.

25. Yi Kwangsu, "Uri ŭi isang," p. 4.

26. Yi Kwangsu, "Ch'ŏnjaeya! ch'ŏnjaeya," *Hak chi kwang*, no. 12 (Apr. 1914): 10.

27. Ch'unwŏn (Yi Kwangsu), "Puhwal ŭi sŏgwang," *Ch'ŏngch'un*, no. 12 (Mar. 1918): 25.

28. Ibid., p. 21.

29. Ibid., p. 26.

30. The titles of the eleven sections are: (1) The Differences in Old and New Meanings; (2) The Definition of Literature; (3) Literature and Emotion; (4) The Materials of Literature; (5) Literature and Morality; (6) The Effect of Literature; (7) Literature and Nationhood; (8) The Types of Literature; (9) Literature and Writing; (10) Literature and Literary Figures; (11) Chosŏn Literature.

31. Yi Kwangsu, "Tuong kwa na," *Chosŏn ilbo*, Jan. 20, 1935, reprinted in *Yi Kwangsu chŏnjip*, 16: 414. For a comparison of Yi Kwangsu's views on art with those of Lu Hsun and Natsume Sōseki, see Kim T'aejun, "Yi Kwangsu ŭi munhangnon: 'Munhak iran hao' rŭl chungsim ŭro," in Yŏnsei taehakkyo, Kukhak yŏnguwŏn, ed., *Ch'unwŏn Yi Kwangsu munhak yŏn'gu*, pp. 123–50.

32. See Yi Kwangsu, "Tuong kwa na," p. 412–13. For a fictionalized account of his initial encounter with Tolstoy's writings, see Yi Kwangsu, *Kŭ ŭi chasŏjŏn*, in *Yi Kwangsu chŏnjip*, 9: 287–93.

33. Yi Kwangsu, "T'olsŭt'oi ŭi insaenggwan," in *Yi Kwangsu chŏnjip*, 16: 236.

34. See, e.g., Yi Kwangsu, "Munhak e ttŭsŭl tunŭn i ege," *Kaebyŏk*, Mar. 1923; reprinted in *Yi Kwangsu chŏnjip*, 16: 46.

35. Yi Kwangsu, "What Is Literature?" p. 507. Page numbers for all future quotations from this article are given directly in the text.

36. Leo N. Tolstoy, *What Is Art?*, trans. Almyer Maude (Indianapolis: Bobbs-Merrill, 1960), p. 49.

37. See, e.g., his "Chanyŏ chungsimnon" (On a child-centered [society]), *Ch'ŏngch'un*, no. 15, Sept. 1918, which was a critique of the negative social effects of filial piety.

38. Tolstoy, *What Is Art?*, pp. 51, 139.

39. Leo N. Tolstoy, *Resurrection*, trans. Aline Delano (New York: Thomas Y. Crowell, 1911), 2: 282. A much abridged translation appeared in the second issue of *Ch'ŏngch'un*.

40. For an early example of such a view, see Kim Tongin, *Chosŏn kŭndae sosŏl ko* (An examination of modern Chosŏn novels), serialized in *Chosŏn ilbo*, July 28–Aug. 16, 1929, reprinted in Kim, *Ch'unwŏn yŏn'gu*, p. 185. See also Yŏm Sangsŏp, "Na wa P'yeho sidae," p. 210.

41. See, e.g., Tolstoy, *What Is Art?*, p. 178.

42. In this chapter, I will not discuss Yi Kwangsu's innovations in language. For an in-depth treatment of this topic, see Ann Sung-hi Lee, "Yi Kwangsu and Early Modern Korean Literature" (Ph.D. diss., Columbia University, 1991), esp. chap. 5: "Language in the Early Writings of Yi Kwangsu." Lee also provides a much more complete analysis of Yi Kwangsu's life and of *Mujŏng* than is attempted here.

43. Yi Kwangsu, "Tuong kwa na," p. 414.

44. As paraphrased in Yi Kwangsu, "Ch'ŏnjaeya! ch'ŏnjaeya!" p. 8. In this article, Yi Kwangsu used the terms "genius" (*ch'ŏnjae*) and "great figure" (*uiin*) interchangeably.

45. This transition can be traced in the following texts: Yi Kwangsu, "Munsa wa suyang" (Authors and cultivation), *Ch'angjo*, no. 8 (Jan. 1921); "Munhak e ttŭsŭl tunŭn i ege" (To those who devote themselves to literature), *Kaebyŏk*, no. 21 (Mar. 1922); "Munhak kangjwa" (Lectures on literature), *Chosŏn mundan*, nos. 1–5 (Nov. 1924–Feb. 1925); all three articles are reprinted in *Yi Kwangsu chŏnjip*, vol. 16.

46. Yi Kwangsu, "Ch'ŏnjaeya! ch'ŏnjaeya!" pp. 10–11.

47. Tolstoy, *What Is Art?*, p. 110.

48. Yi Kwangsu, "Chosŏn minjok ron," *Tonggwang*, June-July, 1933, reprinted in *Yi Kwangsu chŏnjip*, 17: 10.

49. A list of the booksellers that carried the journal appeared in virtually every issue, usually at the very back.

50. *Ch'ŏngch'un* was shut down after the March 1915 issue (no. 6), and Yi Kwangsu left for Japan in September 1915.

51. The notice for the "regular" contest appeared toward the back of each issue, starting from the seventh issue. The notice for the "special" contest appeared in *Ch'ŏngch'un*, no. 7, p. 125.

52. Yi Kwangsu, "Hyŏnsang sosŏl kosŏn yŏŏn," *Ch'ŏngch'un*, no. 12 (Mar. 1918): 97. Yi Kwangsu noted that he did not count an earlier contest in the *Maeil sinbo* because its purpose was not purely literary.

53. For the "regular" contest, the first-place prize for a short story was three wŏn, second place two wŏn, and third place one wŏn; all other prizes were one wŏn or less. For the "special" contest, the amounts were ten, five, and three wŏn for the short story competition, and five, three, and one wŏn for the prose categories. By comparison, the monthly salary for Yi Hyŏngsik, the schoolteacher who is the protagonist of *Mujŏng*, was 35 wŏn. See Yi Kwangsu, *Mujŏng/Kkum* (Seoul: Munhak kwa sasangsa, 1992), p. 86. All quotations from *Mujŏng* are taken from this edition.

54. "Maeho hyŏnsang munye," *Ch'ŏngch'un*, no. 9 (July 1917): 126.

55. Chu Yohan later became famous as a poet and journalist. Although Yi Kwangsu and Chu Yohan were longtime friends, they did not meet until 1919 in Shanghai after the March First movement. At the time of the literary contest, Yi Kwangsu did not know who the author of the story was.

56. For a detailed analysis of this story and the life of Kim Myŏngsun, see Carolyn P. So, "Seeing the Silent Pen: Kim Myongsun, a Pioneering Woman Writer," *Korean Culture*, 15, no. 2 (Summer 1994): 34-40.

57. Chin Sunsŏng was one of the pseudonyms used by Chin Hagmun.

58. *Ch'ŏngch'un*, no. 6 (Mar. 1915).

59. *Ch'ŏngch'un*, no. 13 (Apr. 1918).

60. E.g., the future KAPF critic Pak Yŏnghŭi. See Pak Yŏnghŭi, "Munhaksang ŭro pon Yi Kwangsu," *Kaebyŏk*, Jan. 1925, p. 86.

61. For a detailed discussion of the "I-novel," see Edward Fowler, *The Rhetoric of Confession: Shishōsetsu in Early Twentieth-Century Japanese Fiction* (Berkeley: University of California Press, 1988).

62. See "Yi Kwangsu ssi wa ŭi kyodamnok," *Samchŏlli* (Three thousand *ri*), Sept. 1933, reprinted in *Yi Kwangsu chŏnjip*, 20: 248-49.

63. *Ch'ŏngch'un*, no. 12 (Mar. 1918).

64. *Ch'ŏngch'un*, nos. 9-11 (July-Nov. 1917).

65. Kim Tongin, *Ch'unwŏn yŏn'gu*, pp. 25-26.

66. Ibid., p. 26.

67. *Ch'ŏngch'un*, no. 8 (June 1917).

68. *Ch'ŏngch'un*, no. 7 (May 1917).

69. *Ch'ŏngch'un*, no. 9 (July 1917).

70. The Latin word *translatus* can also mean "transfer," and the root word *latus* means "to carry" or "to bear."

71. The literal meaning of the word "metaphor" is the same as that of "translation": to transport from one place to another. For a discussion of trains as metaphors, see Michel de Certeau, *The Practice of Everyday Life*,

trans. Steven Rendall (Berkeley: University of California Press, 1984), chap. 8, "Railway Navigation and Incarceration."

72. *Söllǔnt'ang* is a kind of beef stew in a milky white broth.

73. According to a note at the end of the story, it was written (or completed—it is not clear) on Jan. 11, 1917. See *Ch'ǒngch'un*, no. 13, p. 82.

74. Published under the pen name *Koju*, or "lonely boat."

75. Yǒm Sangsǒp seems to make the same point in the passage used as an epigraph for this chapter.

76. The translation is from Ann Lee, "Yi Kwangsu and Early Modern Korean Literature," p. 132.

77. Kim Tongin, *Ch'unwǒn yǒn'gu*, p. 23.

78. "To My Young Friend" was written under the pseudonym *Oebae*, which also means "lonely boat."

79. Kim Tongin, *Ch'unwǒn yǒn'gu*, p. 26.

80. In his memoirs, Han Sǔngin, who was a middle school student in the early 1920s, recollected, "In middle school, we fought each other to read *Mujǒng*. . . . [We] did not read other novels because of [our school's] strict rules against [reading novels], but we all read that novel." See Han Sǔngin, *Naega mannan ijilsu ǒmnǔn saramdǔl* (Seoul: Ilwǒl sǒgak, 1988), p. 108.

81. See the advertisements in issues of *Ch'ǒngch'un* from 1918.

82. *Chosǒn mundan* (The Chosǒn literary world) was a literary journal that first appeared in 1924 under the editorship of Yi Kwangsu, and the editorial board included writers such as Kim Tongin, Na Tohyang, and Yǒm Sangsǒp.

83. One such advertisement appeared in the inaugural issue (Nov. 1924).

84. Yi Kwangsu, "Yǒ ǔi chakchajǒk t'aedo," p. 193.

85. Yi Kwangsu, "Chosǒn ǔi munhak," in *Yi Kwangsu chǒnjip*, 16: 199.

86. Yǒm Sangsǒp, "Na wa chayǒnjuǔi," *Sǒul sinmun*, Sept. 30, 1955, reprinted in *Yǒm Sangsǒp chǒnjip*, 12: 219.

87. Kim Yunsik, "Koaǔisik ǔi ch'okǔk kwa chwajǒl," *Munhak sasang*, no. 232 (Feb. 1992).

88. See Ernest Renan, "What Is a Nation?" in Homi Bhabha, ed., *Nation and Narration* (London: Routledge, 1990).

89. For more on this controversy, see Robinson, *Cultural Nationalism in Colonial Korea, 1920–1925*, pp. 64–77, 137–45.

90. Many of the most famous writers of the time participated in the journal, such as Kim Tongin, Chu Yohan, and Yǒm Sangsǒp, and it published now-canonical works such as Kim Tongin's "Kamja" (Potato). Even leftist and left-leaning writers who became famous later in the decade such as Han Sǒrya and Ch'ae Mansik made their debuts in this journal.

91. The short stories were: "Hyǒlsǒ" (Blood writing), *Chosǒn mundan*, no. 1 (Oct. 1924); "H kun ǔl saenggak hago" (Thinking of H), *Chosǒn mundan*, no. 2 (Nov. 1924); "Ǒttǒn ach'im" (One morning), *Chosǒn mundan*, no. 2 (Dec. 1924); and the epistolary story "Sarang e churyǒtt tǒn idǔl" (Those thirsting

for love), *Chosŏn mundan*, no. 4 (Jan. 1925). Even the titles suggest continuities with his earlier stories.

92. Interestingly, Yi Kwangsu's short stories in other publications were very different from those in *Ch'ŏngch'un* and *Chosŏn mundan*, lacking any sign of being a "coded" reflection on writing. For example, "Kasil," *Tonga ilbo*, Feb. 1923, was a fictionalized historical story about a soldier in the Silla period named Kasil, and "Kŏrukhan iŭi chugŭm" (The death of a great man), *Kaebyŏk*, Mar. 1923, was about the execution of Ch'oe Cheu, the founder of the Tonghak peasant movement.

93. See, e.g., the special section on Yi Kwangsu in the Jan. 1925 issue of *Kaebyŏk*.

94. See Roland Barthes, *Writing Degree Zero*, trans. Annette Lavers and Colin Smith (New York: Hill and Wang, 1967), p. 38: "Modernism begins with the search for a Literature which is no longer possible."

*Chapter 10: Clark Sorensen, "National Identity and the Creation of the Category 'Peasant' in Colonial Korea"*

1. By "peasant country" I mean one in which most of the population are small-scale combined subsistence and market cultivators. In 1970 South Korea's population was 59 percent rural; ten years later only 43 percent were. During that decade some three million people moved from rural to urban places, from farming to urban occupations. By 1990 three-quarters of the population lived in urban areas, and only some 15 percent engaged in farming. The rural population has declined steadily in absolute numbers since about 1975.

2. Hwang Sŏgyŏng, *Chang Kilsan* (Seoul: Hyŏnaksa, 1986), set in Hwanghae province during the seventeenth century, is another prominent example of this genre.

3. All quotations in this section come from the first chapter of Pak Kyŏngni's *Land*, in *Pak Kyŏngni chŏnjip 4* (Seoul: Chisik sanŏpsa, 1979), pp. 11–16.

4. The term *nongbu* has the general meaning of "those engaged in agriculture" and is widely used today as equivalent to the English term *peasant* (thus Korean anthropologists render "peasant society" as *nongbu sahoe*). It also has an older, narrower meaning of "hired farmhand," and it is possible that this is the sense Pak intends here.

5. Since the early 1930s Korean literary critics have frequently distinguished between *chŏnwŏn munak* (pastoral literature) and *nongmin munhak* (peasant literature); pastoral literature is written by upper classes to romanticize rural life, whereas peasant literature places the peasants and their bitterness, or *han*, at the center of the work. See, e.g., Han pit, pseud., "Chŏnwŏn munhak kwa nongmin munhak," *Nongmin* 1932, no. 12; and Im Hyŏn'gŭk, "Nongmin munhak ŭi sin kyujŏng," *Nongmin* 1933, no. 2. I have

not used this distinction here partly because this chapter focuses on the earlier period in the 1920s when "peasantry" emerged as a category and before the distinction became popular, and partly because the distinction has often functioned as polemic to dismiss the relevance of literature that certain literary critics have deemed to lack the "proper" social and political consciousness.

6. I use the English term *peasant* here in the sense of people for whom "agriculture is a livelihood and way of life" as opposed to "farmers," who engage in agriculture as "a business for profit" and look upon land simply as capital and commodity. See Robert Redfield, *Peasant Society and Culture* (Chicago: University of Chicago Press, 1956), p. 18. I do not deem peasants a specific class position in the Marxist sense, nor do I mean to imply a low level of culture. I use it as an English gloss for *nongmin* to emphasize the sense of tradition, community, and common way of life implied by that word in twentieth-century Korean; see below for a more detailed discussion of this usage.

7. Kenneth Wells, "The Cultural Construction of Korean History," in his *South Korea's Minjung Movement: The Culture and Politics of Dissidence* (Honolulu: University of Hawaii Press, 1995), p. 25.

8. Cho Tonggöl, *Ilcheha Han'guk nongmin undongsa* (Seoul: Han'gilsa, 1978), p. 19.

9. Pierre Bourdieu, *Distinction: A Social Critique of the Judgement of Taste*, trans. Richard Nice (Cambridge, Mass.: Harvard University Press, 1984), p. 482.

10. Benedict Anderson, *Imagined Communities: Reflections on the Origin and Spread of Nationalism* (London: Verso, 1983).

11. I deliberately use the blunt oral term for commoner (*sangnom*) and base persons (*ch'ŏnnom*) because these are the terms that in my experience peasants most commonly use in frank verbal discourse. Other, more neutral terms obscure the sense of opprobrium that is an integral part of the concepts actually used.

12. Here and throughout the paper I use Koreanized pronunciations of Chinese characters, whether the original text was written in Chinese or Korean.

13. See, e.g., King Sejong's fifteenth-century "Edict for the Promotion of Agriculture," in Peter H. Lee, ed., *Sourcebook of Korean Civilization* (New York: Columbia University Press, 1993), 1: 580.

14. John Stuart Mill, *Principles of Political Economy, Book II: Distribution* (New York: Appleton, 1893), p. 302.

15. James Scarth Gale, *Korea in Transition* (New York: Eaton and Mains, 1909), p. 96.

16. I leave aside here distinctions between families with civil versus military traditions, and between those with access to central government office versus local office, or just those with local prestige. A full analysis of

pre-twentieth-century social stratification in Korea would obviously take these into account.

17. "Chijeŭi," in *Yu Kiljun Nonso sŏ* (Seoul: Iljogak, 1987), pp. 35–63, 83–88.

18. *Maeil sinmun* (Daily news), begun on January 26, 1898, was the first modern daily newspaper published in Korea (there had been weeklies from 1883). It consisted of four pages of editorials, Korean news, foreign news, and cultural commentary written in Korean alphabet without Chinese characters. It lasted a little less than a year, but by the time of its demise other Korean daily newspapers were being published.

19. *Maeil sinmun*, 1898.2.26.

20. Ibid., 1898.4.2.

21. The fact that A-frame Kim was recognized as *yangban* in his local community does not, of course, necessarily mean that he would have been recognized as *yangban* in other contexts.

22. See, e.g., *Maeil sinmun*, 1898.2.26.

23. See Max Weber, *Economy and Society* (Berkeley: University of California Press, 1978), p. 932.

24. Sin Ch'aeho, "Yŏksa wa aeguksim ŭi kwan'gye," in *Tanje Sin Ch'aeho chŏnjip* (Seoul: Ŭryu munhwa sa, 1972), p. 353.

25. *Maeil sinbo* (Daily report) was the daily Korean-language organ of the Japanese colonial government published from August 30, 1910, until 1945. Published in mixed *han'gŭl* and Sino-Korean script, it had been acquired though the forced sale of the independent *Taehan maeil sinbo* (Korean daily report), which had begun in 1905. *Taehan maeil sinbo* had been under the editorship of T. Bethell, who, as a citizen of Britain with whom Japan was allied, had been able to shield the newspaper from too much Japanese interference during the Protectorate (1905–10).

26. The term *hai k'alla* was borrowed from Japan, where it had come to refer in general to those who decked themselves in stylish Western clothes (the exception until after 1945 in Japan). *Gentleman*, however, was not widely used in Japanese, probably because it is phonetically difficult to render in Japanese script.

27. The Japanese term *shina* (pronounced *china* in Korean) was a neologism invented on the model of the English term "China" to refer to what had traditionally been termed *Shūkoku*, "the Middle Kingdom." This was consciously done to decenter China within East Asia. See Stephan Tanaka, *Japan's Orient: Rendering Pasts into History* (Berkeley: University of California Press, 1993), pp. 5–7.

28. See Zenshō Eisuke, *Chōsen kosaku kanshū* (Keijō: Chōsen sōtokufu, 1929), p. 28.

29. Suh Sang-ch'ul, *Growth and Structural Changes in the Korean Economy, 1910–1940* (Cambridge, Mass.: Harvard University, Council on East Asian Studies, 1978), pp. 6–12.

30. Status groups in the terminology used in this chapter.

31. Yi Kwangsu, "Kŭnil Chosŏn yesu kyohoe ŭi kyŏltchŏm," *Ch'ŏng-ch'un,* no. 1 (1917); reprinted in *Yi Kwangsu chŏnjip* (Seoul: Samjungdang, 1962), 17: 20.

32 *Yi Kwangsu chŏnjip,* 17: 170–71.

33. Lee Kwang-rin has documented not only that Yan Fu's Chinese-language translations of Spencer were available in Korea, but that Liang's magazine, *Xinmin congbao,* was also known and available. Several of Liang's important articles and books were translated and published in Korea in the period between 1900 and 1910, and editorials of the period frequently cite Liang's writings. See Lee Kwang-rin, "Korea's Responses to Social Darwin-ism—I," *Korea Journal* 18 (April 1978): 36–47.

34. Pak Talsŏng, "Sigŭp i haegyŏrhal Chosŏn ŭi i tae munje," *Kaebyŏk,* no. 1 (June 1920): 23–29.

35. See, e.g., Yi Kwangsu, "Chungch'u kyegŭp kwa sahoe," *Kaebyŏk,* July 1921, in which he argued for building a progressive intelligentsia.

36. Reprinted in Sin Kyŏngnim, ed., *Nongmin munhangnon* (Seoul: On-nuri, 1983), pp. 353–56.

37. Very approximate translations for "kŭ kkajit nonggunnomdŭl, kŭ kkajit ch'onnomdŭl, kŭ kkajit paessagongnomdŭl" (*Chosŏn nongmin* 1, no. 1 [Dec. 1925]: 4).

38. I remember a discussion among villagers early on during my field-work in rural Kangwŏn province in 1977 in which my host told a group of men I was okay because I did not go around saying "*paeksŏng* this and *paek-sŏng* that."

39. A literal translation for this term would be "coming from the same womb," but it is always used in the sense of brethren or compatriots.

40. *Chosŏn nongmin* 1, no. 1: 18.

41. Serfdom is treated as intermediate between agricultural slavery and free peasantry. (Korean farmers of this period were a free peasantry operat-ing under conditions of high tenancy, in which many did various kinds of paid agricultural labor as well as ran independent farm households, al-though traces of the former system of agricultural slavery could still be found in certain rural villages well into the twentieth century). There is no suggestion in *Chosŏn nongmin* that serfdom is appropriate for describing Ko-rea, and the thrust of this section is to describe a confusing and strange in-stitution albeit a theoretically important one.

42. These terms are the Korean pronunciation of Chinese characters used to write the Japanese words *kosaku* and *kosakujin.* See Kim Pyŏngha, *Han'guk nongŏp kyŏngyŏng sa yŏn'gu* (Seoul: Han'guk chŏngsin munhwa yŏn'guwŏn, 1993), pp. 4–14.

43 *Chosŏn nongmin,* 2, no. 1 (Jan. 1926): 14.

44. Irene Taeuber, *The Population of Japan* (Princeton: Princeton University Press, 1958). Although this was only about 3 percent of the total population of 24 million, the Japanese residents of Korea were concentrated in the cities,

and the Koreans in the countryside. Seoul had about 150,000 Japanese residents (16.3 percent of the population), and most Korean cities had similar proportions of Japanese residents. The Japanese residents usually lived in the most modern, developed sectors of the city.

45 Myron L. Cohen, "Cultural and Political Inventions in Modern China: The Case of the Chinese 'Peasant,'" *Daedalus*, Spring 1993, pp. 151–70.

46. A "return graphic loan" is a term that existed in Classical Chinese that was borrowed in Japanese to express new, usually Western, concepts and then taken up in this new meaning in China. Some of these neologisms actually originated in China before being popularized in Japan and returning to China. See Lydia H. Liu, *Translingual Practice: Literature, National Culture, and Translated Modernity – China, 1900–1937* (Stanford: Stanford University Press, 1995), pp. 33–34; *nongmin* is listed explicitly on p. 329.

47. *Zhonghua nongmin* was published by the Peasant Institute of the Guomindang in Canton in 1926 and 1927.

48. "Important Points the Peasant Movement Should Heed," *Zhongguo nongmin*, no. 1 (1926): 13–19.

49. The discourse outlined in this chapter was contested early on by committed Marxists, who saw the peasants as producers and thus the natural allies of the workers in the anti-imperialist struggle. This discourse, perhaps because of the influence of Comintern on both the Chinese and the Korean Communist movements, is closer to the Chinese discourse and does not problematize Korean ethnicity. Since it has been amply treated in the literature on Korean communism, I have not dealt with it here.

50. Sŏ Sŏkchae, *Yŏngwŏnhan ch'onnom* (Seoul: Munhak sasangsa, 1995).

### Chapter 11: Joong-Seop Kim, "In Search of Human Rights: The Paekchŏng Movement in Colonial Korea"

I am very grateful to Gi-Wook Shin and Michael Robinson for their thoughtful comments on earlier versions of this chapter.

1. For a detailed discussion of the Hyŏngp'yŏngsa, see Joong-Seop Kim, "Social Equity and Collective Action: The Social History of the Korean *Paekjong* Under Japanese Colonial Rule" (Ph.D. diss., Hull University, 1989). For a revised version in Korean, see Kim Joong-Seop, *Hyŏngp'yŏng undong yŏn'gu: ilche ch'imnyaggi paekchŏng ŭi sahoesa* (Seoul: Minyŏngsa, 1994).

2. For a discussion of the *paekchŏng* in English, see Herbert Passin, "The *Paekchŏng* of Korea: A Brief Social History," *Monumenta Nipponica* 12, nos. 1–2 (1956): 27–72; Soon Man Rhim, "The *Paekjong*: Untouchables of Korea," *Journal of Oriental Studies* (Hong Kong) 12 (1974): 30–40; and Ian Neary, "The *Paekjong* and the Hyŏngp'yŏngsa: The Untouchables of Korea and Their Struggle for Liberation," *Immigrants and Minorities* 6, no. 2 (July 1987): 117–50.

3. See Kim Joong-Seop, *Hyŏngp'yŏng undong yŏn'gu*, pp. 41–52; Ch'a Ch'onja, "Paekchŏng sahoe ŭi amdamhan saenghwalsang ŭl kŏron haya

hyŏngp'yŏng chŏnsŏn ŭi t'ongil ŭl ch'okham," *Kaebyŏk* 5, no. 7 (July 1924): 39–45.

4. Sin Yongha, "1894 nyŏn ŭi sahoe sinbunje ŭi p'yeji," in *Han'guk kŭndae sahoesa yŏn'gu* (Seoul: Ilchisa, 1987); Kim Inhwan, "19 segi tonghak sasang ŭi sŏnggyŏk," in Chin Tŏkkyu et al., *19 segi Han'guk chŏnt'ong sahoe ŭi pyŏnmo wa minjung ŭisik* (Seoul: Korea University Press, 1982), pp. 91–150.

5. L. G. Paik, *The History of Protestant Missions in Korea, 1832–1910* (Seoul: Yonsei University Press, 1970).

6. S. F. Moore, "The Butchers of Korea," *Korean Repository* 5 (Apr. 1898): 127–32; Im Sunman (Soon Man Rhim), "Kidokkyŏ chŏnp'aga paekchŏng kongdongch'e e mich'in yŏnghyang," in Hyŏngp'yŏng undong 70 chunyŏn kinyŏm saophoe, ed., *Hyŏngp'yŏng undong ŭi chaeinsik* (Seoul: Sol Publishing, 1993), 65–102.

7. Chinju kyohoesa yŏnhyŏk wiwŏnhoe, *Chinju'myŏn okpongni Yesukyo changnohoe yŏnhyŏksa* (Chinju, 1930).

8. *Hwangsŏng sinmun*, Feb. 28, 1900, Oct. 20, 1900.

9. Ibid., Feb. 8, 1901, May 16, 1901.

10. See Kim Joong-Seop, "Sahoe undong punsŏk ŭi taeanjŏk chŏpkŭn pangbŏp," *Sahoehak yŏn'gu* 3 (1985): 188–211; J. Craig Jenkins, "Resource Mobilization Theory and the Study of Social Movements," *Annual Review of Sociology* 9 (1983): 527–53.

11. See Neil J. Smelser, *Theory of Collective Behavior* (London: Routledge and Kegan Paul, 1962); Ted Robert Gurr, *Why Men Rebel* (Princeton: Princeton University Press, 1970).

12. *Tongnip sinmun*, Nov. 3, 1896, Mar. 13 and 19, 1897, July 8, 1899.

13. *Maeil sinbo*, May 11, 1922.

14. Kim Chŏngmi, "19 segimal esŏ 20 segi ch'ogi e ittŏsŏ ŭi paekchŏng," in Kang Chaeŏn et al., eds., *Han'guk kŭndae sahoe wa sasang* (Seoul: Chungwŏn munhwa, 1984), pp. 191–226; Ko Sukhwa, "Hyŏngpy'ŏngsa e taehan il yŏn'gu," *Sahak yŏn'gu* 38 (Dec. 1984): 645–90.

15. *Kyŏngnam ilbo*, Jan. 5, 7 and 15, 1910.

16. Kim Ŭihwan, "Ilche ch'iha ŭi hyŏngp'yŏng undong ko," *Hyangt'o Seoul* 31 (1967): 66.

17. *Maeil sinbo*, Mar. 12, 1921, Aug. 21, 1922.

18. *Tonga ilbo*, May 22, 1925.

19. For personal backgrounds of the activists and interviews with their descendents, see Kim Joong-Seop, "1920 nyŏndae hyŏngp'yŏng undong ŭi hyŏngsŏng kwajŏng: Chinju chiyŏk ŭl chungsim ŭro," *Tongbang hakchi* 59 (1988): 231–73.

20. Kim Joong-Seop, "Ilcheha 3.1 undong kwa chiyŏk sahoe undong ŭi palchŏn: Chinju chiyŏk ŭl chungsim ŭro," *Han'guk sahoehak* 30 (Summer 1996): 359–87.

21. *Tonga ilbo*, Jan. 1–16, 1929; *Kyŏngnam ilbo*, Jan. 15, 1910.

22. See *Tonga ilbo*, May 20, 1923.

23. *Chosŏn ilbo*, May 19, 1923; *Tonga ilbo*, May 17, 1923.

24. When the national headquarters is included in the count, the number of organizations becomes 80; see Chōsen sōtokufu, *Chōsen no kunshu* (Keijō, 1926), p. 183.

25. Chosŏn hyŏngp'yŏngsa, Sohombu, "Chōsen kohei undō no kogai," *Chōsen oyobi Chōsen mizoku* 1 (1927): 166–69.

26. Chōsen sōtokufu, Keimukyoku, *Chōsen no chian jōkyō* (annual publication) (Seoul, 1927, 1930).

27. See Kim Joong-Seop, *Hyŏngp'yŏng undong yŏn'gu*, chap. 5.

28. *Tonga ilbo*, Sept. 8, 1925.

29. See Kim Joong-Seop, "Ilcheha 3.1 undong kwa chiyŏk sahoe undong ŭi palchŏn."

30. See Kim Joong-Seop, *Hyŏngp'yŏng undong yŏn'gu*, chap. 4.

31. *Tonga ilbo*, Apr. 22 and 26, 1924; *Chosŏn ilbo*, Apr. 22, 1924; *Sidae ilbo*, Apr. 22, 1924.

32. *Tonga ilbo*, Aug. 12 and 20, 1925; *Chosŏn ilbo*, Aug. 10 and 19, 1925; *Sidae ilbo*, Aug. 11 and 22, 1925.

33. See Kim Joong-Seop, *Hyŏngp'yŏng undong yŏn'gu*, pp. 213–29.

34. Kim Joong-Seop, "Hyŏngp'yŏng undong ŭi chihyang kwa chŏllyak," in Hyŏngp'yŏng undong 70 chunyŏn kinyŏm saophoe, ed., *Hyŏngp'yŏng undong ŭi chaeinsik*, pp. 103–36.

35. Constitution of the Hyŏngp'yŏngsa, article 3.

36. Prospectus of the Hyŏngp'yŏngsa, reported in *Chosŏn ilbo*, Aug. 30, 1923.

37. Declaration of the Sŏkwanghoe (later transformed into Kimje branch of the Hyŏngp'yŏngsa), reported in *Chosŏn ilbo*, May 23, 1923; *Tonga ilbo*, May 23, 1923.

38. *Tonga ilbo*, May 14, 1923.

39. Constitution of the Hyŏngp'yŏngsa, articles 3 and 6.

40. Rhonda E. Howard, *Human Rights and the Search for Community* (Boulder, Colo.: Westview Press, 1995).

41. It is presumed they first sought to publish their own journal in 1924, with several attempts thereafter, but no copy of a journal published by the association can be found except *Chŏngjin* (Right progress), published in 1929.

42. *Tonga ilbo*, Nov. 23, 1925; *Chosŏn ilbo*, Jan. 7, 1926.

43. *Chosŏn ilbo*, Mar. 8, 1929.

44. *Maeil sinbo*, Sept. 28, 1926.

45. Kim Joong-Seop, *Hyŏngp'yŏng undong yŏn'gu*, chap. 5.

46. See Ko Sukhwa, "Yech'ŏn sagŏn ŭl t'onghae pon ilcheha ŭi hyŏngp'yŏng undong," in *Such'on Pak Yŏngsŏk kyosu hoegap kimyŏn hanminjok tongnip undongsa nonch'ong* (Seoul, 1992), pp. 275–92.

47. *Tonga ilbo*, July 7, 11, Aug. 30, Nov. 8, 23, and 28, 1938; *Chosŏn ilbo*, Mar. 27, 1940.

48. See Kim Joong-Seop, *Hyŏngp'yŏng undong yŏn'gu*, pp. 250–56.

49. Ko Sukhwa, "Ilcheha hyŏngp'yŏngsa yŏn'gu" (Ph.D. diss., Ehwa Women's University, 1996).

50. Yi Pansong (pseud. of Tsubo Senji), *Chōsen shakai shiso undō enkaku ryakushi* (Seoul, 1934), 84–93.

51. *Tonga ilbo*, Aug. 14, 1931.

52. Yi Tonghwan, "Hyŏngp'yŏngsa che 9hoe chŏn'guk taehoe p'yŏng," *Pip'an* 1, no. 2 (June 1931): 36–43; *Tonga ilbo*, July 11, 1931.

53. *Tonga ilbo*, Aug. 26 and 27, 1928, Aug. 25, 1932, and Aug. 25 and 28, 1933; *Chosŏn chungwoe ilbo*, Aug. 25 and 28, 1933; *Chosŏn ilbo*, Aug. 25 and 28, 1928, and Aug. 27, 1933.

54. *Tonga ilbo*, July 28, 1932.

55. See Kim Joong-Seop, *Hyŏngp'yŏng undong yŏn'gu*, pp. 279–85.

56. Chōsen sōtokufu, Keimukyoku, *Saikin ni okeru Chōsen chian jōkyō* (1933), pp. 134–35.

57. *Chosŏn ilbo*, Nov. 22 and 27, 1936.

*Chapter 12: Henry H. Em, "Minjok as a Modern and Democratic Construct: Sin Ch'aeho's Historiography"*

1. As Prasenjit Duara points out, understanding the process by which narratives get transmitted over time requires that we understand how narratives break down over time: "Transmission of a trace or a narrative is premised upon repression, contestation, and negotiation of other, dispersed traces and narratives. For the historian, it is methodologically necessary to grasp this bifurcation of history as linear transmission and dispersion; only then can we keep in view the heterogeneity of the past upon which both our historical narratives and the representations from the past—the traces, our sources—have been constructed"; see Prasenjit Duara, "Bifurcating Linear History: Nation and Histories in China and India," *positions: east asia cultures critique* 1, no. 3 (Winter 1993). In other words, it is only through the violence of historiography (both premodern and modern) that "Korean history" (or any other national history) can be understood as a single coherent narrative.

2. Following Lydia Liu, I do not assume that languages are commensurate or that equivalents exist naturally between them. Depending on the context, I will translate *minjok* as "people," "Koreans," or as an ethnically defined "nation." When Korean (and Chinese and Japanese) nationalists wrote in English in the first half of the twentieth century, the English word they generally utilized for *minjok* was "race." In the nineteenth and early twentieth centuries, as Walker Connor points out, numerous writers in the West (incorrectly) employed "race" as a synonym for "nation." In those cases in which I employ the word "nation" for *minjok*, I *do* mean to convey the idea of common blood ties as suggested in the Latin noun "natio" (from which the word "nation" is derived). On the etymology of words like "nation" and "ethnicity," and the conflation of "state" and "nation," see Walker Conner,

"A Nation Is a Nation, Is a State, Is an Ethnic Group, Is a . . . ," _Ethnic and Racial Studies_ 1, no. 4 (1978): 379–88.

3. Yasuda Hiroshi, "Kindai Nihon ni okeru 'minzoku' kannen no keisei," _Shisō to gendai_ 31 (Sept. 1992); cited in Kevin Doak, "Ethnic Nationalism and Romanticism in Early Twentieth-Century Japan," _Journal of Japanese Studies_ 22, no. 1 (1996). In this article, Doak also cites Yun Koncha, "Minzoku gensō no satetsu: 'Nihon minzoku' to iu jiko teiji," _Shisō_, no. 834 (Dec. 1993). Contrary to Yasuda, Yun argues that ethnic consciousness (_minzoku ishiki_) was not fully established in Japan until the turn of the twentieth century. For further discussion on national narratives and the ethnic imagination in twentieth-century Japan, see Doak, "What Is a Nation and Who Belongs?" _American Historical Review_ 102, no. 2 (Apr. 1997).

4. Sin Ilch'ŏl makes this point: "It must be kept in mind that [the word] '_minjok_,' as it is commonly used in our country, is not congruent to either 'nation' or 'race' in English. Rather, it is analogous to 'Volk' or 'Volkschaft' in German." Having attained ethnic homogeneity quite early in its history, Sin argues, the Korean _minjok_ or _kyŏre_ in premodern times constituted a _chun minjokchŏk kongdongch'e_ (a proto-national community) comparable to the _Volkschaft_, or to the _narodnosti_ as conceptualized in Stalin's later writings on the national question. In an interesting twist, Sin argues that the emergence of modern (_Gesellschaft_) nationalism in Korea was made difficult precisely because traditional society in Korea had such a strong _Gemeinschaft_ (community) consciousness. See Sin Ilch'ŏl, "Sin Ch'aeho ŭi kŭndae kukkagwan," in Kang Man'gil, ed., _Sin Ch'aeho_ (Seoul: Koryŏ taehakkyo ch'ulp'anbu, 1990), pp. 1–3. See also Joseph Stalin, _Marxism and Linguistics_ (New York: International Publishers, 1951).

5. Andre Schmid, "Rediscovering Manchuria: Sin Ch'aeho and the Politics of Territorial History in Korea," _Journal of Asian Studies_ 56, no. 1 (Feb. 1997). Schmid cites two sources on how the term _minzoku_ was appropriated by Chinese intellectuals in the early years of the twentieth century: Han Jinchun and Li Yinfun, "Hanwen 'minzu' yici chuxian ji qi chuji shiyong qingkuang," _Minzu yanjiu_ 1984, no. 2, pp. 36–43; and Peng Yingming, "Guanyu woguo minzu gainian lishi de chubu kaocha," _Minzu yanjiu_ 1985, no. 2, pp. 5–11.

6. Such a model—which implies that "a word in language A must equal a word or a phrase in language B; otherwise one of the languages is lacking"—will lead the observer to form mistaken opinions about other peoples and, conversely, about the observer's own totalized identity; see Lydia H. Liu, _Translingual Practice: Literature, National Culture, and Translated Modernity, China, 1900–1937_ (Stanford: Stanford University Press, 1995), p. 4.

7. Son Chint'ae, _Chosŏn minjoksa kaeron_ (Seoul: Ŭryu munhwasa, 1948). The quotation is from his "Introduction" and can be found in _Yŏktae Han'guksa nonsŏn_, compiled by Yi Kibaek (Seoul: Saemunsa, 1993), p. 241. Son's introduction to _Chosŏn minjoksa kaeron_ (Outline of Korean national

history) was written in the post-liberation context of divided occupation (Soviet forces north and U.S. forces south of the 38th parallel), and violent struggle between the left and the right that led to the establishment of separate states (DPRK and ROK) in 1948. As an anti-communist, Son nonetheless extended high praise to the Marxist historiography of Paek Namun, but then criticized him for discovering only a part of "ourselves" (*uri chasin*). That is to say, Son Chint'ae's privileging of the *minjok* as the totality of "ourselves" that transcends class divisions attests to how the category of *minjok* was implicated in ideological struggles during and after the colonial period. Son became South Korea's vice-minister of education in 1950, and he was forcibly taken to North Korea during the Korean War.

8. Cho Tonggŏl, "Kŭndae ch'ogi ŭi yŏksa insik," in Cho Tonggŏl, Han Yŏngu, and Pak Ch'ansŭng, eds., *Han'guk ŭi yŏksaga wa yŏksa insik* (Seoul: Ch'angjak kwa pip'yŏngsa, 1994), 2: 19.

9. Eugen Weber, *Peasants into Frenchmen: The Modernization of Rural France, 1870-1914* (Stanford: Stanford University Press, 1976). Ernest Gellner makes a similar argument. Nationalism, Gellner writes, "claims to defend folk culture while in fact it is forging a high [i.e., *yangban*] culture; it claims to protect an old folk society while in fact helping to build up an anonymous mass society; . . . it preaches and defends continuity, but owes everything to a decisive and unutterably profound break in human history [the development of industrial society]"; Gellner, *Nations and Nationalism* (Ithaca: Cornell University Press, 1983), pp. 124–25.

10. As Fujiya Kawashima has shown, by the eighteenth century the *yangban* elite in the countryside has succeeded in constructing diverse local cultures based on Confucian ethics, a culture that structured the daily lives of not just *yangban*, but also *chungin*, commoners, and slaves. This "cultural localism" was upheld as being "universal" in that Confucian ethics and morality were applicable to everyone everywhere, even as it accentuated a shared sense of self-discipline, self-rule, and self-sufficiency. But this shared local culture did not transgress status distinctions. This culture assumed that the social hierarchy separating the different status groups (*myŏngbun*) was natural and commonsensical. See Fujiya Kawashima, "Cultural Localism in the Late Chosŏn Dynasty and Its Significance in Modern Korea," *Bulletin of Hiroshima Jogakuin University*, no. 45 (Dec. 1995).

11. Carter Eckert, *Offspring of Empire: The Koch'ang Kims and the Colonial Origins of Korean Capitalism, 1876-1945* (Seattle: University of Washington Press, 1991), pp. 226–27.

12. Although Chinese dynasties viewed their interaction with peoples and kingdoms beyond their borders in terms of the "tribute system," Peter Yun points out that this system encompassed a wide range of political relationships that ranged from total subjugation to virtual equality. Yun argues that from the fourth century until the Mongol conquest of the whole region in the thirteenth century, a triangular balance of power among China,

Manchuria, and Korea had prevailed in Northeast Asia. By destroying this triangular balance of power, the Mongols for the first time forced Korea (Koryŏ) to perform all the duties of a "model tributary." It was not until the sixteenth century, however, that Korean Confucian elites developed a strong ideological commitment to the moral correctness of the tribute system. See Peter Yun, "Rethinking the Tribute System: Northeast Asian Interstate Relations, 600–1600." Ph.D. diss., UCLA, 1998.

13. There are, of course, other factors behind Chosŏn's remarkable longevity. The most important treatment of this issue is James Palais's "Stability in Yi Dynasty Korea," *Occasional Papers on Korea* 3 (June 1975): 1–18.

14. Benedict Anderson, *Imagined Communities: Reflections on the Origin and Spread of Nationalism* (London: Verso, 1983), pp. 15–16.

15. The categories of "nationalist historians" and "nationalist historiography" during the colonial period, as commonly defined in contemporary South Korean historiography, encompass a wide range of historical writing by writers who embraced quite different, sometimes opposing philosophical, political, and methodological positions. By "nationalist historiography," I mean histories written as a narrative of resistance to colonial rule, devoted to countering the pernicious effects of colonialist historiography and to empowering Koreans to join the struggle for Korea's independence. Representative historians are Sin Ch'aeho, Pak Ŭnsik, An Chaehong, Mun Ilp'yŏng, and Chŏng Inbo. Historians such as Han Yŏngu carefully distinguish national historiography (*minjok sahak*) and nationalist historiography (*minjokchuŭi yŏksahak*). That is, almost all histories written today are national histories (e.g., histories of Korean women, religion, literature, music, art—not to mention politics), but not all are nationalist histories.

16. Sin Ch'aeho was born in 1880, in South Ch'ungch'ŏng province. He received a classical education from his grandfather and at the age of eighteen entered the Sŏnggyun'gwan, the government-run Confucian academy. In 1905, Sin received his *paksa* degree and at the invitation of Chang Chiyŏn joined the editorial staff of the *Hwangsŏng sinmun* (Capital gazette). When the Japanese authorities forced the *Hwangsŏng sinmun* to close, Sin moved to the *Taehan maeil sinbo* (Korea daily news) and became its editor in chief. In 1907, with the intention of inspiring Korean youth to become heroes themselves, Sin translated Liang Qichao's (Liang Ch'i-ch'ao) biographical sketches of Mazzini, Garibaldi, and Cavour (*Itali kŏn'guk samgŏljŏn*) and, in the following year, wrote biographic sketches of the Koguryŏ general Ŭlchi Mundŏk and Chosŏn admiral Yi Sunsin. In 1907, Sin also helped organize the Sinminhoe (New people's association, a clandestine nationalist organization) and, through his editorials, publicized Sinminhoe views. Until Korea's annexation in 1910, Sin published a magazine for women (*Kajŏng chapchi*: Family magazine) and wrote essays on nationalism, Korean linguistics, Korean history, and poetry. Sin left Korea just before the annexation to continue his nationalist activities abroad, and with the exception of a brief trip home in 1916, he never set foot in Korea again. In 1919,

when the March First movement erupted in Korea, Sin took part in organizing the Korean Provisional Government (KPG) in Shanghai. By 1920, however, Sin was so disgusted with the diplomatic and gradualist strategies advocated by Syngman Rhee and An Ch'angho that he turned his back on the KPG. Although active in revolutionary nationalist politics, Sin also immersed himself in historical study. Sin's writings in the 1910s and 1920s were influenced by Liang Qichao's historical methodology (1910s) and by Chinese anarchist intellectuals (early 1920s). In 1923, Sin Ch'aeho wrote the "Declaration of Korean Revolution" for the Korean revolutionary organization Ŭiyŏldan. By 1925, Sin Ch'aeho had become an anarchist. In 1927 Sin joined the Eastern Anarchist Association, and in the following year he was arrested by the Japanese military in connection with a forgery scheme to raise funds for anarchist activities. In 1936, he died in a Japanese prison in Port Arthur.

17. The Tan'gun legend is a prototypical foundation myth that explains the creation of the people, the state, and the culture of Old Chosŏn. As narrated by Iryŏn in the *Samguk yusa*, Hwanin, the Supreme Spirit, sent down his son, Hwanung, to the peak of T'aebaeksan. A bear and a tiger, which lived together in a cave, prayed to Hwanung to be transformed into human form. Hwanin then gave them mugwort and garlic to eat and told them not to see light for one hundred days. The tiger could not endure the ordeal; the bear persevered and became a woman. Hwanung married her, and she bore a son who was called Tan'gun wanggŏm. Iryŏn goes on to say that in the fiftieth year of the Emperor Yao, Tan'gun established a city at P'yŏngyang and called his country Chosŏn. This would date the establishment of Old Chosŏn at 2306 B.C.E., but the Tan'gun calendar traditionally begins with Tan'gun's birth, which is said to have occurred in 2333 B.C.E. For concise analyses of the Tan'gun myth as narrated in the *Samguk yusa*, see James H. Grayson, *Korea, a Religious History* (Oxford: Oxford University Press, 1989), pp. 281–84; Peter H. Lee, ed., *Sourcebook of Korean Civilization* (New York: Columbia University Press, 1993), 1: 3–8.; and Sarah M. Nelson, *The Archaeology of Korea* (Cambridge, Eng.: Cambridge University Press, 1993), pp. 155–56.

18. Although no longer extant, state histories were compiled by each of the Three Kingdoms: by Yi Munjin for Koguryŏ (600); by Kohŭng for Paekche (375) (and as noted by Peter Lee — judging from quotations in the *Nihon shoki* — other Paekche histories must have existed); and by Kŏch'ilbu (fl. 545–76) for Silla (Peter Lee, *Sourcebook of Korean Civilization*, 1: 119). It is thought that *Samguksa* (History of the Three Kingdoms), written at the beginning of the Koryŏ period but no longer extant, did mention the Tan'gun legend. But according to Han Yŏngu, the *Samguksa* probably was not a sophisticated Confucian history and was probably not written in the annal-biography (*kijŏnch'e*) style; See Han Yŏngu, "Uri nara yŏksahak ŭi hŭrŭm," in Cho Tonggŏl et al., eds., *Han'guk ŭi yŏksaga wa yŏksahak*, 1: 15.

19. A Buddhist monk versed in geomancy, Myoch'ŏng (?–1135) contended that the topographical vigor of Kaegyŏng (Kaesŏng), the capital of

Koryŏ, was depleted. Myoch'ŏng's proposal to move the capital to Sŏgyŏng (P'yŏngyang) would have weakened the power of aristocratic families entrenched in Kaegyŏng and would have instated a more aggressive policy toward the Jurchen Chin in the north. Conservatives like Kim Pusik opposed Myoch'ŏng's plan because moving the capital to a more "propitious" area would have also sanctioned an extensive (and expansive) program of reconstructing the physical and social order. In 1135, after years of fruitless polemic, Myoch'ŏng raised an army in revolt, a revolt that ended in defeat to forces led by Kim Pusik.

20. According to Song Kiho, the core of Parhae's ruling class was made up of Koguryŏ émigrés and the subject population was mostly Malgal people. "Unified" Silla regarded Parhae as a state founded by the descendents of Koguryŏ, and, in its dealings with "Japan," Parhae referred to itself as Koryŏ (i.e., Koguryŏ). There are passages in the *Samguk sagi* and in Ch'oe Ch'iwŏn's writings (857–?: a scholar-official of late Silla) that refer to Parhae as "the Northern State" (*pukkuk*), and Song infers that Parhae for its part might have regarded Silla as "the Southern State" (*namguk*). Song then reasons that Parhae and Silla saw themselves as forming a single ethnic group. See Song Kiho, "Silla chungdae sahoe wa Parhae," in Han'guksa t'ŭkkang p'yŏnch'an wiwŏnhoe, ed., *Han'guksa t'ŭkkang* (Seoul: Sŏul taehakkyo ch'ulp'anbu, 1990), pp. 67–81. I think it is entirely possible that, when convenient, i.e., for political reasons (to seek asylum, or as justification for territorial ambitions), the ruling classes of Parhae and Silla might have articulated their relationship to one another in terms of clientship and kinship ties. But I think it is doubtful that they even thought about their own subjects (the people from whom they extracted tribute and labor) in terms of a deep, horizontal comradeship that is the hallmark of the ethnic nation.

21. Han Yŏngu, "Uri nara yŏksahak ŭi hŭrŭm," pp. 14–17.

22. The Tan'gun legend in *Samguk yusa* might have been based on much earlier sources such as the *Wei shu* and *Tan'gun kogi*. The Tan'gun legend also appears in later (Chosŏn) court-sponsored works like the *Ŭngjesi chu* (Commentary on poems written at royal command) by Kwŏn Nam (1416–65), the monograph on geography in the *Sejong sillok*, and the *Tongguk yŏji sŭngnam* (1481).

23. Ki-baik Lee (Yi Kibaek), *A New History of Korea*, trans. Edward W. Wagner (Cambridge, Mass.: Harvard-Yenching Institute, 1984), p. 167.

24. As Peter Yun ("Rethinking the Tribute System: Northeast Asian Interstate Relations") points out, successive Koryŏ kings had princesses of the Yuan imperial house as their primary consorts, and the throne was reserved for the princes born to Mongol queens.

25. Iryŏn writes, "It is written in an old book, 'In ancient times, Hwanung, the son of Hwanin (this means Chesŏk), desired to descend from Heaven and to live among men. . . . Together with his ministers of wind, rain, and cloud, Hwanung instructed mankind about agriculture, the pres-

ervation of life, the curing of disease, punishments, the difference between right and wrong.'" This translation by James H. Grayson can be found in Grayson, *Korea, a Religious History*, p. 282. See also Peter Lee's translation in *Sourcebook of Korean Civilization*, 1: 4–7. For Iryŏn, Koryŏ was the land wherein the Buddha dwells (thus culturally superior to the Mongols), and it was Buddhism that could safeguard the land and the people. This was why he equated Hwanin, the Ruler of Heaven, with Chesŏk, a rendering of Indra, one of the three great deities of Vedic Hinduism.

26. There were histories written in the epic style, most notably the vernacular translation of the *Sanguozhi tongsu yanyi* (Romance of the Three Kingdoms: *Samgukchi t'ongsok yŏnŭi* in Korean). Confucian historians considered such popular histories fiction rather than history proper. But, much to their dismay, *Samgukchi t'ongsok yŏnŭi* was widely read in late Chosŏn. As Emanuel Pastreich points out, Yi Ik (1681–1763), for example, lamented the fact that the *Samgukchi t'ongsok yŏnŭi* was being read aloud in every home and even quoted in the civil service examination questions. The earliest complaint on record seems to be a memorial written by the scholar Ki Taesŭng to King Sŏnjo in 1569 in which he rebukes the king for drawing a reference from *Samgukchi t'ongsok yŏnŭi*. Without having to read it, Ki Taesŭng was able to compare its extreme ludicrousness to books on astrology. Emanuel Pastreich argues that the literary style of *Samgukji t'ongsok yŏnŭi* set some of the basic conventions for the vernacular novel in late Chosŏn. See Emanuel Pastreich, "The Reception of Chinese Vernacular Narrative in Korea and Japan" (Ph.D. diss., Harvard University, 1997), pp. 49–52. But it is not clear what influence, if any, literary conventions in late Chosŏn vernacular literature had on history writing in the modern period. In the case of Sin Ch'aeho, Thomas Carlyle's *On Heroes, Hero-Worship, and the Heroic in History* and Liang Qichao's biographical sketches of Mazzini, Garibaldi, and Cavour (which Sin translated in 1907 as *Itali kŏn'guk samgŏljŏn*) stimulated him to write biographic sketches of the Koguryŏ general Ŭlchi Mundŏk (mid-sixth century–early seventh century) and Yi Sunsin (1545–98). (*Ŭlchi Mundŏk* was published as a booklet in 1908, and *Yi Sunsin-jŏn* was serialized in the *Taehan maeil sinbo* in the same year.) As Michael Robinson points out, Sin Ch'aeho's motive for writing these biographies was to exhort Korean youth to emulate the purity of spirit and patriotic example of these military heroes in Korean history; see "National Identity and the Thought of Sin Ch'ae-ho: Sadaejuŭi and Chuch'e in History and Politics," *Journal of Korean Studies* 5 (1984): 134.

27. Private histories were sometimes free of some of the restraints that inhibited official historiography. However, because the authors were either potential or actual officeholders, there was a strong similarity in outlook between private historiography and official historiography.

28. After at least 1178, the literati had access to the *Chobo*, which was written by lower functionaries and noted decrees and orders from the king,

appointments and dismissals of officials, palace affairs, and the particulars of reports from local officials. See Suh Chung-Woo, "Enlightenment Period Newspapers and Fiction," *Korean Studies* 18 (1994): 16. However, only a small circle of scholar-officials had access to documents such as the *Records of the Royal Secretariat, Record for Daily Reflection,* or the *Record of the Border Defense Command,* sources that recorded the daily activities of the central government and were used for the compilation of the *Sillok* (Veritable records). See James B. Palais, "Records and Record-keeping in Nineteenth-Century Korea," *Journal of Asian Studies* 30 (1971). In a 1984 interview, Yi Pyŏngdo (1896–1989) recalled how he saw the *Chosŏn wangjo sillok* for the first time in the home of Ikeuchi Hiroshi, professor of Korean history at Tokyo Imperial University. This was during his student days at Waseda University (1916–19). During the Chosŏn period, copies of the *Sillok* were kept at four separate archives in remote mountainous areas in addition to the central archive in Seoul. The *Sillok* kept by Ikeuchi was destroyed during the Tokyo earthquake of 1923. The interview, conducted by Chŏng Hongjun, appears in Chindan hakhoe, ed., *Yŏksaga ŭi yuhyang* (Seoul: Ilchokak, 1991), pp. 264–76.

29. Sinminhoe was a secret society organized in 1907 by An Ch'angho, with Yi Tonghwi, Yang Kit'ak, Yi Kap, Yi Sŭnghun, Chŏn Tŏkki, An T'aeguk, Yi Tongnyŏng, Sin Ch'aeho, and others (Sin Ch'aeho wrote its prospectus: "Ch'wijimun"). It consisted of patriots, each of whom committed his life and property to the organization in the cause of promoting nationalist consciousness, Korean independence, and a republican form of government. With the start of the Russo-Japanese War, Japanese suppression of Korean nationalist groups intensified. To preserve the security of the organization, Sinminhoe members were grouped into columns (so that a member would know the identity of only the person above and below himself). At one point the membership grew to about 800 men, many of whom were journalists, religious leaders, military men, and businessmen. To promote education, the Sinminhoe founded schools in P'yŏngyang and Chŏngju; to promote modern industry, it established a ceramics factory in P'yŏngyang; and to promote nationalist politics in the public sphere, it established the bilingual newspaper *Korea Daily News* (*Taehan maeil sinbo*).

30. In a later essay, when Sin continued his polemic against Kim Pusik, Kim's many faults were condensed to *sadaejuŭi,* or a mentality of subservience. This essay, "Chosŏn yŏksasang ilch'ŏnnyŏnlae cheil taesakkŏn" (The most disastrous event in the past one thousand years of Korean history), was serialized in the *Tonga ilbo* from October 1924 through March 1925. For Sin Ch'aeho, the defeat of Myoch'ŏng by Kim Pusik in 1135 and the subsequent erasure of Tan'gun and Parhae (and thus Manchuria) from Korean history was *the* disastrous turning point in Korean history and ushered in a thousand-year legacy of *sadaejuŭi,* or a culture of subservience. The historical context for this polemic (early 1920s) had to do with Sin's denunciation of

those Koreans who were lobbying for an "independent domestic administration" (*naejŏng tongnip*), "participatory government" (*ch'am chŏnggwŏn*), or "self-rule" (*chach'i*) within colonial Korea. Sin understood these moves as capitulation to Japan's claim over Korea, a capitulation that emanated from the mentality of subservience begun by Kim Pusik.

31. Han Yŏngu identifies Sin Ch'aeho as the initiator (*sŏnch'angja*) of modern nationalist historiography in Korea. According to Han Yŏngu, Sin Ch'aeho's "Toksa sillon," written in 1908, was a pioneering work in modern nationalist historiography because its epistemology was informed by three tenets: nation (*minjok*), democracy (*minju*), and science (*kwahak*); see Han Yŏngu, *Han'guk minjokchuŭi yŏksahak* (Seoul: Ilchokak, 1994), pp. 4, 6.

32. I would like to acknowledge Michael Robinson's "National Identity and the Thought of Sin Ch'ae-ho," pp. 121–42. This article by Robinson and two articles by Andre Schmid were very important to me in writing this article. See Schmid, "Rediscovering Manchuria," pp. 26–46, and "Decentering the Middle Kingdom: China in Korean Nationalist Thought," unpublished paper. In Korean, I learned a great deal from studies on Korean nationalist historiography written by Cho Kwang, Cho Tonggŏl, Han Yŏngu, Kang Mangil, Kim Yongsŏp, Pak Ch'ansŭng, Sin Ilch'ŏl, Sin Yongha, and Yi Manyŏl. One very important issue not discussed in my essay is the relationship between Taejonggyo (Religion of the great ancestors) and Sin Ch'aeho's focus on Tan'gun (in his early work). On this issue, see Han Yŏngu, *Han'guk minjokchuŭi yŏksahak*.

33. Here Sin Ch'aeho is criticizing the lack of constancy in the new history textbooks regarding the question of Korean national origins. Inconstancy is exemplified by the vacillations of the Warring States–period kingdom of Wei (Wi in Korean) between an alliance with Liang in the morning and Ch'u in the evening.

34. Sin Ch'aeho, "Toksa sillon," *TSCHC*, 1: 471–72. In translating this passage from "Toksa sillon," I have consulted the han'gŭl text in *Sin Ch'aeho yŏksa nonsŏlchip*, trans. Chŏng Haeryŏm (Seoul: Hyŏndae silhaksa, 1995), as well as the English translation by Han-kyo Kim in Peter Lee, ed., *Sourcebook of Korean Civilization*, vol. 2.

35. For the list of history textbooks used in this period, see Han Yŏngu, *Han'guk minjokchuŭi yŏksahak*, p. 43. Hyŏn Ch'ae's *Tongguk saryak* (1906), for example, was all but a translation of Hayashi Taisuke's *Chōsenshi* (1892). It is not clear to what extent Sin Ch'aeho had direct access to Japanese writings on Korea. But in other essays, he does cite a number of Japanese texts: for example, *Chōsen no ichi* (Korea's position); see "Tongyang itaeli (The Italy of the Orient)," in *TSCHC*, 4: 184.

36. "Kukka ranŭn kŏtsi il kaein ŭi soyumul i aniyo, modŭn inmin ŭi konggong chaesan [ida]." Sin Ch'aeho, "Toksa sillon," in *TSCHC*, 1: 482.

37. Vipan Chandra contrasts this with the situation in China and Japan: "Unlike China, where revolutionists could draw on 'Han nationalism' against

'alien' Manchu rule, or Japan, where the Meiji Restorationists . . . could paint the shogunate as a usurper of imperial sovereignty, Korea offered no such rationale for radical activists"; see Vipan Chandra, *Imperialism, Resistance, and Reform in Late Nineteenth-Century Korea: Enlightenment and the Independence Club* (Berkeley, Calif.: Institute of East Asian Studies, 1988), p. 215.

38. See the preface by Kang Man'gil, "Ilche sidae ŭi pan-singmin sahangnon," in Han'guksa yŏn'guhoe, ed., *Han'guk sahaksa ŭi yŏn'gu* (Seoul: Ŭlyu munhwasa, 1985), pp. 231–32.

39. As Schmid notes, Sin Ch'aeho's lament over the erasure of Parhae from official historiography, along with his irredentism, had historical precedent. In *Parhae ko*, completed in 1784, Yu Tŭkkong (1748–1807) lamented the fact that Koryŏ did not compile a history of Parhae. (In the Confucian historiographic tradition, it is the duty of successive dynasties to compile the history of preceding dynasties from the material left by their predecessors.) Because the *Samguk sagi* did not include Parhae's history, tracing Koryŏ's legitimacy via Unified Silla, Koryŏ had in effect given up its claim over the territory Parhae had once controlled. To reclaim Parhae's history as part of Korean history, Yu argued that Parhae and Unified Silla should be seen as forming the Northern and Southern states. This argument was repeated by Kim Chŏngho in his *Taedong chiji* (1864). During the colonial period, this way of periodizing Korean history was adopted by Chang Tobin, An Hwak, and Kwŏn Tŏkkyu. After liberation, in North Korea, Pak Sihyŏng, Chu Yŏnghŏn, and others characterized Parhae as the successor state of Koguryŏ, but they did not refer to this era as the Period of Northern and Southern States (*Nam-Pukguk sidae*). In South Korea, Yi Usŏng has been the strongest promoter of this term; see his "Nam-Pukguk sidae wa Ch'oe Ch'iwŏn," in *Han'guk ŭi yŏksasang* (Seoul: Ch'angjak kwa pip'yŏngsa, 1982). For an overview of historiographical issues surrounding Parhae, see essays by Song Kiho in *Han'guksa t'ŭkkang*, pp. 67–81; and his essay on Yu Tŭkkong in Cho Tonggŏl et al., eds., *Han'guk ŭi yŏksaga wa yŏksahak*, 1: 296–309.

40. See Schmid, "Rediscovering Manchuria," p. 27.

41. In *Chosŏn sanggosa* (History of ancient Korea), written sixteen years later (1924), Sin Ch'aeho praised Han Paekkyŏm's *Tongguk chiriji* (Korea's topographic record) as having inaugurated (proper) historiography. Completed in 1615, Han narrated two lines of descent for Korean history: in the north, from Tan'gun and Kija down through Koguryŏ; in the south, from Samhan down through Paekche, Silla, and Kaya. Han Paekkyŏm's narrative privileged the northern line of descent over the southern one. Writing at a time when another invasion from the south (from Japan) seemed unlikely, a time when the Ming seemed weak even as the Jurchens were gathering their forces in the north, Han had argued for a strong policy toward the Jurchens and included (reinstated) Manchuria within the territorial boundaries of Korea's ancient past. Adopting Han's narrative strategy, Sin Ch'aeho panegyrized the northern line of descent.

42. The reference is to Kume Kunitake, "Nihon fukuin no enkaku," *Shigakkai zasshi* 1 (Dec. 1889). According to Stefan Tanaka, in making the argument that Japan before Jinmu (the mythical first emperor) was a sort of thalassocracy encompassing Kyūshū, Korea, and southeastern China, Kume used passages from the *Nihon shoki* and *Kojiki*, not as actual facts, but as allegorical data that describe historical events. See Stefan Tanaka, *Japan's Orient: Rendering Pasts into History* (Berkeley: University of California Press, 1993), pp. 71–75. In 1891, Kume published an article in *Shigaku zasshi* in which he referred to Shinto as "a primitive custom of sacrifice to heaven." Kume came under such heavy attack from Shintoists and nationalists that he was obliged to relinquish his post at Tokyo Imperial University (i.e., two years after his "Nihon fukuin no enkaku" essay). See Jiro Numata, "Shigeno Yasutsugu and the Modern Tokyo Tradition of Historical Writing," in W. G. Beasley and E. G. Pulleyblank, eds., *Historians of China and Japan* (London: Oxford University Press, 1961), p. 272.

43. As Schmid points out, the depiction of Korea as encompassing nearly all of Manchuria reveals an irredentism in Sin Ch'aeho's thought that has not been adequately addressed in mainstream Korean historiography. Irredentism does loom large in the imaginations of right-wing nationalists in South Korea today, who dream about reclaiming Korea's "ancestral lands" (*kut'o hoebok*). See Schmid, "Rediscovering a Korean Manchuria: Irredentism in the Thought of Sin Ch'aeho," unpublished paper.

44. By "colonialist historiography," I mean historiography written before, during, and after the colonial period whose ultimate *political* aim was to justify Japan's colonization of Korea in 1910. See Song Ch'ansŏp, "Ilche ŭi singminsahak," in Cho Tonggŏl et al., eds., *Han'guk ŭi yŏksaga wa yŏksahak.*

45. The history department at Tokyo Imperial University was established in 1887. *Nihon shiryaku* (An outline of Japanese history) was also published in the same year (*Kokushi gan* was a revision of *Nihon shiryaku*). See Hatada Takashi, *Nihonjin no Chōsenkan* (Tokyo: Chikuma shobō, 1969).

46. Shigeno Yasutsugu, Kume Kunitake, and Hoshino Hisashi were all on the faculty of Tokyo Imperial University. Numata ("Shigeno Yasutsugu," p. 281) writes, "As a result of this superimposition of Western historical methods on the existing ones of *kōshō-gaku*, there was established a positivist method according to which only facts verified in reliable original sources could be regarded as objective historical facts; and this it would be fair to call the birth of modern historical science in Japan." It can be argued that this "tradition" was reproduced in colonial Korea by historians like Yi Pyŏngdo and the positivist school (*silchŭng sahak*). During his student days at Waseda University (1916–19), Yi received private instruction in historical methodology from Ikeuchi Hiroshi (who taught Korean history at Tokyo Imperial University) and Tsuda Sōkichi (Waseda University). After returning to Korea, Yi worked on and off for the Chōsenshi henshūkai, whose work was directed and funded by the Government-General. In 1934, Yi Pyŏngdo,

along with Yi Sangbaek, organized the Chindan hakhoe (Chindan society) for the study of Korean history and literature. After liberation, when Keijō Imperial University was reorganized as Seoul National University under the direction of the United States Army Military Government in Korea (USAM-GIK), all the Korean history faculty were recruited from Chindan hakhoe. Both before and after the Korean War, Chindan hakhoe received financial support from the Rockefeller Foundation. It was not until the April 19 student revolution in 1960, which toppled the Syngman Rhee regime, that the Chindan hakhoe's grip on South Korean historiography was challenged by nationalist historians of a younger generation.

47. Hatada, *Nihonjin no Chōsenkan*, p. 232.

48. Much archaeological evidence suggests a very different dynamic between "Japan" and "Korea" during the Three Kingdoms period. Succinctly put, émigrés from Koguryŏ, Paekche, and Silla played decisive roles (cultural and political) in the formative period of "Japanese" history. For example, one of the early emperors, Ōjin, was probably a member of the Puyŏ ruling house of Paekche.

49. Besides Hyŏn Ch'ae, Kim T'aeyŏng's *Tongsa chimnyak* (1902) and even Chang Chiyŏn in his *Taehan kangyŏkko* repeated the colonialist claims about Mimana (Kaya). In 1901, Hayashi published the sequel *Chōsen kinseishi*, which covered Korean history up to 1895. This work more explicitly advocated Japan's control over Korea.

50. When Paek Namun wrote his *Chōsen shakai keizaishi* (The socioeconomic history of Korea; 1933), his polemical target was Fukuda Tokuzō and the "stagnation theory" then prevalent in Japanese historiography on Korea. Paek Namun studied at Tōkyō Kōshō (today Hitotsubashi University) from 1919 to 1924, where Fukuda Tokuzō taught economics.

51. Stefan Tanaka, *Japan's Orient*, p. 4.

52. Shiratori Kurakichi was a professor at Tokyo Imperial University from 1904 to 1925 and, according to Stefan Tanaka (ibid., p. 4), the scholar primarily responsible for the formation and formulation of Tōyōshi as an academic field of study. Tanaka notes that many consider the Tōyōshi of the prewar era and Shiratori's career as synonymous.

53. Schmid, "Decentering the Middle Kingdom," p. 4.

54. One could perhaps locate the emergence of Japan's Orientalism in the early years of the Meiji period when Fukuzawa Yukichi argued that Japan must "leave Asia" (*datsu-A*). But this ideological system really established itself in Japanese popular discourse around the turn of the century—especially after Japan's victory over Russia in the Russo-Japanese War—when an army of cartoonists, novelists, and pundits conceptualized East Asia as Tōyō, and China not as Chūgoku but Shina, a name now connoting backwardness and corruption.

55. Tanaka, *Japan's Orient*, p. 47.

56. Ibid., p. 17.

57. Partha Chatterjee, *Nationalist Thought and the Colonial World: A Derivative Discourse* (Minneapolis: University of Minnesota Press, 1986).

58. Elie Kedourie, *Nationalism* (London: Hutchinson, 1960), pp. 71–81.

59. Prasenjit Duara, *Rescuing History from the Nation* (Chicago: University of Chicago Press, 1995), p. 4.

60. I thank my colleague John Duncan for allowing me to quote from his paper "Proto-nationalism in Premodern Korea," presented at the Third Pacific-Asia Conference on Korean Studies held in Sydney, Australia, in the summer of 1996. In this paper, Duncan rejects the premise (common in Korean national histories) that the nation (*minjok*) was already in existence at the dawn of historical time, as well as the interpretation that the contest among the Three Kingdoms (Koguryŏ, Paekche, and Silla) represented a struggle for the political unification of the nation (*minjok*). On the other hand, Duncan points out that the formation of a homogeneous, country-wide elite class was well under way by the mid-Koryŏ. Moreover, Duncan argues that we should not rule out the possibility that state-organized corvée and military service could have created a wider sense of identification with the state, "however negative that may have been at times," and a certain homogenizing of the populace. To what extent the premodern state, or other forces, could have broken down local cultural and linguistic barriers, I will have to address in another forum. Suffice it to say at this point, Duncan's conclusion somewhat parallels my own in that nationalist historiography seeks to project into the past "a modern nationalist discourse which seeks to elide potentially competitive forms of identification such as class, region, or gender in favor of a totalizing national identity."

61. See Etienne Balibar's "The Nation Form: History and Ideology," in Balibar and Immanuel Wallerstein, eds., *Race, Nation, Class: Ambiguous Identities* (New York: Verso, 1991), p. 86.

62. The same holds for North Korean historiography—except that Koguryŏ/Parhae would be substituted for Unified Silla in tracing the development of subsequent "mainstream" Korean history. The reason for the discrepancy is quite simple: the kingdom of Koguryŏ, and subsequently Parhae, encompassed northern Korea and southern Manchuria, whereas Unified Silla (after causing Koguryŏ's collapse with the aid of Tang China) encompassed the southern two-thirds of the Korean peninsula. Unified Silla's northern boundary with Parhae ran east along the Taedong River to the Bay of Wŏnsan.

63. See Balibar, in Balibar and Wallerstein, *Race, Nation, Class*, p. 88.

64. In *Han'guk kodaesa sanch'aek*, the authors (a younger generation of historians) begin their narrative with an admission of uncertainty: "When did people begin to live in the Korean peninsula? And who are our ancestors? These questions engross many people, but the reader cannot expect clear-cut answers. And this situation will remain the same. Clear-cut answers will not be forthcoming because it was so long ago, and because there

is such a dearth of historical evidence. . . . Habitually calling ourselves a homogeneous nation (*tanil minjok*), there is a tendency to stress the purity of our bloodline. But the bloodline of contemporary Koreans was not homogenous nor constant from the beginning." See *Han'guk kodaesa sanch'aek* (Seoul: Yŏksa pip'yŏngsa, 1994), pp. 11, 15. As suggested by *Han'guk kodaesa sanch'aek*, the essentialist, totalizing strategy does get problematized by Korean historians. But it seems to me that this undertaking needs to be theorized in a more rigorous way.

65. See Prasenjit Duara, "Rescuing History from the Nation-State," Working Papers and Proceedings of the Center for Psychosocial Studies (Chicago: Center for Psychosocial Studies, 1991), p. 7.

66. Almost all general histories of Korea begin with the Bronze Age, if not earlier, suggesting that the people who used bronze daggers and built dolmen tombs more than 2,500 years ago were early Koreans. A cursory survey can illustrate this essentialist tendency. The university-level general Korean history textbook *Han'guksa kaesŏl* (Outline of Korean history), authored by South Korea's Compilation Committee for National History Textbooks, begins the narrative of Korean history with: "The Korean nation (*minjok*) emerged from the Neolithic period and the Bronze Age as an exceptional, homogeneous people possessing a unique culture and established a tradition that was different from that of the Chinese"; see *Han'guksa kaesŏl* (Seoul: Kuksa kyojae p'yŏnch'an wiwŏnhoe, 1983), p. 15. In *Chosŏn t'ongsa*, vol. 1, published in P'yŏngyang by the Social Science Academy, the narrative begins with the appearance of "primitive bands" in Northeast Asia and the Korean peninsula during the Paleolithic era about a million years ago; see Son Yŏngjong et al., *Chosŏn t'ongsa* (P'yŏngyang: Sahoe kwahak ch'ulp'ansa, 1991), 1: 2.

67. For Immanuel Wallerstein, the interstate system emerged as the political superstructure of a capitalist world-economy. The interstate system is competitive because nation-states in the periphery may succeed in attaining core status, and core nations can slip to semi-periphery status. See his essay "The Construction of Peoplehood," in Balibar and Wallerstein, *Race, Nation, Class*.

68. Etienne Balibar (Balibar and Wallerstein, *Race, Nation, Class*, pp. 96–97) writes, "No nation possesses an ethnic base naturally, but as social formations are nationalized, the populations included within them . . . are ethnicized."

69. See Yi Kimun, "Han'gŭl ŭi yŏn'gu wa pogŭp," in Kuksa p'yŏnch'an wiwŏnhoe, ed., *Han minjok tongnip undongsa* (Seoul: Kuksa p'yŏnch'an wiwŏnhoe, 1987), vol. 2.

70. Ibid., p. 108. According to An Pyŏnghŭi, ŏnmun (han'gŭl) does not appear in any legal documents after King Sejong's time. From the latter half of the eighteenth century, moreover, ŏnmun was specifically prohibited

from appearing in legal documents. See An Pyŏnghŭi, *Kugŏsa yŏn'gu* (Seoul: Munhak kwa chisŏngsa, 1992), p. 254.

71. About print capitalism and how it makes possible the production of "homogenous time" and "homogenous space," see Anderson, *Imagined Communities*.

72. Here, I would include movements ranging from the failed coup d'état by "progressives" in 1884 to the Tonghak peasant rebellion in 1894, which had the potential of toppling the dynasty.

73. Unable to suppress the Tonghak forces, the Korean government had turned to China for help. When China dispatched 3,000 troops, Japan sent 8,000. Japan suggested that the two powers jointly sponsor reform in Korea, a proposal that China rejected. The ensuing Sino-Japanese War lasted ten months, from July 1894 to April 1895, with Japan emerging victorious. But even before the war with China, Japan had made demands that the Korean government carry out reform measures. See Carter Eckert, Ki-baik Lee, et al., *Korea, Old and New: A History* (Cambridge, Mass.: Harvard University, Korea Institute, 1990).

74. The transformation of Japanese peasants into Japanese (*kokumin*) had begun several decades earlier—after the consolidation of the Meiji Restoration and the establishment of a strong central state. By the time of Korea's annexation, the Japanese state had accumulated substantial experience with the technologies of nation-building—including the production of national consciousness. In addition, those who became colonial administrators (e.g., Gōtō Shinpei) made a careful study of Western colonial institutions and methods.

75. I am indebted to Ted Hughes for his discussion of *naisen ittai*. Hughes writes: "The nation can figure itself as plenitude, presence, originary self-identity only by means of a supplementary racism which, as supplement, necessarily points to the structural lack, absence, dispersal of this self-identity. Japan as 'Interior' can only figure itself as inside, as nation, by adding to itself the supplement of its 'inferior' racial Other" (unpublished paper). For discussion of racism not as an "expression" of nationalism but as its "supplement," see Etienne Balibar, "Racism and Nationalism," in Balibar and Wallerstein, *Race, Nation, Class*.

76. Contemporary South Korean historians usually divide historiography in the colonial period into four different categories. (1) *Colonialist historiography*: its ultimate political aim was to justify Japan's annexation of Korea; it portrayed Korean history as stagnant and determined by external forces. (2) *Nationalist historiography*: this was a narrative of resistance, devoted to countering the pernicious effects of colonialist historiography and to empowering Koreans to join the struggle for Korea's independence; representative historians are Sin Ch'aeho, Pak Ŭnsik, An Chaehong, Mun Ilp'yŏng, and Chŏng Inbo. (3) *Empiricist historiography*: it claimed to take an objective,

positivist approach to historiography, but its chief practitioners were usually employed by the colonial state—Yi Pyŏngdo, for example. (4) *Marxist historiography*: it sought to narrate Korean history as part of world history, unfolding in accordance with historical laws and by way of universal stages of development—representative historians are Paek Namun and Yi Ch'ŏngwŏn. There are problems with creating a typology such as this, a basic shortcoming being that a number of historians and their work do not fit into any of these categories, e.g., Hae Wŏn, Hwang Ŭidon, Ch'oe Namsŏn, An Hwak, Kwŏn Tŏkkyu, and Chang Tobin. But for sake of convenience, the categories of colonialist and nationalist historiography used in this essay follow conventional usage.

77. By this I mean starvation alongside plenty, brutal oppression alongside new forms of pleasure and new objects of desire (made possible by a new popular/consumer culture). These contradictions, experienced in radically different ways by Korean and Japanese residents of Korea, endlessly reproduced the politics of identity and difference.

78. Military advantage, conventionally thought to be crucial to hegemony, merely "locks in" hegemony for a limited period. Rather than military advantage, the critical element in maintaining hegemony is "productive advantage," which conditions the other two elements—commerce and finance. But productive advantage is ephemeral—thus the rise and fall of the British (and American) empire. See Terence K. Hopkins and Immanuel Wallerstein, "Patterns of Development of the Modern World-System," *Review* 1, no. 2 (Fall 1977): 120–21; cited in Bruce Cumings, "Archaeology, Descent, Emergence: Japan in British/American Hegemony, 1900–1950," in Masao Miyoshi and H. D. Harootunian, eds., *Japan in the World* (Durham: Duke University Press, 1993), p. 102.

79. See his essay "The Construction of Peoplehood," in Balibar and Wallerstein, *Race, Nation, Class*.

80. Bruce Cumings, "Archaeology, Descent, Emergence," p. 87.

81. Ibid., p. 86.

82. Balibar and Wallerstein, eds., *Race, Nation, Class*, p. 89.

83. Ibid., p. 90.

84. Ibid., p. 84.

85. Robert Young asserts that, if poststructuralism is the product of a single historical moment, then that moment is probably not May 1968 but rather the Algerian War of Independence. Suggesting that there is a link between subversive tendencies in poststructuralism and resistance to colonialism in the periphery (Algeria), Young notes that Sartre, Althusser, Derrida, and Lyotard, among others, were all either born in Algeria or personally involved with the events of the war. See Robert Young, *White Mythologies: Writing History and the West* (London: Routledge, 1990), p. 1.

86. In 1932, after ten years of work, SCKH published the first five volumes of what became the 38-volume *Chōsenshi* (Korean history). In addition, SCKH went on to publish a 3-volume *Chōsen shiryō shushin* (Collection of

Korean documents), and a 21-volume *Chōsen shiryō sōkan* (Archive of Korean documents). The SCKH was clearly an organ of the Japanese colonial state, but its members included Korean historians like Ch'oe Namsŏn, the man who drafted the "Korean Declaration of Independence" in 1919 and Yi Nŭnghwa, a renowned historian of Korean Buddhism. Yi Nŭnghwa was one of the original fourteen members when the SCKH was organized in 1922 by Arikishi Tadaichi, and Ch'oe Namsŏn joined in 1928. SCKH began as Chō-senshi hensan iinkai and was renamed the Chōsenshi henshūkai in 1925. See Yi Manyŏl's chapter on "colonialist historiography" in his *Han'guk kŭndae yŏksahak ŭi ihae* (Seoul: Ch'angjak kwa pip'yŏngsa, 1981).

87. The series began in June 1931 and ended in October of the same year. Sin Ch'aeho probably wrote the Introduction to *CS* in Beijing around 1924. When *CS* was published in the *Chosŏn ilbo*, it was entitled "Chosŏnsa." After Liberation, *CS* was republished as a monograph (in 1948) under the title *Chosŏn sanggosa*.

88. Before graduating from Waseda University in 1914, An Chaehong traveled to China and met Sin Ch'aeho in Shanghai. The powerlessness of the Korean independence movement in China (especially its weak financial base) in the early 1910s seems to have persuaded him not to go into exile. After returning to Korea, An served as the vice-principal of Chungang Middle School and organized the Taehan ch'ŏngnyŏn oegyodan (Korean youth diplomatic corps)—for which he spent three years in jail. Upon release, he served as president and chief editor of *Chosŏn ilbo*. When the Sin'ganhoe was organized in 1927, he became its secretary—and was jailed for eight months. In 1931, An opposed the socialists' call for the dissolution of the Sin'ganhoe, and after its break-up he aligned himself with moderate and conservative nationalists. After Liberation, An tried to create a left-right coalition, but when this effort failed, he accepted the position of chief civil administrator in USAMGIK. Thereafter, he allied himself with anti-communist forces who argued for the creation of a separate state in southern Korea. During the Korean War, An was taken to North Korea, and he died in P'yŏngyang in 1965.

89. In translating these paragraphs, I have consulted J. Michael Allen's translation in "In the Beginning: National Origins and National Identity in Korea"—a paper he presented at the conference on "Korea's Minjung Movement" in Bloomington, Indiana (Nov. 1989). Sin Ch'aeho, *Chosŏn sang-gosa, TSCHC*, 1: 31–32.

90. Sin Ch'aeho (*Chosŏn sanggosa, TSCHC*, 1: 70) writes: "Where is the self-identity (*chasŏng*: inner essence, true nature, in-itself) of individuals? If neither individuals nor societies possess a self-identity, then where is the motive force of history? In looking at this problem, I think self-identity comes to be constituted by way of the environment (*hwan'gyŏng*) and the epoch (*sidae*)."

91. Young, *White Mythologies*, p. 3.

92. When the KPG in Shanghai elected Syngman Rhee as president in absentia and proved unwilling to take up armed struggle against Japanese

colonialism, Sin Chaeho denounced it in the newspaper *Sin Taehan* (New Korea) and returned to Beijing in 1920. In 1923, when Sin wrote the "Declaration of the Korean Revolution" for the Korean revolutionary organization Ŭiyŏldan, he did so in consultation with Yu Chamyŏng who was an anarchist and the leading theorist in the ŭiyŏldan. According to Sin Yongha, Yu Chamyŏng's anarchist ideas were influenced by Li Shizeng and Wu Zhihui. See Sin Yongha, "Sin Ch'aeho ŭi mujŏngbujuŭi tongnip sasang," in Kang Mangil, ed., *Sin Ch'aeho* (Seoul: Koryŏ taehakkyo ch'ulp'anbu, 1990), p. 106. Li Shizeng and Wu Zhihui were among the doyens of Chinese anarchism. Both Li and Wu were important members of the Guomindang, and according to Arif Dirlik, both played important roles in anarchist anti-communism in the early 1920s; see Arif Dirlik, *Anarchism in the Chinese Revolution* (Berkeley: University of California Press, 1991), pp. 12–14. Although I know of no evidence of a direct relationship between Sin Ch'aeho and the Chinese anarchist thinkers Li Shizeng and Wu Zhihui, it is clear that anarchist ideals were broadly diffused in radical circles in Beijing and Shanghai in the early 1920s. One very apparent commonality between Li, Wu, and Sin was their admiration of Peter Kropotkin. In his 1925 essay "Nanggaek ŭi sinnyŏn manp'il," Sin called on the Korean youth to "become baptized" by Peter Kropotkin's essay "An Appeal to the Young"; see *Sin Ch'aeho yŏksa nonsŏljip* (Seoul: Hyŏndae silhaksa, 1995), p. 350.

93. Sin Ch'aeho, "Introduction" to *CS*, in *TSCHC*, 1: 31–32.

94. Sin Ch'aeho, "Chosŏn hyŏngmyŏng sŏnŏn," *TSCHC*, 3: 35–46. See also the han'gŭl text in *Sin Ch'aeho yŏksa nonsŏlchip*, pp. 329–39.

95. Unlike other conservative nationalist intellectuals, Sin Yongha acknowledges Sin Ch'aeho's turn toward anarchism. According to Sin Yongha, Sin Ch'aeho turned to anarchism because he had become estranged from the nationalists in the KPG and because he was persuaded by Kropotkin's critique of Social Darwinism. For Kropotkin, mutual aid (i.e., cooperation) was as central to animal and human evolution as the struggle of the fittest. In Sin Ch'aeho's earlier nationalist writings, there had been a tension between Sin's program of strengthening national power and his critique of Japanese imperialism. That is, if survival depended on national power, what could be the ethical basis for criticizing imperialism? As Sin Yongha notes, this tension emanated from Social Darwinist assumptions that emphasized competition but not mutual aid. In Kropotkin, then, Sin Ch'aeho found a more ethical way to understand human evolution. Repelled by the antics of nationalist politicians, Sin turned to anarchism that placed so much faith on the cooperative spirit of the *minjung* while at the same time taking direct action against imperialism. See Sin Yongha, "Sin Ch'aeho ŭi mujŏngbujuŭi tongnip sasang," in Kang Man'gil, ed., *Sin Ch'aeho*, pp. 78–147.

96. In a later Declaration ("Sŏnŏnmun," *TSCHC*, 3: 47–50), Sin Ch'aeho uses "propertyless masses" (*musan taejung*), "propertyless *minjung*" (*musan minjung*), and "*minjung*" interchangeably.

97. Sin Ch'aeho, "Chosŏn hyŏngmyŏng sŏnŏn," *TSCHC*, 3: 44.

98. Sin Ilch'ŏl suggests that anarchism was a mere tool for Sin Ch'aeho's nationalist goals; see his *Sin Ch'aeho ŭi sahoe sasang yŏn'gu* (Seoul: Han'gilsa, 1984), p. 328. The dismissal of Sin Ch'aeho's anarchism is difficult to fathom in light of the textual evidence. Sin Yongha, who acknowledges Sin Ch'aeho's turn to anarchism in the mid-1920s, argues that Sin would have abandoned his anarchism after Korea's liberation from Japanese colonial rule. But this is just another way of erasing the tension between Sin Ch'aeho's earlier writings on *minjok* and his later emphasis on *minjung*. By erasing this tension, what is being repressed is the radically egalitarian, anti-authoritarian, and open-ended character of Sin Ch'aeho's later writings.

99. Sin Ch'aeho, "Chosŏn hyŏngmyŏng sŏnŏn," *TSCHC*, 3: 43–44.

*Epilogue: Carter J. Eckert, "Exorcising Hegel's Ghosts: Toward a Postnationalist Historiography of Korea"*

1. Hyon Kilon, "Substance and Shadow," trans. by Sol Soonbong, in *Manoa: A Pacific Journal of International Writing* 2.2 (Fall 1990): 155–74. The original title in Korean, "Kkŏpchil kwa soksal," literally means something like "husk and pith," or "shell and meat." See Hyŏn Kirŏn, "Kkŏpchil kwa soksal," *Munye chungang* (Spring 1986): 204–26.

2. Hyon, p. 159.

3. Ibid., p. 156.

4. Ibid., p. 173.

5. Ibid., p. 173.

6. Ibid., p. 173.

7. Ibid., p. 171.

8. See G. W. F. Hegel, *Introduction to the Philosophy of History*, trans. Leo Rauch (Indianapolis and Cambridge: Hackett, 1988), pp. 40–42, 101–3.

9. Yu Kilchun, *Sŏyu kyŏnmun*, in *Yu Kilchun chŏnsŏ* (Seoul: Ilchogak, 1971), 1: 323–34; Sin Ch'aeho, "Toksa sillon," in *Pŏmje Sin Ch'aeho chŏnjip* (Seoul: Pŏmje Sin Ch'aeho sŏnsaeng kinyŏm saŏphoe, 1972; rev. ed. 1982), 1: 471. See also Chapter 12 by Henry Em, pp. 336–61 in this volume.

10. See Carter J. Eckert, "Will to Greatness: An Historical Note on Korea's Transition to Modernity," in *Historical Perspectives on Contemporary East Asia*, ed. by Merle Goldman and Andrew Gordon (Cambridge, Mass.: Harvard University Press, forthcoming).

11. Yu Kilchun, *Sŏyu kyŏnmun*, p. 399.

12. In a famous essay on prewar Japanese "ultra-nationalism" originally published in 1946, Maruyama Masao described a phenomenon that seems eerily similar to postwar Korean nationalism, minus, of course, the Japanese imperial cult: "Until the day in 1946 when the divinity of the Emperor was formally denied in an Imperial Rescript, there was in principle no basis in Japan for freedom of belief. Since the nation includes in its 'national polity' all the internal values of truth, morality, and beauty, neither scholarship nor

art could exist apart from these national values" (Masao Maruyama, *Thought and Behavior in Japanese Politics*, ed. by Ivan Morris [London: Oxford University Press, 1963], p. 6).

13. Quoted in Isaiah Berlin, "Political Ideas in the Twentieth Century," in his *Four Essays on Liberty* (Oxford: Oxford University Press, 1969), p. 39. Berlin, who was an eloquent advocate of intellectual and political pluralism, frequently quoted this remark by Kant in his writings.

14. See David Brewster, *Memoirs of the Life, Writings, and Discoveries of Sir Isaac Newton* (Edinburgh: T. Constable, 1855), 2: 407.

15. As James Palais notes, this practice turned out to be impossible to uphold in the case of the Chosŏn dynasty, not through any rejection of the principle itself, but simply because the dynasty lasted so long (over five hundred years, from 1392 to 1910), and because there was no succeeding dynasty to write the history. See James B. Palais, "Records and Record-keeping in Nineteenth-Century Korea," *Journal of Asian Studies* 30 (1971): 584–85.

16. Simon Schama, "Clio at the Multiplex," *New Yorker*, Jan. 19, 1998, p. 41.

17. Ibid.

18. See "Tarnished Laureate: Nobel Winner Accused of Stretching the Truth," *New York Times on the Web* (Books), Dec. 15, 1998. See also Peter Canby, "The Truth About Rigoberta Menchú," *New York Review of Books*, Apr., 1999, pp. 28–33.

19. From Johnson's 1753 "Dedication" to *Shakespear Illustrated: or the Novels and Histories, On which the Plays of Shakespear Are Founded*, reprinted in D. Nichol Smith, ed., *Shakespeare Criticism* (London: Oxford University Press, 1946 [1916]), pp. 75–76.

20. Isaiah Berlin, "John Stuart Mill and the Ends of Life," in his *Four Essays in Freedom*, pp. 198–99.

# Index

*Harvard East Asian Monographs*
(* out-of-print)

# Harvard East Asian Monographs

# Harvard East Asian Monographs

172. Charles Shiro Inouye, *The Similitude of Blossoms: A Critical Biography of Izumi Kyōka (1873–1939), Japanese Novelist and Playwright*

173. Aviad E. Raz, *Riding the Black Ship: Japan and Tokyo Disneyland*

174. Deborah J. Milly, *Poverty, Equality and the Growth: The Politics of Economic Need in Postwar Japan*

175. See Heng Teow, *Japan's Cultural Policy Toward China, 1918–1931: A Comparative Perspective*

176. Michael A. Fuller, *An Introduction to Literary Chinese*

177. Frederick R. Dickinson, *War and National Reinvention: Japan in the Great War, 1914–1919*

178. John Solt, *Shredding the Tapestry of Meaning: The Poetry and Poetics of Kitasono Katue (1902–1978)*

179. Edward Pratt, *Japan's Protoindustrial Elite: The Economic Foundations of the Gōnō*

180. Atsuko Sakaki, *Recontextualizing Texts: Narrative Performance in Modern Japanese Fiction*

181. Soon-Won Park, *Colonial Industrialization and Labor in Korea: The Onoda Cement Factory*

182. JaHyun Kim Haboush and Martina Deuchler, *Culture and the State in Late Chosŏn Korea*

183. John W. Chaffee, *Branches of Heaven: A History of the Imperial Clan of Sung China*

184. Gi-Wook Shin and Michael Robinson, eds., *Colonial Modernity in Korea*

185. Nam-lin Hur, *Prayer and Play in Late Tokugawa Japan: Asakusa Sensōji and Edo Society*